ADAAG — ADA and ABA ACCESSIBILITY GUIDELINES FOR BUILDINGS AND FACILITIES

U.S Access Board
July 2004

Printed and
Distributed By:

BUILDER'S BOOK, INC.
CONTRACTOR'S BOOK CENTER
BOOKSTORE

8001 Canoga Ave.
Canoga Park, CA 91304

1-800-273-7375 • 818-887-7828
www.buildersbook.com

Printed by Builder's Book, Inc., Bookstore · www.buildersbook.com

Printed by Builder's Book, Inc., Bookstore · www.buildersbook.com

Printed by Builder's Book, Inc., Bookstore · www.buildersbook.com

4

ADA CHAPTER 1: APPLICATION AND ADMINISTRATION

101 Purpose

101.1 General. This document contains scoping and technical requirements for *accessibility* to *sites*, *facilities*, *buildings*, and *elements* by individuals with disabilities. The requirements are to be applied during the design, construction, *additions* to, and *alteration* of *sites*, *facilities*, *buildings*, and *elements* to the extent required by regulations issued by Federal agencies under the Americans with Disabilities Act of 1990 (ADA).

> **Advisory 101.1 General.** In addition to these requirements, covered entities must comply with the regulations issued by the Department of Justice and the Department of Transportation under the Americans with Disabilities Act. There are issues affecting individuals with disabilities which are not addressed by these requirements, but which are covered by the Department of Justice and the Department of Transportation regulations.

101.2 Effect on Removal of Barriers in Existing Facilities. This document does not address existing *facilities* unless *altered* at the discretion of a covered entity. The Department of Justice has authority over existing *facilities* that are subject to the requirement for removal of barriers under title III of the ADA. Any determination that this document applies to existing *facilities* subject to the barrier removal requirement is solely within the discretion of the Department of Justice and is effective only to the extent required by regulations issued by the Department of Justice.

102 Dimensions for Adults and Children

The technical requirements are based on adult dimensions and anthropometrics. In addition, this document includes technical requirements based on children's dimensions and anthropometrics for drinking fountains, water closets, toilet compartments, lavatories and sinks, dining surfaces, and work surfaces.

103 Equivalent Facilitation

Nothing in these requirements prevents the use of designs, products, or technologies as alternatives to those prescribed, provided they result in substantially equivalent or greater *accessibility* and usability.

> **Advisory 103 Equivalent Facilitation.** The responsibility for demonstrating equivalent facilitation in the event of a challenge rests with the covered entity. With the exception of transit facilities, which are covered by regulations issued by the Department of Transportation, there is no process for certifying that an alternative design provides equivalent facilitation.

104 Conventions

104.1 Dimensions. Dimensions that are not stated as "maximum" or "minimum" are absolute.

5

104.1.1 Construction and Manufacturing Tolerances. All dimensions are subject to conventional industry tolerances except where the requirement is stated as a range with specific minimum and maximum end points.

> **Advisory 104.1.1 Construction and Manufacturing Tolerances.** Conventional industry tolerances recognized by this provision include those for field conditions and those that may be a necessary consequence of a particular manufacturing process. Recognized tolerances are not intended to apply to design work.
>
> It is good practice when specifying dimensions to avoid specifying a tolerance where dimensions are absolute. For example, if this document requires "1½ inches," avoid specifying "1½ inches plus or minus X inches."
>
> Where the requirement states a specified range, such as in Section 609.4 where grab bars must be installed between 33 inches and 36 inches above the floor, the range provides an adequate tolerance and therefore no tolerance outside of the range at either end point is permitted.
>
> Where a requirement is a minimum or a maximum dimension that does not have two specific minimum and maximum end points, tolerances may apply. Where an element is to be installed at the minimum or maximum permitted dimension, such as "15 inches minimum" or "5 pounds maximum", it would not be good practice to specify "5 pounds (plus X pounds) or 15 inches (minus X inches)." Rather, it would be good practice to specify a dimension less than the required maximum (or more than the required minimum) by the amount of the expected field or manufacturing tolerance and not to state any tolerance in conjunction with the specified dimension.
>
> Specifying dimensions in design in the manner described above will better ensure that facilities and elements accomplish the level of accessibility intended by these requirements. It will also more often produce an end result of strict and literal compliance with the stated requirements and eliminate enforcement difficulties and issues that might otherwise arise. Information on specific tolerances may be available from industry or trade organizations, code groups and building officials, and published references.

104.2 Calculation of Percentages. Where the required number of *elements* or *facilities* to be provided is determined by calculations of ratios or percentages and remainders or fractions result, the next greater whole number of such *elements* or *facilities* shall be provided. Where the determination of the required size or dimension of an *element* or *facility* involves ratios or percentages, rounding down for values less than one half shall be permitted.

104.3 Figures. Unless specifically stated otherwise, figures are provided for informational purposes only.

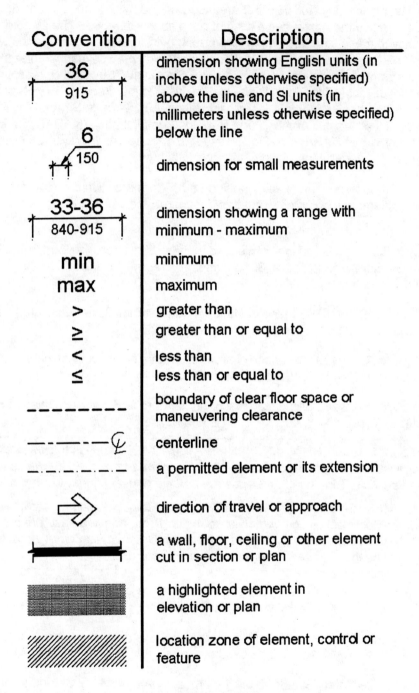

Convention	Description
36 / 915	dimension showing English units (in inches unless otherwise specified) above the line and SI units (in millimeters unless otherwise specified) below the line
6 / 150	dimension for small measurements
33-36 / 840-915	dimension showing a range with minimum - maximum
min	minimum
max	maximum
>	greater than
≥	greater than or equal to
<	less than
≤	less than or equal to
– – – – –	boundary of clear floor space or maneuvering clearance
– · – · – ₵	centerline
– · – · –	a permitted element or its extension
⇒	direction of travel or approach
▬	a wall, floor, ceiling or other element cut in section or plan
▓	a highlighted element in elevation or plan
▨	location zone of element, control or feature

Figure 104
Graphic Convention for Figures

Printed by Builder's Book, Inc., Bookstore · www.buildersbook.com

105 Referenced Standards

105.1 General. The standards listed in 105.2 are incorporated by reference in this document and are part of the requirements to the prescribed extent of each such reference. The Director of the Federal Register has approved these standards for incorporation by reference in accordance with 5 U.S.C. 552(a) and 1 CFR part 51. Copies of the referenced standards may be inspected at the Architectural and Transportation Barriers Compliance Board, 1331 F Street, NW, Suite 1000, Washington, DC 20004; at the Department of Justice, Civil Rights Division, Disability Rights Section, 1425 New York Avenue, NW, Washington, DC; at the Department of Transportation, 400 Seventh Street, SW, Room 10424, Washington DC; or at the National Archives and Records Administration (NARA). For information on the availability of this material at NARA, call (202) 741-6030, or go to http://www.archives.gov/federal_register/code_of_federal_regulations/ibr_locations.html.

105.2 Referenced Standards. The specific edition of the standards listed below are referenced in this document. Where differences occur between this document and the referenced standards, this document applies.

105.2.1 ANSI/BHMA. Copies of the referenced standards may be obtained from the Builders Hardware Manufacturers Association, 355 Lexington Avenue, 17th floor, New York, NY 10017 (http://www.buildershardware.com).

ANSI/BHMA A156.10-1999 American National Standard for Power Operated Pedestrian Doors (see 404.3).

ANSI/BHMA A156.19-1997 American National Standard for Power Assist and Low Energy Power Operated Doors (see 404.3, 408.3.2.1, and 409.3.1).

ANSI/BHMA A156.19-2002 American National Standard for Power Assist and Low Energy Power Operated Doors (see 404.3, 408.3.2.1, and 409.3.1).

> **Advisory 105.2.1 ANSI/BHMA.** ANSI/BHMA A156.10-1999 applies to power operated doors for pedestrian use which open automatically when approached by pedestrians. Included are provisions intended to reduce the chance of user injury or entrapment.
>
> ANSI/BHMA A156.19-1997 and A156.19-2002 applies to power assist doors, low energy power operated doors or low energy power open doors for pedestrian use not provided for in ANSI/BHMA A156.10 for Power Operated Pedestrian Doors. Included are provisions intended to reduce the chance of user injury or entrapment.

105.2.2 ASME. Copies of the referenced standards may be obtained from the American Society of Mechanical Engineers, Three Park Avenue, New York, New York 10016 (http://www.asme.org).

ASME A17.1- 2000 Safety Code for Elevators and Escalators, including ASME A17.1a-2002 Addenda and ASME A17.1b-2003 Addenda (see 407.1, 408.1, 409.1, and 810.9).

ASME A18.1-1999 Safety Standard for Platform Lifts and Stairway Chairlifts, including ASME A18.1a-2001 Addenda and ASME A18.1b-2001 Addenda (see 410.1).

ASME A18.1-2003 Safety Standard for Platform Lifts and Stairway Chairlifts, (see 410.1).

Advisory 105.2.2 ASME. ASME A17.1-2000 is used by local jurisdictions throughout the United States for the design, construction, installation, operation, inspection, testing, maintenance, alteration, and repair of elevators and escalators. The majority of the requirements apply to the operational machinery not seen or used by elevator passengers. ASME A17.1 requires a two-way means of emergency communications in passenger elevators. This means of communication must connect with emergency or authorized personnel and not an automated answering system. The communication system must be push button activated. The activation button must be permanently identified with the word "HELP." A visual indication acknowledging the establishment of a communications link to authorized personnel must be provided. The visual indication must remain on until the call is terminated by authorized personnel. The building location, the elevator car number, and the need for assistance must be provided to authorized personnel answering the emergency call. The use of a handset by the communications system is prohibited. Only the authorized personnel answering the call can terminate the call. Operating instructions for the communications system must be provided in the elevator car.

The provisions for escalators require that at least two flat steps be provided at the entrance and exit of every escalator and that steps on escalators be demarcated by yellow lines 2 inches wide maximum along the back and sides of steps.

ASME A18.1-1999 and ASME A18.1-2003 address the design, construction, installation, operation, inspection, testing, maintenance and repair of lifts that are intended for transportation of persons with disabilities. Lifts are classified as: vertical platform lifts, inclined platform lifts, inclined stairway chairlifts, private residence vertical platform lifts, private residence inclined platform lifts, and private residence inclined stairway chairlifts.

This document does not permit the use of inclined stairway chairlifts which do not provide platforms because such lifts require the user to transfer to a seat.

ASME A18.1 contains requirements for runways, which are the spaces in which platforms or seats move. The standard includes additional provisions for runway enclosures, electrical equipment and wiring, structural support, headroom clearance (which is 80 inches minimum), lower level access ramps and pits. The enclosure walls not used for entry or exit are required to have a grab bar the full length of the wall on platform lifts. Access ramps are required to meet requirements similar to those for ramps in Chapter 4 of this document.

Each of the lift types addressed in ASME A18.1 must meet requirements for capacity, load, speed, travel, operating devices, and control equipment. The maximum permitted height for operable parts is consistent with Section 308 of this document. The standard also addresses attendant operation. However, Section 410.1 of this document does not permit attendant operation.

105.2.3 ASTM. Copies of the referenced standards may be obtained from the American Society for Testing and Materials, 100 Bar Harbor Drive, West Conshohocken, Pennsylvania 19428 (http://www.astm.org).

ASTM F 1292-99 Standard Specification for Impact Attenuation of Surface Systems Under and Around Playground Equipment (see 1008.2.6.2).

ASTM F 1292-04 Standard Specification for Impact Attenuation of Surfacing Materials Within the Use Zone of Playground Equipment (see 1008.2.6.2).

ASTM F 1487-01 Standard Consumer Safety Performance Specification for Playground Equipment for Public Use (see 106.5).

ASTM F 1951-99 Standard Specification for Determination of Accessibility of Surface Systems Under and Around Playground Equipment (see 1008.2.6.1).

> **Advisory 105.2.3 ASTM.** ASTM F 1292-99 and ASTM F 1292-04 establish a uniform means to measure and compare characteristics of surfacing materials to determine whether materials provide a safe surface under and around playground equipment. These standards are referenced in the play areas requirements of this document when an accessible surface is required inside a play area use zone where a fall attenuating surface is also required. The standards cover the minimum impact attenuation requirements, when tested in accordance with Test Method F 355, for surface systems to be used under and around any piece of playground equipment from which a person may fall.
>
> ASTM F 1487-01 establishes a nationally recognized safety standard for public playground equipment to address injuries identified by the U.S. Consumer Product Safety Commission. It defines the use zone, which is the ground area beneath and immediately adjacent to a play structure or play equipment designed for unrestricted circulation around the equipment and on whose surface it is predicted that a user would land when falling from or exiting a play structure or equipment. The play areas requirements in this document reference the ASTM F 1487 standard when defining accessible routes that overlap use zones requiring fall attenuating surfaces. If the use zone of a playground is not entirely surfaced with an accessible material, at least one accessible route within the use zone must be provided from the perimeter to all accessible play structures or components within the playground.
>
> ASTM F 1951-99 establishes a uniform means to measure the characteristics of surface systems in order to provide performance specifications to select materials for use as an accessible surface under and around playground equipment. Surface materials that comply with this standard and are located in the use zone must also comply with ASTM F 1292. The test methods in this standard address access for children and adults who may traverse the surfacing to aid children who are playing. When a surface is tested it must have an average work per foot value for straight propulsion and for turning less than the average work per foot values for straight propulsion and for turning, respectively, on a hard, smooth surface with a grade of 7% (1:14).

105.2.4 ICC/IBC. Copies of the referenced standard may be obtained from the International Code Council, 5203 Leesburg Pike, Suite 600, Falls Church, Virginia 22041 (www.iccsafe.org).

International Building Code, 2000 Edition (see 207.1, 207.2, 216.4.2, 216.4.3, and 1005.2.1).

International Building Code, 2001 Supplement (see 207.1 and 207.2).

International Building Code, 2003 Edition (see 207.1, 207.2, 216.4.2, 216.4.3, and 1005.2.1).

Advisory 105.2.4 ICC/IBC. International Building Code (IBC)-2000 (including 2001 Supplement to the International Codes) and IBC-2003 are referenced for means of egress, areas of refuge, and railings provided on fishing piers and platforms. At least one accessible means of egress is required for every accessible space and at least two accessible means of egress are required where more than one means of egress is required. The technical criteria for accessible means of egress allow the use of exit stairways and evacuation elevators when provided in conjunction with horizontal exits or areas of refuge. While typical elevators are not designed to be used during an emergency evacuation, evacuation elevators are designed with standby power and other features according to the elevator safety standard and can be used for the evacuation of individuals with disabilities. The IBC also provides requirements for areas of refuge, which are fire-rated spaces on levels above or below the exit discharge levels where people unable to use stairs can go to register a call for assistance and wait for evacuation.

The recreation facilities requirements of this document references two sections in the IBC for fishing piers and platforms. An exception addresses the height of the railings, guards, or handrails where a fishing pier or platform is required to include a guard, railing, or handrail higher than 34 inches (865 mm) above the ground or deck surface.

105.2.5 NFPA. Copies of the referenced standards may be obtained from the National Fire Protection Association, 1 Batterymarch Park, Quincy, Massachusetts 02169-7471, (http://www.nfpa.org).

NFPA 72 National Fire Alarm Code, 1999 Edition (see 702.1 and 809.5.2).

NFPA 72 National Fire Alarm Code, 2002 Edition (see 702.1 and 809.5.2).

Advisory 105.2.5 NFPA. NFPA 72-1999 and NFPA 72-2002 address the application, installation, performance, and maintenance of protective signaling systems and their components. The NFPA 72 incorporates Underwriters Laboratory (UL) 1971 by reference. The standard specifies the characteristics of audible alarms, such as placement and sound levels. However, Section 702 of these requirements limits the volume of an audible alarm to 110 dBA, rather than the maximum 120 dBA permitted by NFPA 72-1999.

NFPA 72 specifies characteristics for visible alarms, such as flash frequency, color, intensity, placement, and synchronization. However, Section 702 of this document requires that visual alarm appliances be permanently installed. UL 1971 specifies intensity dispersion requirements for visible alarms. In particular, NFPA 72 requires visible alarms to have a light source that is clear or white and has polar dispersion complying with UL 1971.

106 Definitions

106.1 General. For the purpose of this document, the terms defined in 106.5 have the indicated meaning.

> **Advisory 106.1 General.** Terms defined in Section 106.5 are italicized in the text of this document.

106.2 Terms Defined in Referenced Standards. Terms not defined in 106.5 or in regulations issued by the Department of Justice and the Department of Transportation to implement the Americans with Disabilities Act, but specifically defined in a referenced standard, shall have the specified meaning from the referenced standard unless otherwise stated.

106.3 Undefined Terms. The meaning of terms not specifically defined in 106.5 or in regulations issued by the Department of Justice and the Department of Transportation to implement the Americans with Disabilities Act or in referenced standards shall be as defined by collegiate dictionaries in the sense that the context implies.

106.4 Interchangeability. Words, terms and phrases used in the singular include the plural and those used in the plural include the singular.

106.5 Defined Terms.

Accessible. A *site*, *building*, *facility*, or portion thereof that complies with this part.

Accessible Means of Egress. A continuous and unobstructed way of egress travel from any point in a *building* or *facility* that provides an *accessible* route to an area of refuge, a horizontal exit, or a *public way*.

Addition. An expansion, extension, or increase in the gross floor area or height of a *building* or *facility*.

Administrative Authority. A governmental agency that adopts or enforces regulations and guidelines for the design, construction, or *alteration* of *buildings* and *facilities*.

Alteration. A change to a *building* or *facility* that affects or could affect the usability of the *building* or *facility* or portion thereof. *Alterations* include, but are not limited to, remodeling, renovation, rehabilitation, reconstruction, historic restoration, resurfacing of *circulation paths* or *vehicular ways*, changes or rearrangement of the structural parts or *elements*, and changes or rearrangement in the plan configuration of walls and full-height partitions. Normal maintenance, reroofing, painting or wallpapering, or changes to mechanical and electrical systems are not *alterations* unless they affect the usability of the *building* or *facility*.

Amusement Attraction. Any *facility*, or portion of a *facility*, located within an amusement park or theme park which provides amusement without the use of an amusement device. Amusement attractions include, but are not limited to, fun houses, barrels, and other attractions without seats.

12

Amusement Ride. A system that moves persons through a fixed course within a defined area for the purpose of amusement.

Amusement Ride Seat. A seat that is built-in or mechanically fastened to an *amusement ride* intended to be occupied by one or more passengers.

Area of Sport Activity. That portion of a room or *space* where the play or practice of a sport occurs.

Assembly Area. A *building* or *facility*, or portion thereof, used for the purpose of entertainment, educational or civic gatherings, or similar purposes. For the purposes of these requirements, *assembly areas* include, but are not limited to, classrooms, lecture halls, courtrooms, public meeting rooms, public hearing rooms, legislative chambers, motion picture houses, auditoria, theaters, playhouses, dinner theaters, concert halls, centers for the performing arts, amphitheaters, arenas, stadiums, grandstands, or convention centers.

Assistive Listening System (ALS). An amplification system utilizing transmitters, receivers, and coupling devices to bypass the acoustical *space* between a sound source and a listener by means of induction loop, radio frequency, infrared, or direct-wired equipment.

Boarding Pier. A portion of a pier where a boat is temporarily secured for the purpose of embarking or disembarking.

Boat Launch Ramp. A sloped surface designed for launching and retrieving trailered boats and other water craft to and from a body of water.

Boat Slip. That portion of a pier, main pier, finger pier, or float where a boat is moored for the purpose of berthing, embarking, or disembarking.

Building. Any structure used or intended for supporting or sheltering any use or occupancy.

Catch Pool. A pool or designated section of a pool used as a terminus for water slide flumes.

Characters. Letters, numbers, punctuation marks and typographic symbols.

Children's Use. Describes *spaces* and *elements* specifically designed for use primarily by people 12 years old and younger.

Circulation Path. An exterior or interior way of passage provided for pedestrian travel, including but not limited to, *walks*, hallways, courtyards, elevators, platform lifts, *ramps*, stairways, and landings.

Closed-Circuit Telephone. A telephone with a dedicated line such as a house phone, courtesy phone or phone that must be used to gain entry to a *facility*.

Common Use. Interior or exterior *circulation paths*, rooms, *spaces*, or *elements* that are not for *public use* and are made available for the shared use of two or more people.

Cross Slope. The slope that is perpendicular to the direction of travel (see *running slope*).

Curb Ramp. A short *ramp* cutting through a curb or built up to it.

Detectable Warning. A standardized surface feature built in or applied to walking surfaces or other *elements* to warn of hazards on a *circulation path*.

Element. An architectural or mechanical component of a *building*, *facility*, *space*, or *site*.

Elevated Play Component. A *play component* that is approached above or below grade and that is part of a composite play structure consisting of two or more *play components* attached or functionally linked to create an integrated unit providing more than one play activity.

Employee Work Area. All or any portion of a *space* used only by employees and used only for work. Corridors, toilet rooms, kitchenettes and break rooms are not *employee work areas*.

Entrance. Any access point to a *building* or portion of a *building* or *facility* used for the purpose of entering. An *entrance* includes the approach *walk*, the vertical access leading to the *entrance* platform, the *entrance* platform itself, vestibule if provided, the entry door or gate, and the hardware of the entry door or gate.

Facility. All or any portion of *buildings*, structures, *site* improvements, *elements*, and pedestrian routes or *vehicular ways* located on a *site*.

Gangway. A variable-sloped pedestrian walkway that links a fixed structure or land with a floating structure. *Gangways* that connect to vessels are not addressed by this document.

Golf Car Passage. A continuous passage on which a motorized golf car can operate.

Ground Level Play Component. A *play component* that is approached and exited at the ground level.

Key Station. Rapid and light rail stations, and commuter rail stations, as defined under criteria established by the Department of Transportation in 49 CFR 37.47 and 49 CFR 37.51, respectively.

Mail Boxes. Receptacles for the receipt of documents, packages, or other deliverable matter. *Mail boxes* include, but are not limited to, post office boxes and receptacles provided by commercial mail-receiving agencies, apartment *facilities*, or schools.

Marked Crossing. A crosswalk or other identified path intended for pedestrian use in crossing a *vehicular way*.

Mezzanine. An intermediate level or levels between the floor and ceiling of any *story* with an aggregate floor area of not more than one-third of the area of the room or *space* in which the level or levels are located. *Mezzanines* have sufficient elevation that *space* for human occupancy can be provided on the floor below.

Occupant Load. The number of persons for which the means of egress of a *building* or portion of a *building* is designed.

Operable Part. A component of an *element* used to insert or withdraw objects, or to activate, deactivate, or adjust the *element*.

14

Pictogram. A pictorial symbol that represents activities, *facilities*, or concepts.

Play Area. A portion of a *site* containing *play components* designed and constructed for children.

Play Component. An *element* intended to generate specific opportunities for play, socialization, or learning. *Play components* are manufactured or natural; and are stand-alone or part of a composite play structure.

Private Building or Facility. A place of public accommodation or a commercial *building* or *facility* subject to title III of the ADA and 28 CFR part 36 or a transportation *building* or *facility* subject to title III of the ADA and 49 CFR 37.45.

Public Building or Facility. A *building* or *facility* or portion of a *building* or *facility* designed, constructed, or *altered* by, on behalf of, or for the use of a public entity subject to title II of the ADA and 28 CFR part 35 or to title II of the ADA and 49 CFR 37.41 or 37.43.

Public Entrance. An *entrance* that is not a *service entrance* or a *restricted entrance*.

Public Use. Interior or exterior rooms, *spaces*, or *elements* that are made available to the public. *Public use* may be provided at a *building* or *facility* that is privately or publicly owned.

Public Way. Any street, alley or other parcel of land open to the outside air leading to a public street, which has been deeded, dedicated or otherwise permanently appropriated to the public for *public use* and which has a clear width and height of not less than 10 feet (3050 mm).

Qualified Historic Building or Facility. A *building* or *facility* that is listed in or eligible for listing in the National Register of Historic Places, or designated as historic under an appropriate State or local law.

Ramp. A walking surface that has a *running slope* steeper than 1:20.

Residential Dwelling Unit. A unit intended to be used as a residence, that is primarily long-term in nature. *Residential dwelling units* do not include *transient lodging*, inpatient medical care, licensed long-term care, and detention or correctional *facilities*.

Restricted Entrance. An *entrance* that is made available for *common use* on a controlled basis but not *public use* and that is not a *service entrance*.

Running Slope. The slope that is parallel to the direction of travel (see *cross slope*).

Self-Service Storage. *Building* or *facility* designed and used for the purpose of renting or leasing individual storage *spaces* to customers for the purpose of storing and removing personal property on a self-service basis.

Service Entrance. An *entrance* intended primarily for delivery of goods or services.

Site. A parcel of land bounded by a property line or a designated portion of a public right-of-way.

Soft Contained Play Structure. A play structure made up of one or more *play components* where the user enters a fully enclosed play environment that utilizes pliable materials, such as plastic, netting, or fabric.

Space. A definable area, such as a room, toilet room, hall, *assembly area*, *entrance*, storage room, alcove, courtyard, or lobby.

Story. That portion of a *building* or *facility* designed for human occupancy included between the upper surface of a floor and upper surface of the floor or roof next above. A *story* containing one or more *mezzanines* has more than one floor level.

Structural Frame. The columns and the girders, beams, and trusses having direct connections to the columns and all other members that are essential to the stability of the *building* or *facility* as a whole.

Tactile. An object that can be perceived using the sense of touch.

Technically Infeasible. With respect to an *alteration* of a *building* or a *facility*, something that has little likelihood of being accomplished because existing structural conditions would require removing or *altering* a load-bearing member that is an essential part of the *structural frame*; or because other existing physical or *site* constraints prohibit modification or *addition* of *elements*, *spaces*, or features that are in full and strict compliance with the minimum requirements.

Teeing Ground. In golf, the starting place for the hole to be played.

Transfer Device. Equipment designed to facilitate the transfer of a person from a wheelchair or other mobility aid to and from an *amusement ride seat*.

Transient Lodging. A *building* or *facility* containing one or more guest room(s) for sleeping that provides accommodations that are primarily short-term in nature. *Transient lodging* does not include *residential dwelling units* intended to be used as a residence, inpatient medical care *facilities*, licensed long-term care *facilities*, detention or correctional *facilities*, or *private buildings or facilities* that contain not more than five rooms for rent or hire and that are actually occupied by the proprietor as the residence of such proprietor.

Transition Plate. A sloping pedestrian walking surface located at the end(s) of a *gangway*.

TTY. An abbreviation for teletypewriter. Machinery that employs interactive text-based communication through the transmission of coded signals across the telephone network. *TTYs* may include, for example, devices known as TDDs (telecommunication display devices or telecommunication devices for deaf persons) or computers with special modems. *TTYs* are also called text telephones.

Use Zone. The ground level area beneath and immediately adjacent to a play structure or play equipment that is designated by ASTM F 1487 (incorporated by reference, see "Referenced Standards" in Chapter 1) for unrestricted circulation around the play equipment and where it is predicted that a user would land when falling from or exiting the play equipment.

Vehicular Way. A route provided for vehicular traffic, such as in a street, driveway, or parking *facility*.

Walk. An exterior prepared surface for pedestrian use, including pedestrian areas such as plazas and courts.

Wheelchair Space. *Space* for a single wheelchair and its occupant.

Work Area Equipment. Any machine, instrument, engine, motor, pump, conveyor, or other apparatus used to perform work. As used in this document, this term shall apply only to equipment that is permanently installed or built-in in *employee work areas*. *Work area equipment* does not include passenger elevators and other accessible means of vertical transportation.

Printed by Builder's Book, Inc., Bookstore · www.buildersbook.com

ADA CHAPTER 2: SCOPING REQUIREMENTS

201 Application

201.1 Scope. All areas of newly designed and newly constructed *buildings* and *facilities* and *altered* portions of existing *buildings* and *facilities* shall comply with these requirements.

> **Advisory 201.1 Scope.** These requirements are to be applied to all areas of a facility unless exempted, or where scoping limits the number of multiple elements required to be accessible. For example, not all medical care patient rooms are required to be accessible; those that are not required to be accessible are not required to comply with these requirements. However, common use and public use spaces such as recovery rooms, examination rooms, and cafeterias are not exempt from these requirements and must be accessible.

201.2 Application Based on Building or Facility Use. Where a *site*, *building*, *facility*, room, or *space* contains more than one use, each portion shall comply with the applicable requirements for that use.

201.3 Temporary and Permanent Structures. These requirements shall apply to temporary and permanent *buildings* and *facilities*.

> **Advisory 201.3 Temporary and Permanent Structures.** Temporary buildings or facilities covered by these requirements include, but are not limited to, reviewing stands, temporary classrooms, bleacher areas, stages, platforms and daises, fixed furniture systems, wall systems, and exhibit areas, temporary banking facilities, and temporary health screening facilities. Structures and equipment directly associated with the actual processes of construction are not required to be accessible as permitted in 203.2.

202 Existing Buildings and Facilities

202.1 General. *Additions* and *alterations* to existing *buildings* or *facilities* shall comply with 202.

202.2 Additions. Each *addition* to an existing *building* or *facility* shall comply with the requirements for new construction. Each *addition* that affects or could affect the usability of or access to an area containing a primary function shall comply with 202.4.

202.3 Alterations. Where existing *elements* or *spaces* are *altered*, each *altered element* or *space* shall comply with the applicable requirements of Chapter 2.
EXCEPTIONS: 1. Unless required by 202.4, where *elements* or *spaces* are *altered* and the *circulation path* to the *altered element* or *space* is not *altered*, an *accessible* route shall not be required.
2. In *alterations*, where compliance with applicable requirements is *technically infeasible*, the *alteration* shall comply with the requirements to the maximum extent feasible.

3. *Residential dwelling units* not required to be *accessible* in compliance with a standard issued pursuant to the Americans with Disabilities Act or Section 504 of the Rehabilitation Act of 1973, as amended, shall not be required to comply with 202.3.

> **Advisory 202.3 Alterations.** Although covered entities are permitted to limit the scope of an alteration to individual elements, the alteration of multiple elements within a room or space may provide a cost-effective opportunity to make the entire room or space accessible. Any elements or spaces of the building or facility that are required to comply with these requirements must be made accessible within the scope of the alteration, to the maximum extent feasible. If providing accessibility in compliance with these requirements for people with one type of disability (e.g., people who use wheelchairs) is not feasible, accessibility must still be provided in compliance with the requirements for people with other types of disabilities (e.g., people who have hearing impairments or who have vision impairments) to the extent that such accessibility is feasible.

202.3.1 Prohibited Reduction in Access. An *alteration* that decreases or has the effect of decreasing the *accessibility* of a *building* or *facility* below the requirements for new construction at the time of the *alteration* is prohibited.

202.3.2 Extent of Application. An *alteration* of an existing *element*, *space*, or area of a *building* or *facility* shall not impose a requirement for *accessibility* greater than required for new construction.

202.4 Alterations Affecting Primary Function Areas. In addition to the requirements of 202.3, an *alteration* that affects or could affect the usability of or access to an area containing a primary function shall be made so as to ensure that, to the maximum extent feasible, the path of travel to the *altered* area, including the rest rooms, telephones, and drinking fountains serving the *altered* area, are readily *accessible* to and usable by individuals with disabilities, unless such *alterations* are disproportionate to the overall *alterations* in terms of cost and scope as determined under criteria established by the Attorney General. In existing transportation *facilities*, an area of primary function shall be as defined under regulations published by the Secretary of the Department of Transportation or the Attorney General.

    EXCEPTION: *Residential dwelling units* shall not be required to comply with 202.4.

> **Advisory 202.4 Alterations Affecting Primary Function Areas.** An area of a building or facility containing a major activity for which the building or facility is intended is a primary function area. Department of Justice ADA regulations state, "Alterations made to provide an accessible path of travel to the altered area will be deemed disproportionate to the overall alteration when the cost exceeds 20% of the cost of the alteration to the primary function area." (28 CFR 36.403 (f)(1)). See also Department of Transportation ADA regulations, which use similar concepts in the context of public sector transportation facilities (49 CFR 37.43 (e)(1)).
>
> There can be multiple areas containing a primary function in a single building. Primary function areas are not limited to public use areas. For example, both a bank lobby and the bank's employee areas such as the teller areas and walk-in safe are primary function areas.

Printed by Builder's Book, Inc., Bookstore · www.buildersbook.com

> **Advisory 202.4 Alterations Affecting Primary Function Areas (Continued).** Also, mixed use facilities may include numerous primary function areas for each use. Areas containing a primary function do not include: mechanical rooms, boiler rooms, supply storage rooms, employee lounges or locker rooms, janitorial closets, entrances, corridors, or restrooms.

202.5 Alterations to Qualified Historic Buildings and Facilities. *Alterations* to a *qualified historic building* or *facility* shall comply with 202.3 and 202.4.

EXCEPTION: Where the State Historic Preservation Officer or Advisory Council on Historic Preservation determines that compliance with the requirements for *accessible* routes, *entrances*, or toilet *facilities* would threaten or destroy the historic significance of the *building* or *facility*, the exceptions for *alterations* to *qualified historic buildings or facilities* for that *element* shall be permitted to apply.

> **Advisory 202.5 Alterations to Qualified Historic Buildings and Facilities Exception.** State Historic Preservation Officers are State appointed officials who carry out certain responsibilities under the National Historic Preservation Act. State Historic Preservation Officers consult with Federal and State agencies, local governments, and private entities on providing access and protecting significant elements of qualified historic buildings and facilities. There are exceptions for alterations to qualified historic buildings and facilities for accessible routes (206.2.1 Exception 1 and 206.2.3 Exception 7); entrances (206.4 Exception 2); and toilet facilities (213.2 Exception 2). When an entity believes that compliance with the requirements for any of these elements would threaten or destroy the historic significance of the building or facility, the entity should consult with the State Historic Preservation Officer. If the State Historic Preservation Officer agrees that compliance with the requirements for a specific element would threaten or destroy the historic significance of the building or facility, use of the exception is permitted. Public entities have an additional obligation to achieve program accessibility under the Department of Justice ADA regulations. See 28 CFR 35.150. These regulations require public entities that operate historic preservation programs to give priority to methods that provide physical access to individuals with disabilities. If alterations to a qualified historic building or facility to achieve program accessibility would threaten or destroy the historic significance of the building or facility, fundamentally alter the program, or result in undue financial or administrative burdens, the Department of Justice ADA regulations allow alternative methods to be used to achieve program accessibility. In the case of historic preservation programs, such as an historic house museum, alternative methods include using audio-visual materials to depict portions of the house that cannot otherwise be made accessible. In the case of other qualified historic properties, such as an historic government office building, alternative methods include relocating programs and services to accessible locations. The Department of Justice ADA regulations also allow public entities to use alternative methods when altering qualified historic buildings or facilities in the rare situations where the State Historic Preservation Officer determines that it is not feasible to provide physical access using the exceptions permitted in Section 202.5 without threatening or destroying the historic significance of the building or facility. See 28 CFR 35.151(d).

20

Advisory 202.5 Alterations to Qualified Historic Buildings and Facilities Exception (Continued). The AccessAbility Office at the National Endowment for the Arts (NEA) provides a variety of resources for museum operators and historic properties including: the Design for Accessibility Guide and the Disability Symbols. Contact NEA about these and other resources at (202) 682-5532 or www.arts.gov.

203 General Exceptions

203.1 General. *Sites, buildings, facilities,* and *elements* are exempt from these requirements to the extent specified by 203.

203.2 Construction Sites. Structures and *sites* directly associated with the actual processes of construction, including but not limited to, scaffolding, bridging, materials hoists, materials storage, and construction trailers shall not be required to comply with these requirements or to be on an *accessible* route. Portable toilet units provided for use exclusively by construction personnel on a construction *site* shall not be required to comply with 213 or to be on an *accessible* route.

203.3 Raised Areas. Areas raised primarily for purposes of security, life safety, or fire safety, including but not limited to, observation or lookout galleries, prison guard towers, fire towers, or life guard stands shall not be required to comply with these requirements or to be on an *accessible* route.

203.4 Limited Access Spaces. *Spaces* accessed only by ladders, catwalks, crawl *spaces*, or very narrow passageways shall not be required to comply with these requirements or to be on an *accessible* route.

203.5 Machinery Spaces. *Spaces* frequented only by service personnel for maintenance, repair, or occasional monitoring of equipment shall not be required to comply with these requirements or to be on an *accessible* route. Machinery *spaces* include, but are not limited to, elevator pits or elevator penthouses; mechanical, electrical or communications equipment rooms; piping or equipment catwalks; water or sewage treatment pump rooms and stations; electric substations and transformer vaults; and highway and tunnel utility *facilities*.

203.6 Single Occupant Structures. Single occupant structures accessed only by passageways below grade or elevated above standard curb height, including but not limited to, toll booths that are accessed only by underground tunnels, shall not be required to comply with these requirements or to be on an *accessible* route.

203.7 Detention and Correctional Facilities. In detention and correctional *facilities, common use* areas that are used only by inmates or detainees and security personnel and that do not serve holding cells or housing cells required to comply with 232, shall not be required to comply with these requirements or to be on an *accessible* route.

203.8 Residential Facilities. In residential *facilities, common use* areas that do not serve *residential dwelling units* required to provide mobility features complying with 809.2 through 809.4 shall not be required to comply with these requirements or to be on an *accessible* route.

203.9 Employee Work Areas. *Spaces* and *elements* within *employee work areas* shall only be required to comply with 206.2.8, 207.1, and 215.3 and shall be designed and constructed so that individuals with disabilities can approach, enter, and exit the *employee work area. Employee work areas,* or portions of *employee work areas,* that are less than 300 square feet (28 m²) and elevated 7 inches (180 mm) or more above the finish floor or ground where the elevation is essential to the function of the *space* shall not be required to comply with these requirements or to be on an *accessible* route.

> **Advisory 203.9 Employee Work Areas.** Although areas used exclusively by employees for work are not required to be fully accessible, consider designing such areas to include non-required turning spaces, and provide accessible elements whenever possible. Under the ADA, employees with disabilities are entitled to reasonable accommodations in the workplace; accommodations can include alterations to spaces within the facility. Designing employee work areas to be more accessible at the outset will avoid more costly retrofits when current employees become temporarily or permanently disabled, or when new employees with disabilities are hired. Contact the Equal Employment Opportunity Commission (EEOC) at www.eeoc.gov for information about title I of the ADA prohibiting discrimination against people with disabilities in the workplace.

203.10 Raised Refereeing, Judging, and Scoring Areas. Raised structures used solely for refereeing, judging, or scoring a sport shall not be required to comply with these requirements or to be on an *accessible* route.

203.11 Water Slides. Water slides shall not be required to comply with these requirements or to be on an *accessible* route.

203.12 Animal Containment Areas. Animal containment areas that are not for *public use* shall not be required to comply with these requirements or to be on an *accessible* route.

> **Advisory 203.12 Animal Containment Areas.** Public circulation routes where animals may travel, such as in petting zoos and passageways alongside animal pens in State fairs, are not eligible for the exception.

203.13 Raised Boxing or Wrestling Rings. Raised boxing or wrestling rings shall not be required to comply with these requirements or to be on an *accessible* route.

203.14 Raised Diving Boards and Diving Platforms. Raised diving boards and diving platforms shall not be required to comply with these requirements or to be on an *accessible* route.

204 Protruding Objects

204.1 General. Protruding objects on *circulation paths* shall comply with 307.
    EXCEPTIONS: 1. Within *areas of sport activity*, protruding objects on *circulation paths* shall not be required to comply with 307.
    2. Within *play areas*, protruding objects on *circulation paths* shall not be required to comply with 307 provided that ground level *accessible* routes provide vertical clearance in compliance with 1008.2.

205 Operable Parts

205.1 General. *Operable parts* on *accessible elements, accessible* routes, and in *accessible* rooms and *spaces* shall comply with 309.
   EXCEPTIONS: 1. *Operable parts* that are intended for use only by service or maintenance personnel shall not be required to comply with 309.
   2. Electrical or communication receptacles serving a dedicated use shall not be required to comply with 309.
   3. Where two or more outlets are provided in a kitchen above a length of counter top that is uninterrupted by a sink or appliance, one outlet shall not be required to comply with 309.
   4. Floor electrical receptacles shall not be required to comply with 309.
   5. HVAC diffusers shall not be required to comply with 309.
   6. Except for light switches, where redundant controls are provided for a single *element*, one control in each *space* shall not be required to comply with 309.
   7. Cleats and other boat securement devices shall not be required to comply with 309.3.
   8. Exercise machines and exercise equipment shall not be required to comply with 309.

> **Advisory 205.1 General.** Controls covered by 205.1 include, but are not limited to, light switches, circuit breakers, duplexes and other convenience receptacles, environmental and appliance controls, plumbing fixture controls, and security and intercom systems.

206 Accessible Routes

206.1 General. *Accessible* routes shall be provided in accordance with 206 and shall comply with Chapter 4.

206.2 Where Required. *Accessible* routes shall be provided where required by 206.2.

   206.2.1 Site Arrival Points. At least one *accessible* route shall be provided within the *site* from *accessible* parking *spaces* and *accessible* passenger loading zones; public streets and sidewalks; and public transportation stops to the *accessible building* or *facility entrance* they serve.
      EXCEPTIONS: 1. Where exceptions for *alterations* to *qualified historic buildings or facilities* are permitted by 202.5, no more than one *accessible* route from a *site* arrival point to an *accessible entrance* shall be required.
      2. An *accessible* route shall not be required between *site* arrival points and the *building* or *facility entrance* if the only means of access between them is a *vehicular way* not providing pedestrian access.

> **Advisory 206.2.1 Site Arrival Points.** Each site arrival point must be connected by an accessible route to the accessible building entrance or entrances served. Where two or more similar site arrival points, such as bus stops, serve the same accessible entrance or entrances, both bus stops must be on accessible routes. In addition, the accessible routes must serve all of the accessible entrances on the site.

Advisory 206.2.1 Site Arrival Points Exception 2. Access from site arrival points may include vehicular ways. Where a vehicular way, or a portion of a vehicular way, is provided for pedestrian travel, such as within a shopping center or shopping mall parking lot, this exception does not apply.

206.2.2 Within a Site. At least one *accessible* route shall connect *accessible buildings, accessible facilities, accessible elements*, and *accessible spaces* that are on the same *site*.
  EXCEPTION: An *accessible* route shall not be required between *accessible buildings, accessible facilities, accessible elements,* and *accessible spaces* if the only means of access between them is a *vehicular way* not providing pedestrian access.

Advisory 206.2.2 Within a Site. An accessible route is required to connect to the boundary of each area of sport activity. Examples of areas of sport activity include: soccer fields, basketball courts, baseball fields, running tracks, skating rinks, and the area surrounding a piece of gymnastic equipment. While the size of an area of sport activity may vary from sport to sport, each includes only the space needed to play. Where multiple sports fields or courts are provided, an accessible route is required to each field or area of sport activity.

206.2.3 Multi-Story Buildings and Facilities. At least one *accessible* route shall connect each *story* and *mezzanine* in multi-*story buildings* and *facilities*.
  EXCEPTIONS: 1. In *private buildings or facilities* that are less than three *stories* or that have less than 3000 square feet (279 m^2) per *story*, an *accessible* route shall not be required to connect *stories* provided that the *building* or *facility* is not a shopping center, a shopping mall, the professional office of a health care provider, a terminal, depot or other station used for specified public transportation, an airport passenger terminal, or another type of *facility* as determined by the Attorney General.
  2. Where a two *story public building or facility* has one *story* with an *occupant load* of five or fewer persons that does not contain *public use space*, that *story* shall not be required to be connected to the *story* above or below.
  3. In detention and correctional *facilities*, an *accessible* route shall not be required to connect *stories* where cells with mobility features required to comply with 807.2, all *common use* areas serving cells with mobility features required to comply with 807.2, and all *public use* areas are on an *accessible* route.
  4. In residential *facilities*, an *accessible* route shall not be required to connect *stories* where *residential dwelling units* with mobility features required to comply with 809.2 through 809.4, all *common use* areas serving *residential dwelling units* with mobility features required to comply with 809.2 through 809.4, and *public use* areas serving *residential dwelling units* are on an *accessible* route.
  5. Within multi-*story transient lodging* guest rooms with mobility features required to comply with 806.2, an *accessible* route shall not be required to connect *stories* provided that *spaces* complying with 806.2 are on an *accessible* route and sleeping accommodations for two persons minimum are provided on a *story* served by an accessible route.
  6. In air traffic control towers, an *accessible* route shall not be required to serve the cab and the floor immediately below the cab.

7. Where exceptions for *alterations* to *qualified historic buildings or facilities* are permitted by 202.5, an *accessible* route shall not be required to *stories* located above or below the *accessible story*.

> **Advisory 206.2.3 Multi-Story Buildings and Facilities.** Spaces and elements located on a level not required to be served by an accessible route must fully comply with this document. While a mezzanine may be a change in level, it is not a story. If an accessible route is required to connect stories within a building or facility, the accessible route must serve all mezzanines.
>
> **Advisory 206.2.3 Multi-Story Buildings and Facilities Exception 4.** Where common use areas are provided for the use of residents, it is presumed that all such common use areas "serve" accessible dwelling units unless use is restricted to residents occupying certain dwelling units. For example, if all residents are permitted to use all laundry rooms, then all laundry rooms "serve" accessible dwelling units. However, if the laundry room on the first floor is restricted to use by residents on the first floor, and the second floor laundry room is for use by occupants of the second floor, then first floor accessible units are "served" only by laundry rooms on the first floor. In this example, an accessible route is not required to the second floor provided that all accessible units and all common use areas serving them are on the first floor.

206.2.3.1 Stairs and Escalators in Existing Buildings. In *alterations* and *additions*, where an escalator or stair is provided where none existed previously and major structural modifications are necessary for the installation, an *accessible* route shall be provided between the levels served by the escalator or stair unless exempted by 206.2.3 Exceptions 1 through 7.

206.2.4 Spaces and Elements. At least one *accessible* route shall connect *accessible building* or *facility entrances* with all *accessible spaces* and *elements* within the *building* or *facility* which are otherwise connected by a *circulation path* unless exempted by 206.2.3 Exceptions 1 through 7.

EXCEPTIONS: 1. Raised courtroom stations, including judges' benches, clerks' stations, bailiffs' stations, deputy clerks' stations, and court reporters' stations shall not be required to provide vertical access provided that the required clear floor *space*, maneuvering *space*, and, if appropriate, electrical service are installed at the time of initial construction to allow future installation of a means of vertical access complying with 405, 407, 408, or 410 without requiring substantial reconstruction of the *space*.

2. In *assembly areas* with fixed seating required to comply with 221, an *accessible* route shall not be required to serve fixed seating where *wheelchair spaces* required to be on an *accessible* route are not provided.

3. *Accessible* routes shall not be required to connect *mezzanines* where *buildings* or *facilities* have no more than one story. In addition, *accessible* routes shall not be required to connect stories or *mezzanines* where multi-story *buildings* or *facilities* are exempted by 206.2.3 Exceptions 1 through 7.

Advisory 206.2.4 Spaces and Elements. Accessible routes must connect all spaces and elements required to be accessible including, but not limited to, raised areas and speaker platforms.

Advisory 206.2.4 Spaces and Elements Exception 1. The exception does not apply to areas that are likely to be used by members of the public who are not employees of the court such as jury areas, attorney areas, or witness stands.

206.2.5 Restaurants and Cafeterias. In restaurants and cafeterias, an *accessible* route shall be provided to all dining areas, including raised or sunken dining areas, and outdoor dining areas.
EXCEPTIONS: 1. In *buildings or facilities* not required to provide an *accessible* route between *stories*, an *accessible* route shall not be required to a *mezzanine* dining area where the *mezzanine* contains less than 25 percent of the total combined area for seating and dining and where the same decor and services are provided in the *accessible* area.
2. In *alterations*, an *accessible* route shall not be required to existing raised or sunken dining areas, or to all parts of existing outdoor dining areas where the same services and decor are provided in an *accessible space* usable by the public and not restricted to use by people with disabilities.
3. In sports *facilities*, tiered dining areas providing seating required to comply with 221 shall be required to have *accessible* routes serving at least 25 percent of the dining area provided that *accessible* routes serve seating complying with 221 and each tier is provided with the same services.

Advisory 206.2.5 Restaurants and Cafeterias Exception 2. Examples of "same services" include, but are not limited to, bar service, rooms having smoking and non-smoking sections, lotto and other table games, carry-out, and buffet service. Examples of "same decor" include, but are not limited to, seating at or near windows and railings with views, areas designed with a certain theme, party and banquet rooms, and rooms where entertainment is provided.

206.2.6 Performance Areas. Where a *circulation path* directly connects a performance area to an assembly seating area, an *accessible* route shall directly connect the assembly seating area with the performance area. An *accessible* route shall be provided from performance areas to ancillary areas or *facilities* used by performers unless exempted by 206.2.3 Exceptions 1 through 7.

206.2.7 Press Boxes. Press boxes in *assembly areas* shall be on an *accessible* route.
EXCEPTIONS: 1. An *accessible* route shall not be required to press boxes in bleachers that have points of entry at only one level provided that the aggregate area of all press boxes is 500 square feet (46 m^2) maximum.
2. An *accessible* route shall not be required to free-standing press boxes that are elevated above grade 12 feet (3660 mm) minimum provided that the aggregate area of all press boxes is 500 square feet (46 m^2) maximum.

Advisory 206.2.7 Press Boxes Exception 2. Where a facility contains multiple assembly areas, the aggregate area of the press boxes in each assembly area is to be calculated separately. For example, if a university has a soccer stadium with three press boxes elevated 12 feet (3660 mm) or more above grade and each press box is 150 square feet (14 m^2), then the aggregate area of the soccer stadium press boxes is less than 500 square feet (46 m^2) and Exception 2 applies to the soccer stadium. If that same university also has a football stadium with two press boxes elevated 12 feet (3660 mm) or more above grade and one press box is 250 square feet (23 m^2), and the second is 275 square feet (26 m^2), then the aggregate area of the football stadium press boxes is more than 500 square feet (46 m^2) and Exception 2 does not apply to the football stadium.

206.2.8 Employee Work Areas. *Common use circulation paths* within *employee work areas* shall comply with 402.

    EXCEPTIONS: 1. *Common use circulation paths* located within *employee work areas* that are less than 1000 square feet (93 m^2) and defined by permanently installed partitions, counters, casework, or furnishings shall not be required to comply with 402.

    2. *Common use circulation paths* located within *employee work areas* that are an integral component of *work area equipment* shall not be required to comply with 402.

    3. *Common use circulation paths* located within exterior *employee work areas* that are fully exposed to the weather shall not be required to comply with 402.

Advisory 206.2.8 Employee Work Areas Exception 1. Modular furniture that is not permanently installed is not directly subject to these requirements. The Department of Justice ADA regulations provide additional guidance regarding the relationship between these requirements and elements that are not part of the built environment. Additionally, the Equal Employment Opportunity Commission (EEOC) implements title I of the ADA which requires non-discrimination in the workplace. EEOC can provide guidance regarding employers' obligations to provide reasonable accommodations for employees with disabilities.

Advisory 206.2.8 Employee Work Areas Exception 2. Large pieces of equipment, such as electric turbines or water pumping apparatus, may have stairs and elevated walkways used for overseeing or monitoring purposes which are physically part of the turbine or pump. However, passenger elevators used for vertical transportation between stories are not considered "work area equipment" as defined in Section 106.5.

206.2.9 Amusement Rides. *Amusement rides* required to comply with 234 shall provide *accessible* routes in accordance with 206.2.9. *Accessible* routes serving *amusement rides* shall comply with Chapter 4 except as modified by 1002.2.

    206.2.9.1 Load and Unload Areas. Load and unload areas shall be on an *accessible* route. Where load and unload areas have more than one loading or unloading position, at least one loading and unloading position shall be on an *accessible* route.

27

206.2.9.2 Wheelchair Spaces, Ride Seats Designed for Transfer, and Transfer Devices. When *amusement rides* are in the load and unload position, *wheelchair spaces* complying with 1002.4, *amusement ride seats* designed for transfer complying with 1002.5, and *transfer devices* complying with 1002.6 shall be on an *accessible* route.

206.2.10 Recreational Boating Facilities. *Boat slips* required to comply with 235.2 and *boarding piers* at *boat launch ramps* required to comply with 235.3 shall be on an *accessible* route. *Accessible* routes serving recreational boating *facilities* shall comply with Chapter 4, except as modified by 1003.2.

206.2.11 Bowling Lanes. Where bowling lanes are provided, at least 5 percent, but no fewer than one of each type of bowling lane, shall be on an *accessible* route.

206.2.12 Court Sports. In court sports, at least one *accessible* route shall directly connect both sides of the court.

206.2.13 Exercise Machines and Equipment. Exercise machines and equipment required to comply with 236 shall be on an *accessible* route.

206.2.14 Fishing Piers and Platforms. Fishing piers and platforms shall be on an *accessible* route. *Accessible* routes serving fishing piers and platforms shall comply with Chapter 4 except as modified by 1005.1.

206.2.15 Golf Facilities. At least one *accessible* route shall connect *accessible elements* and *spaces* within the boundary of the golf course. In addition, *accessible* routes serving golf car rental areas; bag drop areas; course weather shelters complying with 238.2.3; course toilet rooms; and practice putting greens, practice *teeing grounds*, and teeing stations at driving ranges complying with 238.3 shall comply with Chapter 4 except as modified by 1006.2.
   EXCEPTION: *Golf car passages* complying with 1006.3 shall be permitted to be used for all or part of *accessible* routes required by 206.2.15.

206.2.16 Miniature Golf Facilities. Holes required to comply with 239.2, including the start of play, shall be on an *accessible* route. *Accessible* routes serving miniature golf *facilities* shall comply with Chapter 4 except as modified by 1007.2.

206.2.17 Play Areas. *Play areas* shall provide *accessible* routes in accordance with 206.2.17. *Accessible* routes serving *play areas* shall comply with Chapter 4 except as modified by 1008.2.

206.2.17.1 Ground Level and Elevated Play Components. At least one *accessible* route shall be provided within the *play area*. The *accessible* route shall connect *ground level play components* required to comply with 240.2.1 and *elevated play components* required to comply with 240.2.2, including entry and exit points of the *play components*.

206.2.17.2 Soft Contained Play Structures. Where three or fewer entry points are provided for *soft contained play structures*, at least one entry point shall be on an *accessible* route. Where four or more entry points are provided for *soft contained play structures*, at least two entry points shall be on an *accessible* route.

206.3 Location. *Accessible* routes shall coincide with or be located in the same area as general *circulation paths*. Where *circulation paths* are interior, required *accessible* routes shall also be interior.

> **Advisory 206.3 Location.** The accessible route must be in the same area as the general circulation path. This means that circulation paths, such as vehicular ways designed for pedestrian traffic, walks, and unpaved paths that are designed to be routinely used by pedestrians must be accessible or have an accessible route nearby. Additionally, accessible vertical interior circulation must be in the same area as stairs and escalators, not isolated in the back of the facility.

206.4 Entrances. *Entrances* shall be provided in accordance with 206.4. *Entrance* doors, doorways, and gates shall comply with 404 and shall be on an *accessible* route complying with 402.
    EXCEPTIONS: 1. Where an *alteration* includes *alterations* to an *entrance*, and the *building* or *facility* has another *entrance* complying with 404 that is on an *accessible* route, the *altered entrance* shall not be required to comply with 206.4 unless required by 202.4.
    2. Where exceptions for *alterations* to *qualified historic buildings or facilities* are permitted by 202.5, no more than one *public entrance* shall be required to comply with 206.4. Where no *public entrance* can comply with 206.4 under criteria established in 202.5 Exception, then either an unlocked *entrance* not used by the public shall comply with 206.4; or a locked *entrance* complying with 206.4 with a notification system or remote monitoring shall be provided.

206.4.1 Public Entrances. In addition to *entrances* required by 206.4.2 through 206.4.9, at least 60 percent of all *public entrances* shall comply with 404.

206.4.2 Parking Structure Entrances. Where direct access is provided for pedestrians from a parking structure to a *building* or *facility entrance*, each direct access to the *building* or *facility entrance* shall comply with 404.

206.4.3 Entrances from Tunnels or Elevated Walkways. Where direct access is provided for pedestrians from a pedestrian tunnel or elevated walkway to a *building* or *facility*, at least one direct *entrance* to the *building* or *facility* from each tunnel or walkway shall comply with 404.

206.4.4 Transportation Facilities. In addition to the requirements of 206.4.2, 206.4.3, and 206.4.5 through 206.4.9, transportation *facilities* shall provide *entrances* in accordance with 206.4.4.

    206.4.4.1 Location. In transportation *facilities*, where different *entrances* serve different transportation fixed routes or groups of fixed routes, at least one *public entrance* shall comply with 404.
        EXCEPTION: *Entrances* to *key stations* and existing intercity rail stations retrofitted in accordance with 49 CFR 37.49 or 49 CFR 37.51 shall not be required to comply with 206.4.4.1.

206.4.4.2 Direct Connections. Direct connections to other *facilities* shall provide an *accessible* route complying with 404 from the point of connection to boarding platforms and all transportation system *elements* required to be *accessible*. Any *elements* provided to facilitate future direct connections shall be on an *accessible* route connecting boarding platforms and all transportation system *elements* required to be *accessible*.

> **EXCEPTION:** In *key stations* and existing intercity rail stations, existing direct connections shall not be required to comply with 404.

206.4.4.3 Key Stations and Intercity Rail Stations. *Key stations* and existing intercity rail stations required by Subpart C of 49 CFR part 37 to be *altered*, shall have at least one *entrance* complying with 404.

206.4.5 Tenant Spaces. At least one *accessible entrance* to each tenancy in a *facility* shall comply with 404.

> **EXCEPTION:** *Self-service storage facilities* not required to comply with 225.3 shall not be required to be on an accessible route.

206.4.6 Residential Dwelling Unit Primary Entrance. In *residential dwelling units*, at least one primary *entrance* shall comply with 404. The primary *entrance* to a *residential dwelling unit* shall not be to a bedroom.

206.4.7 Restricted Entrances. Where *restricted entrances* are provided to a *building* or *facility*, at least one *restricted entrance* to the *building* or *facility* shall comply with 404.

206.4.8 Service Entrances. If a *service entrance* is the only *entrance* to a *building* or to a tenancy in a *facility*, that *entrance* shall comply with 404.

206.4.9 Entrances for Inmates or Detainees. Where *entrances* used only by inmates or detainees and security personnel are provided at judicial *facilities*, detention *facilities*, or correctional *facilities*, at least one such *entrance* shall comply with 404.

206.5 Doors, Doorways, and Gates. Doors, doorways, and gates providing user passage shall be provided in accordance with 206.5.

206.5.1 Entrances. Each *entrance* to a *building* or *facility* required to comply with 206.4 shall have at least one door, doorway, or gate complying with 404.

206.5.2 Rooms and Spaces. Within a *building* or *facility*, at least one door, doorway, or gate serving each room or *space* complying with these requirements shall comply with 404.

206.5.3 Transient Lodging Facilities. In *transient lodging facilities*, *entrances*, doors, and doorways providing user passage into and within guest rooms that are not required to provide mobility features complying with 806.2 shall comply with 404.2.3.

> **EXCEPTION:** Shower and sauna doors in guest rooms that are not required to provide mobility features complying with 806.2 shall not be required to comply with 404.2.3.

206.5.4 Residential Dwelling Units. In *residential dwelling units* required to provide mobility features complying with 809.2 through 809.4, all doors and doorways providing user passage shall comply with 404.

206.6 Elevators. Elevators provided for passengers shall comply with 407. Where multiple elevators are provided, each elevator shall comply with 407.
  EXCEPTIONS: 1. In a *building* or *facility* permitted to use the exceptions to 206.2.3 or permitted by 206.7 to use a platform lift, elevators complying with 408 shall be permitted.
  2. Elevators complying with 408 or 409 shall be permitted in multi-*story residential dwelling units*.

206.6.1 Existing Elevators. Where *elements* of existing elevators are *altered*, the same *element* shall also be *altered* in all elevators that are programmed to respond to the same hall call control as the *altered* elevator and shall comply with the requirements of 407 for the *altered element*.

206.7 Platform Lifts. Platform lifts shall comply with 410. Platform lifts shall be permitted as a component of an *accessible* route in new construction in accordance with 206.7. Platform lifts shall be permitted as a component of an *accessible* route in an existing *building* or *facility*.

206.7.1 Performance Areas and Speakers' Platforms. Platform lifts shall be permitted to provide *accessible* routes to performance areas and speakers' platforms.

206.7.2 Wheelchair Spaces. Platform lifts shall be permitted to provide an *accessible* route to comply with the *wheelchair space* dispersion and line-of-sight requirements of 221 and 802.

206.7.3 Incidental Spaces. Platform lifts shall be permitted to provide an *accessible* route to incidental *spaces* which are not *public use spaces* and which are occupied by five persons maximum.

206.7.4 Judicial Spaces. Platform lifts shall be permitted to provide an *accessible* route to: jury boxes and witness stands; raised courtroom stations including, judges' benches, clerks' stations, bailiffs' stations, deputy clerks' stations, and court reporters' stations; and to depressed areas such as the well of a court.

206.7.5 Existing Site Constraints. Platform lifts shall be permitted where existing exterior *site* constraints make use of a *ramp* or elevator infeasible.

> **Advisory 206.7.5 Existing Site Constraints.** This exception applies where topography or other similar existing site constraints necessitate the use of a platform lift as the only feasible alternative. While the site constraint must reflect exterior conditions, the lift can be installed in the interior of a building. For example, a new building constructed between and connected to two existing buildings may have insufficient space to coordinate floor levels and also to provide ramped entry from the public way. In this example, an exterior or interior platform lift could be used to provide an accessible entrance or to coordinate one or more interior floor levels.

206.7.6 Guest Rooms and Residential Dwelling Units. Platform lifts shall be permitted to connect levels within *transient lodging* guest rooms required to provide mobility features complying with 806.2 or *residential dwelling units* required to provide mobility features complying with 809.2 through 809.4.

206.7.7 Amusement Rides. Platform lifts shall be permitted to provide *accessible* routes to load and unload areas serving *amusement rides.*

206.7.8 Play Areas. Platform lifts shall be permitted to provide *accessible* routes to *play components* or *soft contained play structures.*

206.7.9 Team or Player Seating. Platform lifts shall be permitted to provide *accessible* routes to team or player seating areas serving *areas of sport activity.*

> **Advisory 206.7.9 Team or Player Seating.** While the use of platform lifts is allowed, ramps are recommended to provide access to player seating areas serving an area of sport activity.

206.7.10 Recreational Boating Facilities and Fishing Piers and Platforms. Platform lifts shall be permitted to be used instead of *gangways* that are part of *accessible* routes serving recreational boating *facilities* and fishing piers and platforms.

206.8 Security Barriers. Security barriers, including but not limited to, security bollards and security check points, shall not obstruct a required *accessible* route or *accessible means of egress.*
   EXCEPTION: Where security barriers incorporate *elements* that cannot comply with these requirements such as certain metal detectors, fluoroscopes, or other similar devices, the *accessible* route shall be permitted to be located adjacent to security screening devices. The *accessible* route shall permit persons with disabilities passing around security barriers to maintain visual contact with their personal items to the same extent provided others passing through the security barrier.

207 Accessible Means of Egress

207.1 General. Means of egress shall comply with section 1003.2.13 of the International Building Code (2000 edition and 2001 Supplement) or section 1007 of the International Building Code (2003 edition) (incorporated by reference, see "Referenced Standards" in Chapter 1).
   EXCEPTIONS: 1. Where means of egress are permitted by local *building* or life safety codes to share a common path of egress travel, *accessible means of egress* shall be permitted to share a common path of egress travel.
   2. Areas of refuge shall not be required in detention and correctional *facilities.*

207.2 Platform Lifts. Standby power shall be provided for platform lifts permitted by section 1003.2.13.4 of the International Building Code (2000 edition and 2001 Supplement) or section 1007.5 of the International Building Code (2003 edition) (incorporated by reference, see "Referenced Standards" in Chapter 1) to serve as a part of an *accessible means of egress.*

208 Parking Spaces

208.1 General. Where parking *spaces* are provided, parking *spaces* shall be provided in accordance with 208.

EXCEPTION: Parking *spaces* used exclusively for buses, trucks, other delivery vehicles, law enforcement vehicles, or vehicular impound shall not be required to comply with 208 provided that lots accessed by the public are provided with a passenger loading zone complying with 503.

208.2 Minimum Number. Parking *spaces* complying with 502 shall be provided in accordance with Table 208.2 except as required by 208.2.1, 208.2.2, and 208.2.3. Where more than one parking *facility* is provided on a *site*, the number of *accessible spaces* provided on the *site* shall be calculated according to the number of *spaces* required for each parking *facility*.

Table 208.2 Parking Spaces

Total Number of Parking Spaces Provided in Parking Facility	Minimum Number of Required Accessible Parking Spaces
1 to 25	1
26 to 50	2
51 to 75	3
76 to 100	4
101 to 150	5
151 to 200	6
201 to 300	7
301 to 400	8
401 to 500	9
501 to 1000	2 percent of total
1001 and over	20, plus 1 for each 100, or fraction thereof, over 1000

Advisory 208.2 Minimum Number. The term "parking facility" is used Section 208.2 instead of the term "parking lot" so that it is clear that both parking lots and parking structures are required to comply with this section. The number of parking spaces required to be accessible is to be calculated separately for each parking facility; the required number is not to be based on the total number of parking spaces provided in all of the parking facilities provided on the site.

208.2.1 Hospital Outpatient Facilities. Ten percent of patient and visitor parking *spaces* provided to serve hospital outpatient *facilities* shall comply with 502.

> **Advisory 208.2.1 Hospital Outpatient Facilities.** The term "outpatient facility" is not defined in this document but is intended to cover facilities or units that are located in hospitals and that provide regular and continuing medical treatment without an overnight stay. Doctors' offices, independent clinics, or other facilities not located in hospitals are not considered hospital outpatient facilities for purposes of this document.

208.2.2 Rehabilitation Facilities and Outpatient Physical Therapy Facilities. Twenty percent of patient and visitor parking *spaces* provided to serve rehabilitation *facilities* specializing in treating conditions that affect mobility and outpatient physical therapy *facilities* shall comply with 502.

> **Advisory 208.2.2 Rehabilitation Facilities and Outpatient Physical Therapy Facilities.** Conditions that affect mobility include conditions requiring the use or assistance of a brace, cane, crutch, prosthetic device, wheelchair, or powered mobility aid; arthritic, neurological, or orthopedic conditions that severely limit one's ability to walk; respiratory diseases and other conditions which may require the use of portable oxygen; and cardiac conditions that impose significant functional limitations.

208.2.3 Residential Facilities. Parking *spaces* provided to serve residential facilities shall comply with 208.2.3.

208.2.3.1 Parking for Residents. Where at least one parking *space* is provided for each *residential dwelling unit*, at least one parking *space* complying with 502 shall be provided for each *residential dwelling unit* required to provide mobility features complying with 809.2 through 809.4.

208.2.3.2 Additional Parking Spaces for Residents. Where the total number of parking *spaces* provided for each *residential dwelling unit* exceeds one parking *space* per *residential dwelling unit*, 2 percent, but no fewer than one *space,* of all the parking *spaces* not covered by 208.2.3.1 shall comply with 502.

208.2.3.3 Parking for Guests, Employees, and Other Non-Residents. Where parking spaces are provided for persons other than residents, parking shall be provided in accordance with Table 208.2.

208.2.4 Van Parking Spaces. For every six or fraction of six parking *spaces* required by 208.2 to comply with 502, at least one shall be a van parking *space* complying with 502.

208.3 Location. Parking *facilities* shall comply with 208.3

208.3.1 General. Parking *spaces* complying with 502 that serve a particular *building* or *facility* shall be located on the shortest *accessible* route from parking to an *entrance* complying with 206.4. Where parking serves more than one *accessible entrance*, parking *spaces* complying with 502 shall be dispersed and located on the shortest *accessible* route to the *accessible entrances*. In parking

34

facilities that do not serve a particular *building* or *facility*, parking *spaces* complying with 502 shall be located on the shortest *accessible* route to an *accessible* pedestrian *entrance* of the parking *facility*.

    EXCEPTIONS: 1. All van parking *spaces* shall be permitted to be grouped on one level within a multi-*story* parking *facility*.

    2. Parking *spaces* shall be permitted to be located in different parking *facilities* if substantially equivalent or greater *accessibility* is provided in terms of distance from an *accessible entrance* or *entrances*, parking fee, and user convenience.

> **Advisory 208.3.1 General Exception 2.** Factors that could affect "user convenience" include, but are not limited to, protection from the weather, security, lighting, and comparative maintenance of the alternative parking site.

208.3.2 Residential Facilities. In residential *facilities* containing *residential dwelling units* required to provide mobility features complying with 809.2 through 809.4, parking *spaces* provided in accordance with 208.2.3.1 shall be located on the shortest *accessible* route to the *residential dwelling unit entrance* they serve. *Spaces* provided in accordance with 208.2.3.2 shall be dispersed throughout all types of parking provided for the *residential dwelling units*.

    EXCEPTION: Parking *spaces* provided in accordance with 208.2.3.2 shall not be required to be dispersed throughout all types of parking if substantially equivalent or greater *accessibility* is provided in terms of distance from an *accessible entrance*, parking fee, and user convenience.

> **Advisory 208.3.2 Residential Facilities Exception.** Factors that could affect "user convenience" include, but are not limited to, protection from the weather, security, lighting, and comparative maintenance of the alternative parking site.

209 Passenger Loading Zones and Bus Stops

209.1 General. Passenger loading zones shall be provided in accordance with 209.

209.2 Type. Where provided, passenger loading zones shall comply with 209.2.

209.2.1 Passenger Loading Zones. Passenger loading zones, except those required to comply with 209.2.2 and 209.2.3, shall provide at least one passenger loading zone complying with 503 in every continuous 100 linear feet (30 m) of loading zone *space*, or fraction thereof.

209.2.2 Bus Loading Zones. In bus loading zones restricted to use by designated or specified public transportation vehicles, each bus bay, bus stop, or other area designated for lift or *ramp* deployment shall comply with 810.2.

> **Advisory 209.2.2 Bus Loading Zones.** The terms "designated public transportation" and "specified public transportation" are defined by the Department of Transportation at 49 CFR 37.3 in regulations implementing the Americans with Disabilities Act. These terms refer to public transportation services provided by public or private entities, respectively. For example, designated public transportation vehicles include buses and vans operated by public transit agencies, while specified public transportation vehicles include tour and charter buses, taxis and limousines, and hotel shuttles operated by private entities.

35

209.2.3 On-Street Bus Stops. On-street bus stops shall comply with 810.2 to the maximum extent practicable.

209.3 Medical Care and Long-Term Care Facilities. At least one passenger loading zone complying with 503 shall be provided at an *accessible entrance* to licensed medical care and licensed long-term care *facilities* where the period of stay exceeds twenty-four hours.

209.4 Valet Parking. Parking *facilities* that provide valet parking services shall provide at least one passenger loading zone complying with 503.

209.5 Mechanical Access Parking Garages. Mechanical access parking garages shall provide at least one passenger loading zone complying with 503 at vehicle drop-off and vehicle pick-up areas.

210 Stairways

210.1 General. Interior and exterior stairs that are part of a means of egress shall comply with 504.
    EXCEPTIONS: 1. In detention and correctional *facilities*, stairs that are not located in *public use* areas shall not be required to comply with 504.
    2. In *alterations*, stairs between levels that are connected by an *accessible* route shall not be required to comply with 504, except that handrails complying with 505 shall be provided when the stairs are *altered*.
    3. In *assembly areas*, aisle stairs shall not be required to comply with 504.
    4. Stairs that connect *play components* shall not be required to comply with 504.

> **Advisory 210.1 General.** Although these requirements do not mandate handrails on stairs that are not part of a means of egress, State or local building codes may require handrails or guards.

211 Drinking Fountains

211.1 General. Where drinking fountains are provided on an exterior *site*, on a floor, or within a secured area they shall be provided in accordance with 211.
    EXCEPTION: In detention or correctional *facilities*, drinking fountains only serving holding or housing cells not required to comply with 232 shall not be required to comply with 211.

211.2 Minimum Number. No fewer than two drinking fountains shall be provided. One drinking fountain shall comply with 602.1 through 602.6 and one drinking fountain shall comply with 602.7.
    EXCEPTION: Where a single drinking fountain complies with 602.1 through 602.6 and 602.7, it shall be permitted to be substituted for two separate drinking fountains.

211.3 More Than Minimum Number. Where more than the minimum number of drinking fountains specified in 211.2 are provided, 50 percent of the total number of drinking fountains provided shall comply with 602.1 through 602.6, and 50 percent of the total number of drinking fountains provided shall comply with 602.7.

EXCEPTION: Where 50 percent of the drinking fountains yields a fraction, 50 percent shall be permitted to be rounded up or down provided that the total number of drinking fountains complying with 211 equals 100 percent of drinking fountains.

212 Kitchens, Kitchenettes, and Sinks

212.1 General. Where provided, kitchens, kitchenettes, and sinks shall comply with 212.

212.2 Kitchens and Kitchenettes. Kitchens and kitchenettes shall comply with 804.

212.3 Sinks. Where sinks are provided, at least 5 percent, but no fewer than one, of each type provided in each *accessible* room or *space* shall comply with 606.
    EXCEPTION: Mop or service sinks shall not be required to comply with 212.3.

213 Toilet Facilities and Bathing Facilities

213.1 General. Where toilet *facilities* and bathing *facilities* are provided, they shall comply with 213. Where toilet *facilities* and bathing *facilities* are provided in *facilities* permitted by 206.2.3 Exceptions 1 and 2 not to connect *stories* by an *accessible* route, toilet *facilities* and bathing *facilities* shall be provided on a *story* connected by an *accessible* route to an *accessible entrance*.

213.2 Toilet Rooms and Bathing Rooms. Where toilet rooms are provided, each toilet room shall comply with 603. Where bathing rooms are provided, each bathing room shall comply with 603.
    EXCEPTIONS: 1. In *alterations* where it is *technically infeasible* to comply with 603, *altering* existing toilet or bathing rooms shall not be required where a single unisex toilet room or bathing room complying with 213.2.1 is provided and located in the same area and on the same floor as existing inaccessible toilet or bathing rooms.
    2. Where exceptions for *alterations* to *qualified historic buildings or facilities* are permitted by 202.5, no fewer than one toilet room for each sex complying with 603 or one unisex toilet room complying with 213.2.1 shall be provided.
    3. Where multiple single user portable toilet or bathing units are clustered at a single location, no more than 5 percent of the toilet units and bathing units at each cluster shall be required to comply with 603. Portable toilet units and bathing units complying with 603 shall be identified by the International Symbol of *Accessibility* complying with 703.7.2.1.
    4. Where multiple single user toilet rooms are clustered at a single location, no more than 50 percent of the single user toilet rooms for each use at each cluster shall be required to comply with 603.

> **Advisory 213.2 Toilet Rooms and Bathing Rooms.** These requirements allow the use of unisex (or single-user) toilet rooms in alterations when technical infeasibility can be demonstrated. Unisex toilet rooms benefit people who use opposite sex personal care assistants. For this reason, it is advantageous to install unisex toilet rooms in addition to accessible single-sex toilet rooms in new facilities.
>
> **Advisory 213.2 Toilet Rooms and Bathing Rooms Exceptions 3 and 4.** A "cluster" is a group of toilet rooms proximate to one another. Generally, toilet rooms in a cluster are within sight of, or adjacent to, one another.

Printed by Builder's Book, Inc., Bookstore · www.buildersbook.com

213.2.1 Unisex (Single-Use or Family) Toilet and Unisex Bathing Rooms. Unisex toilet rooms shall contain not more than one lavatory, and two water closets without urinals or one water closet and one urinal. Unisex bathing rooms shall contain one shower or one shower and one bathtub, one lavatory, and one water closet. Doors to unisex toilet rooms and unisex bathing rooms shall have privacy latches.

213.3 Plumbing Fixtures and Accessories. Plumbing fixtures and accessories provided in a toilet room or bathing room required to comply with 213.2 shall comply with 213.3.

213.3.1 Toilet Compartments. Where toilet compartments are provided, at least one toilet compartment shall comply with 604.8.1. In addition to the compartment required to comply with 604.8.1, at least one compartment shall comply with 604.8.2 where six or more toilet compartments are provided, or where the combination of urinals and water closets totals six or more fixtures.

> **Advisory 213.3.1 Toilet Compartments.** A toilet compartment is a partitioned space that is located within a toilet room, and that normally contains no more than one water closet. A toilet compartment may also contain a lavatory. A lavatory is a sink provided for hand washing. Full-height partitions and door assemblies can comprise toilet compartments where the minimum required spaces are provided within the compartment.

213.3.2 Water Closets. Where water closets are provided, at least one shall comply with 604.

213.3.3 Urinals. Where more than one urinal is provided, at least one shall comply with 605.

213.3.4 Lavatories. Where lavatories are provided, at least one shall comply with 606 and shall not be located in a toilet compartment.

213.3.5 Mirrors. Where mirrors are provided, at least one shall comply with 603.3.

213.3.6 Bathing Facilities. Where bathtubs or showers are provided, at least one bathtub complying with 607 or at least one shower complying with 608 shall be provided.

213.3.7 Coat Hooks and Shelves. Where coat hooks or shelves are provided in toilet rooms without toilet compartments, at least one of each type shall comply with 603.4. Where coat hooks or shelves are provided in toilet compartments, at least one of each type complying with 604.8.3 shall be provided in toilet compartments required to comply with 213.3.1. Where coat hooks or shelves are provided in bathing *facilities*, at least one of each type complying with 603.4 shall serve fixtures required to comply with 213.3.6.

214 Washing Machines and Clothes Dryers

214.1 General. Where provided, washing machines and clothes dryers shall comply with 214.

214.2 Washing Machines. Where three or fewer washing machines are provided, at least one shall comply with 611. Where more than three washing machines are provided, at least two shall comply with 611.

38

214.3 Clothes Dryers. Where three or fewer clothes dryers are provided, at least one shall comply with 611. Where more than three clothes dryers are provided, at least two shall comply with 611.

215 Fire Alarm Systems

215.1 General. Where fire alarm systems provide audible alarm coverage, alarms shall comply with 215.

> **EXCEPTION:** In existing *facilities*, visible alarms shall not be required except where an existing fire alarm system is upgraded or replaced, or a new fire alarm system is installed.

> **Advisory 215.1 General.** Unlike audible alarms, visible alarms must be located within the space they serve so that the signal is visible. Facility alarm systems (other than fire alarm systems) such as those used for tornado warnings and other emergencies are not required to comply with the technical criteria for alarms in Section 702. Every effort should be made to ensure that such alarms can be differentiated in their signal from fire alarms systems and that people who need to be notified of emergencies are adequately safeguarded. Consult local fire departments and prepare evacuation plans taking into consideration the needs of every building occupant, including people with disabilities.

215.2 Public and Common Use Areas. Alarms in *public use* areas and *common use* areas shall comply with 702.

215.3 Employee Work Areas. Where *employee work areas* have audible alarm coverage, the wiring system shall be designed so that visible alarms complying with 702 can be integrated into the alarm system.

215.4 Transient Lodging. Guest rooms required to comply with 224.4 shall provide alarms complying with 702.

215.5 Residential Facilities. Where provided in *residential dwelling units* required to comply with 809.5, alarms shall comply with 702.

216 Signs

216.1 General. Signs shall be provided in accordance with 216 and shall comply with 703.
> **EXCEPTIONS: 1.** *Building* directories, menus, seat and row designations in *assembly areas*, occupant names, *building* addresses, and company names and logos shall not be required to comply with 216.
> **2.** In parking *facilities*, signs shall not be required to comply with 216.2, 216.3, and 216.6 through 216.12.
> **3.** Temporary, 7 days or less, signs shall not be required to comply with 216.
> **4.** In detention and correctional *facilities*, signs not located in *public use* areas shall not be required to comply with 216.

216.2 Designations. Interior and exterior signs identifying permanent rooms and *spaces* shall comply with 703.1, 703.2, and 703.5. Where *pictograms* are provided as designations of permanent interior rooms and *spaces*, the *pictograms* shall comply with 703.6 and shall have text descriptors complying with 703.2 and 703.5.

> **EXCEPTION:** Exterior signs that are not located at the door to the *space* they serve shall not be required to comply with 703.2.

> **Advisory 216.2 Designations.** Section 216.2 applies to signs that provide designations, labels, or names for interior rooms or spaces where the sign is not likely to change over time. Examples include interior signs labeling restrooms, room and floor numbers or letters, and room names. Tactile text descriptors are required for pictograms that are provided to label or identify a permanent room or space. Pictograms that provide information about a room or space, such as "no smoking," occupant logos, and the International Symbol of Accessibility, are not required to have text descriptors.

216.3 Directional and Informational Signs. Signs that provide direction to or information about interior *spaces* and *facilities* of the *site* shall comply with 703.5.

> **Advisory 216.3 Directional and Informational Signs.** Information about interior spaces and facilities includes rules of conduct, occupant load, and similar signs. Signs providing direction to rooms or spaces include those that identify egress routes.

216.4 Means of Egress. Signs for means of egress shall comply with 216.4.

216.4.1 Exit Doors. Doors at exit passageways, exit discharge, and exit stairways shall be identified by *tactile* signs complying with 703.1, 703.2, and 703.5.

> **Advisory 216.4.1 Exit Doors.** An exit passageway is a horizontal exit component that is separated from the interior spaces of the building by fire-resistance-rated construction and that leads to the exit discharge or public way. The exit discharge is that portion of an egress system between the termination of an exit and a public way.

216.4.2 Areas of Refuge. Signs required by section 1003.2.13.5.4 of the International Building Code (2000 edition) or section 1007.6.4 of the International Building Code (2003 edition) (incorporated by reference, see "Referenced Standards" in Chapter 1) to provide instructions in areas of refuge shall comply with 703.5.

216.4.3 Directional Signs. Signs required by section 1003.2.13.6 of the International Building Code (2000 edition) or section 1007.7 of the International Building Code (2003 edition) (incorporated by reference, see "Referenced Standards" in Chapter 1) to provide directions to *accessible means of egress* shall comply with 703.5.

216.5 Parking. Parking *spaces* complying with 502 shall be identified by signs complying with 502.6.
EXCEPTIONS: 1. Where a total of four or fewer parking *spaces*, including *accessible* parking *spaces*, are provided on a *site*, identification of *accessible* parking *spaces* shall not be required.
2. In residential *facilities*, where parking *spaces* are assigned to specific *residential dwelling units*, identification of *accessible* parking *spaces* shall not be required.

216.6 Entrances. Where not all *entrances* comply with 404, *entrances* complying with 404 shall be identified by the International Symbol of *Accessibility* complying with 703.7.2.1. Directional signs complying with 703.5 that indicate the location of the nearest *entrance* complying with 404 shall be provided at *entrances* that do not comply with 404.

> **Advisory 216.6 Entrances.** Where a directional sign is required, it should be located to minimize backtracking. In some cases, this could mean locating a sign at the beginning of a route, not just at the inaccessible entrances to a building.

216.7 Elevators. Where existing elevators do not comply with 407, elevators complying with 407 shall be clearly identified with the International Symbol of *Accessibility* complying with 703.7.2.1.

216.8 Toilet Rooms and Bathing Rooms. Where existing toilet rooms or bathing rooms do not comply with 603, directional signs indicating the location of the nearest toilet room or bathing room complying with 603 within the *facility* shall be provided. Signs shall comply with 703.5 and shall include the International Symbol of *Accessibility* complying with 703.7.2.1. Where existing toilet rooms or bathing rooms do not comply with 603, the toilet rooms or bathing rooms complying with 603 shall be identified by the International Symbol of *Accessibility* complying with 703.7.2.1. Where clustered single user toilet rooms or bathing *facilities* are permitted to use exceptions to 213.2, toilet rooms or bathing *facilities* complying with 603 shall be identified by the International Symbol of *Accessibility* complying with 703.7.2.1 unless all toilet rooms and bathing *facilities* comply with 603.

216.9 TTYs. Identification and directional signs for public *TTYs* shall be provided in accordance with 216.9.

216.9.1 Identification Signs. Public *TTYs* shall be identified by the International Symbol of *TTY* complying with 703.7.2.2.

216.9.2 Directional Signs. Directional signs indicating the location of the nearest public *TTY* shall be provided at all banks of public pay telephones not containing a public *TTY*. In addition, where signs provide direction to public pay telephones, they shall also provide direction to public *TTYs*. Directional signs shall comply with 703.5 and shall include the International Symbol of *TTY* complying with 703.7.2.2.

216.10 Assistive Listening Systems. Each *assembly area* required by 219 to provide *assistive listening systems* shall provide signs informing patrons of the availability of the *assistive listening system*. Assistive listening signs shall comply with 703.5 and shall include the International Symbol of Access for Hearing Loss complying with 703.7.2.4.

EXCEPTION: Where ticket offices or windows are provided, signs shall not be required at each *assembly area* provided that signs are displayed at each ticket office or window informing patrons of the availability of *assistive listening systems*.

216.11 Check-Out Aisles. Where more than one check-out aisle is provided, check-out aisles complying with 904.3 shall be identified by the International Symbol of *Accessibility* complying with 703.7.2.1. Where check-out aisles are identified by numbers, letters, or functions, signs identifying check-out aisles complying with 904.3 shall be located in the same location as the check-out aisle identification.

> **EXCEPTION:** Where all check-out aisles serving a single function comply with 904.3, signs complying with 703.7.2.1 shall not be required.

216.12 Amusement Rides. Signs identifying the type of access provided on *amusement rides* shall be provided at entries to queues and waiting lines. In addition, where *accessible* unload areas also serve as *accessible* load areas, signs indicating the location of the *accessible* load and unload areas shall be provided at entries to queues and waiting lines.

> **Advisory 216.12 Amusement Rides.** Amusement rides designed primarily for children, amusement rides that are controlled or operated by the rider, and amusement rides without seats, are not required to provide wheelchair spaces, transfer seats, or transfer systems, and need not meet the sign requirements in 216.12. The load and unload areas of these rides must, however, be on an accessible route and must provide turning space.

217 Telephones

217.1 General. Where coin-operated public pay telephones, coinless public pay telephones, public *closed-circuit telephones*, public courtesy phones, or other types of public telephones are provided, public telephones shall be provided in accordance with 217 for each type of public telephone provided. For purposes of this section, a bank of telephones shall be considered to be two or more adjacent telephones.

> **Advisory 217.1 General.** These requirements apply to all types of public telephones including courtesy phones at airports and rail stations that provide a free direct connection to hotels, transportation services, and tourist attractions.

217.2 Wheelchair Accessible Telephones. Where public telephones are provided, wheelchair *accessible* telephones complying with 704.2 shall be provided in accordance with Table 217.2.

> **EXCEPTION:** Drive-up only public telephones shall not be required to comply with 217.2.

Table 217.2 Wheelchair Accessible Telephones

Number of Telephones Provided on a Floor, Level, or Exterior Site	Minimum Number of Required Wheelchair Accessible Telephones
1 or more single units	1 per floor, level, and exterior *site*
1 bank	1 per floor, level, and exterior *site*
2 or more banks	1 per bank

217.3 Volume Controls. All public telephones shall have volume controls complying with 704.3.

217.4 TTYs. *TTYs* complying with 704.4 shall be provided in accordance with 217.4.

42

> **Advisory 217.4 TTYs.** Separate requirements are provided based on the number of public pay telephones provided at a bank of telephones, within a floor, a building, or on a site. In some instances one TTY can be used to satisfy more than one of these requirements. For example, a TTY required for a bank can satisfy the requirements for a building. However, the requirement for at least one TTY on an exterior site cannot be met by installing a TTY in a bank inside a building. Consideration should be given to phone systems that can accommodate both digital and analog transmissions for compatibility with digital and analog TTYs.

217.4.1 Bank Requirement. Where four or more public pay telephones are provided at a bank of telephones, at least one public *TTY* complying with 704.4 shall be provided at that bank.

> **EXCEPTION:** *TTYs* shall not be required at banks of telephones located within 200 feet (61 m) of, and on the same floor as, a bank containing a public *TTY*.

217.4.2 Floor Requirement. *TTYs* in *public buildings* shall be provided in accordance with 217.4.2.1. *TTYs* in *private buildings* shall be provided in accordance with 217.4.2.2.

217.4.2.1 Public Buildings. Where at least one public pay telephone is provided on a floor of a *public building*, at least one public *TTY* shall be provided on that floor.

217.4.2.2 Private Buildings. Where four or more public pay telephones are provided on a floor of a *private building*, at least one public *TTY* shall be provided on that floor.

217.4.3 Building Requirement. *TTYs* in *public buildings* shall be provided in accordance with 217.4.3.1. *TTYs* in *private buildings* shall be provided in accordance with 217.4.3.2.

217.4.3.1 Public Buildings. Where at least one public pay telephone is provided in a *public building*, at least one public *TTY* shall be provided in the *building*. Where at least one public pay telephone is provided in a *public use* area of a *public building*, at least one public *TTY* shall be provided in the *public building* in a *public use* area.

217.4.3.2 Private Buildings. Where four or more public pay telephones are provided in a *private building*, at least one public *TTY* shall be provided in the *building*.

217.4.4 Exterior Site Requirement. Where four or more public pay telephones are provided on an exterior *site*, at least one public *TTY* shall be provided on the *site*.

217.4.5 Rest Stops, Emergency Roadside Stops, and Service Plazas. Where at least one public pay telephone is provided at a public rest stop, emergency roadside stop, or service plaza, at least one public *TTY* shall be provided.

217.4.6 Hospitals. Where at least one public pay telephone is provided serving a hospital emergency room, hospital recovery room, or hospital waiting room, at least one public *TTY* shall be provided at each location.

Printed by Builder's Book, Inc., Bookstore · www.buildersbook.com

217.4.7 Transportation Facilities. In transportation *facilities*, in addition to the requirements of 217.4.1 through 217.4.4, where at least one public pay telephone serves a particular *entrance* to a bus or rail *facility*, at least one public *TTY* shall be provided to serve that *entrance*. In airports, in addition to the requirements of 217.4.1 through 217.4.4, where four or more public pay telephones are located in a terminal outside the security areas, a concourse within the security areas, or a baggage claim area in a terminal, at least one public *TTY* shall be provided in each location.

217.4.8 Detention and Correctional Facilities. In detention and correctional *facilities*, where at least one pay telephone is provided in a secured area used only by detainees or inmates and security personnel, at least one *TTY* shall be provided in at least one secured area.

217.5 Shelves for Portable TTYs. Where a bank of telephones in the interior of a *building* consists of three or more public pay telephones, at least one public pay telephone at the bank shall be provided with a shelf and an electrical outlet in accordance with 704.5.
> **EXCEPTIONS: 1.** Secured areas of detention and correctional *facilities* where shelves and outlets are prohibited for purposes of security or safety shall not be required to comply with 217.5.
> **2.** The shelf and electrical outlet shall not be required at a bank of telephones with a *TTY*.

218 Transportation Facilities

218.1 General. Transportation *facilities* shall comply with 218.

218.2 New and Altered Fixed Guideway Stations. New and *altered* stations in rapid rail, light rail, commuter rail, intercity rail, high speed rail, and other fixed guideway systems shall comply with 810.5 through 810.10.

218.3 Key Stations and Existing Intercity Rail Stations. *Key stations* and existing intercity rail stations shall comply with 810.5 through 810.10.

218.4 Bus Shelters. Where provided, bus shelters shall comply with 810.3.

218.5 Other Transportation Facilities. In other transportation *facilities*, public address systems shall comply with 810.7 and clocks shall comply with 810.8.

219 Assistive Listening Systems

219.1 General. *Assistive listening systems* shall be provided in accordance with 219 and shall comply with 706.

219.2 Required Systems. In each *assembly area* where audible communication is integral to the use of the *space*, an *assistive listening system* shall be provided.
> **EXCEPTION:** Other than in courtrooms, *assistive listening systems* shall not be required where audio amplification is not provided.

219.3 Receivers. Receivers complying with 706.2 shall be provided for *assistive listening systems* in each *assembly area* in accordance with Table 219.3. Twenty-five percent minimum of receivers provided, but no fewer than two, shall be hearing-aid compatible in accordance with 706.3.

44

EXCEPTIONS: 1. Where a *building* contains more than one *assembly area* and the *assembly areas* required to provide *assistive listening systems* are under one management, the total number of required receivers shall be permitted to be calculated according to the total number of seats in the *assembly areas* in the *building* provided that all receivers are usable with all systems.

2. Where all seats in an *assembly area* are served by an induction loop *assistive listening system*, the minimum number of receivers required by Table 219.3 to be hearing-aid compatible shall not be required to be provided.

Table 219.3 Receivers for Assistive Listening Systems

Capacity of Seating in Assembly Area	Minimum Number of Required Receivers	Minimum Number of Required Receivers Required to be Hearing-aid Compatible
50 or less	2	2
51 to 200	2, plus 1 per 25 seats over 50 seats[1]	2
201 to 500	2, plus 1 per 25 seats over 50 seats[1]	1 per 4 receivers[1]
501 to 1000	20, plus 1 per 33 seats over 500 seats[1]	1 per 4 receivers[1]
1001 to 2000	35, plus 1 per 50 seats over 1000 seats[1]	1 per 4 receivers[1]
2001 and over	55 plus 1 per 100 seats over 2000 seats[1]	1 per 4 receivers[1]

1. Or fraction thereof.

220 Automatic Teller Machines and Fare Machines

220.1 General. Where automatic teller machines or self-service fare vending, collection, or adjustment machines are provided, at least one of each type provided at each location shall comply with 707. Where bins are provided for envelopes, waste paper, or other purposes, at least one of each type shall comply with 811.

> **Advisory 220.1 General.** If a bank provides both interior and exterior ATMs, each such installation is considered a separate location. Accessible ATMs, including those with speech and those that are within reach of people who use wheelchairs, must provide all the functions provided to customers at that location at all times. For example, it is unacceptable for the accessible ATM only to provide cash withdrawals while inaccessible ATMs also sell theater tickets.

221 Assembly Areas

221.1 General. *Assembly areas* shall provide *wheelchair spaces*, companion seats, and designated aisle seats complying with 221 and 802. In addition, lawn seating shall comply with 221.5.

221.2 Wheelchair Spaces. *Wheelchair spaces* complying with 221.2 shall be provided in *assembly areas* with fixed seating.

221.2.1 Number and Location. *Wheelchair spaces* shall be provided complying with 221.2.1.

221.2.1.1 General Seating. *Wheelchair spaces* complying with 802.1 shall be provided in accordance with Table 221.2.1.1.

Table 221.2.1.1 Number of Wheelchair Spaces in Assembly Areas

Number of Seats	Minimum Number of Required Wheelchair Spaces
4 to 25	1
26 to 50	2
51 to 150	4
151 to 300	5
301 to 500	6
501 to 5000	6, plus 1 for each 150, or fraction thereof, between 501 through 5000
5001 and over	36, plus 1 for each 200, or fraction thereof, over 5000

221.2.1.2 Luxury Boxes, Club Boxes, and Suites in Arenas, Stadiums, and Grandstands. In each luxury box, club box, and suite within arenas, stadiums, and grandstands, *wheelchair spaces* complying with 802.1 shall be provided in accordance with Table 221.2.1.1.

> **Advisory 221.2.1.2 Luxury Boxes, Club Boxes, and Suites in Arenas, Stadiums, and Grandstands.** The number of wheelchair spaces required in luxury boxes, club boxes, and suites within an arena, stadium, or grandstand is to be calculated box by box and suite by suite.

221.2.1.3 Other Boxes. In boxes other than those required to comply with 221.2.1.2, the total number of *wheelchair spaces* required shall be determined in accordance with Table 221.2.1.1. *Wheelchair spaces* shall be located in not less than 20 percent of all boxes provided. *Wheelchair spaces* shall comply with 802.1.

Advisory 221.2.1.3 Other Boxes. The provision for seating in "other boxes" includes box seating provided in facilities such as performing arts auditoria where tiered boxes are designed for spatial and acoustical purposes. The number of wheelchair spaces required in boxes covered by 221.2.1.3 is calculated based on the total number of seats provided in these other boxes. The resulting number of wheelchair spaces must be located in no fewer than 20% of the boxes covered by this section. For example, a concert hall has 20 boxes, each of which contains 10 seats, totaling 200 seats. In this example, 5 wheelchair spaces would be required, and they must be placed in at least 4 of the boxes. Additionally, because the wheelchair spaces must also meet the dispersion requirements of 221.2.3, the boxes containing these wheelchair spaces cannot all be located in one area unless an exception to the dispersion requirements applies.

221.2.1.4 Team or Player Seating. At least one *wheelchair space* complying with 802.1 shall be provided in team or player seating areas serving *areas of sport activity.*

    EXCEPTION: *Wheelchair spaces* shall not be required in team or player seating areas serving bowling lanes not required to comply with 206.2.11.

221.2.2 Integration. *Wheelchair spaces* shall be an integral part of the seating plan.

Advisory 221.2.2 Integration. The requirement that wheelchair spaces be an "integral part of the seating plan" means that wheelchair spaces must be placed within the footprint of the seating area. Wheelchair spaces cannot be segregated from seating areas. For example, it would be unacceptable to place only the wheelchair spaces, or only the wheelchair spaces and their associated companion seats, outside the seating areas defined by risers in an assembly area.

221.2.3 Lines of Sight and Dispersion. *Wheelchair spaces* shall provide lines of sight complying with 802.2 and shall comply with 221.2.3. In providing lines of sight, *wheelchair spaces* shall be dispersed. *Wheelchair spaces* shall provide spectators with choices of seating locations and viewing angles that are substantially equivalent to, or better than, the choices of seating locations and viewing angles available to all other spectators. When the number of *wheelchair spaces* required by 221.2.1 has been met, further dispersion shall not be required.

    EXCEPTION: *Wheelchair spaces* in team or player seating areas serving *areas of sport activity* shall not be required to comply with 221.2.3.

Advisory 221.2.3 Lines of Sight and Dispersion. Consistent with the overall intent of the ADA, individuals who use wheelchairs must be provided equal access so that their experience is substantially equivalent to that of other members of the audience. Thus, while individuals who use wheelchairs need not be provided with the best seats in the house, neither may they be relegated to the worst.

221.2.3.1 Horizontal Dispersion. *Wheelchair spaces* shall be dispersed horizontally.

    EXCEPTIONS: 1. Horizontal dispersion shall not be required in *assembly areas* with 300 or fewer seats if the companion seats required by 221.3 and *wheelchair spaces* are located within the 2nd or 3rd quartile of the total row length. Intermediate aisles shall be included in

47

determining the total row length. If the row length in the 2nd and 3rd quartile of a row is insufficient to accommodate the required number of companion seats and *wheelchair spaces*, the additional companion seats and *wheelchair spaces* shall be permitted to be located in the 1st and 4th quartile of the row.

2. In row seating, two *wheelchair spaces* shall be permitted to be located side-by-side.

> **Advisory 221.2.3.1 Horizontal Dispersion.** Horizontal dispersion of wheelchair spaces is the placement of spaces in an assembly facility seating area from side-to-side or, in the case of an arena or stadium, around the field of play or performance area.

221.2.3.2 Vertical Dispersion. *Wheelchair spaces* shall be dispersed vertically at varying distances from the screen, performance area, or playing field. In addition, *wheelchair spaces* shall be located in each balcony or *mezzanine* that is located on an *accessible* route.

EXCEPTIONS: 1. Vertical dispersion shall not be required in *assembly areas* with 300 or fewer seats if the *wheelchair spaces* provide viewing angles that are equivalent to, or better than, the average viewing angle provided in the *facility*.

2. In bleachers, *wheelchair spaces* shall not be required to be provided in rows other than rows at points of entry to bleacher seating.

> **Advisory 221.2.3.2 Vertical Dispersion.** When wheelchair spaces are dispersed vertically in an assembly facility they are placed at different locations within the seating area from front-to-back so that the distance from the screen, stage, playing field, area of sports activity, or other focal point is varied among wheelchair spaces.
>
> **Advisory 221.2.3.2 Vertical Dispersion Exception 2.** Points of entry to bleacher seating may include, but are not limited to, cross aisles, concourses, vomitories, and entrance ramps and stairs. Vertical, center, or side aisles adjoining bleacher seating that are stepped or tiered are not considered entry points.

221.3 Companion Seats. At least one companion seat complying with 802.3 shall be provided for each *wheelchair space* required by 221.2.1.

221.4 Designated Aisle Seats. At least 5 percent of the total number of aisle seats provided shall comply with 802.4 and shall be the aisle seats located closest to *accessible* routes.

EXCEPTION: Team or player seating areas serving *areas of sport activity* shall not be required to comply with 221.4.

> **Advisory 221.4 Designated Aisle Seats.** When selecting which aisle seats will meet the requirements of 802.4, those aisle seats which are closest to, not necessarily on, accessible routes must be selected first. For example, an assembly area has two aisles (A and B) serving seating areas with an accessible route connecting to the top and bottom of Aisle A only. The aisle seats chosen to meet 802.4 must be those at the top and bottom of Aisle A, working toward the middle. Only when all seats on Aisle A would not meet the five percent minimum would seats on Aisle B be designated.

48

221.5 Lawn Seating. Lawn seating areas and exterior overflow seating areas, where fixed seats are not provided, shall connect to an *accessible* route.

222 Dressing, Fitting, and Locker Rooms

222.1 General. Where dressing rooms, fitting rooms, or locker rooms are provided, at least 5 percent, but no fewer than one, of each type of use in each cluster provided shall comply with 803.
   EXCEPTION: In *alterations*, where it is *technically infeasible* to provide rooms in accordance with 222.1, one room for each sex on each level shall comply with 803. Where only unisex rooms are provided, unisex rooms shall be permitted.

> **Advisory 222.1 General.** A "cluster" is a group of rooms proximate to one another. Generally, rooms in a cluster are within sight of, or adjacent to, one another. Different styles of design provide users varying levels of privacy and convenience. Some designs include private changing facilities that are close to core areas of the facility, while other designs use space more economically and provide only group dressing facilities. Regardless of the type of facility, dressing, fitting, and locker rooms should provide people with disabilities rooms that are equally private and convenient to those provided others. For example, in a physician's office, if people without disabilities must traverse the full length of the office suite in clothing other than their street clothes, it is acceptable for people with disabilities to be asked to do the same.

222.2 Coat Hooks and Shelves. Where coat hooks or shelves are provided in dressing, fitting or locker rooms without individual compartments, at least one of each type shall comply with 803.5. Where coat hooks or shelves are provided in individual compartments at least one of each type complying with 803.5 shall be provided in individual compartments in dressing, fitting, or locker rooms required to comply with 222.1.

223 Medical Care and Long-Term Care Facilities

223.1 General. In licensed medical care *facilities* and licensed long-term care *facilities* where the period of stay exceeds twenty-four hours, patient or resident sleeping rooms shall be provided in accordance with 223.
   EXCEPTION: Toilet rooms that are part of critical or intensive care patient sleeping rooms shall not be required to comply with 603.

> **Advisory 223.1 General.** Because medical facilities frequently reconfigure spaces to reflect changes in medical specialties, Section 223.1 does not include a provision for dispersion of accessible patient or resident sleeping rooms. The lack of a design requirement does not mean that covered entities are not required to provide services to people with disabilities where accessible rooms are not dispersed in specialty areas. Locate accessible rooms near core areas that are less likely to change over time. While dispersion is not required, the flexibility it provides can be a critical factor in ensuring cost effective compliance with applicable civil rights laws, including titles II and III of the ADA and Section 504 of the Rehabilitation Act of 1973, as amended.

> **Advisory 223.1 General (Continued).** Additionally, all types of features and amenities should be dispersed among accessible sleeping rooms to ensure equal access to and a variety of choices for all patients and residents.

223.1.1 Alterations. Where sleeping rooms are *altered* or *added*, the requirements of 223 shall apply only to the sleeping rooms being *altered* or *added* until the number of sleeping rooms complies with the minimum number required for new construction.

> **Advisory 223.1.1 Alterations.** In alterations and additions, the minimum required number is based on the total number of sleeping rooms altered or added instead of on the total number of sleeping rooms provided in a facility. As a facility is altered over time, every effort should be made to disperse accessible sleeping rooms among patient care areas such as pediatrics, cardiac care, maternity, and other units. In this way, people with disabilities can have access to the full-range of services provided by a medical care facility.

223.2 Hospitals, Rehabilitation Facilities, Psychiatric Facilities and Detoxification Facilities. Hospitals, rehabilitation *facilities*, psychiatric *facilities* and detoxification *facilities* shall comply with 223.2.

223.2.1 Facilities Not Specializing in Treating Conditions That Affect Mobility. In *facilities* not specializing in treating conditions that affect mobility, at least 10 percent, but no fewer than one, of the patient sleeping rooms shall provide mobility features complying with 805.

223.2.2 Facilities Specializing in Treating Conditions That Affect Mobility. In *facilities* specializing in treating conditions that affect mobility, 100 percent of the patient sleeping rooms shall provide mobility features complying with 805.

> **Advisory 223.2.2 Facilities Specializing in Treating Conditions That Affect Mobility.** Conditions that affect mobility include conditions requiring the use or assistance of a brace, cane, crutch, prosthetic device, wheelchair, or powered mobility aid; arthritic, neurological, or orthopedic conditions that severely limit one's ability to walk; respiratory diseases and other conditions which may require the use of portable oxygen; and cardiac conditions that impose significant functional limitations. Facilities that may provide treatment for, but that do not specialize in treatment of such conditions, such as general rehabilitation hospitals, are not subject to this requirement but are subject to Section 223.2.1.

223.3 Long-Term Care Facilities. In licensed long-term care *facilities*, at least 50 percent, but no fewer than one, of each type of resident sleeping room shall provide mobility features complying with 805.

224 Transient Lodging Guest Rooms

224.1 General. *Transient lodging facilities* shall provide guest rooms in accordance with 224.

Advisory 224.1 General. Certain facilities used for transient lodging, including time shares, dormitories, and town homes may be covered by both these requirements and the Fair Housing Amendments Act. The Fair Housing Amendments Act requires that certain residential structures having four or more multi-family dwelling units, regardless of whether they are privately owned or federally assisted, include certain features of accessible and adaptable design according to guidelines established by the U.S. Department of Housing and Urban Development (HUD). This law and the appropriate regulations should be consulted before proceeding with the design and construction of residential housing.

224.1.1 Alterations. Where guest rooms are *altered* or *added*, the requirements of 224 shall apply only to the guest rooms being *altered* or *added* until the number of guest rooms complies with the minimum number required for new construction.

Advisory 224.1.1 Alterations. In alterations and additions, the minimum required number of accessible guest rooms is based on the total number of guest rooms altered or added instead of the total number of guest rooms provided in a facility. Typically, each alteration of a facility is limited to a particular portion of the facility. When accessible guest rooms are added as a result of subsequent alterations, compliance with 224.5 (Dispersion) is more likely to be achieved if all of the accessible guest rooms are not provided in the same area of the facility.

224.1.2 Guest Room Doors and Doorways. *Entrances,* doors, and doorways providing user passage into and within guest rooms that are not required to provide mobility features complying with 806.2 shall comply with 404.2.3.
   EXCEPTION: Shower and sauna doors in guest rooms that are not required to provide mobility features complying with 806.2 shall not be required to comply with 404.2.3.

Advisory 224.1.2 Guest Room Doors and Doorways. Because of the social interaction that often occurs in lodging facilities, an accessible clear opening width is required for doors and doorways to and within all guest rooms, including those not required to be accessible. This applies to all doors, including bathroom doors, that allow full user passage. Other requirements for doors and doorways in Section 404 do not apply to guest rooms not required to provide mobility features.

224.2 Guest Rooms with Mobility Features. In *transient lodging facilities,* guest rooms with mobility features complying with 806.2 shall be provided in accordance with Table 224.2.

Printed by Builder's Book, Inc., Bookstore · www.buildersbook.com

Table 224.2 Guest Rooms with Mobility Features

Total Number of Guest Rooms Provided	Minimum Number of Required Rooms Without Roll-in Showers	Minimum Number of Required Rooms With Roll-in Showers	Total Number of Required Rooms
1 to 25	1	0	1
26 to 50	2	0	2
51 to 75	3	1	4
76 to 100	4	1	5
101 to 150	5	2	7
151 to 200	6	2	8
201 to 300	7	3	10
301 to 400	8	4	12
401 to 500	9	4	13
501 to 1000	2 percent of total	1 percent of total	3 percent of total
1001 and over	20, plus 1 for each 100, or fraction thereof, over 1000	10, plus 1 for each 100, or fraction thereof, over 1000	30, plus 2 for each 100, or fraction thereof, over 1000

224.3 Beds. In guest rooms having more than 25 beds, 5 percent minimum of the beds shall have clear floor *space* complying with 806.2.3.

224.4 Guest Rooms with Communication Features. In *transient lodging facilities*, guest rooms with communication features complying with 806.3 shall be provided in accordance with Table 224.4.

Table 224.4 Guest Rooms with Communication Features

Total Number of Guest Rooms Provided	Minimum Number of Required Guest Rooms With Communication Features
2 to 25	2
26 to 50	4
51 to 75	7
76 to 100	9
101 to 150	12

Table 224.4 Guest Rooms with Communication Features

Total Number of Guest Rooms Provided	Minimum Number of Required Guest Rooms With Communication Features
151 to 200	14
201 to 300	17
301 to 400	20
401 to 500	22
501 to 1000	5 percent of total
1001 and over	50, plus 3 for each 100 over 1000

224.5 Dispersion. Guest rooms required to provide mobility features complying with 806.2 and guest rooms required to provide communication features complying with 806.3 shall be dispersed among the various classes of guest rooms, and shall provide choices of types of guest rooms, number of beds, and other amenities comparable to the choices provided to other guests. Where the minimum number of guest rooms required to comply with 806 is not sufficient to allow for complete dispersion, guest rooms shall be dispersed in the following priority: guest room type, number of beds, and amenities. At least one guest room required to provide mobility features complying with 806.2 shall also provide communication features complying with 806.3. Not more than 10 percent of guest rooms required to provide mobility features complying with 806.2 shall be used to satisfy the minimum number of guest rooms required to provide communication features complying with 806.3.

> **Advisory 224.5 Dispersion.** Factors to be considered in providing an equivalent range of options may include, but are not limited to, room size, bed size, cost, view, bathroom fixtures such as hot tubs and spas, smoking and nonsmoking, and the number of rooms provided.

225 Storage

225.1 General. Storage *facilities* shall comply with 225.

225.2 Storage. Where storage is provided in accessible *spaces*, at least one of each type shall comply with 811.

> **Advisory 225.2 Storage.** Types of storage include, but are not limited to, closets, cabinets, shelves, clothes rods, hooks, and drawers. Where provided, at least one of each type of storage must be within the reach ranges specified in 308; however, it is permissible to install additional storage outside the reach ranges.

225.2.1 Lockers. Where lockers are provided, at least 5 percent, but no fewer than one of each type, shall comply with 811.

> **Advisory 225.2.1 Lockers.** Different types of lockers may include full-size and half-size lockers, as well as those specifically designed for storage of various sports equipment.

225.2.2 Self-Service Shelving. Self-service shelves shall be located on an *accessible* route complying with 402. Self-service shelving shall not be required to comply with 308.

> **Advisory 225.2.2 Self-Service Shelving.** Self-service shelves include, but are not limited to, library, store, or post office shelves.

225.3 Self-Service Storage Facilities. *Self-service storage facilities* shall provide individual *self-service storage spaces* complying with these requirements in accordance with Table 225.3.

Table 225.3 Self-Service Storage Facilities

Total Spaces in Facility	Minimum Number of Spaces Required to be Accessible
1 to 200	5 percent, but no fewer than 1
201 and over	10, plus 2 percent of total number of units over 200

> **Advisory 225.3 Self-Service Storage Facilities.** Although there are no technical requirements that are unique to self-service storage facilities, elements and spaces provided in facilities containing self-service storage spaces required to comply with these requirements must comply with this document where applicable. For example: the number of storage spaces required to comply with these requirements must provide Accessible Routes complying with Section 206; Accessible Means of Egress complying with Section 207; Parking Spaces complying with Section 208; and, where provided, other pubic use or common use elements and facilities such as toilet rooms, drinking fountains, and telephones must comply with the applicable requirements of this document.

225.3.1 Dispersion. Individual *self-service storage spaces* shall be dispersed throughout the various classes of *spaces* provided. Where more classes of *spaces* are provided than the number required to be *accessible*, the number of *spaces* shall not be required to exceed that required by Table 225.3. *Self-service storage spaces* complying with Table 225.3 shall not be required to be dispersed among *buildings* in a multi-*building facility*.

226 Dining Surfaces and Work Surfaces

226.1 General. Where dining surfaces are provided for the consumption of food or drink, at least 5 percent of the seating *spaces* and standing *spaces* at the dining surfaces shall comply with 902. In addition, where work surfaces are provided for use by other than employees, at least 5 percent shall comply with 902.
  EXCEPTIONS: 1. Sales counters and service counters shall not be required to comply with 902.

2. Check writing surfaces provided at check-out aisles not required to comply with 904.3 shall not be required to comply with 902.

> **Advisory 226.1 General.** In facilities covered by the ADA, this requirement does not apply to work surfaces used only by employees. However, the ADA and, where applicable, Section 504 of the Rehabilitation Act of 1973, as amended, provide that employees are entitled to "reasonable accommodations." With respect to work surfaces, this means that employers may need to procure or adjust work stations such as desks, laboratory and work benches, fume hoods, reception counters, teller windows, study carrels, commercial kitchen counters, and conference tables to accommodate the individual needs of employees with disabilities on an "as needed" basis. Consider work surfaces that are flexible and permit installation at variable heights and clearances.

226.2 Dispersion. Dining surfaces and work surfaces required to comply with 902 shall be dispersed throughout the *space* or *facility* containing dining surfaces and work surfaces.

227 Sales and Service

227.1 General. Where provided, check-out aisles, sales counters, service counters, food service lines, queues, and waiting lines shall comply with 227 and 904.

227.2 Check-Out Aisles. Where check-out aisles are provided, check-out aisles complying with 904.3 shall be provided in accordance with Table 227.2. Where check-out aisles serve different functions, check-out aisles complying with 904.3 shall be provided in accordance with Table 227.2 for each function. Where check-out aisles are dispersed throughout the *building* or *facility*, check-out aisles complying with 904.3 shall be dispersed.

EXCEPTION: Where the selling *space* is under 5000 square feet (465 m^2) no more than one check-out aisle complying with 904.3 shall be required.

Table 227.2 Check-Out Aisles

Number of Check-Out Aisles of Each Function	Minimum Number of Check-Out Aisles of Each Function Required to Comply with 904.3
1 to 4	1
5 to 8	2
9 to 15	3
16 and over	3, plus 20 percent of additional aisles

227.2.1 Altered Check-Out Aisles. Where check-out aisles are *altered*, at least one of each check-out aisle serving each function shall comply with 904.3 until the number of check-out aisles complies with 227.2.

227.3 Counters. Where provided, at least one of each type of sales counter and service counter shall comply with 904.4. Where counters are dispersed throughout the *building* or *facility*, counters complying with 904.4 also shall be dispersed.

> **Advisory 227.3 Counters.** Types of counters that provide different services in the same facility include, but are not limited to, order, pick-up, express, and returns. One continuous counter can be used to provide different types of service. For example, order and pick-up are different services. It would not be acceptable to provide access only to the part of the counter where orders are taken when orders are picked-up at a different location on the same counter. Both the order and pick-up section of the counter must be accessible.

227.4 Food Service Lines. Food service lines shall comply with 904.5. Where self-service shelves are provided, at least 50 percent, but no fewer than one, of each type provided shall comply with 308.

227.5 Queues and Waiting Lines. Queues and waiting lines servicing counters or check-out aisles required to comply with 904.3 or 904.4 shall comply with 403.

228 Depositories, Vending Machines, Change Machines, Mail Boxes, and Fuel Dispensers

228.1 General. Where provided, at least one of each type of depository, vending machine, change machine, and fuel dispenser shall comply with 309.
    EXCEPTION: Drive-up only depositories shall not be required to comply with 309.

> **Advisory 228.1 General.** Depositories include, but are not limited to, night receptacles in banks, post offices, video stores, and libraries.

228.2 Mail Boxes. Where *mail boxes* are provided in an interior location, at least 5 percent, but no fewer than one, of each type shall comply with 309. In residential *facilities*, where *mail boxes* are provided for each *residential dwelling unit*, *mail boxes* complying with 309 shall be provided for each *residential dwelling unit* required to provide mobility features complying with 809.2 through 809.4.

229 Windows

229.1 General. Where glazed openings are provided in *accessible* rooms or *spaces* for operation by occupants, at least one opening shall comply with 309. Each glazed opening required by an *administrative authority* to be operable shall comply with 309.
    EXCEPTION: 1. Glazed openings in *residential dwelling units* required to comply with 809 shall not be required to comply with 229.
    2. Glazed openings in guest rooms required to provide communication features and in guest rooms required to comply with 206.5.3 shall not be required to comply with 229.

230 Two-Way Communication Systems

230.1 General. Where a two-way communication system is provided to gain admittance to a *building* or *facility* or to restricted areas within a *building* or *facility*, the system shall comply with 708.

Advisory 230.1 General. This requirement applies to facilities such as office buildings, courthouses, and other facilities where admittance to the building or restricted spaces is dependent on two-way communication systems.

231 Judicial Facilities

231.1 General. Judicial *facilities* shall comply with 231.

231.2 Courtrooms. Each courtroom shall comply with 808.

231.3 Holding Cells. Where provided, central holding cells and court-floor holding cells shall comply with 231.3.

231.3.1 Central Holding Cells. Where separate central holding cells are provided for adult male, juvenile male, adult female, or juvenile female, one of each type shall comply with 807.2. Where central holding cells are provided and are not separated by age or sex, at least one cell complying with 807.2 shall be provided.

231.3.2 Court-Floor Holding Cells. Where separate court-floor holding cells are provided for adult male, juvenile male, adult female, or juvenile female, each courtroom shall be served by one cell of each type complying with 807.2. Where court-floor holding cells are provided and are not separated by age or sex, courtrooms shall be served by at least one cell complying with 807.2. Cells may serve more than one courtroom.

231.4 Visiting Areas. Visiting areas shall comply with 231.4.

231.4.1 Cubicles and Counters. At least 5 percent, but no fewer than one, of cubicles shall comply with 902 on both the visitor and detainee sides. Where counters are provided, at least one shall comply with 904.4.2 on both the visitor and detainee sides.
   EXCEPTION: The detainee side of cubicles or counters at non-contact visiting areas not serving holding cells required to comply with 231 shall not be required to comply with 902 or 904.4.2.

231.4.2 Partitions. Where solid partitions or security glazing separate visitors from detainees at least one of each type of cubicle or counter partition shall comply with 904.6.

232 Detention Facilities and Correctional Facilities

232.1 General. *Buildings*, *facilities*, or portions thereof, in which people are detained for penal or correction purposes, or in which the liberty of the inmates is restricted for security reasons shall comply with 232.

Advisory 232.1 General. Detention facilities include, but are not limited to, jails, detention centers, and holding cells in police stations. Correctional facilities include, but are not limited to, prisons, reformatories, and correctional centers.

57

232.2 General Holding Cells and General Housing Cells. General holding cells and general housing cells shall be provided in accordance with 232.2.

EXCEPTION: *Alterations* to cells shall not be required to comply except to the extent determined by the Attorney General.

> **Advisory 232.2 General Holding Cells and General Housing Cells.** Accessible cells or rooms should be dispersed among different levels of security, housing categories, and holding classifications (e.g., male/female and adult/juvenile) to facilitate access. Many detention and correctional facilities are designed so that certain areas (e.g., "shift" areas) can be adapted to serve as different types of housing according to need. For example, a shift area serving as a medium-security housing unit might be redesignated for a period of time as a high-security housing unit to meet capacity needs. Placement of accessible cells or rooms in shift areas may allow additional flexibility in meeting requirements for dispersion of accessible cells or rooms.
>
> **Advisory 232.2 General Holding Cells and General Housing Cells Exception.** Although these requirements do not specify that cells be accessible as a consequence of an alteration, title II of the ADA requires that each service, program, or activity conducted by a public entity, when viewed in its entirety, be readily accessible to and usable by individuals with disabilities. This requirement must be met unless doing so would fundamentally alter the nature of a service, program, or activity or would result in undue financial and administrative burdens.

232.2.1 Cells with Mobility Features. At least 2 percent, but no fewer than one, of the total number of cells in a *facility* shall provide mobility features complying with 807.2.

232.2.1.1 Beds. In cells having more than 25 beds, at least 5 percent of the beds shall have clear floor *space* complying with 807.2.3.

232.2.2 Cells with Communication Features. At least 2 percent, but no fewer than one, of the total number of general holding cells and general housing cells equipped with audible emergency alarm systems and permanently installed telephones within the cell shall provide communication features complying with 807.3.

232.3 Special Holding Cells and Special Housing Cells. Where special holding cells or special housing cells are provided, at least one cell serving each purpose shall provide mobility features complying with 807.2. Cells subject to this requirement include, but are not limited to, those used for purposes of orientation, protective custody, administrative or disciplinary detention or segregation, detoxification, and medical isolation.

EXCEPTION: *Alterations* to cells shall not be required to comply except to the extent determined by the Attorney General.

232.4 Medical Care Facilities. Patient bedrooms or cells required to comply with 223 shall be provided in addition to any medical isolation cells required to comply with 232.3.

232.5 Visiting Areas. Visiting areas shall comply with 232.5.

Printed by Builder's Book, Inc., Bookstore · www.buildersbook.com

232.5.1 Cubicles and Counters. At least 5 percent, but no fewer than one, of cubicles shall comply with 902 on both the visitor and detainee sides. Where counters are provided, at least one shall comply with 904.4.2 on both the visitor and detainee or inmate sides.

> **EXCEPTION:** The inmate or detainee side of cubicles or counters at non-contact visiting areas not serving holding cells or housing cells required to comply with 232 shall not be required to comply with 902 or 904.4.2.

232.5.2 Partitions. Where solid partitions or security glazing separate visitors from detainees or inmates at least one of each type of cubicle or counter partition shall comply with 904.6.

233 Residential Facilities

233.1 General. *Facilities* with *residential dwelling units* shall comply with 233.

> **Advisory 233.1 General.** Section 233 outlines the requirements for residential facilities subject to the Americans with Disabilities Act of 1990. The facilities covered by Section 233, as well as other facilities not covered by this section, may still be subject to other Federal laws such as the Fair Housing Act and Section 504 of the Rehabilitation Act of 1973, as amended. For example, the Fair Housing Act requires that certain residential structures having four or more multi-family dwelling units, regardless of whether they are privately owned or federally assisted, include certain features of accessible and adaptable design according to guidelines established by the U.S. Department of Housing and Urban Development (HUD). These laws and the appropriate regulations should be consulted before proceeding with the design and construction of residential facilities.
>
> Residential facilities containing residential dwelling units provided by entities subject to HUD's Section 504 regulations and residential dwelling units covered by Section 233.3 must comply with the technical and scoping requirements in Chapters 1 through 10 included this document. Section 233 is not a stand-alone section; this section only addresses the minimum number of residential dwelling units within a facility required to comply with Chapter 8. However, residential facilities must also comply with the requirements of this document. For example: Section 206.5.4 requires all doors and doorways providing user passage in residential dwelling units providing mobility features to comply with Section 404; Section 206.7.6 permits platform lifts to be used to connect levels within residential dwelling units providing mobility features; Section 208 provides general scoping for accessible parking and Section 208.2.3.1 specifies the required number of accessible parking spaces for each residential dwelling unit providing mobility features; Section 228.2 requires mail boxes to be within reach ranges when they serve residential dwelling units providing mobility features; play areas are addressed in Section 240; and swimming pools are addressed in Section 242. There are special provisions applicable to facilities containing residential dwelling units at: Exception 3 to 202.3; Exception to 202.4; 203.8; and Exception 4 to 206.2.3.

233.2 Residential Dwelling Units Provided by Entities Subject to HUD Section 504 Regulations. Where *facilities* with *residential dwelling units* are provided by entities subject to regulations issued by the Department of Housing and Urban Development (HUD) under Section 504 of the Rehabilitation Act of 1973, as amended, such entities shall provide *residential dwelling units* with mobility features complying with 809.2 through 809.4 in a number required by the applicable HUD regulations. *Residential dwelling units* required to provide mobility features complying with 809.2 through 809.4 shall be on an *accessible* route as required by 206. In addition, such entities shall provide *residential dwelling units* with communication features complying with 809.5 in a number required by the applicable HUD regulations. Entities subject to 233.2 shall not be required to comply with 233.3.

> **Advisory 233.2 Residential Dwelling Units Provided by Entities Subject to HUD Section 504 Regulations.** Section 233.2 requires that entities subject to HUD's regulations implementing Section 504 of the Rehabilitation Act of 1973, as amended, provide residential dwelling units containing mobility features and residential dwelling units containing communication features complying with these regulations in a number specified in HUD's Section 504 regulations. Further, the residential dwelling units provided must be dispersed according to HUD's Section 504 criteria. In addition, Section 233.2 defers to HUD the specification of criteria by which the technical requirements of this document will apply to alterations of existing facilities subject to HUD's Section 504 regulations.

233.3 Residential Dwelling Units Provided by Entities Not Subject to HUD Section 504 Regulations. *Facilities* with *residential dwelling units* provided by entities not subject to regulations issued by the Department of Housing and Urban Development (HUD) under Section 504 of the Rehabilitation Act of 1973, as amended, shall comply with 233.3.

233.3.1 Minimum Number: New Construction. Newly constructed *facilities* with *residential dwelling units* shall comply with 233.3.1.

> **EXCEPTION:** Where *facilities* contain 15 or fewer *residential dwelling units*, the requirements of 233.3.1.1 and 233.3.1.2 shall apply to the total number of *residential dwelling units* that are constructed under a single contract, or are developed as a whole, whether or not located on a common *site*.

233.3.1.1 Residential Dwelling Units with Mobility Features. In *facilities* with *residential dwelling units*, at least 5 percent, but no fewer than one unit, of the total number of *residential dwelling units* shall provide mobility features complying with 809.2 through 809.4 and shall be on an *accessible* route as required by 206.

233.3.1.2 Residential Dwelling Units with Communication Features. In *facilities* with *residential dwelling units*, at least 2 percent, but no fewer than one unit, of the total number of *residential dwelling units* shall provide communication features complying with 809.5.

233.3.2 Residential Dwelling Units for Sale. *Residential dwelling units* offered for sale shall provide *accessible* features to the extent required by regulations issued by Federal agencies under the Americans with Disabilities Act or Section 504 of the Rehabilitation Act of 1973, as amended.

> **Advisory 233.3.2 Residential Dwelling Units for Sale.** A public entity that conducts a program to build housing for purchase by individual home buyers must provide access according to the requirements of the ADA regulations and a program receiving Federal financial assistance must comply with the applicable Section 504 regulation.

233.3.3 Additions. Where an *addition* to an existing *building* results in an increase in the number of *residential dwelling units,* the requirements of 233.3.1 shall apply only to the *residential dwelling units* that are *added* until the total number of *residential dwelling units* complies with the minimum number required by 233.3.1. *Residential dwelling units* required to comply with 233.3.1.1 shall be on an *accessible* route as required by 206.

233.3.4 Alterations. *Alterations* shall comply with 233.3.4.

    EXCEPTION: Where compliance with 809.2, 809.3, or 809.4 is *technically infeasible*, or where it is *technically infeasible* to provide an *accessible* route to a *residential dwelling unit*, the entity shall be permitted to *alter* or construct a comparable *residential dwelling unit* to comply with 809.2 through 809.4 provided that the minimum number of *residential dwelling units* required by 233.3.1.1 and 233.3.1.2, as applicable, is satisfied.

> **Advisory 233.3.4 Alterations Exception.** A substituted dwelling unit must be comparable to the dwelling unit that is not made accessible. Factors to be considered in comparing one dwelling unit to another should include the number of bedrooms; amenities provided within the dwelling unit; types of common spaces provided within the facility; and location with respect to community resources and services, such as public transportation and civic, recreational, and mercantile facilities.

233.3.4.1 Alterations to Vacated Buildings. Where a *building* is vacated for the purposes of *alteration*, and the *altered building* contains more than 15 *residential dwelling units*, at least 5 percent of the *residential dwelling units* shall comply with 809.2 through 809.4 and shall be on an *accessible* route as required by 206. In addition, at least 2 percent of the *residential dwelling units* shall comply with 809.5.

> **Advisory 233.3.4.1 Alterations to Vacated Buildings.** This provision is intended to apply where a building is vacated with the intent to alter the building. Buildings that are vacated solely for pest control or asbestos removal are not subject to the requirements to provide residential dwelling units with mobility features or communication features.

233.3.4.2 Alterations to Individual Residential Dwelling Units. In individual *residential dwelling units*, where a bathroom or a kitchen is substantially *altered*, and at least one other room is *altered*, the requirements of 233.3.1 shall apply to the *altered residential dwelling units* until the total number of *residential dwelling units* complies with the minimum number required by 233.3.1.1 and 233.3.1.2. *Residential dwelling units* required to comply with 233.3.1.1 shall be on an *accessible* route as required by 206.

    EXCEPTION: Where *facilities* contain 15 or fewer *residential dwelling units*, the requirements of 233.3.1.1 and 233.3.1.2 shall apply to the total number of *residential dwelling units* that are *altered* under a single contract, or are developed as a whole, whether or not located on a common *site*.

Advisory 233.3.4.2 Alterations to Individual Residential Dwelling Units. Section 233.3.4.2 uses the terms "substantially altered" and "altered." A substantial alteration to a kitchen or bathroom includes, but is not limited to, alterations that are changes to or rearrangements in the plan configuration, or replacement of cabinetry. Substantial alterations do not include normal maintenance or appliance and fixture replacement, unless such maintenance or replacement requires changes to or rearrangements in the plan configuration, or replacement of cabinetry. The term "alteration" is defined both in Section 106 of these requirements and in the Department of Justice ADA regulations.

233.3.5 Dispersion. *Residential dwelling units* required to provide mobility features complying with 809.2 through 809.4 and *residential dwelling units* required to provide communication features complying with 809.5 shall be dispersed among the various types of *residential dwelling units* in the *facility* and shall provide choices of *residential dwelling units* comparable to, and integrated with, those available to other residents.

> **EXCEPTION:** Where multi-*story residential dwelling units* are one of the types of *residential dwelling units* provided, one-*story residential dwelling units* shall be permitted as a substitute for multi-*story residential dwelling units* where equivalent *spaces* and amenities are provided in the one-*story residential dwelling unit*.

234 Amusement Rides

234.1 General. A*musement rides* shall comply with 234.

> **EXCEPTION:** Mobile or portable *amusement rides* shall not be required to comply with 234.

Advisory 234.1 General. These requirements apply generally to newly designed and constructed amusement rides and attractions. A custom designed and constructed ride is new upon its first use, which is the first time amusement park patrons take the ride. With respect to amusement rides purchased from other entities, new refers to the first permanent installation of the ride, whether it is used off the shelf or modified before it is installed. Where amusement rides are moved after several seasons to another area of the park or to another park, the ride would not be considered newly designed or newly constructed.

Some amusement rides and attractions that have unique designs and features are not addressed by these requirements. In those situations, these requirements are to be applied to the extent possible. An example of an amusement ride not specifically addressed by these requirements includes "virtual reality" rides where the device does not move through a fixed course within a defined area. An accessible route must be provided to these rides. Where an attraction or ride has unique features for which there are no applicable scoping provisions, then a reasonable number, but at least one, of the features must be located on an accessible route. Where there are appropriate technical provisions, they must be applied to the elements that are covered by the scoping provisions.

Advisory 234.1 General Exception. Mobile or temporary rides are those set up for short periods of time such as traveling carnivals, State and county fairs, and festivals. The amusement rides that are covered by 234.1 are ones that are not regularly assembled and disassembled.

234.2 Load and Unload Areas. Load and unload areas serving *amusement rides* shall comply with 1002.3.

234.3 Minimum Number. *Amusement rides* shall provide at least one *wheelchair space* complying with 1002.4, or at least one *amusement ride seat* designed for transfer complying with 1002.5, or at least one *transfer device* complying with 1002.6.

   EXCEPTIONS: 1. *Amusement rides* that are controlled or operated by the rider shall not be required to comply with 234.3.

   2. *Amusement rides* designed primarily for children, where children are assisted on and off the ride by an adult, shall not be required to comply with 234.3.

   3. *Amusement rides* that do not provide *amusement ride seats* shall not be required to comply with 234.3.

> **Advisory 234.3 Minimum Number Exceptions 1 through 3.** Amusement rides controlled or operated by the rider, designed for children, or rides without ride seats are not required to comply with 234.3. These rides are not exempt from the other provisions in 234 requiring an accessible route to the load and unload areas and to the ride. The exception does not apply to those rides where patrons may cause the ride to make incidental movements, but where the patron otherwise has no control over the ride.
>
> **Advisory 234.3 Minimum Number Exception 2.** The exception is limited to those rides designed "primarily" for children, where children are assisted on and off the ride by an adult. This exception is limited to those rides designed for children and not for the occasional adult user. An accessible route to and turning space in the load and unload area will provide access for adults and family members assisting children on and off these rides.

234.4 Existing Amusement Rides. Where existing *amusement rides* are *altered*, the *alteration* shall comply with 234.4.

> **Advisory 234.4 Existing Amusement Rides.** Routine maintenance, painting, and changing of theme boards are examples of activities that do not constitute an alteration subject to this section.

234.4.1 Load and Unload Areas. Where load and unload areas serving existing *amusement rides* are newly designed and constructed, the load and unload areas shall comply with 1002.3.

234.4.2 Minimum Number. Where the structural or operational characteristics of an *amusement ride* are *altered* to the extent that the *amusement ride*'s performance differs from that specified by the manufacturer or the original design, the *amusement ride* shall comply with 234.3.

235 Recreational Boating Facilities

235.1 General. Recreational boating *facilities* shall comply with 235.

235.2 Boat Slips. *Boat slips* complying with 1003.3.1 shall be provided in accordance with Table 235.2. Where the number of *boat slips* is not identified, each 40 feet (12 m) of *boat slip* edge provided along the perimeter of the pier shall be counted as one *boat slip* for the purpose of this section.

Table 235.2 Boat Slips

Total Number of Boat Slips Provided in Facility	Minimum Number of Required Accessible Boat Slips
1 to 25	1
26 to 50	2
51 to 100	3
101 to 150	4
151 to 300	5
301 to 400	6
401 to 500	7
501 to 600	8
601 to 700	9
701 to 800	10
801 to 900	11
901 to 1000	12
1001 and over	12, plus 1 for every 100, or fraction thereof, over 1000

Advisory 235.2 Boat Slips. The requirement for boat slips also applies to piers where boat slips are not demarcated. For example, a single pier 25 feet (7620 mm) long and 5 feet (1525 mm) wide (the minimum width specified by Section 1003.3) allows boats to moor on three sides. Because the number of boat slips is not demarcated, the total length of boat slip edge (55 feet, 17 m) must be used to determine the number of boat slips provided (two). This number is based on the specification in Section 235.2 that each 40 feet (12 m) of boat slip edge, or fraction thereof, counts as one boat slip. In this example, Table 235.2 would require one boat slip to be accessible.

235.2.1 Dispersion. *Boat slips* complying with 1003.3.1 shall be dispersed throughout the various types of *boat slips* provided. Where the minimum number of *boat slips* required to comply with 1003.3.1 has been met, no further dispersion shall be required.

Advisory 235.2.1 Dispersion. Types of boat slips are based on the size of the boat slips; whether single berths or double berths, shallow water or deep water, transient or longer-term lease, covered or uncovered; and whether slips are equipped with features such as telephone, water, electricity or cable connections. The term "boat slip" is intended to cover any pier area other than launch ramp boarding piers where recreational boats are moored for purposes of berthing, embarking, or disembarking. For example, a fuel pier may contain boat slips, and this type of short term slip would be included in determining compliance with 235.2.

235.3 Boarding Piers at Boat Launch Ramps. Where *boarding piers* are provided at *boat launch ramps*, at least 5 percent, but no fewer than one, of the *boarding piers* shall comply with 1003.3.2.

236 Exercise Machines and Equipment

236.1 General. At least one of each type of exercise machine and equipment shall comply with 1004.

Advisory 236.1 General. Most strength training equipment and machines are considered different types. Where operators provide a biceps curl machine and cable-cross-over machine, both machines are required to meet the provisions in this section, even though an individual may be able to work on their biceps through both types of equipment.

Similarly, there are many types of cardiovascular exercise machines, such as stationary bicycles, rowing machines, stair climbers, and treadmills. Each machine provides a cardiovascular exercise and is considered a different type for purposes of these requirements.

237 Fishing Piers and Platforms

237.1 General. Fishing piers and platforms shall comply with 1005.

238 Golf Facilities

238.1 General. Golf *facilities* shall comply with 238.

238.2 Golf Courses. Golf courses shall comply with 238.2.

238.2.1 Teeing Grounds. Where one *teeing ground* is provided for a hole, the *teeing ground* shall be designed and constructed so that a golf car can enter and exit the *teeing ground*. Where two *teeing grounds* are provided for a hole, the forward *teeing ground* shall be designed and constructed so that a golf car can enter and exit the *teeing ground*. Where three or more *teeing grounds* are provided for a hole, at least two *teeing grounds*, including the forward *teeing ground*, shall be designed and constructed so that a golf car can enter and exit each *teeing ground*.

EXCEPTION: In existing golf courses, the forward *teeing ground* shall not be required to be one of the *teeing grounds* on a hole designed and constructed so that a golf car can enter and exit the *teeing ground* where compliance is not feasible due to terrain.

238.2.2 Putting Greens. Putting greens shall be designed and constructed so that a golf car can enter and exit the putting green.

238.2.3 Weather Shelters. Where provided, weather shelters shall be designed and constructed so that a golf car can enter and exit the weather shelter and shall comply with 1006.4.

238.3 Practice Putting Greens, Practice Teeing Grounds, and Teeing Stations at Driving Ranges. At least 5 percent, but no fewer than one, of practice putting greens, practice *teeing grounds*, and teeing stations at driving ranges shall be designed and constructed so that a golf car can enter and exit the practice putting greens, practice *teeing grounds*, and teeing stations at driving ranges.

239 Miniature Golf Facilities

239.1 General. Miniature golf *facilities* shall comply with 239.

239.2 Minimum Number. At least 50 percent of holes on miniature golf courses shall comply with 1007.3.

> **Advisory 239.2 Minimum Number.** Where possible, providing access to all holes on a miniature golf course is recommended. If a course is designed with the minimum 50 percent accessible holes, designers or operators are encouraged to select holes which provide for an equivalent experience to the maximum extent possible.

239.3 Miniature Golf Course Configuration. Miniature golf courses shall be configured so that the holes complying with 1007.3 are consecutive. Miniature golf courses shall provide an *accessible* route from the last hole complying with 1007.3 to the course *entrance* or exit without requiring travel through any other holes on the course.

EXCEPTION: One break in the sequence of consecutive holes shall be permitted provided that the last hole on the miniature golf course is the last hole in the sequence.

> **Advisory 239.3 Miniature Golf Course Configuration.** Where only the minimum 50 percent of the holes are accessible, an accessible route from the last accessible hole to the course exit or entrance must not require travel back through other holes. In some cases, this may require an additional accessible route. Other options include increasing the number of accessible holes in a way that limits the distance needed to connect the last accessible hole with the course exit or entrance.

240 Play Areas

240.1 General. *Play areas* for children ages 2 and over shall comply with 240. Where separate *play areas* are provided within a *site* for specific age groups, each *play area* shall comply with 240.

EXCEPTIONS: 1. *Play areas* located in family child care *facilities* where the proprietor actually resides shall not be required to comply with 240.

2. In existing *play areas*, where *play components* are relocated for the purposes of creating safe *use zones* and the ground surface is not *altered* or extended for more than one *use zone*, the *play area* shall not be required to comply with 240.

3. *Amusement attractions* shall not be required to comply with 240.

4. Where *play components* are *altered* and the ground surface is not *altered*, the ground surface shall not be required to comply with 1008.2.6 unless required by 202.4.

> **Advisory 240.1 General.** Play areas may be located on exterior sites or within a building. Where separate play areas are provided within a site for children in specified age groups (e.g., preschool (ages 2 to 5) and school age (ages 5 to 12)), each play area must comply with this section. Where play areas are provided for the same age group on a site but are geographically separated (e.g., one is located next to a picnic area and another is located next to a softball field), they are considered separate play areas and each play area must comply with this section.

240.1.1 Additions. Where *play areas* are designed and constructed in phases, the requirements of 240 shall apply to each successive *addition* so that when the *addition* is completed, the entire *play area* complies with all the applicable requirements of 240.

> **Advisory 240.1.1 Additions.** These requirements are to be applied so that when each successive addition is completed, the entire play area complies with all applicable provisions. For example, a play area is built in two phases. In the first phase, there are 10 elevated play components and 10 elevated play components are added in the second phase for a total of 20 elevated play components in the play area. When the first phase was completed, at least 5 elevated play components, including at least 3 different types, were to be provided on an accessible route. When the second phase is completed, at least 10 elevated play components must be located on an accessible route, and at least 7 ground level play components, including 4 different types, must be provided on an accessible route. At the time the second phase is complete, ramps must be used to connect at least 5 of the elevated play components and transfer systems are permitted to be used to connect the rest of the elevated play components required to be located on an accessible route.

240.2 Play Components. Where provided, *play components* shall comply with 240.2.

240.2.1 Ground Level Play Components. *Ground level play components* shall be provided in the number and types required by 240.2.1. *Ground level play components* that are provided to comply with 240.2.1.1 shall be permitted to satisfy the additional number required by 240.2.1.2 if the minimum required types of *play components* are satisfied. Where two or more required *ground level play components* are provided, they shall be dispersed throughout the *play area* and integrated with other *play components*.

> **Advisory 240.2.1 Ground Level Play Components.** Examples of ground level play components may include spring rockers, swings, diggers, and stand-alone slides. When distinguishing between the different types of ground level play components, consider the general experience provided by the play component. Examples of different types of experiences include, but are not limited to, rocking, swinging, climbing, spinning, and sliding.

Printed by Builder's Book, Inc., Bookstore · www.buildersbook.com

Advisory 240.2.1 Ground Level Play Components (Continued). A spiral slide may provide a slightly different experience from a straight slide, but sliding is the general experience and therefore a spiral slide is not considered a different type of play component from a straight slide.

Ground level play components accessed by children with disabilities must be integrated into the play area. Designers should consider the optimal layout of ground level play components accessed by children with disabilities to foster interaction and socialization among all children. Grouping all ground level play components accessed by children with disabilities in one location is not considered integrated.

Where a stand-alone slide is provided, an accessible route must connect the base of the stairs at the entry point to the exit point of the slide. A ramp or transfer system to the top of the slide is not required. Where a sand box is provided, an accessible route must connect to the border of the sand box. Accessibility to the sand box would be enhanced by providing a transfer system into the sand or by providing a raised sand table with knee clearance complying with 1008.4.3.

Ramps are preferred over transfer systems since not all children who use wheelchairs or other mobility devices may be able to use, or may choose not to use, transfer systems. Where ramps connect elevated play components, the maximum rise of any ramp run is limited to 12 inches (305 mm). Where possible, designers and operators are encouraged to provide ramps with a slope less than the 1:12 maximum. Berms or sculpted dirt may be used to provide elevation and may be part of an accessible route to composite play structures.

Platform lifts are permitted as a part of an accessible route. Because lifts must be independently operable, operators should carefully consider the appropriateness of their use in unsupervised settings.

240.2.1.1 Minimum Number and Types. Where *ground level play components* are provided, at least one of each type shall be on an *accessible* route and shall comply with 1008.4.

240.2.1.2 Additional Number and Types. Where *elevated play components* are provided, *ground level play components* shall be provided in accordance with Table 240.2.1.2 and shall comply with 1008.4.

EXCEPTION: If at least 50 percent of the *elevated play components* are connected by a *ramp* and at least 3 of the *elevated play components* connected by the *ramp* are different types of *play components*, the *play area* shall not be required to comply with 240.2.1.2.

Printed by Builder's Book, Inc., Bookstore · www.buildersbook.com

Table 240.2.1.2 Number and Types of Ground Level Play Components Required to be on Accessible Routes

Number of Elevated Play Components Provided	Minimum Number of Ground Level Play Components Required to be on an Accessible Route	Minimum Number of Different Types of Ground Level Play Components Required to be on an Accessible Route
1	Not applicable	Not applicable
2 to 4	1	1
5 to 7	2	2
8 to 10	3	3
11 to 13	4	3
14 to 16	5	3
17 to 19	6	3
20 to 22	7	4
23 to 25	8	4
26 and over	8, plus 1 for each additional 3, or fraction thereof, over 25	5

Advisory 240.2.1.2 Additional Number and Types. Where a large play area includes two or more composite play structures designed for the same age group, the total number of elevated play components on all the composite play structures must be added to determine the additional number and types of ground level play components that must be provided on an accessible route.

240.2.2 Elevated Play Components. Where *elevated play components* are provided, at least 50 percent shall be on an *accessible* route and shall comply with 1008.4.

Advisory 240.2.2 Elevated Play Components. A double or triple slide that is part of a composite play structure is one elevated play component. For purposes of this section, ramps, transfer systems, steps, decks, and roofs are not considered elevated play components. Although socialization and pretend play can occur on these elements, they are not primarily intended for play.

Some play components that are attached to a composite play structure can be approached or exited at the ground level or above grade from a platform or deck. For example, a climber attached to a composite play structure can be approached or exited at the ground level or above grade from a platform or deck on a composite play structure.

Printed by Builder's Book, Inc., Bookstore · www.buildersbook.com

Advisory 240.2.2 Elevated Play Components (Continued). Play components that are attached to a composite play structure and can be approached from a platform or deck (e.g., climbers and overhead play components) are considered elevated play components. These play components are not considered ground level play components and do not count toward the requirements in 240.2.1.2 regarding the number of ground level play components that must be located on an accessible route.

241 Saunas and Steam Rooms

241 General. Where provided, saunas and steam rooms shall comply with 612.
EXCEPTION: Where saunas or steam rooms are clustered at a single location, no more than 5 percent of the saunas and steam rooms, but no fewer than one, of each type in each cluster shall be required to comply with 612.

242 Swimming Pools, Wading Pools, and Spas

242.1 General. Swimming pools, wading pools, and spas shall comply with 242.

242.2 Swimming Pools. At least two *accessible* means of entry shall be provided for swimming pools. *Accessible* means of entry shall be swimming pool lifts complying with 1009.2; sloped entries complying with 1009.3; transfer walls complying with 1009.4; transfer systems complying with 1009.5; and pool stairs complying with 1009.6. At least one *accessible* means of entry provided shall comply with 1009.2 or 1009.3.
EXCEPTIONS: 1. Where a swimming pool has less than 300 linear feet (91 m) of swimming pool wall, no more than one *accessible* means of entry shall be required provided that the *accessible* means of entry is a swimming pool lift complying with 1009.2 or sloped entry complying with 1009.3.
2. Wave action pools, leisure rivers, sand bottom pools, and other pools where user access is limited to one area shall not be required to provide more than one *accessible* means of entry provided that the *accessible* means of entry is a swimming pool lift complying with 1009.2, a sloped entry complying with 1009.3, or a transfer system complying with 1009.5.
3. *Catch pools* shall not be required to provide an *accessible* means of entry provided that the *catch pool* edge is on an *accessible* route.

Advisory 242.2 Swimming Pools. Where more than one means of access is provided into the water, it is recommended that the means be different. Providing different means of access will better serve the varying needs of people with disabilities in getting into and out of a swimming pool. It is also recommended that where two or more means of access are provided, they not be provided in the same location in the pool. Different locations will provide increased options for entry and exit, especially in larger pools.

Advisory 242.2 Swimming Pools Exception 1. Pool walls at diving areas and areas along pool walls where there is no pool entry because of landscaping or adjacent structures are to be counted when determining the number of accessible means of entry required.

242.3 Wading Pools. At least one *accessible* means of entry shall be provided for wading pools. Accessible means of entry shall comply with sloped entries complying with 1009.3.

242.4 Spas. At least one *accessible* means of entry shall be provided for spas. *Accessible* means of entry shall comply with swimming pool lifts complying with 1009.2; transfer walls complying with 1009.4; or transfer systems complying with 1009.5.

    EXCEPTION: Where spas are provided in a cluster, no more than 5 percent, but no fewer than one, spa in each cluster shall be required to comply with 242.4.

243 Shooting Facilities with Firing Positions

243.1 General. Where shooting *facilities* with firing positions are designed and constructed at a *site*, at least 5 percent, but no fewer than one, of each type of firing position shall comply with 1010.

ABA CHAPTER 1: APPLICATION AND ADMINISTRATION

F101 Purpose

This document contains scoping and technical requirements for *accessibility* to *sites*, *facilities*, *buildings*, and *elements* by individuals with disabilities. The requirements are to be applied during the design, construction, *addition* to, *alteration,* and *lease* of *sites*, *facilities*, *buildings*, and *elements* to the extent required by regulations issued by Federal agencies under the Architectural Barriers Act of 1968 (ABA).

F102 Dimensions for Adults and Children

The technical requirements are based on adult dimensions and anthropometrics. In addition, this document includes technical requirements based on children's dimensions and anthropometrics for drinking fountains, water closets, toilet compartments, lavatories and sinks, dining surfaces, and work surfaces.

F103 Modifications and Waivers

The Architectural Barriers Act authorizes the Administrator of the General Services Administration, the Secretary of the Department of Housing and Urban Development, the Secretary of the Department of Defense, and the United States Postal Service to modify or waive the *accessibility* standards for *buildings* and *facilities* covered by the Architectural Barriers Act on a case-by-case basis, upon application made by the head of the department, agency, or instrumentality of the United States concerned. The General Services Administration, the Department of Housing and Urban Development, the Department of Defense, and the United States Postal Service may grant a modification or waiver only upon a determination that it is clearly necessary. Section 502(b)(1) of the Rehabilitation Act of 1973 authorizes the Access Board to ensure that modifications and waivers are based on findings of fact and are not inconsistent with the Architectural Barriers Act.

> **Advisory F103 Modifications and Waivers.** The provisions for modifications and waivers differ from the requirement issued under the Americans with Disabilities Act in that "equivalent facilitation" does not apply. There is a formal procedure for Federal agencies to request a waiver or modification of applicable standards under the Architectural Barriers Act.

F104 Conventions

F104.1 Dimensions. Dimensions that are not stated as "maximum" or "minimum" are absolute.

F104.1.1 Construction and Manufacturing Tolerances. All dimensions are subject to conventional industry tolerances except where the requirement is stated as a range with specific minimum and maximum end points.

72

Advisory F104.1.1 Construction and Manufacturing Tolerances. Conventional industry tolerances recognized by this provision include those for field conditions and those that may be a necessary consequence of a particular manufacturing process. Recognized tolerances are not intended to apply to design work.

It is good practice when specifying dimensions to avoid specifying a tolerance where dimensions are absolute. For example, if this document requires "1½ inches," avoid specifying "1½ inches plus or minus X inches."

Where the requirement states a specified range, such as in Section 609.4 where grab bars must be installed between 33 inches and 36 inches above the floor, the range provides an adequate tolerance and therefore no tolerance outside of the range at either end point is permitted.

Where a requirement is a minimum or a maximum dimension that does not have two specific minimum and maximum end points, tolerances may apply. Where an element is to be installed at the minimum or maximum permitted dimension, such as "15 inches minimum" or "5 pounds maximum", it would not be good practice to specify "5 pounds (plus X pounds) or 15 inches (minus X inches)." Rather, it would be good practice to specify a dimension less than the required maximum (or more than the required minimum) by the amount of the expected field or manufacturing tolerance and not to state any tolerance in conjunction with the specified dimension.

Specifying dimensions in design in the manner described above will better ensure that facilities and elements accomplish the level of accessibility intended by these requirements. It will also more often produce an end result of strict and literal compliance with the stated requirements and eliminate enforcement difficulties and issues that might otherwise arise. Information on specific tolerances may be available from industry or trade organizations, code groups and building officials, and published references.

F104.2 Calculation of Percentages. Where the required number of *elements* or *facilities* to be provided is determined by calculations of ratios or percentages and remainders or fractions result, the next greater whole number of such *elements* or *facilities* shall be provided. Where the determination of the required size or dimension of an *element* or *facility* involves ratios or percentages, rounding down for values less than one half shall be permitted.

F104.3 Figures. Unless specifically stated otherwise, figures are provided for informational purposes only.

Convention	Description
36 / 915	dimension showing English units (in inches unless otherwise specified) above the line and SI units (in millimeters unless otherwise specified) below the line
6 / 150	dimension for small measurements
33-36 / 840-915	dimension showing a range with minimum - maximum
min	minimum
max	maximum
>	greater than
≥	greater than or equal to
<	less than
≤	less than or equal to
– – – – –	boundary of clear floor space or maneuvering clearance
— — — — ₵	centerline
— ·· — ·· —	a permitted element or its extension
⇒	direction of travel or approach
▬▬▬▬	a wall, floor, ceiling or other element cut in section or plan
▓▓▓▓	a highlighted element in elevation or plan
▨▨▨▨	location zone of element, control or feature

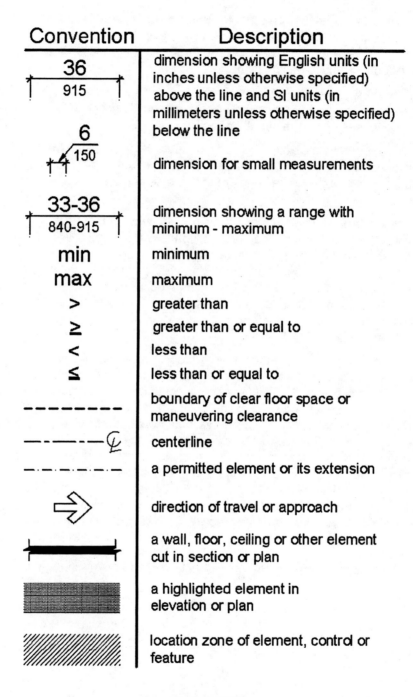

Figure F104
Graphic Convention for Figures

74

F105 Referenced Standards

F105.1 General. The standards listed in F105.2 are incorporated by reference in this document and are part of the requirements to the prescribed extent of each such reference. The Director of the Federal Register has approved these standards for incorporation by reference in accordance with 5 U.S.C. 552(a) and 1 CFR part 51. Copies of the referenced standards may be inspected at the Architectural and Transportation Barriers Compliance Board, 1331 F Street, NW, Suite 1000, Washington, DC 20004; at the Department of Justice, Civil Rights Division, Disability Rights Section, 1425 New York Avenue, NW, Washington, DC; at the Department of Transportation, 400 Seventh Street, SW, Room 10424, Washington DC; or at the National Archives and Records Administration (NARA). For information on the availability of this material at NARA, call (202) 741-6030, or go to http://www.archives.gov/federal_register/code_of_federal_regulations/ibr_locations.html.

F105.2 Referenced Standards. The specific edition of the standards listed below are referenced in this document. Where differences occur between this document and the referenced standards, this document applies.

F105.2.1 ANSI/BHMA. Copies of the referenced standards may be obtained from the Builders Hardware Manufacturers Association, 355 Lexington Avenue, 17th floor, New York, NY 10017 (http://www.buildershardware.com).

ANSI/BHMA A156.10-1999 American National Standard for Power Operated Pedestrian Doors (see 404.3).

ANSI/BHMA A156.19-1997 American National Standard for Power Assist and Low Energy Power Operated Doors (see 404.3, 408.3.2.1, and 409.3.1).

ANSI/BHMA A156.19-2002 American National Standard for Power Assist and Low Energy Power Operated Doors (see 404.3, 408.3.2.1, and 409.3.1).

> **Advisory F105.2.1 ANSI/BHMA.** ANSI/BHMA A156.10-1999 applies to power operated doors for pedestrian use which open automatically when approached by pedestrians. Included are provisions intended to reduce the chance of user injury or entrapment.
>
> ANSI/BHMA A156.19-1997 and A156.19-2002 applies to power assist doors, low energy power operated doors or low energy power open doors for pedestrian use not provided for in ANSI/BHMA A156.10 for Power Operated Pedestrian Doors. Included are provisions intended to reduce the chance of user injury or entrapment.

F105.2.2 ASME. Copies of the referenced standards may be obtained from the American Society of Mechanical Engineers, Three Park Avenue, New York, New York 10016 (http://www.asme.org).

ASME A17.1- 2000 Safety Code for Elevators and Escalators, including ASME A17.1a-2002 Addenda and ASME A17.1b-2003 Addenda (see 407.1, 408.1, 409.1, and 810.9).

ASME A18.1-1999 Safety Standard for Platform Lifts and Stairway Chairlifts, including ASME A18.1a-2001 Addenda and ASME A18.1b-2001 Addenda (see 410.1).

ASME A18.1-2003 Safety Standard for Platform Lifts and Stairway Chairlifts, (see 410.1).

Advisory F105.2.2 ASME. ASME A17.1-2000 is used by local jurisdictions throughout the United States for the design, construction, installation, operation, inspection, testing, maintenance, alteration, and repair of elevators and escalators. The majority of the requirements apply to the operational machinery not seen or used by elevator passengers. ASME A17.1 requires a two-way means of emergency communications in passenger elevators. This means of communication must connect with emergency or authorized personnel and not an automated answering system. The communication system must be push button activated. The activation button must be permanently identified with the word "HELP." A visual indication acknowledging the establishment of a communications link to authorized personnel must be provided. The visual indication must remain on until the call is terminated by authorized personnel. The building location, the elevator car number, and the need for assistance must be provided to authorized personnel answering the emergency call. The use of a handset by the communications system is prohibited. Only the authorized personnel answering the call can terminate the call. Operating instructions for the communications system must be provided in the elevator car.

The provisions for escalators require that at least two flat steps be provided at the entrance and exit of every escalator and that steps on escalators be demarcated by yellow lines 2 inches wide maximum along the back and sides of steps.

ASME A18.1-1999 and ASME A18.1-2003 address the design, construction, installation, operation, inspection, testing, maintenance and repair of lifts that are intended for transportation of persons with disabilities. Lifts are classified as: vertical platform lifts, inclined platform lifts, inclined stairway chairlifts, private residence vertical platform lifts, private residence inclined platform lifts, and private residence inclined stairway chairlifts.

This document does not permit the use of inclined stairway chairlifts which do not provide platforms because such lifts require the user to transfer to a seat.

ASME A18.1 contains requirements for runways, which are the spaces in which platforms or seats move. The standard includes additional provisions for runway enclosures, electrical equipment and wiring, structural support, headroom clearance (which is 80 inches minimum), lower level access ramps and pits. The enclosure walls not used for entry or exit are required to have a grab bar the full length of the wall on platform lifts. Access ramps are required to meet requirements similar to those for ramps in Chapter 4 of this document.

Each of the lift types addressed in ASME A18.1 must meet requirements for capacity, load, speed, travel, operating devices, and control equipment. The maximum permitted height for operable parts is consistent with Section 308 of this document. The standard also addresses attendant operation. However, Section 410.1 of this document does not permit attendant operation.

F105.2.3 ASTM. Copies of the referenced standards may be obtained from the American Society for Testing and Materials, 100 Bar Harbor Drive, West Conshohocken, Pennsylvania 19428 (http://www.astm.org).

ASTM F 1292-99 Standard Specification for Impact Attenuation of Surface Systems Under and Around Playground Equipment (see 1008.2.6.2).

ASTM F 1292-04 Standard Specification for Impact Attenuation of Surfacing Materials Within the Use Zone of Playground Equipment (see 1008.2.6.2).

ASTM F 1487-01 Standard Consumer Safety Performance Specification for Playground Equipment for Public Use (see F106.5).

ASTM F 1951-99 Standard Specification for Determination of Accessibility of Surface Systems Under and Around Playground Equipment (see 1008.2.6.1).

Advisory F105.2.3 ASTM. ASTM F 1292-99 and ASTM F 1292-04 establish a uniform means to measure and compare characteristics of surfacing materials to determine whether materials provide a safe surface under and around playground equipment. These standards are referenced in the play areas requirements of this document when an accessible surface is required inside a play area use zone where a fall attenuating surface is also required. The standards cover the minimum impact attenuation requirements, when tested in accordance with Test Method F 355, for surface systems to be used under and around any piece of playground equipment from which a person may fall.

ASTM F 1487-01 establishes a nationally recognized safety standard for public playground equipment to address injuries identified by the U.S. Consumer Product Safety Commission. It defines the use zone, which is the ground area beneath and immediately adjacent to a play structure or play equipment designed for unrestricted circulation around the equipment and on whose surface it is predicted that a user would land when falling from or exiting a play structure or equipment. The play areas requirements in this document reference the ASTM F 1487 standard when defining accessible routes that overlap use zones requiring fall attenuating surfaces. If the use zone of a playground is not entirely surfaced with an accessible material, at least one accessible route within the use zone must be provided from the perimeter to all accessible play structures or components within the playground.

ASTM F 1951-99 establishes a uniform means to measure the characteristics of surface systems in order to provide performance specifications to select materials for use as an accessible surface under and around playground equipment. Surface materials that comply with this standard and are located in the use zone must also comply with ASTM F 1292. The test methods in this standard address access for children and adults who may traverse the surfacing to aid children who are playing. When a surface is tested it must have an average work per foot value for straight propulsion and for turning less than the average work per foot values for straight propulsion and for turning, respectively, on a hard, smooth surface with a grade of 7% (1:14).

F105.2.4 ICC/IBC. Copies of the referenced standard may be obtained from the International Code Council, 5203 Leesburg Pike, Suite 600, Falls Church, Virginia 22041 (www.iccsafe.org).

International Building Code, 2000 Edition (see F207.1, F207.2, F216.4.2, F216.4.3, and 1005.2.1).

International Building Code, 2001 Supplement (see F207.1 and F207.2).

International Building Code, 2003 Edition (see F207.1, F207.2, F216.4.2, F216.4.3, and 1005.2.1).

Advisory F105.2.4 ICC/IBC. International Building Code (IBC)-2000 (including 2001 Supplement to the International Codes) and IBC-2003 are referenced for means of egress, areas of refuge, and railings provided on fishing piers and platforms. At least one accessible means of egress is required for every accessible space and at least two accessible means of egress are required where more than one means of egress is required. The technical criteria for accessible means of egress allow the use of exit stairways and evacuation elevators when provided in conjunction with horizontal exits or areas of refuge. While typical elevators are not designed to be used during an emergency evacuation, evacuation elevators are designed with standby power and other features according to the elevator safety standard and can be used for the evacuation of individuals with disabilities. The IBC also provides requirements for areas of refuge, which are fire-rated spaces on levels above or below the exit discharge levels where people unable to use stairs can go to register a call for assistance and wait for evacuation.

The recreation facilities requirements of this document references two sections in the IBC for fishing piers and platforms. An exception addresses the height of the railings, guards, or handrails where a fishing pier or platform is required to include a guard, railing, or handrail higher than 34 inches (865 mm) above the ground or deck surface.

F105.2.5 NFPA. Copies of the referenced standards may be obtained from the National Fire Protection Association, 1 Batterymarch Park, Quincy, Massachusetts 02169-7471, (http://www.nfpa.org).

NFPA 72 National Fire Alarm Code, 1999 Edition (see 702.1 and 809.5.2).

NFPA 72 National Fire Alarm Code, 2002 Edition (see 702.1 and 809.5.2).

Advisory F105.2.5 NFPA. NFPA 72-1999 and NFPA 72-2002 address the application, installation, performance, and maintenance of protective signaling systems and their components. The NFPA 72 incorporates Underwriters Laboratory (UL) 1971 by reference. The standard specifies the characteristics of audible alarms, such as placement and sound levels. However, Section 702 of these requirements limits the volume of an audible alarm to 110 dBA, rather than the maximum 120 dBA permitted by NFPA 72-1999.

NFPA 72 specifies characteristics for visible alarms, such as flash frequency, color, intensity, placement, and synchronization. However, Section 702 of this document requires that visual alarm appliances be permanently installed. UL 1971 specifies intensity dispersion requirements for visible alarms. In particular, NFPA 72 requires visible alarms to have a light source that is clear or white and has polar dispersion complying with UL 1971.

F106 Definitions

F106.1 General. For the purpose of this document, the terms defined in F106.5 have the indicated meaning.

> **Advisory F106.1 General.** Terms defined in Section 106.5 are italicized in the text of this document.

F106.2 Terms Defined in Referenced Standard. Terms not defined in F106.5 or in regulations issued by the Administrator of the General Services Administration, the Secretary of Defense, the Secretary of Housing and Urban Development, or the United States Postal Service to implement the Architectural Barriers Act but specifically defined in a referenced standard, shall have the specified meaning from the referenced standard unless otherwise stated

F106.3 Undefined Terms. The meaning of terms not specifically defined in F106.5 or in regulations issued by the Administrator of the General Services Administration, the Secretary of Defense, the Secretary of Housing and Urban Development, or the United States Postal Service

to implement the Architectural Barriers Act or in referenced standards shall be as defined by collegiate dictionaries in the sense that the context implies.

F106.4 Interchangeability. Words, terms and phrases used in the singular include the plural and those used in the plural include the singular.

F106.5 Defined Terms.

Accessible. A *site*, *building*, *facility*, or portion thereof that complies with this part.

Accessible Means of Egress. A continuous and unobstructed way of egress travel from any point in a *building* or *facility* that provides an *accessible* route to an area of refuge, a horizontal exit, or a *public way*.

Addition. An expansion, extension, or increase in the gross floor area or height of a *building* or *facility*.

Administrative Authority. A governmental agency that adopts or enforces regulations and guidelines for the design, construction, or *alteration* of *buildings* and *facilities*.

Alteration. A change to a *building* or *facility* that affects or could affect the usability of the *building* or *facility* or portion thereof. *Alterations* include, but are not limited to, remodeling, renovation, rehabilitation, reconstruction, historic restoration, resurfacing of *circulation paths* or *vehicular ways*, changes or rearrangement of the structural parts or *elements*, and changes or rearrangement in the plan configuration of walls and full-height partitions. Normal maintenance, reroofing, painting or wallpapering, or changes to mechanical and electrical systems are not *alterations* unless they affect the usability of the *building* or *facility*.

Amusement Attraction. Any *facility*, or portion of a *facility*, located within an amusement park or theme park which provides amusement without the use of an amusement device. Amusement attractions include, but are not limited to, fun houses, barrels, and other attractions without seats.

Amusement Ride. A system that moves persons through a fixed course within a defined area for the purpose of amusement.

Amusement Ride Seat. A seat that is built-in or mechanically fastened to an *amusement ride* intended to be occupied by one or more passengers.

Area of Sport Activity. That portion of a room or *space* where the play or practice of a sport occurs.

Assembly Area. A *building* or *facility*, or portion thereof, used for the purpose of entertainment, worship, educational or civic gatherings, or similar purposes. For the purposes of these requirements, *assembly areas* include, but are not limited to, classrooms, lecture halls, courtrooms, public meeting rooms, public hearing rooms, legislative chambers, motion picture houses, auditoria, theaters, playhouses, dinner theaters, concert halls, centers for the performing arts, amphitheaters, arenas, stadiums, grandstands, or convention centers.

Assistive Listening System (ALS). An amplification system utilizing transmitters, receivers, and coupling devices to bypass the acoustical *space* between a sound source and a listener by means of induction loop, radio frequency, infrared, or direct-wired equipment.

Boarding Pier. A portion of a pier where a boat is temporarily secured for the purpose of embarking or disembarking.

Boat Launch Ramp. A sloped surface designed for launching and retrieving trailered boats and other water craft to and from a body of water.

Boat Slip. That portion of a pier, main pier, finger pier, or float where a boat is moored for the purpose of berthing, embarking, or disembarking.

Building. Any structure used or intended for supporting or sheltering any use or occupancy.

Catch Pool. A pool or designated section of a pool used as a terminus for water slide flumes.

Characters. Letters, numbers, punctuation marks and typographic symbols.

Children's Use. Describes *spaces* and *elements* specifically designed for use primarily by people 12 years old and younger.

Circulation Path. An exterior or interior way of passage provided for pedestrian travel, including but not limited to, *walks*, hallways, courtyards, elevators, platform lifts, *ramps*, stairways, and landings.

Closed-Circuit Telephone. A telephone with a dedicated line such as a house phone, courtesy phone or phone that must be used to gain entry to a *facility*.

Common Use. Interior or exterior *circulation paths*, rooms, *spaces*, or *elements* that are not for *public use* and are made available for the shared use of two or more people.

Cross Slope. The slope that is perpendicular to the direction of travel (see *running slope*).

Curb Ramp. A short *ramp* cutting through a curb or built up to it.

Detectable Warning. A standardized surface feature built in or applied to walking surfaces or other *elements* to warn of hazards on a *circulation path*.

Element. An architectural or mechanical component of a *building*, *facility*, *space*, or *site*.

Elevated Play Component. A *play component* that is approached above or below grade and that is part of a composite play structure consisting of two or more *play components* attached or functionally linked to create an integrated unit providing more than one play activity.

Employee Work Area. All or any portion of a *space* used only by employees and used only for work. Corridors, toilet rooms, kitchenettes and break rooms are not *employee work areas*.

Entrance. Any access point to a *building* or portion of a *building* or *facility* used for the purpose of entering. An *entrance* includes the approach *walk*, the vertical access leading to the *entrance* platform, the *entrance* platform itself, vestibule if provided, the entry door or gate, and the hardware of the entry door or gate.

Facility. All or any portion of *buildings*, structures, *site* improvements, *elements*, and pedestrian routes or *vehicular ways* located on a *site*.

Gangway. A variable-sloped pedestrian walkway that links a fixed structure or land with a floating structure. *Gangways* that connect to vessels are not addressed by this document.

Golf Car Passage. A continuous passage on which a motorized golf car can operate.

Ground Level Play Component. A *play component* that is approached and exited at the ground level.

Joint Use. Interior or exterior rooms, *spaces*, or *elements* that are common *space* available for use by all occupants of the *building*. *Joint use* does not include mechanical or custodial rooms, or areas occupied by other tenants.

Lease. Any agreement which establishes the relationship of landlord and tenant.

Mail Boxes. Receptacles for the receipt of documents, packages, or other deliverable matter. *Mail boxes* include, but are not limited to, post office boxes and receptacles provided by commercial mail-receiving agencies, apartment *facilities*, or schools.

Marked Crossing. A crosswalk or other identified path intended for pedestrian use in crossing a *vehicular way*.

Mezzanine. An intermediate level or levels between the floor and ceiling of any *story* with an aggregate floor area of not more than one-third of the area of the room or *space* in which the level or levels are located. *Mezzanines* have sufficient elevation that *space* for human occupancy can be provided on the floor below.

Military Installation. A base, camp, post, station, yard, center, homeport *facility* for any ship, or other activity or operation under the jurisdiction of the Department of Defense, including any *leased facility*. *Military installation* does not include any *facility* used primarily for civil works, rivers and harbors projects, or flood control projects. Multiple, contiguous, or collocated bases, camps, posts, stations, yards, centers, or home ports shall not be considered as constituting a single *military installation*.

Occupant Load. The number of persons for which the means of egress of a *building* or portion of a *building* is designed.

Operable Part. A component of an *element* used to insert or withdraw objects, or to activate, deactivate, or adjust the *element*.

Pictogram. A pictorial symbol that represents activities, *facilities*, or concepts.

Play Area. A portion of a *site* containing *play components* designed and constructed for children.

Play Component. An *element* intended to generate specific opportunities for play, socialization, or learning. *Play components* are manufactured or natural; and are stand-alone or part of a composite play structure.

Public Entrance. An *entrance* that is not a *service entrance* or a *restricted entrance*.

Public Use. Interior or exterior rooms, *spaces*, or *elements* that are made available to the public. *Public use* may be provided at a *building* or *facility* that is privately or publicly owned.

Public Way. Any street, alley or other parcel of land open to the outside air leading to a public street, which has been deeded, dedicated or otherwise permanently appropriated to the public for *public use*, and which has a clear width and height of not less than 10 feet (3050 mm).

Qualified Historic Building or Facility. A *building* or *facility* that is listed in or eligible for listing in the National Register of Historic Places, or designated as historic under an appropriate State or local law.

Ramp. A walking surface that has a *running slope* steeper than 1:20.

Residential Dwelling Unit. A unit intended to be used as a residence, that is primarily long-term in nature. *Residential dwelling units* do not include *transient lodging*, inpatient medical care, licensed long-term care, and detention or correctional *facilities*.

Restricted Entrance. An *entrance* that is made available for *common use* on a controlled basis but not *public use* and that is not a *service entrance*.

Running Slope. The slope that is parallel to the direction of travel (see *cross slope*).

Self-Service Storage. *Building* or *facility* designed and used for the purpose of renting or *leasing* individual storage *spaces* to customers for the purpose of storing and removing personal property on a self-service basis.

Service Entrance. An *entrance* intended primarily for delivery of goods or services.

Site. A parcel of land bounded by a property line or a designated portion of a public right-of-way.

Soft Contained Play Structure. A play structure made up of one or more *play components* where the user enters a fully enclosed play environment that utilizes pliable materials, such as plastic, netting, or fabric.

Space. A definable area, such as a room, toilet room, hall, *assembly area*, *entrance*, storage room, alcove, courtyard, or lobby.

Story. That portion of a *building* or *facility* designed for human occupancy included between the upper surface of a floor and upper surface of the floor or roof next above. A *story* containing one or more *mezzanines* has more than one floor level.

Structural Frame. The columns and the girders, beams, and trusses having direct connections to the columns and all other members that are essential to the stability of the *building* or *facility* as a whole.

Tactile. An object that can be perceived using the sense of touch.

Technically Infeasible. With respect to an *alteration* of a *building* or a *facility*, something that has little likelihood of being accomplished because existing structural conditions would require removing or *altering* a load-bearing member that is an essential part of the *structural frame*; or because other existing physical or *site* constraints prohibit modification or *addition* of *elements*, *spaces*, or features that are in full and strict compliance with the minimum requirements.

Teeing Ground. In golf, the starting place for the hole to be played.

Transfer Device. Equipment designed to facilitate the transfer of a person from a wheelchair or other mobility aid to and from an *amusement ride seat*.

Transient Lodging. A *building* or *facility* containing one or more guest room(s) for sleeping that provides accommodations that are primarily short-term in nature. *Transient lodging* does not include *residential dwelling units* intended to be used as a residence, inpatient medical care *facilities*, licensed long-term care *facilities*, detention or correctional *facilities*, or *private buildings or facilities* that contain not more than five rooms for rent or hire and that are actually occupied by the proprietor as the residence of such proprietor.

Transition Plate. A sloping pedestrian walking surface located at the end(s) of a *gangway*.

TTY. An abbreviation for teletypewriter. Machinery that employs interactive text-based communication through the transmission of coded signals across the telephone network. *TTYs* may include, for example, devices known as TDDs (telecommunication display devices or telecommunication devices for deaf persons) or computers with special modems. *TTYs* are also called text telephones.

Use Zone. The ground level area beneath and immediately adjacent to a play structure or play equipment that is designated by ASTM F 1487 (incorporated by reference, see "Referenced Standards" in Chapter 1) for unrestricted circulation around the play equipment and where it is predicted that a user would land when falling from or exiting the play equipment.

Vehicular Way. A route provided for vehicular traffic, such as in a street, driveway, or parking *facility*.

Walk. An exterior prepared surface for pedestrian use, including pedestrian areas such as plazas and courts.

Wheelchair Space. *Space* for a single wheelchair and its occupant.

Work Area Equipment. Any machine, instrument, engine, motor, pump, conveyor, or other apparatus used to perform work. As used in this document, this term shall apply only to equipment that is permanently installed or built-in in *employee work areas* subject to the Americans with Disabilities Act of 1990 (ADA). *Work area equipment* does not include passenger elevators and other accessible means of vertical transportation.

ABA CHAPTER 2: SCOPING REQUIREMENTS

F201 Application

F201.1 Scope. All areas of newly designed and newly constructed *buildings* and *facilities* and *altered* or *leased* portions of existing *buildings* and *facilities* shall comply with these requirements.

> **Advisory F201.1 Scope.** The requirements are to be applied to all areas of a facility unless exempted, or where scoping limits the number of multiple elements required to be accessible. For example, not all medical care patient rooms are required to be accessible; those that are not required to be accessible are not required to comply with these requirements. However, common use and public use spaces such as recovery rooms, examination rooms, and cafeterias are not exempt from these requirements and must be accessible.

F201.2 Application Based on Building or Facility Use. Where a *site*, *building*, *facility*, room, or *space* contains more than one use, each portion shall comply with the applicable requirements for that use.

F201.3 Temporary and Permanent Structures. These requirements shall apply to temporary and permanent *buildings* and *facilities*.

> **Advisory F201.3 Temporary and Permanent Structures.** Temporary buildings or facilities covered by these requirements include, but are not limited to, reviewing stands, temporary classrooms, bleacher areas, stages, platforms and daises, fixed furniture systems, wall systems, and exhibit areas, temporary banking facilities, and temporary health screening facilities. Structures and equipment directly associated with the actual processes of construction are not required to be accessible as permitted in F203.3.

F202 Existing Buildings and Facilities

F202.1 General. *Additions* and *alterations* to existing *buildings* or *facilities*, including *leased buildings* or *facilities*, shall comply with F202.

F202.2 Additions. Each *addition* to an existing *building* or *facility* shall comply with the requirements for new construction.

F202.2.1 Accessible Route. At least one *accessible* route shall be provided within the *site* from *accessible* parking *spaces* and *accessible* passenger loading zones; public streets and sidewalks; and public transportation stops to an *accessible entrance* serving the *addition*. If the only *accessible entrances* serving the *addition* are provided in the existing *building* or *facility*, the *accessible* route shall connect at least one existing *entrance* to all *accessible spaces* and *elements* within the *addition*. In addition, *elements* and *spaces* specified in F202.2.2 through F202.2.5 shall be on an *accessible* route.

F202.2.2 Entrance. Where an *entrance* is not provided in an *addition*, at least one *entrance* in the existing *building* or *facility* shall comply with F206.4 and shall serve the *addition*.

F202.2.3 Toilet and Bathing Facilities. Where toilet *facilities* and bathing *facilities* are not provided in an *addition* but are provided in the existing *building* or *facility* to serve the *addition*, the toilet *facilities* and bathing *facilities* shall comply with F202.2.3.

    EXCEPTION: In *alterations* to areas serving *additions* where it is *technically infeasible* to comply with 603, *altering* existing toilet or bathing rooms is not required where a single unisex toilet room or bathing room complying with F213.2.1 is provided to serve the *addition*.

F202.2.3.1 Existing Toilet Facility. Where existing toilet *facilities* are provided in the existing *building* or *facility*, at least one toilet *facility* for men and at least one toilet *facility* for women shall comply with F213.2 and F213.3 and shall serve the *addition*.

    EXCEPTION: Where only one toilet *facility* is provided in the existing *building* or *facility*, one toilet *facility* shall comply with F213.2 and F213.3 and shall serve the *addition*.

F202.2.3.2 Existing Bathing Facility. Where existing bathing *facilities* are provided in the existing *building* or *facility*, at least one bathing *facility* for men and at least one bathing *facility* for women shall comply with F213.2 and F213.3 and shall serve the *addition*.

    EXCEPTION: Where only one bathing *facility* is provided in the existing *building* or *facility*, one bathing *facility* shall comply with F213.2 and F213.3 and shall serve the *addition*.

F202.2.4 Public Telephone. Where a public telephone is not provided in an *addition* but is provided in the existing *building* or *facility* to serve the *addition*, at least one public telephone in the existing *building* or *facility* shall comply with F217.

F202.2.5 Drinking Fountain. Where a drinking fountain is not provided in an *addition* but is provided in the existing *building* or *facility* to serve the *addition*, at least one drinking fountain in the existing *building* or *facility* shall comply with 602.1 through 602.6.

F202.3 Alterations. Where existing *elements* or *spaces* are *altered*, each *altered element* or *space* shall comply with the applicable requirements of Chapter 2.

    EXCEPTIONS: 1. Unless required by F202.4, where *elements* or *spaces* are *altered* and the *circulation path* to the *altered element* or *space* is not *altered*, an *accessible* route shall not be required.

    2. In *alterations*, where compliance with applicable requirements is *technically infeasible*, the *alteration* shall comply with the requirements to the maximum extent feasible.

    3. *Residential dwelling units* not required to be *accessible* in compliance with a standard issued pursuant to the Architectural Barriers Act or Section 504 of the Rehabilitation Act of 1973, as amended, shall not be required to comply with F202.3.

> **Advisory F202.3 Alterations.** Although covered entities are permitted to limit the scope of an alteration to individual elements, the alteration of multiple elements within a room or space may provide a cost-effective opportunity to make the entire room or space accessible. Any elements or spaces of the building or facility that are required to comply with these requirements must be made accessible within the scope of the alteration, to the maximum extent feasible. If providing accessibility in compliance with these requirements for people with one type of disability (e.g., people who use wheelchairs) is not feasible, accessibility must still be provided in compliance with the requirements for people with other types of disabilities (e.g., people who have hearing impairments or who have vision impairments) to the extent that such accessibility is feasible.

F202.3.1 Prohibited Reduction in Access. An *alteration* that decreases or has the effect of decreasing the *accessibility* of a *building* or *facility* below the requirements for new construction at the time of the *alteration* is prohibited.

F202.3.2 Extent of Application. An *alteration* of an existing *element, space,* or area of a *building* or *facility* shall not impose a requirement for *accessibility* greater than required for new construction.

F202.4 Alterations Affecting Primary Function Areas. In addition to the requirements of F202.3, an *alteration* that affects or could affect the usability of or access to an area containing a primary function shall be made so as to ensure that, to the maximum extent feasible, the path of travel to the *altered* area, including the rest rooms, telephones, and drinking fountains serving the *altered* area, are readily *accessible* to and usable by individuals with disabilities, unless such *alterations* are disproportionate to the overall *alterations* in terms of cost and scope as determined under criteria established by the Administrator of the General Services Administration, the Secretary of Defense, the Secretary of Housing and Urban Development, or the United States Postal Service.
EXCEPTION: *Residential dwelling units* shall not be required to comply with F202.4.

> **Advisory F202.4 Alterations Affecting Primary Function Areas.** An area of a building or facility containing a major activity for which the building or facility is intended is a primary function area. There can be multiple areas containing a primary function in a single building. Primary function areas are not limited to public use areas. For example, both a bank lobby and the bank's employee areas such as the teller areas and walk-in safe are primary function areas. Also, mixed use facilities may include numerous primary function areas for each use. Areas containing a primary function do not include: mechanical rooms, boiler rooms, supply storage rooms, employee lounges or locker rooms, janitorial closets, entrances, corridors, or restrooms.

F202.5 Alterations to Qualified Historic Buildings and Facilities. *Alterations* to a *qualified historic building* or *facility* shall comply with F202.3 and F202.4.
EXCEPTION: Where the State Historic Preservation Officer or Advisory Council on Historic Preservation determines that compliance with the requirements for *accessible* routes, *entrances,* or toilet *facilities* would threaten or destroy the historic significance of the *building* or *facility,* the exceptions for *alterations* to *qualified historic buildings or facilities* for that *element* shall be permitted to apply.

Printed by Builder's Book, Inc., Bookstore · www.buildersbook.com

> **Advisory F202.5 Alterations to Qualified Historic Buildings and Facilities Exception.** Section 106 of the National Historic Preservation Act requires that a Federal agency with jurisdiction over a proposed Federal or federally assisted undertaking consider the effect of the action on buildings and facilities listed in or eligible for listing in the National Register of Historic Places prior to approving the expenditure of any Federal funds. The Advisory Council on Historic Preservation has established procedures for Federal agencies to meet this statutory responsibility. See 36 CFR Part 800. The procedures require Federal agencies to consult with the State Historic Preservation Officer, and provide for involvement by the Advisory Council on Historic Preservation in certain cases. There are exceptions for alterations to qualified historic buildings and facilities for accessible routes (F206.2.1 Exception 1 and F206.2.3 Exception 6); entrances (F206.4 Exception 2); and toilet facilities (F213.2 Exception 2). These exceptions apply only when the State Historic Preservation Officer or the Advisory Council on Historic Preservation agrees that compliance with requirements for the specific element would threaten or destroy the historic significance of the building or facility.
>
> The AccessAbility Office at the National Endowment for the Arts (NEA) provides a variety of resources for museum operators and historic properties including: the Design for Accessibility Guide and the Disability Symbols. Contact NEA about these and other resources at (202) 682-5532 or www.arts.gov.

F202.6 Leases. *Buildings* or *facilities* for which new *leases* are negotiated by the Federal government after the effective date of the revised standards issued pursuant to the Architectural Barriers Act, including new *leases* for *buildings* or *facilities* previously occupied by the Federal government, shall comply with F202.6.

    EXCEPTIONS: 1. *Buildings* or *facilities leased* for use by officials servicing disasters on a temporary, emergency basis shall not be required to comply with F202.6.
    2. *Buildings* or *facilities leased* for 12 months or less shall not be required to comply with F202.6 provided that the *lease* may not be extended or renewed.

    F202.6.1 Joint Use Areas. *Joint use* areas serving the *leased space* shall comply with F202.6.
        EXCEPTION: *Alterations* and *additions* to *joint use* areas serving the *leased space* shall not be required to comply with F202.2, F202.3, and F202.5 provided that the *alterations* are not undertaken by or on behalf of the Federal government.

> **Advisory F202.6.1 Joint Use Areas Exception.** When negotiating a lease, ensure that joint use areas are accessible. Inaccessible joint use areas may prevent access to and from leased space.

    F202.6.2 Accessible Route. Primary function areas, as defined by Administrator of the General Services Administration, the Secretary of Defense, the Secretary of Housing and Urban Development, and the United States Postal Service, shall be served by at least one *accessible* route complying with F206. *Elements* and *spaces* required to be *accessible* by F202.6 shall be on an *accessible* route complying with F206.

EXCEPTION: Fire alarms required by F202.6.5.2 and *assistive listening systems* required by F202.6.5.5 shall not be required to be on an *accessible* route.

F202.6.3 Toilet and Bathing Facilities. Where provided, toilet *facilities* and bathing *facilities* shall comply with F202.6.3.

F202.6.3.1 Multiple Facilities. At least one toilet *facility* or bathing *facility* for each sex on each floor that has toilet *facilities* or bathing *facilities* shall comply with F213.2 and F213.3.

F202.6.3.2 Single Facilities. Where only one toilet or bathing *facility* is provided in a *building* or *facility* for each sex, either one unisex toilet or bathing *facility*, or one toilet or bathing *facility* for each sex, shall comply with F213.2 and F213.3.

F202.6.4 Parking. Parking shall comply with F208.

F202.6.5 Other Elements and Spaces. Where provided, the following *elements* and *spaces* shall comply with F202.6.5.

F202.6.5.1 Drinking Fountains. Drinking fountains shall comply with F211.

F202.6.5.2 Fire Alarms. Fire alarms shall comply with F215.
EXCEPTION: Fire alarms shall not be required to comply with 702 where existing power sources must be upgraded to meet the requirement.

F202.6.5.3 Public Telephones. Public telephones shall comply with F217.

F202.6.5.4 Dining Surfaces and Work Surfaces. Dining surfaces and work surfaces shall comply with F226.

F202.6.5.5 Assembly Areas. *Assistive listening systems* shall comply with F219 and assembly seating shall comply with F221.

F202.6.5.6 Sales and Service Counters. Sales and service counters shall comply with F227.

F202.6.5.7 Depositories, Vending Machines, Change Machines, and Mail Boxes. Depositories, vending machines, change machines, and *mail boxes* shall comply with F228.

F202.6.5.8 Residential Facilities. *Residential dwelling units* shall comply with F233.

F203 General Exceptions

F203.1 General. *Sites, buildings, facilities,* and *elements* are exempt from these requirements to the extent specified by F203.

F203.2 Existing Elements. *Elements* in compliance with an earlier standard issued pursuant to the Architectural Barriers Act or Section 504 of the Rehabilitation Act of 1973, as amended shall not be required to comply with these requirements unless *altered.*

89

Advisory F203.2 Existing Elements. The exception at F203.2 does not obviate or limit in any way a federal agency's obligation to provide reasonable accommodations pursuant to the Rehabilitation Act of 1973. Federal employees with disabilities are entitled to reasonable accommodations in the workplace. Such accommodations may include modifications to workstations or to other areas of the workplace, including the common areas such as toilet rooms, meeting rooms, or break rooms. Reasonable accommodations are always provided on a case-by-case basis and are specific to the unique needs of a person. As such, an accommodation may be consistent with, or depart from, the specific technical requirements of this, or any other, document.

In addition, the exception at F203.2 provides that compliance with an earlier standard issued under Section 504 of the Rehabilitation Act satisfies the requirements of the Architectural Barriers Act; the exception does not obviate or limit a Federal agency's authority to enforce requirements issued pursuant to Section 504 of the Rehabilitation Act, including requirements for making reasonable modifications to policies, practices, and procedures, or making structural changes to facilities in order to make a program or activity accessible to and usable by persons with disabilities.

F203.3 Construction Sites. Structures and *sites* directly associated with the actual processes of construction, including but not limited to, scaffolding, bridging, materials hoists, materials storage, and construction trailers shall not be required to comply with these requirements or to be on an *accessible* route. Portable toilet units provided for use exclusively by construction personnel on a construction *site* shall not be required to comply with F213 or to be on an *accessible* route.

F203.4 Raised Areas. Areas raised primarily for purposes of security, life safety, or fire safety, including but not limited to, observation or lookout galleries, prison guard towers, fire towers, or life guard stands shall not be required to comply with these requirements or to be on an *accessible* route.

F203.5 Limited Access Spaces. *Spaces* accessed only by ladders, catwalks, crawl *spaces*, or very narrow passageways shall not be required to comply with these requirements or to be on an *accessible* route.

F203.6 Machinery Spaces. *Spaces* frequented only by service personnel for maintenance, repair, or occasional monitoring of equipment shall not be required to comply with these requirements or to be on an *accessible* route. Machinery *spaces* include, but are not limited to, elevator pits or elevator penthouses; mechanical, electrical or communications equipment rooms; piping or equipment catwalks; water or sewage treatment pump rooms and stations; electric substations and transformer vaults; and highway and tunnel utility *facilities*.

F203.7 Single Occupant Structures. Single occupant structures accessed only by passageways below grade or elevated above standard curb height, including but not limited to, toll booths that are accessed only by underground tunnels, shall not be required to comply with these requirements or to be on an *accessible* route.

F203.8 Detention and Correctional Facilities. In detention and correctional *facilities*, *common use* areas that are used only by inmates or detainees and security personnel and that do not serve holding cells or housing cells required to comply with F232, shall not be required to comply with these requirements or to be on an *accessible* route.

F203.9 Residential Facilities. In residential *facilities, common use* areas that do not serve *residential dwelling units* required to provide mobility features complying with 809.2 through 809.4 shall not be required to comply with these requirements or to be on an *accessible* route.

F203.10 Raised Refereeing, Judging, and Scoring Areas. Raised structures used solely for refereeing, judging, or scoring a sport shall not be required to comply with these requirements or to be on an *accessible* route.

F203.11 Water Slides. Water slides shall not be required to comply with these requirements or to be on an *accessible* route.

F203.12 Animal Containment Areas. Animal containment areas that are not for *public use* shall not be required to comply with these requirements or to be on an *accessible* route.

> **Advisory F203.12 Animal Containment Areas.** Public circulation routes where animals may travel, such as in petting zoos and passageways alongside animal pens in State fairs, are not eligible for the exception.

F203.13 Raised Boxing or Wrestling Rings. Raised boxing or wrestling rings shall not be required to comply with these requirements or to be on an *accessible* route.

F203.14 Raised Diving Boards and Diving Platforms. Raised diving boards and diving platforms shall not be required to comply with these requirements or to be on an *accessible* route.

F204 Protruding Objects

F204.1 General. Protruding objects on *circulation paths* shall comply with 307.
EXCEPTIONS: **1.** Within *areas of sport activity*, protruding objects on *circulation paths* shall not be required to comply with 307.
2. Within *play areas*, protruding objects on *circulation paths* shall not be required to comply with 307 provided that ground level *accessible* routes provide vertical clearance in compliance with 1008.2.

F205 Operable Parts

F205.1 General. *Operable parts* on *accessible elements, accessible* routes, and in *accessible* rooms and *spaces* shall comply with 309.
EXCEPTIONS: **1.** *Operable parts* that are intended for use only by service or maintenance personnel shall not be required to comply with 309.
2. Electrical or communication receptacles serving a dedicated use shall not be required to comply with 309.
3. Where two or more outlets are provided in a kitchen above a length of counter top that is uninterrupted by a sink or appliance, one outlet shall not be required to comply with 309.
4. Floor electrical receptacles shall not be required to comply with 309.

5. HVAC diffusers shall not be required to comply with 309.

6. Except for light switches, where redundant controls are provided for a single *element*, one control in each *space* shall not be required to comply with 309.

7. Cleats and other boat securement devices shall not be required to comply with 309.3.

8. Exercise machines and exercise equipment shall not be required to comply with 309.

> **Advisory F205.1 General.** Controls covered by F205.1 include, but are not limited to, light switches, circuit breakers, duplexes and other convenience receptacles, environmental and appliance controls, plumbing fixture controls, and security and intercom systems.

F206 Accessible Routes

F206.1 General. *Accessible* routes shall be provided in accordance with F206 and shall comply with Chapter 4 except that the exemptions at 403.5, 405.5, and 405.8 shall not apply.

F206.2 Where Required. *Accessible* routes shall be provided where required by F206.2.

F206.2.1 Site Arrival Points. At least one *accessible* route shall be provided within the *site* from *accessible* parking *spaces* and *accessible* passenger loading zones; public streets and sidewalks; and public transportation stops to the *accessible building* or *facility entrance* they serve.

EXCEPTIONS: 1. Where exceptions for *alterations* to *qualified historic buildings or facilities* are permitted by F202.5, no more than one *accessible* route from a *site* arrival point to an *accessible entrance* shall be required.

2. An *accessible* route shall not be required between *site* arrival points and the *building* or *facility entrance* if the only means of access between them is a *vehicular way* not providing pedestrian access.

> **Advisory F206.2.1 Site Arrival Points.** Each site arrival point must be connected by an accessible route to the accessible building entrance or entrances served. Where two or more similar site arrival points, such as bus stops, serve the same accessible entrance or entrances, both bus stops must be on accessible routes. In addition, the accessible routes must serve all of the accessible entrances on the site.
>
> **Advisory F206.2.1 Site Arrival Points Exception 2.** Access from site arrival points may include vehicular ways. Where a vehicular way, or a portion of a vehicular way, is provided for pedestrian travel, such as within a shopping center or shopping mall parking lot, this exception does not apply.

F206.2.2 Within a Site. At least one *accessible* route shall connect *accessible buildings*, *accessible facilities*, *accessible elements*, and *accessible spaces* that are on the same *site*.

EXCEPTION: An *accessible* route shall not be required between *accessible buildings*, *accessible facilities*, *accessible elements* and *accessible spaces* if the only means of access between them is a *vehicular way* not providing pedestrian access.

Advisory F206.2.2 Within a Site. An accessible route is required to connect to the boundary of each area of sport activity. Examples of areas of sport activity include: soccer fields, basketball courts, baseball fields, running tracks, skating rinks, and the area surrounding a piece of gymnastic equipment. While the size of an area of sport activity may vary from sport to sport, each includes only the space needed to play. Where multiple sports fields or courts are provided, an accessible route is required to each field or area of sport activity.

F206.2.3 Multi-Story Buildings and Facilities. At least one *accessible* route shall connect each *story* and *mezzanine* in multi-*story buildings* and *facilities*.

EXCEPTIONS: 1. Where a two *story building or facility* has one *story* with an *occupant load* of five or fewer persons that does not contain *public use space*, that *story* shall not be required to be connected to the *story* above or below.

2. In detention and correctional *facilities*, an *accessible* route shall not be required to connect *stories* where cells with mobility features required to comply with 807.2, all *common use* areas serving cells with mobility features required to comply with 807.2, and all *public use* areas are on an *accessible* route.

3. In residential *facilities,* an *accessible* route shall not be required to connect *stories* where *residential dwelling units* with mobility features required to comply with 809.2 through 809.4, all *common use* areas serving *residential dwelling units* with mobility features required to comply with 809.2 through 809.4, and *public use* areas serving *residential dwelling units* are on an *accessible* route.

4. Within multi-*story transient lodging* guest rooms with mobility features required to comply with 806.2, an *accessible* route shall not be required to connect *stories* provided that *spaces* complying with 806.2 are on an *accessible* route and sleeping accommodations for two persons minimum are provided on a *story* served by an accessible route.

5. In air traffic control towers, an *accessible* route shall not be required to serve the cab and the floor immediately below the cab.

6. Where exceptions for *alterations* to *qualified historic buildings or facilities* are permitted by F202.5, an *accessible* route shall not be required to *stories* located above or below the *accessible story*.

Advisory F206.2.3 Multi-Story Buildings and Facilities. Spaces and elements located on a level not required to be served by an accessible route must fully comply with this document. While a mezzanine may be a change in level, it is not a story. If an accessible route is required to connect stories within a building or facility, the accessible route must serve all mezzanines.

Advisory F206.2.3 Multi-Story Buildings and Facilities Exception 3. Where common use areas are provided for the use of residents, it is presumed that all such common use areas "serve" accessible dwelling units unless use is restricted to residents occupying certain dwelling units. For example, if all residents are permitted to use all laundry rooms, then all laundry rooms "serve" accessible dwelling units.

Advisory F206.2.3 Multi-Story Buildings and Facilities Exception 3 (Continued).
However, if the laundry room on the first floor is restricted to use by residents on the first floor, and the second floor laundry room is for use by occupants of the second floor, then first floor accessible units are "served" only by laundry rooms on the first floor. In this example, an accessible route is not required to the second floor provided that all accessible units and all common use areas serving them are on the first floor.

F206.2.3.1 Stairs and Escalators in Existing Buildings. In *alterations* and *additions*, where an escalator or stair is provided where none existed previously and major structural modifications are necessary for the installation, an *accessible* route shall be provided between the levels served by the escalator or stair unless exempted by F206.2.3 Exceptions 1 through 6.

F206.2.4 Spaces and Elements. At least one *accessible* route shall connect *accessible building* or *facility entrances* with all *accessible spaces* and *elements* within the *building* or *facility* which are otherwise connected by a *circulation path* unless exempted by F206.2.3 Exceptions 1 through 6.

EXCEPTIONS: 1. Raised courtroom stations, including judges' benches, clerks' stations, bailiffs' stations, deputy clerks' stations, and court reporters' stations shall not be required to provide vertical access provided that the required clear floor *space*, maneuvering *space*, and, if appropriate, electrical service are installed at the time of initial construction to allow future installation of a means of vertical access complying with 405, 407, 408, or 410 without requiring substantial reconstruction of the *space*.

2. In *assembly areas* with fixed seating required to comply with F221, an *accessible* route shall not be required to serve fixed seating where *wheelchair spaces* required to be on an *accessible* route are not provided.

3. *Accessible* routes shall not be required to connect *mezzanines* where *buildings* or *facilities* have no more than one story. In addition, *accessible* routes shall not be required to connect stories or *mezzanines* where multi-story *buildings* or *facilities* are exempted by F206.2.3 Exceptions 1 through 6.

Advisory F206.2.4 Spaces and Elements. Accessible routes must connect all spaces and elements required to be accessible including, but not limited to, raised areas and speaker platforms.

Advisory F206.2.4 Spaces and Elements Exception 1. The exception does not apply to areas that are likely to be used by members of the public who are not employees of the court such as jury areas, attorney areas, or witness stands.

F206.2.5 Restaurants and Cafeterias. In restaurants and cafeterias, an *accessible* route shall be provided to all dining areas, including raised or sunken dining areas, and outdoor dining areas.

EXCEPTIONS: 1. In *alterations*, an *accessible* route shall not be required to existing raised or sunken dining areas, or to all parts of existing outdoor dining areas where the same services and decor are provided in an *accessible space* usable by the public and not restricted to use by people with disabilities.

2. In sports *facilities,* tiered dining areas providing seating required to comply with F221 shall be required to have *accessible* routes serving at least 25 percent of the dining area provided that *accessible* routes serve seating complying with F221 and each tier is provided with the same services.

> **Advisory F206.2.5 Restaurants and Cafeterias Exception 1.** Examples of "same services" include, but are not limited to, bar service, rooms having smoking and non-smoking sections, lotto and other table games, carry-out, and buffet service. Examples of "same decor" include, but are not limited to, seating at or near windows and railings with views, areas designed with a certain theme, party and banquet rooms, and rooms where entertainment is provided.

F206.2.6 Performance Areas. Where a *circulation path* directly connects a performance area to an assembly seating area, an *accessible* route shall directly connect the assembly seating area with the performance area. An *accessible* route shall be provided from performance areas to ancillary areas or *facilities* used by performers unless exempted by F206.2.3 Exceptions 1 through 6.

F206.2.7 Press Boxes. Press boxes in *assembly areas* shall be on an *accessible* route.
    EXCEPTIONS: 1. An *accessible* route shall not be required to press boxes in bleachers that have points of entry at only one level provided that the aggregate area of all press boxes is 500 square feet (46 m^2) maximum.
    2. An *accessible* route shall not be required to free-standing press boxes that are elevated above grade 12 feet (3660 mm) minimum provided that the aggregate area of all press boxes is 500 square feet (46 m^2) maximum.

> **Advisory F206.2.7 Press Boxes Exception 2.** Where a facility contains multiple assembly areas, the aggregate area of the press boxes in each assembly area is to be calculated separately. For example, if a university has a soccer stadium with three press boxes elevated 12 feet (3660 mm) or more above grade and each press box is 150 square feet (14 m^2), then the aggregate area of the soccer stadium press boxes is less than 500 square feet (465 m^2) and Exception 2 applies to the soccer stadium. If that same university also has a football stadium with two press boxes elevated 12 feet (3660 mm) or more above grade and one press box is 250 square feet (23 m^2), and the second is 275 square feet (26 m^2), then the aggregate area of the football stadium press boxes is more than 500 square feet (465 m^2) and Exception 2 does not apply to the football stadium.

F206.2.8 Amusement Rides. *Amusement rides* required to comply with F234 shall provide *accessible* routes in accordance with F206.2.8. *Accessible* routes serving *amusement rides* shall comply with Chapter 4 except as modified by 1002.2.

    F206.2.8.1 Load and Unload Areas. Load and unload areas shall be on an *accessible* route. Where load and unload areas have more than one loading or unloading position, at least one loading and unloading position shall be on an *accessible* route.

    F206.2.8.2 Wheelchair Spaces, Ride Seats Designed for Transfer, and Transfer Devices. When *amusement rides* are in the load and unload position, *wheelchair spaces* complying with

1002.4, *amusement ride seats* designed for transfer complying with 1002.5, and *transfer devices* complying with 1002.6 shall be on an *accessible* route.

F206.2.9 Recreational Boating Facilities. *Boat slips* required to comply with F235.2 and *boarding piers* at *boat launch ramps* required to comply with F235.3 shall be on an *accessible* route. *Accessible* routes serving recreational boating *facilities* shall comply with Chapter 4 except as modified by 1003.2.

F206.2.10 Bowling Lanes. Where bowling lanes are provided, at least 5 percent, but no fewer than one of each type of bowling lane, shall be on an *accessible* route.

F206.2.11 Court Sports. In court sports, at least one *accessible* route shall directly connect both sides of the court.

F206.2.12 Exercise Machines and Equipment. Exercise machines and equipment required to comply with F236 shall be on an *accessible* route.

F206.2.13 Fishing Piers and Platforms. Fishing piers and platforms shall be on an *accessible* route. *Accessible* routes serving fishing piers and platforms shall comply with Chapter 4 except as modified by 1005.1.

F206.2.14 Golf Facilities. At least one *accessible* route shall connect *accessible elements* and *spaces* within the boundary of the golf course. In addition, *accessible* routes serving golf car rental areas; bag drop areas; course weather shelters complying with F238.2.3; course toilet rooms; and practice putting greens, practice *teeing grounds*, and teeing stations at driving ranges complying with F238.3 shall comply with Chapter 4 except as modified by 1006.2.

    EXCEPTION: *Golf car passages* complying with 1006.3 shall be permitted to be used for all or part of *accessible* routes required by F206.2.14.

F206.2.15 Miniature Golf Facilities. Holes required to comply with F239.2, including the start of play, shall be on an *accessible* route. *Accessible* routes serving miniature golf *facilities* shall comply with Chapter 4 except as modified by 1007.2.

F206.2.16 Play Areas. *Play areas* shall provide *accessible* routes in accordance with F206.2.16. *Accessible* routes serving *play areas* shall comply with Chapter 4 except as modified by 1008.2.

    F206.2.16.1 Ground Level and Elevated Play Components. At least one *accessible* route shall be provided within the *play area*. The *accessible* route shall connect *ground level play components* required to comply with F240.2.1 and *elevated play components* required to comply with F240.2.2, including entry and exit points of the *play components*.

    F206.2.16.2 Soft Contained Play Structures. Where three or fewer entry points are provided for *soft contained play structures*, at least one entry point shall be on an *accessible* route. Where four or more entry points are provided for *soft contained play structures*, at least two entry points shall be on an *accessible* route.

F206.3 Location. *Accessible* routes shall coincide with or be located in the same area as general *circulation paths*. Where *circulation paths* are interior, required *accessible* routes shall also be interior.

> **Advisory F206.3 Location.** The accessible route must be in the same area as the general circulation path. This means that circulation paths, such as vehicular ways designed for pedestrian traffic, walks, and unpaved paths that are designed to be routinely used by pedestrians must be accessible or have an accessible route nearby. Additionally, accessible vertical interior circulation must be in the same area as stairs and escalators, not isolated in the back of the facility.

F206.4 Entrances. *Entrances* shall be provided in accordance with F206.4. *Entrance* doors, doorways, and gates shall comply with 404 and shall be on an *accessible* route complying with 402.

    EXCEPTIONS: 1. Where an *alteration* includes *alterations* to an *entrance*, and the *building* or *facility* has another *entrance* complying with 404 that is on an *accessible* route, the *altered entrance* shall not be required to comply with F206.4 unless required by F202.4.

    2. Where exceptions for *alterations* to *qualified historic buildings or facilities* are permitted by F202.5, no more than one *public entrance* shall be required to comply with F206.4. Where no *public entrance* can comply with F206.4 under criteria established in F202.5 Exception, then either an unlocked *entrance* not used by the public shall comply with F206.4; or a locked *entrance* complying with F206.4 with a notification system or remote monitoring shall be provided.

F206.4.1 Public Entrances. In addition to *entrances* required by F206.4.2 through F206.4.9, at least 60 percent of all *public entrances* shall comply with 404.

F206.4.2 Parking Structure Entrances. Where direct access is provided for pedestrians from a parking structure to a *building* or *facility entrance*, each direct access to the *building* or *facility entrance* shall comply with 404.

F206.4.3 Entrances from Tunnels or Elevated Walkways. Where direct access is provided for pedestrians from a pedestrian tunnel or elevated walkway to a *building* or *facility*, at least one direct *entrance* to the *building* or *facility* from each tunnel or walkway shall comply with 404.

F206.4.4 Transportation Facilities. In addition to the requirements of F206.4.2, F206.4.3, and F206.4.5 through F206.4.9, transportation *facilities* shall provide *entrances* in accordance with F206.4.4.

    F206.4.4.1 Location. In transportation *facilities*, where different *entrances* serve different transportation fixed routes or groups of fixed routes, at least one *public entrance* shall comply with 404.

    F206.4.4.2 Direct Connections. Direct connections to other *facilities* shall provide an *accessible* route complying with 404 from the point of connection to boarding platforms and all transportation system *elements* required to be *accessible*. Any *elements* provided to facilitate future direct connections shall be on an *accessible* route connecting boarding platforms and all transportation system *elements* required to be *accessible*.

F206.4.5 Tenant Spaces. At least one *accessible entrance* to each tenancy in a *facility* shall comply with 404.

> **EXCEPTION:** *Self-service storage* facilities not required to comply with F225.3 shall not be required to be on an *accessible* route.

F206.4.6 Residential Dwelling Unit Primary Entrance. In *residential dwelling units*, at least one primary *entrance* shall comply with 404. The primary *entrance* to a *residential dwelling unit* shall not be to a bedroom.

F206.4.7 Restricted Entrances. Where *restricted entrances* are provided to a *building* or *facility*, at least one *restricted entrance* to the *building* or *facility* shall comply with 404.

F206.4.8 Service Entrances. If a *service entrance* is the only *entrance* to a *building* or to a tenancy in a *facility*, that *entrance* shall comply with 404.

F206.4.9 Entrances for Inmates or Detainees. Where *entrances* used only by inmates or detainees and security personnel are provided at judicial *facilities,* detention *facilities,* or correctional *facilities*, at least one such *entrance* shall comply with 404.

F206.5 Doors, Doorways, and Gates. Doors, doorways, and gates providing user passage shall be provided in accordance with F206.5.

F206.5.1 Entrances. Each *entrance* to a *building* or *facility* required to comply with F206.4 shall have at least one door, doorway, or gate complying with 404.

F206.5.2 Rooms and Spaces. Within a *building* or *facility*, at least one door, doorway, or gate serving each room or *space* complying with these requirements shall comply with 404.

F206.5.3 Transient Lodging Facilities. In *transient lodging facilities, entrances,* doors, and doorways providing user passage into and within guest rooms that are not required to provide mobility features complying with 806.2 shall comply with 404.2.3.

> **EXCEPTION:** Shower and sauna doors in guest rooms that are not required to provide mobility features complying with 806.2 shall not be required to comply with 404.2.3.

F206.5.4 Residential Dwelling Units. In *residential dwelling units* required to provide mobility features complying with 809.2 through 809.4, all doors and doorways providing user passage shall comply with 404.

F206.6 Elevators. Elevators provided for passengers shall comply with 407. Where multiple elevators are provided, each elevator shall comply with 407.

> **EXCEPTIONS: 1.** In a *building* or *facility* permitted to use the exceptions to F206.2.3 or permitted by F206.7 to use a platform lift, elevators complying with 408 shall be permitted.
> **2.** Elevators complying with 408 or 409 shall be permitted in multi-*story residential dwelling units*.

F206.6.1 Existing Elevators. Where *elements* of existing elevators are *altered*, the same *element* shall also be *altered* in all elevators that are programmed to respond to the same hall call control as the *altered* elevator and shall comply with the requirements of 407 for the *altered element*.

F206.7 Platform Lifts. Platform lifts shall comply with 410. Platform lifts shall be permitted as a component of an *accessible* route in new construction in accordance with F206.7. Platform lifts shall be permitted as a component of an *accessible* route in an existing *building* or *facility*.

F206.7.1 Performance Areas and Speakers' Platforms. Platform lifts shall be permitted to provide *accessible* routes to performance areas and speakers' platforms.

F206.7.2 Wheelchair Spaces. Platform lifts shall be permitted to provide an *accessible* route to comply with the *wheelchair space* dispersion and line-of-sight requirements of F221 and 802.

F206.7.3 Incidental Spaces. Platform lifts shall be permitted to provide an *accessible* route to incidental *spaces* which are not *public use spaces* and which are occupied by five persons maximum.

F206.7.4 Judicial Spaces. Platform lifts shall be permitted to provide an *accessible* route to: jury boxes and witness stands; raised courtroom stations including, judges' benches, clerks' stations, bailiffs' stations, deputy clerks' stations, and court reporters' stations; and to depressed areas such as the well of a court.

F206.7.5 Existing Site Constraints. Platform lifts shall be permitted where existing exterior *site* constraints make use of a *ramp* or elevator infeasible.

> **Advisory F206.7.5 Existing Site Constraints.** This exception applies where topography or other similar existing site constraints necessitate the use of a platform lift as the only feasible alternative. While the site constraint must reflect exterior conditions, the lift can be installed in the interior of a building. For example, a new building constructed between and connected to two existing buildings may have insufficient space to coordinate floor levels and also to provide ramped entry from the public way. In this example, an exterior or interior platform lift could be used to provide an accessible entrance or to coordinate one or more interior floor levels.

F206.7.6 Guest Rooms and Residential Dwelling Units. Platform lifts shall be permitted to connect levels within *transient lodging* guest rooms required to provide mobility features complying with 806.2 or *residential dwelling units* required to provide mobility features complying with 809.2 through 809.4.

F206.7.7 Amusement Rides. Platform lifts shall be permitted to provide *accessible* routes to load and unload areas serving *amusement rides*.

F206.7.8 Play Areas. Platform lifts shall be permitted to provide *accessible* routes to *play components* or *soft contained play structures*.

F206.7.9 Team or Player Seating. Platform lifts shall be permitted to provide *accessible* routes to team or player seating areas serving *areas of sport activity*.

> **Advisory F206.7.9 Team or Player Seating.** While the use of platform lifts is allowed, ramps are recommended to provide access to player seating areas serving an area of sport activity.

F206.7.10 Recreational Boating Facilities and Fishing Piers and Platforms. Platform lifts shall be permitted to be used instead of *gangways* that are part of *accessible* routes serving recreational boating *facilities* and fishing piers and platforms.

F206.8 Security Barriers. Security barriers, including but not limited to, security bollards and security check points, shall not obstruct a required *accessible* route or *accessible means of egress*.
> **EXCEPTION:** Where security barriers incorporate *elements* that cannot comply with these requirements such as certain metal detectors, fluoroscopes, or other similar devices, the *accessible* route shall be permitted to be located adjacent to security screening devices. The *accessible* route shall permit persons with disabilities passing around security barriers to maintain visual contact with their personal items to the same extent provided others passing through the security barrier.

F207 Accessible Means of Egress

F207.1 General. Means of egress shall comply with section 1003.2.13 of the International Building Code (2000 edition and 2001 Supplement) or section 1007 of the International Building Code (2003 edition) (incorporated by reference, see "Referenced Standards" in Chapter 1).
> **EXCEPTIONS: 1.** Where means of egress are permitted by local *building* or life safety codes to share a common path of egress travel, *accessible means of egress* shall be permitted to share a common path of egress travel.
> **2.** Areas of refuge shall not be required in detention and correctional *facilities*.

F207.2 Platform Lifts. Standby power shall be provided for platform lifts permitted by section 1003.2.13.4 of the International Building Code (2000 edition and 2001 Supplement) or section 1007.5 of the International Building Code (2003 edition) (incorporated by reference, see "Referenced Standards" in Chapter 1) to serve as a part of an *accessible means of egress*.

F208 Parking Spaces

F208.1 General. Where parking *spaces* are provided, parking *spaces* shall be provided in accordance with F208.
> **EXCEPTION:** Parking *spaces* used exclusively for buses, trucks, other delivery vehicles, law enforcement vehicles, or vehicular impound shall not be required to comply with F208 provided that lots accessed by the public are provided with a passenger loading zone complying with 503.

F208.2 Minimum Number. Parking *spaces* complying with 502 shall be provided in accordance with Table F208.2 except as required by F208.2.1, F208.2.2, and F208.2.3. Where more than one parking *facility* is provided on a *site*, the number of *accessible spaces* provided on the *site* shall be calculated according to the number of *spaces* required for each parking *facility*.

Table F208.2 Parking Spaces

Total Number of Parking Spaces Provided in Parking Facility	Minimum Number of Required Accessible Parking Spaces
1 to 25	1
26 to 50	2
51 to 75	3
76 to 100	4
101 to 150	5
151 to 200	6
201 to 300	7
301 to 400	8
401 to 500	9
501 to 1000	2 percent of total
1001 and over	20, plus 1 for each 100, or fraction thereof, over 1000

Advisory F208.2 Minimum Number. The term "parking facility" is used Section F208.2 instead of the term "parking lot" so that it is clear that both parking lots and parking structures are required to comply with this section. The number of parking spaces required to be accessible is to be calculated separately for each parking facility; the required number is not to be based on the total number of parking spaces provided in all of the parking facilities provided on the site.

F208.2.1 Hospital Outpatient Facilities. Ten percent of patient and visitor parking *spaces* provided to serve hospital outpatient *facilities* shall comply with 502.

Advisory F208.2.1 Hospital Outpatient Facilities. The term "outpatient facility" is not defined in this document but is intended to cover facilities or units that are located in hospitals and that provide regular and continuing medical treatment without an overnight stay. Doctors' offices, independent clinics, or other facilities not located in hospitals are not considered hospital outpatient facilities for purposes of this document.

F208.2.2 Rehabilitation Facilities and Outpatient Physical Therapy Facilities. Twenty percent of patient and visitor parking *spaces* provided to serve rehabilitation *facilities* specializing in treating conditions that affect mobility and outpatient physical therapy *facilities* shall comply with 502.

> **Advisory F208.2.2 Rehabilitation Facilities and Outpatient Physical Therapy Facilities.** Conditions that affect mobility include conditions requiring the use or assistance of a brace, cane, crutch, prosthetic device, wheelchair, or powered mobility aid; arthritic, neurological, or orthopedic conditions that severely limit one's ability to walk; respiratory diseases and other conditions which may require the use of portable oxygen; and cardiac conditions that impose significant functional limitations.

F208.2.3 Residential Facilities. Parking *spaces* provided to serve residential facilities shall comply with F208.2.3.

F208.2.3.1 Parking for Residents. Where at least one parking *space* is provided for each *residential dwelling unit*, at least one parking *space* complying with 502 shall be provided for each *residential dwelling unit* required to provide mobility features complying with 809.2 through 809.4.

F208.2.3.2 Additional Parking Spaces for Residents. Where the total number of parking *spaces* provided for each *residential dwelling unit* exceeds one parking *space* per *residential dwelling unit*, 2 percent, but no fewer than one *space*, of all the parking *spaces* not covered by F208.2.3.1 shall comply with 502.

F208.2.3.3 Parking for Guests, Employees, and Other Non-Residents. Where parking spaces are provided for persons other than residents, parking shall be provided in accordance with Table F208.2.

F208.2.4 Van Parking Spaces. For every six or fraction of six parking *spaces* required by F208.2 to comply with 502, at least one shall be a van parking *space* complying with 502.

F208.3 Location. Parking *facilities* shall comply with F208.3

F208.3.1 General. Parking *spaces* complying with 502 that serve a particular *building* or *facility* shall be located on the shortest *accessible* route from parking to an *entrance* complying with F206.4. Where parking serves more than one *accessible entrance*, parking *spaces* complying with 502 shall be dispersed and located on the shortest *accessible* route to the *accessible entrances*. In parking *facilities* that do not serve a particular *building* or *facility*, parking *spaces* complying with 502 shall be located on the shortest *accessible* route to an *accessible* pedestrian *entrance* of the parking *facility*.
EXCEPTIONS: 1. All van parking *spaces* shall be permitted to be grouped on one level within a multi-*story* parking *facility*.
2. Parking *spaces* shall be permitted to be located in different parking *facilities* if substantially equivalent or greater *accessibility* is provided in terms of distance from an *accessible entrance* or *entrances*, parking fee, and user convenience.

> **Advisory F208.3.1 General Exception 2.** Factors that could affect "user convenience" include, but are not limited to, protection from the weather, security, lighting, and comparative maintenance of the alternative parking site.

F208.3.2 Residential Facilities. In residential *facilities* containing *residential dwelling units* required to provide mobility features complying with 809.2 through 809.4, parking *spaces* provided in accordance with F208.2.3.1 shall be located on the shortest *accessible* route to the *residential dwelling unit entrance* they serve. *Spaces* provided in accordance with F208.2.3.2 shall be dispersed throughout all types of parking provided for the *residential dwelling units*.

    EXCEPTION: Parking *spaces* provided in accordance with F208.2.3.2 shall not be required to be dispersed throughout all types of parking if substantially equivalent or greater *accessibility* is provided in terms of distance from an *accessible entrance*, parking fee, and user convenience.

> **Advisory F208.3.2 Residential Facilities Exception.** Factors that could affect "user convenience" include, but are not limited to, protection from the weather, security, lighting, and comparative maintenance of the alternative parking site.

F209 Passenger Loading Zones and Bus Stops

F209.1 General. Passenger loading zones shall be provided in accordance with F209.

F209.2 Type. Where provided, passenger loading zones shall comply with F209.2.

    F209.2.1 Passenger Loading Zones. Passenger loading zones, except those required to comply with F209.2.2 and F209.2.3, shall provide at least one passenger loading zone complying with 503 in every continuous 100 linear feet (30 m) of loading zone *space*, or fraction thereof.

    F209.2.2 Bus Loading Zones. In bus loading zones restricted to use by designated or specified public transportation vehicles, each bus bay, bus stop, or other area designated for lift or *ramp* deployment shall comply with 810.2.

> **Advisory F209.2.2 Bus Loading Zones.** The terms "designated public transportation" and "specified public transportation" are defined by the Department of Transportation at 49 CFR 37.3 in regulations implementing the Americans with Disabilities Act. These terms refer to public transportation services provided by public or private entities, respectively. For example, designated public transportation vehicles include buses and vans operated by public transit agencies, while specified public transportation vehicles include tour and charter buses, taxis and limousines, and hotel shuttles operated by private entities.

    F209.2.3 On-Street Bus Stops. On-street bus stops shall comply with 810.2 to the maximum extent practicable.

F209.3 Medical Care and Long-Term Care Facilities. At least one passenger loading zone complying with 503 shall be provided at an *accessible entrance* to licensed medical care and licensed long-term care *facilities* where the period of stay exceeds twenty-four hours.

F209.4 Valet Parking. Parking *facilities* that provide valet parking services shall provide at least one passenger loading zone complying with 503.

F209.5 Mechanical Access Parking Garages. Mechanical access parking garages shall provide at least one passenger loading zone complying with 503 at vehicle drop-off and vehicle pick-up areas.

F210 Stairways

F210.1 General. Interior and exterior stairs that are part of a means of egress shall comply with 504.
    EXCEPTIONS: 1. In detention and correctional *facilities*, stairs that are not located in *public use* areas shall not be required to comply with 504.
    2. In *alterations*, stairs between levels that are connected by an *accessible* route shall not be required to comply with 504, except that handrails complying with 505 shall be provided when the stairs are *altered*.
    3. In *assembly areas*, aisle stairs shall not be required to comply with 504.
    4. Stairs that connect *play components* shall not be required to comply with 504.

> **Advisory F210.1 General.** Although these requirements do not mandate handrails on stairs that are not part of a means of egress, State or local building codes may require handrails or guards.

F211 Drinking Fountains

F211.1 General. Where drinking fountains are provided on an exterior *site*, on a floor, and within a secured area they shall be provided in accordance with F211.
    EXCEPTION: In detention or correctional *facilities*, drinking fountains only serving holding or housing cells not required to comply with F232 shall not be required to comply with F211.

F211.2 Minimum Number. No fewer than two drinking fountains shall be provided. One drinking fountain shall comply with 602.1 through 602.6 and one drinking fountain shall comply with 602.7.
    EXCEPTION: Where a single drinking fountain complies with 602.1 through 602.6 and 602.7, it shall be permitted to be substituted for two separate drinking fountains.

F211.3 More Than Minimum Number. Where more than the minimum number of drinking fountains specified in F211.2 are provided, 50 percent of the total number of drinking fountains provided shall comply with 602.1 through 602.6, and 50 percent of the total number of drinking fountains provided shall comply with 602.7.
    EXCEPTION: Where 50 percent of the drinking fountains yields a fraction, 50 percent shall be permitted to be rounded up or down provided that the total number of drinking fountains complying with F211 equals 100 percent of drinking fountains.

F212 Kitchens, Kitchenettes, and Sinks

F212.1 General. Where provided, kitchens, kitchenettes, and sinks shall comply with F212.

F212.2 Kitchens and Kitchenettes. Kitchens and kitchenettes shall comply with 804.

F212.3 Sinks. Where sinks are provided, at least 5 percent, but no fewer than one, of each type provided in each *accessible* room or *space* shall comply with 606.

104

EXCEPTION: Mop or service sinks shall not be required to comply with F212.3.

F213 Toilet Facilities and Bathing Facilities

F213.1 General. Where toilet *facilities* and bathing *facilities* are provided, they shall comply with F213. Where toilet *facilities* and bathing *facilities* are provided in *facilities* permitted by F206.2.3 Exceptions 1 and 2 not to connect *stories* by an *accessible* route, toilet *facilities* and bathing *facilities* shall be provided on a *story* connected by an *accessible* route to an *accessible entrance*.

F213.2 Toilet Rooms and Bathing Rooms. Where toilet rooms are provided, each toilet room shall comply with 603. Where bathing rooms are provided, each bathing room shall comply with 603.

EXCEPTIONS: 1. In *alterations* where it is *technically infeasible* to comply with 603, *altering* existing toilet or bathing rooms shall not be required where a single unisex toilet room or bathing room complying with F213.2.1 is provided and located in the same area and on the same floor as existing inaccessible toilet or bathing rooms.

2. Where exceptions for *alterations* to *qualified historic buildings or facilities* are permitted by F202.5 and toilet rooms are provided, no fewer than one toilet room for each sex complying with 603 or one unisex toilet room complying with F213.2.1 shall be provided.

3. Where multiple single user portable toilet or bathing units are clustered at a single location, no more than 5 percent of the toilet units and bathing units at each cluster shall be required to comply with 603. Portable toilet units and bathing units complying with 603 shall be identified by the International Symbol of *Accessibility* complying with 703.7.2.1.

4. Where multiple single user toilet rooms are clustered at a single location, no more than 50 percent of the single user toilet rooms for each use at each cluster shall be required to comply with 603.

> **Advisory F213.2 Toilet Rooms and Bathing Rooms.** These requirements allow the use of unisex (or single-user) toilet rooms in alterations when technical infeasibility can be demonstrated. Unisex toilet rooms benefit people who use opposite sex personal care assistants. For this reason, it is advantageous to install unisex toilet rooms in addition to accessible single-sex toilet rooms in new facilities.
>
> **Advisory F213.2 Toilet Rooms and Bathing Rooms Exceptions 3 and 4.** A "cluster" is a group of toilet rooms proximate to one another. Generally, toilet rooms in a cluster are within sight of, or adjacent to, one another.

F213.2.1 Unisex (Single-Use or Family) Toilet and Bathing Rooms. Unisex toilet rooms shall contain not more than one lavatory, and two water closets without urinals or one water closet and one urinal. Unisex bathing rooms shall contain one shower or one shower and one bathtub, one lavatory, and one water closet. Doors to unisex toilet rooms and unisex bathing rooms shall have privacy latches.

F213.3 Plumbing Fixtures and Accessories. Plumbing fixtures and accessories provided in a toilet room or bathing room required to comply with F213.2 shall comply with F213.3.

F213.3.1 Toilet Compartments. Where toilet compartments are provided, at least one toilet compartment shall comply with 604.8.1. In addition to the compartment required to comply with

604.8.1, at least one compartment shall comply with 604.8.2 where six or more toilet compartments are provided, or where the combination of urinals and water closets totals six or more fixtures.

> **Advisory F213.3.1 Toilet Compartments.** A toilet compartment is a partitioned space that is located within a toilet room, and that normally contains no more than one water closet. A toilet compartment may also contain a lavatory. A lavatory is a sink provided for hand washing. Full-height partitions and door assemblies can comprise toilet compartments where the minimum required spaces are provided within the compartment.

F213.3.2 Water Closets. Where water closets are provided at least one shall comply with 604.

F213.3.3 Urinals. Where more than one urinal is provided, at least one shall comply with 605.

F213.3.4 Lavatories. Where lavatories are provided, at least one shall comply with 606 and shall not be located in a toilet compartment.

F213.3.5 Mirrors. Where mirrors are provided, at least one shall comply with 603.3.

F213.3.6 Bathing Facilities. Where bathtubs or showers are provided, at least one bathtub complying with 607 or at least one shower complying with 608 shall be provided.

F213.3.7 Coat Hooks and Shelves. Where coat hooks or shelves are provided in toilet rooms without toilet compartments, at least one of each type shall comply with 603.4. Where coat hooks or shelves are provided in toilet compartments, at least one of each type complying with 604.8.3 shall be provided in toilet compartments required to comply with F213.3.1. Where coat hooks or shelves are provided in bathing *facilities*, at least one of each type complying with 603.4 shall serve fixtures required to comply with F213.3.6.

F214 Washing Machines and Clothes Dryers

F214.1 General. Where provided, washing machines and clothes dryers shall comply with F214.
EXCEPTION: Washing machines and clothes dryers provided in *employee work areas* shall not be required to comply with F214.

> **Advisory F214.1 General Exception.** Washers and dryers provided for use by employees during non-work hours are not considered to be provided in employee work areas. For example, if trainees are housed in a dormitory and provided access to washers and dryers, those facilities are not considered part of the employee work area. Examples of washing machines and clothes dryers provided in employee work areas include, but are not limited to, employee only laundries in hospitals, hotels, and prisons.

F214.2 Washing Machines. Where three or fewer washing machines are provided, at least one shall comply with 611. Where more than three washing machines are provided, at least two shall comply with 611.

F214.3 Clothes Dryers. Where three or fewer clothes dryers are provided, at least one shall comply with 611. Where more than three clothes dryers are provided, at least two shall comply with 611.

F215 Fire Alarm Systems

F215.1 General. Where fire alarm systems provide audible alarm coverage, alarms shall comply with F215.
    EXCEPTION: In existing *facilities*, visible alarms shall not be required except where an existing fire alarm system is upgraded or replaced, or a new fire alarm system is installed.

> **Advisory F215.1 General.** Unlike audible alarms, visible alarms must be located within the space they serve so that the signal is visible. Facility alarm systems (other than fire alarm systems) such as those used for tornado warnings and other emergencies are not required to comply with the technical criteria for alarms in Section 702. Every effort should be made to ensure that such alarms can be differentiated in their signal from fire alarms systems and that people who need to be notified of emergencies are adequately safeguarded. Consult local fire departments and prepare evacuation plans taking into consideration the needs of every building occupant, including people with disabilities.

F215.2 Public and Common Use Areas. Alarms in *public use* areas and *common use* areas shall comply with 702.

F215.3 Employee Work Areas. Where *employee work areas* have audible alarm coverage, the wiring system shall be designed so that visible alarms complying with 702 can be integrated into the alarm system.

F215.4 Transient Lodging. Guest rooms required to comply with F224.4 shall provide alarms complying with 702.

F215.5 Residential Facilities. Where provided in *residential dwelling units* required to comply with 809.5, alarms shall comply with 702.

F216 Signs

F216.1 General. Signs shall be provided in accordance with F216 and shall comply with 703.
    EXCEPTIONS: 1. *Building* directories, menus, seat and row designations in *assembly areas*, occupant names, *building* addresses, and company names and logos shall not be required to comply with F216.
    2. In parking *facilities,* signs shall not be required to comply with F216.2, F216.3, and F216.6 through F216.12.
    3. Temporary, 7 days or less, signs shall not be required to comply with F216.
    4. In detention and correctional *facilities*, signs not located in *public use* areas shall not be required to comply with F216.

F216.2 Designations. Interior and exterior signs identifying permanent rooms and *spaces* shall comply with 703.1, 703.2, and 703.5. Where *pictograms* are provided as designations of permanent interior rooms and *spaces*, the *pictograms* shall comply with 703.6 and shall have text descriptors complying with 703.2 and 703.5.

EXCEPTION: Exterior signs that are not located at the door to the *space* they serve shall not be required to comply with 703.2.

> **Advisory F216.2 Designations.** Section F216.2 applies to signs that provide designations, labels, or names for interior rooms or spaces where the sign is not likely to change over time. Examples include interior signs labeling restrooms, room and floor numbers or letters, and room names. Tactile text descriptors are required for pictograms that are provided to label or identify a permanent room or space. Pictograms that provide information about a room or space, such as "no smoking," occupant logos, and the International Symbol of Accessibility, are not required to have text descriptors.

F216.3 Directional and Informational Signs. Signs that provide direction to or information about interior *spaces* and *facilities* of the *site* shall comply with 703.5.

> **Advisory F216.3 Directional and Informational Signs.** Information about interior spaces and facilities includes rules of conduct, occupant load, and similar signs. Signs providing direction to rooms or spaces include those that identify egress routes.

F216.4 Means of Egress. Signs for means of egress shall comply with F216.4.

F216.4.1 Exit Doors. Doors at exit passageways, exit discharge, and exit stairways shall be identified by *tactile* signs complying with 703.1, 703.2, and 703.5.

> **Advisory F216.4.1 Exit Doors.** An exit passageway is a horizontal exit component that is separated from the interior spaces of the building by fire-resistance-rated construction and that leads to the exit discharge or public way. The exit discharge is that portion of an egress system between the termination of an exit and a public way.

F216.4.2 Areas of Refuge. Signs required by section 1003.2.13.5.4 of the International Building Code (2000 edition) or section 1007.6.4 of the International Building Code (2003 edition) (incorporated by reference, see "Referenced Standards" in Chapter 1) to provide instructions in areas of refuge shall comply with 703.5.

F216.4.3 Directional Signs. Signs required by section 1003.2.13.6 of the International Building Code (2000 edition) or section 1007.7 of the International Building Code (2003 edition) (incorporated by reference, see "Referenced Standards" in Chapter 1) to provide directions to *accessible means of egress* shall comply with 703.5.

F216.5 Parking. Parking *spaces* complying with 502 shall be identified by signs complying with 502.6.
EXCEPTIONS: 1. Where a total of four or fewer parking *spaces*, including *accessible* parking *spaces*, are provided on a *site*, identification of *accessible* parking *spaces* shall not be required.
2. In residential *facilities*, where parking *spaces* are assigned to specific *residential dwelling units*, identification of *accessible* parking *spaces* shall not be required.

F216.6 Entrances. Where not all *entrances* comply with 404, *entrances* complying with 404 shall be identified by the International Symbol of *Accessibility* complying with 703.7.2.1. Directional signs complying with 703.5 that indicate the location of the nearest *entrance* complying with 404 shall be provided at *entrances* that do not comply with 404.

> **Advisory F216.6 Entrances.** Where a directional sign is required, it should be located to minimize backtracking. In some cases, this could mean locating a sign at the beginning of a route, not just at the inaccessible entrances to a building.

F216.7 Elevators. Where existing elevators do not comply with 407, elevators complying with 407 shall be clearly identified with the International Symbol of *Accessibility* complying with 703.7.2.1.

F216.8 Toilet Rooms and Bathing Rooms. Where existing toilet rooms or bathing rooms do not comply with 603, directional signs indicating the location of the nearest toilet room or bathing room complying with 603 within the *facility* shall be provided. Signs shall comply with 703.5 and shall include the International Symbol of *Accessibility* complying with 703.7.2.1. Where existing toilet rooms or bathing rooms do not comply with 603, the toilet rooms or bathing rooms complying with 603 shall be identified by the International Symbol of *Accessibility* complying with 703.7.2.1. Where clustered single user toilet rooms or bathing *facilities* are permitted to use exception to F213.2, toilet rooms or bathing *facilities* complying with 603 shall be identified by the International Symbol of *Accessibility* complying with 703.7.2.1 unless all toilet rooms and bathing *facilities* comply with 603.

F216.9 TTYs. Identification and directional signs for public *TTYs* shall be provided in accordance with F216.9.

F216.9.1 Identification Signs. Public *TTYs* shall be identified by the International Symbol of *TTY* complying with 703.7.2.2.

F216.9.2 Directional Signs. Directional signs indicating the location of the nearest public *TTY* shall be provided at all banks of public pay telephones not containing a public *TTY*. In addition, where signs provide direction to public pay telephones, they shall also provide direction to public *TTYs*. Directional signs shall comply with 703.5 and shall include the International Symbol of *TTY* complying with 703.7.2.2.

F216.10 Assistive Listening Systems. Each *assembly area* required by F219 to provide *assistive listening systems* shall provide signs informing patrons of the availability of the *assistive listening system*. Assistive listening signs shall comply with 703.5 and shall include the International Symbol of Access for Hearing Loss complying with 703.7.2.4.

EXCEPTION: Where ticket offices or windows are provided, signs shall not be required at each *assembly area* provided that signs are displayed at each ticket office or window informing patrons of the availability of *assistive listening systems*.

F216.11 Check-Out Aisles. Where more than one check-out aisle is provided, check-out aisles complying with 904.3 shall be identified by the International Symbol of *Accessibility* complying with 703.7.2.1. Where check-out aisles are identified by numbers, letters, or functions, signs identifying check-out aisles complying with 904.3 shall be located in the same location as the check-out aisle identification.

   EXCEPTION: Where all check-out aisles serving a single function comply with 904.3, signs complying with 703.7.2.1 shall not be required.

F216.12 Amusement Rides. Signs identifying the type of access provided on *amusement rides* shall be provided at entries to queues and waiting lines. In addition, where *accessible* unload areas also serve as *accessible* load areas, signs indicating the location of the *accessible* load and unload areas shall be provided at entries to queues and waiting lines.

> **Advisory F216.12 Amusement Rides.** Amusement rides designed primarily for children, amusement rides that are controlled or operated by the rider, and amusement rides without seats, are not required to provide wheelchair spaces, transfer seats, or transfer systems, and need not meet the sign requirements in 216.12. The load and unload areas of these rides must, however, be on an accessible route and must provide turning space.

F217 Telephones

F217.1 General. Where coin-operated public pay telephones, coinless public pay telephones, public *closed-circuit telephones*, public courtesy phones, or other types of public telephones are provided, public telephones shall be provided in accordance with F217 for each type of public telephone provided. For purposes of this section, a bank of telephones shall be considered to be two or more adjacent telephones.

> **Advisory F217.1 General.** These requirements apply to all types of public telephones including courtesy phones at airports and rail stations that provide a free direct connection to hotels, transportation services, and tourist attractions.

F217.2 Wheelchair Accessible Telephones. Where public telephones are provided, wheelchair *accessible* telephones complying with 704.2 shall be provided in accordance with Table F217.2.

   EXCEPTION: Drive-up only public telephones shall not be required to comply with F217.2.

Table F217.2 Wheelchair Accessible Telephones

Number of Telephones Provided on a Floor, Level, or Exterior Site	Minimum Number of Required Wheelchair Accessible Telephones
1 or more single units	1 per floor, level, and exterior *site*
1 bank	1 per floor, level, and exterior *site*
2 or more banks	1 per bank

F217.3 Volume Controls. All public telephones shall have volume controls complying with 704.3.

F217.4 TTYs. *TTYs* complying with 704.4 shall be provided in accordance with F217.4.

110

Advisory F217.4 TTYs. Separate requirements are provided based on the number of public pay telephones provided at a bank of telephones, within a floor, a building, or on a site. In some instances one TTY can be used to satisfy more than one of these requirements. For example, a TTY required for a bank can satisfy the requirements for a building. However, the requirement for at least one TTY on an exterior site cannot be met by installing a TTY in a bank inside a building. Consideration should be given to phone systems that can accommodate both digital and analog transmissions for compatibility with digital and analog TTYs.

F217.4.1 Bank Requirement. Where four or more public pay telephones are provided at a bank of telephones, at least one public *TTY* complying with 704.4 shall be provided at that bank.
   EXCEPTION: *TTYs* shall not be required at banks of telephones located within 200 feet (61 m) of, and on the same floor as, a bank containing a public *TTY.*

F217.4.2 Floor Requirement. Where at least one public pay telephone is provided on a floor of a *building*, at least one public *TTY* shall be provided on that floor.

F217.4.3 Building Requirement. Where at least one public pay telephone is provided in a *public use* area of a *building*, at least one public *TTY* shall be provided in the *building* in a *public use* area.

F217.4.4 Exterior Site Requirement. Where four or more public pay telephones are provided on an exterior *site*, at least one public *TTY* shall be provided on the *site*.

F217.4.5 Rest Stops, Emergency Roadside Stops, and Service Plazas. Where at least one public pay telephone is provided at a public rest stop, emergency roadside stop, or service plaza, at least one public *TTY* shall be provided.

F217.4.6 Hospitals. Where at least one public pay telephone is provided serving a hospital emergency room, hospital recovery room, or hospital waiting room, at least one public *TTY* shall be provided at each location.

F217.4.7 Transportation Facilities. In transportation *facilities*, in addition to the requirements of F217.4.1 through F217.4.4, where at least one public pay telephone serves a particular *entrance* to a bus or rail *facility*, at least one public *TTY* shall be provided to serve that *entrance*. In airports, in addition to the requirements of F217.4.1 through F217.4.4, where four or more public pay telephones are located in a terminal outside the security areas, a concourse within the security areas, or a baggage claim area in a terminal, at least one public *TTY* shall be provided in each location.

F217.4.8 Detention and Correctional Facilities. In detention and correctional *facilities*, where at least one pay telephone is provided in a secured area used only by detainees or inmates and security personnel, at least one *TTY* shall be provided in at least one secured area.

F217.5 Shelves for Portable TTYs. Where a bank of telephones in the interior of a *building* consists of three or more public pay telephones, at least one public pay telephone at the bank shall be provided with a shelf and an electrical outlet in accordance with 704.5.

EXCEPTIONS: 1. Secured areas of detention and correctional *facilities* where shelves and outlets are prohibited for purposes of security or safety shall not be required to comply with F217.5.
2. The shelf and electrical outlet shall not be required at a bank of telephones with a *TTY*.

F218 Transportation Facilities

F218.1 General. Transportation *facilities* shall comply with F218.

F218.2 New and Altered Fixed Guideway Stations. New and altered stations in rapid rail, light rail, commuter rail, intercity rail, high speed rail, and other fixed guideway systems shall comply with 810.5 through 810.10.

F218.3 Bus Shelters. Where provided, bus shelters shall comply with 810.3 and 810.4.

F218.4 Other Transportation Facilities. In other transportation *facilities*, public address systems shall comply with 810.7 and clocks shall comply with 810.8.

F219 Assistive Listening Systems

F219.1 General. *Assistive listening systems* shall be provided in accordance with F219 and shall comply with 706.

F219.2 Required Systems. In each *assembly area* where audible communication is integral to the use of the *space*, an *assistive listening system* shall be provided.
   EXCEPTION: Other than in courtrooms, *assistive listening systems* shall not be required where audio amplification is not provided.

F219.3 Receivers. Receivers complying with 706.2 shall be provided for *assistive listening systems* in each *assembly area* in accordance with Table F219.3. Twenty-five percent minimum of receivers provided, but no fewer than two, shall be hearing-aid compatible in accordance with 706.3.
   EXCEPTIONS: 1. Where a *building* contains more than one *assembly area* and the *assembly areas* required to provide *assistive listening systems* are under one management, the total number of required receivers shall be permitted to be calculated according to the total number of seats in the *assembly areas* in the *building* provided that all receivers are usable with all systems.
   2. Where all seats in an *assembly area* are served by an induction loop *assistive listening system*, the minimum number of receivers required by Table F219.3 to be hearing-aid compatible shall not be required to be provided.

Table F219.3 Receivers for Assistive Listening Systems

Capacity of Seating in Assembly Area	Minimum Number of Required Receivers	Minimum Number of Required Receivers Required to be Hearing-aid Compatible
50 or less	2	2
51 to 200	2, plus 1 per 25 seats over 50 seats[1]	2
201 to 500	2, plus 1 per 25 seats over 50 seats[1]	1 per 4 receivers[1]
501 to 1000	20, plus 1 per 33 seats over 500 seats[1]	1 per 4 receivers[1]
1001 to 2000	35, plus 1 per 50 seats over 1000 seats[1]	1 per 4 receivers[1]
2001 and over	55, plus 1 per 100 seats over 2000 seats[1]	1 per 4 receivers[1]

1. Or fraction thereof.

F220 Automatic Teller Machines and Fare Machines

F220.1 General. Where automatic teller machines or self-service fare vending, collection, or adjustment machines are provided, at least one of each type provided at each location shall comply with 707. Where bins are provided for envelopes, waste paper, or other purposes, at least one of each type shall comply with 811.

> **Advisory F220.1 General.** If a bank provides both interior and exterior ATMs, each such installation is considered a separate location. Accessible ATMs, including those with speech and those that are within reach of people who use wheelchairs, must provide all the functions provided to customers at that location at all times. For example, it is unacceptable for the accessible ATM only to provide cash withdrawals while inaccessible ATMs also sell theater tickets.

F221 Assembly Areas

F221.1 General. *Assembly areas* shall provide *wheelchair spaces*, companion seats, and designated aisle seats complying with F221 and 802. In addition, lawn seating shall comply with F221.5.

F221.2 Wheelchair Spaces. *Wheelchair spaces* complying with F221.2 shall be provided in *assembly areas* with fixed seating.

F221.2.1 Number and Location. *Wheelchair spaces* shall be provided complying with F221.2.1.

F221.2.1.1 General Seating. *Wheelchair spaces* complying with 802.1 shall be provided in accordance with Table F221.2.1.1.

Table F221.2.1.1 Number of Wheelchair Spaces in Assembly Areas

Number of Seats	Minimum Number of Required Wheelchair Spaces
4 to 25	1
26 to 50	2
51 to 150	4
151 to 300	5
301 to 500	6
501 to 5000	6, plus 1 for each 150, or fraction thereof, between 501 through 5000
5001 and over	36, plus 1 for each 200, or fraction thereof, over 5000

F221.2.1.2 Luxury Boxes, Club Boxes, and Suites in Arenas, Stadiums, and Grandstands. In each luxury box, club box, and suite within arenas, stadiums, and grandstands, *wheelchair spaces* complying with 802.1 shall be provided in accordance with Table F221.2.1.1.

> **Advisory F221.2.1.2 Luxury Boxes, Club Boxes, and Suites in Arenas, Stadiums, and Grandstands.** The number of wheelchair spaces required in luxury boxes, club boxes, and suites within an arena, stadium, or grandstand is to be calculated box by box and suite by suite.

F221.2.1.3 Other Boxes. In boxes other than those required to comply with F221.2.1.2, the total number of *wheelchair spaces* required shall be determined in accordance with Table F221.2.1.1. *Wheelchair spaces* shall be located in not less than 20 percent of all boxes provided. *Wheelchair spaces* shall comply with 802.1.

Printed by Builder's Book, Inc., Bookstore · www.buildersbook.com

> **Advisory F221.2.1.3 Other Boxes.** The provision for seating in "other boxes" includes box seating provided in facilities such as performing arts auditoria where tiered boxes are designed for spatial and acoustical purposes. The number of wheelchair spaces required in boxes covered by 221.2.1.3 is calculated based on the total number of seats provided in these other boxes. The resulting number of wheelchair spaces must be located in no fewer than 20% of the boxes covered by this section. For example, a concert hall has 20 boxes, each of which contains 10 seats, totaling 200 seats. In this example, 5 wheelchair spaces would be required, and they must be placed in at least 4 of the boxes. Additionally, because the wheelchair spaces must also meet the dispersion requirements of 221.2.3, the boxes containing these wheelchair spaces cannot all be located in one area unless an exception to the dispersion requirements applies.

F221.2.1.4 Team or Player Seating. At least one *wheelchair space* complying with 802.1 shall be provided in team or player seating areas serving *areas of sport activity*.

    EXCEPTION: *Wheelchair spaces* shall not be required in team or player seating areas serving bowling lanes not required to comply with F206.2.10.

F221.2.2 Integration. *Wheelchair spaces* shall be an integral part of the seating plan.

> **Advisory F221.2.2 Integration.** The requirement that wheelchair spaces be an "integral part of the seating plan" means that wheelchair spaces must be placed within the footprint of the seating area. Wheelchair spaces cannot be segregated from seating areas. For example, it would be unacceptable to place only the wheelchair spaces, or only the wheelchair spaces and their associated companion seats, outside the seating areas defined by risers in an assembly area.

F221.2.3 Lines of Sight and Dispersion. *Wheelchair spaces* shall provide lines of sight complying with 802.2 and shall comply with F221.2.3. In providing lines of sight, *wheelchair spaces* shall be dispersed. *Wheelchair spaces* shall provide spectators with choices of seating locations and viewing angles that are substantially equivalent to, or better than, the choices of seating locations and viewing angles available to all other spectators. When the number of *wheelchair spaces* required by F221.2.1 has been met, further dispersion shall not be required.

    EXCEPTION: *Wheelchair spaces* in team or player seating areas serving *areas of sport activity* shall not be required to comply with F221.2.3.

> **Advisory F221.2.3 Lines of Sight and Dispersion.** Consistent with the overall intent of the ADA, individuals who use wheelchairs must be provided equal access so that their experience is substantially equivalent to that of other members of the audience. Thus, while individuals who use wheelchairs need not be provided with the best seats in the house, neither may they be relegated to the worst.

F221.2.3.1 Horizontal Dispersion. *Wheelchair spaces* shall be dispersed horizontally.
    EXCEPTIONS: 1. Horizontal dispersion shall not be required in *assembly areas* with 300 or fewer seats if the companion seats required by F221.3 and *wheelchair spaces* are located within the 2nd or 3rd quartile of the total row length. Intermediate aisles shall be included in

determining the total row length. If the row length in the 2nd and 3rd quartile of a row is insufficient to accommodate the required number of companion seats and *wheelchair spaces*, the additional companion seats and *wheelchair spaces* shall be permitted to be located in the 1st and 4th quartile of the row.

2. In row seating, two *wheelchair spaces* shall be permitted to be located side-by-side.

> **Advisory F221.2.3.1 Horizontal Dispersion.** Horizontal dispersion of wheelchair spaces is the placement of spaces in an assembly facility seating area from side-to-side or, in the case of an arena or stadium, around the field of play or performance area.

F221.2.3.2 Vertical Dispersion. *Wheelchair spaces* shall be dispersed vertically at varying distances from the screen, performance area, or playing field. In addition, *wheelchair spaces* shall be located in each balcony or *mezzanine* that is located on an *accessible* route.

EXCEPTIONS: 1. Vertical dispersion shall not be required in *assembly areas* with 300 or fewer seats if the *wheelchair spaces* provide viewing angles that are equivalent to, or better than, the average viewing angle provided in the *facility*.

2. In bleachers, *wheelchair spaces* shall not be required to be provided in rows other than rows at points of entry to bleacher seating.

> **Advisory F221.2.3.2 Vertical Dispersion.** When wheelchair spaces are dispersed vertically in an assembly facility they are placed at different locations within the seating area from front-to-back so that the distance from the screen, stage, playing field, area of sports activity, or other focal point is varied among wheelchair spaces.
>
> **Advisory F221.2.3.2 Vertical Dispersion Exception 2.** Points of entry to bleacher seating may include, but are not limited to, cross aisles, concourses, vomitories, and entrance ramps and stairs. Vertical, center, or side aisles adjoining bleacher seating that are stepped or tiered are not considered entry points.

F221.3 Companion Seats. At least one companion seat complying with 802.3 shall be provided for each *wheelchair space* required by F221.2.1.

F221.4 Designated Aisle Seats. At least 5 percent of the total number of aisle seats provided shall comply with 802.4 and shall be the aisle seats located closest to *accessible* routes.

EXCEPTION: Team or player seating areas serving *areas of sport activity* shall not be required to comply with F221.4.

> **Advisory F221.4 Designated Aisle Seats.** When selecting which aisle seats will meet the requirements of 802.4, those aisle seats which are closest to, not necessarily on, accessible routes must be selected first. For example, an assembly area has two aisles (A and B) serving seating areas with an accessible route connecting to the top and bottom of Aisle A only. The aisle seats chosen to meet 802.4 must be those at the top and bottom of Aisle A, working toward the middle. Only when all seats on Aisle A would not meet the five percent minimum would seats on Aisle B be designated.

F221.5 Lawn Seating. Lawn seating areas and exterior overflow seating areas, where fixed seats are not provided, shall connect to an *accessible* route.

F222 Dressing, Fitting, and Locker Rooms

F222.1 General. Where dressing rooms, fitting rooms, or locker rooms are provided, at least 5 percent, but no fewer than one, of each type of use in each cluster provided shall comply with 803.
> **EXCEPTION:** In *alterations*, where it is *technically infeasible* to provide rooms in accordance with F222.1, one room for each sex on each level shall comply with 803. Where only unisex rooms are provided, unisex rooms shall be permitted.

> **Advisory F222.1 General.** A "cluster" is a group of rooms proximate to one another. Generally, rooms in a cluster are within sight of, or adjacent to, one another. Different styles of design provide users varying levels of privacy and convenience. Some designs include private changing facilities that are close to core areas of the facility, while other designs use space more economically and provide only group dressing facilities. Regardless of the type of facility, dressing, fitting, and locker rooms should provide people with disabilities rooms that are equally private and convenient to those provided others. For example, in a physician's office, if people without disabilities must traverse the full length of the office suite in clothing other than their street clothes, it is acceptable for people with disabilities to be asked to do the same.

F222.2 Coat Hooks and Shelves. Where coat hooks or shelves are provided in dressing, fitting or locker rooms without individual compartments, at least one of each type shall comply with 803.5. Where coat hooks or shelves are provided in individual compartments at least one of each type complying with 803.5 shall be provided in individual compartments in dressing, fitting, or locker rooms required to comply with F222.1.

F223 Medical Care and Long-Term Care Facilities

F223.1 General. In licensed medical care *facilities* and licensed long-term care *facilities* where the period of stay exceeds twenty-four hours, patient or resident sleeping rooms shall be provided in accordance with F223.
> **EXCEPTION:** Toilet rooms that are part of critical or intensive care patient sleeping rooms shall not be required to comply with 603.

> **Advisory F223.1 General.** Because medical facilities frequently reconfigure spaces to reflect changes in medical specialties, Section F223.1 does not include a provision for dispersion of accessible patient or resident sleeping rooms. The lack of a design requirement does not mean that covered entities are not required to provide services to people with disabilities where accessible rooms are not dispersed in specialty areas. Locate accessible rooms near core areas that are less likely to change over time. While dispersion is not required, the flexibility it provides can be a critical factor in ensuring cost effective compliance with applicable civil rights laws, including Sections 501 and 504 of the Rehabilitation Act of 1973, as amended.

Advisory F223.1 General (Continued). Additionally, all types of features and amenities should be dispersed among accessible sleeping rooms to ensure equal access to and a variety of choices for all patients and residents.

F223.1.1 Alterations. Where sleeping rooms are *altered* or *added*, the requirements of F223 shall apply only to the sleeping rooms being *altered* or *added* until the number of sleeping rooms complies with the minimum number required for new construction.

Advisory F223.1.1 Alterations. In alterations and additions, the minimum required number is based on the total number of sleeping rooms altered or added instead of on the total number of sleeping rooms provided in a facility. As a facility is altered over time, every effort should be made to disperse accessible sleeping rooms among patient care areas such as pediatrics, cardiac care, maternity, and other units. In this way, people with disabilities can have access to the full-range of services provided by a medical care facility.

F223.2 Hospitals, Rehabilitation Facilities, Psychiatric Facilities and Detoxification Facilities. Hospitals, rehabilitation *facilities*, psychiatric *facilities* and detoxification *facilities* shall comply with F223.2.

F223.2.1 Facilities Not Specializing in Treating Conditions That Affect Mobility. In *facilities* not specializing in treating conditions that affect mobility, at least 10 percent, but no fewer than one, of the patient sleeping rooms shall provide mobility features complying with 805.

F223.2.2 Facilities Specializing in Treating Conditions That Affect Mobility. In *facilities* specializing in treating conditions that affect mobility, 100 percent of the patient sleeping rooms shall provide mobility features complying with 805.

Advisory F223.2.2 Facilities Specializing in Treating Conditions That Affect Mobility. Conditions that affect mobility include conditions requiring the use or assistance of a brace, cane, crutch, prosthetic device, wheelchair, or powered mobility aid; arthritic, neurological, or orthopedic conditions that severely limit one's ability to walk; respiratory diseases and other conditions which may require the use of portable oxygen; and cardiac conditions that impose significant functional limitations. Facilities that may provide treatment for, but that do not specialize in treatment of such conditions, such as general rehabilitation hospitals, are not subject to this requirement but are subject to Section F223.2.1.

F223.3 Long-Term Care Facilities. In licensed long-term care *facilities*, at least 50 percent, but no fewer than one, of each type of resident sleeping room shall provide mobility features complying with 805.

F224 Transient Lodging Guest Rooms

F224.1 General. *Transient lodging facilities* shall provide guest rooms in accordance with F224.

Advisory F224.1 General. Certain facilities used for transient lodging including time shares, dormitories, and town homes may be covered by both these requirements and the Fair Housing Amendments Act. The Fair Housing Amendments Act requires that certain residential structures having four or more multi-family dwelling units, regardless of whether they are privately owned or federally assisted, include certain features of accessible and adaptable design according to guidelines established by the U.S. Department of Housing and Urban Development (HUD). This law and the appropriate regulations should be consulted before proceeding with the design and construction of residential housing.

F224.1.1 Alterations. Where guest rooms are *altered* or *added*, the requirements of F224 shall apply only to the guest rooms being *altered* or *added* until the number of guest rooms complies with the minimum number required for new construction.

Advisory F224.1.1 Alterations. In alterations and additions, the minimum required number of accessible guest rooms is based on the total number of guest rooms altered or added instead of the total number of guest rooms provided in a facility. Typically, each alteration of a facility is limited to a particular portion of the facility. When accessible guest rooms are added as a result of subsequent alterations, compliance with 224.5 (Dispersion) is more likely to be achieved if all of the accessible guest rooms are not provided in the same area of the facility.

F224.1.2 Guest Room Doors and Doorways. *Entrances,* doors, and doorways providing user passage into and within guest rooms that are not required to provide mobility features complying with 806.2 shall comply with 404.2.3.

    EXCEPTION: Shower and sauna doors in guest rooms that are not required to provide mobility features complying with 806.2 shall not be required to comply with 404.2.3.

Advisory F224.1.2 Guest Room Doors and Doorways. Because of the social interaction that often occurs in lodging facilities, an accessible clear opening width is required for doors and doorways to and within all guest rooms, including those not required to be accessible. This applies to all doors, including bathroom doors, that allow full user passage. Other requirements for doors and doorways in Section 404 do not apply to guest rooms not required to provide mobility features.

F224.2 Guest Rooms with Mobility Features. In *transient lodging facilities*, guest rooms with mobility features complying with 806.2 shall be provided in accordance with Table F224.2.

Table F224.2 Guest Rooms with Mobility Features

Total Number of Guest Rooms Provided	Minimum Number of Required Rooms Without Roll-in Showers	Minimum Number of Required Rooms With Roll-in Showers	Total Number of Required Rooms
1 to 25	1	0	1
26 to 50	2	0	2
51 to 75	3	1	4
76 to 100	4	1	5
101 to 150	5	2	7
151 to 200	6	2	8
201 to 300	7	3	10
301 to 400	8	4	12
401 to 500	9	4	13
501 to 1000	2 percent of total	1 percent of total	3 percent of total
1001 and over	20, plus 1 for each 100, or fraction thereof, over 1000	10, plus 1 for each 100, or fraction thereof, over 1000	30, plus 2 for each 100, or fraction thereof, over 1000

F224.3 Beds. In guest rooms having more than 25 beds, 5 percent minimum of the beds shall have clear floor *space* complying with 806.2.3.

F224.4 Guest Rooms with Communication Features. In *transient lodging facilities*, guest rooms with communication features complying with 806.3 shall be provided in accordance with Table F224.4.

Table F224.4 Guest Rooms with Communication Features

Total Number of Guest Rooms Provided	Minimum Number of Required Guest Rooms With Communication Features
2 to 25	2
26 to 50	4
51 to 75	7
76 to 100	9
101 to 150	12

Printed by Builder's Book, Inc., Bookstore · www.buildersbook.com

Table F224.4 Guest Rooms with Communication Features

Total Number of Guest Rooms Provided	Minimum Number of Required Guest Rooms With Communication Features
151 to 200	14
201 to 300	17
301 to 400	20
401 to 500	22
501 to 1000	5 percent of total
1001 and over	50, plus 3 for each 100 over 1000

F224.5 Dispersion. Guest rooms required to provide mobility features complying with 806.2 and guest rooms required to provide communication features complying with 806.3 shall be dispersed among the various classes of guest rooms, and shall provide choices of types of guest rooms, number of beds, and other amenities comparable to the choices provided to other guests. Where the minimum number of guest rooms required to comply with 806 is not sufficient to allow for complete dispersion, guest rooms shall be dispersed in the following priority: guest room type, number of beds, and amenities. At least one guest room required to provide mobility features complying with 806.2 shall also provide communication features complying with 806.3. Not more than 10 percent of guest rooms required to provide mobility features complying with 806.2 shall be used to satisfy the minimum number of guest rooms required to provide communication features complying with 806.3.

> **Advisory F224.5 Dispersion.** Factors to be considered in providing an equivalent range of options may include, but are not limited to, room size, bed size, cost, view, bathroom fixtures such as hot tubs and spas, smoking and nonsmoking, and the number of rooms provided.

F225 Storage

F225.1 General. Storage *facilities* shall comply with F225.

F225.2 Storage. Where storage is provided in *accessible spaces*, at least one of each type shall comply with 811.

> **Advisory F225.2 Storage.** Types of storage include, but are not limited to, closets, cabinets, shelves, clothes rods, hooks, and drawers. Where provided, at least one of each type of storage must be within the reach ranges specified in 308; however, it is permissible to install additional storage outside the reach ranges.

F225.2.1 Lockers. Where lockers are provided, at least 5 percent, but no fewer than one of each type, shall comply with 811.

> **Advisory F225.2.1 Lockers.** Different types of lockers may include full-size and half-size lockers, as well as those specifically designed for storage of various sports equipment.

F225.2.2 Self-Service Shelving. Self-service shelves shall be located on an *accessible* route complying with 402. Self-service shelving shall not be required to comply with 308.

> **Advisory F225.2.2 Self-Service Shelving.** Self-service shelves include, but are not limited to, library, store, or post office shelves.

F225.3 Self-Service Storage Facilities. *Self-service storage facilities* shall provide individual *self-service storage spaces* complying with these requirements in accordance with Table F225.3.

Table F225.3 Self-Service Storage Facilities

Total Spaces in Facility	Minimum Number of Spaces Required to be Accessible
1 to 200	5 percent, but no fewer than 1
201 and over	10, plus 2 percent of total number of units over 200

> **Advisory F225.3 Self-Service Storage Facilities.** Although there are no technical requirements that are unique to self-service storage facilities, elements and spaces provided in facilities containing self-service storage spaces required to comply with these requirements must comply with this document where applicable. For example: the number of storage spaces required to comply with these requirements must provide Accessible Routes complying with Section F206; Accessible Means of Egress complying with Section F207; Parking Spaces complying with Section F208; and, where provided, other pubic use or common use elements and facilities such as toilet rooms, drinking fountains, and telephones must comply with the applicable requirements of this document.

F225.3.1 Dispersion. Individual *self-service storage spaces* shall be dispersed throughout the various classes of *spaces* provided. Where more classes of *spaces* are provided than the number required to be *accessible*, the number of *spaces* shall not be required to exceed that required by Table F225.3. *Self-service storage spaces* complying with Table F225.3 shall not be required to be dispersed among *buildings* in a multi-*building facility*.

F226 Dining Surfaces and Work Surfaces

F226.1 General. Where dining surfaces are provided for the consumption of food or drink, at least 5 percent of the seating *spaces* and standing *spaces* at the dining surfaces shall comply with 902. In addition, where work surfaces are provided, at least 5 percent shall comply with 902.

EXCEPTIONS: 1. Sales counters and service counters shall not be required to comply with 902.

2. Check writing surfaces provided at check-out aisles not required to comply with 904.3 shall not be required to comply with 902.

> **Advisory F226.1 General.** In facilities covered by the ABA, this requirement applies to work surfaces used by employees. Five percent, but not less than one, of permanently installed work surfaces in each work area must be accessible. Permanently installed work surfaces include, but are not limited to, laboratory and work benches, fume hoods, reception counters, teller windows, study carrels, commercial kitchen counters, writing surfaces, and fixed conference tables. Where furnishings are not fixed, Sections 501, 503, and 504 of the Rehabilitation Act of 1973, as amended provides that Federal employees, employees of Federal contractors, and certain other employees, are entitled to "reasonable accommodations." This means that employers may need to procure or adjust furnishings to accommodate the individual needs of employees with disabilities on an "as needed" basis. Consider work surfaces that are flexible and permit installation at variable heights and clearances.

F226.2 Dispersion. Dining surfaces and work surfaces required to comply with 902 shall be dispersed throughout the *space* or *facility* containing dining surfaces and work surfaces.

F227 Sales and Service

F227.1 General. Where provided, check-out aisles, sales counters, service counters, food service lines, queues, and waiting lines shall comply with F227 and 904.

F227.2 Check-Out Aisles. Where check-out aisles are provided, check-out aisles complying with 904.3 shall be provided in accordance with Table F227.2. Where check-out aisles serve different functions, check-out aisles complying with 904.3 shall be provided in accordance with Table F227.2 for each function. Where check-out aisles are dispersed throughout the *building* or *facility*, check-out aisles complying with 904.3 shall be dispersed.

EXCEPTION: Where the selling *space* is under 5000 square feet (465 m^2) no more than one check-out aisle complying with 904.3 shall be required.

Table F227.2 Check-Out Aisles

Number of Check-Out Aisles of Each Function	Minimum Number of Check-Out Aisles of Each Function Required to Comply with 904.3
1 to 4	1
5 to 8	2
9 to 15	3
16 and over	3, plus 20 percent of additional aisles

123

F227.2.1 Altered Check-Out Aisles. Where check-out aisles are *altered*, at least one of each check-out aisle serving each function shall comply with 904.3 until the number of check-out aisles complies with F227.2.

F227.3 Counters. Where provided, at least one of each type of sales counter and service counter shall comply with 904.4. Where counters are dispersed throughout the *building* or *facility*, counters complying with 904.4 also shall be dispersed.

> **Advisory F227.3 Counters.** Types of counters that provide different services in the same facility include, but are not limited to, order, pick-up, express, and returns. One continuous counter can be used to provide different types of service. For example, order and pick-up are different services. It would not be acceptable to provide access only to the part of the counter where orders are taken when orders are picked-up at a different location on the same counter. Both the order and pick-up section of the counter must be accessible.

F227.4 Food Service Lines. Food service lines shall comply with 904.5. Where self-service shelves are provided, at least 50 percent, but no fewer than one, of each type provided shall comply with 308.

F227.5 Queues and Waiting Lines. Queues and waiting lines servicing counters or check-out aisles required to comply with 904.3 or 904.4 shall comply with 403.

F228 Depositories, Vending Machines, Change Machines, Mail Boxes, and Fuel Dispensers

F228.1 General. Where provided, at least one of each type of depository, vending machine, change machine, and fuel dispenser shall comply with 309.
   EXCEPTIONS: **1.** Drive-up only depositories shall not be required to comply with 309.
   2. Fuel dispensers provided for fueling official government vehicles shall not be required to comply with 309.

> **Advisory F228.1 General.** Depositories include, but are not limited to, night receptacles in banks, post offices, video stores, and libraries.

F228.2 Mail Boxes. Where *mail boxes* are provided in an interior location, at least 5 percent, but no fewer than one, of each type shall comply with 309. In residential *facilities*, where *mail boxes* are provided for each *residential dwelling unit*, *mail boxes* complying with 309 shall be provided for each *residential dwelling unit* required to provide mobility features complying with 809.2 through 809.4.

F229 Windows

F229.1 General. Where glazed openings are provided in *accessible* rooms or *spaces* for operation by occupants, excluding employees, at least one opening shall comply with 309. In *accessible* rooms or *spaces*, each glazed opening required by an *administrative authority* to be operable shall comply with 309.
   EXCEPTION: **1.** Glazed openings in *residential dwelling units* required to comply with 809 shall not be required to comply with F229.

2. Glazed openings in guest rooms required to provide communication features and in guest rooms required to comply with F206.5.3 shall not be required to comply with F229.

F230 Two-Way Communication Systems

F230.1 General. Where a two-way communication system is provided to gain admittance to a *building* or *facility* or to restricted areas within a *building* or *facility*, the system shall comply with 708.

> **Advisory F230.1 General.** This requirement applies to facilities such as office buildings, courthouses, and other facilities where admittance to the building or restricted spaces is dependent on two-way communication systems.

F231 Judicial Facilities

F231.1 General. Judicial *facilities* shall comply with F231.

F231.2 Courtrooms. Each courtroom shall comply with 808.

F231.3 Holding Cells. Where provided, central holding cells and court-floor holding cells shall comply with F231.3.

F231.3.1 Central Holding Cells. Where separate central holding cells are provided for adult male, juvenile male, adult female, or juvenile female, one of each type shall comply with 807.2. Where central holding cells are provided and are not separated by age or sex, at least one cell complying with 807.2 shall be provided.

F231.3.2 Court-Floor Holding Cells. Where separate court-floor holding cells are provided for adult male, juvenile male, adult female, or juvenile female, each courtroom shall be served by one cell of each type complying with 807.2. Where court-floor holding cells are provided and are not separated by age or sex, courtrooms shall be served by at least one cell complying with 807.2. Cells may serve more than one courtroom.

F231.4 Visiting Areas. Visiting areas shall comply with F231.4.

F231.4.1 Cubicles and Counters. At least 5 percent, but no fewer than one, of cubicles shall comply with 902 on both the visitor and detainee sides. Where counters are provided, at least one shall comply with 904.4.2 on both the visitor and detainee sides.
EXCEPTION: The detainee side of cubicles or counters at non-contact visiting areas not serving holding cells required to comply with F231 shall not be required to comply with 902 or 904.4.2.

F231.4.2 Partitions. Where solid partitions or security glazing separate visitors from detainees at least one of each type of cubicle or counter partition shall comply with 904.6.

F232 Detention Facilities and Correctional Facilities

F232.1 General. *Buildings, facilities,* or portions thereof, in which people are detained for penal or correction purposes, or in which the liberty of the inmates is restricted for security reasons shall comply with F232.

> **Advisory F232.1 General.** Detention facilities include, but are not limited to, jails, detention centers, and holding cells in police stations. Correctional facilities include, but are not limited to, prisons, reformatories, and correctional centers.

F232.2 General Holding Cells and General Housing Cells. General holding cells and general housing cells shall be provided in accordance with F232.2.

> **EXCEPTION:** *Alterations* to cells shall not be required to comply except to the extent determined by regulations issued by the appropriate Federal agency having authority under section 504 of the Rehabilitation Act of 1973.

> **Advisory F232.2 General Holding Cells and General Housing Cells.** Accessible cells or rooms should be dispersed among different levels of security, housing categories, and holding classifications (e.g., male/female and adult/juvenile) to facilitate access. Many detention and correctional facilities are designed so that certain areas (e.g., "shift" areas) can be adapted to serve as different types of housing according to need. For example, a shift area serving as a medium-security housing unit might be redesignated for a period of time as a high-security housing unit to meet capacity needs. Placement of accessible cells or rooms in shift areas may allow additional flexibility in meeting requirements for dispersion of accessible cells or rooms.
>
> **Advisory F232.2 General Holding Cells and General Housing Cells Exception.** Although these requirements do not specify that cells be accessible as a consequence of an alteration, Section 504 of the Rehabilitation Act of 1973, as amended requires that each service, program, or activity conducted by a Federal agency, when viewed in its entirety, be readily accessible to and usable by individuals with disabilities. This requirement must be met unless doing so would fundamentally alter the nature of a service, program, or activity or would result in undue financial and administrative burdens.

F232.2.1 Cells with Mobility Features. At least 2 percent, but no fewer than one, of the total number of cells in a *facility* shall provide mobility features complying with 807.2.

> **F232.2.1.1 Beds.** In cells having more than 25 beds, at least 5 percent of the beds shall have clear floor *space* complying with 807.2.3.

F232.2.2 Cells with Communication Features. At least 2 percent, but no fewer than one, of the total number of general holding cells and general housing cells equipped with audible emergency alarm systems and permanently installed telephones within the cell shall provide communication features complying with 807.3.

F232.3 Special Holding Cells and Special Housing Cells. Where special holding cells or special housing cells are provided, at least one cell serving each purpose shall provide mobility features complying with 807.2. Cells subject to this requirement include, but are not limited to, those used for purposes of orientation, protective custody, administrative or disciplinary detention or segregation, detoxification, and medical isolation.

> **EXCEPTION:** *Alterations* to cells shall not be required to comply except to the extent determined by regulations issued by the appropriate Federal agency having authority under section 504 of the Rehabilitation Act of 1973.

F232.4 Medical Care Facilities. Patient bedrooms or cells required to comply with F223 shall be provided in addition to any medical isolation cells required to comply with F232.3.

F232.5 Visiting Areas. Visiting areas shall comply with F232.5.

> **F232.5.1 Cubicles and Counters.** At least 5 percent, but no fewer than one, of cubicles shall comply with 902 on both the visitor and detainee sides. Where counters are provided, at least one shall comply with 904.4.2 on both the visitor and detainee or inmate sides.
>
> > **EXCEPTION:** The inmate or detainee side of cubicles or counters at non-contact visiting areas not serving holding cells or housing cells required to comply with F232 shall not be required to comply with 902 or 904.4.2.
>
> **F232.5.2 Partitions.** Where solid partitions or security glazing separate visitors from detainees or inmates at least one of each type of cubicle or counter partition shall comply with 904.6.

F233 Residential Facilities

> **F233.1 General.** *Facilities* with *residential dwelling units* shall comply with F233.

> **Advisory F233.1 General.** Section F233 outlines the requirements for residential facilities subject to the Architectural Barriers Act. The facilities covered by Section F233, as well as other facilities not covered by this section, may still be subject to other Federal laws such as the Fair Housing Act and Section 504 of the Rehabilitation Act of 1973, as amended. For example, the Fair Housing Act requires that certain residential structures having four or more multi-family dwelling units, regardless of whether they are privately owned or federally assisted, include certain features of accessible and adaptable design according to guidelines established by the U.S. Department of Housing and Urban Development (HUD). These laws and the appropriate regulations should be consulted before proceeding with the design and construction of residential facilities.
>
> Residential facilities containing residential dwelling units provided by entities subject to HUD's Section 504 regulations and residential dwelling units covered by Section F233.3 must comply with the technical and scoping requirements in Chapters 1 through 10 included this document. Section F233 is not a stand-alone section; this section only addresses the minimum number of residential dwelling units within a facility required to comply with Chapter 8. However, residential facilities must also comply with the requirements of this document. For example: Section F206.5.4 requires all doors and doorways providing user

> **Advisory F233.1 General (Continued).** passage in residential dwelling units providing mobility features to comply with Section 404; Section F206.7.6 permits platform lifts to be used to connect levels within residential dwelling units providing mobility features; Section F208 provides general scoping for accessible parking and Section F208.2.3.1 specifies the required number of accessible parking spaces for each residential dwelling unit providing mobility features; Section F228.2 requires mail boxes to be within reach ranges when they serve residential dwelling units providing mobility features; play areas are addressed in Section F240; and swimming pools are addressed in Section F242. There are special provisions applicable to facilities containing residential dwelling units at: Exception 3 to F202.3; Exception to F202.4; F203.9; and Exception 3 to F206.2.3.

F233.2 Residential Dwelling Units Provided by HUD or Through Grant or Loan Programs Administered by HUD. Where *facilities* with *residential dwelling units* are provided by the Department of Housing and Urban Development (HUD), or through a grant or loan program administered by HUD, *residential dwelling units* with mobility features complying with 809.2 through 809.4 shall be provided in a number required by the regulations issued by HUD under Section 504 of the Rehabilitation Act of 1973, as amended. *Residential dwelling units* required to provide mobility features complying with 809.2 through 809.4 shall be on an *accessible* route as required by F206. In addition, *residential dwelling units* with communication features complying with 809.5 shall be provided in a number required by the applicable HUD regulations. *Residential dwelling units* subject to F233.2 shall not be required to comply with F233.3 or F233.4.

> **Advisory F233.2 Residential Dwelling Units Provided by HUD or Through Grant or Loan Programs Administered by HUD.** Section F233.2 requires that entities subject to HUD's regulations implementing Section 504 of the Rehabilitation Act of 1973, as amended, provide residential dwelling units containing mobility features and residential dwelling units containing communication features complying with these regulations in a number specified in HUD's Section 504 regulations. Further, the residential dwelling units provided must be dispersed according to HUD's Section 504 criteria. In addition, Section F233.2 defers to HUD the specification of criteria by which the technical requirements of this document will apply to alterations of existing facilities subject to HUD's Section 504 regulations.

F233.3 Residential Dwelling Units Provided on Military Installations. *Military installations* with *residential dwelling units* shall comply with F233.3. *Residential dwelling units* on *military installations* subject to F233.3 shall not be required to comply with F233.2 or F233.4.

F233.3.1 Minimum Number: New Construction. Newly constructed *facilities* with *residential dwelling units* shall comply with F233.3.1.

F233.3.1.1 Residential Dwelling Units with Mobility Features. On *military installations* with *residential dwelling units*, at least 5 percent, but no fewer than one unit, of the total number of *residential dwelling units* shall provide mobility features complying with 809.2 through 809.4 and shall be on an *accessible* route as required by F206.

Printed by Builder's Book, Inc., Bookstore · www.buildersbook.com

F233.3.1.2 Residential Dwelling Units with Communication Features. On *military installations* with *residential dwelling units*, at least 2 percent, but no fewer than one unit, of the total number of *residential dwelling units* shall provide communication features complying with 809.5.

F233.3.2 Additions. Where an *addition* to an existing *building* results in an increase in the number of *residential dwelling units,* the requirements of F233.3.1 shall apply only to the *residential dwelling units* that are *added* until the total number of *residential dwelling units* complies with the minimum number required by F233.3.1. *Residential dwelling units* required to comply with F233.3.1.1 shall be on an *accessible* route as required by F206.

F233.3.3 Alterations. *Alterations* shall comply with F233.3.3.
EXCEPTION: Where compliance with 809.2, 809.3, or 809.4 is *technically infeasible*, or where it is *technically infeasible* to provide an *accessible* route to a *residential dwelling unit*, the Department of Defense shall be permitted to *alter* or construct a comparable *residential dwelling unit* to comply with 809.2 through 809.4 provided that the minimum number of *residential dwelling units* required by F233.3.1.1 and F233.3.1.2, as applicable, is satisfied.

F233.3.3.1 Alterations to Vacated Buildings. Where a *building* is vacated for the purposes of *alteration*, at least 5 percent of the *residential dwelling units* shall comply with 809.2 through 809.4 and shall be on an *accessible* route as required by F206. In addition, at least 2 percent of the *residential dwelling units* shall comply with 809.5.

F233.3.3.2 Alterations to Individual Residential Dwelling Units. In individual *residential dwelling units*, where a bathroom or a kitchen is substantially *altered*, and at least one other room is *altered*, the requirements of F233.3.1 shall apply to the *altered residential dwelling units* until the total number of *residential dwelling units* complies with the minimum number required by F233.3.1.1 and F233.3.1.2. *Residential dwelling units* required to comply with F233.3.1.1 shall be on an *accessible* route as required by F206.

F233.3.4 Dispersion. *Residential dwelling units* required to provide mobility features complying with 809.2 through 809.4 and *residential dwelling units* required provide communication features complying with 809.5 shall be dispersed among the various types of *residential dwelling units* on the *military installation*, and shall provide choices of *residential dwelling units* comparable to, and integrated with, those available to other residents.
EXCEPTION: Where multi-*story residential dwelling units* are one of the types of *residential dwelling units* provided, one-*story residential dwelling units* shall be permitted as a substitute for multi-*story residential dwelling units* where equivalent *spaces* and amenities are provided in the one-*story residential dwelling unit*.

F233.4 Residential Dwelling Units Provided by Other Federal Agencies or Through Grant or Loan Programs Administered by Other Federal Agencies. *Facilities* with *residential dwelling units* provided by other federal agencies or through grant or loan programs administered by other federal agencies shall comply with F233.4. *Residential dwelling units* subject to F233.4 shall not be required to comply with F233.2 or F233.3.

F233.4.1 Minimum Number: New Construction. Newly constructed *facilities* with *residential dwelling units* shall comply with F233.4.1.

> **EXCEPTION:** Where *facilities* contain 15 or fewer *residential dwelling units*, the requirements of F233.4.1.1 and F233.4.1.2 shall apply to the total number of *residential dwelling units* that are constructed under a single contract, or are developed as a whole, whether or not located on a common *site*.

F233.4.1.1 Residential Dwelling Units with Mobility Features. In *facilities* with *residential dwelling units*, at least 5 percent, but no fewer than one unit, of the total number of *residential dwelling units* shall provide mobility features complying with 809.2 through 809.4 and shall be on an *accessible* route as required by F206.

F233.4.1.2 Residential Dwelling Units with Communication Features. In *facilities* with *residential dwelling units*, at least 2 percent, but no fewer than one unit, of the total number of *residential dwelling units* shall provide communication features complying with 809.5.

F233.4.2 Residential Dwelling Units for Sale. *Residential dwelling units* offered for sale shall provide *accessible* features to the extent required by regulations issued by Federal agencies under Section 504 of the Rehabilitation Act of 1973, as amended.

> **Advisory F233.4.2 Residential Dwelling Units for Sale.** An agency that uses federal funds or an entity that receives federal financial assistance to build housing for purchase by individual home buyers must provide access according to the requirements of the applicable Section 504 regulations.

F233.4.3 Additions. Where an *addition* to an existing *building* results in an increase in the number of *residential dwelling units,* the requirements of F233.4.1 shall apply only to the *residential dwelling units* that are *added* until the total number of *residential dwelling units* complies with the minimum number required by F233.4.1. *Residential dwelling units* required to comply with F233.4.1.1 shall be on an *accessible* route as required by F206.

F233.4.4 Alterations. *Alterations* shall comply with F233.4.4.

> **EXCEPTION:** Where compliance with 809.2, 809.3, or 809.4 is *technically infeasible*, or where it is *technically infeasible* to provide an *accessible* route to a *residential dwelling unit*, the entity shall be permitted to *alter* or construct a comparable *residential dwelling unit* to comply with 809.2 through 809.4 provided that the minimum number of *residential dwelling units* required by F233.4.1.1 and F233.4.1.2, as applicable, is satisfied.

> **Advisory F233.4.4 Alterations Exception.** A substituted dwelling unit must be comparable to the dwelling unit that is not made accessible. Factors to be considered in comparing one dwelling unit to another should include the number of bedrooms; amenities provided within the dwelling unit; types of common spaces provided within the facility; and location with respect to community resources and services, such as public transportation and civic, recreational, and mercantile facilities.

130

F233.4.4.1 Alterations to Vacated Buildings. Where a *building* is vacated for the purposes of *alteration* and the *altered building* contains more than 15 *residential dwelling units*, at least 5 percent of the *residential dwelling units* shall comply with 809.2 through 809.4 and shall be on an *accessible* route as required by F206. In addition, at least 2 percent of the *residential dwelling units* shall comply with 809.5.

> **Advisory F233.4.4.1 Alterations to Vacated Buildings.** This provision is intended to apply where a building is vacated with the intent to alter the building. Buildings that are vacated solely for pest control or asbestos removal are not subject to the requirements to provide residential dwelling units with mobility features or communication features.

F233.4.4.2 Alterations to Individual Residential Dwelling Units. In individual *residential dwelling units*, where a bathroom or a kitchen is substantially *altered*, and at least one other room is *altered* the requirements of F233.4.1 shall apply to the *altered residential dwelling units* until the total number of *residential dwelling units* complies with the minimum number required by F233.4.1.1 and F233.4.1.2. *Residential dwelling units* required to comply with F233.4.1.1 shall be on an *accessible* route as required by F206.
> **EXCEPTION:** Where *facilities* contain 15 or fewer *residential dwelling units*, the requirements of F233.4.1.1 and F233.4.1.2 shall apply to the total number of *residential dwelling units* that are *altered* under a single contract, or are developed as a whole, whether or not located on a common *site*.

> **Advisory F233.4.4.2 Alterations to Individual Residential Dwelling Units.** Section F233.4.4.2 uses the terms "substantially altered" and "altered." A substantial alteration to a kitchen or bathroom includes, but is not limited to, alterations that are changes to or rearrangements in the plan configuration, or replacement of cabinetry. Substantial alterations do not include normal maintenance or appliance and fixture replacement, unless such maintenance or replacement requires changes to or rearrangements in the plan configuration, or replacement of cabinetry. The term "alteration" is defined in Section F106 of these requirements.

F233.4.5 Dispersion. *Residential dwelling units* required to provide mobility features complying with 809.2 through 809.4 and *residential dwelling units* required to provide communication features complying with 809.5 shall be dispersed among the various types of *residential dwelling units* in the *facility* and shall provide choices of *residential dwelling units* comparable to, and integrated with, those available to other residents.
> **EXCEPTION:** Where multi-*story residential dwelling units* are one of the types of *residential dwelling units* provided, one-*story residential dwelling units* shall be permitted as a substitute for multi-*story residential dwelling units* where equivalent *spaces* and amenities are provided in the one-*story residential dwelling unit*.

F234 Amusement Rides

F234.1 General. *Amusement rides* shall comply with F234.
> **EXCEPTION:** Mobile or portable *amusement rides* shall not be required to comply with F234.

Advisory F234.1 General. These requirements apply generally to newly designed and constructed amusement rides and attractions. A custom designed and constructed ride is new upon its first use, which is the first time amusement park patrons take the ride. With respect to amusement rides purchased from other entities, new refers to the first permanent installation of the ride, whether it is used off the shelf or modified before it is installed. Where amusement rides are moved after several seasons to another area of the park or to another park, the ride would not be considered newly designed or newly constructed.

Some amusement rides and attractions that have unique designs and features are not addressed by these requirements. In those situations, these requirements are to be applied to the extent possible. An example of an amusement ride not specifically addressed by these requirements includes "virtual reality" rides where the device does not move through a fixed course within a defined area. An accessible route must be provided to these rides. Where an attraction or ride has unique features for which there are no applicable scoping provisions, then a reasonable number, but at least one, of the features must be located on an accessible route. Where there are appropriate technical provisions, they must be applied to the elements that are covered by the scoping provisions.

Advisory F234.1 General Exception. Mobile or temporary rides are those set up for short periods of time such as traveling carnivals, State and county fairs, and festivals. The amusement rides that are covered by F234.1 are ones that are not regularly assembled and disassembled.

F234.2 Load and Unload Areas. Load and unload areas serving *amusement rides* shall comply with 1002.3.

F234.3 Minimum Number. *Amusement rides* shall provide at least one *wheelchair space* complying with 1002.4, or at least one *amusement ride seat* designed for transfer complying with 1002.5, or at least one *transfer device* complying with 1002.6.

EXCEPTIONS: 1. *Amusement rides* that are controlled or operated by the rider shall not be required to comply with F234.3.

2. *Amusement rides* designed primarily for children, where children are assisted on and off the ride by an adult, shall not be required to comply with F234.3.

3. *Amusement rides* that do not provide *amusement ride seats* shall not be required to comply with F234.3.

Advisory F234.3 Minimum Number Exceptions 1 through 3. Amusement rides controlled or operated by the rider, designed for children, or rides without ride seats are not required to comply with F234.3. These rides are not exempt from the other provisions in F234 requiring an accessible route to the load and unload areas and to the ride. The exception does not apply to those rides where patrons may cause the ride to make incidental movements, but where the patron otherwise has no control over the ride.

Advisory F234.3 Minimum Number Exception 2. The exception is limited to those rides designed "primarily" for children, where children are assisted on and off the ride by an adult. This exception is limited to those rides designed for children and not for the occasional adult user. An accessible route to and turning space in the load and unload area will provide access for adults and family members assisting children on and off these rides.

F234.4 Existing Amusement Rides. Where existing *amusement rides* are *altered*, the *alteration* shall comply with F234.4.

Advisory F234.4 Existing Amusement Rides. Routine maintenance, painting, and changing of theme boards are examples of activities that do not constitute an alteration subject to this section.

F234.4.1 Load and Unload Areas. Where load and unload areas serving existing *amusement rides* are newly designed and constructed, the load and unload areas shall comply with 1002.3.

F234.4.2 Minimum Number. Where the structural or operational characteristics of an *amusement ride* are *altered* to the extent that the *amusement ride*'s performance differs from that specified by the manufacturer or the original design, the *amusement ride* shall comply with F234.3.

F235 Recreational Boating Facilities

F235.1 General. Recreational boating *facilities* shall comply with F235.

F235.2 Boat Slips. *Boat slips* complying with 1003.3.1 shall be provided in accordance with Table F235.2. Where the number of *boat slips* is not identified, each 40 feet (12 m) of *boat slip* edge provided along the perimeter of the pier shall be counted as one *boat slip* for the purpose of this section.

Table F235.2 Boat Slips

Total Number of Boat Slips Provided in Facility	Minimum Number of Required Accessible Boat Slips
1 to 25	1
26 to 50	2
51 to 100	3
101 to 150	4
151 to 300	5
301 to 400	6
401 to 500	7
501 to 600	8

Table F235.2 Boat Slips

Total Number of Boat Slips Provided in Facility	Minimum Number of Required Accessible Boat Slips
601 to 700	9
701 to 800	10
801 to 900	11
901 to 1000	12
1001 and over	12, plus 1 for every 100, or fraction thereof, over 1000

Advisory F235.2 Boat Slips. The requirement for boat slips also applies to piers where boat slips are not demarcated. For example, a single pier 25 feet (7620 mm) long and 5 feet (1525 mm) wide (the minimum width specified by Section 1003.3) allows boats to moor on three sides. Because the number of boat slips is not demarcated, the total length of boat slip edge (55 feet, 17 m) must be used to determine the number of boat slips provided (two). This number is based on the specification in Section F235.2 that each 40 feet (12 m) of boat slip edge, or fraction thereof, counts as one boat slip. In this example, Table F235.2 would require one boat slip to be accessible.

F235.2.1 Dispersion. *Boat slips* complying with 1003.3.1 shall be dispersed throughout the various types of *boat slips* provided. Where the minimum number of *boat slips* required to comply with 1003.3.1 has been met, no further dispersion shall be required.

Advisory F235.2.1 Dispersion. Types of boat slips are based on the size of the boat slips; whether single berths or double berths, shallow water or deep water, transient or longer-term lease, covered or uncovered; and whether slips are equipped with features such as telephone, water, electricity or cable connections. The term "boat slip" is intended to cover any pier area other than launch ramp boarding piers where recreational boats are moored for purposes of berthing, embarking, or disembarking. For example, a fuel pier may contain boat slips, and this type of short term slip would be included in determining compliance with F235.2.

F235.3 Boarding Piers at Boat Launch Ramps. Where *boarding piers* are provided at *boat launch ramps*, at least 5 percent, but no fewer than one, of the *boarding piers* shall comply with 1003.3.2.

F236 Exercise Machines and Equipment

F236.1 General. At least one of each type of exercise machine and equipment shall comply with 1004.

134

Advisory F236.1 General. Most strength training equipment and machines are considered different types. Where operators provide a biceps curl machine and cable cross-over machine, both machines are required to meet the provisions in this section, even though an individual may be able to work on their biceps through both types of equipment.

Similarly, there are many types of cardiovascular exercise machines, such as stationary bicycles, rowing machines, stair climbers, and treadmills. Each machine provides a cardiovascular exercise and is considered a different type for purposes of these requirements.

F237 Fishing Piers and Platforms

F237.1 General. Fishing piers and platforms shall comply with 1005.

F238 Golf Facilities

F238.1 General. Golf *facilities* shall comply with F238.

F238.2 Golf Courses. Golf courses shall comply with F238.2.

F238.2.1 Teeing Grounds. Where one *teeing ground* is provided for a hole, the *teeing ground* shall be designed and constructed so that a golf car can enter and exit the *teeing ground*. Where two *teeing grounds* are provided for a hole, the forward *teeing ground* shall be designed and constructed so that a golf car can enter and exit the *teeing ground*. Where three or more *teeing grounds* are provided for a hole, at least two *teeing grounds*, including the forward *teeing ground*, shall be designed and constructed so that a golf car can enter and exit each *teeing ground*.

EXCEPTION: In existing golf courses, the forward *teeing ground* shall not be required to be one of the *teeing grounds* on a hole designed and constructed so that a golf car can enter and exit the *teeing ground* where compliance is not feasible due to terrain.

F238.2.2 Putting Greens. Putting greens shall be designed and constructed so that a golf car can enter and exit the putting green.

F238.2.3 Weather Shelters. Where provided, weather shelters shall be designed and constructed so that a golf car can enter and exit the weather shelter and shall comply with 1006.4.

F238.3 Practice Putting Greens, Practice Teeing Grounds, and Teeing Stations at Driving Ranges. At least 5 percent, but no fewer than one, of practice putting greens, practice *teeing grounds*, and teeing stations at driving ranges shall be designed and constructed so that a golf car can enter and exit the practice putting greens, practice *teeing grounds*, and teeing stations at driving ranges.

F239 Miniature Golf Facilities

F239.1 General. Miniature golf *facilities* shall comply with F239.

F239.2 Minimum Number. At least 50 percent of holes on miniature golf courses shall comply with 1007.3.

> **Advisory F239.2 Minimum Number.** Where possible, providing access to all holes on a miniature golf course is recommended. If a course is designed with the minimum 50 percent accessible holes, designers or operators are encouraged to select holes which provide for an equivalent experience to the maximum extent possible.

F239.3 Miniature Golf Course Configuration. Miniature golf courses shall be configured so that the holes complying with 1007.3 are consecutive. Miniature golf courses shall provide an *accessible* route from the last hole complying with 1007.3 to the course *entrance* or exit without requiring travel through any other holes on the course.

    EXCEPTION: One break in the sequence of consecutive holes shall be permitted provided that the last hole on the miniature golf course is the last hole in the sequence.

> **Advisory F239.3 Miniature Golf Course Configuration.** Where only the minimum 50 percent of the holes are accessible, an accessible route from the last accessible hole to the course exit or entrance must not require travel back through other holes. In some cases, this may require an additional accessible route. Other options include increasing the number of accessible holes in a way that limits the distance needed to connect the last accessible hole with the course exit or entrance.

F240 Play Areas

F240.1 General. *Play areas* for children ages 2 and over shall comply with F240. Where separate *play areas* are provided within a *site* for specific age groups, each *play area* shall comply with F240.

    EXCEPTIONS: 1. *Play areas* located in family child care *facilities* where the proprietor actually resides shall not be required to comply with F240.

    2. In existing *play areas*, where *play components* are relocated for the purposes of creating safe *use zones* and the ground surface is not *altered* or extended for more than one *use zone*, the *play area* shall not be required to comply with F240.

    3. *Amusement attractions* shall not be required to comply with F240.

    4. Where *play components* are *altered* and the ground surface is not *altered*, the ground surface shall not be required to comply with 1008.2.6 unless required by F202.4.

> **Advisory F240.1 General.** Play areas may be located on exterior sites or within a building. Where separate play areas are provided within a site for children in specified age groups (e.g., preschool (ages 2 to 5) and school age (ages 5 to 12)), each play area must comply with this section. Where play areas are provided for the same age group on a site but are geographically separated (e.g., one is located next to a picnic area and another is located next to a softball field), they are considered separate play areas and each play area must comply with this section.

F240.1.1 Additions. Where *play areas* are designed and constructed in phases, the requirements of F240 shall apply to each successive *addition* so that when the *addition* is completed, the entire *play area* complies with all the applicable requirements of F240.

Advisory F240.1.1 Additions. These requirements are to be applied so that when each successive addition is completed, the entire play area complies with all applicable provisions. For example, a play area is built in two phases. In the first phase, there are 10 elevated play components and 10 elevated play components are added in the second phase for a total of 20 elevated play components in the play area. When the first phase was completed, at least 5 elevated play components, including at least 3 different types, were to be provided on an accessible route. When the second phase is completed, at least 10 elevated play components must be located on an accessible route, and at least 7 ground level play components, including 4 different types, must be provided on an accessible route. At the time the second phase is complete, ramps must be used to connect at least 5 of the elevated play components and transfer systems are permitted to be used to connect the rest of the elevated play components required to be located on an accessible route.

F240.2 Play Components. Where provided, *play components* shall comply with F240.2.

F240.2.1 Ground Level Play Components. *Ground level play components* shall be provided in the number and types required by F240.2.1. *Ground level play components* that are provided to comply with F240.2.1.1 shall be permitted to satisfy the additional number required by F240.2.1.2 if the minimum required types of *play components* are satisfied. Where two or more required *ground level play components* are provided, they shall be dispersed throughout the *play area* and integrated with other *play components*.

Advisory F240.2.1 Ground Level Play Components. Examples of ground level play components may include spring rockers, swings, diggers, and stand-alone slides. When distinguishing between the different types of ground level play components, consider the general experience provided by the play component. Examples of different types of experiences include, but are not limited to, rocking, swinging, climbing, spinning, and sliding. A spiral slide may provide a slightly different experience from a straight slide, but sliding is the general experience and therefore a spiral slide is not considered a different type of play component from a straight slide.

Ground level play components accessed by children with disabilities must be integrated into the play area. Designers should consider the optimal layout of ground level play components accessed by children with disabilities to foster interaction and socialization among all children. Grouping all ground level play components accessed by children with disabilities in one location is not considered integrated.

Where a stand-alone slide is provided, an accessible route must connect the base of the stairs at the entry point to the exit point of the slide. A ramp or transfer system to the top of the slide is not required. Where a sand box is provided, an accessible route must connect to the border of the sand box. Accessibility to the sand box would be enhanced by providing a transfer system into the sand or by providing a raised sand table with knee clearance complying with 1008.4.3.

Ramps are preferred over transfer systems since not all children who use wheelchairs or other mobility devices may be able to use, or may choose not to use, transfer systems.

Advisory F240.2.1 Ground Level Play Components (Continued). Where ramps connect elevated play components, the maximum rise of any ramp run is limited to 12 inches (305 mm). Where possible, designers and operators are encouraged to provide ramps with a slope less than the 1:12 maximum. Berms or sculpted dirt may be used to provide elevation and may be part of an accessible route to composite play structures.

Platform lifts are permitted as a part of an accessible route. Because lifts must be independently operable, operators should carefully consider the appropriateness of their use in unsupervised settings.

F240.2.1.1 Minimum Number and Types. Where *ground level play components* are provided, at least one of each type shall be on an *accessible* route and shall comply with 1008.4.

F240.2.1.2 Additional Number and Types. Where *elevated play components* are provided, *ground level play components* shall be provided in accordance with Table F240.2.1.2 and shall comply with 1008.4.

  EXCEPTION: If at least 50 percent of the *elevated play components* are connected by a *ramp* and at least 3 of the *elevated play components* connected by the *ramp* are different types of *play components*, the *play area* shall not be required to comply with F240.2.1.2.

Table F240.2.1.2 Number and Types of Ground Level Play Components Required to be on Accessible Routes

Number of Elevated Play Components Provided	Minimum Number of Ground Level Play Components Required to be on an Accessible Route	Minimum Number of Different Types of Ground Level Play Components Required to be on an Accessible Route
1	Not applicable	Not applicable
2 to 4	1	1
5 to 7	2	2
8 to 10	3	3
11 to 13	4	3
14 to 16	5	3
17 to 19	6	3
20 to 22	7	4
23 to 25	8	4
26 and over	8, plus 1 for each additional 3, or fraction thereof, over 25	5

Advisory F240.2.1.2 Additional Number and Types. Where a large play area includes two or more composite play structures designed for the same age group, the total number of elevated play components on all the composite play structures must be added to determine the additional number and types of ground level play components that must be provided on an accessible route.

F240.2.2 Elevated Play Components. Where *elevated play components* are provided, at least 50 percent shall be on an *accessible* route and shall comply with 1008.4.

Advisory F240.2.2 Elevated Play Components. A double or triple slide that is part of a composite play structure is one elevated play component. For purposes of this section, ramps, transfer systems, steps, decks, and roofs are not considered elevated play components. Although socialization and pretend play can occur on these elements, they are not primarily intended for play.

Some play components that are attached to a composite play structure can be approached or exited at the ground level or above grade from a platform or deck. For example, a climber attached to a composite play structure can be approached or exited at the ground level or above grade from a platform or deck on a composite play structure. Play components that are attached to a composite play structure and can be approached from a platform or deck (e.g., climbers and overhead play components) are considered elevated play components. These play components are not considered ground level play components and do not count toward the requirements in F240.2.1.2 regarding the number of ground level play components that must be located on an accessible route.

F241 Saunas and Steam Rooms

F241.1 General. Where provided, saunas and steam rooms shall comply with 612.
   EXCEPTION: Where saunas or steam rooms are clustered at a single location, no more than 5 percent of the saunas and steam rooms, but no fewer than one, of each type in each cluster shall be required to comply with 612.

F242 Swimming Pools, Wading Pools, and Spas

F242.1 General. Swimming pools, wading pools, and spas shall comply with F242.

F242.2 Swimming Pools. At least two *accessible* means of entry shall be provided for swimming pools. *Accessible* means of entry shall be swimming pool lifts complying with 1009.2; sloped entries complying with 1009.3; transfer walls complying with 1009.4; transfer systems complying with 1009.5; and pool stairs complying with 1009.6. At least one *accessible* means of entry provided shall comply with 1009.2 or 1009.3.
   EXCEPTIONS: 1. Where a swimming pool has less than 300 linear feet (91 m) of swimming pool wall, no more than one *accessible* means of entry shall be required provided that the *accessible* means of entry is a swimming pool lift complying with 1009.2 or sloped entry complying with 1009.3.
   2. Wave action pools, leisure rivers, sand bottom pools, and other pools where user access is limited to one area shall not be required to provide more than one *accessible* means of entry provided that

the *accessible* means of entry is a swimming pool lift complying with 1009.2, a sloped entry complying with 1009.3, or a transfer system complying with 1009.5.

3. *Catch pools* shall not be required to provide an *accessible* means of entry provided that the *catch pool* edge is on an *accessible* route.

Advisory F242.2 Swimming Pools. Where more than one means of access is provided into the water, it is recommended that the means be different. Providing different means of access will better serve the varying needs of people with disabilities in getting into and out of a swimming pool. It is also recommended that where two or more means of access are provided, they not be provided in the same location in the pool. Different locations will provide increased options for entry and exit, especially in larger pools.

Advisory F242.2 Swimming Pools Exception 1. Pool walls at diving areas and areas along pool walls where there is no pool entry because of landscaping or adjacent structures are to be counted when determining the number of accessible means of entry required.

F242.3 Wading Pools. At least one *accessible* means of entry shall be provided for wading pools. *Accessible* means of entry shall comply with sloped entries complying with 1009.3.

F242.4 Spas. At least one *accessible* means of entry shall be provided for spas. *Accessible* means of entry shall comply with swimming pool lifts complying with 1009.2; transfer walls complying with 1009.4; or transfer systems complying with 1009.5.

    EXCEPTION: Where spas are provided in a cluster, no more than 5 percent, but no fewer than one, spa in each cluster shall be required to comply with F242.4.

F243 Shooting Facilities with Firing Positions

F243.1 General. Where shooting *facilities* with firing positions are designed and constructed at a *site*, at least 5 percent, but no fewer than one, of each type of firing position shall comply with 1010.

140

CHAPTER 3: BUILDING BLOCKS

301 General

301.1 Scope. The provisions of Chapter 3 shall apply where required by Chapter 2 or where referenced by a requirement in this document.

302 Floor or Ground Surfaces

302.1 General. Floor and ground surfaces shall be stable, firm, and slip resistant and shall comply with 302.

EXCEPTIONS: 1. Within animal containment areas, floor and ground surfaces shall not be required to be stable, firm, and slip resistant.

2. *Areas of sport activity* shall not be required to comply with 302.

> **Advisory 302.1 General.** A stable surface is one that remains unchanged by contaminants or applied force, so that when the contaminant or force is removed, the surface returns to its original condition. A firm surface resists deformation by either indentations or particles moving on its surface. A slip-resistant surface provides sufficient frictional counterforce to the forces exerted in walking to permit safe ambulation.

302.2 Carpet. Carpet or carpet tile shall be securely attached and shall have a firm cushion, pad, or backing or no cushion or pad. Carpet or carpet tile shall have a level loop, textured loop, level cut pile, or level cut/uncut pile texture. Pile height shall be ½ inch (13 mm) maximum. Exposed edges of carpet shall be fastened to floor surfaces and shall have trim on the entire length of the exposed edge. Carpet edge trim shall comply with 303.

> **Advisory 302.2 Carpet.** Carpets and permanently affixed mats can significantly increase the amount of force (roll resistance) needed to propel a wheelchair over a surface. The firmer the carpeting and backing, the lower the roll resistance. A pile thickness up to ½ inch (13 mm) (measured to the backing, cushion, or pad) is allowed, although a lower pile provides easier wheelchair maneuvering. If a backing, cushion or pad is used, it must be firm. Preferably, carpet pad should not be used because the soft padding increases roll resistance.

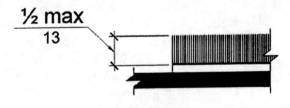

Figure 302.2
Carpet Pile Height

302.3 Openings. Openings in floor or ground surfaces shall not allow passage of a sphere more than ½ inch (13 mm) diameter except as allowed in 407.4.3, 409.4.3, 410.4, 810.5.3 and 810.10. Elongated openings shall be placed so that the long dimension is perpendicular to the dominant direction of travel.

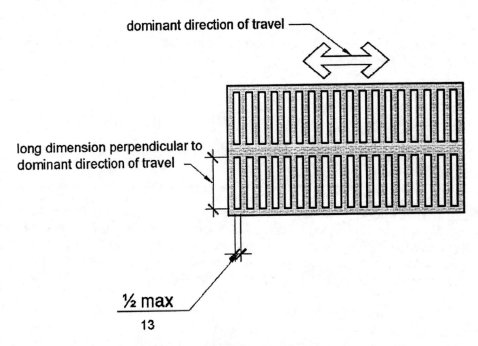

Figure 302.3
Elongated Openings in Floor or Ground Surfaces

303 Changes in Level

303.1 General. Where changes in level are permitted in floor or ground surfaces, they shall comply with 303.

  EXCEPTIONS: 1. Animal containment areas shall not be required to comply with 303.
  2. *Areas of sport activity* shall not be required to comply with 303.

303.2 Vertical. Changes in level of ¼ inch (6.4 mm) high maximum shall be permitted to be vertical.

Figure 303.2
Vertical Change in Level

142

303.3 Beveled. Changes in level between ¼ inch (6.4 mm) high minimum and ½ inch (13 mm) high maximum shall be beveled with a slope not steeper than 1:2.

> **Advisory 303.3 Beveled.** A change in level of ½ inch (13 mm) is permitted to be ¼ inch (6.4 mm) vertical plus ¼ inch (6.4 mm) beveled. However, in no case may the combined change in level exceed ½ inch (13 mm). Changes in level exceeding ½ inch (13 mm) must comply with 405 (Ramps) or 406 (Curb Ramps).

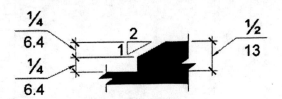

Figure 303.3
Beveled Change in Level

303.4 Ramps. Changes in level greater than ½ inch (13 mm) high shall be *ramped*, and shall comply with 405 or 406.

304 Turning Space

304.1 General. Turning *space* shall comply with 304.

304.2 Floor or Ground Surfaces. Floor or ground surfaces of a turning *space* shall comply with 302. Changes in level are not permitted.
    EXCEPTION: Slopes not steeper than 1:48 shall be permitted.

> **Advisory 304.2 Floor or Ground Surface Exception.** As used in this section, the phrase "changes in level" refers to surfaces with slopes and to surfaces with abrupt rise exceeding that permitted in Section 303.3. Such changes in level are prohibited in required clear floor and ground spaces, turning spaces, and in similar spaces where people using wheelchairs and other mobility devices must park their mobility aids such as in wheelchair spaces, or maneuver to use elements such as at doors, fixtures, and telephones. The exception permits slopes not steeper than 1:48.

304.3 Size. Turning *space* shall comply with 304.3.1 or 304.3.2.

304.3.1 Circular Space. The turning *space* shall be a *space* of 60 inches (1525 mm) diameter minimum. The *space* shall be permitted to include knee and toe clearance complying with 306.

304.3.2 T-Shaped Space. The turning *space* shall be a T-shaped *space* within a 60 inch (1525 mm) square minimum with arms and base 36 inches (915 mm) wide minimum. Each arm of the T shall be clear of obstructions 12 inches (305 mm) minimum in each direction and the base shall be clear of obstructions 24 inches (610 mm) minimum. The *space* shall be permitted to include knee and toe clearance complying with 306 only at the end of either the base or one arm.

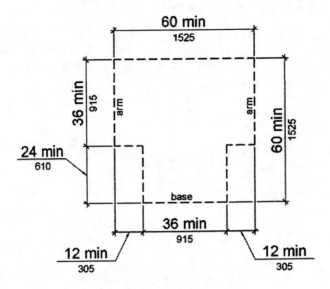

Figure 304.3.2
T-Shaped Turning Space

304.4 Door Swing. Doors shall be permitted to swing into turning *spaces*.

305 Clear Floor or Ground Space

305.1 General. Clear floor or ground *space* shall comply with 305.

305.2 Floor or Ground Surfaces. Floor or ground surfaces of a clear floor or ground *space* shall comply with 302. Changes in level are not permitted.
   EXCEPTION: Slopes not steeper than 1:48 shall be permitted.

305.3 Size. The clear floor or ground *space* shall be 30 inches (760 mm) minimum by 48 inches (1220 mm) minimum.

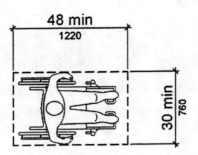

Figure 305.3
Clear Floor or Ground Space

305.4 Knee and Toe Clearance. Unless otherwise specified, clear floor or ground *space* shall be permitted to include knee and toe clearance complying with 306.

305.5 Position. Unless otherwise specified, clear floor or ground *space* shall be positioned for either forward or parallel approach to an *element*.

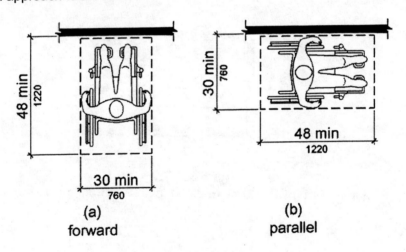

(a)
forward

(b)
parallel

Figure 305.5
Position of Clear Floor or Ground Space

305.6 Approach. One full unobstructed side of the clear floor or ground *space* shall adjoin an *accessible* route or adjoin another clear floor or ground *space*.

305.7 Maneuvering Clearance. Where a clear floor or ground *space* is located in an alcove or otherwise confined on all or part of three sides, additional maneuvering clearance shall be provided in accordance with 305.7.1 and 305.7.2.

Printed by Builder's Book, Inc., Bookstore · www.buildersbook.com

305.7.1 Forward Approach. Alcoves shall be 36 inches (915 mm) wide minimum where the depth exceeds 24 inches (610 mm).

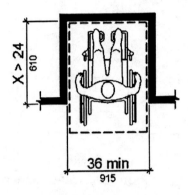

Figure 305.7.1
Maneuvering Clearance in an Alcove, Forward Approach

305.7.2 Parallel Approach. Alcoves shall be 60 inches (1525 mm) wide minimum where the depth exceeds 15 inches (380 mm).

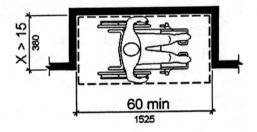

Figure 305.7.2
Maneuvering Clearance in an Alcove, Parallel Approach

306 Knee and Toe Clearance

306.1 General. Where *space* beneath an *element* is included as part of clear floor or ground *space* or turning *space*, the *space* shall comply with 306. Additional *space* shall not be prohibited beneath an *element* but shall not be considered as part of the clear floor or ground *space* or turning *space*.

> **Advisory 306.1 General.** Clearances are measured in relation to the usable clear floor space, not necessarily to the vertical support for an element. When determining clearance under an object for required turning or maneuvering space, care should be taken to ensure the space is clear of any obstructions.

306.2 Toe Clearance.

306.2.1 General. *Space* under an *element* between the finish floor or ground and 9 inches (230 mm) above the finish floor or ground shall be considered toe clearance and shall comply with 306.2.

306.2.2 Maximum Depth. Toe clearance shall extend 25 inches (635 mm) maximum under an *element*.

306.2.3 Minimum Required Depth. Where toe clearance is required at an *element* as part of a clear floor *space*, the toe clearance shall extend 17 inches (430 mm) minimum under the *element*.

306.2.4 Additional Clearance. *Space* extending greater than 6 inches (150 mm) beyond the available knee clearance at 9 inches (230 mm) above the finish floor or ground shall not be considered toe clearance.

306.2.5 Width. Toe clearance shall be 30 inches (760 mm) wide minimum.

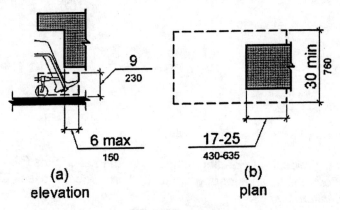

(a)
elevation

(b)
plan

**Figure 306.2
Toe Clearance**

306.3 Knee Clearance.

306.3.1 General. *Space* under an *element* between 9 inches (230 mm) and 27 inches (685 mm) above the finish floor or ground shall be considered knee clearance and shall comply with 306.3.

306.3.2 Maximum Depth. Knee clearance shall extend 25 inches (635 mm) maximum under an *element* at 9 inches (230 mm) above the finish floor or ground.

306.3.3 Minimum Required Depth. Where knee clearance is required under an *element* as part of a clear floor *space*, the knee clearance shall be 11 inches (280 mm) deep minimum at 9 inches (230 mm) above the finish floor or ground, and 8 inches (205 mm) deep minimum at 27 inches (685 mm) above the finish floor or ground.

306.3.4 Clearance Reduction. Between 9 inches (230 mm) and 27 inches (685 mm) above the finish floor or ground, the knee clearance shall be permitted to reduce at a rate of 1 inch (25 mm) in depth for each 6 inches (150 mm) in height.

306.3.5 Width. Knee clearance shall be 30 inches (760 mm) wide minimum.

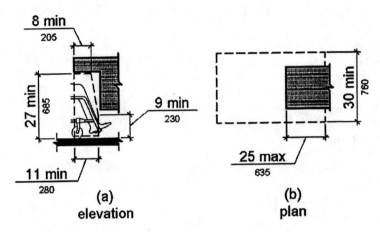

(a)
elevation

(b)
plan

**Figure 306.3
Knee Clearance**

307 Protruding Objects

307.1 General. Protruding objects shall comply with 307.

307.2 Protrusion Limits. Objects with leading edges more than 27 inches (685 mm) and not more than 80 inches (2030 mm) above the finish floor or ground shall protrude 4 inches (100 mm) maximum horizontally into the *circulation path*.

    EXCEPTION: Handrails shall be permitted to protrude 4½ inches (115 mm) maximum.

> **Advisory 307.2 Protrusion Limits.** When a cane is used and the element is in the detectable range, it gives a person sufficient time to detect the element with the cane before there is body contact. Elements located on circulation paths, including operable elements, must comply with requirements for protruding objects. For example, awnings and their supporting structures cannot reduce the minimum required vertical clearance. Similarly, casement windows, when open, cannot encroach more than 4 inches (100 mm) into circulation paths above 27 inches (685 mm).

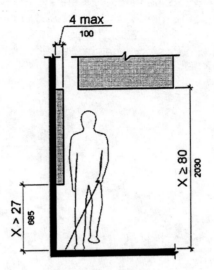

Figure 307.2
Limits of Protruding Objects

307.3 Post-Mounted Objects. Free-standing objects mounted on posts or pylons shall overhang *circulation paths* 12 inches (305 mm) maximum when located 27 inches (685 mm) minimum and 80 inches (2030 mm) maximum above the finish floor or ground. Where a sign or other obstruction is mounted between posts or pylons and the clear distance between the posts or pylons is greater than 12 inches (305 mm), the lowest edge of such sign or obstruction shall be 27 inches (685 mm) maximum or 80 inches (2030 mm) minimum above the finish floor or ground.

EXCEPTION: The sloping portions of handrails serving stairs and *ramps* shall not be required to comply with 307.3.

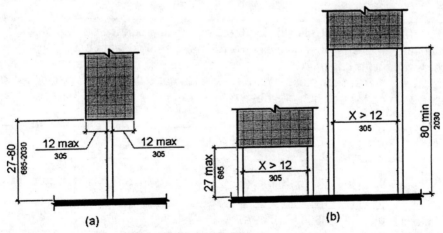

Figure 307.3
Post-Mounted Protruding Objects

307.4 Vertical Clearance. Vertical clearance shall be 80 inches (2030 mm) high minimum. Guardrails or other barriers shall be provided where the vertical clearance is less than 80 inches (2030 mm) high. The leading edge of such guardrail or barrier shall be located 27 inches (685 mm) maximum above the finish floor or ground.

    EXCEPTION: Door closers and door stops shall be permitted to be 78 inches (1980 mm) minimum above the finish floor or ground.

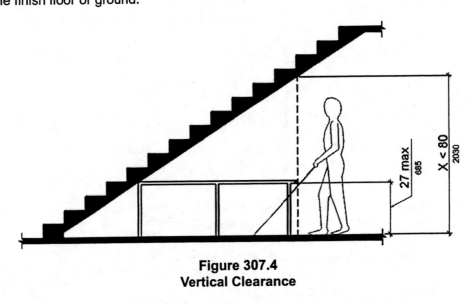

Figure 307.4
Vertical Clearance

307.5 Required Clear Width. Protruding objects shall not reduce the clear width required for *accessible* routes.

308 Reach Ranges

308.1 General. Reach ranges shall comply with 308.

Advisory 308.1 General. The following table provides guidance on reach ranges for children according to age where building elements such as coat hooks, lockers, or operable parts are designed for use primarily by children. These dimensions apply to either forward or side reaches. Accessible elements and operable parts designed for adult use or children over age 12 can be located outside these ranges but must be within the adult reach ranges required by 308.

Children's Reach Ranges			
Forward or Side Reach	Ages 3 and 4	Ages 5 through 8	Ages 9 through 12
High (maximum)	36 in (915 mm)	40 in (1015 mm)	44 in (1120 mm)
Low (minimum)	20 in (510 mm)	18 in (455 mm)	16 in (405 mm)

308.2 Forward Reach.

308.2.1 Unobstructed. Where a forward reach is unobstructed, the high forward reach shall be 48 inches (1220 mm) maximum and the low forward reach shall be 15 inches (380 mm) minimum above the finish floor or ground.

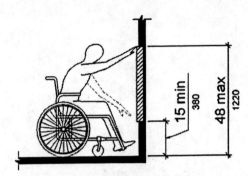

Figure 308.2.1
Unobstructed Forward Reach

308.2.2 Obstructed High Reach. Where a high forward reach is over an obstruction, the clear floor *space* shall extend beneath the *element* for a distance not less than the required reach depth over the obstruction. The high forward reach shall be 48 inches (1220 mm) maximum where the reach depth is 20 inches (510 mm) maximum. Where the reach depth exceeds 20 inches (510 mm), the high forward reach shall be 44 inches (1120 mm) maximum and the reach depth shall be 25 inches (635 mm) maximum.

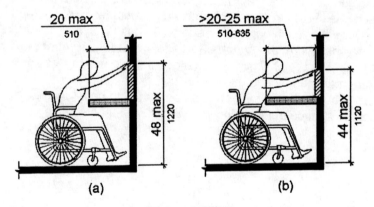

Figure 308.2.2
Obstructed High Forward Reach

308.3 Side Reach.

308.3.1 Unobstructed. Where a clear floor or ground *space* allows a parallel approach to an *element* and the side reach is unobstructed, the high side reach shall be 48 inches (1220 mm) maximum and the low side reach shall be 15 inches (380 mm) minimum above the finish floor or ground.

    EXCEPTIONS: 1. An obstruction shall be permitted between the clear floor or ground *space* and the *element* where the depth of the obstruction is 10 inches (255 mm) maximum.

    2. *Operable parts* of fuel dispensers shall be permitted to be 54 inches (1370 mm) maximum measured from the surface of the *vehicular way* where fuel dispensers are installed on existing curbs.

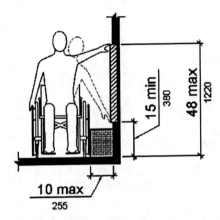

Figure 308.3.1
Unobstructed Side Reach

308.3.2 Obstructed High Reach. Where a clear floor or ground *space* allows a parallel approach to an *element* and the high side reach is over an obstruction, the height of the obstruction shall be 34 inches (865 mm) maximum and the depth of the obstruction shall be 24 inches (610 mm) maximum. The high side reach shall be 48 inches (1220 mm) maximum for a reach depth of 10 inches (255 mm) maximum. Where the reach depth exceeds 10 inches (255 mm), the high side reach shall be 46 inches (1170 mm) maximum for a reach depth of 24 inches (610 mm) maximum.

    EXCEPTIONS: 1. The top of washing machines and clothes dryers shall be permitted to be 36 inches (915 mm) maximum above the finish floor.

    2. *Operable parts* of fuel dispensers shall be permitted to be 54 inches (1370 mm) maximum measured from the surface of the *vehicular way* where fuel dispensers are installed on existing curbs.

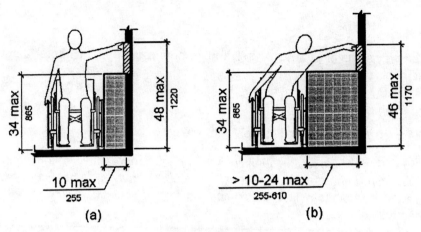

Figure 308.3.2
Obstructed High Side Reach

309 Operable Parts

309.1 General. *Operable parts* shall comply with 309.

309.2 Clear Floor Space. A clear floor or ground *space* complying with 305 shall be provided.

309.3 Height. *Operable parts* shall be placed within one or more of the reach ranges specified in 308.

309.4 Operation. *Operable parts* shall be operable with one hand and shall not require tight grasping, pinching, or twisting of the wrist. The force required to activate *operable parts* shall be 5 pounds (22.2 N) maximum.

    EXCEPTION: Gas pump nozzles shall not be required to provide *operable parts* that have an activating force of 5 pounds (22.2 N) maximum.

CHAPTER 4: ACCESSIBLE ROUTES

401 General

401.1 Scope. The provisions of Chapter 4 shall apply where required by Chapter 2 or where referenced by a requirement in this document.

402 Accessible Routes

402.1 General. *Accessible* routes shall comply with 402.

402.2 Components. *Accessible* routes shall consist of one or more of the following components: walking surfaces with a *running slope* not steeper than 1:20, doorways, *ramps*, *curb ramps* excluding the flared sides, elevators, and platform lifts. All components of an *accessible* route shall comply with the applicable requirements of Chapter 4.

> **Advisory 402.2 Components.** Walking surfaces must have running slopes not steeper than 1:20, see 403.3. Other components of accessible routes, such as ramps (405) and curb ramps (406), are permitted to be more steeply sloped.

403 Walking Surfaces

403.1 General. Walking surfaces that are a part of an *accessible* route shall comply with 403.

403.2 Floor or Ground Surface. Floor or ground surfaces shall comply with 302.

403.3 Slope. The *running slope* of walking surfaces shall not be steeper than 1:20. The *cross slope* of walking surfaces shall not be steeper than 1:48.

403.4 Changes in Level. Changes in level shall comply with 303.

403.5 Clearances. Walking surfaces shall provide clearances complying with 403.5.
  EXCEPTION: Within *employee work area*s, clearances on *common use circulation path*s shall be permitted to be decreased by *work area equipment* provided that the decrease is essential to the function of the work being performed.

  403.5.1 Clear Width. Except as provided in 403.5.2 and 403.5.3, the clear width of walking surfaces shall be 36 inches (915 mm) minimum.
    EXCEPTION: The clear width shall be permitted to be reduced to 32 inches (815 mm) minimum for a length of 24 inches (610 mm) maximum provided that reduced width segments are separated by segments that are 48 inches (1220 mm) long minimum and 36 inches (915 mm) wide minimum.

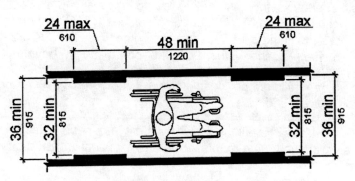

Figure 403.5.1
Clear Width of an Accessible Route

403.5.2 Clear Width at Turn. Where the *accessible* route makes a 180 degree turn around an *element* which is less than 48 inches (1220 mm) wide, clear width shall be 42 inches (1065 mm) minimum approaching the turn, 48 inches (1220 mm) minimum at the turn and 42 inches (1065 mm) minimum leaving the turn.

EXCEPTION: Where the clear width at the turn is 60 inches (1525 mm) minimum compliance with 403.5.2 shall not be required.

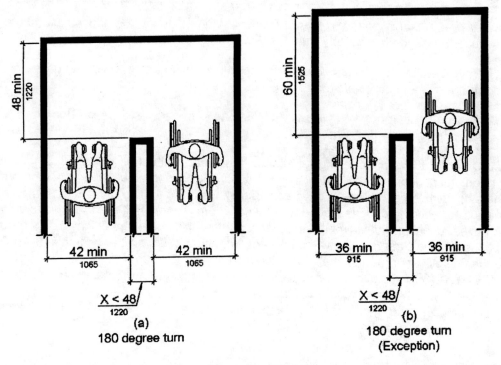

Figure 403.5.2
Clear Width at Turn

Printed by Builder's Book, Inc., Bookstore · www.buildersbook.com

403.5.3 Passing Spaces. An *accessible* route with a clear width less than 60 inches (1525 mm) shall provide passing *spaces* at intervals of 200 feet (61 m) maximum. Passing *spaces* shall be either: a *space* 60 inches (1525 mm) minimum by 60 inches (1525 mm) minimum; or, an intersection of two walking surfaces providing a T-shaped *space* complying with 304.3.2 where the base and arms of the T-shaped *space* extend 48 inches (1220 mm) minimum beyond the intersection.

403.6 Handrails. Where handrails are provided along walking surfaces with *running slopes* not steeper than 1:20 they shall comply with 505.

> **Advisory 403.6 Handrails.** Handrails provided in elevator cabs and platform lifts are not required to comply with the requirements for handrails on walking surfaces.

404 Doors, Doorways, and Gates

404.1 General. Doors, doorways, and gates that are part of an *accessible* route shall comply with 404.
  EXCEPTION: Doors, doorways, and gates designed to be operated only by security personnel shall not be required to comply with 404.2.7, 404.2.8, 404.2.9, 404.3.2 and 404.3.4 through 404.3.7.

> **Advisory 404.1 General Exception.** Security personnel must have sole control of doors that are eligible for the Exception at 404.1. It would not be acceptable for security personnel to operate the doors for people with disabilities while allowing others to have independent access.

404.2 Manual Doors, Doorways, and Manual Gates. Manual doors and doorways and manual gates intended for user passage shall comply with 404.2.

404.2.1 Revolving Doors, Gates, and Turnstiles. Revolving doors, revolving gates, and turnstiles shall not be part of an *accessible* route.

404.2.2 Double-Leaf Doors and Gates. At least one of the active leaves of doorways with two leaves shall comply with 404.2.3 and 404.2.4.

404.2.3 Clear Width. Door openings shall provide a clear width of 32 inches (815 mm) minimum. Clear openings of doorways with swinging doors shall be measured between the face of the door and the stop, with the door open 90 degrees. Openings more than 24 inches (610 mm) deep shall provide a clear opening of 36 inches (915 mm) minimum. There shall be no projections into the required clear opening width lower than 34 inches (865 mm) above the finish floor or ground. Projections into the clear opening width between 34 inches (865 mm) and 80 inches (2030 mm) above the finish floor or ground shall not exceed 4 inches (100 mm).
  EXCEPTIONS: 1. In *alterations*, a projection of 5/8 inch (16 mm) maximum into the required clear width shall be permitted for the latch side stop.
  2. Door closers and door stops shall be permitted to be 78 inches (1980 mm) minimum above the finish floor or ground.

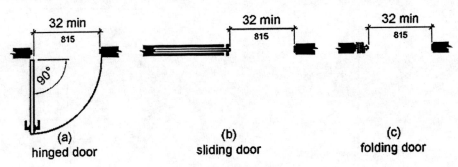

Figure 404.2.3
Clear Width of Doorways

404.2.4 Maneuvering Clearances. Minimum maneuvering clearances at doors and gates shall comply with 404.2.4. Maneuvering clearances shall extend the full width of the doorway and the required latch side or hinge side clearance.

EXCEPTION: Entry doors to hospital patient rooms shall not be required to provide the clearance beyond the latch side of the door.

404.2.4.1 Swinging Doors and Gates. Swinging doors and gates shall have maneuvering clearances complying with Table 404.2.4.1.

Table 404.2.4.1 Maneuvering Clearances at Manual Swinging Doors and Gates

Type of Use		Minimum Maneuvering Clearance	
Approach Direction	**Door or Gate Side**	**Perpendicular to Doorway**	**Parallel to Doorway (beyond latch side unless noted)**
From front	Pull	60 inches (1525 mm)	18 inches (455 mm)
From front	Push	48 inches (1220 mm)	0 inches (0 mm)[1]
From hinge side	Pull	60 inches (1525 mm)	36 inches (915 mm)
From hinge side	Pull	54 inches (1370 mm)	42 inches (1065 mm)
From hinge side	Push	42 inches (1065 mm)[2]	22 inches (560 mm)[3]
From latch side	Pull	48 inches (1220 mm)[4]	24 inches (610 mm)
From latch side	Push	42 inches (1065 mm)[4]	24 inches (610 mm)

1. Add 12 inches (305 mm) if closer and latch are provided.
2. Add 6 inches (150 mm) if closer and latch are provided.
3. Beyond hinge side.
4. Add 6 inches (150 mm) if closer is provided.

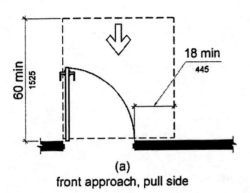

(a)
front approach, pull side

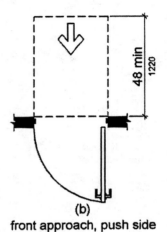

(b)
front approach, push side

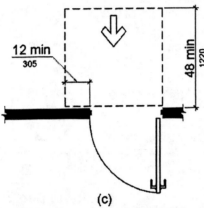

(c)
front approach, push side, door
provided with both closer and latch

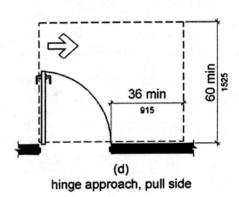

(d)
hinge approach, pull side

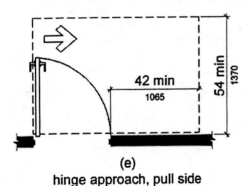

(e)
hinge approach, pull side

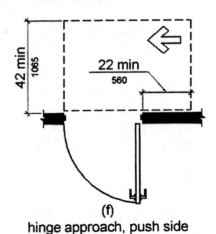

(f)
hinge approach, push side

Figure 404.2.4.1
Maneuvering Clearances at Manual Swinging Doors and Gates

158

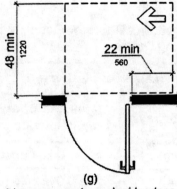

(g)
hinge approach, push side, door
provided with both closer and latch

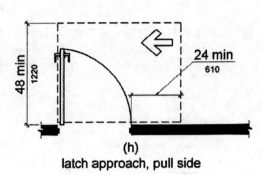

(h)
latch approach, pull side

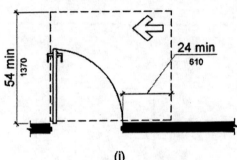

(i)
latch approach, pull side,
door provided with closer

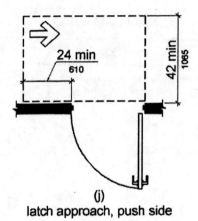

(j)
latch approach, push side

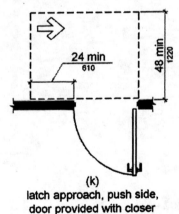

(k)
latch approach, push side,
door provided with closer

Figure 404.2.4.1
Maneuvering Clearances at Manual Swinging Doors and Gates

404.2.4.2 Doorways without Doors or Gates, Sliding Doors, and Folding Doors. Doorways less than 36 inches (915 mm) wide without doors or gates, sliding doors, or folding doors shall have maneuvering clearances complying with Table 404.2.4.2.

Table 404.2.4.2 Maneuvering Clearances at Doorways without Doors or Gates, Manual Sliding Doors, and Manual Folding Doors

Approach Direction	Minimum Maneuvering Clearance	
	Perpendicular to Doorway	Parallel to Doorway (beyond stop/latch side unless noted)
From Front	48 inches (1220 mm)	0 inches (0 mm)
From side[1]	42 inches (1065 mm)	0 inches (0 mm)
From pocket/hinge side	42 inches (1065 mm)	22 inches (560 mm)[2]
From stop/latch side	42 inches (1065 mm)	24 inches (610 mm)

1. Doorway with no door only.
2. Beyond pocket/hinge side.

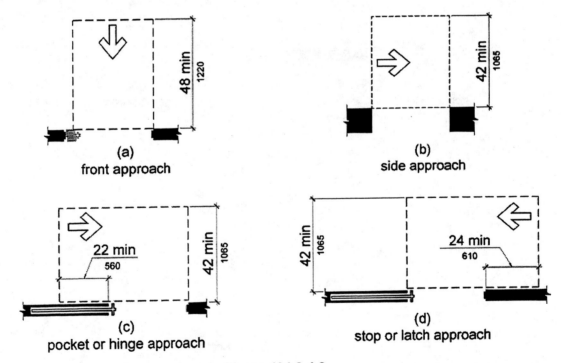

(a)
front approach

(b)
side approach

(c)
pocket or hinge approach

(d)
stop or latch approach

Figure 404.2.4.2
Maneuvering Clearances at Doorways without Doors, Sliding Doors, Gates, and Folding Doors

160

404.2.4.3 Recessed Doors and Gates. Maneuvering clearances for forward approach shall be provided when any obstruction within 18 inches (455 mm) of the latch side of a doorway projects more than 8 inches (205 mm) beyond the face of the door, measured perpendicular to the face of the door or gate.

> **Advisory 404.2.4.3 Recessed Doors and Gates.** A door can be recessed due to wall thickness or because of the placement of casework and other fixed elements adjacent to the doorway. This provision must be applied wherever doors are recessed.

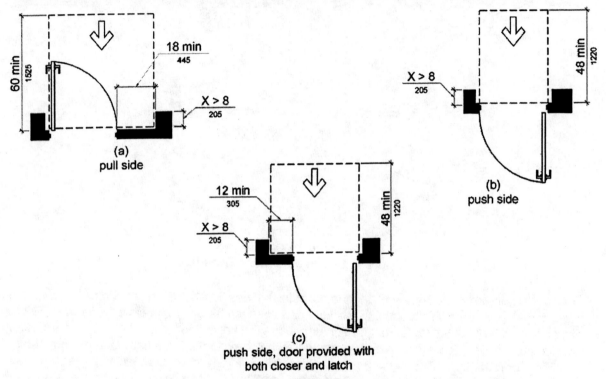

Figure 404.2.4.3
Maneuvering Clearances at Recessed Doors and Gates

404.2.4.4 Floor or Ground Surface. Floor or ground surface within required maneuvering clearances shall comply with 302. Changes in level are not permitted.
   EXCEPTIONS: 1. Slopes not steeper than 1:48 shall be permitted.
   2. Changes in level at thresholds complying with 404.2.5 shall be permitted.

404.2.5 Thresholds. Thresholds, if provided at doorways, shall be ½ inch (13 mm) high maximum. Raised thresholds and changes in level at doorways shall comply with 302 and 303.
   EXCEPTION: Existing or *altered* thresholds ¾ inch (19 mm) high maximum that have a beveled edge on each side with a slope not steeper than 1:2 shall not be required to comply with 404.2.5.

404.2.6 Doors in Series and Gates in Series. The distance between two hinged or pivoted doors in series and gates in series shall be 48 inches (1220 mm) minimum plus the width of doors or gates swinging into the *space*.

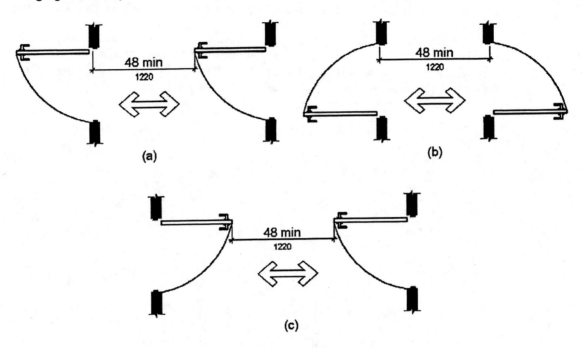

(a)　　　　(b)

(c)

Figure 404.2.6
Doors in Series and Gates in Series

404.2.7 Door and Gate Hardware. Handles, pulls, latches, locks, and other *operable parts* on doors and gates shall comply with 309.4. *Operable parts* of such hardware shall be 34 inches (865 mm) minimum and 48 inches (1220 mm) maximum above the finish floor or ground. Where sliding doors are in the fully open position, operating hardware shall be exposed and usable from both sides.

EXCEPTIONS: 1. Existing locks shall be permitted in any location at existing glazed doors without stiles, existing overhead rolling doors or grilles, and similar existing doors or grilles that are designed with locks that are activated only at the top or bottom rail.

2. Access gates in barrier walls and fences protecting pools, spas, and hot tubs shall be permitted to have *operable parts* of the release of latch on self-latching devices at 54 inches (1370 mm) maximum above the finish floor or ground provided the self-latching devices are not also self-locking devices and operated by means of a key, electronic opener, or integral combination lock.

Advisory 404.2.7 Door and Gate Hardware. Door hardware that can be operated with a closed fist or a loose grip accommodates the greatest range of users. Hardware that requires simultaneous hand and finger movements require greater dexterity and coordination, and is not recommended.

404.2.8 Closing Speed. Door and gate closing speed shall comply with 404.2.8.

404.2.8.1 Door Closers and Gate Closers. Door closers and gate closers shall be adjusted so that from an open position of 90 degrees, the time required to move the door to a position of 12 degrees from the latch is 5 seconds minimum.

404.2.8.2 Spring Hinges. Door and gate spring hinges shall be adjusted so that from the open position of 70 degrees, the door or gate shall move to the closed position in 1.5 seconds minimum.

404.2.9 Door and Gate Opening Force. Fire doors shall have a minimum opening force allowable by the appropriate *administrative authority*. The force for pushing or pulling open a door or gate other than fire doors shall be as follows:
1. Interior hinged doors and gates: 5 pounds (22.2 N) maximum.
2. Sliding or folding doors: 5 pounds (22.2 N) maximum.

These forces do not apply to the force required to retract latch bolts or disengage other devices that hold the door or gate in a closed position.

> **Advisory 404.2.9 Door and Gate Opening Force.** The maximum force pertains to the continuous application of force necessary to fully open a door, not the initial force needed to overcome the inertia of the door. It does not apply to the force required to retract bolts or to disengage other devices used to keep the door in a closed position.

404.2.10 Door and Gate Surfaces. Swinging door and gate surfaces within 10 inches (255 mm) of the finish floor or ground measured vertically shall have a smooth surface on the push side extending the full width of the door or gate. Parts creating horizontal or vertical joints in these surfaces shall be within 1/16 inch (1.6 mm) of the same plane as the other. Cavities created by added kick plates shall be capped.

EXCEPTIONS: 1. Sliding doors shall not be required to comply with 404.2.10.
2. Tempered glass doors without stiles and having a bottom rail or shoe with the top leading edge tapered at 60 degrees minimum from the horizontal shall not be required to meet the 10 inch (255 mm) bottom smooth surface height requirement.
3. Doors and gates that do not extend to within 10 inches (255 mm) of the finish floor or ground shall not be required to comply with 404.2.10.
4. Existing doors and gates without smooth surfaces within 10 inches (255 mm) of the finish floor or ground shall not be required to provide smooth surfaces complying with 404.2.10 provided that if added kick plates are installed, cavities created by such kick plates are capped.

404.2.11 Vision Lights. Doors, gates, and side lights adjacent to doors or gates, containing one or more glazing panels that permit viewing through the panels shall have the bottom of at least one glazed panel located 43 inches (1090 mm) maximum above the finish floor.

EXCEPTION: Vision lights with the lowest part more than 66 inches (1675 mm) from the finish floor or ground shall not be required to comply with 404.2.11.

404.3 Automatic and Power-Assisted Doors and Gates. Automatic doors and automatic gates shall comply with 404.3. Full-powered automatic doors shall comply with ANSI/BHMA A156.10 (incorporated by reference, see "Referenced Standards" in Chapter 1). Low-energy and power-assisted doors shall comply with ANSI/BHMA A156.19 (1997 or 2002 edition) (incorporated by reference, see "Referenced Standards" in Chapter 1).

404.3.1 Clear Width. Doorways shall provide a clear opening of 32 inches (815 mm) minimum in power-on and power-off mode. The minimum clear width for automatic door systems in a doorway shall be based on the clear opening provided by all leaves in the open position.

404.3.2 Maneuvering Clearance. Clearances at power-assisted doors and gates shall comply with 404.2.4. Clearances at automatic doors and gates without standby power and serving an *accessible means of egress* shall comply with 404.2.4.
  EXCEPTION: Where automatic doors and gates remain open in the power-off condition, compliance with 404.2.4 shall not be required.

404.3.3 Thresholds. Thresholds and changes in level at doorways shall comply with 404.2.5.

404.3.4 Doors in Series and Gates in Series. Doors in series and gates in series shall comply with 404.2.6.

404.3.5 Controls. Manually operated controls shall comply with 309. The clear floor *space* adjacent to the control shall be located beyond the arc of the door swing.

404.3.6 Break Out Opening. Where doors and gates without standby power are a part of a means of egress, the clear break out opening at swinging or sliding doors and gates shall be 32 inches (815 mm) minimum when operated in emergency mode.
  EXCEPTION: Where manual swinging doors and gates comply with 404.2 and serve the same means of egress compliance with 404.3.6 shall not be required.

404.3.7 Revolving Doors, Revolving Gates, and Turnstiles. Revolving doors, revolving gates, and turnstiles shall not be part of an *accessible* route.

405 Ramps

405.1 General. *Ramps* on *accessible* routes shall comply with 405.
  EXCEPTION: In *assembly areas*, aisle *ramps* adjacent to seating and not serving *elements* required to be on an *accessible* route shall not be required to comply with 405.

405.2 Slope. *Ramp* runs shall have a *running slope* not steeper than 1:12.
  EXCEPTION: In existing *sites*, *buildings*, and *facilities*, *ramps* shall be permitted to have *running slopes* steeper than 1:12 complying with Table 405.2 where such slopes are necessary due to *space* limitations.

Table 405.2 Maximum Ramp Slope and Rise for Existing Sites, Buildings, and Facilities

Slope[1]	Maximum Rise
Steeper than 1:10 but not steeper than 1:8	3 inches (75 mm)
Steeper than 1:12 but not steeper than 1:10	6 inches (150 mm)

1. A slope steeper than 1:8 is prohibited.

> **Advisory 405.2 Slope.** To accommodate the widest range of users, provide ramps with the least possible running slope and, wherever possible, accompany ramps with stairs for use by those individuals for whom distance presents a greater barrier than steps, e.g., people with heart disease or limited stamina.

405.3 Cross Slope. *Cross slope* of *ramp* runs shall not be steeper than 1:48.

> **Advisory 405.3 Cross Slope.** Cross slope is the slope of the surface perpendicular to the direction of travel. Cross slope is measured the same way as slope is measured (i.e., the rise over the run).

405.4 Floor or Ground Surfaces. Floor or ground surfaces of *ramp* runs shall comply with 302. Changes in level other than the *running slope* and *cross slope* are not permitted on *ramp* runs.

405.5 Clear Width. The clear width of a *ramp* run and, where handrails are provided, the clear width between handrails shall be 36 inches (915 mm) minimum.

   EXCEPTION: Within *employee work area*s, the required clear width of *ramps* that are a part of *common use circulation path*s shall be permitted to be decreased by *work area equipment* provided that the decrease is essential to the function of the work being performed.

405.6 Rise. The rise for any *ramp* run shall be 30 inches (760 mm) maximum.

405.7 Landings. *Ramps* shall have landings at the top and the bottom of each *ramp* run. Landings shall comply with 405.7.

> **Advisory 405.7 Landings.** Ramps that do not have level landings at changes in direction can create a compound slope that will not meet the requirements of this document. Circular or curved ramps continually change direction. Curvilinear ramps with small radii also can create compound cross slopes and cannot, by their nature, meet the requirements for accessible routes. A level landing is needed at the accessible door to permit maneuvering and simultaneously door operation.

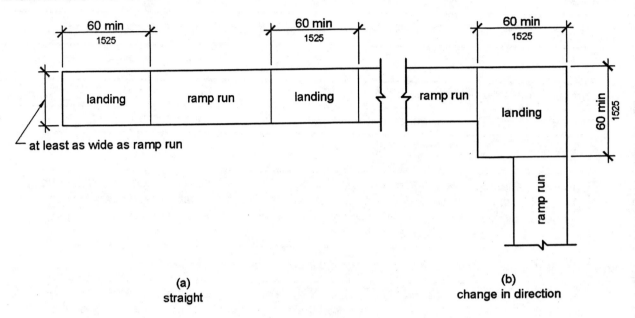

Figure 405.7
Ramp Landings

405.7.1 Slope. Landings shall comply with 302. Changes in level are not permitted.
EXCEPTION: Slopes not steeper than 1:48 shall be permitted.

405.7.2 Width. The landing clear width shall be at least as wide as the widest *ramp* run leading to the landing.

405.7.3 Length. The landing clear length shall be 60 inches (1525 mm) long minimum.

405.7.4 Change in Direction. *Ramps* that change direction between runs at landings shall have a clear landing 60 inches (1525 mm) minimum by 60 inches (1525 mm) minimum.

405.7.5 Doorways. Where doorways are located adjacent to a *ramp* landing, maneuvering clearances required by 404.2.4 and 404.3.2 shall be permitted to overlap the required landing area.

405.8 Handrails. *Ramp* runs with a rise greater than 6 inches (150 mm) shall have handrails complying with 505.
EXCEPTION: Within *employee work areas*, handrails shall not be required where *ramps* that are part of *common use circulation paths* are designed to permit the installation of handrails complying with 505. *Ramps* not subject to the exception to 405.5 shall be designed to maintain a 36 inch (915 mm) minimum clear width when handrails are installed.

405.9 Edge Protection. Edge protection complying with 405.9.1 or 405.9.2 shall be provided on each side of *ramp* runs and at each side of *ramp* landings.

166

EXCEPTIONS: 1. Edge protection shall not be required on *ramps* that are not required to have handrails and have sides complying with 406.3.

2. Edge protection shall not be required on the sides of *ramp* landings serving an adjoining *ramp* run or stairway.

3. Edge protection shall not be required on the sides of *ramp* landings having a vertical drop-off of ½ inch (13 mm) maximum within 10 inches (255 mm) horizontally of the minimum landing area specified in 405.7.

405.9.1 Extended Floor or Ground Surface. The floor or ground surface of the *ramp* run or landing shall extend 12 inches (305 mm) minimum beyond the inside face of a handrail complying with 505.

> **Advisory 405.9.1 Extended Floor or Ground Surface.** The extended surface prevents wheelchair casters and crutch tips from slipping off the ramp surface.

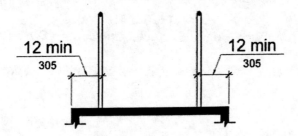

Figure 405.9.1
Extended Floor or Ground Surface Edge Protection

405.9.2 Curb or Barrier. A curb or barrier shall be provided that prevents the passage of a 4 inch (100 mm) diameter sphere, where any portion of the sphere is within 4 inches (100 mm) of the finish floor or ground surface.

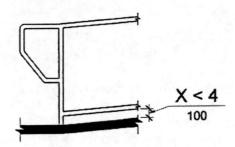

Figure 405.9.2
Curb or Barrier Edge Protection

405.10 Wet Conditions. Landings subject to wet conditions shall be designed to prevent the accumulation of water.

406 Curb Ramps

406.1 General. *Curb ramps* on *accessible* routes shall comply with 406, 405.2 through 405.5, and 405.10.

406.2 Counter Slope. Counter slopes of adjoining gutters and road surfaces immediately adjacent to the *curb ramp* shall not be steeper than 1:20. The adjacent surfaces at transitions at *curb ramps* to *walks*, gutters, and streets shall be at the same level.

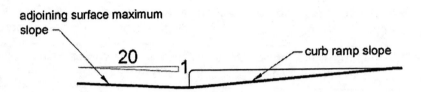

Figure 406.2
Counter Slope of Surfaces Adjacent to Curb Ramps

406.3 Sides of Curb Ramps. Where provided, *curb ramp* flares shall not be steeper than 1:10.

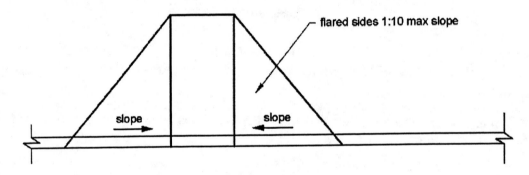

Figure 406.3
Sides of Curb Ramps

406.4 Landings. Landings shall be provided at the tops of *curb ramps*. The landing clear length shall be 36 inches (915 mm) minimum. The landing clear width shall be at least as wide as the *curb ramp*, excluding flared sides, leading to the landing.
    EXCEPTION: In *alterations*, where there is no landing at the top of *curb ramps*, *curb ramp* flares shall be provided and shall not be steeper than 1:12.

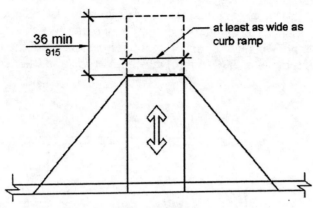

Figure 406.4
Landings at the Top of Curb Ramps

406.5 Location. *Curb ramps* and the flared sides of *curb ramps* shall be located so that they do not project into vehicular traffic lanes, parking *spaces*, or parking access aisles. *Curb ramps* at *marked crossings* shall be wholly contained within the markings, excluding any flared sides.

406.6 Diagonal Curb Ramps. Diagonal or corner type *curb ramps* with returned curbs or other well-defined edges shall have the edges parallel to the direction of pedestrian flow. The bottom of diagonal *curb ramps* shall have a clear *space* 48 inches (1220 mm) minimum outside active traffic lanes of the roadway. Diagonal *curb ramps* provided at *marked crossings* shall provide the 48 inches (1220 mm) minimum clear *space* within the markings. Diagonal *curb ramps* with flared sides shall have a segment of curb 24 inches (610 mm) long minimum located on each side of the *curb ramp* and within the *marked crossing*.

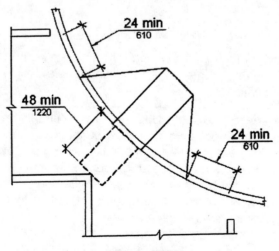

Figure 406.6
Diagonal or Corner Type Curb Ramps

169

406.7 Islands. Raised islands in crossings shall be cut through level with the street or have *curb ramps* at both sides. Each *curb ramp* shall have a level area 48 inches (1220 mm) long minimum by 36 inches (915 mm) wide minimum at the top of the *curb ramp* in the part of the island intersected by the crossings. Each 48 inch (1220 mm) minimum by 36 inch (915 mm) minimum area shall be oriented so that the 48 inch (1220 mm) minimum length is in the direction of the *running slope* of the *curb ramp* it serves. The 48 inch (1220 mm) minimum by 36 inch (915 mm) minimum areas and the *accessible* route shall be permitted to overlap.

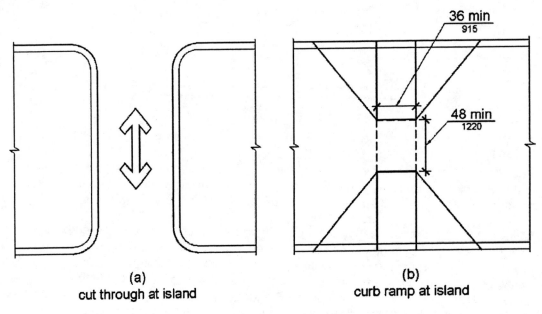

(a)
cut through at island

(b)
curb ramp at island

Figure 406.7
Islands in Crossings

407 Elevators

407.1 General. Elevators shall comply with 407 and with ASME A17.1 (incorporated by reference, see "Referenced Standards" in Chapter 1). They shall be passenger elevators as classified by ASME A17.1. Elevator operation shall be automatic.

> **Advisory 407.1 General.** The ADA and other Federal civil rights laws require that accessible features be maintained in working order so that they are accessible to and usable by those people they are intended to benefit. Building owners should note that the ASME Safety Code for Elevators and Escalators requires routine maintenance and inspections. Isolated or temporary interruptions in service due to maintenance or repairs may be unavoidable; however, failure to take prompt action to effect repairs could constitute a violation of Federal laws and these requirements.

407.2 Elevator Landing Requirements. Elevator landings shall comply with 407.2.

407.2.1 Call Controls. Where elevator call buttons or keypads are provided, they shall comply with 407.2.1 and 309.4. Call buttons shall be raised or flush.
EXCEPTION: Existing elevators shall be permitted to have recessed call buttons.

407.2.1.1 Height. Call buttons and keypads shall be located within one of the reach ranges specified in 308, measured to the centerline of the highest *operable part*.
EXCEPTION: Existing call buttons and existing keypads shall be permitted to be located at 54 inches (1370 mm) maximum above the finish floor, measured to the centerline of the highest *operable part*.

407.2.1.2 Size. Call buttons shall be ¾ inch (19 mm) minimum in the smallest dimension.
EXCEPTION: Existing elevator call buttons shall not be required to comply with 407.2.1.2.

407.2.1.3 Clear Floor or Ground Space. A clear floor or ground *space* complying with 305 shall be provided at call controls.

Advisory 407.2.1.3 Clear Floor or Ground Space. The clear floor or ground space required at elevator call buttons must remain free of obstructions including ashtrays, plants, and other decorative elements that prevent wheelchair users and others from reaching the call buttons. The height of the clear floor or ground space is considered to be a volume from the floor to 80 inches (2030 mm) above the floor. Recessed ashtrays should not be placed near elevator call buttons so that persons who are blind or visually impaired do not inadvertently contact them or their contents as they reach for the call buttons.

407.2.1.4 Location. The call button that designates the up direction shall be located above the call button that designates the down direction.
EXCEPTION: Destination-oriented elevators shall not be required to comply with 407.2.1.4.

Advisory 407.2.1.4 Location Exception. A destination-oriented elevator system provides lobby controls enabling passengers to select floor stops, lobby indicators designating which elevator to use, and a car indicator designating the floors at which the car will stop. Responding cars are programmed for maximum efficiency by reducing the number of stops any passenger experiences.

407.2.1.5 Signals. Call buttons shall have visible signals to indicate when each call is registered and when each call is answered.
EXCEPTIONS: 1. Destination-oriented elevators shall not be required to comply with 407.2.1.5 provided that visible and audible signals complying with 407.2.2 indicating which elevator car to enter are provided.
2. Existing elevators shall not be required to comply with 407.2.1.5.

407.2.1.6 Keypads. Where keypads are provided, keypads shall be in a standard telephone keypad arrangement and shall comply with 407.4.7.2.

407.2.2 Hall Signals. Hall signals, including in-car signals, shall comply with 407.2.2.

407.2.2.1 Visible and Audible Signals. A visible and audible signal shall be provided at each hoistway entrance to indicate which car is answering a call and the car's direction of travel. Where in-car signals are provided, they shall be visible from the floor area adjacent to the hall call buttons.

> **EXCEPTIONS: 1.** Visible and audible signals shall not be required at each destination-oriented elevator where a visible and audible signal complying with 407.2.2 is provided indicating the elevator car designation information.
> **2.** In existing elevators, a signal indicating the direction of car travel shall not be required.

407.2.2.2 Visible Signals. Visible signal fixtures shall be centered at 72 inches (1830 mm) minimum above the finish floor or ground. The visible signal *elements* shall be 2-½ inches (64 mm) minimum measured along the vertical centerline of the *element*. Signals shall be visible from the floor area adjacent to the hall call button.

> **EXCEPTIONS: 1.** Destination-oriented elevators shall be permitted to have signals visible from the floor area adjacent to the hoistway entrance.
> **2.** Existing elevators shall not be required to comply with 407.2.2.2.

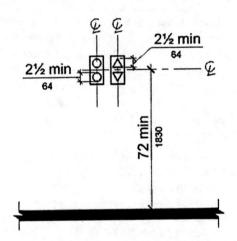

Figure 407.2.2.2
Visible Hall Signals

407.2.2.3 Audible Signals. Audible signals shall sound once for the up direction and twice for the down direction, or shall have verbal annunciators that indicate the direction of elevator car travel. Audible signals shall have a frequency of 1500 Hz maximum. Verbal annunciators shall have a frequency of 300 Hz minimum and 3000 Hz maximum. The audible signal and verbal annunciator shall be 10 dB minimum above ambient, but shall not exceed 80 dB, measured at the hall call button.

> **EXCEPTIONS: 1.** Destination-oriented elevators shall not be required to comply with 407.2.2.3 provided that the audible tone and verbal announcement is the same as those given at the call button or call button keypad.
> **2.** Existing elevators shall not be required to comply with the requirements for frequency and dB range of audible signals.

172

407.2.2.4 Differentiation. Each destination-oriented elevator in a bank of elevators shall have audible and visible means for differentiation.

407.2.3 Hoistway Signs. Signs at elevator hoistways shall comply with 407.2.3.

407.2.3.1 Floor Designation. Floor designations complying with 703.2 and 703.4.1 and shall be provided on both jambs of elevator hoistway entrances. Floor designations shall be provided in both *tactile characters* and braille. *Tactile characters* shall be 2 inches (51 mm) high minimum. A *tactile* star shall be provided on both jambs at the main entry level.

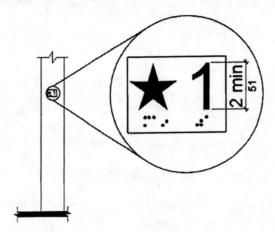

Figure 407.2.3.1
Floor Designations on Jambs of Elevator Hoistway Entrances

407.2.3.2 Car Designations. Destination-oriented elevators shall provide *tactile* car identification complying with 703.2 on both jambs of the hoistway immediately below the floor designation. Car designations shall be provided in both *tactile characters* and braille. *Tactile characters* shall be 2 inches (51 mm) high minimum.

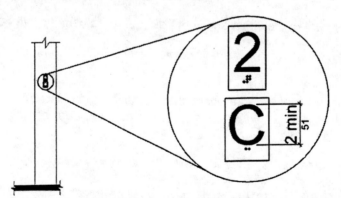

Figure 407.2.3.2
Car Designations on Jambs of Destination-Oriented Elevator Hoistway Entrances

173

407.3 Elevator Door Requirements. Hoistway and car doors shall comply with 407.3.

407.3.1 Type. Elevator doors shall be the horizontal sliding type. Car gates shall be prohibited.

407.3.2 Operation. Elevator hoistway and car doors shall open and close automatically.
EXCEPTION: Existing manually operated hoistway swing doors shall be permitted provided that they comply with 404.2.3 and 404.2.9. Car door closing shall not be initiated until the hoistway door is closed.

407.3.3 Reopening Device. Elevator doors shall be provided with a reopening device complying with 407.3.3 that shall stop and reopen a car door and hoistway door automatically if the door becomes obstructed by an object or person.
EXCEPTION: Existing elevators with manually operated doors shall not be required to comply with 407.3.3.

407.3.3.1 Height. The device shall be activated by sensing an obstruction passing through the opening at 5 inches (125 mm) nominal and 29 inches (735 mm) nominal above the finish floor.

407.3.3.2 Contact. The device shall not require physical contact to be activated, although contact is permitted to occur before the door reverses.

407.3.3.3 Duration. Door reopening devices shall remain effective for 20 seconds minimum.

407.3.4 Door and Signal Timing. The minimum acceptable time from notification that a car is answering a call or notification of the car assigned at the means for the entry of destination information until the doors of that car start to close shall be calculated from the following equation:

T = D/(1.5 ft/s) or T = D/(455 mm/s) = 5 seconds minimum where T equals the total time in seconds and D equals the distance (in feet or millimeters) from the point in the lobby or corridor 60 inches (1525 mm) directly in front of the farthest call button controlling that car to the centerline of its hoistway door.
EXCEPTIONS: 1. For cars with in-car lanterns, T shall be permitted to begin when the signal is visible from the point 60 inches (1525 mm) directly in front of the farthest hall call button and the audible signal is sounded.
2. Destination-oriented elevators shall not be required to comply with 407.3.4.

407.3.5 Door Delay. Elevator doors shall remain fully open in response to a car call for 3 seconds minimum.

407.3.6 Width. The width of elevator doors shall comply with Table 407.4.1.
EXCEPTION: In existing elevators, a power-operated car door complying with 404.2.3 shall be permitted.

407.4 Elevator Car Requirements. Elevator cars shall comply with 407.4.

407.4.1 Car Dimensions. Inside dimensions of elevator cars and clear width of elevator doors shall comply with Table 407.4.1.

EXCEPTION: Existing elevator car configurations that provide a clear floor area of 16 square feet (1.5 m^2) minimum and also provide an inside clear depth 54 inches (1370 mm) minimum and a clear width 36 inches (915 mm) minimum shall be permitted.

Table 407.4.1 Elevator Car Dimensions

Door Location	Minimum Dimensions			
	Door Clear Width	Inside Car, Side to Side	Inside Car, Back Wall to Front Return	Inside Car, Back Wall to Inside Face of Door
Centered	42 inches (1065 mm)	80 inches (2030 mm)	51 inches (1295 mm)	54 inches (1370 mm)
Side (off-centered)	36 inches (915 mm)[1]	68 inches (1725 mm)	51 inches (1295 mm)	54 inches (1370 mm)
Any	36 inches (915 mm)[1]	54 inches (1370 mm)	80 inches (2030 mm)	80 inches (2030 mm)
Any	36 inches (915 mm)[1]	60 inches (1525 mm)[2]	60 inches (1525 mm)[2]	60 inches (1525 mm)[2]

1. A tolerance of minus 5/8 inch (16 mm) is permitted.
2. Other car configurations that provide a turning *space* complying with 304 with the door closed shall be permited.

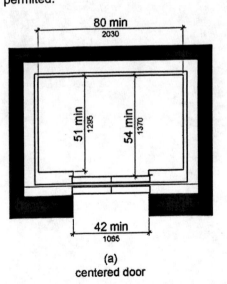

(a)
centered door

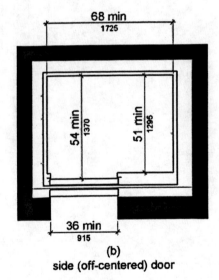

(b)
side (off-centered) door

**Figure 407.4.1
Elevator Car Dimensions**

175

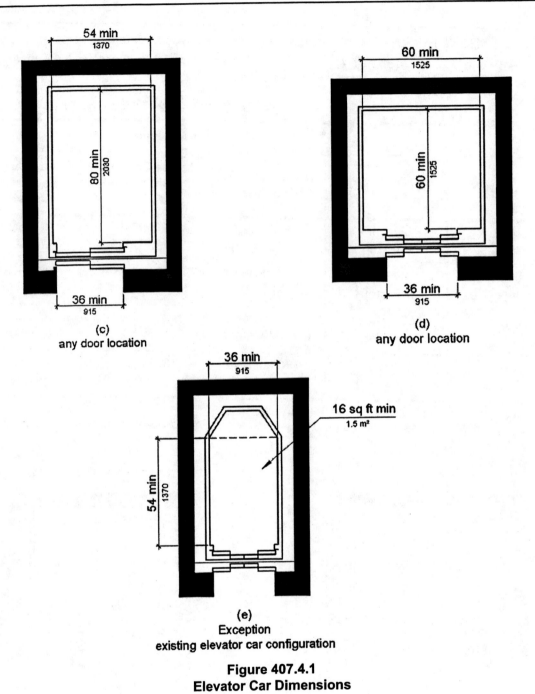

54 min
1370

80 min
2030

36 min
915

(c)
any door location

60 min
1525

60 min
1525

36 min
915

(d)
any door location

36 min
915

16 sq ft min
1.5 m²

54 min
1370

(e)
Exception
existing elevator car configuration

Figure 407.4.1
Elevator Car Dimensions

407.4.2 Floor Surfaces. Floor surfaces in elevator cars shall comply with 302 and 303.

407.4.3 Platform to Hoistway Clearance. The clearance between the car platform sill and the edge of any hoistway landing shall be 1¼ inch (32 mm) maximum.

407.4.4 Leveling. Each car shall be equipped with a self-leveling feature that will automatically bring and maintain the car at floor landings within a tolerance of ½ inch (13 mm) under rated loading to zero loading conditions.

407.4.5 Illumination. The level of illumination at the car controls, platform, car threshold and car landing sill shall be 5 foot candles (54 lux) minimum.

407.4.6 Elevator Car Controls. Where provided, elevator car controls shall comply with 407.4.6 and 309.4.
  EXCEPTION: In existing elevators, where a new car operating panel complying with 407.4.6 is provided, existing car operating panels shall not be required to comply with 407.4.6.

  407.4.6.1 Location. Controls shall be located within one of the reach ranges specified in 308.
    EXCEPTIONS: 1. Where the elevator panel serves more than 16 openings and a parallel approach is provided, buttons with floor designations shall be permitted to be 54 inches (1370 mm) maximum above the finish floor.
    2. In existing elevators, car control buttons with floor designations shall be permitted to be located 54 inches (1370 mm) maximum above the finish floor where a parallel approach is provided.

  407.4.6.2 Buttons. Car control buttons with floor designations shall comply with 407.4.6.2 and shall be raised or flush.
    EXCEPTION: In existing elevators, buttons shall be permitted to be recessed.

    407.4.6.2.1 Size. Buttons shall be 3/4 inch (19 mm) minimum in their smallest dimension.

    407.4.6.2.2 Arrangement. Buttons shall be arranged with numbers in ascending order. When two or more columns of buttons are provided they shall read from left to right.

  407.4.6.3 Keypads. Car control keypads shall be in a standard telephone keypad arrangement and shall comply with 407.4.7.2.

  407.4.6.4 Emergency Controls. Emergency controls shall comply with 407.4.6.4.

    407.4.6.4.1 Height. Emergency control buttons shall have their centerlines 35 inches (890 mm) minimum above the finish floor.

    407.4.6.4.2 Location. Emergency controls, including the emergency alarm, shall be grouped at the bottom of the panel.

407.4.7 Designations and Indicators of Car Controls. Designations and indicators of car controls shall comply with 407.4.7.

EXCEPTION: In existing elevators, where a new car operating panel complying with 407.4.7 is provided, existing car operating panels shall not be required to comply with 407.4.7.

407.4.7.1 Buttons. Car control buttons shall comply with 407.4.7.1.

407.4.7.1.1 Type. Control buttons shall be identified by *tactile characters* complying with 703.2.

407.4.7.1.2 Location. Raised *character* and braille designations shall be placed immediately to the left of the control button to which the designations apply.
EXCEPTION: Where *space* on an existing car operating panel precludes *tactile* markings to the left of the controls, markings shall be placed as near to the control as possible.

407.4.7.1.3 Symbols. The control button for the emergency stop, alarm, door open, door close, main entry floor, and phone, shall be identified with *tactile* symbols as shown in Table 407.4.7.1.3.

Table 407.4.7.1.3 Elevator Control Button Identification

Control Button	Tactile Symbol	Braille Message
Emergency Stop	⊗	"ST"OP" Three cells
Alarm	🔔	AL"AR"M Four cells
Door Open	◀▮▶	OP"EN" Three cells
Door Close	▶◀	CLOSE Five cells
Main Entry Floor	★	MA"IN" Three cells
Phone	☎	PH"ONE" Four cells

407.4.7.1.4 Visible Indicators. Buttons with floor designations shall be provided with visible indicators to show that a call has been registered. The visible indication shall extinguish when the car arrives at the designated floor.

407.4.7.2 Keypads. Keypads shall be identified by *characters* complying with 703.5 and shall be centered on the corresponding keypad button. The number five key shall have a single raised dot. The dot shall be 0.118 inch (3 mm) to 0.120 inch (3.05 mm) base diameter and in other aspects comply with Table 703.3.1.

407.4.8 Car Position Indicators. Audible and visible car position indicators shall be provided in elevator cars.

407.4.8.1 Visible Indicators. Visible indicators shall comply with 407.4.8.1.

407.4.8.1.1 Size. *Characters* shall be ½ inch (13 mm) high minimum.

407.4.8.1.2 Location. Indicators shall be located above the car control panel or above the door.

407.4.8.1.3 Floor Arrival. As the car passes a floor and when a car stops at a floor served by the elevator, the corresponding *character* shall illuminate.
  EXCEPTION: Destination-oriented elevators shall not be required to comply with 407.4.8.1.3 provided that the visible indicators extinguish when the call has been answered.

407.4.8.1.4 Destination Indicator. In destination-oriented elevators, a display shall be provided in the car with visible indicators to show car destinations.

407.4.8.2 Audible Indicators. Audible indicators shall comply with 407.4.8.2.

407.4.8.2.1 Signal Type. The signal shall be an automatic verbal annunciator which announces the floor at which the car is about to stop.
  EXCEPTION: For elevators other than destination-oriented elevators that have a rated speed of 200 feet per minute (1 m/s) or less, a non-verbal audible signal with a frequency of 1500 Hz maximum which sounds as the car passes or is about to stop at a floor served by the elevator shall be permitted.

407.4.8.2.2 Signal Level. The verbal annunciator shall be 10 dB minimum above ambient, but shall not exceed 80 dB, measured at the annunciator.

407.4.8.2.3 Frequency. The verbal annunciator shall have a frequency of 300 Hz minimum to 3000 Hz maximum.

407.4.9 Emergency Communication. Emergency two-way communication systems shall comply with 308. *Tactile* symbols and *characters* shall be provided adjacent to the device and shall comply with 703.2.

408 Limited-Use/Limited-Application Elevators

408.1 General. Limited-use/limited-application elevators shall comply with 408 and with ASME A17.1 (incorporated by reference, see "Referenced Standards" in Chapter 1). They shall be passenger elevators as classified by ASME A17.1. Elevator operation shall be automatic.

408.2 Elevator Landings. Landings serving limited-use/limited-application elevators shall comply with 408.2.

408.2.1 Call Buttons. Elevator call buttons and keypads shall comply with 407.2.1.

408.2.2 Hall Signals. Hall signals shall comply with 407.2.2.

408.2.3 Hoistway Signs. Signs at elevator hoistways shall comply with 407.2.3.1.

408.3 Elevator Doors. Elevator hoistway doors shall comply with 408.3.

408.3.1 Sliding Doors. Sliding hoistway and car doors shall comply with 407.3.1 through 407.3.3 and 408.4.1.

408.3.2 Swinging Doors. Swinging hoistway doors shall open and close automatically and shall comply with 404, 407.3.2 and 408.3.2.

408.3.2.1 Power Operation. Swinging doors shall be power-operated and shall comply with ANSI/BHMA A156.19 (1997 or 2002 edition) (incorporated by reference, see "Referenced Standards" in Chapter 1).

408.3.2.2 Duration. Power-operated swinging doors shall remain open for 20 seconds minimum when activated.

408.4 Elevator Cars. Elevator cars shall comply with 408.4.

408.4.1 Car Dimensions and Doors. Elevator cars shall provide a clear width 42 inches (1065 mm) minimum and a clear depth 54 inches (1370 mm) minimum. Car doors shall be positioned at the narrow ends of cars and shall provide 32 inches (815 mm) minimum clear width.
EXCEPTIONS: 1. Cars that provide a clear width 51 inches (1295 mm) minimum shall be permitted to provide a clear depth 51 inches (1295 mm) minimum provided that car doors provide a clear opening 36 inches (915 mm) wide minimum.
2. Existing elevator cars shall be permitted to provide a clear width 36 inches (915 mm) minimum, clear depth 54 inches (1370 mm) minimum, and a net clear platform area 15 square feet (1.4 m^2) minimum.

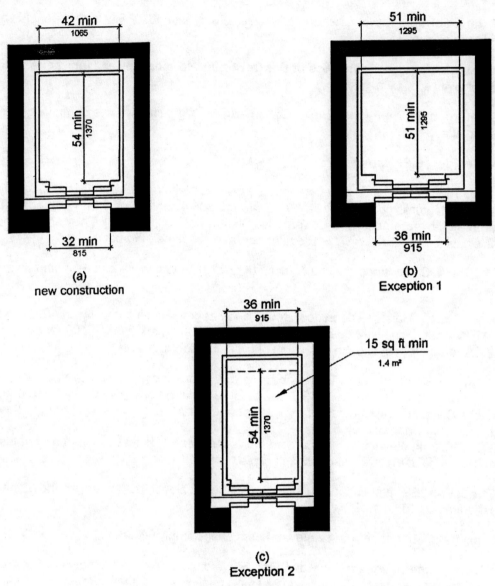

(a)
new construction

(b)
Exception 1

(c)
Exception 2

Figure 408.4.1
Limited-Use/Limited-Application (LULA) Elevator Car Dimensions

408.4.2 Floor Surfaces. Floor surfaces in elevator cars shall comply with 302 and 303.

408.4.3 Platform to Hoistway Clearance. The platform to hoistway clearance shall comply with 407.4.3.

408.4.4 Leveling. Elevator car leveling shall comply with 407.4.4.

408.4.5 Illumination. Elevator car illumination shall comply with 407.4.5.

408.4.6 Car Controls. Elevator car controls shall comply with 407.4.6. Control panels shall be centered on a side wall.

408.4.7 Designations and Indicators of Car Controls. Designations and indicators of car controls shall comply with 407.4.7.

408.4.8 Emergency Communications. Car emergency signaling devices complying with 407.4.9 shall be provided.

409 Private Residence Elevators

409.1 General. Private residence elevators that are provided within a *residential dwelling unit* required to provide mobility features complying with 809.2 through 809.4 shall comply with 409 and with ASME A17.1 (incorporated by reference, see "Referenced Standards" in Chapter 1). They shall be passenger elevators as classified by ASME A17.1. Elevator operation shall be automatic.

409.2 Call Buttons. Call buttons shall be ¾ inch (19 mm) minimum in the smallest dimension and shall comply with 309.

409.3 Elevator Doors. Hoistway doors, car doors, and car gates shall comply with 409.3 and 404.
   EXCEPTION: Doors shall not be required to comply with the maneuvering clearance requirements in 404.2.4.1 for approaches to the push side of swinging doors.

409.3.1 Power Operation. Elevator car and hoistway doors and gates shall be power operated and shall comply with ANSI/BHMA A156.19 (1997 or 2002 edition) (incorporated by reference, see "Referenced Standards" in Chapter 1). Power operated doors and gates shall remain open for 20 seconds minimum when activated.
   EXCEPTION: In elevator cars with more than one opening, hoistway doors and gates shall be permitted to be of the manual-open, self-close type.

409.3.2 Location. Elevator car doors or gates shall be positioned at the narrow end of the clear floor *spaces* required by 409.4.1.

409.4 Elevator Cars. Private residence elevator cars shall comply with 409.4.

409.4.1 Inside Dimensions of Elevator Cars. Elevator cars shall provide a clear floor *space* of 36 inches (915 mm) minimum by 48 inches (1220 mm) minimum and shall comply with 305.

409.4.2 Floor Surfaces. Floor surfaces in elevator cars shall comply with 302 and 303.

409.4.3 Platform to Hoistway Clearance. The clearance between the car platform and the edge of any landing sill shall be 1½ inch (38 mm) maximum.

409.4.4 Leveling. Each car shall automatically stop at a floor landing within a tolerance of ½ inch (13 mm) under rated loading to zero loading conditions.

409.4.5 Illumination Levels. Elevator car illumination shall comply with 407.4.5.

409.4.6 Car Controls. Elevator car control buttons shall comply with 409.4.6, 309.3, 309.4, and shall be raised or flush.

409.4.6.1 Size. Control buttons shall be 3/4 inch (19 mm) minimum in their smallest dimension.

409.4.6.2 Location. Control panels shall be on a side wall, 12 inches (305 mm) minimum from any adjacent wall.

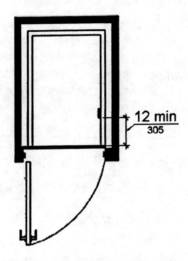

12 min
305

Figure 409.4.6.2
Location of Private Residence Elevator Control Panel

409.4.7 Emergency Communications. Emergency two-way communication systems shall comply with 409.4.7.

409.4.7.1 Type. A telephone and emergency signal device shall be provided in the car.

409.4.7.2 Operable Parts. The telephone and emergency signaling device shall comply with 309.3 and 309.4.

409.4.7.3 Compartment. If the telephone or device is in a closed compartment, the compartment door hardware shall comply with 309.

409.4.7.4 Cord. The telephone cord shall be 29 inches (735 mm) long minimum.

410 Platform Lifts

410.1 General. Platform lifts shall comply with ASME A18.1 (1999 edition or 2003 edition) (incorporated by reference, see "Referenced Standards" in Chapter 1). Platform lifts shall not be attendant-operated and shall provide unassisted entry and exit from the lift.

> **Advisory 410.1 General.** Inclined stairway chairlifts and inclined and vertical platform lifts are available for short-distance vertical transportation. Because an accessible route requires an 80 inch (2030 mm) vertical clearance, care should be taken in selecting lifts as they may not be equally suitable for use by people using wheelchairs and people standing. If a lift does not provide 80 inch (2030 mm) vertical clearance, it cannot be considered part of an accessible route in new construction.
>
> The ADA and other Federal civil rights laws require that accessible features be maintained in working order so that they are accessible to and usable by those people they are intended to benefit. Building owners are reminded that the ASME A18 Safety Standard for Platform Lifts and Stairway Chairlifts requires routine maintenance and inspections. Isolated or temporary interruptions in service due to maintenance or repairs may be unavoidable; however, failure to take prompt action to effect repairs could constitute a violation of Federal laws and these requirements.

410.2 Floor Surfaces. Floor surfaces in platform lifts shall comply with 302 and 303.

410.3 Clear Floor Space. Clear floor *space* in platform lifts shall comply with 305.

410.4 Platform to Runway Clearance. The clearance between the platform sill and the edge of any runway landing shall be 1¼ inch (32 mm) maximum.

410.5 Operable Parts. Controls for platform lifts shall comply with 309.

410.6 Doors and Gates. Platform lifts shall have low-energy power-operated doors or gates complying with 404.3. Doors shall remain open for 20 seconds minimum. End doors and gates shall provide a clear width 32 inches (815 mm) minimum. Side doors and gates shall provide a clear width 42 inches (1065 mm) minimum.
   EXCEPTION: Platform lifts serving two landings maximum and having doors or gates on opposite sides shall be permitted to have self-closing manual doors or gates.

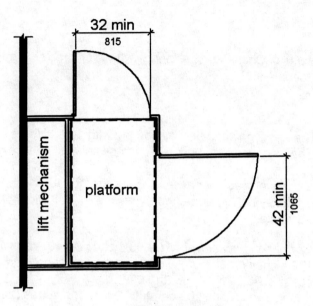

Figure 410.6
Platform Lift Doors and Gates

CHAPTER 5: GENERAL SITE AND BUILDING ELEMENTS

501 General

501.1 Scope. The provisions of Chapter 5 shall apply where required by Chapter 2 or where referenced by a requirement in this document.

502 Parking Spaces

502.1 General. Car and van parking *spaces* shall comply with 502. Where parking *spaces* are marked with lines, width measurements of parking *spaces* and access aisles shall be made from the centerline of the markings.

> **EXCEPTION:** Where parking *spaces* or access aisles are not adjacent to another parking *space* or access aisle, measurements shall be permitted to include the full width of the line defining the parking *space* or access aisle.

502.2 Vehicle Spaces. Car parking *spaces* shall be 96 inches (2440 mm) wide minimum and van parking *spaces* shall be 132 inches (3350 mm) wide minimum, shall be marked to define the width, and shall have an adjacent access aisle complying with 502.3.

> **EXCEPTION:** Van parking *spaces* shall be permitted to be 96 inches (2440 mm) wide minimum where the access aisle is 96 inches (2440 mm) wide minimum.

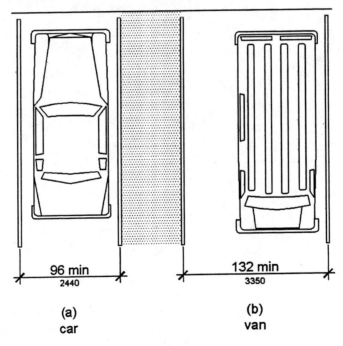

(a)
car

(b)
van

Figure 502.2
Vehicle Parking Spaces

502.3 Access Aisle. Access aisles serving parking *spaces* shall comply with 502.3. Access aisles shall adjoin an *accessible* route. Two parking *spaces* shall be permitted to share a common access aisle.

> **Advisory 502.3 Access Aisle.** Accessible routes must connect parking spaces to accessible entrances. In parking facilities where the accessible route must cross vehicular traffic lanes, marked crossings enhance pedestrian safety, particularly for people using wheelchairs and other mobility aids. Where possible, it is preferable that the accessible route not pass behind parked vehicles.

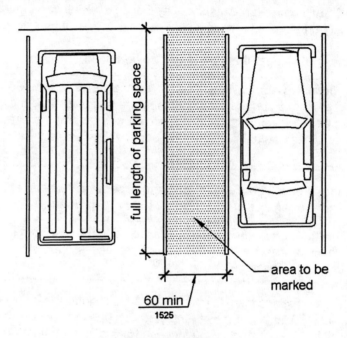

Figure 502.3
Parking Space Access Aisle

502.3.1 Width. Access aisles serving car and van parking *spaces* shall be 60 inches (1525 mm) wide minimum.

502.3.2 Length. Access aisles shall extend the full length of the parking *spaces* they serve.

502.3.3 Marking. Access aisles shall be marked so as to discourage parking in them.

> **Advisory 502.3.3 Marking.** The method and color of marking are not specified by these requirements but may be addressed by State or local laws or regulations. Because these requirements permit the van access aisle to be as wide as a parking space, it is important that the aisle be clearly marked.

502.3.4 Location. Access aisles shall not overlap the *vehicular way.* Access aisles shall be permitted to be placed on either side of the parking *space* except for angled van parking *spaces* which shall have access aisles located on the passenger side of the parking *spaces.*

> **Advisory 502.3.4 Location.** Wheelchair lifts typically are installed on the passenger side of vans. Many drivers, especially those who operate vans, find it more difficult to back into parking spaces than to back out into comparatively unrestricted vehicular lanes. For this reason, where a van and car share an access aisle, consider locating the van space so that the access aisle is on the passenger side of the van space.

502.4 Floor or Ground Surfaces. Parking *spaces* and access aisles serving them shall comply with 302. Access aisles shall be at the same level as the parking *spaces* they serve. Changes in level are not permitted.

   EXCEPTION: Slopes not steeper than 1:48 shall be permitted.

> **Advisory 502.4 Floor or Ground Surfaces.** Access aisles are required to be nearly level in all directions to provide a surface for wheelchair transfer to and from vehicles. The exception allows sufficient slope for drainage. Built-up curb ramps are not permitted to project into access aisles and parking spaces because they would create slopes greater than 1:48.

502.5 Vertical Clearance. Parking *spaces* for vans and access aisles and vehicular routes serving them shall provide a vertical clearance of 98 inches (2490 mm) minimum.

> **Advisory 502.5 Vertical Clearance.** Signs provided at entrances to parking facilities informing drivers of clearances and the location of van accessible parking spaces can provide useful customer assistance.

502.6 Identification. Parking *space* identification signs shall include the International Symbol of *Accessibility* complying with 703.7.2.1. Signs identifying van parking *spaces* shall contain the designation "van accessible." Signs shall be 60 inches (1525 mm) minimum above the finish floor or ground surface measured to the bottom of the sign.

> **Advisory 502.6 Identification.** The required "van accessible" designation is intended to be informative, not restrictive, in identifying those spaces that are better suited for van use. Enforcement of motor vehicle laws, including parking privileges, is a local matter.

502.7 Relationship to Accessible Routes. Parking *spaces* and access aisles shall be designed so that cars and vans, when parked, cannot obstruct the required clear width of adjacent *accessible* routes.

> **Advisory 502.7 Relationship to Accessible Routes.** Wheel stops are an effective way to prevent vehicle overhangs from reducing the clear width of accessible routes.

503 Passenger Loading Zones

503.1 General. Passenger loading zones shall comply with 503.

503.2 Vehicle Pull-Up Space. Passenger loading zones shall provide a vehicular pull-up *space* 96 inches (2440 mm) wide minimum and 20 feet (6100 mm) long minimum.

503.3 Access Aisle. Passenger loading zones shall provide access aisles complying with 503 adjacent to the vehicle pull-up space. Access aisles shall adjoin an *accessible* route and shall not overlap the *vehicular way.*

503.3.1 Width. Access aisles serving vehicle pull-up *spaces* shall be 60 inches (1525 mm) wide minimum.

503.3.2 Length. Access aisles shall extend the full length of the vehicle pull-up *spaces* they serve.

503.3.3 Marking. Access aisles shall be marked so as to discourage parking in them.

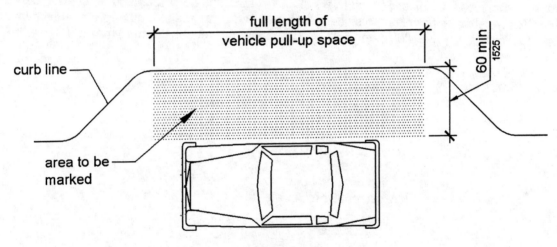

Figure 503.3
Passenger Loading Zone Access Aisle

503.4 Floor and Ground Surfaces. Vehicle pull-up *spaces* and access aisles serving them shall comply with 302. Access aisles shall be at the same level as the vehicle pull-up *space* they serve. Changes in level are not permitted.
EXCEPTION: Slopes not steeper than 1:48 shall be permitted.

503.5 Vertical Clearance. Vehicle pull-up *spaces*, access aisles serving them, and a vehicular route from an *entrance* to the passenger loading zone, and from the passenger loading zone to a vehicular exit shall provide a vertical clearance of 114 inches (2895 mm) minimum.

504 Stairways

504.1 General. Stairs shall comply with 504.

504.2 Treads and Risers. All steps on a flight of stairs shall have uniform riser heights and uniform tread depths. Risers shall be 4 inches (100 mm) high minimum and 7 inches (180 mm) high maximum. Treads shall be 11 inches (280 mm) deep minimum.

504.3 Open Risers. Open risers are not permitted.

504.4 Tread Surface. Stair treads shall comply with 302. Changes in level are not permitted.
   EXCEPTION: Treads shall be permitted to have a slope not steeper than 1:48.

> **Advisory 504.4 Tread Surface.** Consider providing visual contrast on tread nosings, or at the leading edges of treads without nosings, so that stair treads are more visible for people with low vision.

504.5 Nosings. The radius of curvature at the leading edge of the tread shall be ½ inch (13 mm) maximum. Nosings that project beyond risers shall have the underside of the leading edge curved or beveled. Risers shall be permitted to slope under the tread at an angle of 30 degrees maximum from vertical. The permitted projection of the nosing shall extend 1½ inches (38 mm) maximum over the tread below.

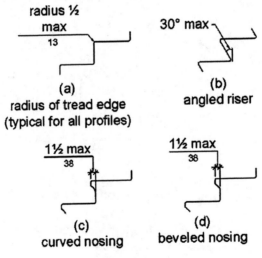

(a)
radius of tread edge
(typical for all profiles)

(b)
angled riser

(c)
curved nosing

(d)
beveled nosing

Figure 504.5
Stair Nosings

504.6 Handrails. Stairs shall have handrails complying with 505.

504.7 Wet Conditions. Stair treads and landings subject to wet conditions shall be designed to prevent the accumulation of water.

190

505 Handrails

505.1 General. Handrails provided along walking surfaces complying with 403, required at *ramps* complying with 405, and required at stairs complying with 504 shall comply with 505.

> **Advisory 505.1 General.** Handrails are required on ramp runs with a rise greater than 6 inches (150 mm) (see 405.8) and on certain stairways (see 504). Handrails are not required on walking surfaces with running slopes less than 1:20. However, handrails are required to comply with 505 when they are provided on walking surfaces with running slopes less than 1:20 (see 403.6). Sections 505.2, 505.3, and 505.10 do not apply to handrails provided on walking surfaces with running slopes less than 1:20 as these sections only reference requirements for ramps and stairs.

505.2 Where Required. Handrails shall be provided on both sides of stairs and *ramps*.
   EXCEPTION: In *assembly areas*, handrails shall not be required on both sides of aisle *ramps* where a handrail is provided at either side or within the aisle width.

505.3 Continuity. Handrails shall be continuous within the full length of each stair flight or *ramp* run. Inside handrails on switchback or dogleg stairs and *ramps* shall be continuous between flights or runs.
   EXCEPTION: In *assembly areas*, handrails on *ramps* shall not be required to be continuous in aisles serving seating.

505.4 Height. Top of gripping surfaces of handrails shall be 34 inches (865 mm) minimum and 38 inches (965 mm) maximum vertically above walking surfaces, stair nosings, and *ramp* surfaces. Handrails shall be at a consistent height above walking surfaces, stair nosings, and *ramp* surfaces.

> **Advisory 505.4 Height.** The requirements for stair and ramp handrails in this document are for adults. When children are the principle users in a building or facility (e.g., elementary schools), a second set of handrails at an appropriate height can assist them and aid in preventing accidents. A maximum height of 28 inches (710 mm) measured to the top of the gripping surface from the ramp surface or stair nosing is recommended for handrails designed for children. Sufficient vertical clearance between upper and lower handrails, 9 inches (230 mm) minimum, should be provided to help prevent entrapment.

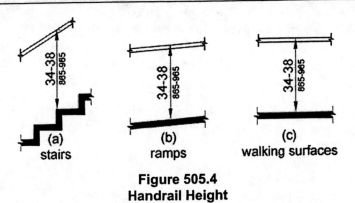

Figure 505.4
Handrail Height

505.5 Clearance. Clearance between handrail gripping surfaces and adjacent surfaces shall be 1½ inches (38 mm) minimum.

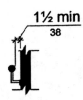

Figure 505.5
Handrail Clearance

505.6 Gripping Surface. Handrail gripping surfaces shall be continuous along their length and shall not be obstructed along their tops or sides. The bottoms of handrail gripping surfaces shall not be obstructed for more than 20 percent of their length. Where provided, horizontal projections shall occur 1½ inches (38 mm) minimum below the bottom of the handrail gripping surface.
    EXCEPTIONS: 1. Where handrails are provided along walking surfaces with slopes not steeper than 1:20, the bottoms of handrail gripping surfaces shall be permitted to be obstructed along their entire length where they are integral to crash rails or bumper guards.
    2. The distance between horizontal projections and the bottom of the gripping surface shall be permitted to be reduced by 1/8 inch (3.2 mm) for each ½ inch (13 mm) of additional handrail perimeter dimension that exceeds 4 inches (100 mm).

> **Advisory 505.6 Gripping Surface.** People with disabilities, older people, and others benefit from continuous gripping surfaces that permit users to reach the fingers outward or downward to grasp the handrail, particularly as the user senses a loss of equilibrium or begins to fall.

Figure 505.6
Horizontal Projections Below Gripping Surface

505.7 Cross Section. Handrail gripping surfaces shall have a cross section complying with 505.7.1 or 505.7.2.

    505.7.1 Circular Cross Section. Handrail gripping surfaces with a circular cross section shall have an outside diameter of 1¼ inches (32 mm) minimum and 2 inches (51 mm) maximum.

505.7.2 Non-Circular Cross Sections. Handrail gripping surfaces with a non-circular cross section shall have a perimeter dimension of 4 inches (100 mm) minimum and 6¼ inches (160 mm) maximum, and a cross-section dimension of 2¼ inches (57 mm) maximum.

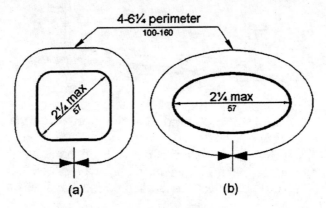

Figure 505.7.2
Handrail Non-Circular Cross Section

505.8 Surfaces. Handrail gripping surfaces and any surfaces adjacent to them shall be free of sharp or abrasive *elements* and shall have rounded edges.

505.9 Fittings. Handrails shall not rotate within their fittings.

505.10 Handrail Extensions. Handrail gripping surfaces shall extend beyond and in the same direction of stair flights and *ramp* runs in accordance with 505.10.
    EXCEPTIONS: 1. Extensions shall not be required for continuous handrails at the inside turn of switchback or dogleg stairs and *ramps*.
    2. In *assembly areas*, extensions shall not be required for *ramp* handrails in aisles serving seating where the handrails are discontinuous to provide access to seating and to permit crossovers within aisles.
    3. In *alterations*, full extensions of handrails shall not be required where such extensions would be hazardous due to plan configuration.

505.10.1 Top and Bottom Extension at Ramps. *Ramp* handrails shall extend horizontally above the landing for 12 inches (305 mm) minimum beyond the top and bottom of *ramp* runs. Extensions shall return to a wall, guard, or the landing surface, or shall be continuous to the handrail of an adjacent *ramp* run.

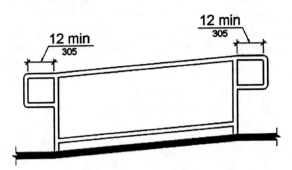

Figure 505.10.1
Top and Bottom Handrail Extension at Ramps

505.10.2 Top Extension at Stairs. At the top of a stair flight, handrails shall extend horizontally above the landing for 12 inches (305 mm) minimum beginning directly above the first riser nosing. Extensions shall return to a wall, guard, or the landing surface, or shall be continuous to the handrail of an adjacent stair flight.

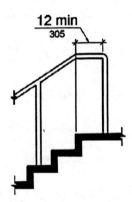

Figure 505.10.2
Top Handrail Extension at Stairs

505.10.3 Bottom Extension at Stairs. At the bottom of a stair flight, handrails shall extend at the slope of the stair flight for a horizontal distance at least equal to one tread depth beyond the last riser nosing. Extension shall return to a wall, guard, or the landing surface, or shall be continuous to the handrail of an adjacent stair flight.

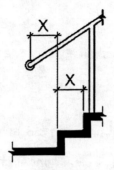

Note: X = tread depth

Figure 505.10.3
Bottom Handrail Extension at Stairs

CHAPTER 6: PLUMBING ELEMENTS AND FACILITIES

601 General

601.1 Scope. The provisions of Chapter 6 shall apply where required by Chapter 2 or where referenced by a requirement in this document.

602 Drinking Fountains

602.1 General. Drinking fountains shall comply with 307 and 602.

602.2 Clear Floor Space. Units shall have a clear floor or ground *space* complying with 305 positioned for a forward approach and centered on the unit. Knee and toe clearance complying with 306 shall be provided.
    EXCEPTION: A parallel approach complying with 305 shall be permitted at units for *children's use* where the spout is 30 inches (760 mm) maximum above the finish floor or ground and is 3½ inches (90 mm) maximum from the front edge of the unit, including bumpers.

602.3 Operable Parts. *Operable parts* shall comply with 309.

602.4 Spout Height. Spout outlets shall be 36 inches (915 mm) maximum above the finish floor or ground.

602.5 Spout Location. The spout shall be located 15 inches (380 mm) minimum from the vertical support and 5 inches (125 mm) maximum from the front edge of the unit, including bumpers.

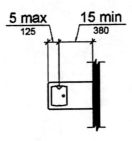

Figure 602.5
Drinking Fountain Spout Location

602.6 Water Flow. The spout shall provide a flow of water 4 inches (100 mm) high minimum and shall be located 5 inches (125 mm) maximum from the front of the unit. The angle of the water stream shall be measured horizontally relative to the front face of the unit. Where spouts are located less than 3 inches (75 mm) of the front of the unit, the angle of the water stream shall be 30 degrees maximum. Where spouts are located between 3 inches (75 mm) and 5 inches (125 mm) maximum from the front of the unit, the angle of the water stream shall be 15 degrees maximum.

196

Advisory 602.6 Water Flow. The purpose of requiring the drinking fountain spout to produce a flow of water 4 inches (100 mm) high minimum is so that a cup can be inserted under the flow of water to provide a drink of water for an individual who, because of a disability, would otherwise be incapable of using the drinking fountain.

602.7 Drinking Fountains for Standing Persons. Spout outlets of drinking fountains for standing persons shall be 38 inches (965 mm) minimum and 43 inches (1090 mm) maximum above the finish floor or ground.

603 Toilet and Bathing Rooms

603.1 General. Toilet and bathing rooms shall comply with 603.

603.2 Clearances. Clearances shall comply with 603.2.

603.2.1 Turning Space. Turning *space* complying with 304 shall be provided within the room.

603.2.2 Overlap. Required clear floor *spaces*, clearance at fixtures, and turning *space* shall be permitted to overlap.

603.2.3 Door Swing. Doors shall not swing into the clear floor *space* or clearance required for any fixture. Doors shall be permitted to swing into the required turning *space*.
EXCEPTIONS: 1. Doors to a toilet room or bathing room for a single occupant accessed only through a private office and not for *common use* or *public use* shall be permitted to swing into the clear floor *space* or clearance provided the swing of the door can be reversed to comply with 603.2.3.
2. Where the toilet room or bathing room is for individual use and a clear floor *space* complying with 305.3 is provided within the room beyond the arc of the door swing, doors shall be permitted to swing into the clear floor *space* or clearance required for any fixture.

Advisory 603.2.3 Door Swing Exception 1. At the time the door is installed, and if the door swing is reversed in the future, the door must meet all the requirements specified in 404. Additionally, the door swing cannot reduce the required width of an accessible route. Also, avoid violating other building or life safety codes when the door swing is reversed.

603.3 Mirrors. Mirrors located above lavatories or countertops shall be installed with the bottom edge of the reflecting surface 40 inches (1015 mm) maximum above the finish floor or ground. Mirrors not located above lavatories or countertops shall be installed with the bottom edge of the reflecting surface 35 inches (890 mm) maximum above the finish floor or ground.

Advisory 603.3 Mirrors. A single full-length mirror can accommodate a greater number of people, including children. In order for mirrors to be usable by people who are ambulatory and people who use wheelchairs, the top edge of mirrors should be 74 inches (1880 mm) minimum from the floor or ground.

603.4 Coat Hooks and Shelves. Coat hooks shall be located within one of the reach ranges specified in 308. Shelves shall be located 40 inches (1015 mm) minimum and 48 inches (1220 mm) maximum above the finish floor.

604 Water Closets and Toilet Compartments

604.1 General. Water closets and toilet compartments shall comply with 604.2 through 604.8.
   EXCEPTION: Water closets and toilet compartments for *children's use* shall be permitted to comply with 604.9.

604.2 Location. The water closet shall be positioned with a wall or partition to the rear and to one side. The centerline of the water closet shall be 16 inches (405 mm) minimum to 18 inches (455 mm) maximum from the side wall or partition, except that the water closet shall be 17 inches (430 mm) minimum and 19 inches (485 mm) maximum from the side wall or partition in the ambulatory *accessible* toilet compartment specified in 604.8.2. Water closets shall be arranged for a left-hand or right-hand approach.

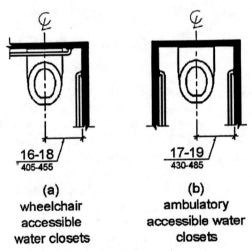

(a)
wheelchair
accessible
water closets

(b)
ambulatory
accessible water
closets

Figure 604.2
Water Closet Location

604.3 Clearance. Clearances around water closets and in toilet compartments shall comply with 604.3.

604.3.1 Size. Clearance around a water closet shall be 60 inches (1525 mm) minimum measured perpendicular from the side wall and 56 inches (1420 mm) minimum measured perpendicular from the rear wall.

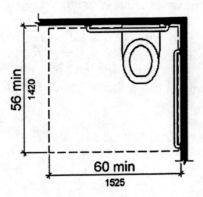

Figure 604.3.1
Size of Clearance at Water Closets

604.3.2 Overlap. The required clearance around the water closet shall be permitted to overlap the water closet, associated grab bars, dispensers, sanitary napkin disposal units, coat hooks, shelves, *accessible* routes, clear floor *space* and clearances required at other fixtures, and the turning *space*. No other fixtures or obstructions shall be located within the required water closet clearance.

> **EXCEPTION:** In *residential dwelling units*, a lavatory complying with 606 shall be permitted on the rear wall 18 inches (455 mm) minimum from the water closet centerline where the clearance at the water closet is 66 inches (1675 mm) minimum measured perpendicular from the rear wall.

Advisory 604.3.2 Overlap. When the door to the toilet room is placed directly in front of the water closet, the water closet cannot overlap the required maneuvering clearance for the door inside the room.

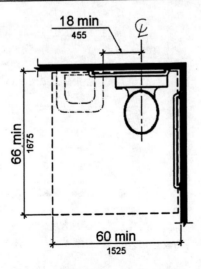

Figure 604.3.2 (Exception)
Overlap of Water Closet Clearance in Residential Dwelling Units

604.4 Seats. The seat height of a water closet above the finish floor shall be 17 inches (430 mm) minimum and 19 inches (485 mm) maximum measured to the top of the seat. Seats shall not be sprung to return to a lifted position.

> **EXCEPTIONS: 1.** A water closet in a toilet room for a single occupant accessed only through a private office and not for *common use* or *public use* shall not be required to comply with 604.4.
> **2.** In *residential dwelling units*, the height of water closets shall be permitted to be 15 inches (380 mm) minimum and 19 inches (485 mm) maximum above the finish floor measured to the top of the seat.

604.5 Grab Bars. Grab bars for water closets shall comply with 609. Grab bars shall be provided on the side wall closest to the water closet and on the rear wall.

> **EXCEPTIONS: 1.** Grab bars shall not be required to be installed in a toilet room for a single occupant accessed only through a private office and not for *common use* or *public use* provided that reinforcement has been installed in walls and located so as to permit the installation of grab bars complying with 604.5.
> **2.** In *residential dwelling units*, grab bars shall not be required to be installed in toilet or bathrooms provided that reinforcement has been installed in walls and located so as to permit the installation of grab bars complying with 604.5.
> **3.** In detention or correction *facilities*, grab bars shall not be required to be installed in housing or holding cells that are specially designed without protrusions for purposes of suicide prevention.

> **Advisory 604.5 Grab Bars Exception 2.** Reinforcement must be sufficient to permit the installation of rear and side wall grab bars that fully meet all accessibility requirements including, but not limited to, required length, installation height, and structural strength.

604.5.1 Side Wall. The side wall grab bar shall be 42 inches (1065 mm) long minimum, located 12 inches (305 mm) maximum from the rear wall and extending 54 inches (1370 mm) minimum from the rear wall.

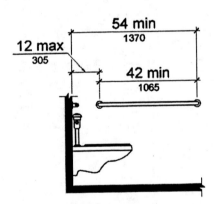

Figure 604.5.1
Side Wall Grab Bar at Water Closets

604.5.2 Rear Wall. The rear wall grab bar shall be 36 inches (915 mm) long minimum and extend from the centerline of the water closet 12 inches (305 mm) minimum on one side and 24 inches (610 mm) minimum on the other side.

EXCEPTIONS: 1. The rear grab bar shall be permitted to be 24 inches (610 mm) long minimum, centered on the water closet, where wall *space* does not permit a length of 36 inches (915 mm) minimum due to the location of a recessed fixture adjacent to the water closet.

2. Where an *administrative authority* requires flush controls for flush valves to be located in a position that conflicts with the location of the rear grab bar, then the rear grab bar shall be permitted to be split or shifted to the open side of the toilet area.

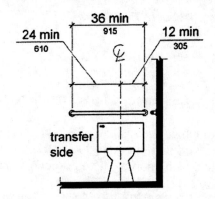

Figure 604.5.2
Rear Wall Grab Bar at Water Closets

604.6 Flush Controls. Flush controls shall be hand operated or automatic. Hand operated flush controls shall comply with 309. Flush controls shall be located on the open side of the water closet except in ambulatory *accessible* compartments complying with 604.8.2.

> **Advisory 604.6 Flush Controls.** If plumbing valves are located directly behind the toilet seat, flush valves and related plumbing can cause injury or imbalance when a person leans back against them. To prevent causing injury or imbalance, the plumbing can be located behind walls or to the side of the toilet; or if approved by the local authority having jurisdiction, provide a toilet seat lid.

604.7 Dispensers. Toilet paper dispensers shall comply with 309.4 and shall be 7 inches (180 mm) minimum and 9 inches (230 mm) maximum in front of the water closet measured to the centerline of the dispenser. The outlet of the dispenser shall be 15 inches (380 mm) minimum and 48 inches (1220 mm) maximum above the finish floor and shall not be located behind grab bars. Dispensers shall not be of a type that controls delivery or that does not allow continuous paper flow.

> **Advisory 604.7 Dispensers.** If toilet paper dispensers are installed above the side wall grab bar, the outlet of the toilet paper dispenser must be 48 inches (1220 mm) maximum above the finish floor and the top of the gripping surface of the grab bar must be 33 inches (840 mm) minimum and 36 inches (915 mm) maximum above the finish floor.

201

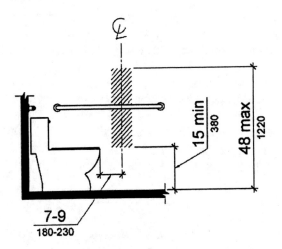

Figure 604.7
Dispenser Outlet Location

604.8 Toilet Compartments. Wheelchair *accessible* toilet compartments shall meet the requirements of 604.8.1 and 604.8.3. Compartments containing more than one plumbing fixture shall comply with 603. Ambulatory *accessible* compartments shall comply with 604.8.2 and 604.8.3.

604.8.1 Wheelchair Accessible Compartments. Wheelchair *accessible* compartments shall comply with 604.8.1.

604.8.1.1 Size. Wheelchair *accessible* compartments shall be 60 inches (1525 mm) wide minimum measured perpendicular to the side wall, and 56 inches (1420 mm) deep minimum for wall hung water closets and 59 inches (1500 mm) deep minimum for floor mounted water closets measured perpendicular to the rear wall. Wheelchair *accessible* compartments for *children's use* shall be 60 inches (1525 mm) wide minimum measured perpendicular to the side wall, and 59 inches (1500 mm) deep minimum for wall hung and floor mounted water closets measured perpendicular to the rear wall.

Advisory 604.8.1.1 Size. The minimum space required in toilet compartments is provided so that a person using a wheelchair can maneuver into position at the water closet. This space cannot be obstructed by baby changing tables or other fixtures or conveniences, except as specified at 604.3.2 (Overlap). If toilet compartments are to be used to house fixtures other than those associated with the water closet, they must be designed to exceed the minimum space requirements. Convenience fixtures such as baby changing tables must also be accessible to people with disabilities as well as to other users. Toilet compartments that are designed to meet, and not exceed, the minimum space requirements may not provide adequate space for maneuvering into position at a baby changing table.

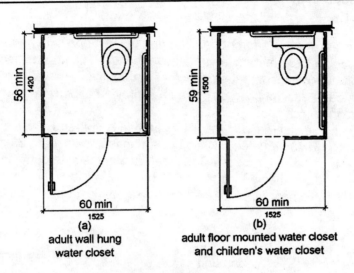

Figure 604.8.1.1
Size of Wheelchair Accessible Toilet Compartment

604.8.1.2 Doors. Toilet compartment doors, including door hardware, shall comply with 404 except that if the approach is to the latch side of the compartment door, clearance between the door side of the compartment and any obstruction shall be 42 inches (1065 mm) minimum. Doors shall be located in the front partition or in the side wall or partition farthest from the water closet. Where located in the front partition, the door opening shall be 4 inches (100 mm) maximum from the side wall or partition farthest from the water closet. Where located in the side wall or partition, the door opening shall be 4 inches (100 mm) maximum from the front partition. The door shall be self-closing. A door pull complying with 404.2.7 shall be placed on both sides of the door near the latch. Toilet compartment doors shall not swing into the minimum required compartment area.

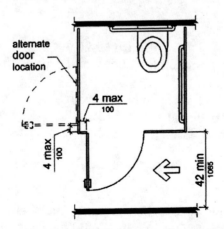

Figure 604.8.1.2
Wheelchair Accessible Toilet Compartment Doors

203

604.8.1.3 Approach. Compartments shall be arranged for left-hand or right-hand approach to the water closet.

604.8.1.4 Toe Clearance. The front partition and at least one side partition shall provide a toe clearance of 9 inches (230 mm) minimum above the finish floor and 6 inches (150 mm) deep minimum beyond the compartment-side face of the partition, exclusive of partition support members. Compartments for *children's use* shall provide a toe clearance of 12 inches (305 mm) minimum above the finish floor.

> **EXCEPTION:** Toe clearance at the front partition is not required in a compartment greater than 62 inches (1575 mm) deep with a wall-hung water closet or 65 inches (1650 mm) deep with a floor-mounted water closet. Toe clearance at the side partition is not required in a compartment greater than 66 inches (1675 mm) wide. Toe clearance at the front partition is not required in a compartment for *children's use* that is greater than 65 inches (1650 mm) deep.

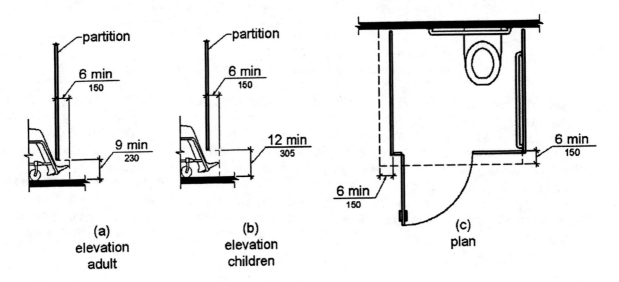

Figure 604.8.1.4
Wheelchair Accessible Toilet Compartment Toe Clearance

604.8.1.5 Grab Bars. Grab bars shall comply with 609. A side-wall grab bar complying with 604.5.1 shall be provided and shall be located on the wall closest to the water closet. In addition, a rear-wall grab bar complying with 604.5.2 shall be provided.

604.8.2 Ambulatory Accessible Compartments. Ambulatory *accessible* compartments shall comply with 604.8.2.

604.8.2.1 Size. Ambulatory *accessible* compartments shall have a depth of 60 inches (1525 mm) minimum and a width of 35 inches (890 mm) minimum and 37 inches (940 mm) maximum.

Printed by Builder's Book, Inc., Bookstore · www.buildersbook.com

604.8.2.2 Doors. Toilet compartment doors, including door hardware, shall comply with 404, except that if the approach is to the latch side of the compartment door, clearance between the door side of the compartment and any obstruction shall be 42 inches (1065 mm) minimum. The door shall be self-closing. A door pull complying with 404.2.7 shall be placed on both sides of the door near the latch. Toilet compartment doors shall not swing into the minimum required compartment area.

604.8.2.3 Grab Bars. Grab bars shall comply with 609. A side-wall grab bar complying with 604.5.1 shall be provided on both sides of the compartment.

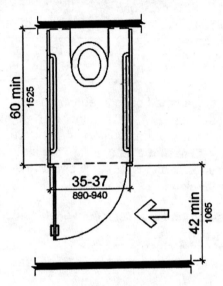

Figure 604.8.2
Ambulatory Accessible Toilet Compartment

604.8.3 Coat Hooks and Shelves. Coat hooks shall be located within one of the reach ranges specified in 308. Shelves shall be located 40 inches (1015 mm) minimum and 48 inches (1220 mm) maximum above the finish floor.

604.9 Water Closets and Toilet Compartments for Children's Use. Water closets and toilet compartments for *children's use* shall comply with 604.9.

> **Advisory 604.9 Water Closets and Toilet Compartments for Children's Use.** The requirements in 604.9 are to be followed where the exception for children's water closets in 604.1 is used. The following table provides additional guidance in applying the specifications for water closets for children according to the age group served and reflects the differences in the size, stature, and reach ranges of children ages 3 through 12. The specifications chosen should correspond to the age of the primary user group. The specifications of one age group should be applied consistently in the installation of a water closet and related elements.

Advisory Specifications for Water Closets Serving Children Ages 3 through 12			
	Ages 3 and 4	Ages 5 through 8	Ages 9 through 12
Water Closet Centerline	12 inches (305 mm)	12 to 15 inches (305 to 380 mm)	15 to 18 inches (380 to 455 mm)
Toilet Seat Height	11 to 12 inches (280 to 305 mm)	12 to 15 inches (305 to 380 mm)	15 to 17 inches (380 to 430 mm)
Grab Bar Height	18 to 20 inches (455 to 510 mm)	20 to 25 inches (510 to 635 mm)	25 to 27 inches (635 to 685 mm)
Dispenser Height	14 inches (355 mm)	14 to 17 inches (355 to 430 mm)	17 to 19 inches (430 to 485 mm)

604.9.1 Location. The water closet shall be located with a wall or partition to the rear and to one side. The centerline of the water closet shall be 12 inches (305 mm) minimum and 18 inches (455 mm) maximum from the side wall or partition, except that the water closet shall be 17 inches (430 mm) minimum and 19 inches (485 mm) maximum from the side wall or partition in the ambulatory *accessible* toilet compartment specified in 604.8.2. Compartments shall be arranged for left-hand or right-hand approach to the water closet.

604.9.2 Clearance. Clearance around a water closet shall comply with 604.3.

604.9.3 Height. The height of water closets shall be 11 inches (280 mm) minimum and 17 inches (430 mm) maximum measured to the top of the seat. Seats shall not be sprung to return to a lifted position.

604.9.4 Grab Bars. Grab bars for water closets shall comply with 604.5.

604.9.5 Flush Controls. Flush controls shall be hand operated or automatic. Hand operated flush controls shall comply with 309.2 and 309.4 and shall be installed 36 inches (915 mm) maximum above the finish floor. Flush controls shall be located on the open side of the water closet except in ambulatory *accessible* compartments complying with 604.8.2.

604.9.6 Dispensers. Toilet paper dispensers shall comply with 309.4 and shall be 7 inches (180 mm) minimum and 9 inches (230 mm) maximum in front of the water closet measured to the centerline of the dispenser. The outlet of the dispenser shall be 14 inches (355 mm) minimum and 19 inches (485 mm) maximum above the finish floor. There shall be a clearance of 1½ inches (38 mm) minimum below the grab bar. Dispensers shall not be of a type that controls delivery or that does not allow continuous paper flow.

604.9.7 Toilet Compartments. Toilet compartments shall comply with 604.8.

605 Urinals

605.1 General. Urinals shall comply with 605.

> **Advisory 605.1 General.** Stall-type urinals provide greater accessibility for a broader range of persons, including people of short stature.

605.2 Height and Depth. Urinals shall be the stall-type or the wall-hung type with the rim 17 inches (430 mm) maximum above the finish floor or ground. Urinals shall be 13½ inches (345 mm) deep minimum measured from the outer face of the urinal rim to the back of the fixture.

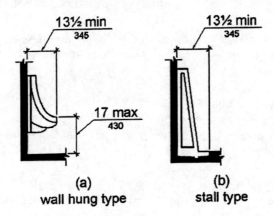

(a)
wall hung type

(b)
stall type

Figure 605.2
Height and Depth of Urinals

605.3 Clear Floor Space. A clear floor or ground *space* complying with 305 positioned for forward approach shall be provided.

605.4 Flush Controls. Flush controls shall be hand operated or automatic. Hand operated flush controls shall comply with 309.

606 Lavatories and Sinks

606.1 General. Lavatories and sinks shall comply with 606.

> **Advisory 606.1 General.** If soap and towel dispensers are provided, they must be located within the reach ranges specified in 308. Locate soap and towel dispensers so that they are conveniently usable by a person at the accessible lavatory.

606.2 Clear Floor Space. A clear floor *space* complying with 305, positioned for a forward approach, and knee and toe clearance complying with 306 shall be provided.
　　EXCEPTIONS: 1. A parallel approach complying with 305 shall be permitted to a kitchen sink in a *space* where a cook top or conventional range is not provided and to wet bars.

207

2. A lavatory in a toilet room or bathing *facility* for a single occupant accessed only through a private office and not for *common use* or *public use* shall not be required to provide knee and toe clearance complying with 306.

3. In *residential dwelling units*, cabinetry shall be permitted under lavatories and kitchen sinks provided that all of the following conditions are met:

    (a) the cabinetry can be removed without removal or replacement of the fixture;

    (b) the finish floor extends under the cabinetry; and

    (c) the walls behind and surrounding the cabinetry are finished.

4. A knee clearance of 24 inches (610 mm) minimum above the finish floor or ground shall be permitted at lavatories and sinks used primarily by children 6 through 12 years where the rim or counter surface is 31 inches (785 mm) maximum above the finish floor or ground.

5. A parallel approach complying with 305 shall be permitted to lavatories and sinks used primarily by children 5 years and younger.

6. The dip of the overflow shall not be considered in determining knee and toe clearances.

7. No more than one bowl of a multi-bowl sink shall be required to provide knee and toe clearance complying with 306.

606.3 Height. Lavatories and sinks shall be installed with the front of the higher of the rim or counter surface 34 inches (865 mm) maximum above the finish floor or ground.

    EXCEPTIONS: 1. A lavatory in a toilet or bathing *facility* for a single occupant accessed only through a private office and not for *common use* or *public use* shall not be required to comply with 606.3.

    2. In *residential dwelling unit* kitchens, sinks that are adjustable to variable heights, 29 inches (735 mm) minimum and 36 inches (915 mm) maximum, shall be permitted where rough-in plumbing permits connections of supply and drain pipes for sinks mounted at the height of 29 inches (735 mm).

606.4 Faucets. Controls for faucets shall comply with 309. Hand-operated metering faucets shall remain open for 10 seconds minimum.

606.5 Exposed Pipes and Surfaces. Water supply and drain pipes under lavatories and sinks shall be insulated or otherwise configured to protect against contact. There shall be no sharp or abrasive surfaces under lavatories and sinks.

607 Bathtubs

607.1 General. Bathtubs shall comply with 607.

607.2 Clearance. Clearance in front of bathtubs shall extend the length of the bathtub and shall be 30 inches (760 mm) wide minimum. A lavatory complying with 606 shall be permitted at the control end of the clearance. Where a permanent seat is provided at the head end of the bathtub, the clearance shall extend 12 inches (305 mm) minimum beyond the wall at the head end of the bathtub.

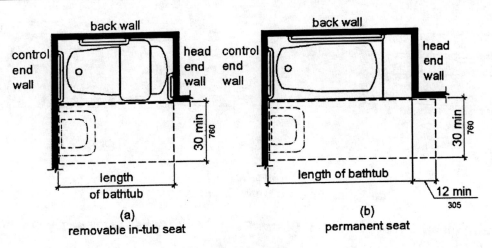

Figure 607.2
Clearance for Bathtubs

607.3 Seat. A permanent seat at the head end of the bathtub or a removable in-tub seat shall be provided. Seats shall comply with 610.

607.4 Grab Bars. Grab bars for bathtubs shall comply with 609 and shall be provided in accordance with 607.4.1 or 607.4.2.

EXCEPTIONS: 1. Grab bars shall not be required to be installed in a bathtub located in a bathing *facility* for a single occupant accessed only through a private office and not for *common use* or *public use* provided that reinforcement has been installed in walls and located so as to permit the installation of grab bars complying with 607.4.

2. In *residential dwelling units*, grab bars shall not be required to be installed in bathtubs located in bathing *facilities* provided that reinforcement has been installed in walls and located so as to permit the installation of grab bars complying with 607.4.

607.4.1 Bathtubs With Permanent Seats. For bathtubs with permanent seats, grab bars shall be provided in accordance with 607.4.1.

607.4.1.1 Back Wall. Two grab bars shall be installed on the back wall, one located in accordance with 609.4 and the other located 8 inches (205 mm) minimum and 10 inches (255 mm) maximum above the rim of the bathtub. Each grab bar shall be installed 15 inches (380 mm) maximum from the head end wall and 12 inches (305 mm) maximum from the control end wall.

607.4.1.2 Control End Wall. A grab bar 24 inches (610 mm) long minimum shall be installed on the control end wall at the front edge of the bathtub.

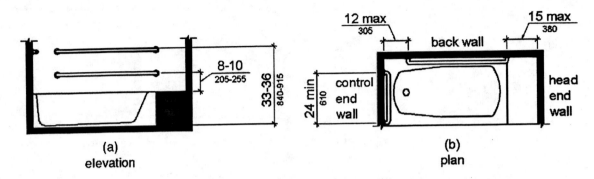

Figure 607.4.1
Grab Bars for Bathtubs with Permanent Seats

607.4.2 Bathtubs Without Permanent Seats. For bathtubs without permanent seats, grab bars shall comply with 607.4.2.

607.4.2.1 Back Wall. Two grab bars shall be installed on the back wall, one located in accordance with 609.4 and other located 8 inches (205 mm) minimum and 10 inches (255 mm) maximum above the rim of the bathtub. Each grab bar shall be 24 inches (610 mm) long minimum and shall be installed 24 inches (610 mm) maximum from the head end wall and 12 inches (305 mm) maximum from the control end wall.

607.4.2.2 Control End Wall. A grab bar 24 inches (610 mm) long minimum shall be installed on the control end wall at the front edge of the bathtub.

607.4.2.3 Head End Wall. A grab bar 12 inches (305 mm) long minimum shall be installed on the head end wall at the front edge of the bathtub.

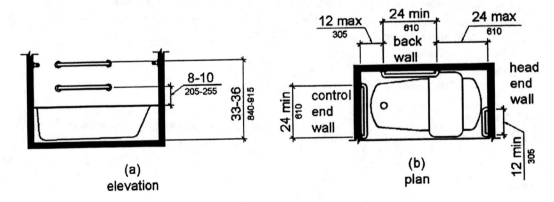

Figure 607.4.2
Grab Bars for Bathtubs with Removable In-Tub Seats

210

607.5 Controls. Controls, other than drain stoppers, shall be located on an end wall. Controls shall be between the bathtub rim and grab bar, and between the open side of the bathtub and the centerline of the width of the bathtub. Controls shall comply with 309.4.

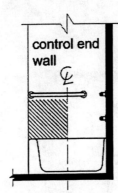

control end wall

Figure 607.5
Bathtub Control Location

607.6 Shower Spray Unit and Water. A shower spray unit with a hose 59 inches (1500 mm) long minimum that can be used both as a fixed-position shower head and as a hand-held shower shall be provided. The shower spray unit shall have an on/off control with a non-positive shut-off. If an adjustable-height shower head on a vertical bar is used, the bar shall be installed so as not to obstruct the use of grab bars. Bathtub shower spray units shall deliver water that is 120°F (49°C) maximum.

> **Advisory 607.6 Shower Spray Unit and Water.** Ensure that hand-held shower spray units are capable of delivering water pressure substantially equivalent to fixed shower heads.

607.7 Bathtub Enclosures. Enclosures for bathtubs shall not obstruct controls, faucets, shower and spray units or obstruct transfer from wheelchairs onto bathtub seats or into bathtubs. Enclosures on bathtubs shall not have tracks installed on the rim of the open face of the bathtub.

608 Shower Compartments

608.1 General. Shower compartments shall comply with 608.

> **Advisory 608.1 General.** Shower stalls that are 60 inches (1525 mm) wide and have no curb may increase the usability of a bathroom because the shower area provides additional maneuvering space.

608.2 Size and Clearances for Shower Compartments. Shower compartments shall have sizes and clearances complying with 608.2.

608.2.1 Transfer Type Shower Compartments. Transfer type shower compartments shall be 36 inches (915 mm) by 36 inches (915 mm) clear inside dimensions measured at the center points of opposing sides and shall have a 36 inch (915 mm) wide minimum entry on the face of the shower

211

compartment. Clearance of 36 inches (915 mm) wide minimum by 48 inches (1220 mm) long minimum measured from the control wall shall be provided.

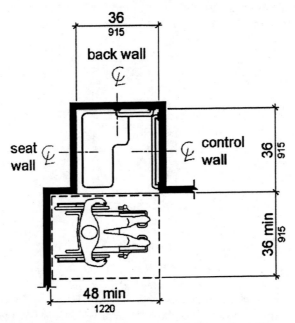

Note: inside finished dimensions measured at the center points
of opposing sides

Figure 608.2.1
Transfer Type Shower Compartment Size and Clearance

608.2.2 Standard Roll-In Type Shower Compartments. Standard roll-in type shower compartments shall be 30 inches (760 mm) wide minimum by 60 inches (1525 mm) deep minimum clear inside dimensions measured at center points of opposing sides and shall have a 60 inches (1525 mm) wide minimum entry on the face of the shower compartment.

608.2.2.1 Clearance. A 30 inch (760 mm) wide minimum by 60 inch (1525 mm) long minimum clearance shall be provided adjacent to the open face of the shower compartment.
EXCEPTION: A lavatory complying with 606 shall be permitted on one 30 inch (760 mm) wide minimum side of the clearance provided that it is not on the side of the clearance adjacent to the controls or, where provided, not on the side of the clearance adjacent to the shower seat.

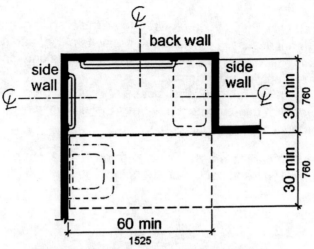

Note: inside finished dimensions measured at the center
points of opposing sides

Figure 608.2.2
Standard Roll-In Type Shower Compartment Size and Clearance

608.2.3 Alternate Roll-In Type Shower Compartments. Alternate roll-in type shower compartments shall be 36 inches (915 mm) wide and 60 inches (1525 mm) deep minimum clear inside dimensions measured at center points of opposing sides. A 36 inch (915 mm) wide minimum entry shall be provided at one end of the long side of the compartment.

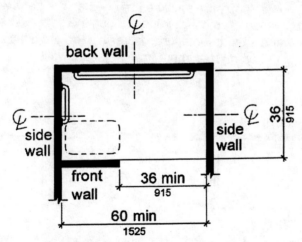

Note: inside finished dimensions measured at the center
points of opposing sides

Figure 608.2.3
Alternate Roll-In Type Shower Compartment Size and Clearance

213

608.3 Grab Bars. Grab bars shall comply with 609 and shall be provided in accordance with 608.3. Where multiple grab bars are used, required horizontal grab bars shall be installed at the same height above the finish floor.

EXCEPTIONS: 1. Grab bars shall not be required to be installed in a shower located in a bathing *facility* for a single occupant accessed only through a private office, and not for *common use* or *public use* provided that reinforcement has been installed in walls and located so as to permit the installation of grab bars complying with 608.3.

2. In *residential dwelling units*, grab bars shall not be required to be installed in showers located in bathing *facilities* provided that reinforcement has been installed in walls and located so as to permit the installation of grab bars complying with 608.3.

608.3.1 Transfer Type Shower Compartments. In transfer type compartments, grab bars shall be provided across the control wall and back wall to a point 18 inches (455 mm) from the control wall.

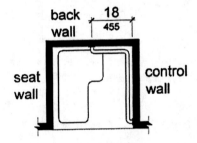

Figure 608.3.1
Grab Bars for Transfer Type Showers

608.3.2 Standard Roll-In Type Shower Compartments. Where a seat is provided in standard roll-in type shower compartments, grab bars shall be provided on the back wall and the side wall opposite the seat. Grab bars shall not be provided above the seat. Where a seat is not provided in standard roll-in type shower compartments, grab bars shall be provided on three walls. Grab bars shall be installed 6 inches (150 mm) maximum from adjacent walls.

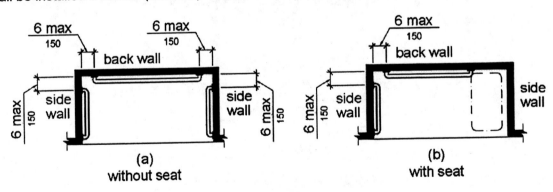

Figure 608.3.2
Grab Bars for Standard Roll-In Type Showers

214

608.3.3 Alternate Roll-In Type Shower Compartments. In alternate roll-in type shower compartments, grab bars shall be provided on the back wall and the side wall farthest from the compartment entry. Grab bars shall not be provided above the seat. Grab bars shall be installed 6 inches (150 mm) maximum from adjacent walls.

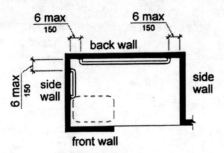

Figure 608.3.3
Grab Bars for Alternate Roll-In Type Showers

608.4 Seats. A folding or non-folding seat shall be provided in transfer type shower compartments. A folding seat shall be provided in roll-in type showers required in *transient lodging* guest rooms with mobility features complying with 806.2. Seats shall comply with 610.

    EXCEPTION: In *residential dwelling units*, seats shall not be required in transfer type shower compartments provided that reinforcement has been installed in walls so as to permit the installation of seats complying with 608.4.

608.5 Controls. Controls, faucets, and shower spray units shall comply with 309.4.

608.5.1 Transfer Type Shower Compartments. In transfer type shower compartments, the controls, faucets, and shower spray unit shall be installed on the side wall opposite the seat 38 inches (965 mm) minimum and 48 inches (1220 mm) maximum above the shower floor and shall be located on the control wall 15 inches (380 mm) maximum from the centerline of the seat toward the shower opening.

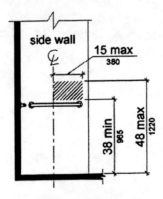

Figure 608.5.1
Transfer Type Shower Compartment Control Location

608.5.2 Standard Roll-In Type Shower Compartments. In standard roll-in type shower compartments, the controls, faucets, and shower spray unit shall be located above the grab bar, but no higher than 48 inches (1220 mm) above the shower floor. Where a seat is provided, the controls, faucets, and shower spray unit shall be installed on the back wall adjacent to the seat wall and shall be located 27 inches (685 mm) maximum from the seat wall.

> **Advisory 608.5.2 Standard Roll-in Type Shower Compartments.** In standard roll-in type showers without seats, the shower head and operable parts can be located on any of the three walls of the shower without adversely affecting accessibility.

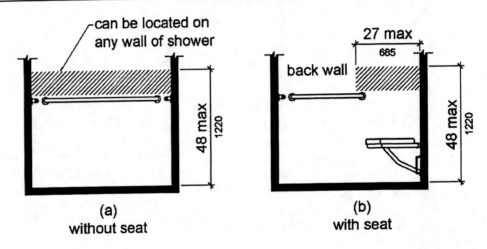

(a)
without seat

(b)
with seat

Figure 608.5.2
Standard Roll-In Type Shower Compartment Control Location

608.5.3 Alternate Roll-In Type Shower Compartments. In alternate roll-in type shower compartments, the controls, faucets, and shower spray unit shall be located above the grab bar, but no higher than 48 inches (1220 mm) above the shower floor. Where a seat is provided, the controls, faucets, and shower spray unit shall be located on the side wall adjacent to the seat 27 inches (685 mm) maximum from the side wall behind the seat or shall be located on the back wall opposite the seat 15 inches (380 mm) maximum, left or right, of the centerline of the seat. Where a seat is not provided, the controls, faucets, and shower spray unit shall be installed on the side wall farthest from the compartment entry.

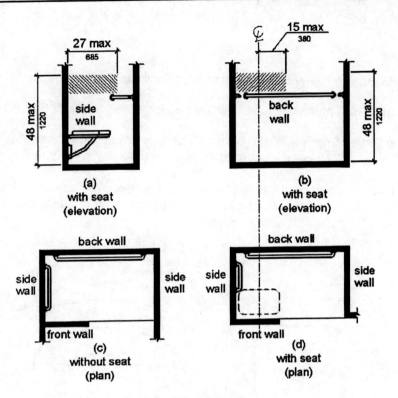

Figure 608.5.3
Alternate Roll-In Type Shower Compartment Control Location

608.6 Shower Spray Unit and Water. A shower spray unit with a hose 59 inches (1500 mm) long minimum that can be used both as a fixed-position shower head and as a hand-held shower shall be provided. The shower spray unit shall have an on/off control with a non-positive shut-off. If an adjustable-height shower head on a vertical bar is used, the bar shall be installed so as not to obstruct the use of grab bars. Shower spray units shall deliver water that is 120°F (49°C) maximum.

> **EXCEPTION:** A fixed shower head located at 48 inches (1220 mm) maximum above the shower finish floor shall be permitted instead of a hand-held spray unit in *facilities* that are not medical care *facilities*, long-term care *facilities*, *transient lodging* guest rooms, or *residential dwelling units*.

> **Advisory 608.6 Shower Spray Unit and Water.** Ensure that hand-held shower spray units are capable of delivering water pressure substantially equivalent to fixed shower heads.

608.7 Thresholds. Thresholds in roll-in type shower compartments shall be ½ inch (13 mm) high maximum in accordance with 303. In transfer type shower compartments, thresholds ½ inch (13 mm) high maximum shall be beveled, rounded, or vertical.

> **EXCEPTION:** A threshold 2 inches (51 mm) high maximum shall be permitted in transfer type shower compartments in existing *facilities* where provision of a ½ inch (13 mm) high threshold would disturb the structural reinforcement of the floor slab.

217

608.8 Shower Enclosures. Enclosures for shower compartments shall not obstruct controls, faucets, and shower spray units or obstruct transfer from wheelchairs onto shower seats.

609 Grab Bars

609.1 General. Grab bars in toilet *facilities* and bathing *facilities* shall comply with 609.

609.2 Cross Section. Grab bars shall have a cross section complying with 609.2.1 or 609.2.2.

609.2.1 Circular Cross Section. Grab bars with circular cross sections shall have an outside diameter of 1¼ inches (32 mm) minimum and 2 inches (51 mm) maximum.

609.2.2 Non-Circular Cross Section. Grab bars with non-circular cross sections shall have a cross-section dimension of 2 inches (51 mm) maximum and a perimeter dimension of 4 inches (100 mm) minimum and 4.8 inches (120 mm) maximum.

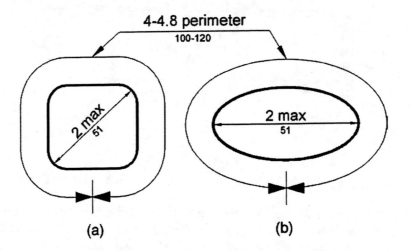

Figure 609.2.2
Grab Bar Non-Circular Cross Section

609.3 Spacing. The *space* between the wall and the grab bar shall be 1½ inches (38 mm). The *space* between the grab bar and projecting objects below and at the ends shall be 1½ inches (38 mm) minimum. The *space* between the grab bar and projecting objects above shall be 12 inches (305 mm) minimum.
    EXCEPTION: The *space* between the grab bars and shower controls, shower fittings, and other grab bars above shall be permitted to be 1½ inches (38 mm) minimum.

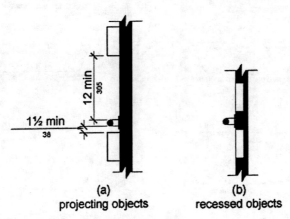

Figure 609.3
Spacing of Grab Bars

609.4 Position of Grab Bars. Grab bars shall be installed in a horizontal position, 33 inches (840 mm) minimum and 36 inches (915 mm) maximum above the finish floor measured to the top of the gripping surface, except that at water closets for *children's use* complying with 604.9, grab bars shall be installed in a horizontal position 18 inches (455 mm) minimum and 27 inches (685 mm) maximum above the finish floor measured to the top of the gripping surface. The height of the lower grab bar on the back wall of a bathtub shall comply with 607.4.1.1 or 607.4.2.1.

609.5 Surface Hazards. Grab bars and any wall or other surfaces adjacent to grab bars shall be free of sharp or abrasive *elements* and shall have rounded edges.

609.6 Fittings. Grab bars shall not rotate within their fittings.

609.7 Installation. Grab bars shall be installed in any manner that provides a gripping surface at the specified locations and that does not obstruct the required clear floor *space*.

609.8 Structural Strength. Allowable stresses shall not be exceeded for materials used when a vertical or horizontal force of 250 pounds (1112 N) is applied at any point on the grab bar, fastener, mounting device, or supporting structure.

610 Seats

610.1 General. Seats in bathtubs and shower compartments shall comply with 610.

610.2 Bathtub Seats. The top of bathtub seats shall be 17 inches (430 mm) minimum and 19 inches (485 mm) maximum above the bathroom finish floor. The depth of a removable in-tub seat shall be 15 inches (380 mm) minimum and 16 inches (405 mm) maximum. The seat shall be capable of secure placement. Permanent seats at the head end of the bathtub shall be 15 inches (380 mm) deep minimum and shall extend from the back wall to or beyond the outer edge of the bathtub.

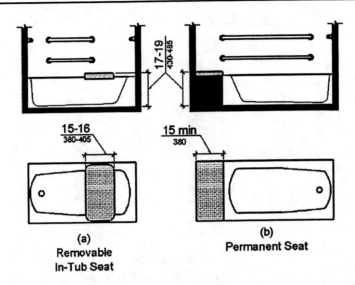

Figure 610.2
Bathtub Seats

610.3 Shower Compartment Seats. Where a seat is provided in a standard roll-in shower compartment, it shall be a folding type, shall be installed on the side wall adjacent to the controls, and shall extend from the back wall to a point within 3 inches (75 mm) of the compartment entry. Where a seat is provided in an alternate roll-in type shower compartment, it shall be a folding type, shall be installed on the front wall opposite the back wall, and shall extend from the adjacent side wall to a point within 3 inches (75 mm) of the compartment entry. In transfer-type showers, the seat shall extend from the back wall to a point within 3 inches (75 mm) of the compartment entry. The top of the seat shall be 17 inches (430 mm) minimum and 19 inches (485 mm) maximum above the bathroom finish floor. Seats shall comply with 610.3.1 or 610.3.2.

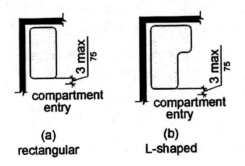

Figure 610.3
Extent of Seat

610.3.1 Rectangular Seats. The rear edge of a rectangular seat shall be 2½ inches (64 mm) maximum and the front edge 15 inches (380 mm) minimum and 16 inches (405 mm) maximum from the seat wall. The side edge of the seat shall be 1½ inches (38 mm) maximum from the adjacent wall.

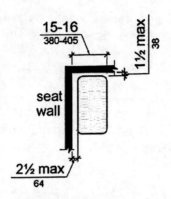

Figure 610.3.1
Rectangular Shower Seat

610.3.2 L-Shaped Seats. The rear edge of an L-shaped seat shall be 2½ inches (64 mm) maximum and the front edge 15 inches (380 mm) minimum and 16 inches (405 mm) maximum from the seat wall. The rear edge of the "L" portion of the seat shall be 1½ inches (38 mm) maximum from the wall and the front edge shall be 14 inches (355 mm) minimum and 15 inches (380 mm) maximum from the wall. The end of the "L" shall be 22 inches (560 mm) minimum and 23 inches maximum (585 mm) from the main seat wall.

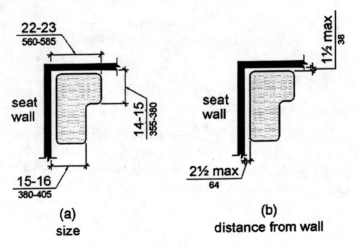

(a)
size

(b)
distance from wall

Figure 610.3.2
L-Shaped Shower Seat

610.4 Structural Strength. Allowable stresses shall not be exceeded for materials used when a vertical or horizontal force of 250 pounds (1112 N) is applied at any point on the seat, fastener, mounting device, or supporting structure.

221

611 Washing Machines and Clothes Dryers

611.1 General. Washing machines and clothes dryers shall comply with 611.

611.2 Clear Floor Space. A clear floor or ground *space* complying with 305 positioned for parallel approach shall be provided. The clear floor or ground *space* shall be centered on the appliance.

611.3 Operable Parts. *Operable parts*, including doors, lint screens, and detergent and bleach compartments shall comply with 309.

611.4 Height. Top loading machines shall have the door to the laundry compartment located 36 inches (915 mm) maximum above the finish floor. Front loading machines shall have the bottom of the opening to the laundry compartment located 15 inches (380 mm) minimum and 36 inches (915 mm) maximum above the finish floor.

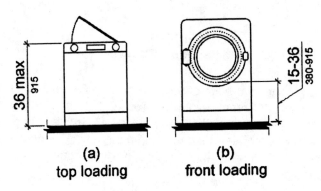

(a)
top loading

(b)
front loading

Figure 611.4
Height of Laundry Compartment Opening

612 Saunas and Steam Rooms

612.1 General. Saunas and steam rooms shall comply with 612.

612.2 Bench. Where seating is provided in saunas and steam rooms, at least one bench shall comply with 903. Doors shall not swing into the clear floor *space* required by 903.2.
   EXCEPTION: A readily removable bench shall be permitted to obstruct the turning *space* required by 612.3 and the clear floor or ground *space* required by 903.2.

612.3 Turning Space. A turning *space* complying with 304 shall be provided within saunas and steam rooms.

CHAPTER 7: COMMUNICATION ELEMENTS AND FEATURES

701 General

701.1 Scope. The provisions of Chapter 7 shall apply where required by Chapter 2 or where referenced by a requirement in this document.

702 Fire Alarm Systems

702.1 General. Fire alarm systems shall have permanently installed audible and visible alarms complying with NFPA 72 (1999 or 2002 edition) (incorporated by reference, see "Referenced Standards" in Chapter 1), except that the maximum allowable sound level of audible notification appliances complying with section 4-3.2.1 of NFPA 72 (1999 edition) shall have a sound level no more than 110 dB at the minimum hearing distance from the audible appliance. In addition, alarms in guest rooms required to provide communication features shall comply with sections 4-3 and 4-4 of NFPA 72 (1999 edition) or sections 7.4 and 7.5 of NFPA 72 (2002 edition).

> **EXCEPTION:** Fire alarm systems in medical care *facilities* shall be permitted to be provided in accordance with industry practice.

703 Signs

703.1 General. Signs shall comply with 703. Where both visual and *tactile characters* are required, either one sign with both visual and *tactile characters*, or two separate signs, one with visual, and one with *tactile characters*, shall be provided.

703.2 Raised Characters. Raised *characters* shall comply with 703.2 and shall be duplicated in braille complying with 703.3. Raised *characters* shall be installed in accordance with 703.4.

> **Advisory 703.2 Raised Characters.** Signs that are designed to be read by touch should not have sharp or abrasive edges.

703.2.1 Depth. Raised *characters* shall be 1/32 inch (0.8 mm) minimum above their background.

703.2.2 Case. *Characters* shall be uppercase.

703.2.3 Style. *Characters* shall be sans serif. *Characters* shall not be italic, oblique, script, highly decorative, or of other unusual forms.

703.2.4 Character Proportions. *Characters* shall be selected from fonts where the width of the uppercase letter "O" is 55 percent minimum and 110 percent maximum of the height of the uppercase letter "I".

703.2.5 Character Height. *Character* height measured vertically from the baseline of the *character* shall be 5/8 inch (16 mm) minimum and 2 inches (51 mm) maximum based on the height of the uppercase letter "I".

EXCEPTION: Where separate raised and visual *characters* with the same information are provided, raised *character* height shall be permitted to be ½ inch (13 mm) minimum.

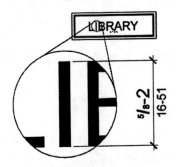

Figure 703.2.5
Height of Raised Characters

703.2.6 Stroke Thickness. Stroke thickness of the uppercase letter "I" shall be 15 percent maximum of the height of the *character*.

703.2.7 Character Spacing. *Character* spacing shall be measured between the two closest points of adjacent raised *characters* within a message, excluding word *spaces*. Where *characters* have rectangular cross sections, spacing between individual raised *characters* shall be 1/8 inch (3.2 mm) minimum and 4 times the raised *character* stroke width maximum. Where *characters* have other cross sections, spacing between individual raised *characters* shall be 1/16 inch (1.6 mm) minimum and 4 times the raised *character* stroke width maximum at the base of the cross sections, and 1/8 inch (3.2 mm) minimum and 4 times the raised *character* stroke width maximum at the top of the cross sections. *Characters* shall be separated from raised borders and decorative *elements* 3/8 inch (9.5 mm) minimum.

703.2.8 Line Spacing. Spacing between the baselines of separate lines of raised *characters* within a message shall be 135 percent minimum and 170 percent maximum of the raised *character* height.

703.3 Braille. Braille shall be contracted (Grade 2) and shall comply with 703.3 and 703.4.

703.3.1 Dimensions and Capitalization. Braille dots shall have a domed or rounded shape and shall comply with Table 703.3.1. The indication of an uppercase letter or letters shall only be used before the first word of sentences, proper nouns and names, individual letters of the alphabet, initials, and acronyms.

Table 703.3.1 Braille Dimensions

Measurement Range	Minimum in Inches Maximum in Inches
Dot base diameter	0.059 (1.5 mm) to 0.063 (1.6 mm)
Distance between two dots in the same cell[1]	0.090 (2.3 mm) to 0.100 (2.5 mm)
Distance between corresponding dots in adjacent cells[1]	0.241 (6.1 mm) to 0.300 (7.6 mm)
Dot height	0.025 (0.6 mm) to 0.037 (0.9 mm)
Distance between corresponding dots from one cell directly below[1]	0.395 (10 mm) to 0.400 (10.2 mm)

1. Measured center to center.

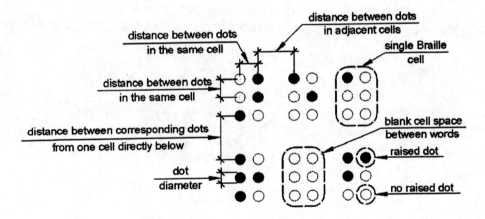

Figure 703.3.1
Braille Measurement

703.3.2 Position. Braille shall be positioned below the corresponding text. If text is multi-lined, braille shall be placed below the entire text. Braille shall be separated 3/8 inch (9.5 mm) minimum from any other *tactile characters* and 3/8 inch (9.5 mm) minimum from raised borders and decorative *elements*.

225

EXCEPTION: Braille provided on elevator car controls shall be separated 3/16 inch (4.8 mm) minimum and shall be located either directly below or adjacent to the corresponding raised *characters* or symbols.

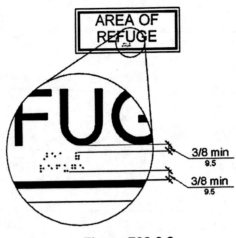

Figure 703.3.2
Position of Braille

703.4 Installation Height and Location. Signs with *tactile characters* shall comply with 703.4.

703.4.1 Height Above Finish Floor or Ground. *Tactile characters* on signs shall be located 48 inches (1220 mm) minimum above the finish floor or ground surface, measured from the baseline of the lowest *tactile character* and 60 inches (1525 mm) maximum above the finish floor or ground surface, measured from the baseline of the highest *tactile character*.

EXCEPTION: *Tactile characters* for elevator car controls shall not be required to comply with 703.4.1.

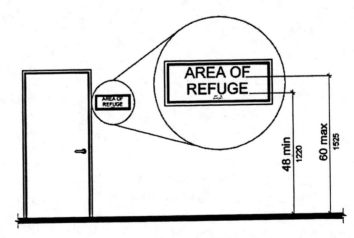

Figure 703.4.1
Height of Tactile Characters Above Finish Floor or Ground

226

703.4.2 Location. Where a *tactile* sign is provided at a door, the sign shall be located alongside the door at the latch side. Where a *tactile* sign is provided at double doors with one active leaf, the sign shall be located on the inactive leaf. Where a *tactile* sign is provided at double doors with two active leafs, the sign shall be located to the right of the right hand door. Where there is no wall *space* at the latch side of a single door or at the right side of double doors, signs shall be located on the nearest adjacent wall. Signs containing *tactile characters* shall be located so that a clear floor *space* of 18 inches (455 mm) minimum by 18 inches (455 mm) minimum, centered on the *tactile characters*, is provided beyond the arc of any door swing between the closed position and 45 degree open position.

> **EXCEPTION:** Signs with *tactile characters* shall be permitted on the push side of doors with closers and without hold-open devices.

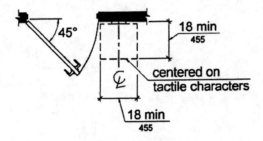

Figure 703.4.2
Location of Tactile Signs at Doors

703.5 Visual Characters. Visual *characters* shall comply with 703.5.
> **EXCEPTION:** Where visual *characters* comply with 703.2 and are accompanied by braille complying with 703.3, they shall not be required to comply with 703.5.2 through 703.5.9.

703.5.1 Finish and Contrast. *Characters* and their background shall have a non-glare finish. *Characters* shall contrast with their background with either light *characters* on a dark background or dark *characters* on a light background.

> **Advisory 703.5.1 Finish and Contrast.** Signs are more legible for persons with low vision when characters contrast as much as possible with their background. Additional factors affecting the ease with which the text can be distinguished from its background include shadows cast by lighting sources, surface glare, and the uniformity of the text and its background colors and textures.

703.5.2 Case. *Characters* shall be uppercase or lowercase or a combination of both.

703.5.3 Style. *Characters* shall be conventional in form. *Characters* shall not be italic, oblique, script, highly decorative, or of other unusual forms.

703.5.4 Character Proportions. *Characters* shall be selected from fonts where the width of the uppercase letter "O" is 55 percent minimum and 110 percent maximum of the height of the uppercase letter "I".

227

703.5.5 Character Height. Minimum *character* height shall comply with Table 703.5.5. Viewing distance shall be measured as the horizontal distance between the *character* and an obstruction preventing further approach towards the sign. *Character* height shall be based on the uppercase letter "I".

Table 703.5.5 Visual Character Height

Height to Finish Floor or Ground From Baseline of Character	Horizontal Viewing Distance	Minimum Character Height
40 inches (1015 mm) to less than or equal to 70 inches (1780 mm)	less than 72 inches (1830 mm)	5/8 inch (16 mm)
	72 inches (1830 mm) and greater	5/8 inch (16 mm), plus 1/8 inch (3.2 mm) per foot (305 mm) of viewing distance above 72 inches (1830 mm)
Greater than 70 inches (1780 mm) to less than or equal to 120 inches (3050 mm)	less than 180 inches (4570 mm)	2 inches (51 mm)
	180 inches (4570 mm) and greater	2 inches (51 mm), plus 1/8 inch (3.2 mm) per foot (305 mm) of viewing distance above 180 inches (4570 mm)
greater than 120 inches (3050 mm)	less than 21 feet (6400 mm)	3 inches (75 mm)
	21 feet (6400 mm) and greater	3 inches (75 mm), plus 1/8 inch (3.2 mm) per foot (305 mm) of viewing distance above 21 feet (6400 mm)

703.5.6 Height From Finish Floor or Ground. Visual *characters* shall be 40 inches (1015 mm) minimum above the finish floor or ground.

EXCEPTION: Visual *characters* indicating elevator car controls shall not be required to comply with 703.5.6.

703.5.7 Stroke Thickness. Stroke thickness of the uppercase letter "I" shall be 10 percent minimum and 30 percent maximum of the height of the *character*.

703.5.8 Character Spacing. *Character* spacing shall be measured between the two closest points of adjacent *characters*, excluding word *spaces*. Spacing between individual *characters* shall be 10 percent minimum and 35 percent maximum of *character* height.

703.5.9 Line Spacing. Spacing between the baselines of separate lines of *characters* within a message shall be 135 percent minimum and 170 percent maximum of the *character* height.

703.6 Pictograms. *Pictograms* shall comply with 703.6.

703.6.1 Pictogram Field. *Pictograms* shall have a field height of 6 inches (150 mm) minimum. *Characters* and braille shall not be located in the *pictogram* field.

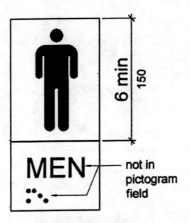

Figure 703.6.1
Pictogram Field

703.6.2 Finish and Contrast. *Pictograms* and their field shall have a non-glare finish. *Pictograms* shall contrast with their field with either a light *pictogram* on a dark field or a dark *pictogram* on a light field.

> **A703.6.2 Finish and Contrast.** Signs are more legible for persons with low vision when characters contrast as much as possible with their background. Additional factors affecting the ease with which the text can be distinguished from its background include shadows cast by lighting sources, surface glare, and the uniformity of the text and background colors and textures.

703.6.3 Text Descriptors. *Pictograms* shall have text descriptors located directly below the *pictogram* field. Text descriptors shall comply with 703.2, 703.3 and 703.4.

703.7 Symbols of Accessibility. Symbols of *accessibility* shall comply with 703.7.

703.7.1 Finish and Contrast. Symbols of *accessibility* and their background shall have a non-glare finish. Symbols of *accessibility* shall contrast with their background with either a light symbol on a dark background or a dark symbol on a light background.

> **Advisory 703.7.1 Finish and Contrast.** Signs are more legible for persons with low vision when characters contrast as much as possible with their background. Additional factors affecting the ease with which the text can be distinguished from its background include shadows cast by lighting sources, surface glare, and the uniformity of the text and background colors and textures.

703.7.2 Symbols.

703.7.2.1 International Symbol of Accessibility. The International Symbol of *Accessibility* shall comply with Figure 703.7.2.1.

Figure 703.7.2.1
International Symbol of Accessibility

703.7.2.2 International Symbol of TTY. The International Symbol of *TTY* shall comply with Figure 703.7.2.2.

Figure 703.7.2.2
International Symbol of TTY

703.7.2.3 Volume Control Telephones. Telephones with a volume control shall be identified by a *pictogram* of a telephone handset with radiating sound waves on a square field such as shown in Figure 703.7.2.3.

Figure 703.7.2.3
Volume Control Telephone

Printed by Builder's Book, Inc., Bookstore · www.buildersbook.com

703.7.2.4 Assistive Listening Systems. *Assistive listening systems* shall be identified by the International Symbol of Access for Hearing Loss complying with Figure 703.7.2.4.

Figure 703.7.2.4
International Symbol of Access for Hearing Loss

704 Telephones

704.1 General. Public telephones shall comply with 704.

704.2 Wheelchair Accessible Telephones. Wheelchair *accessible* telephones shall comply with 704.2.

704.2.1 Clear Floor or Ground Space. A clear floor or ground *space* complying with 305 shall be provided. The clear floor or ground *space* shall not be obstructed by bases, enclosures, or seats.

> **Advisory 704.2.1 Clear Floor or Ground Space.** Because clear floor and ground space is required to be unobstructed, telephones, enclosures and related telephone book storage cannot encroach on the required clear floor or ground space and must comply with the provisions for protruding objects. (See Section 307).

704.2.1.1 Parallel Approach. Where a parallel approach is provided, the distance from the edge of the telephone enclosure to the face of the telephone unit shall be 10 inches (255 mm) maximum.

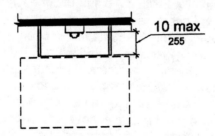

Figure 704.2.1.1
Parallel Approach to Telephone

704.2.1.2 Forward Approach. Where a forward approach is provided, the distance from the front edge of a counter within the telephone enclosure to the face of the telephone unit shall be 20 inches (510 mm) maximum.

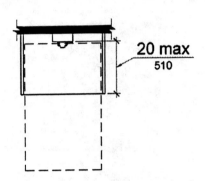

Figure 704.2.1.2
Forward Approach to Telephone

704.2.2 Operable Parts. *Operable parts* shall comply with 309. Telephones shall have push-button controls where such service is available.

704.2.3 Telephone Directories. Telephone directories, where provided, shall be located in accordance with 309.

704.2.4 Cord Length. The cord from the telephone to the handset shall be 29 inches (735 mm) long minimum.

704.3 Volume Control Telephones. Public telephones required to have volume controls shall be equipped with a receive volume control that provides a gain adjustable up to 20 dB minimum. For incremental volume control, provide at least one intermediate step of 12 dB of gain minimum. An automatic reset shall be provided.

Advisory 704.3 Volume Control Telephones. Amplifiers on pay phones are located in the base or the handset or are built into the telephone. Most are operated by pressing a button or key. If the microphone in the handset is not being used, a mute button that temporarily turns off the microphone can also reduce the amount of background noise which the person hears in the earpiece. If a volume adjustment is provided that allows the user to set the level anywhere from the base volume to the upper requirement of 20 dB, there is no need to specify a lower limit. If a stepped volume control is provided, one of the intermediate levels must provide 12 dB of gain. Consider compatibility issues when matching an amplified handset with a phone or phone system. Amplified handsets that can be switched with pay telephone handsets are available. Portable and in-line amplifiers can be used with some phones but are not practical at most public phones covered by these requirements.

704.4 TTYs. *TTY*s required at a public pay telephone shall be permanently affixed within, or adjacent to, the telephone enclosure. Where an acoustic coupler is used, the telephone cord shall be sufficiently long to allow connection of the *TTY* and the telephone receiver.

> **Advisory 704.4 TTYs.** Ensure that sufficient electrical service is available where TTYs are to be installed.

704.4.1 Height. When in use, the touch surface of *TTY* keypads shall be 34 inches (865 mm) minimum above the finish floor.
    EXCEPTION: Where seats are provided, *TTY*s shall not be required to comply with 704.4.1.

> **Advisory 704.4.1 Height.** A telephone with a TTY installed underneath cannot also be a wheelchair accessible telephone because the required 34 inches (865 mm) minimum keypad height can causes the highest operable part of the telephone, usually the coin slot, to exceed the maximum permitted side and forward reach ranges. (See Section 308).
>
> **Advisory 704.4.1 Height Exception.** While seats are not required at TTYs, reading and typing at a TTY is more suited to sitting than standing. Facilities that often provide seats at TTY's include, but are not limited to, airports and other passenger terminals or stations, courts, art galleries, and convention centers.

704.5 TTY Shelf. Public pay telephones required to accommodate portable *TTY*s shall be equipped with a shelf and an electrical outlet within or adjacent to the telephone enclosure. The telephone handset shall be capable of being placed flush on the surface of the shelf. The shelf shall be capable of accommodating a *TTY* and shall have 6 inches (150 mm) minimum vertical clearance above the area where the *TTY* is to be placed.

705 Detectable Warnings

705.1 General. *Detectable warnings* shall consist of a surface of truncated domes and shall comply with 705.

705.1.1 Dome Size. Truncated domes in a *detectable warning* surface shall have a base diameter of 0.9 inch (23 mm) minimum and 1.4 inches (36 mm) maximum, a top diameter of 50 percent of the base diameter minimum to 65 percent of the base diameter maximum, and a height of 0.2 inch (5.1 mm).

705.1.2 Dome Spacing. Truncated domes in a *detectable warning* surface shall have a center-to-center spacing of 1.6 inches (41 mm) minimum and 2.4 inches (61 mm) maximum, and a base-to-base spacing of 0.65 inch (17 mm) minimum, measured between the most adjacent domes on a square grid.

705.1.3 Contrast. *Detectable warning* surfaces shall contrast visually with adjacent walking surfaces either light-on-dark, or dark-on-light.

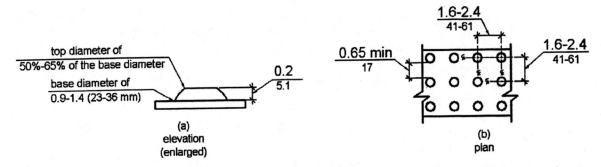

Figure 705.1
Size and Spacing of Truncated Domes

705.2 Platform Edges. *Detectable warning* surfaces at platform boarding edges shall be 24 inches (610 mm) wide and shall extend the full length of the *public use* areas of the platform.

706 Assistive Listening Systems

706.1 General. *Assistive listening systems* required in *assembly areas* shall comply with 706.

> **Advisory 706.1 General.** Assistive listening systems are generally categorized by their mode of transmission. There are hard-wired systems and three types of wireless systems: induction loop, infrared, and FM radio transmission. Each has different advantages and disadvantages that can help determine which system is best for a given application. For example, an FM system may be better than an infrared system in some open-air assemblies since infrared signals are less effective in sunlight. On the other hand, an infrared system is typically a better choice than an FM system where confidential transmission is important because it will be contained within a given space.
>
> The technical standards for assistive listening systems describe minimum performance levels for volume, interference, and distortion. Sound pressure levels (SPL), expressed in decibels, measure output sound volume. Signal-to-noise ratio (SNR or S/N), also expressed in decibels, represents the relationship between the loudness of a desired sound (the signal) and the background noise in a space or piece of equipment. The higher the SNR, the more intelligible the signal. The peak clipping level limits the distortion in signal output produced when high-volume sound waves are manipulated to serve assistive listening devices.
>
> Selecting or specifying an effective assistive listening system for a large or complex venue requires assistance from a professional sound engineer. The Access Board has published technical assistance on assistive listening devices and systems.

706.2 Receiver Jacks. Receivers required for use with an *assistive listening system* shall include a 1/8 inch (3.2 mm) standard mono jack.

706.3 Receiver Hearing-Aid Compatibility. Receivers required to be hearing-aid compatible shall interface with telecoils in hearing aids through the provision of neckloops.

> **Advisory 706.3 Receiver Hearing-Aid Compatibility.** Neckloops and headsets that can be worn as neckloops are compatible with hearing aids. Receivers that are not compatible include earbuds, which may require removal of hearing aids, earphones, and headsets that must be worn over the ear, which can create disruptive interference in the transmission and can be uncomfortable for people wearing hearing aids.

706.4 Sound Pressure Level. *Assistive listening systems* shall be capable of providing a sound pressure level of 110 dB minimum and 118 dB maximum with a dynamic range on the volume control of 50 dB.

706.5 Signal-to-Noise Ratio. The signal-to-noise ratio for internally generated noise in *assistive listening systems* shall be 18 dB minimum.

706.6 Peak Clipping Level. Peak clipping shall not exceed 18 dB of clipping relative to the peaks of speech.

707 Automatic Teller Machines and Fare Machines

> **Advisory 707 Automatic Teller Machines and Fare Machines.** Interactive transaction machines (ITMs), other than ATMs, are not covered by Section 707. However, for entities covered by the ADA, the Department of Justice regulations that implement the ADA provide additional guidance regarding the relationship between these requirements and elements that are not directly addressed by these requirements. Federal procurement law requires that ITMs purchased by the Federal government comply with standards issued by the Access Board under Section 508 of the Rehabilitation Act of 1973, as amended. This law covers a variety of products, including computer hardware and software, websites, phone systems, fax machines, copiers, and similar technologies. For more information on Section 508 consult the Access Board's website at www.access-board.gov.

707.1 General. Automatic teller machines and fare machines shall comply with 707.

> **Advisory 707.1 General.** If farecards have one tactually distinctive corner they can be inserted with greater accuracy. Token collection devices that are designed to accommodate tokens which are perforated can allow a person to distinguish more readily between tokens and common coins. Place accessible gates and fare vending machines in close proximity to other accessible elements when feasible so the facility is easier to use.

707.2 Clear Floor or Ground Space. A clear floor or ground *space* complying with 305 shall be provided.
> **EXCEPTION:** Clear floor or ground *space* shall not be required at drive-up only automatic teller machines and fare machines.

707.3 Operable Parts. *Operable parts* shall comply with 309. Unless a clear or correct key is provided, each *operable part* shall be able to be differentiated by sound or touch, without activation.

> **EXCEPTION:** Drive-up only automatic teller machines and fare machines shall not be required to comply with 309.2 and 309.3.

707.4 Privacy. Automatic teller machines shall provide the opportunity for the same degree of privacy of input and output available to all individuals.

> **Advisory 707.4 Privacy.** In addition to people who are blind or visually impaired, people with limited reach who use wheelchairs or have short stature, who cannot effectively block the ATM screen with their bodies, may prefer to use speech output. Speech output users can benefit from an option to render the visible screen blank, thereby affording them greater personal security and privacy.

707.5 Speech Output. Machines shall be speech enabled. Operating instructions and orientation, visible transaction prompts, user input verification, error messages, and all displayed information for full use shall be *accessible* to and independently usable by individuals with vision impairments. Speech shall be delivered through a mechanism that is readily available to all users, including but not limited to, an industry standard connector or a telephone handset. Speech shall be recorded or digitized human, or synthesized.

> **EXCEPTIONS: 1.** Audible tones shall be permitted instead of speech for visible output that is not displayed for security purposes, including but not limited to, asterisks representing personal identification numbers.
>
> **2.** Advertisements and other similar information shall not be required to be audible unless they convey information that can be used in the transaction being conducted.
>
> **3.** Where speech synthesis cannot be supported, dynamic alphabetic output shall not be required to be audible.

> **Advisory 707.5 Speech Output.** If an ATM provides additional functions such as dispensing coupons, selling theater tickets, or providing copies of monthly statements, all such functions must be available to customers using speech output. To avoid confusion at the ATM, the method of initiating the speech mode should be easily discoverable and should not require specialized training. For example, if a telephone handset is provided, lifting the handset can initiate the speech mode.

707.5.1 User Control. Speech shall be capable of being repeated or interrupted. Volume control shall be provided for the speech function.

> **EXCEPTION:** Speech output for any single function shall be permitted to be automatically interrupted when a transaction is selected.

707.5.2 Receipts. Where receipts are provided, speech output devices shall provide audible balance inquiry information, error messages, and all other information on the printed receipt necessary to complete or verify the transaction.

> **EXCEPTIONS: 1.** Machine location, date and time of transaction, customer account number, and the machine identifier shall not be required to be audible.

2. Information on printed receipts that duplicates information available on-screen shall not be required to be presented in the form of an audible receipt.

3. Printed copies of bank statements and checks shall not be required to be audible.

707.6 Input. Input devices shall comply with 707.6.

707.6.1 Input Controls. At least one *tactilely* discernible input control shall be provided for each function. Where provided, key surfaces not on active areas of display screens, shall be raised above surrounding surfaces. Where membrane keys are the only method of input, each shall be *tactilely* discernable from surrounding surfaces and adjacent keys.

707.6.2 Numeric Keys. Numeric keys shall be arranged in a 12-key ascending or descending telephone keypad layout. The number five key shall be *tactilely* distinct from the other keys.

> **Advisory 707.6.2 Numeric Keys.** Telephone keypads and computer keyboards differ in one significant feature, ascending versus descending numerical order. Both types of keypads are acceptable, provided the computer-style keypad is organized similarly to the number pad located at the right on most computer keyboards, and does not resemble the line of numbers located above the computer keys.

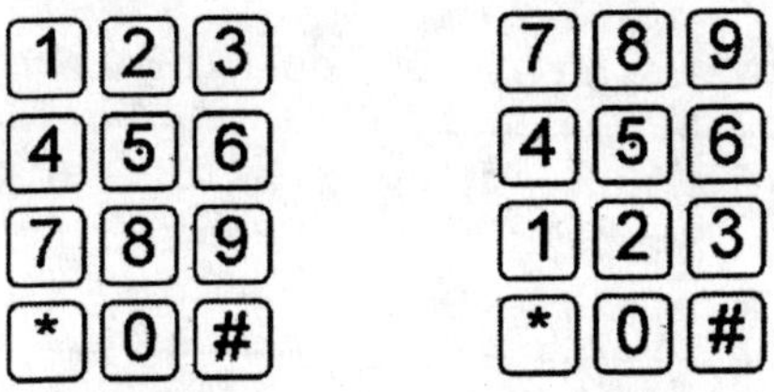

(a)
12-key
ascending

(b)
12-key
descending

Figure 707.6.2
Numeric Key Layout

707.6.3 Function Keys. Function keys shall comply with 707.6.3.

707.6.3.1 Contrast. Function keys shall contrast visually from background surfaces. *Characters* and symbols on key surfaces shall contrast visually from key surfaces. Visual contrast shall be either light-on-dark or dark-on-light.

    EXCEPTION: *Tactile* symbols required by 707.6.3.2 shall not be required to comply with 707.6.3.1.

707.6.3.2 Tactile Symbols. Function key surfaces shall have *tactile* symbols as follows: Enter or Proceed key: raised circle; Clear or Correct key: raised left arrow; Cancel key: raised letter ex; Add Value key: raised plus sign; Decrease Value key: raised minus sign.

707.7 Display Screen. The display screen shall comply with 707.7.
EXCEPTION: Drive-up only automatic teller machines and fare machines shall not be required to comply with 707.7.1.

707.7.1 Visibility. The display screen shall be visible from a point located 40 inches (1015 mm) above the center of the clear floor *space* in front of the machine.

707.7.2 Characters. *Characters* displayed on the screen shall be in a sans serif font. *Characters* shall be 3/16 inch (4.8 mm) high minimum based on the uppercase letter "I". *Characters* shall contrast with their background with either light *characters* on a dark background or dark *characters* on a light background.

707.8 Braille Instructions. Braille instructions for initiating the speech mode shall be provided. Braille shall comply with 703.3.

708 Two-Way Communication Systems

708.1 General. Two-way communication systems shall comply with 708.

> **Advisory 708.1 General.** Devices that do not require handsets are easier to use by people who have a limited reach.

708.2 Audible and Visual Indicators. The system shall provide both audible and visual signals.

> **Advisory 708.2 Audible and Visual Indicators.** A light can be used to indicate visually that assistance is on the way. Signs indicating the meaning of visual signals should be provided.

708.3 Handsets. Handset cords, if provided, shall be 29 inches (735 mm) long minimum.

708.4 Residential Dwelling Unit Communication Systems. Communications systems between a *residential dwelling unit* and a *site*, *building*, or floor *entrance* shall comply with 708.4.

708.4.1 Common Use or Public Use System Interface. The *common use* or *public use* system interface shall include the capability of supporting voice and *TTY* communication with the *residential dwelling unit* interface.

708.4.2 Residential Dwelling Unit Interface. The *residential dwelling unit* system interface shall include a telephone jack capable of supporting voice and *TTY* communication with the *common use* or *public use* system interface.

CHAPTER 8: SPECIAL ROOMS, SPACES, AND ELEMENTS

801 General

801.1 Scope. The provisions of Chapter 8 shall apply where required by Chapter 2 or where referenced by a requirement in this document.

> **Advisory 801.1 Scope.** Facilities covered by these requirements are also subject to the requirements of the other chapters. For example, 806 addresses guest rooms in transient lodging facilities while 902 contains the technical specifications for dining surfaces. If a transient lodging facility contains a restaurant, the restaurant must comply with requirements in other chapters such as those applicable to certain dining surfaces.

802 Wheelchair Spaces, Companion Seats, and Designated Aisle Seats

802.1 Wheelchair Spaces. *Wheelchair spaces* shall comply with 802.1.

802.1.1 Floor or Ground Surface. The floor or ground surface of *wheelchair spaces* shall comply with 302. Changes in level are not permitted.
   EXCEPTION: Slopes not steeper than 1:48 shall be permitted.

802.1.2 Width. A single *wheelchair space* shall be 36 inches (915 mm) wide minimum Where two adjacent *wheelchair spaces* are provided, each *wheelchair space* shall be 33 inches (840 mm) wide minimum.

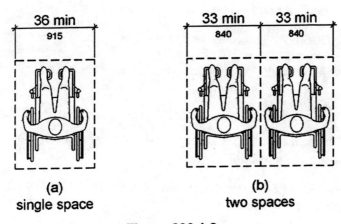

Figure 802.1.2
Width of Wheelchair Spaces

802.1.3 Depth. Where a *wheelchair space* can be entered from the front or rear, the *wheelchair space* shall be 48 inches (1220 mm) deep minimum. Where a *wheelchair space* can be entered only from the side, the *wheelchair space* shall be 60 inches (1525 mm) deep minimum.

239

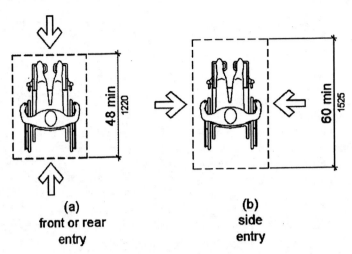

Figure 802.1.3
Depth of Wheelchair Spaces

802.1.4 Approach. *Wheelchair spaces* shall adjoin *accessible* routes. *Accessible* routes shall not overlap *wheelchair spaces*.

> **Advisory 802.1.4 Approach.** Because accessible routes serving wheelchair spaces are not permitted to overlap the clear floor space at wheelchair spaces, access to any wheelchair space cannot be through another wheelchair space.

802.1.5 Overlap. *Wheelchair spaces* shall not overlap *circulation paths*.

> **Advisory 802.1.5 Overlap.** The term "circulation paths" used in Section 802.1.5 means aisle width required by applicable building or life safety codes for the specific assembly occupancy. Where the circulation path provided is wider than the required aisle width, the wheelchair space may intrude into that portion of the circulation path that is provided in excess of the required aisle width.

802.2 Lines of Sight. Lines of sight to the screen, performance area, or playing field for spectators in *wheelchair spaces* shall comply with 802.2.

802.2.1 Lines of Sight Over Seated Spectators. Where spectators are expected to remain seated during events, spectators in *wheelchair spaces* shall be afforded lines of sight complying with 802.2.1.

802.2.1.1 Lines of Sight Over Heads. Where spectators are provided lines of sight over the heads of spectators seated in the first row in front of their seats, spectators seated in *wheelchair spaces* shall be afforded lines of sight over the heads of seated spectators in the first row in front of *wheelchair spaces*.

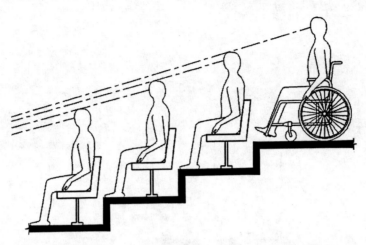

Figure 802.2.1.1
Lines of Sight Over the Heads of Seated Spectators

802.2.1.2 Lines of Sight Between Heads. Where spectators are provided lines of sight over the shoulders and between the heads of spectators seated in the first row in front of their seats, spectators seated in *wheelchair spaces* shall be afforded lines of sight over the shoulders and between the heads of seated spectators in the first row in front of *wheelchair spaces*.

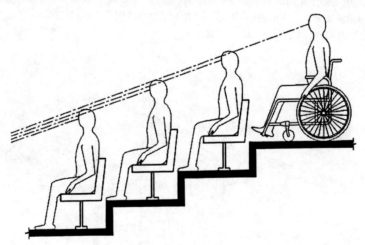

Figure 802.2.1.2
Lines of Sight Between the Heads of Seated Spectators

802.2.2 Lines of Sight Over Standing Spectators. Where spectators are expected to stand during events, spectators in *wheelchair spaces* shall be afforded lines of sight complying with 802.2.2.

802.2.2.1 Lines of Sight Over Heads. Where standing spectators are provided lines of sight over the heads of spectators standing in the first row in front of their seats, spectators seated in *wheelchair spaces* shall be afforded lines of sight over the heads of standing spectators in the first row in front of *wheelchair spaces*.

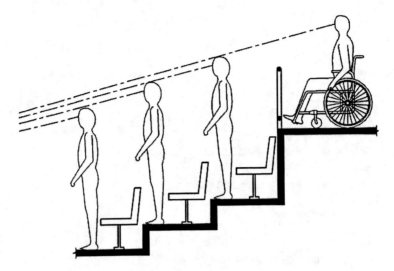

Figure 802.2.2.1
Lines of Sight Over the Heads of Standing Spectators

802.2.2.2 Lines of Sight Between Heads. Where standing spectators are provided lines of sight over the shoulders and between the heads of spectators standing in the first row in front of their seats, spectators seated in *wheelchair spaces* shall be afforded lines of sight over the shoulders and between the heads of standing spectators in the first row in front of *wheelchair spaces*.

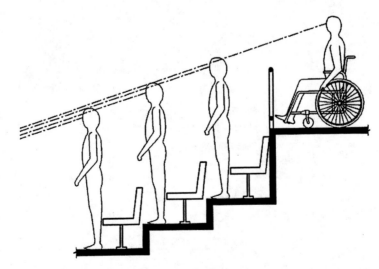

Figure 802.2.2.2
Lines of Sight Between the Heads of Standing Spectators

802.3 Companion Seats. Companion seats shall comply with 802.3.

802.3.1 Alignment. In row seating, companion seats shall be located to provide shoulder alignment with adjacent *wheelchair spaces*. The shoulder alignment point of the *wheelchair space* shall be measured 36 inches (915 mm) from the front of the *wheelchair space*. The floor surface of the companion seat shall be at the same elevation as the floor surface of the *wheelchair space*.

802.3.2 Type. Companion seats shall be equivalent in size, quality, comfort, and amenities to the seating in the immediate area. Companion seats shall be permitted to be movable.

802.4 Designated Aisle Seats. Designated aisle seats shall comply with 802.4.

802.4.1 Armrests. Where armrests are provided on the seating in the immediate area, folding or retractable armrests shall be provided on the aisle side of the seat.

802.4.2 Identification. Each designated aisle seat shall be identified by a sign or marker.

> **Advisory 802.4.2 Identification.** Seats with folding or retractable armrests are intended for use by individuals who have difficulty walking. Consider identifying such seats with signs that contrast (light-on-dark or dark-on-light) and that are also photo luminescent.

803 Dressing, Fitting, and Locker Rooms

803.1 General. Dressing, fitting, and locker rooms shall comply with 803.

> **Advisory 803.1 General.** Partitions and doors should be designed to ensure people using accessible dressing and fitting rooms privacy equivalent to that afforded other users of the facility. Section 903.5 requires dressing room bench seats to be installed so that they are at the same height as a typical wheelchair seat, 17 inches (430 mm) to 19 inches (485 mm). However, wheelchair seats can be lower than dressing room benches for people of short stature or children using wheelchairs.

803.2 Turning Space. Turning *space* complying with 304 shall be provided within the room.

803.3 Door Swing. Doors shall not swing into the room unless a clear floor or ground *space* complying with 305.3 is provided beyond the arc of the door swing.

803.4 Benches. A bench complying with 903 shall be provided within the room.

803.5 Coat Hooks and Shelves. Coat hooks provided within the room shall be located within one of the reach ranges specified in 308. Shelves shall be 40 inches (1015 mm) minimum and 48 inches (1220 mm) maximum above the finish floor or ground.

804 Kitchens and Kitchenettes

804.1 General. Kitchens and kitchenettes shall comply with 804.

804.2 Clearance. Where a pass through kitchen is provided, clearances shall comply with 804.2.1. Where a U-shaped kitchen is provided, clearances shall comply with 804.2.2.

　　EXCEPTION: *Spaces* that do not provide a cooktop or conventional range shall not be required to comply with 804.2.

> **Advisory 804.2 Clearance.** Clearances are measured from the furthest projecting face of all opposing base cabinets, counter tops, appliances, or walls, excluding hardware.

804.2.1 Pass Through Kitchen. In pass through kitchens where counters, appliances or cabinets are on two opposing sides, or where counters, appliances or cabinets are opposite a parallel wall, clearance between all opposing base cabinets, counter tops, appliances, or walls within kitchen work areas shall be 40 inches (1015 mm) minimum. Pass through kitchens shall have two entries.

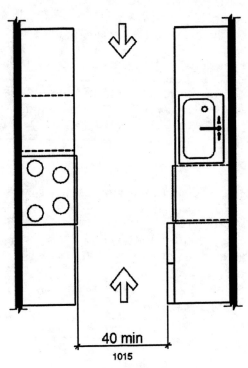

40 min
1015

Figure 804.2.1
Pass Through Kitchens

804.2.2 U-Shaped. In U-shaped kitchens enclosed on three contiguous sides, clearance between all opposing base cabinets, counter tops, appliances, or walls within kitchen work areas shall be 60 inches (1525 mm) minimum.

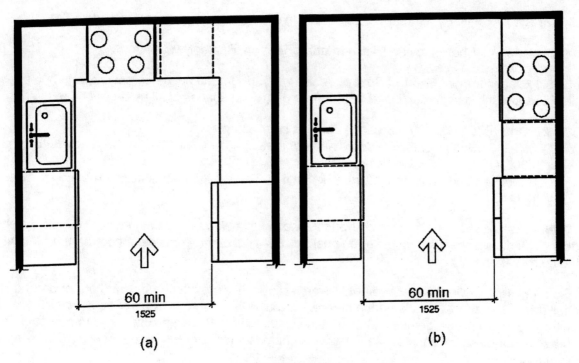

Figure 804.2.2
U-Shaped Kitchens

804.3 Kitchen Work Surface. In *residential dwelling units* required to comply with 809, at least one 30 inches (760 mm) wide minimum section of counter shall provide a kitchen work surface that complies with 804.3.

> **804.3.1 Clear Floor or Ground Space.** A clear floor *space* complying with 305 positioned for a forward approach shall be provided. The clear floor or ground *space* shall be centered on the kitchen work surface and shall provide knee and toe clearance complying with 306.
>   **EXCEPTION:** Cabinetry shall be permitted under the kitchen work surface provided that all of the following conditions are met:
>   (a) the cabinetry can be removed without removal or replacement of the kitchen work surface;
>   (b) the finish floor extends under the cabinetry; and
>   (c) the walls behind and surrounding the cabinetry are finished.

804.3.2 Height. The kitchen work surface shall be 34 inches (865 mm) maximum above the finish floor or ground.
>   **EXCEPTION:** A counter that is adjustable to provide a kitchen work surface at variable heights, 29 inches (735 mm) minimum and 36 inches (915 mm) maximum, shall be permitted.

804.3.3 Exposed Surfaces. There shall be no sharp or abrasive surfaces under the work surface counters.

804.4 Sinks. Sinks shall comply with 606.

804.5 Storage. At least 50 percent of shelf *space* in storage *facilities* shall comply with 811.

804.6 Appliances. Where provided, kitchen appliances shall comply with 804.6.

804.6.1 Clear Floor or Ground Space. A clear floor or ground *space* complying with 305 shall be provided at each kitchen appliance. Clear floor or ground *spaces* shall be permitted to overlap.

804.6.2 Operable Parts. All appliance controls shall comply with 309.
EXCEPTIONS: 1. Appliance doors and door latching devices shall not be required to comply with 309.4.
2. Bottom-hinged appliance doors, when in the open position, shall not be required to comply with 309.3.

804.6.3 Dishwasher. Clear floor or ground *space* shall be positioned adjacent to the dishwasher door. The dishwasher door, in the open position, shall not obstruct the clear floor or ground *space* for the dishwasher or the sink.

804.6.4 Range or Cooktop. Where a forward approach is provided, the clear floor or ground *space* shall provide knee and toe clearance complying with 306. Where knee and toe *space* is provided, the underside of the range or cooktop shall be insulated or otherwise configured to prevent burns, abrasions, or electrical shock. The location of controls shall not require reaching across burners.

804.6.5 Oven. Ovens shall comply with 804.6.5.

804.6.5.1 Side-Hinged Door Ovens. Side-hinged door ovens shall have the work surface required by 804.3 positioned adjacent to the latch side of the oven door.

804.6.5.2 Bottom-Hinged Door Ovens. Bottom-hinged door ovens shall have the work surface required by 804.3 positioned adjacent to one side of the door.

804.6.5.3 Controls. Ovens shall have controls on front panels.

804.6.6 Refrigerator/Freezer. Combination refrigerators and freezers shall have at least 50 percent of the freezer *space* 54 inches (1370 mm) maximum above the finish floor or ground. The clear floor or ground *space* shall be positioned for a parallel approach to the *space* dedicated to a refrigerator/ freezer with the centerline of the clear floor or ground *space* offset 24 inches (610 mm) maximum from the centerline of the dedicated *space*.

805 Medical Care and Long-Term Care Facilities

805.1 General. Medical care *facility* and long-term care *facility* patient or resident sleeping rooms required to provide mobility features shall comply with 805.

805.2 Turning Space. Turning *space* complying with 304 shall be provided within the room.

805.3 Clear Floor or Ground Space. A clear floor *space* complying with 305 shall be provided on each side of the bed. The clear floor *space* shall be positioned for parallel approach to the side of the bed.

805.4 Toilet and Bathing Rooms. Toilet and bathing rooms that are provided as part of a patient or resident sleeping room shall comply with 603. Where provided, no fewer than one water closet, one lavatory, and one bathtub or shower shall comply with the applicable requirements of 603 through 610.

806 Transient Lodging Guest Rooms

806.1 General. *Transient lodging* guest rooms shall comply with 806. Guest rooms required to provide mobility features shall comply with 806.2. Guest rooms required to provide communication features shall comply with 806.3.

806.2 Guest Rooms with Mobility Features. Guest rooms required to provide mobility features shall comply with 806.2.

> **Advisory 806.2 Guest Rooms.** The requirements in Section 806.2 do not include requirements that are common to all accessible spaces. For example, closets in guest rooms must comply with the applicable provisions for storage specified in scoping.

806.2.1 Living and Dining Areas. Living and dining areas shall be *accessible*.

806.2.2 Exterior Spaces. Exterior *spaces*, including patios, terraces and balconies, that serve the guest room shall be *accessible*.

806.2.3 Sleeping Areas. At least one sleeping area shall provide a clear floor *space* complying with 305 on both sides of a bed. The clear floor *space* shall be positioned for parallel approach to the side of the bed.
　　EXCEPTION: Where a single clear floor *space* complying with 305 positioned for parallel approach is provided between two beds, a clear floor or ground space shall not be required on both sides of a bed.

806.2.4 Toilet and Bathing Facilities. No fewer than one water closet, one lavatory, and one bathtub or shower shall comply with 603. In addition, required roll-in shower compartments shall comply with 608.2.2 or 608.2.3.

806.2.4.1 Vanity Counter Top Space. If vanity counter top *space* is provided in non-*accessible* guest toilet or bathing rooms, comparable vanity counter top *space*, in terms of size and proximity to the lavatory, shall also be provided in *accessible* guest toilet or bathing rooms.

> **Advisory 806.2.4.1 Vanity Counter Top Space.** This provision is intended to ensure that accessible guest rooms are provided with comparable vanity counter top space.

806.2.5 Kitchens and Kitchenettes. Kitchens and kitchenettes shall comply with 804.

806.2.6 Turning Space. Turning *space* complying with 304 shall be provided within the guest room.

806.3 Guest Rooms with Communication Features. Guest rooms required to provide communication features shall comply with 806.3.

> **Advisory 806.3 Guest Rooms with Communication Features.** In guest rooms required to have accessible communication features, consider ensuring compatibility with adaptive equipment used by people with hearing impairments. To ensure communication within the facility, as well as on commercial lines, provide telephone interface jacks that are compatible with both digital and analog signal use. If an audio headphone jack is provided on a speaker phone, a cutoff switch can be included in the jack so that insertion of the jack cuts off the speaker. If a telephone-like handset is used, the external speakers can be turned off when the handset is removed from the cradle. For headset or external amplification system compatibility, a standard subminiature jack installed in the telephone will provide the most flexibility.

806.3.1 Alarms. Where emergency warning systems are provided, alarms complying with 702 shall be provided.

806.3.2 Notification Devices. Visible notification devices shall be provided to alert room occupants of incoming telephone calls and a door knock or bell. Notification devices shall not be connected to visible alarm signal appliances. Telephones shall have volume controls compatible with the telephone system and shall comply with 704.3. Telephones shall be served by an electrical outlet complying with 309 located within 48 inches (1220 mm) of the telephone to facilitate the use of a *TTY*.

807 Holding Cells and Housing Cells

807.1 General. Holding cells and housing cells shall comply with 807.

807.2 Cells with Mobility Features. Cells required to provide mobility features shall comply with 807.2.

807.2.1 Turning Space. Turning *space* complying with 304 shall be provided within the cell.

807.2.2 Benches. Where benches are provided, at least one bench shall comply with 903.

807.2.3 Beds. Where beds are provided, clear floor *space* complying with 305 shall be provided on at least one side of the bed. The clear floor *space* shall be positioned for parallel approach to the side of the bed.

807.2.4 Toilet and Bathing Facilities. Toilet *facilities* or bathing *facilities* that are provided as part of a cell shall comply with 603. Where provided, no fewer than one water closet, one lavatory, and one bathtub or shower shall comply with the applicable requirements of 603 through 610.

> **Advisory 807.2.4 Toilet and Bathing Facilities.** In holding cells, housing cells, or rooms required to be accessible, these requirements do not require a separate toilet room.

807.3 Cells with Communication Features. Cells required to provide communication features shall comply with 807.3.

807.3.1 Alarms. Where audible emergency alarm systems are provided to serve the occupants of cells, visible alarms complying with 702 shall be provided.
EXCEPTION: Visible alarms shall not be required where inmates or detainees are not allowed independent means of egress.

807.3.2 Telephones. Telephones, where provided within cells, shall have volume controls complying with 704.3.

808 Courtrooms

808.1 General. Courtrooms shall comply with 808.

808.2 Turning Space. Where provided, areas that are raised or depressed and accessed by *ramps* or platform lifts with entry *ramps* shall provide unobstructed turning *space* complying with 304.

808.3 Clear Floor Space. Each jury box and witness stand shall have, within its defined area, clear floor *space* complying with 305.
EXCEPTION: In *alterations, wheelchair spaces* are not required to be located within the defined area of raised jury boxes or witness stands and shall be permitted to be located outside these *spaces* where *ramp* or platform lift access poses a hazard by restricting or projecting into a means of egress required by the appropriate *administrative authority*.

808.4 Judges' Benches and Courtroom Stations. Judges' benches, clerks' stations, bailiffs' stations, deputy clerks' stations, court reporters' stations and litigants' and counsel stations shall comply with 902.

809 Residential Dwelling Units

809.1 General. *Residential dwelling units* shall comply with 809. *Residential dwelling units* required to provide mobility features shall comply with 809.2 through 809.4. *Residential dwelling units* required to provide communication features shall comply with 809.5.

809.2 Accessible Routes. *Accessible* routes complying with Chapter 4 shall be provided within *residential dwelling units* in accordance with 809.2.
EXCEPTION: *Accessible* routes shall not be required to or within unfinished attics or unfinished basements.

809.2.1 Location. At least one *accessible* route shall connect all *spaces* and *elements* which are a part of the *residential dwelling unit*. Where only one *accessible* route is provided, it shall not pass through bathrooms, closets, or similar *spaces*.

809.2.2 Turning Space. All rooms served by an *accessible* route shall provide a turning *space* complying with 304.

EXCEPTION: Turning *space* shall not be required in exterior *spaces* 30 inches (760 mm) maximum in depth or width.

> **Advisory 809.2.2 Turning Space.** It is generally acceptable to use required clearances to provide wheelchair turning space. For example, in kitchens, 804.3.1 requires at least one work surface with clear floor space complying with 306 to be centered beneath. If designers elect to provide clear floor space that is at least 36 inches (915 mm) wide, as opposed to the required 30 inches (760 mm) wide, that clearance can be part of a T-turn, thereby maximizing efficient use of the kitchen area. However, the overlap of turning space must be limited to one segment of the T-turn so that back-up maneuvering is not restricted. It would, therefore, be unacceptable to use both the clearances under the work surface and the sink as part of a T-turn. See Section 304.3.2 regarding T-turns.

809.3 Kitchen. Where a kitchen is provided, it shall comply with 804.

809.4 Toilet Facilities and Bathing Facilities. At least one toilet *facility* and bathing *facility* shall comply with 603 through 610. At least one of each type of fixture provided shall comply with applicable requirements of 603 through 610. Toilet and bathing fixtures required to comply with 603 through 610 shall be located in the same toilet and bathing area, such that travel between fixtures does not require travel between other parts of the *residential dwelling unit*.

> **Advisory 809.4 Toilet Facilities and Bathing Facilities.** All toilet rooms and bathing rooms in accessible residential dwelling units must be accessible. In addition, at least one of each type of fixture in accessible toilet rooms and bathing rooms must be accessible.
>
> In an effort to promote space efficiency, vanity counter top space in accessible residential dwelling units is often omitted. This omission does not promote equal access or equal enjoyment of the unit. Where comparable units have vanity counter tops, accessible units should also have vanity counter tops located as close as possible to the lavatory for convenient access to toiletries.

809.5 Residential Dwelling Units with Communication Features. *Residential dwelling units* required to provide communication features shall comply with 809.5.

809.5.1 Building Fire Alarm System. Where a *building* fire alarm system is provided, the system wiring shall be extended to a point within the *residential dwelling unit* in the vicinity of the *residential dwelling unit* smoke detection system.

809.5.1.1 Alarm Appliances. Where alarm appliances are provided within a *residential dwelling unit* as part of the *building* fire alarm system, they shall comply with 702.

809.5.1.2 Activation. All visible alarm appliances provided within the *residential dwelling unit* for *building* fire alarm notification shall be activated upon activation of the *building* fire alarm in the portion of the *building* containing the *residential dwelling unit*.

250

809.5.2 Residential Dwelling Unit Smoke Detection System. *Residential dwelling unit* smoke detection systems shall comply with NFPA 72 (1999 or 2002 edition) (incorporated by reference, see "Referenced Standards" in Chapter 1).

809.5.2.2 Activation. All visible alarm appliances provided within the *residential dwelling unit* for smoke detection notification shall be activated upon smoke detection.

809.5.3 Interconnection. The same visible alarm appliances shall be permitted to provide notification of *residential dwelling unit* smoke detection and *building* fire alarm activation.

809.5.4 Prohibited Use. Visible alarm appliances used to indicate *residential dwelling unit* smoke detection or *building* fire alarm activation shall not be used for any other purpose within the *residential dwelling unit*.

809.5.5 Residential Dwelling Unit Primary Entrance. Communication features shall be provided at the *residential dwelling unit* primary *entrance* complying with 809.5.5.

809.5.5.1 Notification. A hard-wired electric doorbell shall be provided. A button or switch shall be provided outside the *residential dwelling unit* primary *entrance*. Activation of the button or switch shall initiate an audible tone and visible signal within the *residential dwelling unit*. Where visible doorbell signals are located in sleeping areas, they shall have controls to deactivate the signal.

809.5.5.2 Identification. A means for visually identifying a visitor without opening the *residential dwelling unit* entry door shall be provided and shall allow for a minimum 180 degree range of view.

> **Advisory 809.5.5.2 Identification.** In doors, peepholes that include prisms clarify the image and should offer a wide-angle view of the hallway or exterior for both standing persons and wheelchair users. Such peepholes can be placed at a standard height and permit a view from several feet from the door.

809.5.6 Site, Building, or Floor Entrance. Where a system, including a closed-circuit system, permitting voice communication between a visitor and the occupant of the *residential dwelling unit* is provided, the system shall comply with 708.4.

810 Transportation Facilities

810.1 General. Transportation *facilities* shall comply with 810.

810.2 Bus Boarding and Alighting Areas. Bus boarding and alighting areas shall comply with 810.2.

> **Advisory 810.2 Bus Boarding and Alighting Areas.** At bus stops where a shelter is provided, the bus stop pad can be located either within or outside of the shelter.

810.2.1 Surface. Bus stop boarding and alighting areas shall have a firm, stable surface.

810.2.2 Dimensions. Bus stop boarding and alighting areas shall provide a clear length of 96 inches (2440 mm) minimum, measured perpendicular to the curb or vehicle roadway edge, and a clear width of 60 inches (1525 mm) minimum, measured parallel to the vehicle roadway.

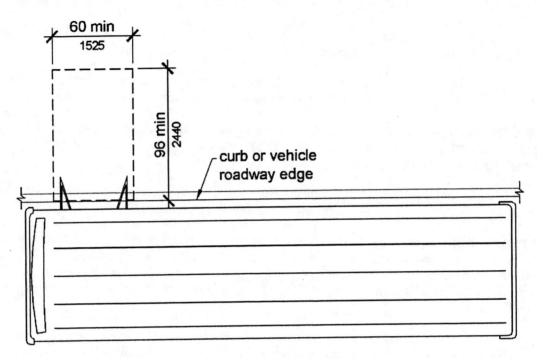

Figure 810.2.2
Dimensions of Bus Boarding and Alighting Areas

810.2.3 Connection. Bus stop boarding and alighting areas shall be connected to streets, sidewalks, or pedestrian paths by an *accessible* route complying with 402.

810.2.4 Slope. Parallel to the roadway, the slope of the bus stop boarding and alighting area shall be the same as the roadway, to the maximum extent practicable. Perpendicular to the roadway, the slope of the bus stop boarding and alighting area shall not be steeper than1:48.

810.3 Bus Shelters. Bus shelters shall provide a minimum clear floor or ground *space* complying with 305 entirely within the shelter. Bus shelters shall be connected by an *accessible* route complying with 402 to a boarding and alighting area complying with 810.2.

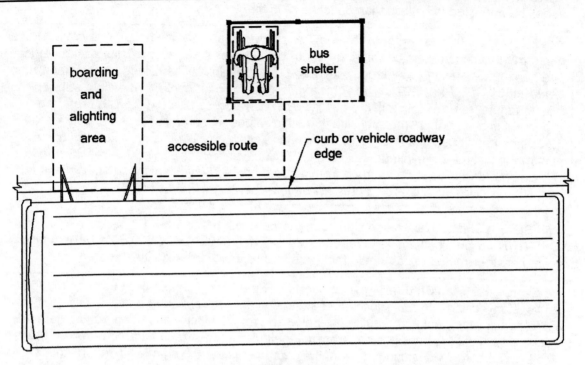

Figure 810.3
Bus Shelters

810.4 Bus Signs. Bus route identification signs shall comply with 703.5.1 through 703.5.4, and 703.5.7 and 703.5.8. In addition, to the maximum extent practicable, bus route identification signs shall comply with 703.5.5.

    EXCEPTION: Bus schedules, timetables and maps that are posted at the bus stop or bus bay shall not be required to comply.

810.5 Rail Platforms. Rail platforms shall comply with 810.5.

    810.5.1 Slope. Rail platforms shall not exceed a slope of 1:48 in all directions.
        EXCEPTION: Where platforms serve vehicles operating on existing track or track laid in existing roadway, the slope of the platform parallel to the track shall be permitted to be equal to the slope (grade) of the roadway or existing track.

    810.5.2 Detectable Warnings. Platform boarding edges not protected by platform screens or guards shall have *detectable warnings* complying with 705 along the full length of the *public use* area of the platform.

    810.5.3 Platform and Vehicle Floor Coordination. Station platforms shall be positioned to coordinate with vehicles in accordance with the applicable requirements of 36 CFR Part 1192. Low-level platforms shall be 8 inches (205 mm) minimum above top of rail.

EXCEPTION: Where vehicles are boarded from sidewalks or street-level, low-level platforms shall be permitted to be less than 8 inches (205 mm).

> **Advisory 810.5.3 Platform and Vehicle Floor Coordination.** The height and position of a platform must be coordinated with the floor of the vehicles it serves to minimize the vertical and horizontal gaps, in accordance with the ADA Accessibility Guidelines for Transportation Vehicles (36 CFR Part 1192). The vehicle guidelines, divided by bus, van, light rail, rapid rail, commuter rail, intercity rail, are available at www.access-board.gov. The preferred alignment is a high platform, level with the vehicle floor. In some cases, the vehicle guidelines permit use of a low platform in conjunction with a lift or ramp. Most such low platforms must have a minimum height of eight inches above the top of the rail. Some vehicles are designed to be boarded from a street or the sidewalk along the street and the exception permits such boarding areas to be less than eight inches high.

810.6 Rail Station Signs. Rail station signs shall comply with 810.6.
EXCEPTION. Signs shall not be required to comply with 810.6.1 and 810.6.2 where audible signs are remotely transmitted to hand-held receivers, or are user- or proximity-actuated.

> **Advisory 810.6 Rail Station Signs Exception.** Emerging technologies such as an audible sign systems using infrared transmitters and receivers may provide greater accessibility in the transit environment than traditional Braille and raised letter signs. The transmitters are placed on or next to print signs and transmit their information to an infrared receiver that is held by a person. By scanning an area, the person will hear the sign. This means that signs can be placed well out of reach of Braille readers, even on parapet walls and on walls beyond barriers. Additionally, such signs can be used to provide wayfinding information that cannot be efficiently conveyed on Braille signs.

810.6.1 Entrances. Where signs identify a station or its *entrance*, at least one sign at each *entrance* shall comply with 703.2 and shall be placed in uniform locations to the maximum extent practicable. Where signs identify a station that has no defined *entrance*, at least one sign shall comply with 703.2 and shall be placed in a central location.

810.6.2 Routes and Destinations. Lists of stations, routes and destinations served by the station which are located on boarding areas, platforms, or *mezzanines* shall comply with 703.5. At least one *tactile* sign identifying the specific station and complying with 703.2 shall be provided on each platform or boarding area. Signs covered by this requirement shall, to the maximum extent practicable, be placed in uniform locations within the system.
EXCEPTION: Where sign *space* is limited, *characters* shall not be required to exceed 3 inches (75 mm).

> **Advisory 810.6.2 Routes and Destinations.** Route maps are not required to comply with the informational sign requirements in this document.

810.6.3 Station Names. Stations covered by this section shall have identification signs complying with 703.5. Signs shall be clearly visible and within the sight lines of standing and sitting passengers from within the vehicle on both sides when not obstructed by another vehicle.

> **Advisory 810.6.3 Station Names.** It is also important to place signs at intervals in the station where passengers in the vehicle will be able to see a sign when the vehicle is either stopped at the station or about to come to a stop in the station. The number of signs necessary may be directly related to the size of the lettering displayed on the sign.

810.7 Public Address Systems. Where public address systems convey audible information to the public, the same or equivalent information shall be provided in a visual format.

810.8 Clocks. Where clocks are provided for use by the public, the clock face shall be uncluttered so that its *elements* are clearly visible. Hands, numerals and digits shall contrast with the background either light-on-dark or dark-on-light. Where clocks are installed overhead, numerals and digits shall comply with 703.5.

810.9 Escalators. Where provided, escalators shall comply with the sections 6.1.3.5.6 and 6.1.3.6.5 of ASME A17.1 (incorporated by reference, see "Referenced Standards" in Chapter 1) and shall have a clear width of 32 inches (815 mm) minimum.
    EXCEPTION: Existing escalators in *key stations* shall not be required to comply with 810.9.

810.10 Track Crossings. Where a *circulation path* serving boarding platforms crosses tracks, it shall comply with 402.
    EXCEPTION: Openings for wheel flanges shall be permitted to be 2½ inches (64 mm) maximum.

Figure 810.10 (Exception)
Track Crossings

811 Storage

811.1 General. Storage shall comply with 811.

811.2 Clear Floor or Ground Space. A clear floor or ground *space* complying with 305 shall be provided.

811.3 Height. Storage *elements* shall comply with at least one of the reach ranges specified in 308.

811.4 Operable Parts. *Operable parts* shall comply with 309.

CHAPTER 9: BUILT-IN ELEMENTS

901 General

901.1 Scope. The provisions of Chapter 9 shall apply where required by Chapter 2 or where referenced by a requirement in this document.

902 Dining Surfaces and Work Surfaces

902.1 General. Dining surfaces and work surfaces shall comply with 902.2 and 902.3.
   EXCEPTION: Dining surfaces and work surfaces for *children's use* shall be permitted to comply with 902.4.

> **Advisory 902.1 General.** Dining surfaces include, but are not limited to, bars, tables, lunch counters, and booths. Examples of work surfaces include writing surfaces, study carrels, student laboratory stations, baby changing and other tables or fixtures for personal grooming, coupon counters, and where covered by the ABA scoping provisions, employee work stations.

902.2 Clear Floor or Ground Space. A clear floor *space* complying with 305 positioned for a forward approach shall be provided. Knee and toe clearance complying with 306 shall be provided.

902.3 Height. The tops of dining surfaces and work surfaces shall be 28 inches (710 mm) minimum and 34 inches (865 mm) maximum above the finish floor or ground.

902.4 Dining Surfaces and Work Surfaces for Children's Use. *Accessible* dining surfaces and work surfaces for *children's use* shall comply with 902.4.
   EXCEPTION: Dining surfaces and work surfaces that are used primarily by children 5 years and younger shall not be required to comply with 902.4 where a clear floor or ground *space* complying with 305 positioned for a parallel approach is provided.

902.4.1 Clear Floor or Ground Space. A clear floor *space* complying with 305 positioned for forward approach shall be provided. Knee and toe clearance complying with 306 shall be provided, except that knee clearance 24 inches (610 mm) minimum above the finish floor or ground shall be permitted.

902.4.2 Height. The tops of tables and counters shall be 26 inches (660 mm) minimum and 30 inches (760 mm) maximum above the finish floor or ground.

903 Benches

903.1 General. Benches shall comply with 903.

903.2 Clear Floor or Ground Space. Clear floor or ground *space* complying with 305 shall be provided and shall be positioned at the end of the bench seat and parallel to the short axis of the bench.

903.3 Size. Benches shall have seats that are 42 inches (1065 mm) long minimum and 20 inches (510 mm) deep minimum and 24 inches (610 mm) deep maximum.

903.4 Back Support. The bench shall provide for back support or shall be affixed to a wall. Back support shall be 42 inches (1065 mm) long minimum and shall extend from a point 2 inches (51 mm) maximum above the seat surface to a point 18 inches (455 mm) minimum above the seat surface. Back support shall be 2½ inches (64 mm) maximum from the rear edge of the seat measured horizontally.

> **Advisory 903.4 Back Support.** To assist in transferring to the bench, consider providing grab bars on a wall adjacent to the bench, but not on the seat back. If provided, grab bars cannot obstruct transfer to the bench.

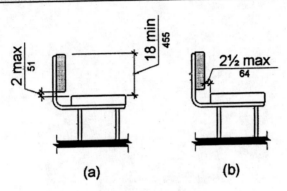

(a)   (b)

**Figure 903.4
Bench Back Support**

903.5 Height. The top of the bench seat surface shall be 17 inches (430 mm) minimum and 19 inches (485 mm) maximum above the finish floor or ground.

903.6 Structural Strength. Allowable stresses shall not be exceeded for materials used when a vertical or horizontal force of 250 pounds (1112 N) is applied at any point on the seat, fastener, mounting device, or supporting structure.

903.7 Wet Locations. Where installed in wet locations, the surface of the seat shall be slip resistant and shall not accumulate water.

904 Check-Out Aisles and Sales and Service Counters

904.1 General. Check-out aisles and sales and service counters shall comply with the applicable requirements of 904.

904.2 Approach. All portions of counters required to comply with 904 shall be located adjacent to a walking surface complying with 403.

Advisory 904.2 Approach. If a cash register is provided at the sales or service counter, locate the accessible counter close to the cash register so that a person using a wheelchair is visible to sales or service personnel and to minimize the reach for a person with a disability.

904.3 Check-Out Aisles. Check-out aisles shall comply with 904.3.

904.3.1 Aisle. Aisles shall comply with 403.

904.3.2 Counter. The counter surface height shall be 38 inches (965 mm) maximum above the finish floor or ground. The top of the counter edge protection shall be 2 inches (51 mm) maximum above the top of the counter surface on the aisle side of the check-out counter.

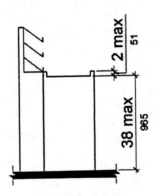

**Figure 904.3.2
Check-Out Aisle Counters**

904.3.3 Check Writing Surfaces. Where provided, check writing surfaces shall comply with 902.3.

904.4 Sales and Service Counters. Sales counters and service counters shall comply with 904.4.1 or 904.4.2. The *accessible* portion of the counter top shall extend the same depth as the sales or service counter top.
EXCEPTION: In *alterations*, when the provision of a counter complying with 904.4 would result in a reduction of the number of existing counters at work stations or a reduction of the number of existing *mail boxes*, the counter shall be permitted to have a portion which is 24 inches (610 mm) long minimum complying with 904.4.1 provided that the required clear floor or ground *space* is centered on the *accessible* length of the counter.

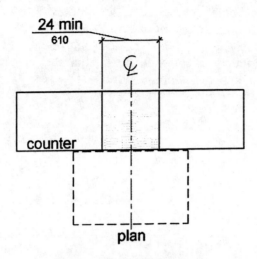

24 min
610

counter

plan

Figure 904.4 (Exception)
Alteration of Sales and Service Counters

904.4.1 Parallel Approach. A portion of the counter surface that is 36 inches (915 mm) long minimum and 36 inches (915 mm) high maximum above the finish floor shall be provided. A clear floor or ground *space* complying with 305 shall be positioned for a parallel approach adjacent to the 36 inch (915 mm) minimum length of counter.

EXCEPTION: Where the provided counter surface is less than 36 inches (915 mm) long, the entire counter surface shall be 36 inches (915 mm) high maximum above the finish floor.

904.4.2 Forward Approach. A portion of the counter surface that is 30 inches (760 mm) long minimum and 36 inches (915 mm) high maximum shall be provided. Knee and toe *space* complying with 306 shall be provided under the counter. A clear floor or ground *space* complying with 305 shall be positioned for a forward approach to the counter.

904.5 Food Service Lines. Counters in food service lines shall comply with 904.5.

904.5.1 Self-Service Shelves and Dispensing Devices. Self-service shelves and dispensing devices for tableware, dishware, condiments, food and beverages shall comply with 308.

904.5.2 Tray Slides. The tops of tray slides shall be 28 inches (710 mm) minimum and 34 inches (865 mm) maximum above the finish floor or ground.

904.6 Security Glazing. Where counters or teller windows have security glazing to separate personnel from the public, a method to facilitate voice communication shall be provided. Telephone handset devices, if provided, shall comply with 704.3.

Advisory 904.6 Security Glazing. Assistive listening devices complying with 706 can facilitate voice communication at counters or teller windows where there is security glazing which promotes distortion in audible information. Where assistive listening devices are installed, place signs complying with 703.7.2.4 to identify those facilities which are so equipped. Other voice communication methods include, but are not limited to, grilles, slats, talk-through baffles, intercoms, or telephone handset devices.

CHAPTER 10: RECREATION FACILITIES

1001 General

1001.1 Scope. The provisions of Chapter 10 shall apply where required by Chapter 2 or where referenced by a requirement in this document.

> **Advisory 1001.1 Scope.** Unless otherwise modified or specifically addressed in Chapter 10, all other ADAAG provisions apply to the design and construction of recreation facilities and elements. The provisions in Section 1001.1 apply wherever these elements are provided. For example, office buildings may contain a room with exercise equipment to which these sections would apply.

1002 Amusement Rides

1002.1 General. *Amusement rides* shall comply with 1002.

1002.2 Accessible Routes. *Accessible* routes serving *amusement rides* shall comply with Chapter 4.
EXCEPTIONS: 1. In load or unload areas and on *amusement rides*, where compliance with 405.2 is not structurally or operationally feasible, *ramp* slope shall be permitted to be 1:8 maximum.
2. In load or unload areas and on *amusement rides*, handrails provided along walking surfaces complying with 403 and required on *ramps* complying with 405 shall not be required to comply with 505 where compliance is not structurally or operationally feasible.

> **Advisory 1002.2 Accessible Routes Exception 1.** Steeper slopes are permitted on accessible routes connecting the amusement ride in the load and unload position where it is "structurally or operationally infeasible." In most cases, this will be limited to areas where the accessible route leads directly to the amusement ride and where there are space limitations on the ride, not the queue line. Where possible, the least possible slope should be used on the accessible route that serves the amusement ride.

1002.3 Load and Unload Areas. A turning *space* complying with 304.2 and 304.3 shall be provided in load and unload areas.

1002.4 Wheelchair Spaces in Amusement Rides. *Wheelchair spaces* in *amusement rides* shall comply with 1002.4.

1002.4.1 Floor or Ground Surface. The floor or ground surface of *wheelchair spaces* shall be stable and firm.

1002.4.2 Slope. The floor or ground surface of *wheelchair spaces* shall have a slope not steeper than 1:48 when in the load and unload position.

1002.4.3 Gaps. Floors of *amusement rides* with *wheelchair spaces* and floors of load and unload areas shall be coordinated so that, when *amusement rides* are at rest in the load and unload

position, the vertical difference between the floors shall be within plus or minus 5/8 inches (16 mm) and the horizontal gap shall be 3 inches (75 mm) maximum under normal passenger load conditions.
EXCEPTION: Where compliance is not operationally or structurally feasible, *ramps*, bridge plates, or similar devices complying with the applicable requirements of 36 CFR 1192.83(c) shall be provided.

> **Advisory 1002.4.3 Gaps Exception.** 36 CFR 1192.83(c) ADA Accessibility Guidelines for Transportation Vehicles - Light Rail Vehicles and Systems - Mobility Aid Accessibility is available at www.access-board.gov. It includes provisions for bridge plates and ramps that can be used at gaps between wheelchair spaces and floors of load and unload areas.

1002.4.4 Clearances. Clearances for *wheelchair spaces* shall comply with 1002.4.4.
EXCEPTIONS: 1. Where provided, securement devices shall be permitted to overlap required clearances.
2. *Wheelchair spaces* shall be permitted to be mechanically or manually repositioned.
3. *Wheelchair spaces* shall not be required to comply with 307.4.

> **Advisory 1002.4.4 Clearances Exception 3.** This exception for protruding objects applies to the ride devices, not to circulation areas or accessible routes in the queue lines or the load and unload areas.

1002.4.4.1 Width and Length. *Wheelchair spaces* shall provide a clear width of 30 inches (760 mm) minimum and a clear length of 48 inches (1220 mm) minimum measured to 9 inches (230 mm) minimum above the floor surface.

1002.4.4.2 Side Entry. Where *wheelchair spaces* are entered only from the side, *amusement rides* shall be designed to permit sufficient maneuvering clearance for individuals using a wheelchair or mobility aid to enter and exit the ride.

> **Advisory 1002.4.4.2 Side Entry.** The amount of clear space needed within the ride, and the size and position of the opening are interrelated. A 32 inch (815 mm) clear opening will not provide sufficient width when entered through a turn into an amusement ride. Additional space for maneuvering and a wider door will be needed where a side opening is centered on the ride. For example, where a 42 inch (1065 mm) opening is provided, a minimum clear space of 60 inches (1525 mm) in length and 36 inches (915mm) in depth is needed to ensure adequate space for maneuvering.

1002.4.4.3 Permitted Protrusions in Wheelchair Spaces. Objects are permitted to protrude a distance of 6 inches (150 mm) maximum along the front of the *wheelchair space*, where located 9 inches (230 mm) minimum and 27 inches (685 mm) maximum above the floor or ground surface of the *wheelchair space*. Objects are permitted to protrude a distance of 25 inches (635 mm) maximum along the front of the *wheelchair space*, where located more than 27 inches (685 mm) above the floor or ground surface of the *wheelchair space*.

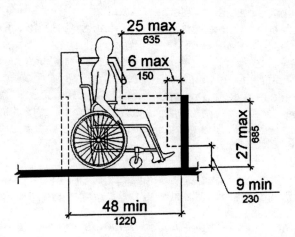

Figure 1002.4.4.3
Protrusions in Wheelchair Spaces in Amusement Rides

1002.4.5 Ride Entry. Openings providing entry to *wheelchair spaces* on *amusement rides* shall be 32 inches (815 mm) minimum clear.

1002.4.6 Approach. One side of the *wheelchair space* shall adjoin an *accessible* route when in the load and unload position.

1002.4.7 Companion Seats. Where the interior width of the *amusement ride* is greater than 53 inches (1345 mm), seating is provided for more than one rider, and the wheelchair is not required to be centered within the *amusement ride*, a companion seat shall be provided for each *wheelchair space*.

1002.4.7.1 Shoulder-to-Shoulder Seating. Where an *amusement ride* provides shoulder-to-shoulder seating, companion seats shall be shoulder-to-shoulder with the adjacent *wheelchair space*.
EXCEPTION: Where shoulder-to-shoulder companion seating is not operationally or structurally feasible, compliance with this requirement shall be required to the maximum extent practicable.

1002.5 Amusement Ride Seats Designed for Transfer. *Amusement ride seats* designed for transfer shall comply with 1002.5 when positioned for loading and unloading.

Advisory 1002.5 Amusement Ride Seats Designed for Transfer. The proximity of the clear floor or ground space next to an element and the height of the element one is transferring to are both critical for a safe and independent transfer. Providing additional clear floor or ground space both in front of and diagonal to the element will provide flexibility and will increase usability for a more diverse population of individuals with disabilities. Ride seats designed for transfer should involve only one transfer. Where possible, designers are encouraged to locate the ride seat no higher than 17 to 19 inches (430 to 485 mm) above the load and unload surface. Where greater distances are required for transfers, providing gripping surfaces, seat padding, and avoiding sharp objects in the path of transfer will facilitate the transfer.

1002.5.1 Clear Floor or Ground Space. A clear floor or ground *space* complying with 305 shall be provided in the load and unload area adjacent to the *amusement ride seats* designed for transfer.

1002.5.2 Transfer Height. The height of *amusement ride seats* designed for transfer shall be 14 inches (355 mm) minimum and 24 inches (610 mm) maximum measured from the surface of the load and unload area.

1002.5.3 Transfer Entry. Where openings are provided for transfer to *amusement ride seats*, the openings shall provide clearance for transfer from a wheelchair or mobility aid to the *amusement ride seat*.

1002.5.4 Wheelchair Storage Space. Wheelchair storage *spaces* complying with 305 shall be provided in or adjacent to unload areas for each required *amusement ride seat* designed for transfer and shall not overlap any required means of egress or *accessible* route.

1002.6 Transfer Devices for Use with Amusement Rides. *Transfer devices* for use with *amusement rides* shall comply with 1002.6 when positioned for loading and unloading.

Advisory 1002.6 Transfer Devices for Use with Amusement Rides. Transfer devices for use with amusement rides should permit individuals to make independent transfers to and from their wheelchairs or mobility devices. There are a variety of transfer devices available that could be adapted to provide access onto an amusement ride. Examples of devices that may provide for transfers include, but are not limited to, transfer systems, lifts, mechanized seats, and custom designed systems. Operators and designers have flexibility in developing designs that will facilitate individuals to transfer onto amusement rides. These systems or devices should be designed to be reliable and sturdy.

Designs that limit the number of transfers required from a wheelchair or mobility device to the ride seat are encouraged. When using a transfer device to access an amusement ride, the least number of transfers and the shortest distance is most usable. Where possible, designers are encouraged to locate the transfer device seat no higher than 17 to 19 inches (430 to 485 mm) above the load and unload surface. Where greater distances are required for transfers, providing gripping surfaces, seat padding, and avoiding sharp objects in the path of transfer will facilitate the transfer. Where a series of transfers are required to reach the amusement ride seat, each vertical transfer should not exceed 8 inches (205 mm).

1002.6.1 Clear Floor or Ground Space. A clear floor or ground *space* complying with 305 shall be provided in the load and unload area adjacent to the *transfer device*.

1002.6.2 Transfer Height. The height of *transfer device* seats shall be 14 inches (355 mm) minimum and 24 inches (610 mm) maximum measured from the load and unload surface.

1002.6.3 Wheelchair Storage Space. Wheelchair storage *spaces* complying with 305 shall be provided in or adjacent to unload areas for each required *transfer device* and shall not overlap any required means of egress or *accessible* route.

1003 Recreational Boating Facilities

1003.1 General. Recreational boating *facilities* shall comply with 1003.

1003.2 Accessible Routes. *Accessible* routes serving recreational boating *facilities*, including *gangways* and floating piers, shall comply with Chapter 4 except as modified by the exceptions in 1003.2.

1003.2.1 Boat Slips. *Accessible* routes serving *boat slips* shall be permitted to use the exceptions in 1003.2.1.

EXCEPTIONS: 1. Where an existing *gangway* or series of *gangways* is replaced or *altered*, an increase in the length of the *gangway* shall not be required to comply with 1003.2 unless required by 202.4.

2. *Gangways* shall not be required to comply with the maximum rise specified in 405.6.

3. Where the total length of a *gangway* or series of *gangways* serving as part of a required *accessible* route is 80 feet (24 m) minimum, *gangways* shall not be required to comply with 405.2.

4. Where *facilities* contain fewer than 25 *boat slips* and the total length of the *gangway* or series of *gangways* serving as part of a required *accessible* route is 30 feet (9145 mm) minimum, *gangways* shall not be required to comply with 405.2.

5. Where *gangways* connect to *transition plates*, landings specified by 405.7 shall not be required.

6. Where *gangways* and *transition plates* connect and are required to have handrails, handrail extensions shall not be required. Where handrail extensions are provided on *gangways* or *transition plates*, the handrail extensions shall not be required to be parallel with the ground or floor surface.

7. The *cross slope* specified in 403.3 and 405.3 for *gangways*, *transition plates*, and floating piers that are part of *accessible* routes shall be measured in the static position.

8. Changes in level complying with 303.3 and 303.4 shall be permitted on the surfaces of *gangways* and *boat launch ramps*.

Advisory 1003.2.1 Boat Slips Exception 3. The following example shows how exception 3 would be applied: A gangway is provided to a floating pier which is required to be on an accessible route. The vertical distance is 10 feet (3050 mm) between the elevation where the gangway departs the landside connection and the elevation of the pier surface at the lowest water level. Exception 3 permits the gangway to be 80 feet (24 m) long. Another design solution would be to have two 40 foot (12 m) plus continuous gangways joined together at a float, where the float (as the water level falls) will stop dropping at an elevation five feet below the landside connection. The length of transition plates would not be included in determining if the gangway(s) meet the requirements of the exception.

1003.2.2 Boarding Piers at Boat Launch Ramps. *Accessible* routes serving *boarding piers* at *boat launch ramps* shall be permitted to use the exceptions in 1003.2.2.

EXCEPTIONS: 1. *Accessible* routes serving floating *boarding piers* shall be permitted to use Exceptions 1, 2, 5, 6, 7 and 8 in 1003.2.1.

2. Where the total length of the *gangway* or series of *gangways* serving as part of a required *accessible* route is 30 feet (9145 mm) minimum, *gangways* shall not be required to comply with 405.2.

3. Where the *accessible* route serving a floating *boarding pier* or skid pier is located within a *boat launch ramp*, the portion of the *accessible* route located within the *boat launch ramp* shall not be required to comply with 405.

1003.3 Clearances. Clearances at *boat slips* and on *boarding piers* at *boat launch ramps* shall comply with 1003.3.

Advisory 1003.3 Clearances. Although the minimum width of the clear pier space is 60 inches (1525 mm), it is recommended that piers be wider than 60 inches (1525 mm) to improve the safety for persons with disabilities, particularly on floating piers.

1003.3.1 Boat Slip Clearance. *Boat slips* shall provide clear pier *space* 60 inches (1525 mm) wide minimum and at least as long as the *boat slips*. Each 10 feet (3050 mm) maximum of linear pier edge serving *boat slips* shall contain at least one continuous clear opening 60 inches (1525 mm) wide minimum.

EXCEPTIONS: 1. Clear pier *space* shall be permitted to be 36 inches (915 mm) wide minimum for a length of 24 inches (610 mm) maximum, provided that multiple 36 inch (915 mm) wide segments are separated by segments that are 60 inches (1525 mm) wide minimum and 60 inches (1525 mm) long minimum.

2. Edge protection shall be permitted at the continuous clear openings, provided that it is 4 inches (100 mm) high maximum and 2 inches (51 mm) wide maximum.

3. In existing piers, clear pier *space* shall be permitted to be located perpendicular to the *boat slip* and shall extend the width of the *boat slip*, where the *facility* has at least one *boat slip* complying with 1003.3, and further compliance with 1003.3 would result in a reduction in the number of *boat slips* available or result in a reduction of the widths of existing slips.

Advisory 1003.3.1 Boat Slip Clearance Exception 3. Where the conditions in exception 3 are satisfied, existing facilities are only required to have one accessible boat slip with a pier clearance which runs the length of the slip. All other accessible slips are allowed to have the required pier clearance at the head of the slip. Under this exception, at piers with perpendicular boat slips, the width of most "finger piers" will remain unchanged. However, where mooring systems for floating piers are replaced as part of pier alteration projects, an opportunity may exist for increasing accessibility. Piers may be reconfigured to allow an increase in the number of wider finger piers, and serve as accessible boat slips.

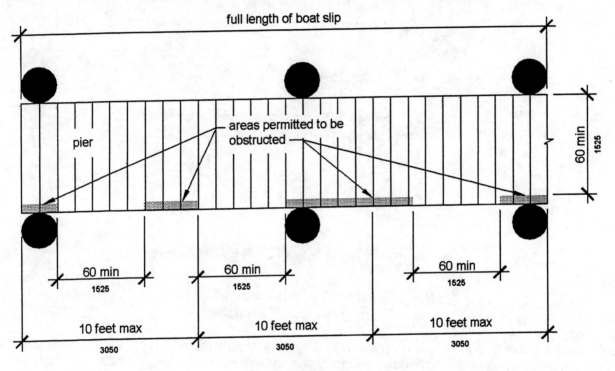

Figure 1003.3.1
Boat Slip Clearance

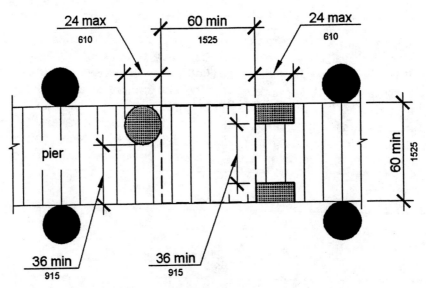

Figure 1003.3.1 (Exception 1)
Clear Pier Space Reduction at Boat Slips

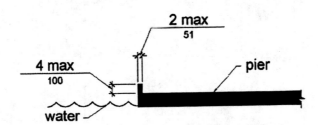

Figure 1003.3.1 (Exception 2)
Edge Protection at Boat Slips

1003.3.2 Boarding Pier Clearances. *Boarding piers* at *boat launch ramps* shall provide clear pier *space* 60 inches (1525 mm) wide minimum and shall extend the full length of the *boarding pier*. Every 10 feet (3050 mm) maximum of linear pier edge shall contain at least one continuous clear opening 60 inches (1525 mm) wide minimum.

EXCEPTIONS: 1. The clear pier *space* shall be permitted to be 36 inches (915 mm) wide minimum for a length of 24 inches (610 mm) maximum provided that multiple 36 inch (915 mm) wide segments are separated by segments that are 60 inches (1525 mm) wide minimum and 60 inches (1525 mm) long minimum.

2. Edge protection shall be permitted at the continuous clear openings provided that it is 4 inches (100 mm) high maximum and 2 inches (51 mm) wide maximum.

Advisory 1003.3.2 Boarding Pier Clearances. These requirements do not establish a minimum length for accessible boarding piers at boat launch ramps. The accessible boarding pier should have a length at least equal to that of other boarding piers provided at the facility. If no other boarding pier is provided, the pier would have a length equal to what would have been provided if no access requirements applied. The entire length of accessible boarding piers would be required to comply with the same technical provisions that apply to accessible boat slips. For example, at a launch ramp, if a 20 foot (6100 mm) long accessible boarding pier is provided, the entire 20 feet (6100 mm) must comply with the pier clearance requirements in 1003.3. Likewise, if a 60 foot (18 m) long accessible boarding pier is provided, the pier clearance requirements in 1003.3 would apply to the entire 60 feet (18 m).

The following example applies to a boat launch ramp boarding pier: A chain of floats is provided on a launch ramp to be used as a boarding pier which is required to be accessible by 1003.3.2. At high water, the entire chain is floating and a transition plate connects the first float to the surface of the launch ramp. As the water level decreases, segments of the chain end up resting on the launch ramp surface, matching the slope of the launch ramp.

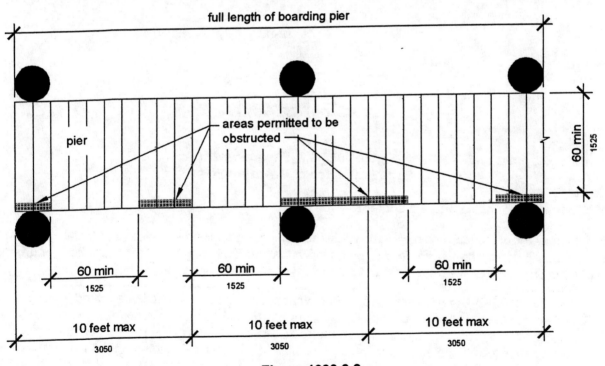

Figure 1003.3.2
Boarding Pier Clearance

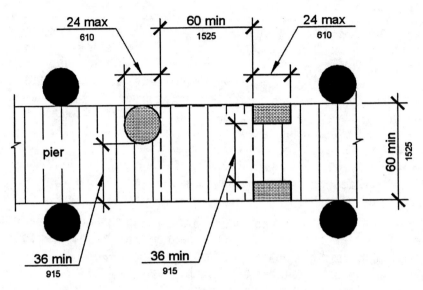

Figure 1003.3.2 (Exception 1)
Clear Pier Space Reduction at Boarding Piers

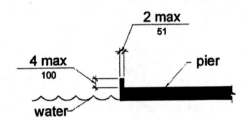

Figure 1003.3.2 (Exception 2)
Edge Protection at Boarding Piers

1004 Exercise Machines and Equipment

1004.1 Clear Floor Space. Exercise machines and equipment shall have a clear floor *space* complying with 305 positioned for transfer or for use by an individual seated in a wheelchair. Clear floor or ground *spaces* required at exercise machines and equipment shall be permitted to overlap.

> **Advisory 1004.1 Clear Floor Space.** One clear floor or ground space is permitted to be shared between two pieces of exercise equipment. To optimize space use, designers should carefully consider layout options such as connecting ends of the row and center aisle spaces. The position of the clear floor space may vary greatly depending on the use of the equipment or machine. For example, to provide access to a shoulder press machine, clear floor space next to the seat would be appropriate to allow for transfer. Clear floor space for a bench press machine designed for use by an individual seated in a wheelchair, however, will most likely be centered on the operating mechanisms.

270

1005 Fishing Piers and Platforms

1005.1 Accessible Routes. *Accessible* routes serving fishing piers and platforms, including *gangways* and floating piers, shall comply with Chapter 4.

EXCEPTIONS: 1. *Accessible* routes serving floating fishing piers and platforms shall be permitted to use Exceptions 1, 2, 5, 6, 7 and 8 in 1003.2.1.

2. Where the total length of the *gangway* or series of *gangways* serving as part of a required *accessible* route is 30 feet (9145 mm) minimum, *gangways* shall not be required to comply with 405.2.

1005.2 Railings. Where provided, railings, guards, or handrails shall comply with 1005.2.

1005.2.1 Height. At least 25 percent of the railings, guards, or handrails shall be 34 inches (865 mm) maximum above the ground or deck surface.

EXCEPTION: Where a guard complying with sections 1003.2.12.1 and 1003.2.12.2 of the International Building Code (2000 edition) or sections 1012.2 and 1012.3 of the International Building Code (2003 edition) (incorporated by reference, see "Referenced Standards" in Chapter 1) is provided, the guard shall not be required to comply with 1005.2.1.

1005.2.1.1 Dispersion. Railings, guards, or handrails required to comply with 1005.2.1 shall be dispersed throughout the fishing pier or platform.

> **Advisory 1005.2.1.1 Dispersion.** Portions of the railings that are lowered to provide fishing opportunities for persons with disabilities must be located in a variety of locations on the fishing pier or platform to give people a variety of locations to fish. Different fishing locations may provide varying water depths, shade (at certain times of the day), vegetation, and proximity to the shoreline or bank.

1005.3 Edge Protection. Where railings, guards, or handrails complying with 1005.2 are provided, edge protection complying with 1005.3.1 or 1005.3.2 shall be provided.

> **Advisory 1005.3 Edge Protection.** Edge protection is required only where railings, guards, or handrails are provided on a fishing pier or platform. Edge protection will prevent wheelchairs or other mobility devices from slipping off the fishing pier or platform. Extending the deck of the fishing pier or platform 12 inches (305 mm) where the 34 inch (865 mm) high railing is provided is an alternative design, permitting individuals using wheelchairs or other mobility devices to pull into a clear space and move beyond the face of the railing. In such a design, curbs or barriers are not required.

1005.3.1 Curb or Barrier. Curbs or barriers shall extend 2 inches (51 mm) minimum above the surface of the fishing pier or platform.

1005.3.2 Extended Ground or Deck Surface. The ground or deck surface shall extend 12 inches (305 mm) minimum beyond the inside face of the railing. Toe clearance shall be provided and shall be 30 inches (760 mm) wide minimum and 9 inches (230 mm) minimum above the ground or deck surface beyond the railing.

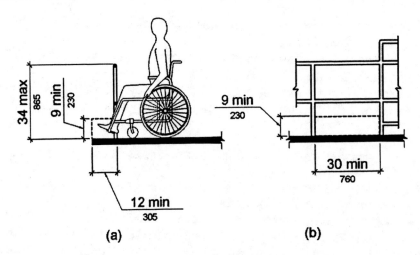

Figure 1005.3.2
Extended Ground or Deck Surface at Fishing Piers and Platforms

1005.4 Clear Floor or Ground Space. At each location where there are railings, guards, or handrails complying with 1005.2.1, a clear floor or ground *space* complying with 305 shall be provided. Where there are no railings, guards, or handrails, at least one clear floor or ground *space* complying with 305 shall be provided on the fishing pier or platform.

1005.5 Turning Space. At least one turning *space* complying with 304.3 shall be provided on fishing piers and platforms.

1006 Golf Facilities

1006.1 General. Golf *facilities* shall comply with 1006.

1006.2 Accessible Routes. *Accessible* routes serving *teeing grounds*, practice *teeing grounds*, putting greens, practice putting greens, teeing stations at driving ranges, course weather shelters, golf car rental areas, bag drop areas, and course toilet rooms shall comply with Chapter 4 and shall be 48 inches (1220 mm) wide minimum. Where handrails are provided, *accessible* routes shall be 60 inches (1525 mm) wide minimum.
　　EXCEPTION: Handrails shall not be required on golf courses. Where handrails are provided on golf courses, the handrails shall not be required to comply with 505.

Advisory 1006.2 Accessible Routes. The 48 inch (1220 mm) minimum width for the accessible route is necessary to ensure passage of a golf car on either the accessible route or the golf car passage. This is important where the accessible route is used to connect the golf car rental area, bag drop areas, practice putting greens, practice teeing grounds, course toilet rooms, and course weather shelters. These are areas outside the boundary of the golf course, but are areas where an individual using an adapted golf car may travel. A golf car passage may not be substituted for other accessible routes to be located outside the boundary of the course. For example, an accessible route connecting an accessible parking space to the entrance of a golf course clubhouse is not covered by this provision.

Providing a golf car passage will permit a person that uses a golf car to practice driving a golf ball from the same position and stance used when playing the game. Additionally, the space required for a person using a golf car to enter and maneuver within the teeing stations required to be accessible should be considered.

1006.3 Golf Car Passages. *Golf car passages* shall comply with 1006.3.

1006.3.1 Clear Width. The clear width of *golf car passages* shall be 48 inches (1220 mm) minimum.

1006.3.2 Barriers. Where curbs or other constructed barriers prevent golf cars from entering a fairway, openings 60 inches (1525 mm) wide minimum shall be provided at intervals not to exceed 75 yards (69 m).

1006.4 Weather Shelters. A clear floor or ground *space* 60 inches (1525 mm) minimum by 96 inches (2440 mm) minimum shall be provided within weather shelters.

1007 Miniature Golf Facilities

1007.1 General. Miniature golf *facilities* shall comply with 1007.

1007.2 Accessible Routes. *Accessible* routes serving holes on miniature golf courses shall comply with Chapter 4. *Accessible* routes located on playing surfaces of miniature golf holes shall be permitted to use the exceptions in 1007.2.

EXCEPTIONS: **1.** Playing surfaces shall not be required to comply with 302.2.
2. Where *accessible* routes intersect playing surfaces of holes, a 1 inch (25 mm) maximum curb shall be permitted for a width of 32 inches (815 mm) minimum.
3. A slope not steeper than 1:4 for a 4 inch (100 mm) maximum rise shall be permitted.
4. *Ramp* landing slopes specified by 405.7.1 shall be permitted to be 1:20 maximum.
5. *Ramp* landing length specified by 405.7.3 shall be permitted to be 48 inches (1220 mm) long minimum.
6. *Ramp* landing size specified by 405.7.4 shall be permitted to be 48 inches (1220 mm) minimum by 60 inches (1525 mm) minimum.
7. Handrails shall not be required on holes. Where handrails are provided on holes, the handrails shall not be required to comply with 505.

1007.3 Miniature Golf Holes. Miniature golf holes shall comply with 1007.3.

1007.3.1 Start of Play. A clear floor or ground *space* 48 inches (1220 mm) minimum by 60 inches (1525 mm) minimum with slopes not steeper than 1:48 shall be provided at the start of play.

1007.3.2 Golf Club Reach Range Area. All areas within holes where golf balls rest shall be within 36 inches (915 mm) maximum of a clear floor or ground *space* 36 inches (915 mm) wide minimum and 48 inches (1220 mm) long minimum having a *running slope* not steeper than 1:20. The clear floor or ground *space* shall be served by an *accessible* route.

> **Advisory 1007.3.2 Golf Club Reach Range Area.** The golf club reach range applies to all holes required to be accessible. This includes accessible routes provided adjacent to or, where provided, on the playing surface of the hole.

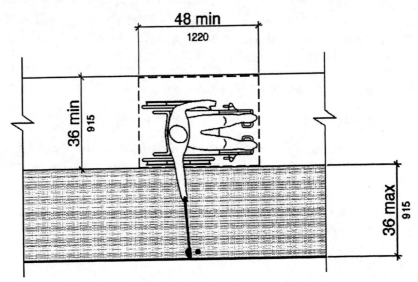

Note: Running Slope of Clear Floor or Ground Space Not Steeper Than 1:20

Figure 1007.3.2
Golf Club Reach Range Area

1008 Play Areas

1008.1 General. *Play areas* shall comply with 1008.

1008.2 Accessible Routes. *Accessible* routes serving *play areas* shall comply with Chapter 4 and 1008.2 and shall be permitted to use the exceptions in 1008.2.1 through 1008.2.3. Where *accessible* routes serve *ground level play components*, the vertical clearance shall be 80 inches high (2030 mm) minimum.

1008.2.1 Ground Level and Elevated Play Components. *Accessible* routes serving *ground level play components* and *elevated play components* shall be permitted to use the exceptions in 1008.2.1.

EXCEPTIONS: 1. Transfer systems complying with 1008.3 shall be permitted to connect *elevated play components* except where 20 or more *elevated play components* are provided no more than 25 percent of the *elevated play components* shall be permitted to be connected by transfer systems.

2. Where transfer systems are provided, an *elevated play component* shall be permitted to connect to another *elevated play component* as part of an *accessible* route.

1008.2.2 Soft Contained Play Structures. *Accessible* routes serving *soft contained play structures* shall be permitted to use the exception in 1008.2.2.

EXCEPTION: Transfer systems complying with 1008.3 shall be permitted to be used as part of an *accessible* route.

1008.2.3 Water Play Components. *Accessible* routes serving water *play components* shall be permitted to use the exceptions in 1008.2.3.

EXCEPTIONS: 1. Where the surface of the *accessible* route, clear floor or ground *spaces*, or turning *spaces* serving water *play components* is submerged, compliance with 302, 403.3, 405.2, 405.3, and 1008.2.6 shall not be required.

2. Transfer systems complying with 1008.3 shall be permitted to connect *elevated play components* in water.

> **Advisory 1008.2.3 Water Play Components.** Personal wheelchairs and mobility devices may not be appropriate for submerging in water when using play components in water. Some may have batteries, motors, and electrical systems that when submerged in water may cause damage to the personal mobility device or wheelchair or may contaminate the water. Providing an aquatic wheelchair made of non-corrosive materials and designed for access into the water will protect the water from contamination and avoid damage to personal wheelchairs.

1008.2.4 Clear Width. *Accessible* routes connecting *play components* shall provide a clear width complying with 1008.2.4.

1008.2.4.1 Ground Level. At ground level, the clear width of *accessible* routes shall be 60 inches (1525 mm) minimum.

EXCEPTIONS: 1. In *play areas* less than 1000 square feet (93 m^2), the clear width of *accessible* routes shall be permitted to be 44 inches (1120 mm) minimum, if at least one turning *space* complying with 304.3 is provided where the restricted *accessible* route exceeds 30 feet (9145 mm) in length.

2. The clear width of *accessible* routes shall be permitted to be 36 inches (915 mm) minimum for a distance of 60 inches (1525 mm) maximum provided that multiple reduced width segments are separated by segments that are 60 inches (1525 mm) wide minimum and 60 inches (1525 mm) long minimum.

1008.2.4.2 Elevated. The clear width of *accessible* routes connecting *elevated play components* shall be 36 inches (915 mm) minimum.

EXCEPTIONS: 1. The clear width of *accessible* routes connecting *elevated play components* shall be permitted to be reduced to 32 inches (815 mm) minimum for a distance of 24 inches (610 mm) maximum provided that reduced width segments are separated by segments that are 48 inches (1220 mm) long minimum and 36 inches (915 mm) wide minimum.
2. The clear width of transfer systems connecting *elevated play components* shall be permitted to be 24 inches (610 mm) minimum.

1008.2.5 Ramps. Within *play areas, ramps* connecting *ground level play components* and *ramps* connecting *elevated play components* shall comply with 1008.2.5.

1008.2.5.1 Ground Level. *Ramp* runs connecting *ground level play components* shall have a *running slope* not steeper than 1:16.

1008.2.5.2 Elevated. The rise for any *ramp* run connecting *elevated play components* shall be 12 inches (305 mm) maximum.

1008.2.5.3 Handrails. Where required on *ramps* serving *play components*, the handrails shall comply with 505 except as modified by 1008.2.5.3.
EXCEPTIONS: 1. Handrails shall not be required on *ramps* located within ground level *use zones.*
2. Handrail extensions shall not be required.

1008.2.5.3.1 Handrail Gripping Surfaces. Handrail gripping surfaces with a circular cross section shall have an outside diameter of 0.95 inch (24 mm) minimum and 1.55 inches (39 mm) maximum. Where the shape of the gripping surface is non-circular, the handrail shall provide an equivalent gripping surface.

1008.2.5.3.2 Handrail Height. The top of handrail gripping surfaces shall be 20 inches (510 mm) minimum and 28 inches (710 mm) maximum above the *ramp* surface.

1008.2.6 Ground Surfaces. Ground surfaces on *accessible* routes, clear floor or ground *spaces*, and turning *spaces* shall comply with 1008.2.6.

Advisory 1008.2.6 Ground Surfaces. Ground surfaces must be inspected and maintained regularly to ensure continued compliance with the ASTM F 1951 standard. The type of surface material selected and play area use levels will determine the frequency of inspection and maintenance activities.

1008.2.6.1 Accessibility. Ground surfaces shall comply with ASTM F 1951 (incorporated by reference, see "Referenced Standards" in Chapter 1). Ground surfaces shall be inspected and maintained regularly and frequently to ensure continued compliance with ASTM F 1951.

1008.2.6.2 Use Zones. Ground surfaces located within *use zones* shall comply with ASTM F 1292 (1999 edition or 2004 edition) (incorporated by reference, see "Referenced Standards" in Chapter 1).

1008.3 Transfer Systems. Where transfer systems are provided to connect to *elevated play components*, transfer systems shall comply with 1008.3.

> **Advisory 1008.3 Transfer Systems.** Where transfer systems are provided, consideration should be given to the distance between the transfer system and the elevated play components. Moving between a transfer platform and a series of transfer steps requires extensive exertion for some children. Designers should minimize the distance between the points where a child transfers from a wheelchair or mobility device and where the elevated play components are located. Where elevated play components are used to connect to another elevated play component instead of an accessible route, careful consideration should be used in the selection of the play components used for this purpose.

1008.3.1 Transfer Platforms. Transfer platforms shall be provided where transfer is intended from wheelchairs or other mobility aids. Transfer platforms shall comply with 1008.3.1.

1008.3.1.1 Size. Transfer platforms shall have level surfaces 14 inches (355 mm) deep minimum and 24 inches (610 mm) wide minimum.

1008.3.1.2 Height. The height of transfer platforms shall be 11 inches (280 mm) minimum and 18 inches (455 mm) maximum measured to the top of the surface from the ground or floor surface.

1008.3.1.3 Transfer Space. A transfer *space* complying with 305.2 and 305.3 shall be provided adjacent to the transfer platform. The 48 inch (1220 mm) long minimum dimension of the transfer *space* shall be centered on and parallel to the 24 inch (610 mm) long minimum side of the transfer platform. The side of the transfer platform serving the transfer *space* shall be unobstructed.

1008.3.1.4 Transfer Supports. At least one means of support for transferring shall be provided.

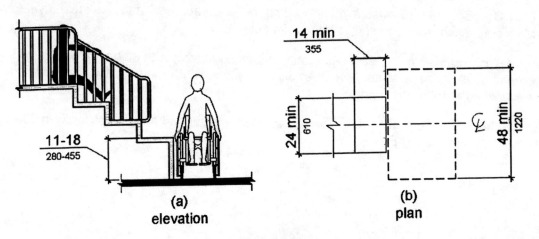

(a) elevation

(b) plan

**Figure 1008.3.1
Transfer Platforms**

1008.3.2 Transfer Steps. Transfer steps shall be provided where movement is intended from transfer platforms to levels with *elevated play components* required to be on *accessible* routes. Transfer steps shall comply with 1008.3.2.

1008.3.2.1 Size. Transfer steps shall have level surfaces 14 inches (355 mm) deep minimum and 24 inches (610 mm) wide minimum.

1008.3.2.2 Height. Each transfer step shall be 8 inches (205 mm) high maximum.

1008.3.2.3 Transfer Supports. At least one means of support for transferring shall be provided.

> **Advisory 1008.3.2.3 Transfer Supports.** Transfer supports are required on transfer platforms and transfer steps to assist children when transferring. Some examples of supports include a rope loop, a loop type handle, a slot in the edge of a flat horizontal or vertical member, poles or bars, or D rings on the corner posts.

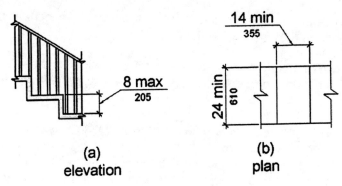

(a)
elevation

(b)
plan

**Figure 1008.3.2
Transfer Steps**

1008.4 Play Components. *Ground level play components* on *accessible* routes and *elevated play components* connected by *ramps* shall comply with 1008.4.

1008.4.1 Turning Space. At least one turning *space* complying with 304 shall be provided on the same level as *play components*. Where swings are provided, the turning *space* shall be located immediately adjacent to the swing.

1008.4.2 Clear Floor or Ground Space. Clear floor or ground *space* complying with 305.2 and 305.3 shall be provided at *play components*.

Advisory 1008.4.2 Clear Floor or Ground Space. Clear floor or ground spaces, turning spaces, and accessible routes are permitted to overlap within play areas. A specific location has not been designated for the clear floor or ground spaces or turning spaces, except swings, because each play component may require that the spaces be placed in a unique location. Where play components include a seat or entry point, designs that provide for an unobstructed transfer from a wheelchair or other mobility device are recommended. This will enhance the ability of children with disabilities to independently use the play component.

When designing play components with manipulative or interactive features, consider appropriate reach ranges for children seated in wheelchairs. The following table provides guidance on reach ranges for children seated in wheelchairs. These dimensions apply to either forward or side reaches. The reach ranges are appropriate for use with those play components that children seated in wheelchairs may access and reach. Where transfer systems provide access to elevated play components, the reach ranges are not appropriate.

Children's Reach Ranges

Forward or Side Reach	Ages 3 and 4	Ages 5 through 8	Ages 9 through 12
High (maximum)	36 in (915 mm)	40 in (1015 mm)	44 in (1120 mm)
Low (minimum)	20 in (510 mm)	18 in (455 mm)	16 in (405 mm)

1008.4.3 Play Tables. Where play tables are provided, knee clearance 24 inches (610 mm) high minimum, 17 inches deep (430 mm) minimum, and 30 inches (760 mm) wide minimum shall be provided. The tops of rims, curbs, or other obstructions shall be 31 inches (785 mm) high maximum.

   EXCEPTION: Play tables designed and constructed primarily for children 5 years and younger shall not be required to provide knee clearance where the clear floor or ground *space* required by 1008.4.2 is arranged for a parallel approach.

1008.4.4 Entry Points and Seats. Where *play components* require transfer to entry points or seats, the entry points or seats shall be 11 inches (280 mm) minimum and 24 inches (610 mm) maximum from the clear floor or ground *space*.

   EXCEPTION: Entry points of slides shall not be required to comply with 1008.4.4.

1008.4.5 Transfer Supports. Where *play components* require transfer to entry points or seats, at least one means of support for transferring shall be provided.

1009 Swimming Pools, Wading Pools, and Spas

1009.1 General. Where provided, pool lifts, sloped entries, transfer walls, transfer systems, and pool stairs shall comply with 1009.

1009.2 Pool Lifts. Pool lifts shall comply with 1009.2.

Advisory 1009.2 Pool Lifts. There are a variety of seats available on pool lifts ranging from sling seats to those that are preformed or molded. Pool lift seats with backs will enable a larger population of persons with disabilities to use the lift. Pool lift seats that consist of materials that resist corrosion and provide a firm base to transfer will be usable by a wider range of people with disabilities. Additional options such as armrests, head rests, seat belts, and leg support will enhance accessibility and better accommodate people with a wide range of disabilities.

1009.2.1 Pool Lift Location. Pool lifts shall be located where the water level does not exceed 48 inches (1220 mm).

EXCEPTIONS: 1. Where the entire pool depth is greater than 48 inches (1220 mm), compliance with 1009.2.1 shall not be required.

2. Where multiple pool lift locations are provided, no more than one pool lift shall be required to be located in an area where the water level is 48 inches (1220 mm) maximum.

1009.2.2 Seat Location. In the raised position, the centerline of the seat shall be located over the deck and 16 inches (405 mm) minimum from the edge of the pool. The deck surface between the centerline of the seat and the pool edge shall have a slope not steeper than 1:48.

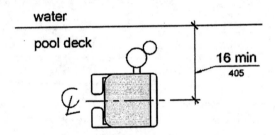

Figure 1009.2.2
Pool Lift Seat Location

1009.2.3 Clear Deck Space. On the side of the seat opposite the water, a clear deck *space* shall be provided parallel with the seat. The *space* shall be 36 inches (915 mm) wide minimum and shall extend forward 48 inches (1220 mm) minimum from a line located 12 inches (305 mm) behind the rear edge of the seat. The clear deck *space* shall have a slope not steeper than 1:48.

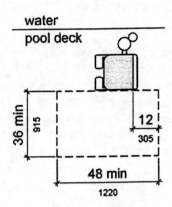

Figure 1009.2.3
Clear Deck Space at Pool Lifts

1009.2.4 Seat Height. The height of the lift seat shall be designed to allow a stop at 16 inches (405 mm) minimum to 19 inches (485 mm) maximum measured from the deck to the top of the seat surface when in the raised (load) position.

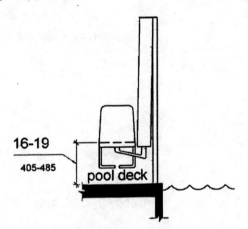

Figure 1009.2.4
Pool Lift Seat Height

1009.2.5 Seat Width. The seat shall be 16 inches (405 mm) wide minimum.

1009.2.6 Footrests and Armrests. Footrests shall be provided and shall move with the seat. If provided, the armrest positioned opposite the water shall be removable or shall fold clear of the seat when the seat is in the raised (load) position.
    EXCEPTION: Footrests shall not be required on pool lifts provided in spas.

281

1009.2.7 Operation. The lift shall be capable of unassisted operation from both the deck and water levels. Controls and operating mechanisms shall be unobstructed when the lift is in use and shall comply with 309.4.

> **Advisory 1009.2.7 Operation.** Pool lifts must be capable of unassisted operation from both the deck and water levels. This will permit a person to call the pool lift when the pool lift is in the opposite position. It is extremely important for a person who is swimming alone to be able to call the pool lift when it is in the up position so he or she will not be stranded in the water for extended periods of time awaiting assistance. The requirement for a pool lift to be independently operable does not preclude assistance from being provided.

1009.2.8 Submerged Depth. The lift shall be designed so that the seat will submerge to a water depth of 18 inches (455 mm) minimum below the stationary water level.

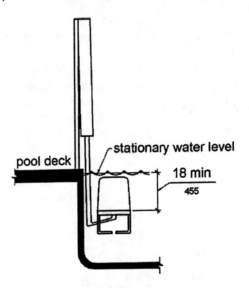

Figure 1009.2.8
Pool Lift Submerged Depth

1009.2.9 Lifting Capacity. Single person pool lifts shall have a weight capacity of 300 pounds. (136 kg) minimum and be capable of sustaining a static load of at least one and a half times the rated load.

> **Advisory 1009.2.9 Lifting Capacity.** Single person pool lifts must be capable of supporting a minimum weight of 300 pounds (136 kg) and sustaining a static load of at least one and a half times the rated load. Pool lifts should be provided that meet the needs of the population they serve. Providing a pool lift with a weight capacity greater than 300 pounds (136 kg) may be advisable.

1009.3 Sloped Entries. Sloped entries shall comply with 1009.3.

> **Advisory 1009.3 Sloped Entries.** Personal wheelchairs and mobility devices may not be appropriate for submerging in water. Some may have batteries, motors, and electrical systems that when submerged in water may cause damage to the personal mobility device or wheelchair or may contaminate the pool water. Providing an aquatic wheelchair made of non-corrosive materials and designed for access into the water will protect the water from contamination and avoid damage to personal wheelchairs or other mobility aids.

1009.3.1 Sloped Entries. Sloped entries shall comply with Chapter 4 except as modified in 1109.3.1 through 1109.3.3.
   EXCEPTION: Where sloped entries are provided, the surfaces shall not be required to be slip resistant.

1009.3.2 Submerged Depth. Sloped entries shall extend to a depth of 24 inches (610 mm) minimum and 30 inches (760 mm) maximum below the stationary water level. Where landings are required by 405.7, at least one landing shall be located 24 inches (610 mm) minimum and 30 inches (760 mm) maximum below the stationary water level.
   EXCEPTION: In wading pools, the sloped entry and landings, if provided, shall extend to the deepest part of the wading pool.

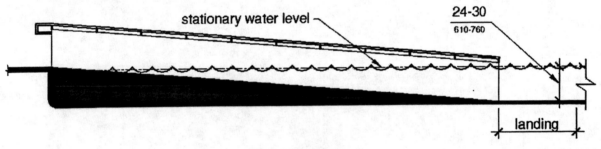

Figure 1009.3.2
Sloped Entry Submerged Depth

1009.3.3 Handrails. At least two handrails complying with 505 shall be provided on the sloped entry. The clear width between required handrails shall be 33 inches (840 mm) minimum and 38 inches (965 mm) maximum.
   EXCEPTIONS: 1. Handrail extensions specified by 505.10.1 shall not be required at the bottom landing serving a sloped entry.
   2. Where a sloped entry is provided for wave action pools, leisure rivers, sand bottom pools, and other pools where user access is limited to one area, the handrails shall not be required to comply with the clear width requirements of 1009.3.3.
   3. Sloped entries in wading pools shall not be required to provide handrails complying with 1009.3.3. If provided, handrails on sloped entries in wading pools shall not be required to comply with 505.

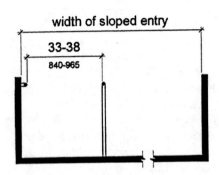

Figure 1009.3.3
Handrails for Sloped Entry

1009.4 Transfer Walls. Transfer walls shall comply with 1009.4.

1009.4.1 Clear Deck Space. A clear deck *space* of 60 inches (1525 mm) minimum by 60 inches (1525 mm) minimum with a slope not steeper than 1:48 shall be provided at the base of the transfer wall. Where one grab bar is provided, the clear deck *space* shall be centered on the grab bar. Where two grab bars are provided, the clear deck *space* shall be centered on the clearance between the grab bars.

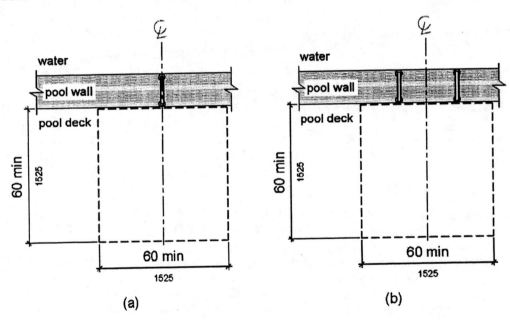

Figure 1009.4.1
Clear Deck Space at Transfer Walls

1009.4.2 Height. The height of the transfer wall shall be 16 inches (405 mm) minimum and 19 inches (485 mm) maximum measured from the deck.

Figure 1009.4.2
Transfer Wall Height

1009.4.3 Wall Depth and Length. The depth of the transfer wall shall be 12 inches (305 mm) minimum and 16 inches (405 mm) maximum. The length of the transfer wall shall be 60 inches (1525 mm) minimum and shall be centered on the clear deck *space*.

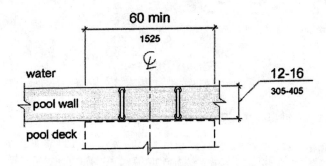

Figure 1009.4.3
Depth and Length of Transfer Walls

1009.4.4 Surface. Surfaces of transfer walls shall not be sharp and shall have rounded edges.

1009.4.5 Grab Bars. At least one grab bar complying with 609 shall be provided on the transfer wall. Grab bars shall be perpendicular to the pool wall and shall extend the full depth of the transfer wall. The top of the gripping surface shall be 4 inches (100 mm) minimum and 6 inches (150 mm) maximum above transfer walls. Where one grab bar is provided, clearance shall be 24 inches (610 mm) minimum on both sides of the grab bar. Where two grab bars are provided, clearance between grab bars shall be 24 inches (610 mm) minimum.

EXCEPTION: Grab bars on transfer walls shall not be required to comply with 609.4.

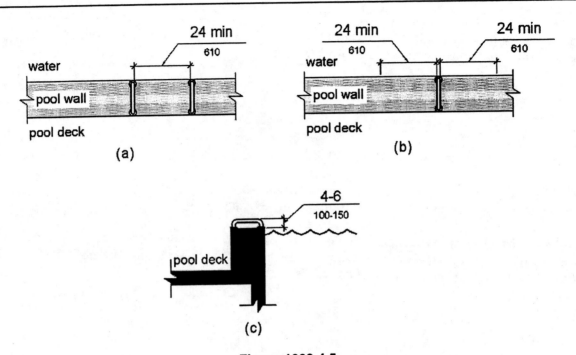

Figure 1009.4.5
Grab Bars for Transfer Walls

1009.5 Transfer Systems. Transfer systems shall comply with 1009.5.

   1009.5.1 Transfer Platform. A transfer platform shall be provided at the head of each transfer system. Transfer platforms shall provide 19 inches (485 mm) minimum clear depth and 24 inches (610 mm) minimum clear width.

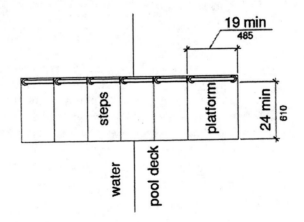

Figure 1009.5.1
Size of Transfer Platform

1009.5.2 Transfer Space. A transfer *space* of 60 inches (1525 mm) minimum by 60 inches (1525 mm) minimum with a slope not steeper than 1:48 shall be provided at the base of the transfer platform surface and shall be centered along a 24 inch (610 mm) minimum side of the transfer platform. The side of the transfer platform serving the transfer *space* shall be unobstructed.

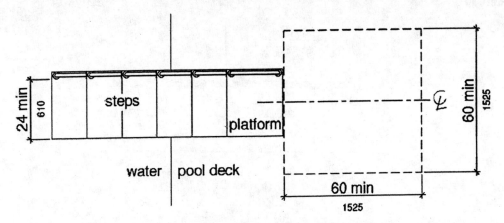

Figure 1009.5.2
Clear Deck Space at Transfer Platform

1009.5.3 Height. The height of the transfer platform shall comply with 1009.4.2.

1009.5.4 Transfer Steps. Transfer step height shall be 8 inches (205 mm) maximum. The surface of the bottom tread shall extend to a water depth of 18 inches (455 mm) minimum below the stationary water level.

Advisory 1009.5.4 Transfer Steps. Where possible, the height of the transfer step should be minimized to decrease the distance an individual is required to lift up or move down to reach the next step to gain access.

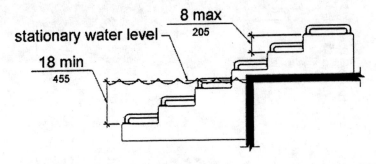

Figure 1009.5.4
Transfer Steps

287

1009.5.5 Surface. The surface of the transfer system shall not be sharp and shall have rounded edges.

1009.5.6 Size. Each transfer step shall have a tread clear depth of 14 inches (355 mm) minimum and 17 inches (430 mm) maximum and shall have a tread clear width of 24 inches (610 mm) minimum.

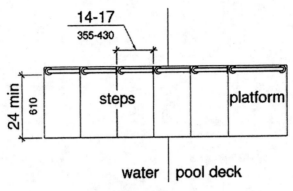

Figure 1009.5.6
Size of Transfer Steps

1009.5.7 Grab Bars. At least one grab bar on each transfer step and the transfer platform or a continuous grab bar serving each transfer step and the transfer platform shall be provided. Where a grab bar is provided on each step, the tops of gripping surfaces shall be 4 inches (100 mm) minimum and 6 inches (150 mm) maximum above each step and transfer platform. Where a continuous grab bar is provided, the top of the gripping surface shall be 4 inches (100 mm) minimum and 6 inches (150 mm) maximum above the step nosing and transfer platform. Grab bars shall comply with 609 and be located on at least one side of the transfer system. The grab bar located at the transfer platform shall not obstruct transfer.

   EXCEPTION: Grab bars on transfer systems shall not be required to comply with 609.4.

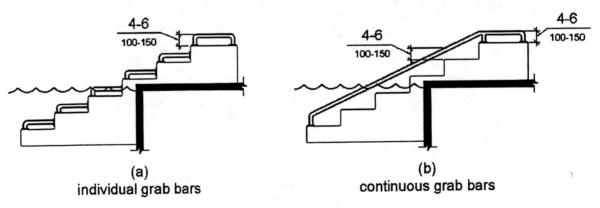

(a)
individual grab bars

(b)
continuous grab bars

Figure 1009.5.7
Grab Bars

1009.6 Pool Stairs. Pool stairs shall comply with 1009.6.

1009.6.1 Pool Stairs. Pool stairs shall comply with 504.
EXCEPTION: Pool step riser heights shall not be required to be 4 inches (100 mm) high minimum and 7 inches (180 mm) high maximum provided that riser heights are uniform.

1009.6.2 Handrails. The width between handrails shall be 20 inches (510 mm) minimum and 24 inches (610 mm) maximum. Handrail extensions required by 505.10.3 shall not be required on pool stairs.

1010 Shooting Facilities with Firing Positions

1010.1 Turning Space. A circular turning *space* 60 inches (1525 mm) diameter minimum with slopes not steeper than 1:48 shall be provided at shooting facilities with firing positions.

Printed by Builder's Book, Inc., Bookstore · www.buildersbook.com

Printed by Builder's Book, Inc., Bookstore · www.buildersbook.com

Printed by Builder's Book, Inc., Bookstore · www.buildersbook.com

297

298

GUIDE to the
NEW ADA and ABA
ACCESSIBILITY
GUIDELINES

A Guide to the New ADA-ABA Accessibility Guidelines

On July 23, 2004, the U.S. Access Board, an independent Federal agency, issued updated accessibility guidelines for new or altered facilities covered by Americans with Disabilities Act and the Architectural Barriers Act. These guidelines address a wide range of facilities in the private and public sectors. Presented here is an overview of the new guidelines that also highlights significant changes.

BACKGROUND

The Americans with Disabilities Act (ADA) of 1990
The ADA, a major civil rights law prohibiting discrimination on the basis of disability, establishes design requirements for the construction or alteration of facilities. It covers facilities in the private sector (places of public accommodation and commercial facilities) and the public sector (state and local government facilities). Under the ADA, the Board is responsible for accessibility guidelines covering newly built and altered facilities. In 1991, the Board published the ADA Accessibility Guidelines (ADAAG) which serve as the basis for standards used to enforce the law. The new guidelines overhaul the original ADAAG.

The Architectural Barriers Act (ABA) of 1968
The ABA requires access to facilities designed, built, altered, or leased with Federal funds. Similar to its responsibility under the ADA, the Board maintains guidelines under the ABA which serve as the basis for enforceable standards. The Board has updated its guidelines for ABA facilities jointly with the new ADA guidelines so that a consistent level of access is specified under both laws.

How the New Guidelines Were Developed
The Board develops and updates its guidelines under a process common to most Federal regulations which provides an opportunity for public comment. In order to get input from a cross section of stakeholders at the outset of this update, the Board established an advisory committee to review the original guidelines and to recommend changes. The ADAAG Review Advisory Committee, which consisted of 22 members representing the design and construction industry, the building code community, and people with disabilities, among others, submitted a report to the Board that detailed recommended revisions to the substance, organization, and format of the guidelines. The finalized guidelines are based largely on these recommendations. The Board published the guidelines in proposed form in November, 1999 and made them available for public comment for six months. During the comment period, the Board held public hearings in Los Angeles and the Washington, D.C. area. The Board received over 2,500 public comments on its proposal and finalized the guidelines based on its review of these comments.

Goals of this Update
Key goals of this update include:
- updating specifications so that they continue to meet the needs of persons with disabilities
- improving the format and usability of the guidelines to facilitate compliance
- harmonizing the guidelines with model building codes and industry standards
- making the requirements for ADA and ABA facilities consistent

Harmonization with Model Building Codes and Industry Standards
Through this update, the Board sought to make its guidelines more consistent with model building codes and industry standards in order to make compliance easier. It coordinated extensively with model code groups and standard-setting bodies so that differences could be reconciled. In particular, the Board sought to harmonize the guidelines with the International

Building Code (IBC) and access standards issued through the American National Standards Institute (ANSI). Used by a growing number of states and local jurisdictions, the IBC contains scoping provisions for accessibility. The ANSI A117.1 standard, a voluntary consensus standard, provides technical criteria referenced by the IBC. A number of revisions were made to the guidelines for consistency with these and other model codes and standards. In addition, the Board worked to resolve remaining differences by advocating changes to the IBC and the ANSI A117.1 standard based on the new guidelines.

When will the new guidelines take effect?

The Board's guidelines are not mandatory on the public, but instead serve as the baseline for enforceable standards (which are) maintained by other Federal agencies. In this respect, they are similar to a model building code in that they are not required to be followed except as adopted by an enforcing authority. Under the ADA, the Department of Justice (and in the case of transit facilities, the Department of Transportation) are responsible for enforceable standards based on the Board's guidelines. These agencies will update their ADA standards based on the new guidelines. In doing so, they will indicate when the new standards are to be followed. Several other agencies (the General Services Administration, Department of Defense, Department of Housing and Urban Development, and the U.S. Postal Service) hold a similar responsibility for standards used to enforce the ABA.

Existing Facilities

The ADA and ABA guidelines cover new construction and planned alterations and generally do not apply to existing facilities except where altered. Facilities built or altered according to earlier versions of the ADA or ABA standards will not necessarily have to meet the updated version except where they are subsequently altered or renovated. The Department of Justice, which regulates requirements for existing facilities under the ADA, intends to address coverage of facilities built or altered according to the original ADA standards in its rulemaking to update the standards. It will also address facilities retrofitted under ADA provisions for existing facilities, such as the requirement for barrier removal in places of public accommodation. With respect to ABA facilities, the Board has clarified in the guidelines that facilities built to earlier ABA standards are subject to the new requirements only in relation to planned alterations.

OVERVIEW

Organization and Format

The updated guidelines feature:

- a new numbering system consistent with model codes
- a more streamlined structure and organization of chapters
- updated scoping and technical provisions, with a greater structural delineation between them
- new figures and commentary (advisory information)
- provision of all figure-based information in written text

A Rule in Three Parts

The Board coordinated its update of the ADA and ABA guidelines into a single rule. The final rule contains updated scoping provisions, which specify what has to be accessible, and technical requirements, which spell out how access is achieved. It contains three parts: a scoping document for ADA facilities (Part I), a scoping document for ABA facilities (Part II), and a common set of technical criteria referenced by both scoping documents (Part III).

2

Supplements to ADAAG
The Board previously developed supplements to the original ADA guidelines that are specific to different types of facilities and elements:

- state and local government facilities, including courthouses and prisons (1998)
- building elements designed for children's use (1998)
- play areas (2000)
- recreation facilities (2002)

These supplements are included in the new guidelines. They have been revised for consistency with the format and approach of the new document, but their substance remains unchanged.

SUMMARY

PART I: ADA APPLICATION AND SCOPING (CHAPTERS 1 AND 2)

Chapter 1: Application and Administration
The guidelines include general provisions that recognize the purpose of the guidelines (101), specifications for adults and children (102), equivalent facilitation, which permits departures providing equal or greater access (103), conventions (104), referenced standards (105), and definitions (106). These provisions include instructions on applying the guidelines, such as conventions concerning specified dimensions. Throughout the guidelines, the Board has replaced absolute dimensions with specified ranges wherever practicable to facilitate compliance.

The guidelines reference several model building codes and industry standards. These include industry standards for powered doors, elevators, platform lifts, and play surfacing and equipment. Requirements for means of egress and fire alarms are addressed through references to the International Building Code (IBC) and the National Fire Alarm Code (NFPA 72). The guidelines reference the most recent editions of these codes and standards.

Chapter 2: Scoping Requirements
Chapter 2 is comprised of provisions that specify which spaces and elements are required to comply. The format and content of the guidelines reinforce the underlying premise that all areas of newly constructed facilities are required to be accessible unless otherwise noted. Consequently, exceptions from the requirements are more thoroughly covered.

The new guidelines enhance coverage of employee work areas. The original ADA guidelines specified that work areas be on an accessible route so that persons with disabilities can approach, enter, and exit the space. In addition to this, the new guidelines also require the accessibility of circulation paths within sizable (1000 square feet or more) work areas (203.9). They also address accessible means of egress from work areas and connections for visual alarms. Another notable revision concerns press boxes, which by their elevation and location have posed challenges to access. The new guidelines include an exception for certain press boxes based on their size, elevation, and location (206.2).

Other revisions include:

- enhanced scoping for public entrances (206.4), van parking (208), passenger loading zones (209), stairways (210), and telecommunication devices (TTYs) at pay phones for persons with hearing or speech impairments (217);

3

- new or clarifying provisions covering access to different types of elevators (destination-oriented, limited-use/ limited application or "LULA," and residential elevators) (206), drinking fountains (211), kitchens, kitchenettes, and sinks (212), washing machines and clothes dryers (214), signs (216), dispersed wheelchair seating (221), windows (229), and residential dwelling units (233);

- reduced scoping for unisex toilet rooms located at a single location (half instead of all) (213), and for wheelchair spaces in large assembly areas (221).

PART II: ABA APPLICATION AND SCOPING (CHAPTERS F1 AND F2)

Application and scoping requirements for ABA facilities are based on those for ADA facilities to ensure a consistent level of access. There are differences in certain areas which stem from variations between the ADA and ABA statutes. For example, the ABA is broader in its coverage of employee work areas, a difference reflected in the updated guidelines. Exceptions for work areas that limit coverage in the ADA scoping document are not included in the ABA counterpart. Other ABA provisions that differ from the ADA document concern modifications and waivers (F103), definitions (F106), additions (F202.2), leased facilities (F202.6), existing elements (F203), and residential facilities (F234).

PART III: TECHNICAL REQUIREMENTS (CHAPTERS 3 – 10)
Part III contains technical chapters referenced by the ADA and ABA scoping documents.

Chapter 3: Building Blocks
Chapter 3 provides criteria for basic elements considered to be the "building blocks" of accessibility as established by the guidelines, including ground and floor surfaces (302), changes in level (303), wheelchair turning space (304), clear floor space (305), knee and toe clearances (306), protruding objects (307), reach ranges (308), and operable parts (309).

The guidelines specify reach ranges according to the approach (forward or side). A significant change of this chapter reduces the maximum side reach range from 54 to 48 inches, the height specified for forward reaches. This change, which was recommended by the ADAAG Review Advisory Committee and strongly supported by public comments, includes exceptions for certain elements, such as gas pumps.

Chapter 4: Accessible Routes
All components of accessible routes have been combined into one chapter that covers walking surfaces (403), doors (404), ramps (405), curb ramps (406), elevators (407 - 409), and platform lifts (410).

New specifications are provided that clarify access at recessed doors, ramps (edge protection), and curb ramps (top landings). Provisions for elevators recognize a greater range of designs and dimensions for standard cars and include new technical criteria for other types of elevators: destination-oriented, limited-use/ limited-application, and residential. Provisions for platform lifts have been updated and reference a new industry standard (ASME A18.1).

The original guidelines required detectable warnings, a distinctive tactile surfacing, on the surface of curb ramps and other areas to alert people with vision impairments of their approach to streets and drop-offs at boarding platforms. The new guidelines do not include a requirement for detectable warnings at curb ramps or hazardous vehicular areas since the Board is revisiting this issue in a separate rulemaking on accessible public rights-of-way. (Under the new

4

guidelines detectable warnings are still required along the edges of boarding platforms in transit facilities.)

Chapter 5: General Site and Building Elements
This chapter contains requirements for parking (502), passenger loading zones (503), stairways (504), and handrails (505). Revisions of this chapter include a new provision specific to angled van parking spaces and revamped specifications for handrails that will permit a greater range of designs and shapes.

Chapter 6: Plumbing Elements and Facilities
Specifications for plumbed fixtures address drinking fountains (602), toilet and bathrooms (603), water closets and compartments (604), urinals (605), lavatories and sinks (606), bathtubs (607), showers (608), grab bars (609), tub and shower seats (610), washing machines and clothes dryers (611), and saunas and steam rooms (612).

Some provisions have been revised to help improve compliance as well as access. For example, an absolute dimension for the centerline placement of toilets (18") has been replaced with a range (16" – 18"). To improve access and allow side transfers at toilets, lavatories are no longer permitted to overlap the required clear space aside toilets.

Other changes of this chapter concern drinking fountains (side approach access is no longer permitted at wheelchair accessible units), shower compartments (specifications for water temperature, spray units, and curbs), and new criteria for washing machines and clothes dryers.

Chapter 7: Communication Elements and Features
This chapter provides technical criteria for communication elements such as fire alarms (702), signs (703), telephones (704), detectable warnings (705), assistive listening systems (706), ATMs and fare machines (707), and two-way communication systems (708). Substantive changes include:

- addressing technical criteria for fire alarms through the National Fire Alarm Code (NFPA 72), which effectively overhauls specifications for visual alarms in a manner that will facilitate compliance while enhancing design and installation options
- revamped specifications for signs
- new specifications for the capabilities and sound quality of assistive listening systems that derive from Board-sponsored research
- improved access at ATMs and fare machines for persons with vision impairments through detailed criteria for audible output and tactile markings
- revised specifications for detectable warnings to allow a greater range of designs and products

Chapter 8: Special Rooms, Spaces, and Elements
Various types of occupancies and spaces are addressed in Chapter 8. These include: assembly areas (802), dressing, fitting, and locker rooms (803), kitchens and kitchenettes (804), medical care facilities (805), transient lodging (806), holding and housing cells (807), courtrooms (808), residential dwelling units (809), transportation facilities (810), and storage (811). The new guidelines are structured to make provisions for certain types of facilities or spaces more integral to the document as a whole. Some provisions specific to these facilities that cover elements also addressed for facilities generally are located in other chapters. For example, Chapter 6 (Plumbing Elements and Facilities) includes provisions specific to toilet and bathing facilities in residential dwelling units.

The requirements found in Chapter 8 were reorganized to clarify the application of requirements for certain types of spaces without respect to the overall occupancy. For example, specifications for kitchens and kitchenettes apply whether such spaces are located in a hotel guest room, a dwelling unit, or an employee break room. This differs from the original guidelines which addressed kitchens and kitchenettes only in relation to transient lodging facilities and, in the case of the ABA guidelines, dwelling units.

Chapter 9: Built-In Furnishings and Equipment
Chapter 9 covers built-in furnishings and equipment and provides specifications for dining and work surfaces (902), benches (903), and sales and service counters, including check-out aisles (904). The guidelines provide revised specifications for benches which include revised criteria for back support.

Chapter 10: Recreation Facilities and Play Areas
Technical provisions for various types of recreation facilities, including play areas the Board developed previously as supplements to the original ADA guidelines are located in Chapter 10. They have been integrated into the new guidelines without substantive change. Requirements are provided for amusement rides (1002), recreational boating facilities (1003), exercise machines (1004), fishing piers and platforms (1005), golf facilities (1006), miniature golf facilities (1007), play areas (1008), swimming pools, wading pools, and spas (1009), and shooting facilities with firing positions (1010).

RESOURCES
Copies of the new ADA and ABA accessibility guidelines, as well as technical assistance and training on them, is available from the Access Board. The Board also enforces design requirements of the ABA which apply to federally funded facilities.

U.S. Access Board
(800) 872-2253 (voice) (800) 993-2822 (TTY)
www.access-board.gov
E-mail:
    pubs@access-board.gov (publication orders)
    ta@access-board.gov (technical assistance)
    training@access-board.gov (training)
    enforce@access-board.gov (ABA enforcement)

Questions about the enforcement of the ADA's design requirements or the update of ADA standards based on the Board's new guidelines should be directed to the U.S. Department of Justice or, in the case of public transit facilities, the U.S. Department of Transportation.

U.S. Department of Justice
(800) 514-0301 (voice) (800) 514-0383 (TTY)
www.ada.gov

Federal Transit Administration
(888) 446-4511 (voice/ relay)
www.fta.dot.gov

July 2004

UNITED STATES ACCESS BOARD
A FEDERAL AGENCY COMMITTED TO ACCESSIBLE DESIGN
1331 F Street, N.W. Suite 1000 Washington, DC 20004-1111
800 872-2253 (v) ■ 800 993-2822 (TTY) ■ Fax: 202 272-0081
www.access-board.gov ■ e-mail: info@access-board.gov

REGULATORY ASSESSMENT
of the
FINAL REVISED ACCESSIBILITY GUIDELINES
for the
AMERICAN WITH DISABILITIES ACT
and
ARCHITECTURAL BARRIERS ACT

Printed by Builder's Book, Inc., Bookstore · www.buildersbook.com

Regulatory Assessment of the Final Revised Accessibility Guidelines for the
Americans with Disabilities Act and Architectural Barriers Act

July 2004

This assessment has been developed and reviewed in accordance with the Access Board's information quality guidelines (www.access-board.gov/infoquality.htm).

CONTENTS

EXECUTIVE SUMMARY

The Access Board prepared this assessment of the final revised accessibility guidelines for the Americans with Disabilities Act and Architectural Barriers Act pursuant to Executive Order 12866. The Americans with Disabilities Act requires newly constructed and altered State and local government facilities, places of public accommodation, and commercial facilities to be accessible to individuals with disabilities. The Architectural Barriers Act requires federally financed facilities to be accessible, including facilities leased by Federal agencies.

The Access Board is required to establish and maintain accessibility guidelines for facilities covered by the Americans with Disabilities Act and Architectural Barriers Act. The guidelines serve as the basis for enforceable standards issued by other agencies under the Americans with Disabilities Act and Architectural Barriers Act. The Access Board initially issued the Minimum Guidelines and Requirements for Accessible Design (MGRAD) for the Architectural Barriers Act in 1982, and the Americans with Disabilities Act Accessibility Guidelines (ADAAG) in 1991.

Since the enactment of the Americans with Disabilities Act, accessibility requirements have been increasingly incorporated in the model codes. The Access Board worked collaboratively with the International Code Council (ICC) and the ANSI A117 Committee to harmonize the final revised guidelines with the International Building Code, which was

1

first published in 2000, and the ICC/ANSI A117.1 Standard on Accessible and Usable Buildings and Facilities, which is referenced in the International Building Code. The International Building Code has been adopted statewide by 28 States and by local governments in another 15 States.

Harmonizing the accessibility guidelines for the Americans with Disabilities Act and Architectural Barriers Act with the International Building Code and the ICC/ANSI A117.1 standard promotes increased compliance, efficiency, and economic growth. It is difficult and time consuming for business owners, builders, developers, and architects to deal with different accessibility requirements at the Federal, State, and local government levels. Differing requirements can contribute to mistakes resulting in litigation and costly retrofitting of facilities after they are constructed. The Americans with Disabilities Act authorizes the Department of Justice to certify State or local codes that meet or exceed Federal accessibility requirements. State and local governments that adopt the International Building Code will find it easier to have their codes certified, and more State and local governments are expected to submit their codes to the Department of Justice for certification. In jurisdictions where codes have been certified by the Department of Justice, business owners, builders, developers, and architects can rely on their State or local government building plan approval and inspection processes as a "check-point" for ensuring that their facilities comply with Federal accessibility requirements. Potential mistakes can be corrected early in the construction process when adjustments can be made easily and inexpensively compared to costly retrofitting after a facility is constructed. Compliance with a certified code is also evidence of compliance with Federal accessibility requirements in litigation to enforce the Americans with Disabilities Act.

The Access Board also revised some requirements in the current guidelines for the Americans with Disabilities Act and Architectural Barriers Act to reduce the impacts on facilities, including lowering the number of wheelchair spaces and assistive listening systems required in large sports facilities; exempting small raised press boxes in sports facilities from the accessible route requirements; exempting parking lots with a few parking spaces from signage requirements for accessible parking spaces; and reducing the number of toilet rooms required to be accessible where multiple single user toilet rooms are clustered at the same location.

The regulatory assessment for the proposed rule estimated that the national costs of the rule would be $87.5 million annually for newly constructed office buildings, hotels, and sports stadiums and arenas. The Board adopted alternatives in the final revised guidelines that eliminate these costs as shown in Table ES.1.

Table ES.1 – Alternatives That Eliminate Costs Estimated for the Proposed Rule
(text version)

Proposed Rule	Final Revised Guidelines
Visible alarms required in all employee work areas, including individual offices. Estimated cost: $16 million annually.	Visible alarms required in public and common use areas, which is consistent with current guidelines. Where employee work areas have audible alarm coverage, wiring system required to be designed so that visible alarms can be added to the system as needed.

2

Communication features required in 50 percent of hotel guest rooms. Estimated cost: $31 million annually.	No change from current guidelines, which require substantially less than 50 percent of hotel guest rooms to provide communication features.
Elevators and platform lifts required to be provided in sufficient number, capacity, and speed so that persons using wheelchair spaces and designated aisle seats have equivalent level of service as persons in the same seating area who can use stairs. Estimated cost: $1.5 million annually.	No change from current guidelines, which require at least one accessible route to connect each story and mezzanine in multi-story facilities.
Wheelchair spaces and designated aisle seats required to be dispersed vertically on each accessible level. Estimated cost: $33.5 million annually.	Wheelchair spaces required to be dispersed vertically at varying distances from the screen, performance area, or playing field, which is consistent with current guidelines.
Companion seats required to be readily removable and to provide additional wheelchair spaces. Estimated cost: $4 million annually.	Companion seats permitted to be removable, but not required to provide additional wheelchair spaces.
One percent of seats required to be designated aisle seats; 25 percent of designated aisle seats required to be on an accessible route; and rest of designated aisle seats required to be not more than two rows from an accessible route. Estimated cost: $1.5 million annually.	Five percent of aisle seats required to be designated aisle seats and to be aisle seats closest to accessible routes.

This assessment compares the final revised guidelines to the current guidelines and the International Building Code in order to evaluate the potential impacts of the revisions. In the absence of the final revised guidelines, newly constructed and altered facilities covered by the Americans with Disabilities Act would have to comply with ADAAG as initially issued in 1991, which has been adopted as enforceable standards by the Department of Justice and Department of Transportation. Many newly constructed and altered facilities covered by the Architectural Barriers Act are also required to comply with ADAAG when it provides a greater level of accessibility compared to the Uniform Federal Accessibility Standards (UFAS). Comparing the final revised guidelines to the current guidelines is the upper bound of the range of potential impacts. The International Building Code has been adopted statewide by 28 States and by local governments in another 15 States. In the absence of the final revised guidelines, newly constructed and altered facilities are required to comply with the International Building Code in jurisdictions that have adopted the model code. Comparing the final revised guidelines to the International Building Code is the lower bound of the range of potential impacts, and assumes that facilities covered by the Americans with Disabilities Act and Architectural Barriers Act are also required to comply with equivalent requirements in the International Building Code. The actual impacts will be between the lower and upper bound of the range.

3

The final revised guidelines reorganize and renumber ADAAG, and rewrite the text to be clearer and easier to understand. Most of the scoping and technical requirements in ADAAG have not been changed. An independent codes expert compared the final revised guidelines and ADAAG to identify revisions that add new features or space to a facility, or present design challenges compared to ADAAG. The codes expert identified 27 revisions that are expected to have minimal impacts on the new construction and alterations of facilities, including adding scoping requirements and exceptions for common use circulation paths in employee work areas; revising scoping requirements for public entrances; referencing the International Building Code for accessible means of egress; adding scoping requirements for dwelling units with mobility features in Federal, State, and local government housing; lowering the high side reach; and adding technical requirements for automated teller machines and fare machines.

The codes expert also identified 14 revisions that are expected to have monetary impacts on the new construction and alterations of facilities. An independent cost estimator prepared cost estimates for these revisions using standard industry procedures. The revisions that are expected to have monetary impacts on the new construction and alterations of facilities are summarized in Table ES.2.

Table ES.2 - Revisions with Monetary Impacts on New Construction and Alterations (text version)

Final Revised Guidelines	Current Guidelines	International Building Code	Unit Cost
Where circulation path directly connects assembly seating area and performing area, accessible route required to directly connect both areas.	Accessible route required to connect assembly seating area and performing area.	IBC 2000 & 2003 have equivalent requirement to final revised guidelines.	Will vary from $0 to $15,674 depending on specific design of facility.
Where platform lift serves as part of accessible means of egress, standby power required.	No requirement.	IBC 2003 has equivalent requirement to final revised guidelines.	Will vary from $0 to $2,353 depending on specific design of facility.
One in every 6 accessible parking spaces required to be van accessible.	One in every 8 accessible parking spaces required to be van accessible.	IBC 2003 has equivalent requirement to final revised guidelines.	$75 to $344
Toilet rooms with 6 or more toilet compartments, or combination of 6 or more water closets and urinals, required to provide ambulatory accessible toilet	Toilet rooms with 6 or more toilet compartments required to provide ambulatory accessible toilet compartment with grab bars.	IBC 2000 & 2003 have equivalent requirement to final revised guidelines.	$145

4

Final Revised Guidelines	Current Guidelines	International Building Code	Unit Cost
compartment with grab bars.			
Private facilities required to provide public TTY in building with 4 or more public telephones, and on floor with 4 or more public telephones. Government facilities required to provide public TTY in building with public telephone, and on floor with public telephone. Private and government facilities required to provide public TTY in bank of 4 or more public telephones. Banks of public telephones located within 200 feet of, and on same floor as, another bank of telephones with public TTY exempt. Private and government facilities required to provide public TTY on exterior site with 4 or more public telephones. Bus or rail stations with public telephone at entrance required to provide public TTY. Public rest stops with public telephone required to provide	Private facilities with 4 or more public telephones required to provide public TTY. Government facilities with public telephone in public use area of building required to provide public TTY. Rail stations with 4 or more public telephones at entrance required to provide public TTY.	IBC 2000 (Appendix E) has equivalent requirement to final revised guidelines for private facilities. IBC 2003 (Appendix E) has equivalent requirement to final revised guidelines for private facilities and government facilities.	$2,320

Final Revised Guidelines	Current Guidelines	International Building Code	Unit Cost
public TTY.			
At least one operable window in accessible rooms required to comply with technical requirements for operable parts. Hotel guest rooms that are not required to provide mobility features and dwelling units are exempt.	No requirement.	IBC2000 & 2003 have equivalent requirement to final revised guidelines for certain occupancies.	$505
Two-way communication systems at entrances required to provide audible and visual signals.	No requirement.		$1,392
Automatic doors serving accessible means of egress required to provide maneuvering clearance or to have standby power.	No requirement.		$2,353
Doors on platform lifts required to be power operated. Platform lifts serving only 2 landings and with self-closing doors on opposite sides exempt.	Doors required to provide maneuvering clearance or to be power operated.	IBC 2000 & 2003 have equivalent requirement to final revised guidelines.	Will vary from $0 to $569 depending on specific design of facility.
Minimum clearance at water closet in accessible single user toilet rooms: 60 x 56 inches.	Minimum clearance at water closet in accessible single user toilet rooms based on approach: Forward: 48 x 60 inches; Parallel: 48 X 56 inches; Both forward and parallel: 60 x 56 inches.	IBC 2000 & 2003 have equivalent requirement to final revised guidelines, except for dwelling units.	$286 for dwelling units $667 for other facilities

6

Final Revised Guidelines	Current Guidelines	International Building Code	Unit Cost
Shower spray unit with on-off control required in bathtubs and shower compartments in accessible toilet and bathing rooms.	Shower spray unit required in bathtubs and shower compartments in accessible toilet and bathing rooms.		$161
Minimum clearance between opposing base cabinets, counter tops, appliances, or walls in accessible galley kitchens where two entries not provided: 60 inches. Kitchens without cooktop or conventional range exempt.	Minimum clearance between opposing base cabinets, counter tops, appliances, or walls in accessible galley kitchens: 40 inches.		$993
Comparable vanity counter top space required in hotel guest rooms with mobility features.	No requirement.		$752
Two percent of dwelling units in Federal, State, and local government housing required to provide communication features.	No requirement.		$96 for visual signal if door bell and peephole provided. $322 for doorbell with visual signal and peephole. $353 for TTY connection if voice communication system provided at entrance.

Office buildings, hotels, hospitals and nursing homes, and Federal, State, and local government housing will be affected by many of the revisions in Table ES.2, and are

7

likely to experience relatively higher costs than other facilities. The assessment estimates the national costs of the revisions for the construction of these facilities. The national costs are summarized in Table ES.3.

Table ES.3 – National Costs for Facilities Likely to Experience Relatively Higher Costs (text version)

Facility	National Costs Compared To	
	Current Guidelines Upper Bound	International Building Code Lower Bound
Office Buildings	$1.5 million	$0.7 million
Hotels	$6.2 million	$4.1 million
Hospitals & Nursing Homes	$13.6 million	$2.4 – $2.9 million
Government Housing	$5.4 million	$5.4 million
Total	**$26.7 million**	**$12.6 - $13.1 million**

The assessment also estimates the additional costs of the revisions for individual facilities as a percentage of total construction costs as shown in Table ES.4.

Table ES.4 – Additional Costs for Individual Facilities (text version)

Facility	Additional Costs as Percentage of Total Construction Costs Compared to	
	Current Guidelines Upper Bound	International Building Code Lower Bound
Office Buildings	0.02 to 0.10 %	0.01 to 0.08 %
Hotels	0.06 to 0.50 %	0.04 to 0.30 %
Hospitals & Nursing Homes	0.02 %	0.00 %
Government Housing	0.01 %	0.01 %

The final revised guidelines will affect the new construction and alterations of other types of facilities. Industry reports estimate $152 billion of non-residential building construction projects were started in 2002; and government reports estimate $264 billion of non-residential building construction work and $6 billion of Federal, State and local government housing construction work was installed in 2002. In order to be considered an economically significant regulatory action with an annual effect on the economy of $100 million or more, the final revised guidelines would need to have impacts ranging from 0.04 percent to 0.07 percent of industry and government construction estimates. The final revised guidelines will have impacts within or above this range on office buildings and hotels, and it is likely that the impacts on some other facilities will be within or above this range. Although the impacts are not significant for an individual facility, when added together across the economy the impacts can be economically significant. Because an extremely low threshold of impacts on individual facilities can render the final revised guidelines economically significant, and because the benefits of the final revised guidelines are unquantifiable but substantial, the Board has classified the final revised guidelines as an economically significant regulatory action.

8

The final revised guidelines will also affect leased postal facilities. When the United States Postal Service enters into a new lease for a postal facility, including previously occupied space, it will have to comply with the accessibility requirements in the final revised guidelines for facilities leased by Federal agencies, including providing accessible customer service counters and van accessible parking spaces. The United States Postal Service leases 27,000 postal facilities, and estimates that it will cost $9,234 per facility to comply with the final revised guidelines. The United States Postal Service enters into an average of 1,661 new leases per year for postal facilities, and estimates it will cost $15.3 million annually for leased postal facilities to comply with the final revised guidelines.

On the basis of this assessment, the Access Board certifies that the final revised guidelines are not expected to have a significant economic impact on the new construction and alterations of facilities by a substantial number of small entities for purposes of the Regulatory Flexibility Act. The final revised guidelines will add 0.01 to 0.5 percent to the total construction costs of facilities compared to the current guidelines; and 0.00 to 0.3 percent to the total construction costs of facilities compared to the International Building Code. These impacts are not significant for an individual facility.

CHAPTER 1: BACKGROUND

1.0 Introduction

Executive Order 12866 requires Federal agencies to submit certain regulatory actions to the Office of Management and Budget for review. The agency must provide the Office of Management and Budget the text of the regulatory action, together with an assessment of the impacts of the regulatory action. The assessment must describe the need for the regulatory action and how the regulatory action will meet that need. The assessment must also explain how the regulatory action is consistent with statutory mandates, promotes the President's priorities, and avoids undue interference with State, local, and tribal governments in the exercise of their governmental functions. The Access Board prepared this assessment of the final revised accessibility guidelines for the Americans with Disabilities Act and Architectural Barriers Act to meet the requirements of Executive Order 12866.

1.1 Statutory Authority

The Access Board is required by statute to establish and maintain minimum guidelines to ensure that facilities covered by the Americans with Disabilities Act and Architectural Barriers Act are accessible, in terms of architecture and design and communication, to individuals with disabilities.[1] These guidelines serve as the basis for enforceable standards issued by other agencies under the Americans with Disabilities Act and Architectural Barriers Act. The requirements of the Americans with Disabilities Act and Architectural Barriers Act with respect to facilities are explained below.

Americans with Disabilities Act

9

The Americans with Disabilities Act was enacted in 1990 based upon the Congress finding that:

"individuals with disabilities continually encounter various forms of discrimination, including . . . the discriminatory effects of architectural, transportation, and communication barriers."

The purpose of the Americans with Disabilities Act is:

"to provide clear, strong, consistent, and enforceable standards addressing discrimination against individuals with disabilities [and] to ensure that the Federal government plays a central role in enforcing the standards."

The Americans with Disabilities Act requires newly constructed State and local government facilities, places of public accommodation, and commercial facilities to be accessible to individuals with disabilities. The Americans with Disabilities Act also requires parts of existing facilities that are altered to be accessible.

Two agencies are responsible for issuing enforceable standards for facilities covered by the Americans with Disabilities Act.

- The Department of Transportation issues enforceable standards for public transportation facilities owned or operated by State and local governments, and the National Railroad Passenger Corporation.

- The Department of Justice issues enforceable standards for all other types of facilities.

Architectural Barriers Act

The Architectural Barriers Act was enacted in 1968 to provide individuals with disabilities access to facilities financed by the Federal government. The Architectural Barriers Act covers facilities constructed, altered, or leased by the Federal government. The Architectural Barriers Act also covers facilities constructed or altered with a Federal grant or loan, where the law authorizing the grant or loan authorizes the administering agency to issue design or construction standards; and facilities constructed by the Washington Metropolitan Area Transit Authority.

Four agencies are responsible for issuing enforceable standards for facilities covered by the Architectural Barriers Act.

- The Department of Housing and Urban Development issues enforceable standards for federally financed residential facilities.
- The Department of Defense issues enforceable standards for military facilities.

10

- The United States Postal Service issues enforceable standards for postal facilities.
- The General Services Administration issues enforceable standards for all other federally financed facilities.

1.2 Current Guidelines and Standards

MGRAD and UFAS

In 1982, the Access Board issued the Minimum Guidelines and Requirements for Accessible Design (MGRAD) to assist the Department of Housing and Urban Development, Department of Defense, United States Postal Service, and General Services Administration in establishing a consistent set of enforceable standards. These four agencies in turn issued the Uniform Federal Accessibility Standards (UFAS) in 1984 as the enforceable standards for facilities covered by the Architectural Barriers Act.

ADAAG

In 1991, the Access Board issued the Americans with Disabilities Act Accessibility Guidelines (ADAAG) to assist the Department of Justice and Department of Transportation in establishing a consistent set of enforceable standards. ADAAG is modeled on UFAS. ADAAG includes provisions for features and facilities that are not addressed in UFAS. For example, ADAAG has provisions for van accessible parking spaces, public TTYs, automated teller machines, and transportation facilities. UFAS does not address these features or facilities. The Access Board prepared a regulatory assessment for ADAAG when the guidelines were initially issued. The Department of Justice and Department of Transportation adopted ADAAG in 1991 as the enforceable standards for facilities covered by the Americans with Disabilities Act. The General Services Administration requires Federal agencies to use ADAAG for facilities covered by the Architectural Barriers Act when it provides a greater level of access compared to UFAS.

11

Children's Facilities Guidelines

In 1998, the Access Board amended ADAAG by adding guidelines for children's facilities. These guidelines add child-sized alternatives to the existing adult dimensions that can be used when designing building elements for children. The Access Board did not prepare a regulatory assessment for the children's facilities guidelines because they do not establish any new requirements. The children's facilities guidelines have not been adopted by the Department of Justice or Department of Transportation.

State and Local Government Facilities Guidelines

In 1998, the Access Board also amended ADAAG by adding guidelines for judicial facilities, and detention and correctional facilities. These guidelines address certain areas within court rooms such as raised judges' benches, and within jails and prisons such as the number of cells required to provide mobility features. The Access Board did not prepare a regulatory assessment for the State and local government facilities guidelines because they do not impose any significant impacts on State and local government facilities. The State and local government facilities guidelines have not been adopted by the Department of Justice or Department of Transportation.

Play Areas Guidelines

In 2000, the Access Board amended ADAAG by adding guidelines for play areas used by children. These guidelines address access to ground level and elevated play components, and ground surfaces. The Access Board prepared a regulatory assessment for the play areas guidelines. The play areas guidelines have not been adopted by the Department of Justice or Department of Transportation.

Recreation Facilities Guidelines

In 2002, the Access Board amended ADAAG by adding guidelines for recreation facilities. These guidelines address access to amusement rides, boating and fishing facilities, golf courses, miniature golf courses, exercise equipment, bowling lanes, shooting facilities, and swimming pools and spas. The Access Board prepared a regulatory assessment for the recreation facilities guidelines. The recreation facilities guidelines have not been adopted by the Department of Justice or Department of Transportation.

The guidelines for play areas and recreation facilities were developed through separate rulemaking processes that involved advisory committees and regulatory negotiation, and were not part of the present rulemaking to revise the guidelines. The guidelines for play areas and recreation facilities are incorporated in the final revised guidelines without any substantive changes.

1.3 Need to Revise Guidelines

Since the enactment of the Americans with Disabilities Act, accessibility requirements have been increasingly incorporated into the model codes. State and local governments adopt the model codes to regulate building construction. The model codes are revised

Printed by Builder's Book, Inc., Bookstore · www.buildersbook.com

every three years. The model codes reference the ICC/ANSI A117.1 Standard on Accessible and Usable Buildings and Facilities for technical requirements. The ICC/ANSI A117.1 standard is revised every five years.

Federal accessibility requirements need to keep pace with the model codes and standards as they are revised. The Access Board has revised the guidelines for the Americans with Disabilities Act and Architectural Barriers Act to harmonize the guidelines with the model codes and standards in order to achieve greater consistency and uniformity in accessibility requirements at the Federal, State, and local government levels. The Access Board has also revised the guidelines to ensure that Federal facilities provide the same level of accessibility as State and local government facilities, and private facilities.

1.4 Rulemaking History

The Access Board established the ADAAG Review Advisory Committee in 1994 to recommend revisions to the guidelines. The advisory committee consisted of 22 organizations representing model codes and standards groups, State and local governments, the building and construction industry, and individuals with disabilities. The advisory committee issued its report, "Recommendations for a New ADAAG," in 1996. The Access Board used the advisory committee's report to develop a proposed rule that was published in 1999. Public hearings were held on the proposed rule in Los Angeles and Washington, DC. Information meetings were also held in Washington, D.C. to hear from industry and disability groups on issues regarding automated teller machines, reach ranges, and captioning equipment for movie theaters. Throughout the rulemaking process, the Access Board worked collaboratively with the International Code Council and ANSI A117 Committee to harmonize the guidelines with the new International Building Code, which was first issued in 2000 and revised in 2003; and the ICC/ANSI A117.1 standard, which was revised in 1998 and 2003. The Access Board released a draft of the final revised guidelines in April 2002 to further promote harmonization with the model codes and standards.

1.5 Final Revised Guidelines

The final revised guidelines consist of three parts which are published as separate appendices to 36 C.F.R. Part 1191.

- Appendix B contains ADA Chapters 1 and 2 of the guidelines, which establish application and scoping requirements for facilities covered by the Americans with Disabilities Act. The scoping requirements specify what features of a newly constructed or altered facility must be accessible. Where multiple features that serve the same function are provided, such as parking spaces in a garage or seats in an assembly area, the scoping requirements specify how many of the features must be accessible.

- Appendix C contains ABA Chapters 1 and 2 of the guidelines, which establish application and scoping requirements for facilities covered by the Architectural

13

Barriers Act. The scoping requirements in Appendix C are mostly the same as those in Appendix B. A few requirements are different based on the Architectural Barriers Act. Appendix C, for example, includes scoping requirements for facilities leased by Federal agencies.

- Appendix D contains Chapters 3 through 10 of the guidelines, which establish common technical requirements for facilities covered by the Americans with Disabilities Act and Architectural Barriers Act. The technical requirements provide dimensions and specifications for making the features of a facility accessible.

Appendix A contains the Table of Contents, and Appendix E contains the List of Figures and Index for the final revised guidelines.

1.6 President's Priorities

On July 26, 2002, President George W. Bush issued a Proclamation on the twelfth anniversary of the Americans with Disabilities Act calling the statute "one of the most compassionate and successful civil rights laws in American history." The President committed his Administration to implementing the Americans with Disabilities Act and "removing the barriers that prevent people with disabilities from realizing their full potential and achieving their dreams." The final revised guidelines will promote the President's priorities by improving implementation of the Americans with Disabilities Act's accessibility requirements.

1.7 Federalism

The Americans with Disabilities Act was enacted "to provide clear, strong, consistent, and enforceable standards addressing discrimination against individuals with disabilities [and] to ensure that the Federal Government plays a central role in enforcing the standards." The Architectural Barriers Act was enacted to provide individuals with disabilities access to federally financed facilities. Ensuring the civil rights of groups who have experienced discrimination has long been recognized as a national issue and a proper function of the Federal government.
The Americans with Disabilities Act recognizes the authority of State and local governments to enact and enforce laws that "provide greater or equal protection for the rights of individuals with disabilities than are afforded by this chapter."

The final revised guidelines serve as the basis for enforceable standards issued by other Federal agencies under the Americans with Disabilities Act and Architectural Barriers Act.
The final revised guidelines adhere to the fundamental federalism principles and policy making criteria in Executive Order 13132. The Access Board consulted with State and local governments throughout the rulemaking process. State and local governments were represented on the ADAAG Review Advisory Committee, participated in public hearings, and submitted comments on the proposed rule. The final revised guidelines

14

are harmonized with model codes that are adopted by State and local governments to regulate building construction.

Regulations that implement statutory rights that prohibit discrimination on the basis of disability are exempt from the Unfunded Mandates Reform Act, which requires agencies to assess the effects of regulatory actions on State and local governments.

CHAPTER 2: METHODOLOGY

2.0 Baseline

Regulatory actions are compared to a baseline to evaluate their potential impacts. The baseline is a reasonable forecast of what would happen in the absence of the regulatory action. As explained below, the final revised guidelines are compared to the current guidelines and the International Building Code. In addition, the final revised guidelines concerning common use circulation paths in employee work areas, accessible means of egress, and visible alarms in hotel guest rooms with communication features are compared to the model fire and life safety codes.

Current Guidelines

In the absence of the final revised guidelines, newly constructed and altered facilities covered by the Americans with Disabilities Act would have to comply with ADAAG as initially issued in 1991, which has been adopted as enforceable standards by the Department of Justice and Department of Transportation. Newly constructed, altered, and leased facilities covered by the Architectural Barriers Act that are subject to standards issued by the General Services Administration are also required to comply with ADAAG, where it provides a greater level of access compared to UFAS.

The final revised guidelines reorganize and renumber ADAAG, and rewrite the text to be clearer and easier to understand. Most of the scoping and technical requirements in ADAAG have not been changed. An independent codes expert compared the final revised guidelines and ADAAG to identify revisions that add new features or space to facilities, or present design challenges compared to ADAAG. The codes expert identified 27 revisions that are expected to have minimal impacts on the new construction and alterations of facilities, which are discussed in Chapter 6; and 14 revisions that are expected to have monetary impacts on the new construction and alterations of facilities, which are discussed in Chapter 7.

Comparing the final revised guidelines to the current guidelines represents the upper bound of the range of potential impacts, and assumes that facilities covered by the Americans with Disabilities Act or Architectural Barriers Act are not required to also comply with equivalent requirements in the International Building Code.

International Building Code

The International Building Code was first issued in 2000 and revised in 2003. The 2000 and 2003 editions of the International Building Code reference the 1998 edition of the

15

ICC/ANSI A117.1 Standard on Accessible and Usable Buildings and Facilities for technical requirements.

In the absence of the final revised guidelines, newly constructed and altered facilities would have to comply with the International Building Code in jurisdictions where the code has been adopted. As shown in Table 2.1, the International Building Code has been adopted statewide in 28 States and by local governments in 15 States. The District of Columbia, the Department of Defense, and the National Park Service have also adopted the International Building Code.

Table 2.1 – State and Local Government Adoption of International Building Code
(text version)

State	Adopted Statewide	Adopted by Local Government*	State	Adopted Statewide	Adopted by Local Government*
Alabama		X (20)	Montana	X	
Alaska	X		Nebraska		X (10)
Arizona		X (33)	Nevada		X (5)
Arkansas	X		New Hampshire	X	
California			New Jersey	X	
Colorado		X (100)	New Mexico		X (6)
Connecticut			New York	X	
Delaware		X (3)	North Carolina	X	
Florida			North Dakota	X	
Georgia	X		Ohio	X	
Hawaii			Oklahoma	X	
Idaho	X		Oregon		
Illinois		X (41)	Pennsylvania	X	
Indiana	X		Rhode Island		
Iowa		X (16)	South Carolina	X	
Kansas		X (17)	South Dakota	X	
Kentucky	X		Tennessee		X (3)
Louisiana	X		Texas		X (117)
Maine		X (21)	Utah	X	
Maryland	X		Vermont		
Massachusetts	X		Virginia	X	
Michigan	X		Washington	X	
Minnesota	X		West Virginia	X	
Mississippi		X (12)	Wisconsin	X	
Missouri		X (39)	Wyoming	X	

* Number of local governments that have adopted the International Building Code is shown in parenthesis

16

The final revised guidelines are compared to the 2000 and 2003 editions of the International Building Code to identify whether the codes contain equivalent requirements. Comparing the final revised guidelines to the International Building Code represents the lower bound of the range of potential impacts, and assumes that facilities covered by the Americans with Disabilities Act or Architectural Barriers Act are required to also comply with equivalent requirements in the International Building Code. The actual impacts will be between the lower and upper bound of the range.

Model Fire and Life Safety Codes

The final revised guidelines concerning common use circulation paths in employee work areas, accessible means of egress, and visible alarms in hotel guest rooms with communication features are also compared to relevant requirements in the 2003 editions of the NFPA 101, Life Safety Code; NFPA 1, Uniform Fire Code; and International Fire Code. As shown in Table 2.2, these model codes have been adopted statewide by 48 States. The other two States, New Jersey and Ohio, have adopted the International Building Code, which contains equivalent requirements to the International Fire Code for means of egress and visible alarms.

Table 2.2 - Statewide Adoption of Model Fire and Life Safety Codes (text version)

State	NFPA 101 Life Safety Code	NFPA 1 Uniform Fire Code	International Fire Code
Alabama	X	X	
Alaska			X
Arizona		X	
Arkansas	X		X
California		X	
Colorado	X	X	
Connecticut	X		
Delaware	X		
Florida	X	X	
Georgia	X		X
Hawaii		X	
Idaho			X
Illinois	X		
Indiana		X	X
Iowa	X		
Kansas	X		
Kentucky	X	X	
Louisiana	X	X	
Maine	X	X	
Maryland	X	X	
Massachusetts	X		
Michigan	X	X	X
Minnesota	X		X
Mississippi	X		

17

State	NFPA 101 Life Safety Code	NFPA 1 Uniform Fire Code	International Fire Code
Missouri	X		
Montana		X	
Nebraska	X	X	
Nevada	X	X	
New Hampshire	X	X	
New Jersey			
New Mexico	X	X	
New York	X		X
North Carolina			X
North Dakota	X	X	
Ohio			
Oklahoma	X		X
Oregon		X	X
Pennsylvania			X
Rhode Island	X	X	
South Carolina	X		X
South Dakota	X	X	X
Tennessee	X	X	
Texas	X		
Utah	X		X
Vermont	X	X	
Virginia	X		X
Washington	X	X	X
West Virginia	X	X	
Wisconsin	X	X	
Wyoming	X	X	X

2.1 Timing of Impacts

The final revised guidelines are not enforceable and will not have any impacts until they are adopted as enforceable standards by the following agencies:

- Department of Justice for State and local government facilities, places of public accommodation, and commercial facilities.

- Department of Transportation for public transportation facilities owned or operated by State and local governments, and the National Railroad Passenger Corporation.

18

- Department of Housing and Urban Development for federally financed residential facilities.

- Department of Defense for military facilities.

- United States Postal Service for postal facilities.

- General Services Administration for all other federally financed facilities.

The Department of Justice, Department of Transportation, Department of Housing and Urban Development, and General Services Administration will have to conduct notice and comment rulemaking to adopt the final revised guidelines as enforceable standards. More State and local governments are expected to adopt the International Building Code by the time the final revised guidelines are adopted as enforceable standards by the above agencies, which will further reduce the potential impacts toward the lower bound of the range.

2.2 Benefits

The Access Board worked collaboratively with the International Code Council and the ANSI A117 Committee to harmonize the final revised guidelines with the 2000 and 2003 editions of the International Building Code and the 1998 and 2003 editions of the ICC/ANSI A117.1 Standard for Accessible and Usable Buildings and Facilities. Harmonization will benefit State and local governments, businesses, architects, and individuals with disabilities. These benefits are discussed in Chapter 3. The Access Board also revised some of the scoping and technical requirements in ADAAG to reduce the impacts on facilities. These revisions are discussed in Chapter 5.

2.3 Alternatives

The regulatory assessment for the proposed rule estimated that the national costs of the rule would be $87.5 million annually for newly constructed office buildings, hotels, and sports stadiums and arenas. The Access Board adopted alternatives in the final revised guidelines that eliminate these costs. These alternatives are discussed in Chapter 4.

2.4 New Construction

Designing facilities to be accessible from the beginning generally has minimal impacts on the total construction costs. Most of the scoping and technical requirements do not add new features or space to facilities, but rather require that features commonly provided meet certain specifications so individuals with disabilities are included. Most designs are produced today with the assistance of computers. Designers can simply

19

incorporate the specifications into their computer assisted design (CAD) programs. This assessment focuses on revisions in the final revised guidelines that either add new features or space to facilities, or present design challenges.

2.5 Alterations to Existing Facilities

There are two general requirements and an exception that apply to alterations to existing facilities:

Element or Space Altered – When an element or space is altered, the altered element or space is required to meet the requirements for new construction. If the circulation path to the altered element or space is not altered, an accessible route is not required to the altered element or space, unless the altered area contains a primary function.

Alterations Affecting Primary Function Areas – If the alterations affect or could affect the usability of or access to an area containing a primary function, the Department of Justice and Department of Transportation regulations implementing the Americans with Disabilities Act require the "path of travel" serving the altered area to be made accessible to the extent that the costs do not exceed 20 percent of the costs of the alterations to the primary function area. A primary function is a major activity for which the facility is intended. The "path of travel" includes an accessible route that connects the altered area with an exterior approach, and the toilet rooms, public telephones, and drinking fountains serving the altered primary function area. When the Department of Justice and Department of Transportation adopt the final revised guidelines as enforceable standards, they will address what an entity's obligations are when elements that are part of the "path of travel" serving an altered primary function area meet earlier standards, and the revised standards change the requirements for the elements.

Technical Infeasibility – If it is not technically feasible to comply with a requirement because existing structural conditions would require removing or altering a load-bearing member that is an essential part of the structural frame or because of other existing physical or site constraints, the alteration is required to meet the requirement to the maximum extent feasible.

The impacts of the revisions on alterations to existing facilities will be facility specific, and will depend on the elements and spaces that are altered. For revisions that have monetary impacts, this assessment examines the impacts of the revisions on alterations to existing facilities by answering three questions:

- Is the element or space typically altered?

- Is the element or space part of the "path of travel" serving a primary function area?

- Does alteration of the element or space involve technical infeasibility?

This assessment also includes alterations projects when estimating the national costs of the final revised guidelines for office buildings, hotels, hospitals and nursing homes, and Federal, State, and local government housing.

2.6 Readily Achievable Barrier Removal

The Americans with Disabilities Act requires places of public accommodation to remove architectural and communication barriers that are structural in nature in existing facilities, where it is readily achievable. Readily achievable is defined as actions that are "easily accomplishable and able to be carried out without much difficulty or expense." The Department of Justice is responsible for issuing regulations to implement the readily achievable "barrier removal" requirement. When the Department of Justice adopts the final revised guidelines as enforceable standards, it will address what an entity's obligations are when an element in an existing facility meets earlier standards, and the revised standards change the requirements for the element. This assessment does not address the impacts of the final revised guidelines on readily achievable "barrier removal" in existing facilities since the Department of Justice will address this issue when it adopts the final revised guidelines as enforceable standards.

CHAPTER 3: HARMONIZATION BENEFITS

3.0 Introduction

The Access Board worked collaboratively with the International Code Council and the ANSI A117 Committee to harmonize the final revised guidelines with the new International Building Code, which was first issued in 2000 and revised in 2003, and the ICC/ANSA A117.1 Standard on Accessible and Usable Buildings and Facilities, which was revised in 1998 and 2003. The 2000 and 2003 editions of the International Building Code reference the 1998 edition of the ICC/ANSI A117.1 standard for technical requirements. As discussed below, harmonization benefits State and local governments, businesses, architects, and individuals with disabilities.

3.1 State and Local Governments

State and local governments that adopt the model codes and standards want accessibility requirements in the model codes and standards and at the Federal level to be harmonized. The Americans with Disabilities Act authorizes the Department of Justice to certify State or local codes that meet or exceed Federal accessibility requirements. State and local governments that adopt the International Building Code will find it easier to have their codes certified, and more State and local governments are expected to submit their codes to the Department of Justice for certification. In jurisdictions where codes have been certified by the Department of Justice, business owners, builders, developers, and architects can rely on their State or local government building plan approval and inspection processes as a "check-point" for ensuring that their facilities comply with Federal accessibility requirements. Potential mistakes can be corrected early in the construction process when adjustments can be made easily and inexpensively compared to costly retrofitting after a facility is constructed. Compliance with a certified code is also evidence of compliance with Federal accessibility requirements in litigation to enforce the Americans with Disabilities Act.

3.2 Businesses

Business owners, builders, and developers want consistent and uniform accessibility requirements adopted by the Federal, State, and local governments. It is difficult and time consuming for them to deal with different accessibility requirements at each layer of government. Dealing with different accessibility requirements at the Federal, State, and local levels can also contribute to mistakes requiring costly corrections after the facilities are constructed. Harmonization of accessibility requirements at the Federal, State, and local levels promotes efficiency and economic growth for businesses.

3.3 Architects

Architects who design buildings also want consistent and uniform accessibility requirements adopted by the Federal, State, and local governments. Architects bear the primary responsibility for designing facilities that meet accessibility requirements and are potentially liable for any mistakes that could result in litigation. Harmonization of accessibility requirements at the Federal, State, and local levels makes it easier for architects to design accessible facilities and reduces the potential for mistakes and litigation.

3.4 Individuals with Disabilities

Individuals with disabilities are the ultimate beneficiaries of harmonization. The U.S. Census Bureau reports that there are 52.5 million Americans with disabilities in the civilian non-institutionalized population age 5 and over. Almost one in five individuals has some type of disability. Among individuals 15 years old and over, 25 million have difficulty walking or using stairs. Harmonization will result in increased compliance with Federal accessibility requirements in jurisdictions that adopt the model codes and standards, and use their plan approval and inspection processes to check for compliance. Increased compliance will result in more accessible facilities for individuals with disabilities.

CHAPTER 4: ALTERNATIVES THAT ELIMINATE COSTS ESTIMATED FOR THE PROPOSED RULE
4.0 Introduction

The regulatory assessment for the proposed rule estimated that the national costs of the rule would be $87.5 million annually for newly constructed office buildings, hotels, and sports stadiums and arenas. The Access Board adopted alternatives in the final revised guidelines that eliminate these costs. This chapter discusses the alternatives that were adopted. The relevant text of the current guidelines, the proposed rule, and the final revised guidelines is presented in tables. Unless otherwise noted, the current guidelines refer to ADAAG. Scoping and technical requirements are presented together, where

22

appropriate. The text of the proposed rule that imposed the cost and the text of the final revised guidelines that eliminates the cost are underlined. Where a new requirement was included in the proposed rule, but is not included in the final revised guidelines, there is no underlined text in the final revised guidelines. Equivalent requirements in the International Building Code and the ICC/ANSI A117.1 Standard on Accessible and Usable Buildings and Facilities are also noted in the tables.

4.1 Office Buildings

The proposed rule added a new scoping requirement for visible alarms in employee work areas. The regulatory assessment for the proposed rule estimated the national costs of the revision for newly constructed office buildings would be $16 million annually. As discussed below, the final revised guidelines eliminate these costs.

Visible Alarms in Employee Work Areas

Table 4.1 shows the relevant text of the current guidelines, the proposed rule, and the final revised guidelines with respect to the scoping requirement for visible alarms in employee work areas.

Table 4.1 - Visible Alarms in Employee Work Areas (text version)

Current Guidelines	Proposed Rule	Final Revised Guidelines
4.1.1(3) Areas Used Only by Employees as Work Areas. Areas that are used only as work areas shall be designed and constructed so that individuals with disabilities can approach, enter, and exit the areas. These guidelines do not require that any areas used only as work areas be constructed to permit maneuvering within the work area or be constructed or equipped (i.e., with racks or shelves) to be accessible. **4.1.3 Accessible Buildings: New Construction.** Accessible buildings and facilities shall meet the following minimum requirements: . . . (14) If emergency warning systems are provided, then they shall include both audible alarms and visual	**203.3 Employee Work Areas.** Employee work areas shall be designed and constructed so that individuals with disabilities can approach enter, and exit the employee work areas. *In addition, visual alarm coverage shall be provided where audible alarm coverage is provided in employee work areas.* This part does not require that employee work areas be constructed to permit maneuvering with the employee work area or be constructed or equipped to be accessible. **215.1 Fire Alarms.** Where fire alarm systems are provided in public use or common use areas, the alarm shall provide a system with both audible and visual signals complying with 702. . . .	**203.9 Employee Work Areas.** Spaces and elements within employee work areas shall only be required to comply with 206.2.8, 207.1, and 215.3 and shall be designed and constructed so that individuals with disabilities can approach, enter, and exit the employee work area. . . . **215.1 General.** Where fire alarm systems provide audible alarm coverage, alarms shall comply with 215. . . . **215.2 Public and Common Use Areas.** Alarms in public and common use areas shall comply with 702. *215.3 Employee Work Areas.* Where employee work areas have audible

Printed by Builder's Book, Inc., Bookstore · www.buildersbook.com

Current Guidelines	Proposed Rule	Final Revised Guidelines
alarms complying with 4.28. . . .		*alarm coverage, the wiring system shall be designed so that visible alarms complying with 702 can be integrated into the alarm system.*
Model Codes & Standards		
IBC 2000: No requirement for visible alarms in employee work areas. **IBC 2003:** Section 907.9.1.2 has an equivalent requirement for visible alarms in employee work areas.		

The current guidelines require visible alarms to be provided where fire alarm systems are provided, but do not require areas used only by employees as work areas to be equipped with accessibility features. As applied to office buildings, the current guidelines require visible alarms to be provided in public and common use areas such as conference rooms, break rooms, and restrooms, where fire alarm systems are provided.

The proposed rule required visible alarm coverage to be provided in employee work areas where audible alarm coverage is provided. Since building codes and fire and life safety codes generally require visible alarms in open-plan office areas, the regulatory assessment for the proposed rule estimated the impact of extending visible alarm coverage to individual offices. The cost of installing a single 15 candela visible alarm appliance in an individual office was estimated at $270. A newly constructed office building with 200,000 square feet in area was estimated to require an additional 250 visible alarm appliances, plus additional power supply and circuits for the alarm system, which would increase the construction cost by $65,375. The regulatory assessment for the proposed rule estimated the national costs of requiring visible alarms in employee work areas would be $16 million annually for 250 newly constructed office buildings.

The final revised guidelines eliminate these costs by requiring the alarm wiring system to be designed so that visible alarms can be added when needed to serve employees who are deaf or hard of hearing. In new construction, alarm systems are typically designed with circuits at 80 percent of their capacity and the alarm wiring is run through the spaces that are provided with alarm coverage. In typical configurations with offices along both sides of a corridor, or with offices on one side and open-plan work areas on the other side, the alarm wiring is commonly run in line with the corridor. This design allows for short wiring "runs" to provide audible and visible alarm appliances in the public and common use areas, and open-plan work areas. This design also places the alarm wiring in a location where it is relatively easy to extend the wiring into an individual office and install a visible alarm appliance when needed.

4.2 Hotels

The proposed rule revised the scoping requirement for guest rooms with communication features. The regulatory assessment for the proposed rule estimated the national costs of the revision for newly constructed hotels would be $31 million annually. As discussed below, the final revised guidelines eliminate these costs.

24

Guest Rooms with Communication Features

Table 4.2 shows the relevant text of the current guidelines, the proposed rule, and the final revised guidelines with respect to the scoping requirement for guest rooms with communications features.

Table 4.2 – Guest Rooms with Communication Features (text version)

Current Guidelines	Proposed Rule	Final Revised Guidelines
9.1.2 Accessible Units, Sleeping Rooms, and Suites. Accessible sleeping rooms or suites that comply with the requirements of 9.2 (Requirements for Accessible Units, Sleeping Rooms, and Suites) shall be provided in accordance with the table below. In addition, in hotels of 50 or more sleeping rooms or suites, additional accessible sleeping rooms or suites that include a roll-in shower shall also be provided in conformance with the table below...	*224.4 Communication Features. In transient lodging facilities, at least fifty percent, but not less than one, of the total number of guest rooms shall have accessible communication features complying with 806.3.*	*224.4 Guest Rooms with Communication Features. In transient lodging facilities, guest rooms with communication features complying with 806.3 shall be provided in accordance with Table 224.4.*

Number of Rooms	Accessible Rooms	Rooms with Roll-in Showers
1 to 25	1	
26 to 50	2	
51 to 75	3	1
766 to 100	4	1
101 to 150	5	2
151 to 200	6	2
201 to 300	7	3
301 to 400	8	4
401 to 500	9	
501 to 1000	2% of total	4 plus 1 for each additional 100 over 400
1001 and over	20 plus 1 for each 100 over 1000	

Table 224.4 Guest Rooms with Communication Features

Total Number of Guest Rooms Provided	Minimum Number of Required Guest Rooms with Communication Features
2 to 25	2
26 to 50	4
51 to 75	7
76 to 100	9
101 to 150	12
151 to 200	14
201 to 300	17
301 to 400	20
401 to 500	22
501 to 1000	5% of total
1001 and over	50, plus 3 for each 100 over 1000

224.5 Dispersion. . . . At least one guest room required to provide mobility features

Printed by Builder's Book, Inc., Bookstore · www.buildersbook.com

Current Guidelines	Proposed Rule	Final Revised Guidelines
9.1.3 Sleeping Accommodations for Persons with Hearing Impairments. In addition to those accessible sleeping rooms and suites required by 9.1.2, sleeping rooms and suites that comply with 9.3 (Visual Alarms, Notification Devices, and Telephones) shall be provided in conformance with the following table:		complying with 806.2 shall also provide communication features complying with 806.3. Not more than 10 percent of guest rooms required to provide mobility features complying with 806.2 shall be used to satisfy the minimum number of guest rooms required to provide communication features complying with 806.3.

Number of Elements	Accessible Elements
1 to 25	1
26 to 50	2
51 to 75	3
76 to 100	4
101 to 150	5
151 to 200	6
201 to 300	7
301 to 400	8
401 to 500	9
501 to 1000	2% of total
1001 and over	20 plus 1 for each 100 over 1000

9.2.2 Minimum Requirements. An accessible unit, sleeping room or suite shall be on an accessible route complying with 4.3 and have the following accessible elements and spaces. . . .

(8) Sleeping room accommodations for persons with hearing impairments required by 9.1 and complying with 9.3 shall be provided in the accessible sleeping room or suite.

Model Codes & Standards
IBC 2000: Section 907.9.1.2 and section E1104.3 of Appendix E have equivalent requirements for the number of guest rooms with communication features in facilities with six or more guest rooms.
IBC 2003: Section 907.9.1.3 and section E104.3 of Appendix E have equivalent

Printed by Builder's Book, Inc., Bookstore · www.buildersbook.com

Current Guidelines	Proposed Rule	Final Revised Guidelines
requirements for the number of guest rooms with communication features in facilities with six or more guest rooms.		

The current guidelines require hotels to provide a minimum number of guest rooms with mobility features based on the total number of guest rooms in the facility. The current guidelines require an additional minimum number of guest rooms to provide roll-in showers. All the guest rooms that are required to provide mobility features and roll-in showers are also required to provide communication features for individuals who are deaf or hard of hearing. The current guidelines also require hotels to provide an additional minimum number of guest rooms with communication features for individuals who are deaf or hard of hearing.

The proposed rule required a minimum of 50 percent of the total number of guest rooms to provide communication features. The regulatory assessment for the proposed rule estimated the cost of providing communication features in a guest room at $556, including $293 for a 110 candela visible alarm appliance and $263 for a notification device. The proposed rule required a newly constructed hotel with 150 guest rooms to provide a minimum of 75 guest rooms with communication features, compared to a minimum of 12 guest rooms under the current guidelines, which would increase the construction cost by $35,028. The regulatory assessment for the proposed rule estimated the national costs of increasing the number of guest rooms required to provide communication features to a minimum of 50 percent of the total number of guest rooms would be $31 million annually for 890 newly constructed hotels.

The final revised guidelines make no change from the current guidelines with respect to the number of guest rooms required to provide communication features. The scoping requirement is consolidated into a single table in the final revised guidelines, instead of appearing in three sections as in the current guidelines. The final revised guidelines also limit the overlap between guest rooms required to provide mobility features and guest rooms required to provide communication features. At least one, but not more than 10 percent, of the guest rooms required to provide mobility features can also provide communication features.

4.3 Sports Stadiums and Arenas

The proposed rule revised the scoping requirements for vertical access, vertical dispersion of wheelchair spaces, companion seats, and designated aisle seats in assembly areas. The regulatory assessment for the proposed rule estimated the national costs of the revisions for newly constructed sports stadiums and arenas would be $40.5 million. As discussed below, the final revised guidelines eliminate these costs.

Vertical Access

Table 4.3 shows the relevant text of the current guidelines, the proposed rule, and the final revised guidelines with respect to the scoping requirement for vertical access.

Table 4.3 - Vertical Access (text version)

Current Guidelines	Proposed Rule	Final Revised Guidelines

27

Current Guidelines	Proposed Rule	Final Revised Guidelines
4.1.3 Accessible Buildings: New Construction. Accessible buildings and facilities shall meet the following minimum requirements: . . . (5) One passenger elevator complying with 4.10 shall serve each level, including mezzanines, in all multi-story buildings and facilities unless exempted below. If more than one elevator is provided, each passenger elevator shall comply with 4.10. . . .	**206.2.3 Multi-Level Buildings and Facilities.** Accessible routes shall connect each level, including mezzanines, in multi-level buildings and facilities. . . . *221.5 Vertical Access. Where wheelchair spaces or designated aisle seats share a common accessible route that includes vertical access by means of elevators or platform lifts, elevators or platform lifts shall be provided in such number, capacity, and speed to provide a level of service equivalent to that provided in the same seating area to patrons who can use stairs or other means of vertical access.*	**206.2.3 Multi-Story Buildings and Facilities.** At least one accessible route shall connect each story and mezzanine in multi-story buildings and facilities. . . . **206.6 Elevators.** Elevators provided for passengers shall comply with 407. Where multiple elevators are provided, each elevator shall comply with 407 . . . .
Model Codes & Standards		
IBC 2000: Section 1104.4 has an equivalent requirement for accessible routes in multi-story facilities. **IBC 2003:** Section 1104.4 has an equivalent requirement for accessible routes in multi-story facilities.		

The current guidelines require one accessible passenger elevator to serve each level in multi-story facilities, unless an exception applies. If more than one elevator is provided, each elevator is required to be accessible.

The proposed rule required elevators or platform lifts to be provided to wheelchair spaces and designated aisle seats in sports stadiums and arenas in sufficient number, capacity, and speed so as to provide a level of service equivalent to that provided in the same seating area to patrons who can use stairs. The regulatory assessment for the proposed rule assumed large sports facilities with 50,000 seats would add 3 more elevators to provide equivalent vertical access to wheelchair spaces and designated aisle seats; medium sports facilities with 20,000 seats would add 2 more elevators; and small sports facilities with 11,000 seats would add 1 more elevator. The cost of installing a 3-stop hydraulic elevator was estimated at $61,794. The regulatory assessment for the proposed rule estimated the national costs of requiring equivalent vertical access to wheelchair spaces and designated aisle seats would be $1.5 million annually for 3 large, 5 medium, and 5 small newly constructed sports facilities.

The final revised guidelines make no change from the current guidelines with respect to accessible routes in multi-story facilities.

Vertical Dispersion of Wheelchair Spaces

Table 4.4 shows the relevant text of the current guidelines, the proposed rule, and the final revised guidelines with respect to the scoping requirement for vertical dispersion of wheelchair spaces in assembly areas.

Table 4.4 – Vertical Dispersion of Wheelchair Spaces (text version)

Current Guidelines	Proposed Rule	Final Revised Guidelines
4.33.3 Placement of Wheelchair Locations. Wheelchair areas . . . shall be provided so as to provide people with physical disabilities a choice of admission prices and lines of sight comparable to those for members of the general public . . . . When the seating capacity exceeds 300, wheelchair spaces shall be provided in more than one location. . . .	*802.6.1 Admission Prices. Wheelchair spaces and designated aisle seats shall be provided in each price level distinguishable by location.* *802.6.3 Vertical Dispersion. Wheelchair spaces and designated aisle seats shall be located at varying distances from the performance area on each accessible level and in each balcony or mezzanine that is located along an accessible route.*	*221.2.3.2 Vertical Dispersion. Wheelchair spaces shall be dispersed vertically at varying distances from the screen, performance area, or playing field. In addition, wheelchair spaces shall be located in each balcony or mezzanine that is located on an accessible route. . . .*
Model Codes & Standards		
IBC 2000: Section 1107.2.3 has a similar requirement for vertical dispersion of wheelchair spaces. **IBC 2003:** Section 1108.2.4 has a similar requirement for vertical dispersion of wheelchair spaces.		

The current guidelines require wheelchair spaces to be located in more than one area where the seating capacity exceeds 300 and to provide a choice of admission prices. Under the current guidelines, sports facilities typically locate some wheelchair spaces on each accessible level of the facilities.

The proposed rule required wheelchair spaces and designated aisle seats to be provided in each price level distinguishable by location, and to be located at varying distances from the performance area on each accessible level and in each balcony or mezzanine that is located along an accessible route. The regulatory assessment for the proposed rule assumed large sports facilities with 50,000 seats would add an additional upper deck concourse to achieve this level of dispersion, which would increase the construction cost by $11 million, and estimated the national costs would be $33 million annually for 3 newly constructed large sports facilities. The regulatory assessment for

29

the proposed rule further assumed medium sports facilities with 20,000 seats would add 4 lifts, and small sports facilities with 11,000 seats would add 2 lifts. The cost of installing a lift was estimated at $14,213, and the national costs would be $0.5 million annually for 5 medium and 5 small newly constructed sports facilities.

The final revised guidelines do not require wheelchair spaces to be dispersed based on admission prices because pricing is not always established at the design phase and may vary by event. Instead of requiring wheelchair spaces to be vertically dispersed on each accessible level, the final revised guidelines require wheelchair spaces to be vertically dispersed at varying distances from the screen, performance area, or playing field. The final revised guidelines also require wheelchair spaces to be located in each balcony or mezzanine served by an accessible route. Sports facilities can meet the requirements by locating some wheelchair spaces on each accessible level of the facilities, which is consistent with the current guidelines.

Companion Seats

Table 4.5 shows the relevant text of the current guidelines, the proposed rule, and the final revised guidelines with respect to the scoping and technical requirements for companion seats in assembly areas.

Table 4.5 - Companion Seats (text version)

Current Guidelines	Proposed Rule	Final Revised Guidelines

Current Guidelines	Proposed Rule	Final Revised Guidelines
4.33.3 Placement of Wheelchair Locations. . . . At least one companion fixed seat shall be provided next to each wheelchair seating area. . . .	*221.3 Readily Removable Companion Seats. One readily removable companion seat complying with 802.7 shall be provided for each wheelchair space. Each required readily removable companion seat shall provide an additional wheelchair space complying with 802.1, 802.2, 802.3, 802.4, 802.5, and 802.9 when removed.*	**221.3 Companion Seats.** At least one companion seat complying with 802.3 shall be provided for each wheelchair space required by 221.2.1. **802.3 Companion Seats.** Companion seats shall comply with 802.3. **802.3.1 Alignment.** In row seating, companion seats shall be located to provide shoulder alignment with adjacent wheelchair spaces. The shoulder alignment point of the wheelchair space shall be measured 36 inches (915mm) from the front of the wheelchair space. The floor surface of the companion seat shall be the same elevation as the floor surface of the wheelchair space. **802.3.2 Type.** Companion seats shall be equivalent in size, quality, comfort, and amenities to the seating in the immediate area. Companion seats shall be permitted to be movable.

Model Codes & Standards
IBC 2000: Section 1107.2.2 has an equivalent requirement for the number of companion seats.
IBC 2003: Section 1108.2.5 has an equivalent requirement for the number of companion seats.

The current guidelines require at least one fixed companion seat to be provided next to each wheelchair space.

The proposed rule required companion seats to be designed so the seat can be readily removed and serve as a wheelchair space. The regulatory assessment for the proposed rule estimated 6 square feet must be added to the companion seat space to make it serve as a wheelchair space; and an anchoring system must be provided to make the seat removable. These requirements would add $1,315 per seat to the construction cost. A newly constructed large sports facility with 50,000 seats must provide 501 companion seats, which would add $661,320 to the construction cost. A newly constructed medium sports facility with 20,000 seats must provide 201 companion seats, which would add $265,320 to the construction cost. A newly constructed small sports facility with 11,000 seats must provide 111 companion seats, which would add $146,520 to the construction cost. The regulatory assessment for the proposed rule estimated the national costs for requiring removable companion seats that can also serve as wheelchair spaces would be $4 million annually for 3 large, 5 medium, and 5 small newly constructed sports facilities.

The final revised guidelines permit companion seats to be readily removable, but do not require the seats to be designed so they can also serve as wheelchair spaces when removed.

Designated Aisle Seats

Table 4.6 shows the relevant text of the current guidelines, the proposed rule, and the final revised guidelines with respect to the scoping and technical requirements for designated aisle seats in assembly areas.

Table 4.6 - Designated Aisle Seats (text version)

Current Guidelines	Proposed Rule	Final Revised Guidelines
4.1.3 Accessible Buildings: New Construction. Accessible buildings and facilities shall meet the following minimum requirements: . . . (19) Assembly areas. (a) ... In addition, one percent but not less than one, of all fixed seats shall be aisle seats with no armrests on the aisle side, or removable or folding armrests on the aisle side. Each such seat shall be identified by a sign or marker.	**221.4 Designated Aisle Seats.** Aisle seats complying with 802.8 shall be provided in all assembly areas. Signs notifying patrons of the availability of such seats shall be posted at the ticket office. **Exception:** Designated aisle seats are not required in luxury boxes, club boxes, or suites. *221.4.1 Number. One designated aisle seat complying with 802.8 per 100 seats, or fraction thereof shall be provided.* *221.4.2 Location. At least one of each four required*	*221.4 Designated Aisle Seats. At least 5 percent of the total number of aisle seats provided shall comply with 802.4 and shall be the aisle seats located closest to accessible routes. . . .* **802.4 Designated Aisle Seats.** Designated aisle seats shall comply with 802.4. **802.4.1 Armrests.** Where armrests are provided on the seating in the immediate area, folding or retractable armrests shall be provided on the aisle side of the seat.

Printed by Builder's Book, Inc., Bookstore · www.buildersbook.com

Signage notifying patrons of the availability of such seats shall be posted at the ticket office. Aisle seats are not be required to comply with 4.33.4.

designated aisle seats shall be located on an accessible route. All other required designated aisle seats shall be located not more than two rows from an accessible route serving such seats.

802.8 Designated Aisle Seats. Removable or folding armrests or no armrests shall be provided on the aisle side of designated aisle seats. Each such seat shall be identified by a sign or marker.

802.4.2 Identification. Each designated aisle seat shall be identified by a sign or marker.

Model Codes & Standards
IBC 2000: No requirement for designated aisle seats.
IBC 2003: Section 1108.2.6 has an equivalent requirement for the number of designated aisle seats.

The current guidelines require 1 percent of fixed seats in assembly areas to be designated aisle seats. Designated aisle seats must have either no armrests or folding or retractable armrests on the aisle side of the seat.

The proposed rule required at least 25 percent of the designated aisle seats to be located on an accessible route, and the rest to be located no more than two rows from an accessible route. The regulatory assessment for the proposed rule assumed large and medium sports facilities would add accessible routes to comply with this requirement. The upper deck concourses added to large sports facilities to comply with the proposed rule's vertical dispersion requirements for wheelchair spaces were assumed to also provide the accessible routes needed to comply with the proposed rule's designated aisle seat requirements. The regulatory assessment for the proposed rule further assumed medium sports facilities with 20,000 seats would add 1,500 square feet to provide accessible routes to the designated aisle seats, and would increase the construction cost by $306,000. The regulatory assessment for the proposed rule estimated the national costs would be $1.5 million annually for 5 medium newly constructed sports facilities.

The final revised guidelines base the number of required designated aisle seats on the number of aisle seats, instead of all the seats in a sports facility as the current guidelines do. At least 5 percent of the aisle seats are required to be designated aisle seats and to be located closest to accessible routes. This revision will almost always result in fewer aisle seats being designated aisle seats compared to the current guidelines. Sports facilities typically locate designated aisle seats on, or as near to, accessible routes as permitted by the configuration of the facilities.

CHAPTER 5: REVISIONS THAT REDUCE IMPACTS
5.0 Introduction

This chapter discusses revisions to the scoping and technical requirements that will reduce impacts on the new construction and alterations of facilities. Some of the revisions will significantly reduce impacts, such as the revised scoping requirements for wheelchair spaces and assistive listening systems in large assembly areas, and the exceptions for accessible routes to small press boxes. The relevant text of the current guidelines and the final revised guidelines is presented in tables. Unless otherwise noted, the current guidelines refer to ADAAG. The requirements are presented in the order in which they appear in the final revised guidelines. Scoping and technical requirements are presented together, where appropriate. The text of the final revised guidelines that will reduce the impacts is underlined. Where the current guidelines contain related text, it is also underlined. Equivalent requirements in the International Building Code and the ICC/ANSI A117.1 Standard on Accessible and Usable Buildings and Facilities are also noted in the tables.

5.1 Limited Access Spaces and Machinery Spaces

Table 5.1 shows the relevant text of the current guidelines and the final revised guidelines with respect to the exceptions for limited access spaces and machinery spaces.

Table 5.1 – Limited Access Spaces and Machinery Spaces (text version)

Current Guidelines	Final Revised Guidelines
4.1.1 Application. . . . (5) General Exceptions. . . . (b) *Accessibility is not required to or in:* . . .	**203.4 Limited Access Spaces.** *Spaces accessed only by ladders, catwalks, crawl spaces, or very narrow passageways shall not be required to comply with these requirements or to be on an accessible route.*
(ii) *non-occupiable spaces accessed only by ladders, catwalks, crawl spaces, very narrow passageways, tunnels, or freight (non-passenger) elevators, and frequented only by service personnel for maintenance, repair, or occasional monitoring of equipment; such spaces may include, but are not limited to, elevator pits, elevator penthouses, piping or equipment catwalks, water or sewage treatment pump rooms and stations, electric substations and transformer vaults, and highway and tunnel facilities; . . .*	**203.5 Machinery Spaces.** *Spaces frequented only by service personnel for maintenance, repair, or occasional monitoring of equipment shall not be required to comply with these requirements or to be on an accessible route. Machinery spaces include, but are not limited to, elevator pits or elevator pent-houses; mechanical, electrical, or communications equipment rooms; piping or equipment catwalks; water or sewage treatment pump rooms and stations; electrical substations and transformer vaults; and highway and traffic tunnel facilities.*
Model Codes & Standards	
IBC 2000: Sections 1103.2.8 and 1103.2.9 have similar exceptions for limited access spaces and machinery spaces.	

34

IBC 2003: Sections 1103.2.8 and 1103.2.9 have similar exceptions for limited access spaces and machinery spaces.

The current guidelines contain an exception that exempts "non-occupiable" spaces that have limited means of access, such as ladders or very narrow passageways, and that are visited only by service personnel for maintenance, repair, or occasional monitoring of equipment from all accessibility requirements. The final revised guidelines expand this exception by removing the condition that the exempt spaces be "non-occupiable," and by separating the other conditions into two independent exceptions: one for spaces with limited means of access, and the other for machinery spaces. More spaces are exempted by these exceptions to the final revised guidelines.

5.2 Operable Parts

Table 5.2 shows the relevant text of the current guidelines and the final revised guidelines with respect to the scoping and technical requirements for operable parts.

Table 5.2 – Operable Parts (text version)

Current Guidelines	Final Revised Guidelines
4.1.3 Accessible Buildings: New Construction. Accessible buildings and facilities shall meet the following minimum requirements: . . . (13) Controls and operating mechanisms in accessible spaces, along accessible routes, or as parts of accessible elements (for example, light switches and dispenser controls) shall comply with 4.27. **4.27.3 Height.** The highest operable part of controls, dispensers, receptacles, and other operable equipment shall be placed within at least one of the reach ranges specified in 4.2.5 and 4.2.6. Electrical and communications systems receptacles on walls shall be mounted no less than 15 in (380 mm) above the floor. *Exception: These requirements do not apply where the use of special equipment dictates otherwise or where electrical and communica-tions systems*	**205.1 General.** Operable parts on accessible elements, accessible routes, and in accessible rooms and spaces shall comply with 309. *Exceptions: 1. Operable parts that are intended for use only by service or maintenance personnel shall not be required to comply with 309.* *2. Electrical or communication receptacles serving a dedicated use shall not be required to comply with 309.* *3. Where two or more outlets are provided in a kitchen above a length of counter top that is uninterrupted by a sink or appliance, one outlet shall not be required to comply with 309.* *4. Floor electrical receptacles shall not be required to comply with 309.* *5. HVAC diffusers shall not be required to comply with 309.* *6. Except for light switches, where redundant controls are provided for a single element, one control in each space shall not be required to comply with 309.* . . . **309.3 Height.** Operable parts shall be placed within one or more of the reach ranges specified in 308.

35

receptacles are not normally intended for use by building occupants. **4.27.4 Operation.** Controls and operating mechanisms shall be operable with one hand and shall not require tight grasping, pinching, or twisting of the wrist. The force required to activate controls shall be no greater than 5 lbf (22.5N).	**309.4 Operation.** Operable parts shall be operable with one hand and shall not require tight grasping, pinching, or twisting of the wrist. The force required to activate operable parts shall be 5 pounds (22.2 N) maximum. *Exception: Gas pump nozzles shall not be required to provide operable parts that have an activating force of 5 pounds (22.2 N) maximum.*

Model Codes & Standards
IBC 2000: Section 1108.13 has an equivalent requirement for operable parts, but no exceptions. Section 1103.2.12 exempts gas pumps from accessibility requirements. **IBC 2003:** Section 1109.13 has an equivalent requirement for operable parts and equivalent exceptions. Section 1103.2.14 requires operable parts on gas pumps to comply with the technical requirement for height.

The current guidelines and the final revised guidelines require operable parts on accessible elements, along accessible routes, and in accessible rooms and spaces to comply with the technical requirements for operable parts, including height and operation. The current guidelines contain an exception that exempts "special equipment [that] dictates otherwise," and electrical and communications systems receptacles not intended for use by building occupants from the technical requirement for height. The final revised guidelines divide this exception into three new exceptions covering operable parts intended only for use by service or maintenance personnel; electrical or communication receptacles serving a dedicated use; and floor electrical receptacles. Operable parts covered by these new exceptions are exempt from all the technical requirements for operable parts. The final revised guidelines add new exceptions that exempt certain outlets at kitchen counters; HVAC diffusers; and redundant controls provided for a single element, other than light switches, from the technical requirements for operable parts. The final revised guidelines also exempt gas pump nozzles from the technical requirement for activating force.

5.3 Accessible Routes from Site Arrival Points and Within Sites

Table 5.3 shows the relevant text of the current guidelines and the final revised guidelines with respect to the scoping requirements for accessible routes from site arrival points and within sites.

Table 5.3 – Accessible Routes from Site Arrival Points and Within Sites (<u>text version</u>)

Current Guidelines	Final Revised Guidelines
4.1.2 Accessible Sites and Exterior Facilities: New Construction. An accessible site shall meet the following minimum requirements:	**206.2.1 Site Arrival Points.** At least one accessible route shall be provided within the site from accessible parking spaces and accessible passenger loading zones; public streets and

36

(1) At least one accessible route complying with 4.3 shall be provided within the boundary of the site from public transportation stops, accessible parking spaces, passenger loading zones if provided, and public streets or sidewalks, to an accessible building entrance.	sidewalks; and public transportation stops to the accessible building or facility entrance they serve. *Exceptions:* ... *2. An accessible route shall not be required between site arrival points and the building or facility entrance if the only means of access between them is a vehicular way not providing pedestrian access.*
(2) At least one accessible route complying with 4.3 shall connect accessible buildings, accessible facilities, accessible elements, and accessible spaces that are on the same site.	**206.2.2 Within a Site.** At least one accessible route shall connect accessible buildings, accessible facilities, accessible elements, and accessible spaces that are on the same site. *Exception: An accessible route shall not be required between accessible buildings, accessible facilities, accessible elements, and accessible spaces if the only means of access between them is a vehicular way not providing pedestrian access.*

Model Codes & Standards
IBC 2000: Sections 1104.1 and 1104.2 have equivalent requirements for accessible routes from site arrival points and within sites, and an equivalent exception for vehicular ways within sites. **IBC 2003:** Sections 1104.1 and 1104.2 have equivalent requirements for accessible routes from site arrival points and within sites, and equivalent exceptions for vehicular ways from site arrival points and within sites.

The current guidelines and the final revised guidelines require at least one accessible route to be provided from site arrival points to an accessible building entrance, and at least one accessible route to connect accessible facilities on the same site. The final revised guidelines add two new exceptions that exempt site arrival points and accessible facilities within a site from the accessible route requirements where the only means of access between them is a vehicular way that does not provide pedestrian access.

5.4 Accessible Routes to Tiered Dining Areas in Sports Facilities

Table 5.4 shows the relevant text of the current guidelines and the final revised guidelines with respect to the scoping requirement for accessible routes to dining areas.

Table 5.4 – Accessible Routes to Dining Areas (text version)

Current Guidelines	Final Revised Guidelines
4.1.3 Accessible Buildings: New Construction. Accessible buildings and facilities shall meet the following	**206.2.5 Restaurants and Cafeterias.** In restaurants and cafeterias, an accessible route shall be provided to all

37

minimum requirements: (1) At least one accessible route complying with 4.3 shall connect accessible building or facility entrances with all accessible spaces and elements within the building or facility. **5.4 Dining Areas.** In new construction, all dining areas, including raised or sunken dining areas, loggias, and outdoor seating areas shall be accessible. . . .	dining areas, including raised or sunken dining areas, and outdoor dining areas. *Exceptions:* . . . *3. In sports facilities, tiered dining areas providing seating required to comply with 221 shall be required to have accessible routes serving at least 25 percent of the dining area provided that accessible routes serve seating complying with 221and each tier is provided with the same services.*

Model Codes & Standards
IBC 2000: Section 1107.2.5 has an equivalent requirement for accessible routes to dining areas, but no exception for tiered dining areas in sports facilities. **IBC 2003:** Section 1108.2.9 has an equivalent requirement for dining areas and an equivalent exception for tiered dining areas in sports facilities.

The current guidelines and the final revised guidelines require an accessible route to be provided to all dining areas, including raised or sunken dining areas. The final revised guidelines add a new exception for tiered dining areas in sports facilities. Dining areas in sports facilities are typically integrated into the seating bowl and are tiered to provide adequate lines of sight. The new exception requires an accessible route to be provided to at least 25 percent of the tiered dining areas in sports facilities. Each tier must have the same services and the accessible route must serve the accessible seating.

5.5 Accessible Routes to Press Boxes

Table 5.5 shows the relevant text of the current guidelines and the final revised guidelines with respect to the scoping requirement for accessible routes to press boxes.

Table 5.5 – Accessible Routes to Press Boxes (text version)

Current Guidelines	Final Revised Guidelines
4.1.1 Application. (1) General. All areas of newly designed or newly constructed buildings and facilities and altered portions of existing buildings and facilities shall comply with section 4, unless otherwise provided in this section or as modified in a special application section. **4.1.3 Accessible Buildings: New Construction.** Accessible buildings and facilities shall meet the following	**206.2.7 Press Boxes.** Press boxes in assembly areas shall be on an accessible route. *Exceptions: 1. An accessible route shall not be required to press boxes in bleachers that have points of entry at only one level provided that the aggregate area of all press boxes is 500 square feet (46 m^2) maximum.* *2. An accessible route shall not be required to free-standing press boxes that are elevated above grade 12 feet (3660 mm) minimum provided that*

38

Current Guidelines	Final Revised Guidelines
and facilities shall meet the following minimum requirements: (1) At least one accessible route complying with 4.3 shall connect accessible building or facility entrances with all accessible spaces and elements within the building or facility.	*the aggregate area of all press boxes is 500 square feet (46 m^2) maximum.*
Model Codes & Standards	
IBC 2000: No requirement for accessible routes to press boxes. **IBC 2003:** Section 1104.3.2 has an equivalent requirement for accessible routes to press boxes and equivalent exceptions for small press boxes.	

The current guidelines require all areas of newly constructed facilities to be accessible, and an accessible route to connect accessible entrances with all accessible spaces and elements within the facility. The final revised guidelines add two new exceptions that exempt small press boxes that are located on bleachers with entrances on only one level, and small press boxes that are free-standing structures elevated more than 12 feet, from the accessible route requirement when the aggregate area of all press boxes in a sports facility does not exceed 500 square feet. These new exceptions significantly reduce the impacts on high school sports facilities.

5.6 Shower and Sauna Doors in Hotel Guest Rooms

Table 5.6 shows the relevant text of the current guidelines and the final revised guidelines with respect to the scoping requirement for doors in hotel guest rooms.

Table 5.6 – Shower and Sauna Doors in Hotel Guest Rooms (text version)

Current Guidelines	Final Revised Guidelines
9.4 Other Sleeping Rooms and Suites. Doors and doorways designed to allow passage into and within all sleeping units or other covered units shall comply with 4.13.5.	**206.5.3 Transient Lodging Facilities.** In transient lodging facilities, entrances, doors, and doorways providing user passage into and within guest rooms that are not required to provide mobility features complying with 806.2 shall comply with 404.2.3. *Exception: Shower and sauna doors in guest rooms that are not required to provide mobility features complying with 806.2 shall not be required to comply with 404.2.3.* **224.1.2 Guest Room Doors and Doorways.** Entrances, doors, and doorways providing user passage into and within guest rooms that are not

39

	required to provide mobility features complying with 806.2 shall comply with 404.2.3. *Exception: Shower and sauna doors in guest rooms that are not required to provide mobility features complying with 806.2 shall not be required to comply with 404.2.3.*
Model Codes & Standards	
No requirement for doors in guest rooms that are not required to provide mobility features.	

The current guidelines and the final revised guidelines require doors in hotel guest rooms that do not provide mobility features to have at least 32 inches clear width. The final revised guidelines add a new exception that exempts shower and sauna doors from the requirement.

5.7 Limited-Use/Limited-Application Elevators and Private Residence Elevators

Table 5.7 shows the relevant text of the current guidelines and the final revised guidelines with respect to the scoping requirements for elevators.

Table 5.7 – Limited-Use/Limited-Application Elevators and Private Residence Elevators (text version)

Current Guidelines	Final Revised Guidelines
4.1.3 Accessible Buildings: New Construction. Accessible buildings and facilities shall meet the following minimum requirements: . . . (5) One passenger elevator complying with 4.10 shall serve each level, including mezzanines, in all multistory buildings and facilities unless exempted below. . . . **Exception 1:** Elevators are not required in: (a) private facilities that are less than three stories or that have less than 3000 square feet per story unless the building is a shopping center, a shopping mall, or the professional office of a health care provider, or another type of facility as determined by the Attorney General; or (b) public facilities that are less than three stories and that are not	**206.2.3 Multi-Story Buildings and Facilities.** At least one accessible route shall connect each story and mezzanine in multi-story buildings and facilities. **Exceptions: 1.** In private buildings or facilities that are less than three stories or that have less than 3000 square feet per story (279 m²), an accessible route shall not be required to connect stories provided the building or facility is not a shopping center, a shopping mall, the professional office of a health care provider, a terminal, depot or other station used for specified public transportation, an airport passenger terminal, or another type of facility as determined by the Attorney General. **2.** Where a two story public building or facility has one story with an occupant load of five or fewer persons that does not contain public use space, that story shall not be required to be connected to the story above or below. . . . **206.6 Elevators.** Elevators provided for

40

open to the general public if the story above or below the accessible ground floor houses no more than five persons and is less than 500 square feet . . . .

In new construction, if a building or facility is eligible for exemption but a passenger elevator is nonetheless planned, that elevator shall meet the requirements of 4.10 and shall serve each level in the building. . . .

passengers shall comply with 407. . . .
Exceptions: 1. *In a building or facility permitted to use the exceptions to 206.2.3 or permitted by 206.7 to use a platform lift, elevators complying with 408 shall be permitted.*
2. Elevators complying with 408 or 409 shall be permitted in multi-story residential dwelling units.

[Note: Section 408 contains technical requirements for limited-use/limited-application (LULA) elevators. Section 409 contains technical requirements for private residence elevators.]

Model Codes & Standards
IBC 2000: No exception permitting LULA elevators. Section 1107.5.4 requires Type A dwelling units to comply with the ICC/ANSI A117.1-1998 standard, which contains technical requirements for private residence elevators in Type A dwelling units.
IBC 2003: No exception permitting LULA elevators. Section 1107.2 requires Type A dwelling units to comply with the ICC/ANSI A117.1-1998 standard, which contains technical requirements for private residence elevators in Type A dwelling units.

The current guidelines and the final revised guidelines include exceptions to the scoping requirement for accessible routes that exempt certain facilities from connecting each story with an elevator. If a facility is exempt from the scoping requirement, but nonetheless installs an elevator, the current guidelines require the elevator to comply with the technical requirements for passenger elevators. The final revised guidelines add a new exception that allows a facility that is exempt from the scoping requirement to install a limited-use/limited-application (LULA) elevator. LULA elevators are typically less expensive than passenger elevators, and are suitable for low-traffic, low-rise facilities. LULA elevators are also permitted as an alternative to platform lifts. The final revised guidelines also add a new exception that permits private residence elevators in multi-story dwelling units. The final revised guidelines contain technical requirements for LULA elevators and private residence elevators.

5.8 Platform Lifts in Hotel Guest Rooms and Dwelling Units

Table 5.8 shows the relevant text of the current guidelines and the final revised guidelines with respect to the scoping requirement for platform lifts.

Table 5.8 – Platform Lifts in Hotel Guest Rooms and Dwelling Units (text version)

Current Guidelines	Final Revised Guidelines
4.1.3 Accessible Buildings: New Construction. Accessible buildings and facilities shall meet the following minimum requirements: . . .	**206.7 Platform Lifts.** . . . Platform lifts shall be permitted as a component of an accessible route in new construction in accordance with 206.7.

41

(5) One passenger elevator complying with 4.10 shall serve each level, including mezzanines, in all multistory buildings and facilities unless exempted below. . . . **Exception 4:** Platform lifts (wheelchair lifts) complying with 4.11 of this guideline and applicable State or local codes may be used in lieu of an elevator only under the following conditions: [Note: No exceptions for hotel guest rooms and dwelling units.]	. . . *206.7.6 Guest Rooms and Residential Dwelling Units.* *Platform lifts shall be permitted to connect levels within transient lodging guest rooms required to provide mobility features complying with 806.2 or residential dwelling units required to provide mobility features complying with 809.2 through 809.4.*

Model Codes & Standards
IBC 2000: Section 1108.7 has an equivalent requirement permitting platform lifts in dwelling units. **IBC 2003:** Section 1109.7 has an equivalent requirement permitting platform lifts in hotel guest rooms and dwelling units.

The current guidelines and the final revised guidelines limit the places where platform lifts are permitted to be used as part of an accessible route in new construction. The final revised guidelines add a new scoping requirement that permits platform lifts to be used in hotel guest rooms and dwelling units with mobility features.

5.9 Parking Spaces

Table 5.9 shows the relevant text of the current guidelines and the final revised guidelines with respect to the scoping requirements for parking spaces.

Table 5.9 – Parking Spaces (text version)

Current Guidelines	Final Revised Guidelines
4.1.2 Accessible Sites and Exterior Facilities: New Construction. An accessible site shall meet the following minimum requirements: . . . (5)(a) If parking spaces are provided for self-parking by employees or visitors, or both, then accessible parking spaces complying with 4.6 shall be provided in each such parking area in conformance with the table below. . . .	**208.1 General.** Where parking spaces are provided, parking spaces shall be provided in accordance with 208. *Exception: Parking spaces used exclusively for buses, trucks, other delivery vehicles, law enforcement vehicles, or vehicular impound shall not be required to comply with 208 provided that lots accessed by the public are provided with a passenger loading zone complying with 503.* **216.5 Parking.** Parking spaces complying with 502 shall be identified by signs complying with 502.6

Current Guidelines	Final Revised Guidelines
(7) Building Signage: . . . Elements and spaces of accessible facilities which shall be identified by the International Symbol of Accessibility and which shall comply with 4.30.7 are: (a) Parking spaces designated as reserved for individuals with disabilities; . . .	*Exceptions: 1. Where a total of four or fewer parking spaces, including accessible parking spaces, are provided on a site, identification of accessible parking spaces shall not be required.* *2. In residential facilities, where parking spaces are assigned to specific residential dwelling units, identification of accessible parking spaces shall not be required.*
Model Codes & Standards	
IBC 2000: Section 1106.1 has an equivalent requirement for the number of accessible parking spaces, but no exception. Section 1109.1 has an equivalent requirement for identification of accessible parking spaces and a similar exception for sites with few parking spaces. **IBC 2003:** Section 1106.1 has an equivalent requirement for the number of accessible parking spaces and a similar exception. Section 1109.1 has an equivalent requirement for identification of accessible parking spaces and an equivalent exception for sites with few parking spaces.	

Where parking spaces are provided, the current guidelines and the final revised guidelines require a certain number of the parking spaces to be accessible. The final revised guidelines add a new exception that exempts parking spaces used exclusively for buses, trucks, delivery vehicles, law enforcement vehicles, or for purposes of vehicular impound from the scoping requirement for parking spaces. If a lot containing parking spaces for these vehicles is used by the public, the lot is required to have an accessible passenger loading zone.

The current guidelines and the final revised guidelines require accessible parking spaces to be identified by signs that display the International Symbol of Accessibility. The final revised guidelines add two new exceptions that exempt accessible parking spaces from the signage requirement. The first exception exempts sites that have four or less parking spaces from the signage requirement. This exception will reduce the impacts on small businesses. The second exception exempts residential facilities where parking spaces are assigned to specific dwelling units from the signage requirement.

5.10 Passenger Loading Zones at Medical Care and Long-Term Care Facilities

Table 5.10 shows the relevant text of the current guidelines and the final revised guidelines with respect to the scoping requirement for passenger loading zones at medical care and long-term care facilities.

Table 5.10 – Passenger Loading Zones at Medical Care and Long-Term Care Facilities (text version)

Current Guidelines	Final Revised Guidelines
6.1 General. Medical care facilities included in this section are those in	*209.3 Medical Care and Long-Term Care Facilities. At least one passenger*

43

Current Guidelines	Final Revised Guidelines
which people receive physical and medical treatment or care and where persons may need assistance in responding to an emergency and where the period of stay may exceed 24 hours. In addition to the requirements of section 4, medical care . . . facilities shall comply with section 6. *6.2 Entrances. At least one accessible entrance that complies with 4.14 shall be protected from the weather by canopy or roof overhang. Such entrances shall incorporate a passenger loading zone that complies with 4.6.6.*	*loading zone complying with 503 shall be provided at an accessible entrance to licensed medical care and licensed long-term care facilities where the period of stay exceeds twenty-four hours.*
Model Codes & Standards	
IBC 2000: Section 1106.6.1 has an equivalent requirement for passenger loading zones at medical care and long-term care facilities. **IBC 2003:** Section 1106.7.2 has an equivalent requirement for passenger loading zones at medical care and long-term care facilities.	

The current guidelines and the final revised guidelines require medical care and long-term care facilities, where the period of stay exceeds 24 hours, to provide at least one passenger loading zone at an accessible entrance. The current guidelines also require a canopy or roof overhang at the passenger loading zone. The final revised guidelines do not require a canopy or roof overhang.

5.11   Aisle Stairs and Ramps in Assembly Areas

Table 5.11 shows the relevant text of the current guidelines and the final revised guidelines with respect to the scoping and technical requirements for aisle stairs and ramps in assembly areas.

Table 5.11 – Aisle Stairs and Ramps in Assembly Areas (text version)

Current Guidelines	Final Revised Guidelines
4.1.3 Accessible Buildings: New Construction. Accessible buildings and facilities shall meet the following minimum requirements: . . . (4) Interior and exterior stairs connecting levels that are not connected by an elevator, ramp, or other accessible means of vertical access shall comply with 4.9.	**210.1 General.** Interior and exterior stairs that are part of a means of egress shall comply with 504. *Exceptions: . . .* *3. In assembly areas, aisle stairs shall not be required to comply with 504.* [Note: Section 504 requires stairs to have handrails complying with 505.] **405.1 General.** Ramps on

Printed by Builder's Book, Inc., Bookstore · www.buildersbook.com

Current Guidelines	Final Revised Guidelines
4.9.4 Handrails. Stairways shall have handrails at both sides of all stairs. Handrails shall comply with 4.26 and shall have the following features: (1) Handrails shall be continuous along both sides of stairs. . . . (2) If handrails are not continuous, they shall extend at least 12 in (305 mm) beyond the top riser and at least 12 in (305 mm) plus the width of one thread beyond the bottom riser. . . . **4.8.1 General.** Any part of an accessible route with a slope greater than 1:20 shall be considered a ramp and shall comply with 4.8. **4.8.5 Handrails.** If a ramp run has a rise greater than 6 in (150 mm) or a horizontal projection greater than 72 in (150 mm), than it shall have handrails on both sides. *Handrails are not required on curb ramps or adjacent to seating in assembly areas.* Handrails shall comply with 4.26 and shall have the following features: (1) Handrails shall be provided along both sides of ramp segments. . . . (2) If handrails are not continuous, they shall extend at least 12 in (305 mm) beyond the top and bottom of the ramp segment and shall be parallel with the floor or ground surface (see Fig. 17). . . .	accessible routes shall comply with 405. *Exception: In assembly areas, aisle ramps adjacent to seating and not serving elements required to be on an accessible route shall not be required to comply with 405.* **405.8 Handrails.** Ramp runs with a rise greater than 6 inches (150 mm) shall have handrails complying with 505. **505.2 Where Required.** Handrails shall be provided on both sides of stairs and ramps. *Exception: In assembly areas, handrails shall not be required on both sides of aisle ramps where a handrail is provided at either side or within the aisle width.* **505.3 Continuity.** Handrails shall be continuous within the full length of each stair flight or ramp run. . . . . *Exception: In assembly areas, handrails on ramps shall not be required to be continuous in aisles serving seating.* **505.10 Handrail Extensions.** Handrail gripping surfaces shall extend beyond and in the same direction of stair flights and ramp runs in accordance with 505.10. *Exceptions:* . . . *2. In assembly areas, extensions shall not be required for ramp handrails in aisles serving seating where the handrails are discontinuous to provide access to seating and to permit crossovers within aisles.* . . .

<table>
<tr><td colspan="2" align="center">Model Codes & Standards</td></tr>
<tr><td colspan="2">ICC/ANSI A117.1-1998: Sections 505.2, 505.3, and 505.10 have equivalent exceptions for aisle ramps in assembly areas with respect to handrail location, continuity, and extensions.</td></tr>
</table>

The current guidelines require stairs that connect levels not served by an elevator, ramp, or platform lift to comply with the technical requirements for stairs. The final revised guidelines require stairs that are part of a means of egress to comply with the technical requirements for stairs. The current guidelines do not contain any exceptions for aisle stairs in assembly areas. The final revised guidelines add a new exception that exempts aisle stairs in assembly areas from the technical requirements for stairs, including handrails.

The current guidelines exempt aisle ramps adjacent to seating in assembly areas only from providing handrails. The final revised guidelines exempt aisle ramps adjacent to seating in assembly areas, which do not serve accessible elements, from all the technical requirements for ramps. Where aisle ramps in assembly areas serve accessible elements, the final revised guidelines exempt the aisle ramps from providing:

- Handrails on both sides of an aisle ramp, where a handrail is provided at one side of the aisle ramp or within the aisle ramp.

- Continuous handrails for the full length of an aisle ramp run.

- Handrail extensions beyond an aisle ramp run, where there are breaks in the handrail to provide access to seating and to permit crossovers within the aisle.

5.12   Multiple Single User Toilet Rooms

Table 5.12 shows the relevant text of the current guidelines and the final revised guidelines with respect to the scoping requirement for toilet rooms.

Table 5.12 – Multiple Single User Toilet Rooms (text version)

Current Guidelines	Final Revised Guidelines
4.1.3 Accessible Buildings: New Construction. Accessible buildings and facilities shall meet the following minimum requirements: . . . (11) Toilet Facilities. If toilet rooms are provided, then each public and common use toilet room shall comply with 4.22. . . .	**213.2 Toilet and Bathing Rooms.** Where toilet rooms are provided, each toilet room shall comply with 603. . . . *Exceptions:* . . . *4. Where multiple single user toilet rooms are clustered at a single location, no more than 50 percent of the single user toilet rooms for each use at each cluster shall be required to comply with 603.*
Model Codes & Standards	
IBC 2000: Section 1108.2 has a similar exception for multiple single user toilet rooms clustered at a single location. **IBC 2003:** Section 1109.2 has a similar exception for multiple single user toilet rooms clustered at a single location.	

The current guidelines and the final revised guidelines require each toilet room to be accessible. The final revised guidelines add a new exception for multiple single user toilet rooms clustered at a single location. The exception requires at least 50 percent of these toilet rooms to be accessible. This exception will reduce the impacts on medical facilities where multiple single user toilet rooms are provided for specimen collection.

46

5.13   Urinals

Table 5.13 shows the relevant text of the current guidelines and the final revised guidelines with respect to the scoping requirement for urinals.

Table 5.13 – Urinals (text version)

Current Guidelines	Final Revised Guidelines
4.22.5 Urinals. If urinals are provided, then at least one shall comply with 4.18.	*213.3.3 Urinals. Where more than one urinal is provided, at least one shall comply with 605.*
Model Codes & Standards	
IBC 2000: Section 1108.2 has a similar requirement for the number of urinals. **IBC 2003:** Section 1109.2 has an equivalent requirement for the number of urinals.	

Where urinals are provided, the current guidelines require at least one to be accessible. The final revised guidelines require at least one urinal to be accessible, where more than one is provided. If a toilet room has only one urinal, an accessible urinal is not required.

5.14   Visible Alarms in Alterations to Existing Facilities

Table 5.14 shows the relevant text of the current guidelines and the final revised guidelines with respect to the scoping requirement for visible alarms in alterations to existing facilities.

Table 5.14 – Visible Alarms and Alterations to Existing Facilities (text version)

Current Guidelines	Final Revised Guidelines
4.1.3 Accessible Buildings: New Construction. Accessible buildings and facilities shall meet the following minimum requirements: . . . (14) If emergency warning systems are provided, then they shall include both audible alarms and visual alarms complying with 4.28. . . . **4.1.6 Accessible Buildings: Alterations.** (1) General. Alterations to existing buildings and facilities shall comply with the following: . . . (b) If existing elements, spaces, or common areas are altered, then each such altered element, space,	**202.3 Alterations.** Where existing elements or spaces are altered, each altered element or space shall comply with the applicable requirements of Chapter 2. **215.1 General.** Where fire alarm systems provide audible alarm coverage, alarms shall comply with 215. *Exception: In existing facilities, visible alarms shall not be required except where an existing fire alarm system is upgraded or replaced, or a new fire alarm system is installed.*

feature, or area shall comply with the applicable provisions of 4.1.1 to 4.1.3 Minimum Requirements (for New Construction). . . .	
Model Codes & Standards	
IBC 2000: Section 907.9.1 has an equivalent exception for visible alarms in alterations to existing facilities.	
IBC 2003: Section 907.9.1 has an equivalent exception for visible alarms in alterations to existing facilities.	

The current guidelines and the final revised guidelines require that when existing elements and spaces of a facility are altered, the alterations must comply with new construction requirements. The final revised guidelines add a new exception to the scoping requirement for visible alarms in alterations to existing facilities. Visible alarms are required only when an existing fire alarm system is upgraded or replaced, or a new fire alarm system is installed.

5.15   Signs

Table 5.15 shows the relevant text of the current guidelines and the final revised guidelines with respect to scoping and technical requirements for signs.

Table 5.15 – Signs (text version)

Current Guidelines	Final Revised Guidelines
4.1.2 Accessible Sites and Exterior Facilities: New Construction. An accessible site shall meet the following minimum requirements: . . . (7) Building Signage. Signs which designate permanent rooms and spaces shall comply with 4.30.1, 4.30.4, 4.30.5, and 4.30.6. Other signs which provide direction to, or information about, functional spaces of the building shall comply with 4.30.1, 4.30.2, 4.30.3, and 4.30.5. . . . **4.1.3 Accessible Buildings: New Construction.** Accessible buildings and facilities shall meet the following minimum requirements: . . . (16) Building Signage. (a) Signs which designate permanent rooms and spaces shall comply with 4.30.1, 4.30.4, 4.30.5, and 4.30.6.	**216.1 General.** Signs shall be provided in accordance with 216 and shall comply with 703. *Exceptions: 1. Building directories, menus, seat and row designations in assembly areas, occupant names, building addresses, and company names and logos shall not be required to comply with 216.* *2. In parking facilities, signs shall not be required to comply with 216.2, 216.3, and 216.6 through 216.12.* *3. Temporary, 7 days or less, signs shall not be required to comply with 216. . . .* **216.2 Designations.** Interior and exterior signs identifying permanent rooms and spaces shall comply with 703.1, 703.2, and 703.5. . . . *Exception: Exterior signs that are not located at the door to the space they serve shall not be required to comply with 703.2.*

48

Current Guidelines	Final Revised Guidelines
(b) Other signs which provide direction to or information about functional spaces of the building shall comply with 4.30.1, 4.30.2, 4.30.3, and 4.30.5. *Exception: Building directories, menus, and all other signs which are temporary are not required to comply.* *4.30.6 Mounting Location and Height. Where permanent identification is provided for rooms and spaces, signs shall be installed on the wall adjacent to the latch side of the door. . . . Mounting height shall be 60 in (1525 mm) above the finish floor to the centerline of the sign. . . .*	**216.3 Directional and Informational Signs.** Signs that provide direction to or information about interior spaces and facilities of the site shall comply with 703.5. *703.4.1 Height Above Finish Floor or Ground. Tactile characters on signs shall be located 48 inches (1220 mm) minimum above the finish floor or ground surface, measured from the baseline of the lowest tactile character and 60 inches (1525 mm) maximum above the finish floor or ground surface, measured from the baseline of the highest tactile character. . . .* **703.4.2 Location.** Where a tactile sign is provided at a door, the sign shall be located alongside the door at the latch side. . . . *Exception: Signs with tactile characters shall be permitted on the push side of doors with closers and without hold-open devices.*

Model Codes & Standards
IBC 2000: Section E1107.3 of Appendix E has similar requirements and exceptions for certain signs. **IBC 2003:** Sections E107.2 and E107.3 of Appendix E has similar requirements and exceptions for certain signs. **ICC/ANSI A117.1-1998:** Section 703.2.7 has an equivalent requirement for the height of tactile characters on signs. Section 703.2.8 has an equivalent exception for the location of signs with tactile characters.

The current guidelines and the final revised guidelines have scoping and technical requirements for certain signs. The current guidelines contain an exception that exempts building directories, menus, and temporary signs from the requirements. The final revised guidelines expand this exception to include seat and row designations in assembly areas, occupant names, building addresses, and company names and logos. The final revised guidelines also exempt signs in parking facilities, other than signs identifying accessible parking spaces and means of egress. The final revised guidelines clarify that the exception for temporary signs applies to signs used for 7 days or less. The final revised guidelines add a new exception that exempts exterior signs identifying permanent rooms and spaces from providing tactile characters, where the exterior signs are not located at the door to the space they serve.

The current guidelines require signs with tactile characters identifying permanent rooms to be located 60 inches above the finish floor along the latch side of the door, measured to the centerline of the sign. The final revised guidelines provide greater flexibility, and require the signs be located between 48 inches above the finish floor, measured from the baseline of the lowest tactile character, and 60 inches above the finish floor, measured from the baseline of the highest tactile character. The final revised guidelines also permit signs with tactile characters to be located on the push side of doors with closers that do not have hold-open devices.

5.16   Drive-Up Public Telephones

Table 5.16 shows the relevant text of the current guidelines and the final revised guidelines with respect to the scoping requirement for wheelchair accessible public telephones.

Table 5.16 – Public Telephones (text version)

Current Guidelines	Final Revised Guidelines
4.1.3 Accessible Buildings: New Construction. Accessible buildings and facilities shall meet the following minimum requirements: . . . (17) Public Telephones. (a) If public pay telephones, public closed circuit telephones, or other public telephones are provided, then they shall comply with 4.31.2 through 4.31.8 to the extent required by the following table: . . .	**217.2 Wheelchair Accessible Telephones.** Where public telephones are provided, wheelchair accessible telephones complying with 704.2 shall be provided in accordance with Table 217.2. *Exception: Drive-up only public telephones shall not be required to comply with 217.2.*
Model Codes & Standards	
IBC 2000: No exception for drive-up only public telephones.	
IBC 2003: No exception for drive-up only public telephones.	

Where public telephones are provided, the current guidelines and the final revised guidelines require a certain number of telephones to be wheelchair accessible. The final revised guidelines add a new exception that exempts drive-up public telephones.

5.17   Assistive Listening Systems

Table 5.17.1 shows the relevant text of the current guidelines and the final revised guidelines with respect to the scoping requirements for assistive listening systems.

Table 5.17.1 – Assistive Listening Systems (text version)

Current Guidelines	Final Revised Guidelines
4.1.3 Accessible Buildings: New Construction. Accessible buildings and facilities shall meet the following minimum	**219.2 Required Systems.** In each assembly area where audible communication is integral to the use of the space, an assistive listening system shall be provided. *Exception: Other than in courtrooms,*

50

Current Guidelines	Final Revised Guidelines
requirements: . . . (19) Assembly Areas. . . . (b) This paragraph applies to assembly areas where audible communications are integral to the use of the space (e.g., concert and lecture halls, playhouses and movie theaters, meeting rooms, etc.). *Such assembly areas, if (1) they accommodate at least 50 persons, or if they have audio-amplification systems, and (2) they have fixed seating, shall have a permanently installed assistive listening system complying with 4.33.* For other assembly areas, a permanently installed assistive listening system, or an adequate number of electrical outlets or other supplementary wiring necessary to support a portable listening system shall be provided. *The minimum number of receivers to be provided shall be equal to 4 percent of the total number of seats, but in no case less than two. . . .* **11.2.1 Courtrooms.** . . . (2) Permanently installed assistive listening systems complying with 4.33 shall be provided in each courtroom. *The minimum number of receivers shall be four percent of the room occupant load, as determined by applicable State or local codes, but not less than two receivers. . . .*	*assistive listening systems shall not be required where audio amplification is not provided.* ***219.3 Receivers.*** *Receivers complying with 706.2 shall be provided for assistive listening systems in each assembly area in accordance with Table 219.3.* Twenty-five percent minimum of receivers provided, but no fewer than two, shall be hearing-aid compatible in accordance with 706.3. ***Exceptions: 1.*** *Where a building contains more than one assembly area and the assembly areas required to provide assistive listening systems are under one management, the total number of required receivers shall be permitted to be calculated according to the total number of seats in the assembly areas in the building provided that all receivers are usable with all systems.* *2. Where all seats in an assembly area are served by an induction loop assistive listening system, the minimum number of receivers required by Table 219.3 to be hearing-aid compatible shall not be required to be provided.*

Table 219.3 Receivers for Assistive Listening Systems

Capacity of Seating in	Minimum Number of Required	Minimum Number of Required Receivers
50 or less	2	2
51 to 200	2, plus 1 per 25 seats over 50	2
201 to 500	2, plus 1 per 25 seats over	1 per 4 receivers[1]
501 to 1000	20, plus 1 per 33 seats over 500 seats[1]	1 per 4 receivers[1]

Current Guidelines	Final Revised Guidelines		
	501 to 1000	20, plus 1 per 33 seats over 500 seats[1]	1 per 4 receivers[1]
	1001 to 2000	35, plus 1 per 50 seats over 1000 seats[1]	1 per 4 receivers[1]
	2001 and over	55, plus 1 per 100 seats over 2000 seats[1]	1 per 4 receivers[1]
	1. Or fraction thereof		
	Model Codes & Standards		
	IBC 2000: Section 1107.2.4 has similar requirements for assistive listening systems and the number of receivers, but no exceptions.		
	IBC 2003: Section 1108.2.7 has equivalent requirements for assistive listening systems and the number of receivers, and an equivalent exception for buildings that contain more than one assembly area.		

The current guidelines require assembly areas where audible communication is integral to the use of the space to provide an assistive listening system if they have an audio amplification system or an occupant load of 50 or more persons. The final revised guidelines exempt assembly areas, other than court rooms, that do not have audio amplification systems from providing assistive listening systems.

The current guidelines require receivers to be provided for at least 4 percent of the seats or room occupant load. The final revised guidelines revise the percentage of receivers required. As Table 5.17.2 shows, the number of receivers is significantly reduced for larger assembly areas.

Table 5.17.2 – Number of Receivers Required (text version)

Seating Capacity	Current Guidelines	Final Revised Guidelines
5,000	200	85
10,000	400	135
25,000	1,000	285
50,000	2,000	535

The final revised guidelines add a new exception that allows multiple assembly areas that are in the same building and under the same management, such as theaters in a multiplex cinema and lecture halls in a college building, to calculate the number of receivers required based on the total number of seats in all the assembly areas, instead of each assembly area separately, where the receivers are compatible with the assistive listening systems used in each of the assembly areas.

52

The final revised guidelines also require at least 25 percent, but no fewer than two, of the receivers to be hearing-aid compatible. Assembly areas served by an induction loop assistive listening system do not have to provide hearing-aid compatible receivers.

5.18   Wheelchair Spaces in Assembly Areas

Table 5.18.1 shows the relevant text of the current guidelines and the final revised guidelines with respect to the scoping requirements for wheelchair spaces in assembly areas.

Table 5.18.1 – Wheelchair Spaces in Assembly Areas (text version)

Current Guidelines	Final Revised Guidelines
4.1.3 Accessible Buildings: New Construction. Accessible buildings and facilities shall meet the following minimum requirements: . . . (19) Assembly Areas. (a) *In places of assembly with fixed seating, accessible wheelchair locations shall comply with 4.33.2, 4.33.3, and 4.33.4 and shall be provided consistent with the following table:*	**221.2 Wheelchair Spaces.** Wheelchair spaces complying with 221.2 shall be provided in assembly areas with fixed seating. ***221.2.1.1 General Seating.*** *Wheelchair spaces complying with 802.1 shall be provided in accordance with Table 221.2.1.1.*

Current Guidelines table:

Capacity of Seating in Assembly Areas	Number of Required Wheelchair Locations
4 to 25	1
26 to 50	2
51 to 300	4
301 to 500	6
over 500 seats	6 plus one additional seat for each total seating capacity increase over 100

. . .

Final Revised Guidelines:

Table 221.2.1.1 Number of Wheelchair Spaces in Assembly Areas

Number of Seats	Minimum Number of Required Wheelchair Spaces
4 to 25	1
26 to 50	2
51 to 150	4
151 to 300	5
301 to 500	6
501 to 5000	6, plus 1 for each 150, or fraction thereof, between 501 through 5000
5001 and over	36, plus 1 for each 200, or fraction thereof, over 5000

221.2.1.2 Luxury Boxes, Club Boxes, and Suites in Arenas, Stadiums, and Grandstands. In each luxury box, club box, and suite within arenas, stadiums, and grandstands, wheelchair spaces

Printed by Builder's Book, Inc., Bookstore · www.buildersbook.com

complying with 802.1 shall be provided in accordance with Table 221.2.1.1.

221.2.1.3 Other Boxes. In boxes other than those required to comply with 221.2.1.2, the total number of wheelchair spaces required shall be determined in accordance with Table 221.2.1.1 Wheelchair spaces shall be located in not less than 20 percent of all boxes provided. Wheelchair spaces shall comply with 802.1.

Model Codes & Standards
IBC 2000: Section 1107.2.2 has similar requirements for the number of wheelchair spaces in assembly areas. **IBC 2003:** Section 1108.2.2 has similar requirements for the number of wheelchair spaces in assembly areas.

The current guidelines and the final revised guidelines require assembly areas with fixed seating to provide wheelchair spaces based on seating capacity. The final revised guidelines revise the number of wheelchair spaces required in assembly areas with more than 500 seats. As Table 5.18.2 shows, the number of wheelchair spaces is significantly reduced for larger assembly areas.

Table 5.18.2 – Number of Wheelchair Spaces Required (text version)

Seating Capacity	Current Guidelines	Final Revised Guidelines
5,000	51	36
10,000	101	61
25,000	251	136
50,000	501	261

The final revised guidelines clarify that the scoping requirements are to be applied separately to general seating areas, and to each luxury box, club box, and suite in stadiums and arenas. In performing arts facilities with tiered boxes, the scoping requirement is applied to the total number of seats in the tiered boxes, and the wheelchair spaces are required to be dispersed among at least 20 percent of the tiered boxes. For example, if a performing arts facility has 20 tiered boxes with 5 fixed seats in each box, at least 4 wheelchair spaces must be provided in the boxes, and they must be dispersed among at least 4 of the 20 boxes.

5.19 Patient Toilet Rooms

Table 5.19 shows the relevant text of the current guidelines and the final revised guidelines with respect to the scoping requirement for patient toilet rooms.

Table 5.19 – Patient Toilet Rooms (text version)

Current Guidelines	Final Revised Guidelines

Printed by Builder's Book, Inc., Bookstore · www.buildersbook.com

Current Guidelines	Final Revised Guidelines
6.4 Patient Toilet Rooms. Where toilet/bathrooms are provided as a part of a patient bedroom, each patient bedroom that is required to be accessible shall have an accessible toilet/bathroom that complies with 4.22 or 4.23 and shall be on an accessible route.	**223.1 General.** In licensed medical care facilities and licensed long-term care facilities where the period of stay exceeds twenty-four hours, patient or resident sleeping rooms shall be provided in accordance with 223. *Exception: Toilet rooms that are part of critical or intensive care patient sleeping rooms shall not be required to comply with 603.*
Model Codes & Standards	
IBC 2000: No exception for toilet rooms serving critical or intensive care patient sleeping rooms. **IBC 2003:** Section 1109.2 has an equivalent exception for toilet rooms serving critical or intensive care patient sleeping rooms.	

The current guidelines and the final revised guidelines require a percentage of patient sleeping rooms to provide mobility features, including accessible toilet rooms. The final revised guidelines add a new exception that exempts toilet rooms serving critical or intensive care patient sleeping rooms.

5.20   Self-Service Storage Facilities

Table 5.20 shows the relevant text of the current guidelines and the final revised guidelines with respect to the scoping requirement for self-service storage facilities.

Table 5.20 – Self-Service Storage Facilities (text version)

Current Guidelines	Final Revised Guidelines	
4.1.1 Application. (1) General. All areas of newly designed or newly constructed buildings and facilities and altered portions of existing buildings and facilities shall comply with section 4, unless otherwise provided in this section or as modified in a special application section.	*225.3 Self-Service Storage Facilities. Self-service storage facilities shall provide individual self-storage spaces complying with these requirements in accordance with Table 225.3.*	
	Table 225.3 Self-Service Storage Facilities	
	Total Spaces in Facility	**Minimum Number of Spaces Required to be Accessible**
	1 to 200	5 percent, but no fewer than 1
	201 and over	10, plus 2 percent of total number of units over 200
Model Codes & Standards		
IBC 2000: Section 1107.6 has an equivalent requirement for the number of accessible storage spaces.		

IBC 2003: Section 1108.3 has an equivalent requirement for the number of accessible storage spaces.

The current guidelines require all areas of newly constructed facilities to be accessible. The final revised guidelines add a new scoping requirement for self-storage facilities. Facilities with 200 or fewer storage spaces are required to make at least 5 percent of the storage spaces accessible. Facilities with more than 200 storage spaces are required to provide 10 accessible storage spaces, plus make at least 2 percent of the storage spaces over 200 accessible.

5.21   Washing Machines and Clothes Dryers

Table 5.21 shows the relevant text of the current guidelines and the final revised guidelines with respect to the scoping and technical requirements for washing machines and clothes dryers.

Table 5.21 Washing Machines and Clothes Dryers (text version)

Current Guidelines	Final Revised Guidelines
4.1.1 Application. (1) General. All areas of newly designed or newly constructed buildings and facilities and altered portions of existing buildings and facilities shall comply with section 4, unless otherwise provided in this section or as modified in a special application section. **4.1.3 Accessible Buildings: New Construction.** Accessible buildings and facilities shall meet the following minimum requirements: . . . (13) Controls and operating mechanisms in accessible spaces, along accessible routes, or as parts of accessible elements (for example, light switches and dispenser controls) shall comply with 4.27. **4.27.3 Height.** The highest operable part of controls, dispensers, receptacles and other operable equipment shall be placed within at least one of the reach ranges specified in 4.2.5 or 4.2.6. **4.2.6 Side Reach. . . .** If the side reach is over an obstruction, the reach and clearances shall be as shown in Fig. 6 (c).	**214.2 Washing Machines.** Where three or fewer washing machines are provided, at least one shall comply with 611. Where more than three washing machines are provided, at least two shall comply with 611. **214.3 Clothes Dryers.** Where three or fewer clothes dryers are provided, at least one shall comply with 611. Where more than three clothes dryers are provided, at least two shall comply with 611. **611.3 Operable Parts.** Operable parts, including doors, lint screens, and detergent and bleach compartments, shall comply with 309. **309.3 Operable Parts.** Operable parts shall be placed within one or more of the reach ranges specified in 308. **308.3.2 Obstructed High Reach.** Where a clear floor or ground space allows a parallel approach to an element and the high side reach is over an obstruction, the height of the obstruction shall be 34 inches (865

56

Current Guidelines	Final Revised Guidelines
[Note: Figure 6 (c) shows an obstruction that is 34 inches maximum in height. The high side reach is 46 inches maximum for a reach depth of 24 inches maximum.]	mm) maximum and the depth of the obstruction shall be 24 inches (610 mm) maximum. . . . Where the reach depth exceeds 10 inches (225 mm), the high side reach shall be 46 inches (1170 mm) maximum for a reach depth of 24 inches (610 mm) maximum. *Exceptions: 1. The top of washing machines and clothes dryers shall be permitted to be 36 inches (915 mm) maximum above the finish floor. . . .*
Model Codes & Standards	
ICC/ANSI A117.1-1998: Section 308.3.2 has an equivalent requirement for an obstructed high reach, but no exception for washing machines and clothes dryers.	

The current guidelines do not contain a specific scoping requirement for washing machines and clothes dryers. The final revised guidelines require at least one of each machine to be accessible, where three or fewer of each machine are provided; and at least two of each machine to be accessible, where more than three of each machine are provided. The current guidelines and the final revised guidelines require the operable parts of accessible equipment to be placed within a forward or side reach; and specify a 34 inch maximum height for an obstruction for a high side reach. The final revised guidelines add a new exception for a high side reach over washing machines and clothes dryers that permit the tops of the machines to be 36 inches maximum above the finish floor to accommodate currently available machines.

5.22   Handrails

Table 5.22 shows the relevant text of the current guidelines and the final revised guidelines with respect to the technical requirements for handrails.

Table 5.22 – Handrails (text version)

Current Guidelines	Final Revised Guidelines
4.8.5 Handrails. If a ramp run has a rise greater than 6 in (150 mm) or a horizontal projection greater than 72 in (150 mm), than it shall have handrails on both sides. . . . Handrails shall comply with 4.26 and shall have the following features: . . . (2) If handrails are not continuous, they shall extend at least 12 in (305 mm) beyond the top and bottom of	*505.5 Clearance. Clearance between handrail gripping surfaces and adjacent surfaces shall be 1½ inches (38 mm) minimum.* *505.6 Gripping Surface. Handrail gripping surfaces shall be continuous along their length and shall not be obstructed along their tops or sides. The bottoms of handrail gripping surfaces shall not be obstructed more than 20 percent of their length. Where provided, horizontal projections shall*

57

Current Guidelines	Final Revised Guidelines
the ramp segment and shall be parallel with the floor or ground surface (see Fig. 17). (3) *The clear space between the handrail and the wall shall be 1½ in (38 mm).* (4) *Gripping surfaces shall be continuous.* **4.9.4 Handrails.** Stairways shall have handrails at both sides of all stairs. Handrails shall comply with 4.26 and shall have the following features: . . . (2) *If handrails are not continuous, they shall extend at least 12 in (305 mm) beyond the top riser and at least 12 in (305 mm) plus the width of one thread beyond the bottom riser.* (3) *The clear space between handrails and wall shall be 1½ in (38 mm).* (4) *Gripping surfaces shall be uninterrupted by newel posts, other construction elements, or obstructions.* ***4.26.2 Size and Spacing of Grab Bars and Handrails.*** *The diameter or width of gripping surfaces of a handrail or grab bar shall be 1¼ in to 1½ in (32 mm to 38 mm), or the shape shall provide an equivalent gripping surface. If handrails or grab bars are mounted adjacent to a wall, the space between the wall and grab bar shall be 1½ in (38 mm) (see Fig. 39(a), (b), (c), and (e)).* **4.26.4 Eliminating Hazards.** A handrail or grab bar and any wall or other surface adjacent to it shall be	*occur 1½ inches (38 mm) minimum below the bottom of the handrail gripping surface.* ***Exceptions:*** *. . .* **2.** *The distance between the horizontal projections and the bottom of the gripping surface shall be permitted to be reduced by ⅛ inch (3mm) for each ½ inch (13 mm) of additional handrail perimeter dimension that exceeds 4 inches (100 mm).* ***505.7 Cross Section.*** *Handrail gripping surfaces shall have a cross section complying with 505.7.1 or 505.7.2.* ***505.7.1 Circular Cross Section.*** *Handrail gripping surfaces with a circular cross section shall have an outside diameter of 1¼ inches (32 mm) minimum and 2 inches (51 mm) maximum.* ***505.7.2 Non-Circular Cross Section.*** *Handrail gripping surfaces with a non-circular cross section shall have a perimeter dimension of 4 inches (100 mm) minimum and 6¼ inches (160 mm) maximum, and a cross section dimension of 2¼ inches (57 mm) maximum.* ***505.8 Surfaces.*** *Handrail gripping surfaces and any surfaces adjacent to them shall be free from sharp or abrasive elements and shall have rounded edges.* **505.10 Handrail Extensions.** Handrail gripping surfaces shall extend beyond and in the same direction of stair flights and ramp runs in accordance with 505.10. ***Exceptions:*** *. . .* **3.** *In alterations, full extensions of handrails shall not be required where such extensions would be hazardous due to plan configuration.* ***505.10.3 Bottom Extension at Stairs.*** *At the bottom of a stair flight, handrails*

58

Current Guidelines	Final Revised Guidelines
free of any sharp or abrasive elements. *Edges shall have a minimum radius of ⅛ in (3.2 mm).*	*shall extend at the slope of the stair flight for a horizontal distance at least equal to one tread depth beyond the last riser nosing. . . .*
Model Codes & Standards	
IBC 2000: Section 1003.3.3.11 has similar requirements for handrails. **IBC 2003:** Section 1009.11 has similar requirements for handrails. **ICC/ANSI A117.1-1998:** Section 505 has similar requirements for handrails.	

The current guidelines and the final revised guidelines contain technical requirements for handrails. The final revised guidelines provide more flexibility than the current guidelines as follows:

- The current guidelines require the clearance between handrail gripping surfaces and adjacent surfaces to be exactly 1½ inches. The final revised guidelines require the clearance to be 1½ inches minimum.

- The current guidelines require handrail gripping surfaces to have edges with a minimum radius of ⅛ inch. The final revised guidelines require handrail gripping surfaces to have rounded edges.

- The current guidelines require handrail gripping surfaces to have a diameter of 1¼ inches to 1½ inches, or to provide an equivalent gripping surface. The final revised guidelines require handrail gripping surfaces with a circular cross section to have an outside diameter of 1¼ inches to 2 inches. Handrail gripping surfaces with a non-circular cross section must have a perimeter dimension of 4 inches to 6¼ inches, and a cross section dimension of 2¼ inches maximum.

- The current guidelines require handrail gripping surfaces to be continuous, and to be uninterrupted by newel posts, other construction elements, or obstructions. The final revised guidelines require handrail gripping surfaces to be continuous along their length and not to be obstructed along their tops or sides. The bottoms of handrail gripping surfaces must not be obstructed more than 20 percent of their length. Where provided, horizontal projections must occur at least 1½ inches below the bottom of the handrail gripping surface. An exception permits the distance between the horizontal projections and the bottom of the gripping surface to be reduced by ⅛ inch for each ½ inch of additional handrail perimeter dimension that exceeds 4 inches.

- The current guidelines require handrails at the bottom of stairs to extend at least 12 inches plus the width of one tread beyond the bottom riser. The final revised guidelines require handrails at the bottom of stairs to extend a horizontal distance at least equal to one tread depth beyond the last riser nosing. The final revised guidelines add a new exception for alterations to existing facilities that exempts handrails at the top and bottom of ramps and stairs from providing full extensions where it would be hazardous due to plan configuration.

5.23 Toilet Room Doors

Table 5.23 shows the relevant text of the current guidelines and the final revised guidelines with respect to the technical requirement for toilet room doors.

Table 5.23 – Toilet Room Doors (text version)

Current Guidelines	Final Revised Guidelines
4.22.2 Doors. All doors to accessible toilet rooms shall comply with 4.13. Doors shall not swing into the clear floor space required for any fixture.	**603.1 General.** Toilet and bathing rooms shall comply with 603. **603.2.3 Door Swing.** Doors shall not swing into the clear floor space or clearance required for any fixture. Doors shall be permitted to swing into the required turning space. *Exceptions: . . .* *2. Where the toilet room or bathing room is for individual use and a clear floor space complying with 305.3 is provided within the room beyond the arc of the door swing, doors shall be permitted to swing into the clear floor space or clearance required for any fixture.*
Model Codes & Standards	
ICC/ANSI A117.1-1998: Section 603.2.3 has an equivalent requirement for toilet room doors and an equivalent exception for single-user toilet rooms.	

The current guidelines and the final revised guidelines prohibit doors from swinging into the clear floor space or clearance required for any fixture in toilet rooms. The final revised guidelines add a new exception for single-user toilet rooms that permits the door to swing into the clear floor space or clearance required for any fixture, where a clear floor space is provided within the room beyond the arc of the door swing. This exception results in at least a 7 square feet reduction in the required size of an accessible single-user toilet room.

5.24 Water Closet Location and Rear Wall Grab Bar

Table 5.24 shows the relevant text of the current guidelines and the final revised guidelines with respect to the technical requirements for the water closet location and rear grab bar.

Table 5.24 – Water Closet Location and Rear Wall Grab Bar (text version)

Current Guidelines	Final Revised Guidelines
4.17.3 Size and Arrangement. The size and arrangement of the standard toilet stall shall comply with Fig. 30(a), Standard Stall. . . .	**604.2 Location.** The water closet shall be positioned with a wall or partition to the rear and to one side. *The centerline of the water closet*

60

Current Guidelines	Final Revised Guidelines
[Note: Figure 30 (a) shows the centerline of the water closet as 18 inches (455 mm) absolute from the side wall.] **4.17.6 Grab Bars.** Grab bars complying with the length and positioning shown in Fig. 30 (a), (b), (c), and (d) shall be provided. . . . [Note: Figures 30 (a), (b), (c), and (d) show the length of the rear grab bar as 36 inches (915 mm) minimum.]	*shall be 16 inches (405 mm) minimum to 18 inches (455 mm) maximum from the side wall or partition. . . .* **604.5.2 Rear Wall.** The rear wall grab bar shall be 36 inches (915 mm) long minimum and extend from the centerline of the water closet 12 inches (305 mm) minimum on one side and 24 inches (610 mm) on the other side. *Exceptions: 1. The rear grab bar shall be permitted to be 24 inches (610 mm) long minimum, centered on the water closet, where wall space does not permit a length of 36 inches (915 mm) minimum due to the location of a recessed fixture adjacent to the water closet. . . .*
colspan-Model Codes & Standards	
ICC/ANSI A117.1-1998: Sections 604.2 has an equivalent requirement for the water closet location. Section 604.5.2 has a similar requirement for the rear wall grab bar.	

The current guidelines and the final revised guidelines contain technical requirements for the location of water closets and the rear wall grab bar. The current guidelines require the centerline of the water closet in accessible toilet rooms and compartments to be located exactly 18 inches from the side wall, and the rear wall grab bar to be at least 36 inches long. The final revised guidelines require the centerline of the water closet to be located between 16 inches and 18 inches from the side wall. The final revised guidelines add a new exception that permits the rear wall grab bar to be at least 24 inches long, where there is not enough wall space for a 36 inch long grab bar because a lavatory is located adjacent to the water closet and the wall behind the lavatory is recessed so that the lavatory does not overlap the clear floor space at the water closet.

5.25   Shower Compartments

Table 5.25 shows the relevant text of the current guidelines and the final revised guidelines with respect to the technical requirements for shower compartments.

Table 5.25 – Shower Compartments (text version)

Current Guidelines	Final Revised Guidelines
4.21.2 Size and Clearances. Except as specified in 9.1.2, shower stall size and clear floor space shall comply with Fig. 35 (a) or (b). The shower stall in Fig. 35 (a) shall be 36 in by 36 in (915 mm by 915 mm). Shower stall required by 9.1.2 shall	**608.1 General.** Shower compartments shall comply with 608. *608.2.1 Transfer Type Shower Compartments. Transfer type shower compartments shall be 36 inches (915 mm) by 36 inches (915 mm) clear*

Current Guidelines	Final Revised Guidelines
comply with Fig. 57 (a) or (b). The shower stall in Fig. 35 (b) will fit into the space required for a bathtub. [Note: Figure 35 (b) shows a roll-in shower compartment that is 30 inches wide and 60 inches long minimum and that has no seat.] **9.1.2 Accessible Units, Sleeping Rooms, and Suites.** *. . . In addition, in hotels of 50 or more sleeping rooms or suites, additional accessible sleeping rooms or suites that include a roll-in shower shall also be provided in conformance with the table below. Such accommodations shall comply with the requirements of 9.2, 4.21, and Figure 57 (a) or (b). . . .* [*Note: Figure 57 (b) shows an alternate roll-in shower compartment that is 36 inches wide and 60 inches long minimum and that has a seat. There is a 36 inch minimum opening on the long side of the compartment. The controls are located on the end wall adjacent to the seat.*] **4.21.5 Controls.** Faucets and other controls complying with 4.27.4 shall be located as shown in Fig. 37. . . . [Note: Figure 37 shows the control area located between 38 inches minimum and 48 inches maximum above the shower floor.] **4.21.7 Curbs.** If provided, curbs in shower stalls 36 in by 36 in (915 mm by 915 mm) shall be no higher than ½ in (13 mm). *Shower stalls that are 30 in by 60 in (760 mm by 1525 mm) minimum shall not have curbs.*	*inside dimensions measured at the center points of opposing sides and shall have a 36 inch (915 mm) wide minimum entry on the face of the shower compartment. . . .* ***608.2.3 Alternate Roll-In Type Shower Compartments.** Alternate roll-in type shower compartments shall be 36 inches (915 mm) wide and 60 inches (1220 mm) deep minimum clear inside dimensions measured at center points of opposing sides. A 36 inch (915 mm) wide minimum entry shall be provided at one end of the long side of the compartment.* ***608.4 Seats.** A folding or non-folding seat shall be provided in transfer type shower compartments. A folding seat shall be provided in roll-in showers required in transient lodging guest rooms required to provide mobility features complying with 806.2. . . .* ***608.5.3 Alternate Roll-In Type Shower Compartments.** In alternate roll-in type shower compartments, the controls, faucets, and shower spray unit shall be located above the grab bar, but no higher than 48 inches (1220 mm) above the shower floor. Where a seat is provided, the controls, faucets, and shower spray unit shall be located on the side wall adjacent to the seat 27 inches (685 mm) maximum from the side wall behind the seat or shall be located on the back wall opposite the seat 15 inches (380 mm) maximum, left or right, of the centerline of the seat. Where a seat is not provided, the controls, faucets, and shower spray unit shall be installed on the side wall farthest from the compartment entry.* ***608.7 Thresholds.** Thresholds in roll-in type shower compartments shall be ½ inch (13 mm) high maximum in accordance with 303. In transfer type*

62

Current Guidelines	Final Revised Guidelines
	shower compartments, thresholds ½ inch (13 mm) high maximum shall be beveled, rounded, or vertical. **Exception:** *A threshold 2 inches (51 mm) high maximum shall be permitted in transfer type shower compartments in existing facilities where provision of a ½ inch (13 mm) high threshold would disturb the structural reinforcement of the floor slab.*
Model Codes & Standards	
ICC/ANSI A117.1-1998: Sections 608.2 through 608.7 have similar requirements for shower compartments.	

The current guidelines and the final revised guidelines contain technical requirements for transfer-type and roll-in shower compartments. The final revised guidelines provide more flexibility than the current guidelines as follows:

- Transfer-type showers are 36 inches by 36 inches and have a folding or non-folding seat. The final revised guidelines specify that these dimensions are measured at the center point of opposing sides to accommodate molded compartments with rounded bottom edges.

- The current guidelines and the final revised guidelines permit a ½ inch maximum curb in transfer-type showers. The final revised guidelines add a new exception that permits a 2 inch maximum curb in transfer-type showers in alterations to existing facilities, where recessing the compartment to achieve a ½ inch curb would disturb the structural reinforcement of the floor slab.

- Roll-in showers are 30 inches minimum by 60 inches minimum. Alternate roll-in showers are 36 inches by 60 inches minimum, and have a 36 inch minimum opening on the long side of the compartment. The current guidelines permit alternate roll-in showers to be used only in hotel guest rooms; require a seat to be provided on the side with the opening; and require the controls to be located on the side adjacent to the seat. The final revised guidelines permit alternate roll-in showers to be used in any facility; only require a seat in hotel guest rooms; and provide more locations for the controls.

- The current guidelines prohibit curbs in roll-in showers. The final revised guidelines permit a ½ inch maximum curb.

5.26   Sales and Service Counters

Table 5.26 shows the relevant text of the current guidelines and the final revised guidelines with respect to the technical requirements for sales and service counters.

Table 5.26 – Sales and Service Counters (text version)

Current Guidelines	Final Revised Guidelines

63

Current Guidelines	Final Revised Guidelines
7.2 Sales and Service Counters . . . (1) In areas used for transactions where counters have cash registers and are provided for sales or distribution of goods or services to the public, at least one of each type shall have a portion of the counter which is at least 36 in (915 mm) in length with a maximum height of 36 in (915 mm) above the finish floor. . . . (2) In areas used for transactions that may not have a cash register but at which goods or services are sold or distributed . . . either: (i) a portion of the main counter which is a minimum of 36 in (915 mm) in length shall be provided with a maximum height of 36 in (915 mm); or (ii) an auxiliary counter with maximum height of 36 in (915 mm) in close proximity to the main counter be provided; or (iii) equivalent facilitation shall be provided . . .	**904.4 Sales and Service Counters.** Sales and service counters shall comply with 904.4.1 or 904.4.2. The accessible portion of the counter top shall extend the same depth as the sales or service counter top. *Exception: In alterations, when the provision of a counter complying with 904.4 would result in a reduction of the number of existing counters at work stations or a reduction of the number of existing mailboxes, the counter shall be permitted to have a portion which is 24 inches (610 mm) long minimum complying with 904.4.1 provided that the required clear floor or ground space is centered on the accessible length of the counter.* **904.4.1 Parallel Approach.** A portion of the counter surface that is 36 inches (915 mm) long minimum and 36 inches (915 mm) high maximum above the finish floor shall be provided. A clear floor or ground space complying with 305 shall be positioned for a parallel approach adjacent to the 36 inch (915 mm) minimum length of the counter. *Exception: Where the provided counter surface is less than 36 inches (915 mm) long, the entire counter surface shall be 36 inches (915 mm) high maximum above the finish floor.* **904.4.2 Forward Approach.** A portion of the counter surface that is 30 inches (760 mm) long minimum and 36 inches (915 mm) high maximum shall be provided. Knee and toe space complying with 306 shall be provided under the counter. A clear floor or ground space complying with 305 shall be positioned for a forward approach to the counter.
Model Codes & Standards	
ICC/ANSI A117.1-1998: Section 904.3 has similar requirements for sales and service counters.	

The current guidelines and the final revised guidelines contain technical requirements for sales and service counters. The current guidelines generally require counters to have an accessible portion at least 36 inches long and no higher than 36 inches. The current guidelines provide some flexibility for counters that do not have cash registers. The final revised guidelines specify different lengths for the accessible portion of counters based on the type of approach. Where a forward approach is provided, the accessible portion of the counter must be at least 30 inches long and no higher than 36 inches, and knee and toe space must be provided under the counter. Where a parallel approach is provided, the accessible portion of the counter must be at least 36 inches long and no higher than 36 inches. The final revised guidelines add a new exception for alterations to counters in existing facilities that permits the accessible portion of the counter to be at least 24 inches long, where providing a longer accessible counter would result in a reduction in the number of existing counters or existing mailboxes.

The final revised guidelines clarify that the accessible portion of the counter must extend the same depth as the sales or service counter top. Where the counter is a single-height counter, this requirement applies across the entire depth of the counter top. Where the counter is a split-height counter, this requirement applies only to the customer side of the counter top. The employee-side of the counter top may be higher or lower than the customer-side of the counter top.

5.27   Detectable Warnings

Table 5.27 shows the relevant text of the current guidelines and the final revised guidelines with respect to the scoping and technical requirements for detectable warnings.

Table 5.27 – Detectable Warnings (text version)

Current Guidelines	Final Revised Guidelines
4.1.3 Accessible Buildings: New Construction. Accessible buildings and facilities shall meet the following minimum requirements: . . . (15) Detectable warnings shall be provided at locations specified in 4.29. *4.7.7 Detectable Warnings. A curb ramp shall have a detectable warning complying with 4.29.2. The detectable warning shall extend the full width and depth of the curb ramp.* **4.29.1 General.** Detectable warnings required by 4.1 and 4.7 shall comply with 4.29. *4.29.2 Detectable Warnings on Walking Surfaces. Detectable*	**218.2 New and Altered Fixed Guideway Stations.** New and altered stations in rapid rail, light rail, commuter rail, intercity rail, high speed rail, and other fixed guideway systems shall comply with 810.5 through 810.10. **218.3 Key Stations and Existing Intercity Rail Stations.** Key stations and existing intercity rail stations shall comply with 810.5 through 810.10. **810.5 Rail Platforms.** Rail platforms shall comply with 810.5. **810.5.2 Detectable Warnings.** Platform boarding edges not protected by platform screens or guards shall have detectable warnings complying with 705 along

Printed by Builder's Book, Inc., Bookstore · www.buildersbook.com

Current Guidelines	Final Revised Guidelines
warnings shall consist of raised truncated domes with a diameter of nominal 0.9 in (23 mm), a height of nominal 0.2 in (5 mm) and a center-to-center spacing of nominal 2.35 in (60 mm) and shall contrast visually with adjoining surfaces, either light-on-dark, or dark-on-light. The material used to provide contrast shall be an integral part of the walking surface. Detectable warnings used on interior surfaces shall differ from adjoining walking surfaces in resiliency or sound-on-cane contact.	the full length of the public use area of the platform.
	705.1 General. Detectable warnings shall consist of a surface of truncated domes and shall comply with 705.
***4.29.5 Detectable Warnings at Hazardous Vehicular Areas.** If a walk crosses or adjoins a vehicular way, and the walking surfaces are not separated by curbs, railings, or other elements between the pedestrian areas and vehicular areas, the boundary between the areas shall be defined by a continuous detectable warning which is 36 in (915 mm) wide, complying with 4.29.2.*	***705.1.1 Dome Size.** Truncated domes in a detectable warning surface shall have a base diameter of 0.9 inch (23 mm) minimum and 1.4 inches (36 mm) maximum, a top diameter of 50 percent of the base diameter minimum to 65 percent of the base diameter maximum, and a height of 0.2 inch (5.1 mm).*
***4.29.6 Detectable Warnings at Reflecting Pools.** The edges of reflecting pools shall be protected by railings, walls, curbs, or detectable warnings complying with 4.29.2.*	***705.1.2 Dome Spacing.** Truncated domes in a detectable warning surface shall have a center-to-center spacing of 1.6 inches (41 mm) minimum and 2.4 inches (61 mm) maximum, and a base-to-base spacing of 0.65 inch (17 mm) minimum, measured between the most adjacent domes on a square grid.*
10.3.1 New Construction. New stations in rapid rail, light rail, commuter rail, intercity bus, intercity rail, high speed rail, and other fixed guideway systems (e.g., automated guideway transit, monorails, etc.) shall comply with the following provisions as applicable: . . .	**705.1.3 Contrast.** Detectable warning surfaces shall contrast visually with adjacent walking surfaces either light-on-dark, or dark-on-light.
(8) Platform edges bordering on a drop-off and not protected by platform screens or guard rails shall have a detectable warning. Such detectable warnings shall comply with 4.29.2 and shall be 24 inches wide running the full length of the platform drop-off.	**705.2 Platform Edges.** Detectable warning surfaces at platform boarding edges shall be 24 inches (610 mm) wide and shall extend the full length of the public use areas of the platform.

66

Current Guidelines	Final Revised Guidelines
Model Codes & Standards	
IBC 2000: Section 1108.9 has an equivalent requirement for detectable warnings at transit platform edges. **IBC 2003:** Section 1109.9 has an equivalent requirement for detectable warnings at transit platform edges. **ICC/ANSI A117.1-1998:** Sections 705.1 through 705.3 have similar requirements for detectable warnings characteristics.	

Detectable warnings are a distinctively textured surface of truncated domes that is identifiable by cane and underfoot. The current guidelines require detectable warnings at curb ramps, hazardous vehicular areas, reflecting pools, and transit platform edges. The final revised guidelines only require detectable warnings at transit platform edges. The final revised guidelines change the specifications for the diameter and spacing of the truncated domes to permit a range of dimensions. The final revised guidelines also delete the requirements for the material used to provide contrast to be an integral part of the truncated domes, and for the truncated domes to contrast in resiliency or sound-on-cane contact from adjoining walking surfaces at interior locations.

CHAPTER 6: REVISIONS THAT HAVE MINIMAL IMPACTS

6.0 Introduction

This chapter discusses revisions to the scoping and technical requirements that will have minimal impacts on the new construction and alteration of facilities. The relevant text of the current guidelines and the final revised guidelines is presented in tables. Unless otherwise noted, the current guidelines refer to ADAAG. The requirements are presented in the order in which they appear in the final revised guidelines. Scoping and technical requirements are presented together, where appropriate. The text of the current guidelines and the final revised guidelines is underlined to highlight the revisions in the scoping and technical requirements. Equivalent requirements in the International Building Code and the ICC/ANSI A117.1 Standard on Accessible and Usable Buildings and Facilities are also noted in the tables.

6.1 Alterations to Primary Function Areas

Table 6.1 shows the relevant text of the current guidelines and the final revised guidelines with respect to the scoping requirement for alterations to primary function areas. The current guidelines refer to UFAS.

Table 6.1 – Alterations to Primary Function Areas (text version)

Current Guidelines	Final Revised Guidelines
4.1.6 Accessible Buildings: Alterations.	*202.4 Alterations Affecting Primary Function Areas. In addition to the requirements of 202.3, an alteration*

67

Current Guidelines	Final Revised Guidelines
(3) Where substantial alteration occurs to a building or facility, then each element or space that is altered or added shall comply with the applicable provisions of 4.1.1 to 4.1.4 of 4.1, Minimum Requirements, except to the extent where it is structurally impracticable. The altered building or facility shall contain:	*that affects or could affect the usability of or access to an area containing a primary function shall be made so as to ensure that, to the maximum extent feasible, the path of travel to the altered area, including the rest rooms, telephones, and drinking fountains serving the altered area, are readily accessible to and usable by individuals with disabilities, unless such alterations are disproportionate to the overall alterations in terms of cost and scope as determined under criteria established by the Attorney General. . . .*
(a) At least one accessible route complying with 4.3, Accessible Route, and 4.1.6(a);	
(b) At least one accessible entrance complying with 4.14, Entrances. If additional entrances are altered then they shall comply with 4.1.6(a); and	*[Note: The Department of Justice defines a "primary function" and "disproportionate" in its regulations at 28 C.F.R. § 36.403. A "primary function" is "a major activity for which a facility is intended." Alterations to provide an accessible path of travel to the altered area are "deemed disproportionate to the overall alteration when the cost exceeds 20 percent of the cost of the alteration to the primary function area."]*
(c) The following toilet facilities, whichever is greater:	
(i) At least one toilet facility for each sex in the altered building complying with 4.22, Toilet Rooms; and 4.23, Bathrooms, Bathing Facilities, and Shower Rooms.	
(ii) At least one toilet facility for each sex on each substantially altered floor, where such facilities are provided, complying with 4.22, Toilet Rooms; and 4.23, Bathrooms, Bathing Facilities, and Shower Rooms.	
(d) In making the determination as to what constitutes "substantial alteration," the agency issuing standards for the facility shall consider the total cost of all alterations (including but not limited to electrical, plumbing, and structural changes) for a building or facility within any twelve (12) month period. For guidance in implementing this provision, an alteration to any building or facility is to be considered substantial if the total cost for this twelve month period amounts to 50 percent or more of the	

Current Guidelines	Final Revised Guidelines
full and fair cash value of the building as defined in 3.5	
Model Codes & Standards	
IBC 2000: Section 3408.6 has an equivalent requirement for alterations to primary function areas.	
IBC 2003: Sections 3409.6 has an equivalent requirement for alterations to primary function areas.	

UFAS requires an accessible route, accessible entrance, and accessible toilets to be provided when alterations amount to 50 percent or more of the value of the facility. When alterations affect a primary function area containing a major activity for which the facility is intended, the final revised guidelines require the path of travel to the altered area and the toilet rooms, public telephones, and drinking fountains serving the altered area to be made accessible, to the extent that the cost of making these elements accessible does not exceeds 20 percent of the cost of the alterations to the primary function area.

The revision affects Federal, State, and local governments. The impacts are expected to be minimal since federally financed facilities subject to standards issued by the General Services Administration are required to comply with ADAAG when it provides an improved level of access compared to UFAS. State and local governments are permitted to use either ADAAG or UFAS. Many State and local governments use ADAAG. The impacts are further minimized by the fact that State and local governments have made many of their existing facilities accessible to comply with separate program accessibility requirements under the Americans with Disabilities Act and section 504 of the Rehabilitation Act.

6.2 Common Use Circulation Paths in Employee Work Areas

Table 6.2.1 shows the relevant text of the current guidelines and the final revised guidelines with respect to the scoping and technical requirements for common use circulation paths in employee work areas.

Table 6.2.1 – Common Use Circulation Paths in Employee Work Areas (text version)

Current Guidelines	Final Revised Guidelines
4.1.1 Application. . . . (3) *Areas Used Only by Employees as Work Areas. Areas that are used only as work areas shall be designed and constructed so that individuals with disabilities can approach, enter, and exit the areas. These guidelines do not require that any areas used only as work areas be constructed to permit maneuvering within the work area or be constructed or equipped (i.e., with racks or shelves) to be accessible.*	***203.9 Employee Work Areas.*** *Spaces and elements within employee work areas shall only be required to comply with 206.2.8, 207.1, and 215.3 and shall be designed and constructed so that individuals with disabilities can approach, enter, and exit the employee work area. Employee work areas, or portions of employee work areas, that are less than 300 square feet (28 m²) in area and elevated 7 inches (178 mm) or more above the finish floor or ground where the elevation is essential to the function of the space shall not be required to comply with these requirements or to be on an accessible route.* ***206.2.8 Employee Work Areas.*** *Common use circulation paths within employee work areas shall comply with 402.* ***Exceptions: 1.*** *Common use circulation paths located within employee work areas that are less than 1000 square feet (93 m²) and defined by permanently installed partitions, counters, casework, or furnishings shall not be required to comply with 402.* ***2.*** *Common use circulation paths located within employee work areas that are an integral component of work area equipment shall not be required to comply with 402.* ***3.*** *Common use circulation paths located within exterior employee work areas that are fully exposed to the weather shall not be required to comply with 402.* **402.1 General.** Accessible routes shall comply with 402. **402.2 Components.** Accessible routes shall consist of one or more of

70

Current Guidelines	Final Revised Guidelines
	the following components: walking surfaces with a running slope not steeper than 1:20, doorways, ramps, curb ramps excluding the flared sides, elevators, and platform lifts. All components of accessible routes shall comply with the applicable requirements of Chapter 4. **403.5 Clearances.** Walking surfaces shall provide clearances complying with 403.5. *Exception: Within employee work areas, clearances on common use circulation paths shall be permitted to be decreased by work area equipment provided that the decrease is essential to the function of the work being performed.* **405.5 Clear Width.** The clear width of a ramp run and, where handrails are provided, the clear width between handrails shall be 36 inches (915 mm) minimum. *Exception: Within employee work areas, the required clear width of ramps that are a part of common use circulation paths shall be permitted to be decreased by work area equipment provided that the decrease is essential to the function of the work being performed.* **405.8 Handrails.** Ramp runs with a rise greater than 6 inches (150 mm) shall have handrails complying with 505. *Exception: Within employee work areas, handrails shall not be required where ramps that are part of common use circulation paths are designed to permit the installation of handrails complying with 505. Ramps not subject to the exception to 405.5 shall be designed to maintain a 36 inch (915 mm) clear width when handrails are installed.*

Model Codes & Standards

71

Current Guidelines	Final Revised Guidelines
IBC 2000: Section 1103.2.3 has similar requirements and exceptions for employee work areas. **IBC 2003:** Section 1104.3.1 has equivalent requirements and similar exceptions for employee work areas.	

The current guidelines and the final revised guidelines require employee work areas to be designed and constructed so that individuals with disabilities can approach, enter, and exit the areas. The work areas themselves are not required to be accessible. The Americans with Disabilities Act requires employers to make reasonable accommodations in the workplace for individuals with disabilities, which may include modifications to work areas when needed.

The final revised guidelines require common use circulation paths within employee works areas to comply with the technical requirements for accessible routes. Individual employee work stations, such as a grocery checkout counter or an automobile service bay designed for use by one person, do not contain common use circulation paths and are not required to comply.

The final revised guidelines contain several exceptions that exempt common use circulation paths in employee work areas where it may be difficult to comply with the technical requirements for accessible routes due to the size or function of the area.

- Employee work areas, or portions of employee work areas, that are less than 300 square feet and are elevated 7 inches or more above the ground or finish floor, where elevation is essential to the function of the space, are exempt. Small work stations in factories are covered by this exception.

- Common use circulation paths within employee work areas that are less than 1,000 square feet and are defined by permanently installed partitions, counters, casework, or furnishings are exempt. Fast food kitchens, cocktail bars, and the employee side of service counters are covered by this exception.

- Common use circulation paths within employee work areas that are an integral component of equipment are exempt. Common use circulation paths within large pieces of equipment in factories, electric power plants, and amusement rides are covered by this exception.

- Common use circulation paths within exterior employee work areas that are fully exposed to the weather are exempt. Farms, ranches, and outdoor maintenance facilities are covered by this exception.

The final revised guidelines also contain exceptions to the technical requirements for accessible routes:

- Machinery and equipment are permitted to reduce the clear width of common use circulation paths where it is essential to the function of the work performed. Machinery and equipment that must be placed a certain way to work properly, or for ergonomics or to prevent workplace injuries are covered by this exception.

72

- Handrails are not required on ramps, provided they can be added in the future.

The model building codes and fire and life safety codes, which are adopted by all the States, require circulation paths in facilities, including employee work areas, to be at least 36 inches wide for purposes of emergency egress. Accessible routes are generally at least 36 inches wide.

Because of the exceptions that exempt common use circulation paths in employee work areas where it may be difficult to comply with the technical requirements for accessible routes due to the size or function of the area, and because the model building codes and fire and life safety codes, which are adopted by all the States, require circulation paths in facilities, including employee work areas, to be at least 36 inches wide for purposes of emergency egress, the revision is expected to have minimal impacts.

6.3 Location of Accessible Routes

Table 6.3 shows the relevant text of the current guidelines and the final revised guidelines with respect to the scoping requirement for the location of accessible routes.

Table 6.3 – Interior Accessible Routes (text version)

Current Guidelines	Final Revised Guidelines
4.3.2 Location. *(1) At least one accessible route within the boundary of the site shall be provided from public transportation stops, accessible parking and accessible passenger loading zones, and public streets or sidewalks to the accessible building entrance they serve. The accessible route shall, to the maximum extent feasible, coincide with the route for the general public.*	*206.3 Location. Accessible routes shall coincide with or be located in the same area as general circulation paths. Where circulation paths are interior, required accessible routes shall also be interior.*
Model Codes & Standards	
IBC 2000: Section 1104.5 has an equivalent requirement for location of accessible routes. **IBC 2003:** Section 1104.5 has an equivalent requirement for location of accessible routes.	

The current guidelines require accessible routes connecting site arrival points and accessible building entrances to coincide with general circulation paths, to the maximum extent feasible. The final revised guidelines require all accessible routes to coincide with or be located in the same general area as general circulation paths. The revision will have no impacts on exterior accessible routes since the requirements in the current guidelines and the final revised guidelines are basically the same. Designing interior accessible routes to coincide with or to be located in the same area as general circulation path will not typically present a difficult design challenge and is expected to have minimal impacts.

73

The final revised guidelines also require accessible routes to be located in the interior of the facility, where general circulation paths are located in the interior of the facility. The revision affects a limited number of buildings. For example, under the current guidelines, a two-story building that is constructed into a hill, has an interior stairway connecting the stories, and is not exempt from providing an accessible route between the stories could provide entrances to each story of the building and connect the entrances with an exterior accessible route. The final revised guidelines would require an elevator to be provided since there is an interior stairway. The revision is expected to have minimal impacts since the cost of providing an elevator would be about the same as constructing an exterior accessible route around the building.

6.4 Public Entrances

Table 6.4 shows the relevant text of the current guidelines and the final revised guidelines with respect to the scoping requirement for public entrances.

Table 6.4 – Public Entrances (text version)

Current Guidelines	Final Revised Guidelines
4.1.3 Accessible Buildings: New Construction. Accessible buildings and facilities shall meet the following minimum requirements: . . .	**206.4 Entrances.** Entrances shall be provided in accordance with 206.4. . . .
	Exceptions: 1. Where an alteration includes alterations to an entrance, and the building or facility has another entrance complying with 404 that is on an accessible route, the altered entrance shall not be required to comply with 206.4 unless required by 202.4. . . .
(8) *The requirements in (a) and (b) below shall be satisfied independently:*	
(a)(i) At least 50 percent of all public entrances (excluding those in (b) below) shall comply with 4.14. . . .	
(ii) Accessible public entrances must be provided in a number at least equivalent to the number of exits required by the applicable building or fire codes. (This paragraph does not require an increase in the total number of public entrances planned for a facility.) . . .	*206.4.1 Public Entrances.* In addition to entrances required by 206.4.2 through 206.4.9, at least 60 percent of all public entrances shall comply with 404.
4.1.6 Accessible Buildings: Alterations.	
(1) General. Alterations to existing buildings and facilities shall comply with the following: . . .	
(h) Entrances. If a planned alteration entails alterations to an entrance, and	

74

the building has an accessible entrance, the entrance being altered is not required to comply with 4.1.3(8), except to the extent required by 4.1.6(2). . . .	
Model Codes & Standards	
IBC 2000: Section 1105.1 has a similar requirement for the number of accessible public entrances.	
IBC 2003: Section 1105.1 has a similar requirement for the number of accessible public entrances.	

The current guidelines require at least 50 percent of public entrances to be accessible. In addition, the current guidelines require the number of accessible public entrances to be equivalent to the number of exits required by applicable building and fire codes. Building and fire codes typically require at least two exits to be provided from a facility. Thus, under the current guidelines where two public entrances are planned in a newly constructed facility, both entrances must be accessible.

Instead of requiring at least 50 percent of public entrances plus a number equal to the number of required exits to be made accessible, the final revised guidelines require at least 60 percent of public entrances to be made accessible. The revision is intended to achieve the same result as the current guidelines. Thus, under the final revised guidelines where two public entrances are planned in a newly constructed facility, both entrances must be accessible.

Where multiple public entrances are planned to serve different site arrival points, the current guidelines and the final revised guidelines require at least one accessible route to be provided from each site arrival point, including accessible parking spaces, accessible passenger loading zones, public streets and sidewalks, and public transportation stops, to an accessible public entrance that serves the site arrival point. Thus, the accessible route requirements will typically result in more than 50 percent of the public entrances being accessible. Requiring at least 60 percent of public entrances to be accessible is not expected to result in a substantial increase in the number of accessible entrances compared to the current guidelines.

On a site with little change in elevation, providing an accessible route to an accessible entrance requires providing a walking surface with a running slope not steeper than 1:20. On a site with a moderate change in elevation, providing an accessible route to an accessible entrance requires providing a ramp with a running slope not steeper than 1:12 along all or part of the accessible route. On a site with extreme changes in elevation, providing an accessible route to an accessible entrance may require adjusting the planned location of an accessible entrance to minimize the amount of ramping, or an elevator or platform lift may be a design solution in rare cases. Where extreme changes in elevation or other site constraints make it too difficult or too costly to make additional public entrances accessible, the likely design solution will be to eliminate redundant public entrances.

The current guidelines and the final revised guidelines contain exceptions that limit the number of accessible entrances required in alterations to existing facilities. When

75

entrances in an existing facility are altered and the facility has an accessible entrance, the entrance being altered is not required to be accessible, unless a primary function area is also altered and then an accessible path of travel must be provided to the primary function area to the extent the cost is not disproportionate.

6.5 Direct Access Entrances from Parking Structures

Table 6.5 shows the relevant text of the current guidelines and the final revised guidelines with respect to the scoping requirement for direct access entrances from parking structures.

Table 6.5 – Direct Access Entrances From Parking Structures (text version)

Current Guidelines	Final Revised Guidelines
4.1.3 Accessible Buildings: New Construction. Accessible buildings and facilities shall meet the following minimum requirements: . . . *(8)(b)(i) In addition, if direct access is provided for pedestrians from an enclosed parking garage to the building, at least one direct entrance from the garage to the building must be accessible. . . .*	***206.4.2 Parking Structure Entrances.** Where direct access is provided for pedestrians from a parking structure to a building or facility entrance, each direct access to the building or facility entrance shall comply with 404.*
Model Codes & Standards	
IBC 2000: Section 1105.2 has a similar requirement for the number of accessible direct access entrances from parking structures. **IBC 2003:** Section 1105.1.1 has an equivalent requirement for the number of accessible direct access entrances from parking structures.	

Where levels in a parking garage have direct connections for pedestrians to another facility, the current guidelines require at least one of the direct connections to be accessible. The final revised guidelines require all of the direct connections to be accessible. The vertical distances between the levels in a parking garage are typically less than the vertical distances between the stories in the facility to which it is connected so that not every level of the parking garage has a direct connection to a story in the facility. For example, a parking garage with five levels may have direct connections to only two or three stories of another facility. Making the direct connections between the parking garage and another facility accessible will not typically present a difficult design challenge and is expected to have minimal impacts.

6.6 Alterations to Existing Elevators

Table 6.6 shows the relevant text of the current guidelines and the final revised guidelines with respect to the scoping requirement for alterations to existing elevators.

Table 6.6 – Alterations to Existing Elevators (text version)

Current Guidelines	Final Revised Guidelines

76

Current Guidelines	Final Revised Guidelines
4.1.6 Accessible Buildings: Alterations. (1) *General. Alterations to existing buildings and facilities shall comply with the following: . . .* (b) *If existing elements, spaces, or common areas are altered, then each such altered element, space, feature, or area shall comply with the applicable provisions of 4.1.1 to 4.1.3 Minimum Requirements (for New Construction). . . .*	***206.6.1 Existing Elevators.** Where elements of existing elevators are altered, the same element shall also be altered in all elevators that are programmed to respond to the same hall call control as the altered elevator and shall comply with the requirements of 407 for the altered element.*
Model Codes & Standards	
IBC 2000: Section 3408.7.1 has an equivalent requirement for alterations to existing elevators. **IBC 2003:** Section 3409.7.2 has an equivalent requirement for alterations to existing elevators.	

When a single space or element is altered, the current guidelines require the space or element to be made accessible. When an element in one elevator is altered, the final revised guidelines require the same element to be altered in all elevators that are programmed to respond to the same call button as the altered elevator to ensure that when an individual with a disability presses a call button, an accessible elevator will arrive, and not an inaccessible one.

The revision is expected to have minimal impacts since all the elevators in a bank are typically upgraded at the same time when elevators are altered as part of a planned modernization project. The final revised guidelines also contain exceptions to the technical requirements for elevators when existing elevators are altered that further minimize the impacts of the revision:

- Existing elevators are permitted to have recessed call buttons.

- Existing call buttons and keypads are permitted to be located at 54 inches above the finish floor, measured to the centerline of the highest operable part.

- Existing call buttons are not required to be ¾ inch minimum in the smallest dimension.

- Existing call buttons are not required to have visible signals to indicate when each call is registered and when each call is answered.

- A visible and audible hall signal is not required to be provided at the hoistway entrance of existing elevators to indicate the direction of car travel.

- Existing visible hall signals are not required to be centered at 72 inches minimum above the finish floor and 2 ½ inches minimum measured along the centerline of the element.

- Existing hall signals are not required to meet the requirements for frequency and range of audible signals.

- Existing manually operated hoistway swing doors are permitted if the door opening provides a clear width of 32 inches minimum, and the force for pushing or pulling open the door is 5 pounds maximum.

- Existing manually operated doors are not required to provide a reopening device that automatically stops and reopens the car door and hoistway door if the doors are obstructed by an object or a person.

- A power operated car door with a door opening that provides a clear width of 32 inches minimum is permitted in an existing elevator.

- Existing elevator car configurations that provide a clear floor area of 16 square feet, and provide 54 inches minimum inside clear depth and 36 inches minimum clear width are permitted.

- Where a new car operating panel with accessible elevator car controls and tactile markings is provided in an existing elevator, existing car operating panels are not required to be made accessible.

- Existing car control buttons with floor designations are permitted to be located 54 inches maximum above the finish floor where a parallel approach is provided.

- Existing car control buttons with floor designations are permitted to be recessed.

- Where space on an existing car operating panel precludes the placement of tactile markings immediately to the left of the control button, the markings are permitted to placed as near to the control button as possible.

6.7 Accessible Means of Egress

Table 6.7 shows the relevant text of the current guidelines and the final revised guidelines with respect to the scoping requirements for accessible means of egress.

Table 6.7 – Accessible Means of Egress (text version)

Current Guidelines	Final Revised Guidelines
4.1.3 Accessible Buildings: New Construction. Accessible buildings and facilities shall meet the following minimum requirements: . . . (9) *In buildings or facilities, or portions of buildings or facilities, required to be*	*207.1 General. Means of egress shall comply with section 1003.2.13 of the International Building Code (2000 edition and 2001 Supplement) or section 1007 of the International Building Code (2003 edition) (incorporated by reference, see*

accessible, accessible means of egress shall be provided in the same number as required for exits by local building/life safety regulations. Where a required exit from an occupiable level above or below a level of accessible exit discharge is not accessible, an area of rescue assistance shall be provided on each such level (in a number equal to that of inaccessible required exits). Areas of rescue assistance shall comply with 4.3.11. A horizontal exit meeting the requirements of local building/life safety regulations, shall satisfy the requirement for an area of rescue assistance.

Exception: Areas of rescue assistance are not required in buildings or facilities having a supervised automatic sprinkler system.

(16) Building Signage. . . .

(b) Other signs which provide direction to or information about functional spaces of the building shall comply with 4.30.1, 4.30.4, 4.30.5, and 4.30.6. . . .

4.1.6 Accessible Buildings: Alterations.

(1) General. Alterations to existing buildings and facilities shall comply with the following: . . .

(g) *In alterations, the requirements of 4.1.3(9) . . . do not apply.*

4.3.10 Egress. *Accessible routes serving any accessible space or element shall also serve as a means of egress for emergencies or connect to an accessible area of rescue assistance.*

"Referenced Standards" in Chapter 1). **Exceptions: 1.** *Where means of egress are permitted by local building or life safety codes to share a common path of egress travel, accessible means of egress shall be permitted to share a common path of egress travel. . . .*

216.4 Means of Egress. *Signs for means of egress shall comply with 216.4.*

216.4.1 Exit Doors. *Doors at exit passageways, exit discharge, and exit stairways shall be identified by tactile signs complying with 703.1, 703.2, and 703.5.*

216.4.2 Areas of Refuge. *Signs required by section 1003.2.13.5.4 of the International Building Code (2000 edition) or section 1007.6.4 of the International Building Code (2003 edition) (incorporated by reference, see "Referenced Standards" in Chapter 1) to provide instructions in areas of refuge shall comply with 703.5.*

216.4.3 Directional Signs. *Signs required by section 1003.2.13.6 of the International Building Code (2000 edition) or section 1007.7 of the International Building Code (2003 edition) (incorporated by reference, see "Referenced Standards" in Chapter 1) to provide directions to accessible means of egress shall comply with 703.5*

Model Codes & Standards
IBC 2000: Section 1003.2.13 has equivalent requirements for accessible means of egress.

79

IBC 2003: Section 1007 has equivalent requirements for accessible means of egress.

The current guidelines establish scoping and technical requirements for accessible means of egress. The final revised guidelines reference the International Building Code for scoping and technical requirements for accessible means of egress.

The current guidelines require the same number of accessible means of egress to be provided as the number of exits required by applicable building and fire codes. The International Building Code requires at least one accessible means of egress; and at least two accessible means of egress, where more than one means of egress is required by other sections of the code. The revision is expected to have minimal impacts since the model fire and life safety codes, which are adopted by all the States, contain equivalent requirements with respect to the number of accessible means of egress.

The current guidelines require areas of rescue assistance or horizontal exits in facilities with stories above or below the exit discharge level. Areas of rescue assistance are spaces, which have direct access to an exit, where individuals who are unable to use stairs can go to register a call for assistance and wait for evacuation. The International Building Code requires an evacuation elevator designed with standby power and other safety features that can be used for emergency evacuation of individuals with disabilities in facilities with four or more stories above or below the exit discharge level, and allows exit stairways and evacuation elevators to be used as an accessible means of egress in conjunction with areas of refuge or horizontal exits. The revision is expected to have minimal impacts since the model fire and life safety codes contain equivalent requirements with respect to evacuation elevators.

The current guidelines exempt facilities equipped with a supervised automatic sprinkler system from providing areas of rescue assistance, and also exempt alterations to existing facilities from providing an accessible means of egress. The International Building Code exempts buildings equipped with a supervised automatic sprinkler system from certain technical requirements for areas of refuge, and also exempts alterations to existing facilities from providing an accessible means of egress.

The current guidelines require signs which provide direction to or information about functional spaces to meet certain technical requirements. Signs used for means of egress are covered by this scoping requirement. The final revised guidelines specifically identify signs used for means of egress and require the signs to meet certain technical requirements.

6.8 Passenger Loading Zones

Table 6.8 shows the relevant text of the current guidelines and the final revised guidelines with respect to the scoping and technical requirements for passenger loading zones.

Table 6.8 – Passenger Loading Zones (text version)

Current Guidelines	Final Revised Guidelines
4.1.2 Accessible Sites and Exterior	*209.2.1 Passenger Loading Zones.*

Current Guidelines	Final Revised Guidelines
Facilities: New Construction. An accessible site shall meet the following minimum requirements: . . . (5) . . . (c) *If passenger loading zones are provided, then at least one passenger loading zone shall comply with 4.6.* **4.6.6 Passenger Loading Zones.** Passenger loading zones shall provide an access aisle at least 60 in (1525 mm) wide and 20 ft (240 in) (6100 mm) long adjacent and parallel to the vehicle pull-up space (see Fig. 10). *If there are curbs between the access aisle and the vehicle pull-up space, then a curb ramp complying with 4.7 shall be provided.* Vehicle standing spaces and access aisles shall be level with surface slopes not exceeding 1:50 (2%) in all directions.	*Passenger loading zones, except those required to comply with 209.2.2 and 209.2.3, shall provide at least one passenger loading zone complying with 503 in every continuous 100 linear feet (30 m) of loading zone space, or fraction thereof.* **503.2 Vehicle Pull-Up Space.** Passenger loading zones shall provide a vehicular pull-up space 96 inches (2440 mm) wide minimum and 20 feet (6100 mm) long minimum. **503.3 Access Aisle.** Passenger loading zones shall provide access aisles complying with 503.3 adjacent to the vehicle pull-up space. Access aisles shall adjoin an accessible route and shall not overlap the vehicular way. **503.3.1 Width.** Access aisles serving vehicle pull-up spaces shall be 60 inches (1525 mm) wide minimum. **503.3.2 Length.** Access aisles shall extend the full length of the vehicle pull-up spaces they serve. **503.3.3 Marking.** Access aisles shall be marked so as to discourage parking in them. **503.4 Floor and Ground Surfaces.** Vehicle pull-up spaces and access aisles serving them shall comply with 302. *Access aisles shall be at the same level as the vehicle pull-up space they serve.* Changes in level are not permitted. **Exception:** Slopes not steeper than 1:48 shall be permitted.
Model Codes & Standards	
IBC 2000: Section 1106.6 has a similar requirement for passenger loading zones. **IBC 2003:** Sections 1106.7.1 and 1106.7.2 have equivalent requirements for	

81

Current Guidelines	Final Revised Guidelines
passenger loading zones. **ICC/ANSI A117.1-1998:** Sections 503.3 and 503.4 have equivalent requirements for vehicle pull-up spaces, access aisles, and floor and ground surfaces.	

Where passenger loading zones are provided, the current guidelines require at least one passenger loading zone to be accessible. The final revised guidelines require facilities such as airport passenger terminals that have long, continuous passenger loading zones to provide one accessible passenger loading zone in every continuous 100 linear feet of loading zone space. The final revised guidelines include technical requirements for the vehicle pull-up space (96 inches wide minimum and 20 feet long minimum). Accessible passenger loading zones must have an access aisle that is 60 inches wide minimum and extends the full length of the vehicle pull-up space. Under the current guidelines, the access aisle may be on the same level as the vehicle pull-up space, or on the sidewalk with a curb ramp. The final revised guidelines require the access aisle to be on the same level as the vehicle pull-up space and to be marked so as to discourage parking in the access aisle.

The revision is expected to have minimal impacts since the overall width of the vehicular way or the pedestrian way does not have to be increased to provide an access aisle. If the sidewalk is wide, the sidewalk can be narrowed 5 feet where the access aisle is provided. If the sidewalk is narrow, the sidewalk can be depressed where the access aisle is provided.

6.9 Valet Parking and Mechanical Access Parking Garages

Table 6.9 shows the relevant text of the current guidelines and the final revised guidelines with respect to the scoping requirements for parking facilities that provide valet parking services and for mechanical access parking garages.

Table 6.9 – Valet Parking and Mechanical Access Parking Garages (text version)

Current Guidelines	Final Revised Guidelines
4.1.2 Accessible Sites and Exterior Facilities: New Construction. An accessible site shall meet the following minimum requirements: . . . (5)(a) If parking spaces are provided for self-parking by employees or visitors, or both, then accessible parking spaces complying with 4.6 shall be provided in each such parking area in conformance with the table below. . . . (e) *Valet Parking. Valet parking facilities shall provide a passenger loading zone complying with 4.6*	**208.2 Minimum Number.** Parking spaces complying with 502 shall be provided in accordance with Table 208.2, except as required by 208.2.1, 208.2.2, and 208.2.3. . . . *209.4 Valet Parking. Parking facilities that provide valet parking services shall provide at least one passenger loading zone complying with 503.* *209.5 Mechanical Access Parking Garages. Mechanical access parking garages shall provide at least one passenger loading zone complying*

82

located on an accessible route to the entrance of the facility. *Paragraphs 5(a), 5(b), and 5(d) of this section do not apply to valet parking facilities.*	with 503 at vehicle drop-off and vehicle pick-up areas.

Model Codes & Standards
IBC 2000: Sections 1106.1 and 1106.6.2 have equivalent requirements for valet parking facilities. **IBC 2003:** Sections 1106.1 and 1106.7.3 have equivalent requirements for valet parking facilities.

The current guidelines and the final revised guidelines require parking facilities that provide valet parking services to have an accessible passenger loading zone. The final revised guidelines also require mechanical access parking garages to have an accessible passenger loading zone. The current guidelines contain an exception that exempts valet parking facilities from providing accessible parking spaces. The final revised guidelines do not include the exception. The revision is expected to have minimal impacts since the exception in the current guidelines applies to facilities that provide valet parking services exclusively and is rarely used.

6.10   Stairs

Table 6.10 shows the relevant text of the current guidelines and the final revised guidelines with respect to the scoping and technical requirements for stairs.

Table 6.10 – Stairs (text version)

Current Guidelines	Final Revised Guidelines
4.1.3 Accessible Buildings: New Construction. Accessible buildings and facilities shall meet the following minimum requirements: . . . (4) *Interior and exterior stairs connecting levels that are not connected by an elevator, ramp, or other accessible means of vertical access shall comply with 4.9.* **4.9.2 Treads and Risers.** *On any given flight of stairs, all steps shall have uniform riser heights and uniform tread widths. Stair treads shall be no less than 11 in (280 mm) wide, measured from riser to riser (see Fig. 18(a)).* . . .	*210.1 General. Interior and exterior stairs that are part of a means of egress shall comply with 504.* ***Exceptions:*** *. . .* *2. In alterations, stairs between levels that are connected by an accessible route shall not be required to comply with 504 except that handrails complying with 505 shall be provided when the stairs are altered. . . .* ***504.2 Treads and Risers.*** *All steps on a flight of stairs shall have uniform riser heights and uniform tread depths. Risers shall be 4 inches (100 mm) high minimum and 7 inches (180 mm) high maximum. Treads shall be 11 inches (280 mm) deep minimum.*
Model Codes & Standards	
IBC 2000: Sections 1003.3.3.3 and 1003.3.3.3.1 have equivalent requirements for stairs that are part of a means of egress.	

Current Guidelines	Final Revised Guidelines
IBC 2003: Sections 1009.3 and 1009.3.1 have equivalent requirements for stairs that are part of a means of egress. **ICC/ANSI A117.1-1998:** Section 504.2 has equivalent requirements for treads and risers.	

The current guidelines require stairs serving levels that are not connected by an accessible route to comply with the technical requirements for stairs. The final revised guidelines require stairs that are part of a means of egress to comply with the technical requirements for stairs, including treads and risers. The current guidelines and the final revised guidelines require uniform riser heights and tread depths. The current guidelines do not specify a riser height. The final revised guidelines specify a riser height of 4 inches minimum and 7 inches maximum. Both the current guidelines and the final revised guidelines specify a tread depth of 11 inches minimum. The revision is expected to have minimal impacts since 7 inch maximum risers and 11 inch minimum treads ("7/11" stairs) are widely accepted as the standard for stairs.

The final revised guidelines include an exception for alterations to existing facilities that exempt stairs serving levels that are connected by an accessible route from the requirements for uniform treads and risers.

6.11   Drinking Fountains

Table 6.11 shows the relevant text of the current guidelines and the final revised guidelines with respect to the scoping and technical requirements for drinking fountains.

Table 6.11 – Drinking Fountains (text version)

Current Guidelines	Final Revised Guidelines
4.1.3 Accessible Buildings: New Construction. Accessible buildings and facilities shall meet the following minimum requirements: . . . (10) Drinking Fountains. (a) Where only one drinking fountain is provided on a floor there shall be a drinking fountain that is accessible to individuals who use wheelchairs in accordance with 4.15 and one accessible to those who have difficulty bending or stooping. . . . (b) Where more than one drinking fountain or water cooler is provided on a floor, 50 percent of those provided shall comply with 4.15	**211.1 General.** Where drinking fountains are provided on an exterior site, on a floor, or within a secured area they shall be provided in accordance with 211. . . . **211.2 Minimum Number.** No fewer than two drinking fountains shall be provided. One drinking fountain shall comply with 602.1 through 602.6 and one drinking fountain shall comply with 602.7. **Exception:** Where a single drinking fountain complies with 602.1 through 602.6 and 602.7, it shall be permitted to be substituted for two separate drinking fountains. **211.3 More Than Minimum Number.** Where more than the

Current Guidelines	Final Revised Guidelines
4.15.2 Spout Height. Spouts shall be no higher than 36 in (915 mm), measured from the floor or ground surfaces to the spout outlet (see Fig. 27 (a)). *4.15.5 Clearances.* *(1) Wall and post-mounted cantilevered units shall have a clear knee space between the bottom of the apron and the floor or ground at least 27 in (685 mm) high, 30 in (760 mm) wide, and 17 in to 19 in (430 mm to 485 mm) deep (see Fig. 27 (a) and (b)). Such units shall also have a minimum clear floor space 30 in by 48 in (760 mm by 1220 mm) to allow a person in a wheelchair to approach the unit facing forward.* ***Exception:** These clearances shall not be required at units used primarily by children ages 12 and younger where clear floor space for a parallel approach complying with 4.2.4 is provided and where the spout is no higher than 30 in (760 mm), measured from the floor or ground surface to the spout outlet.* *(2) Free-standing or built-in units not having a clear space under them shall have a clear floor space at least 30 in by 48 in (760 mm by 1220 mm) that allows a person in a wheelchair to make a parallel approach to the unit (see Fig. 27 (c) and (d)). This clear floor space shall comply with 4.2.4.*	minimum number of drinking fountains specified in 211.2 are provided, 50 percent of the total number of drinking fountains provided shall comply with 602.1 through 602.6, and 50 percent of the total number of drinking fountains provided shall comply with 602.7. **Exception:** Where 50 percent of the drinking fountains yields a fraction, 50 percent shall be permitted to be rounded up or down provided that the total number of drinking fountains complying with 211 equals 100 percent of drinking fountains. *602.2 Clear Floor Space. Units shall have a clear floor or ground clearance complying with 305 positioned for a forward approach and centered on the unit. Knee and toe clearance complying with 306 shall be provided.* ***Exception:** A parallel approach complying with 305 shall be permitted at units for children's use where the spout is 30 inches (760 mm) maximum above the finish floor or ground and is 3½ inches (90 mm) maximum from the front edge of the unit, including bumpers.* **602.4 Spout Height.** Spout outlets shall be 36 inches (915 mm) maximum above the finish floor or ground. *602.7 Drinking Fountains for Standing Persons. Spout outlets for drinking fountains for standing persons shall be 38 inches (965 mm) minimum and 43 inches (1090 m) maximum above the finish floor or ground.*

Model Codes & Standards
IBC 2000: Section 1108.5 has a similar requirement for the number of accessible drinking fountains.
IBC 2003: Section 1109.5 has a similar requirement for the number of accessible drinking fountains.

Current Guidelines	Final Revised Guidelines
ICC/ANSI A117.1-1998: Section 602.2 has a similar requirement for clear floor space at drinking fountains.	

The current guidelines and the final revised guidelines require drinking fountains to be provided at a wheelchair height and at a standing height. The current guidelines require wall and post-mounted cantilevered drinking fountains mounted at a wheelchair height to provide clear floor space for a forward approach with knee and toe clearance, and free-standing or built-in drinking fountains to provide clear floor space for a parallel approach. The final revised guidelines require drinking fountains mounted at a wheelchair height to provide clear floor space for a forward approach with knee and toe clearance, and include an exception for a parallel approach for drinking fountains used by children. The final revised guidelines also include a technical requirement for drinking fountains for standing persons. The revision is expected to have minimal impacts since drinking fountains mounted at a wheelchair height that provide clear floor space for a forward approach with knee and toe clearance are common in new construction, and generally cost less than other types of drinking fountains.

6.12   Sinks

Table 6.12 shows the relevant text of the current guidelines and the final revised guidelines with respect to the scoping and technical requirements for sinks.

Table 6.12 – Sinks (text version)

Current Guidelines	Final Revised Guidelines
4.1.1 Application. (1) General. All areas of newly designed or newly constructed buildings and facilities and altered portions of existing buildings and facilities shall comply with section 4, unless otherwise provided in this section or as modified in a special application section. **4.24.1 General.** Sinks required to be accessible by 4.1 shall comply with 4.24. **4.24.3 Knee Clearance.** Knee clearance that is at least 27 in (685 mm) high, 30 in (760 mm) wide, and 19 in (485 mm) deep shall be provided underneath sinks. **4.24.5 Clear Floor Space.** A clear floor space at least 30 in by 48 in (760	***212.3 Sinks.*** *Where sinks are provided, at least 5 percent, but no fewer than one, of each type provided in each accessible room or space shall comply with 606.* **Exception:** Mop or service sinks shall not be required to comply with 212.3. **606.2 Clear Floor Space.** A clear floor space complying with 305, positioned for a forward approach, and knee and toe clearance complying with 306 shall be provided. ***Exceptions: 1.*** *A parallel approach complying with 305 shall be permitted to a kitchen sink in a space where a cook top or conventional range is not provided and to wet bars. . . .*

mm by 1220 mm) complying with 4.2.4 shall be provided in front of a sink to allow forward approach. The clear floor space shall be on an accessible route and shall extend a maximum of 19 in (485 mm) underneath the sink (see Fig. 32).

9.2.2 Minimum Requirements. An accessible unit, sleeping room or suite shall be on an accessible route complying with 4.3 and have the following accessible elements and spaces. . . .

(7) Kitchens, Kitchenettes, or Wet Bars. When provided as an accessory to a sleeping room or suite, kitchens, kitchenettes, wet bars, or similar amenities shall be accessible. Clear floor space for a front or parallel approach to cabinets, counters, sinks, and appliances shall be provided to comply with 4.2.4. . . .

Model Codes & Standards

IBC 2000: Section 1108.3 has an equivalent requirement for sinks.

IBC 2003: Section 1109.3 has an equivalent requirement for sinks.

ICC/ANSI A117.1-1998: Section 606.2 has an equivalent requirement for clear floor space at sinks and an equivalent exception for sinks without a cook top or conventional range.

The current guidelines contain technical requirements for sinks, but do not have specific scoping requirements for sinks in all accessible spaces. The final revised guidelines require at least 5 percent of sinks in each accessible space to comply with the technical requirements for sinks. The technical requirements address clear floor space, height, faucets, and exposed pipes and surfaces. The current guidelines and the final revised guidelines require the clear floor space at sinks to be positioned for a forward approach, and knee and toe clearance to be provided under the sink. The current guidelines allow the clear floor space at kitchen sinks and wet bars in hotel guest rooms with mobility features to be positioned for either a forward approach with knee and toe clearance, or for a parallel approach because the rooms usually do not have cooking facilities. The final revised guidelines include a broader exception that permits the clear floor space to be positioned for a parallel approach at kitchen sinks in any space where a cook top or conventional range is not provided, and at a wet bar.

The revision is expected to have minimal impacts since the base cabinet under kitchen sinks is usually eliminated to provide knee and toe clearance under the sink when the

87

clear floor space is positioned for a forward approach, which offsets the cost for the lowered sink counter height and the pipe insulation.

6.13   Public Telephone Volume Controls

Table 6.13 shows the relevant text of the current guidelines and the final revised guidelines with respect to the scoping and technical requirements for public telephone volume controls.

Table 6.13 – Public Telephone Volume Controls (text version)

Current Guidelines	Final Revised Guidelines
4.1.3 Accessible Buildings: New Construction. Accessible buildings and facilities shall meet the following minimum requirements: . . . (17) Public Telephones. . . . (b) *All telephones required to be accessible and complying with 4.31.2 through 4.32.8 shall be equipped with a volume control. In addition, 25 percent, but never less than one, of all other public telephones provided shall be equipped with a volume control . . . .* 4.30.7 Symbols of Accessibility. . . . (2) *Volume Control Telephones. Telephones required to have a volume control by 4.1.3 (17) (b) shall be identified by a sign containing a depiction of a telephone handset with radiating sound waves.* **4.31.5 Hearing Aid Compatible and Volume Control Telephones Required by 4.1. . . .** (2) *Volume controls capable of a minimum of 12 dba and a maximum of 18 dba above normal, shall be provided in accordance with 4.1.3. If an automatic reset is provided then 18 dba may be exceeded.*	***217.3 Volume Controls.*** *All public telephones shall have volume controls complying with 704.3.* ***704.3 Volume Control Telephones.*** *Public telephones required to have volume controls shall be equipped with a receive volume control that provides a gain adjustable up to 20 dB minimum. For incremental volume control, provide at least one intermediate step of 12 dB of gain minimum. An automatic reset shall be provided.*
Model Codes & Standards	
IBC 2000: Section E1106.3 of Appendix E has a similar requirement for public telephones with volume controls.	

88

IBC 2003: Section E106.3 of Appendix E has an equivalent requirement for public telephones with volume controls.

ICC/ANSI A117.1-1998: Section 704.3 has an equivalent requirement for level of volume control.

The current guidelines require all wheelchair accessible public telephones and 25 percent of all other public telephones to have volume controls, and to be identified by signs. The final revised guidelines require all public telephones to have volume controls, and delete the requirement for identifying signs. The current guidelines require volume control telephones to provide a minimum gain of 12 dB and a maximum gain of 18 dB. The final revised guidelines require a gain up to 20 dB minimum and an automatic reset.

The revision is expected to have minimal impacts since the scoping and technical requirements in the final revised guidelines are consistent with guidelines and standards issued by the Access Board under section 255 of the Telecommunications Act of 1998 and section 508 of the Rehabilitation Act, which require all new telephones to have volume controls.

6.14 Dispersion of Wheelchair Spaces and Lines of Sight in Assembly Areas

Table 6.14 shows the relevant text of the current guidelines and the final revisions to the guidelines with respect to the scoping and technical requirements for dispersion of wheelchair spaces and lines of sight in assembly areas.

Table 6.14 – Dispersion of Wheelchair Spaces and Lines of Sight in Assembly Areas (text version)

Current Guidelines	Final Revised Guidelines
4.33.3 Placement of Wheelchair Locations. Wheelchair areas shall be an integral part of any fixed seating plan and shall be provided so as to provide people with physical disabilities a choice of admission prices and lines of sight comparable to those for members of the general public. They shall adjoin an accessible route that also serves as a means of egress in case of emergency. . . *When the seating capacity exceeds 300, wheelchair spaces shall be provided in more than one location. . . .* **Exception:** *Accessible viewing positions may be clustered for bleachers, balconies, and other areas having sight lines that require slopes greater than 5 percent. Equivalent accessible viewing positions may be located on levels having accessible*	*221.2.2 Integration. Wheelchair spaces shall be an integral part of the seating plan.* *221.2.3 Lines of Sight and Dispersion. Wheelchair spaces shall provide lines of sight complying with 802.2 and shall comply with 221.2.3. In providing lines of sight, wheelchair spaces shall be dispersed. Wheelchair spaces shall provide spectators with choices of seating locations and viewing angles that are substantially equivalent to, or better than, the choices of seating locations and viewing angles available to all other spectators. When the number of wheelchair spaces required by 221.2.1 has been meet, further dispersion shall not be required. . . .*

89

Current Guidelines	Final Revised Guidelines
egress.	**221.2.3.1 Horizontal Dispersion.** *Wheelchair spaces shall be dispersed horizontally.* **Exceptions: 1.** *Horizontal dispersion shall not be required in assembly areas with 300 or fewer seats if companion seats required by 221.3 and wheelchair spaces are located within the 2nd or 3rd quartile of the total row length. Intermediate aisles shall be included in determining the total row length. If the row length in the 2nd and 3rd quartile of a row is insufficient to accommodate the required number of companion seats and wheelchair spaces, the additional companion seats and wheelchair spaces shall be permitted to be located in the 1st and 4th quartile of the row.* **2.** *In row seating, two wheelchair spaces shall be permitted to be located side-by-side.*
	221.2.3.2 Vertical Dispersion. *Wheelchair spaces shall be dispersed vertically at varying distances from the screen, performance area, or playing field. In addition, wheelchair spaces shall be located in each balcony or mezzanine that is located on an accessible route.* **Exceptions: 1.** *Vertical dispersion shall not be required in assembly areas with 300 or fewer seats if wheelchair spaces provide viewing angles that are equivalent to, or better than, the average viewing angle provided in the facility.* **2.** *In bleachers, wheelchair spaces shall not be required to be provided in rows other than rows at points of entry to bleacher seating.*
	802.2 Lines of Sight. *Lines of sight to the screen, performance area, or playing field for spectators in*

Current Guidelines	Final Revised Guidelines
	wheelchair spaces shall comply with 802.2.

802.2.1 Lines of Sight Over Seated Spectators. *Where spectators are expected to remain seated during events, spectators in wheelchair spaces shall be afforded lines of sight complying with 802.2.1.*

802.2.1.1 Lines of Sight Over Heads. *Where spectators are provided lines of sight over the heads of spectators seated in the first row in front of their seats, spectators seated in wheelchair spaces shall be afforded lines of sight over the heads of seated spectators in the first row in front of wheelchair spaces.*

802.2.1.2 Lines of Sight Between Heads. *Where spectators are provided lines of sight over the shoulders and between the heads of spectators seated in the first row in front of their seats, spectators seated in wheelchair spaces shall be afforded lines of sight over the shoulders and between the heads of seated spectators in the first row in front of wheelchair spaces.*

802.2.2 Lines of Sight Over Standing Spectators. *Where spectators are expected to stand during events, spectators in wheelchair spaces shall be afforded lines of sight complying with 802.2.2.*

802.2.2.1 Lines of Sight Over Heads. *Where standing spectators are provided lines of sight over the heads of spectators standing in the first row in front of their seats, spectators seated in wheelchair spaces shall be afforded lines of sight over the heads of standing spectators in the first row in front of wheelchair spaces.* |

91

Current Guidelines	Final Revised Guidelines
	802.2.2.2 Lines of Sight Between Heads. *Where standing spectators are provided lines of sight over the shoulders and between the heads of spectators standing in the first row in front of their seats, spectators seated in wheelchair spaces shall be afforded lines of sight over the shoulders and between the heads of standing spectators in the first row in front of wheelchair spaces.*

Model Codes & Standards
IBC 2000: Section 1107.2.3 has similar requirements for dispersion of wheelchair spaces.
IBC 2003: Section 1108.2.4 has similar requirements for dispersion of wheelchair spaces.
ICC/ANSI A117.1-1998: Section 802.8 has similar requirements for lines of sight.

The current guidelines require wheelchair spaces to be an integral part of any fixed seating plan in assembly areas and to be dispersed, when the seating capacity exceeds 300. The current guidelines also require wheelchair spaces to provide individuals with disabilities lines of sight comparable to the sightlines available to other spectators in assembly areas. The Department of Justice, which adopted the current guidelines as enforceable standards, interprets comparable sightlines as requiring wheelchair spaces in sports stadiums and arenas to provide lines of sight over standing spectators to the playing field, where spectators are expected to stand during events. The Department of Justice also interprets comparable sightlines as requiring wheelchair spaces in stadium-style movie theaters to provide viewing angles comparable to those provided to other spectators.

The final revised guidelines add specific technical requirements for providing sightlines over seated and standing spectators; and require wheelchair spaces to provide individuals with disabilities choices of seating locations and viewing angles that are substantially equivalent to, or better than, the choices of seating locations and viewing angles available to other spectators. The final revised guidelines also clarify the dispersion requirements. Wheelchair spaces must be dispersed horizontally and vertically. The final revised guidelines include exceptions for assembly areas that have 300 or fewer seats, where the wheelchair spaces are located in the 2nd or 3rd quartile of the total row length and provide viewing angles that are equivalent to, or better than, the average viewing angle provided in the facility. The revisions are expected to have minimal impacts since they are consistent with the Department of Justice's interpretations of the current guidelines.

The current guidelines contain an exception that permits wheelchair spaces to be clustered in steeply sloped bleachers and balconies. The final revised guidelines require wheelchair spaces to be located at the entry points to bleachers, and in each balcony or mezzanine that is on an accessible route.

6.15   Lawn Seating in Assembly Areas

Table 6.15 shows the relevant text of the current guidelines and the final revised guidelines with respect to the scoping requirement for lawn seating in assembly areas.

Table 6.15 – Lawn Seating in Assembly Areas (text version)

Current Guidelines	Final Revised Guidelines
4.1.1 Application. *(1) General. All areas of newly designed or newly constructed buildings and facilities and altered portions of existing buildings and facilities shall comply with section 4, unless otherwise provided in this section or as modified in a special application section.*	*221.5 Lawn Seating. Lawn seating areas and exterior overflow seating areas, where fixed seats are not provided, shall connect to an accessible route.*
Model Codes & Standards	
No requirements for lawn seating in assembly areas.	

The current guidelines require all areas of newly constructed facilities to be accessible, but do not contain a specific scoping requirement for lawn seating in assembly areas. The final revised guidelines specifically require lawn seating areas and exterior overflow seating areas without fixed seats to connect to an accessible route. The revision is expected to have minimal impacts since the requirement can be met by locating an accessible route serving the fixed seating areas along a portion of the lawn seating area. The accessible route does not have to extend through the lawn seating area.

6.16   New Construction of Federal, State, and Local Government Housing

Table 6.16 shows the relevant text of the current guidelines and the final revised guidelines with respect to the scoping requirements for new construction of Federal, State, and local government housing. The current guidelines refer to UFAS.

Table 6.16 – New Construction of Federal, State, and Local Government Housing (text version)

Current Guidelines	Final Revised Guidelines
4.1.4 Occupancy Classifications. Buildings and facilities shall comply with these standards to the extent noted in this section for various occupancy classifications, unless otherwise noted by a special application section. . . . **(11) Residential.** Residential occupancy includes, among others, the	**233.1 General.** Facilities with residential dwelling *units* shall comply with 233. **233.2 Residential Dwelling Units Provided by Entities Subject to HUD Section 504 Regulations.** Where facilities with residential dwelling units are provided by

Printed by Builder's Book, Inc., Bookstore · www.buildersbook.com

use of a building or structure, or portion ~~thereof, for sleeping accommodations~~ when not classed as an institutional occupancy. *Residential occupancies shall comply with the requirements of 4.1 and 4.34 except as follows: . . .*

(b) *Residential occupancies in multiple dwellings where the occupants are primarily permanent in nature, including:*

Facilities	
Federally	5 percent of the total.
Federally	5 percent of the total.
Dormitories	5 percent of the total.

(c) *Residential occupancies in one (1) and two (2) family dwellings where the occupancies are primarily permanent in nature and not classified as preceding residential categories or as institutional.*

entities subject to regulations issued by the Department of Housing and Urban Development (HUD) under Section 504 of the Rehabilitation Act of 1973, as amended, such entities shall provide residential dwelling units with mobility features complying with 809.2 through 809.4 in a number required by the applicable HUD regulations. Residential dwelling units required to provide mobility features complying with 809.2 through 809.4 shall be on an accessible route as required by 206. In addition, such entities shall provide residential dwelling units with communication features complying with 809.5 in a number required by the applicable HUD regulations. Entities subject to 233.2 shall not be required to comply with 233.3.

233.3 Residential Dwelling Units Provided by Entities Not Subject to HUD Section 504 Regulations. Facilities with residential dwelling units provided by entities not subject to regulations issued by the Department of Housing and Urban Development (HUD) under Section 504 of the Rehabilitation Act of 1973, as amended, shall comply with 233.3.

233.3.1 Minimum Number: New Construction. Newly constructed facilities with residential dwelling units shall comply with 233.3.1. Exception: Where facilities contain 15 or fewer residential dwelling units, the requirements of 233.3.1.1 and 233.3.1.2 shall apply to the total number of residential dwelling units that are constructed under a single contract, or are developed as a whole, whether or not located on a common site.

233.3.1.1 Residential Dwelling

94

ownership		
Federally owned	5 percent of the total, or at least one unit, whichever is greater.	

Units with Mobility Features. *In facilities with residential dwelling units, at least 5 percent, but no fewer than one unit, of the total number of residential dwelling units shall provide mobility features complying with 809.2 through 809.4 and shall be on an accessible route as required by 206.*

233.3.1.2 Residential Dwelling Units with Communication Features. *In facilities with residential dwelling units, at least 2 percent, but no fewer than one unit, of the total number of residential dwelling units shall provide communication features complying with 809.5.*

233.3.2 Residential Dwelling Units for Sale. Residential dwelling units offered for sale shall provide accessible features to the extent required by regulations issued by Federal agencies under the Americans with Disabilities Act or Section 504 of the Rehabilitation Act of 1973, as amended.

Model Codes & Standards

IBC 2000: Section 1107.5.4 requires 2 percent of dwelling units in certain multi-family occupancies to comply with the requirements for Type A dwelling units in ICC/ANSI A117.1-1998.

IBC 2003: Section 1107.6.2.1.1 requires 2 percent of dwelling units in certain multi-family occupancies to comply with the requirements for Type A dwelling units in ICC/ANSI A117.1-1998.

The current guidelines contain scoping requirements for the new construction of Federal, State, and local government housing required to comply with the Architectural Barriers Act and Americans with Disabilities Act. For federally owned housing, the current guidelines require 5 percent of newly constructed dwelling units to provide mobility features. For federally assisted housing, the current guidelines require 5 percent of newly constructed dwelling units in projects of 15 or more dwelling units to provide mobility features. The current guidelines do not define the term "project."

The final revised guidelines differentiate between entities subject to the Department of Housing and Urban Development's (HUD) regulations implementing section 504 of the Rehabilitation Act, and entities not subject to the HUD regulations. The HUD regulations apply to recipients of Federal financial assistance through HUD, and require at least 5

95

percent of dwelling units in multi-family projects of five or more dwelling units to provide mobility features and at least 2 percent of the dwelling units to provide communication features. The HUD regulations define a project unique to its programs as "one or more residential structures . . . which are covered by a single contract for Federal financial assistance or application for assistance, or are treated as a whole for processing purposes, whether or not located on a common site." To avoid any potential conflicts with the HUD regulations, the final revised guidelines require entities subject to the HUD regulations to comply with the scoping requirements in the HUD regulations, instead of the scoping requirements in the final revised guidelines.

For entities not subject to the HUD regulations, the final revised guidelines require at least 5 percent of the dwelling units in residential facilities to provide mobility features, and at least 2 percent of the dwelling units to provide communication features. The final revised guidelines define facilities in terms of buildings located on a site. The final revised guidelines permit facilities that contain 15 or fewer dwelling units to apply the scoping requirements to all the dwelling units that are constructed under a single contract, or are developed as whole, whether or not located on a common site.

The final revised guidelines defer to the Department of Justice and agencies responsible for issuing regulations under section 504 of the Rehabilitation Act to determine the extent to which accessible features are to be provided in dwelling units offered for sale.

The scoping requirements in the final revised guidelines for new construction of dwelling units with mobility features are sufficiently similar to the current guidelines that the impacts are expected to be minimal. The technical requirements in the final revised guidelines for dwelling units with communication features will have monetary impacts and are further discussed in Chapter 7.14.

6.17 Alterations to Federal, State, and Local Government Housing

Table 6.17 shows the relevant text of the current guidelines and the final revised guidelines with respect to the scoping requirements for alterations to Federal, State, and local government housing. The current guidelines refer to UFAS.

Table 6.17 – Alterations to Federal, State, and Local Government Housing (text version)

Current Guidelines	Final Revised Guidelines
4.16 Accessible Buildings: Alterations.	**SEQ CHAPTER \h \r 1202.3 Alterations.** Where existing elements or spaces are altered, each altered element or space shall comply with the applicable requirements of Chapter 2.
(1) General. Alterations to existing buildings and facilities shall comply with the following:	*Exceptions: . . .*
	3. Residential dwelling units not required to be accessible in compliance with a standard issued pursuant to the Americans with Disabilities Act or Section 504 of the Rehabilitation Act of 1973, as
(a) If existing elements, spaces, essential features, or common areas are altered, then each such altered element, space, feature, or area shall comply with the applicable provisions of 4.1.1 to 4.1.4 of 4.1, Minimum	

Current Guidelines	Final Revised Guidelines
Requirements. . . . *(c) If alterations of single elements, when considered together, amount to an alteration of a space of a building or facility, the entire space shall be made accessible. . . .* *(2) Where a building or facility is vacated and it is totally altered, then it shall be altered to comply with 4.1.1 to 4.1.5 of 4.1, Minimum Requirements, except to the extent where it is structurally impracticable.* *(3) Where substantial alteration occurs to a building or facility, then each element or space that is altered or added shall comply with the applicable provisions of 4.1.1 to 4.1.4 of 4.1, Minimum Requirements, except to the extent where it is structurally impracticable. The altered building or facility shall contain:* *(a) At least one accessible route complying with 4.3, Accessible Route, and 4.1.6(a);* *(b) At least one accessible entrance complying with 4.14, Entrances. If additional entrances are altered then they shall comply with 4.1.6(a); and* *(c) The following toilet facilities, whichever is greater:* *(i) At least one toilet facility for each sex in the altered building complying with 4.22, Toilet Rooms; and 4.23, Bathrooms, Bathing Facilities, and Shower Rooms.* *(ii) At least one toilet facility for each sex on each substantially altered floor, where such facilities are provided, complying with 4.22, Toilet Rooms; and 4.23, Bathrooms, Bathing Facilities, and Shower Rooms.*	*amended, shall not be required to comply with 202.3.* **202.4 Alterations Affecting Primary Function Areas.** In addition to the requirements of 202.3, an alteration that affects or could affect the usability of or access to an area containing a primary function shall be made so as to ensure that, to the maximum extent feasible, the path of travel to the altered area, including the rest rooms, telephones, and drinking fountains serving the altered area, are readily accessible to and usable by individuals with disabilities, unless such alterations are disproportionate to the overall alterations in terms of cost and scope as determined under criteria established by the Attorney General. . . . *Exception: Residential dwelling units shall not be required to comply with 202.4.* **233.3 Residential Dwelling Units Provided by Entities Not Subject to HUD Section 504 Regulations.** Facilities with residential dwelling units provided by entities not subject to regulations issued by the Department of Housing and Urban Development (HUD) under Section 504 of the Rehabilitation Act of 1973, as amended, shall comply with 233.3. **233.3.4 Alterations.** Alterations shall comply with 233.3.4. **Exception:** Where compliance with 809.2, 809.3, or 809.4 is technically infeasible, or where it is technically infeasible to provide an accessible route to a residential dwelling unit, the entity shall be permitted to alter or construct a comparable residential dwelling unit to comply with 809.2 through 809.4 provided that the minimum number of residential

Current Guidelines	Final Revised Guidelines
	dwelling units required by 233.3.1.1 and 233.3.1.2, as applicable, is satisfied.
(d) In making the determination as to what constitutes "substantial alteration," the agency issuing standards for the facility shall consider the total cost of all alterations (including but not limited to electrical, plumbing, and structural changes) for a building or facility within any twelve (12) month period. For guidance in implementing this provision, an alteration to any building or facility is to be considered substantial if the total cost for this twelve month period amounts to 50 percent or more of the full and fair cash value of the building as defined in 3.5.	***233.3.4.1 Alterations to Vacated Buildings.*** *Where a building is vacated for the purposes of alteration, and the altered building contains more than 15 residential dwelling units, at least 5 percent of the residential dwelling units shall comply with 809.2 through 809.4 and shall be on an accessible route as required by 206. In addition, at least 2 percent of the residential dwelling units shall comply with 809.5.*
	233.3.4.2 Alterations to Individual Residential Dwelling Units. *In individual residential dwelling units, where a bathroom or a kitchen is substantially altered, and at least one other room is altered, the requirements of 233.3.1 shall apply to the altered residential dwelling units until the total number of residential dwelling units complies with the minimum number required by 233.3.1.1 and 233.3.1.2. Residential dwelling units required to comply with 233.3.1.1 shall be on an accessible route as required by 206.* ***Exception:*** *Where facilities contain 15 or fewer residential dwelling units, the requirements of 233.3.1.1 and 233.3.1.2 shall apply to the total number of residential dwelling units that are altered under a single contract, or are developed as a whole, whether or not located on a common site.*
Model Codes & Standards	
No requirements for alterations to dwelling units.	

The current guidelines require Federal, State, and local government housing to comply with the general requirements for alterations to facilities. Applying the general requirements for alterations to housing can result in partially accessible dwelling units where single elements or spaces in dwelling units are altered.

The final revised guidelines contain specific scoping requirements for alterations to dwelling units by entities that are not subject to the Department of Housing and Urban Development's (HUD) regulations implementing section 504 of the Rehabilitation Act. Dwelling units that are not required to be accessible are exempt from the general requirements for alterations to elements and spaces and for alterations to primary function areas.

The scoping requirements for alterations to dwelling units are based on the general requirements in the current guidelines for alterations to facilities that are vacated and for substantially altered facilities, and are expected to have minimal impacts compared to the current guidelines.

- Where a building is vacated for purposes of alterations and has more than 15 dwelling units, at least 5 percent of the altered dwelling units are required to provide mobility features and at least 2 percent of the dwelling units are required to provide communication features.

- Where a bathroom or a kitchen is substantially altered in an individual dwelling unit and at least one other room is also altered, the dwelling unit is required to comply with the scoping requirements for new construction until the total number of dwelling units in the facility required to provide mobility features and communication features is met.

As with new construction, the final revised guidelines permit facilities that contain 15 or fewer dwelling units to apply the scoping requirements to all the dwelling units that are altered under a single contract, or are developed as whole, whether or not located on a common site. The final revised guidelines also permit a comparable dwelling unit to provide mobility features where it is not technically feasible for the altered dwelling unit to comply with the technical requirements.

6.18   Accessible Routes in Dwelling Units with Mobility Features

Table 6.18 shows the relevant text of the current guidelines and the final revised guidelines with respect to the scoping and technical requirements for accessible routes in dwelling units with mobility features. The current guidelines refer to UFAS.

Table 6.18 – Accessible Routes in Dwelling Units with Mobility Features (text version)

Current Guidelines	Final Revised Guidelines
4.34.1 General. The requirements of 4.34 apply to dwelling units required to be accessible by 4.1. *4.34.2 Minimum Requirements. An accessible dwelling unit shall be on an accessible route. An accessible dwelling unit shall have the following accessible elements and spaces as a minimum: . . .*	**233.3.5 Dispersion.** Residential dwelling units required to provide mobility features complying with 809.2 through 809.4 . . . shall be dispersed among the various types of residential dwelling units in the facility and shall provide choices of residential dwelling units comparable to, and integrated with, those available to other residents. *Exception: Where multi-story*

(3) At least one accessible route complying with 4.3 shall connect the accessible entrances with all accessible spaces and elements within the dwelling units. . . .

(12) At least one full bathroom shall comply with 4.34.5. . . .

(13) The kitchen shall comply with 4.34.6.

(14) If laundry facilities are provided, they shall comply with 4.34.7.

(15) The following spaces shall be accessible and shall be on an accessible route:

(a) The living area.

(b) The dining area.

(c) The sleeping area, or the bedroom in one bedroom dwelling areas, or at least two bedrooms or sleeping spaces in dwelling units with two or more bedrooms.

residential dwelling units are one of the types of residential dwelling units provided, one-story residential dwelling units shall be permitted as a substitute for multi-story residential dwelling units where equivalent spaces and amenities are provided in the one-story residential dwelling unit.

809.1 General. . . . Residential dwelling units required to provide mobility features shall comply with 809.2 through 809.4 . . . .

809.2 Accessible Routes.
 Accessible routes complying with Chapter 4 shall be provided within residential dwelling units in accordance with 809.2.
Exception: Accessible routes shall not be required to or within unfinished attics or unfinished basements.

***809.2.1 Location.** At least one accessible route shall connect all spaces and elements which are a part of the residential dwelling unit. Where only one accessible route is provided, it shall not pass through bathrooms, closets, or similar spaces.*

809.4 Toilet Facilities and Bathing Facilities. At least one toilet facility and bathing facility shall comply with 603 through 610. At least one of each type of fixture provided shall comply with applicable requirements of 603 through 610. Toilet and bathing fixtures required to comply with 603 through 610 shall be located in the same toilet and bathing area, such that travel between fixtures does not require travel between other parts of the residential dwelling unit.

Model Codes & Standards
ICC/ANSI A117.1-1998: Section 1002.3 has an equivalent requirement for accessible routes in Type A dwelling units.

100

In dwelling units with mobility features, the current guidelines require the living area, kitchen and dining area, bedroom, bathroom, and laundry area where provided to be on an accessible route. Where dwelling units have two or more bedrooms, at least two bedrooms are required to be on an accessible route.

The final revised guidelines require all spaces and elements within dwelling units with mobility features to be on an accessible route. The final revised guidelines exempt unfinished attics and unfinished basements from the accessible route requirement. The final revised guidelines also include an exception to the dispersion requirement that permits single-story dwelling units or "flats" to be constructed, where multi-story dwelling units are provided. A "flat" eliminates the need to provide a residential elevator or platform lift to connect stories. In multi-family construction, building codes and fire and life safety codes typically require one-hour minimum fire-resistance rated construction between dwelling units regardless of type. There is little difference in the cost of constructing two adjacent two-story dwelling units, and a "flat" and a second dwelling unit on top.

6.19   Side Reach

Table 6.19 shows the relevant text of the current guidelines and the final revised guidelines with respect to the scoping requirements for some of the elements required to be placed within a forward or side reach, and the technical requirements for a side reach.

Table 6.19 – Side Reach (text version)

Current Guidelines	Final Revised Guidelines
4.1.3 Accessible Buildings: New Construction. Accessible buildings and facilities shall meet the following minimum requirements: . . .	**205.1 General.** Operable parts on accessible elements, accessible routes, and in accessible rooms and spaces shall comply with 309.
(13) Controls and operating mechanisms in accessible spaces, along accessible routes, or as parts of accessible elements . . . shall comply with 4.27.	**228.1 General.** Where provided, at least one of each type of depository, vending machine, change machine, and fuel dispenser shall comply with 309. **Exception:** Drive-up only depositories shall not be required to comply with 309.
4.27.3 Height. The highest operable part of controls, dispensers, receptacles, and other operable equipment shall be placed within at least one of the reach ranges specified in 4.2.5 or 4.2.6. . . .	**228.2 Mail Boxes.** Where mailboxes are provided in an interior location, at least 5 percent, but no fewer than one, of each type shall comply with 309. In residential facilities, where mailboxes are provided for each residential unit, mail boxes complying with 309 shall be provided for each residential dwelling unit required to provide mobility features complying with 809.2
4.2.6 Side Reach. If the clear floor space allows a parallel approach by a person in a wheelchair, the maximum high side reach allowed shall be 54 in (1370 mm) and the low side reach shall be no less than 9 in (230 mm)	

101

above the floor (Fig. 6 (a) and (b)).
[Note: Figures 6 (a) and (b) show a
reach depth of 10 inches maximum.]

through 809.4.

309.3 Height. Operable parts shall be placed within one or more of the reach ranges specified in 308.

308.3 Side Reach.

308.3.1 Unobstructed. *Where a clear floor or ground space allows a parallel approach to an element and the side reach is unobstructed, the high side reach shall be 48 inches (1220 mm) maximum and the low side reach shall be 15 inches (380 mm) minimum above the finish floor or ground.*
Exceptions: . . .
2: Operable parts of fuel dispensers shall be permitted to be 54 inches (1370 mm) maximum measured from the surface of the vehicular way where fuel dispensers are installed on existing curbs.

308.3.2 Obstructed High Reach. Where a clear floor or ground space allows a parallel approach to an element and the high side reach is over an obstruction, the height of the obstruction shall be 34 inches (865 mm) maximum and the depth of the obstruction shall be 24 inches (610 mm) maximum. *The high side reach shall be 48 inches (1220 mm) maximum for a reach depth of 10 inches (255 mm) maximum. . . .*

Model Codes & Standards
ICC/ANSI A117.1-1998: Sections 308.3.1 and 308.3.2 have equivalent requirements for a side reach.

The current guidelines and the final revised guidelines require operable parts on accessible elements, along accessible routes, and in accessible rooms and spaces to be placed within a forward or side reach. The final revised guidelines also require at least one of each type of depositories, vending machines, change machines, and gas pumps; and at least 5 percent of mailboxes provided in an interior location to meet the technical requirements for a forward or side reach.

The current guidelines specify a maximum 54 inch high side reach and a minimum 9 inch low side reach for a reach depth of 10 inches maximum. The final revised

102

guidelines specify a maximum 48 inch high side reach and a minimum 15 inch low side reach for an unobstructed reach, and a maximum 48 inch high side reach for a reach depth of 10 inches maximum over an obstruction 34 inches maximum in height.

Changing the side reach will affect a variety of building elements such as light switches, electrical outlets, thermostats, fire-alarm pull stations, card readers, and keypads. Installing the elements at the proper height when a facility is newly constructed or when an element or space is altered typically will involve little or no cost.

The Access Board held public meetings in October 2000 to gather additional information on the impacts of changing the side reach on automated teller machines, gas pumps, and vending machines. Information provided at the public meeting disclosed that the revision will have minimal impacts:

- Most currently available automated teller machines can meet the 48 inch high side reach.

- Fire and life safety codes typically require gas pumps to be protected from vehicular impact either by elevating the equipment on a 6 inch high island, or by providing bollards or other barriers around the equipment. The 6 inch high island is the preferred or required method of protection in many jurisdictions. Many currently available gas pumps can meet the 48 inch high side reach, when installed without a 6 inch high island. These gas pumps can meet the 48 inch high side reach when installed on a 6 inch high island by using add-on buttons and card readers installed at a lower height. The final revised guidelines include an exception for gas pumps installed on existing islands that permit a 54 inch high side reach. Some of the newer model gas pumps can meet the 48 inch high side reach, when installed on a 6 inch high island.

- Only vending machines that are fixed or built-in to a facility are required to meet the 48 inch high side reach. The majority of vending machines are portable. Some vending machines currently meet the 48 inch high side reach. Until more vending machines incorporate a 48 inch high side reach, there may be a limited choice of equipment. Portable vending machines can always be used as an alternative to built-in equipment.

6.20   Handrails Along Walkways

Table 6.20 shows the relevant text of the current guidelines and the final revised guidelines with respect to the technical requirement for handrails along walkways that are not ramps.

Table 6.20 – Handrails Along Walking Surfaces (text version)

Current Guidelines	Final Revised Guidelines
No requirement.	*403.6 Handrails. Where handrails are provided along walking surfaces with running slopes not steeper than 1:20 they shall comply with 505.* [Note: The following requirements in

505 are applicable to handrails along walking surfaces: 505.4 Height; 505.5 Clearance; 505.6 Gripping Surface; 505.7 Cross Section; 505.8 Surfaces; and 505.9 Fittings. An exception to 505.6 permits the handrail gripping surfaces to be obstructed along their entire length where they are integral to crash rails or bumper guards.]
Model Codes & Standards
No requirement for handrails along walking surfaces.

The current guidelines do not contain any technical requirement for handrails provided along walkways that are not ramps. The final revised guidelines require handrails along walkways that are not ramps to comply with certain technical requirements..

The revision is expected to have minimal impacts since handrails provided along walkways that are not ramps are typically installed in accordance with the model codes, which are generally consistent with the final revised guidelines. Certain health care facilities provide handrails in corridors for use by ambulatory patients or residents. Health-care facilities may also provide bumper guards along walls to protect the walls from damage by carts, beds, and other moving equipment. Products that are designed to serve as bumper guards only are not required to comply with the technical requirements for handrails. There are products designed to serve as combination bumper guards and handrails that meet the technical requirements for handrails. Where combination bumper guards and handrails are provided, the final revised guidelines contain an exception that permits the bottom of the gripping surface to be obstructed along the entire length.

6.21   Thresholds at Doorways

Table 6.21 shows the relevant text of the current guidelines and the final revised guidelines with respect to the technical requirement for thresholds at doorways.

Table 6.21 – Thresholds at Doors (text version)

Current Guidelines	Final Revised Guidelines
4.13.8 Thresholds at Doorways. *Thresholds at doorways shall not exceed ¾ in (19 mm) in height for exterior sliding doors or ½ in (13 mm) for other types of doors. Raised thresholds and floor level changes at accessible doorways shall be beveled with a slope no greater than 1:2 (see 4.5.2).* [Note: Section 4.5.2 requires changes in level between ¼ inch and ½ inch to be beveled with a slope not steeper than 1:2.]	**404.1 General.** Doors, doorways, and gates that are part of an accessible route shall comply with 404. ***404.2.5 Thresholds.*** *Thresholds, if provided at doorways, shall be ½ inch (13 mm) high maximum. Raised thresholds and changes in level at doorways shall comply with 302 and 303.* ***EXCEPTION:*** *Existing or altered thresholds ¾ inch (19 mm) high maximum that have a beveled edge on each side with a slope not steeper*

than 1:2 shall not be required to comply with 404.2.5.

Model Codes & Standards

IBC 2000: Section 1003.3.1.6 has an equivalent requirement for thresholds at doorways that are part of an accessible means of egress, except for sliding doors. Section 3408.7.14 has an equivalent exception for existing or altered thresholds.

IBC 2003: Section 1008.1.6 has an equivalent requirement for thresholds at doorways that are part of an accessible means of egress, except for sliding doors. Section 3409.7.12 has an equivalent exception for existing or altered thresholds.

ICC/ANSI A117.1-1998: Section 404.2.5 has an equivalent requirement for thresholds at doorways. Section 1002.5 has an equivalent requirement for thresholds at doorways in Type A dwelling units, except for exterior sliding doors.

The current guidelines require thresholds at doorways not to exceed ½ inch; and thresholds at exterior sliding doors not to exceed ¾ inch. The final revised guidelines require thresholds at all doorways that are part of an accessible route not to exceed ½ inch. The current guidelines and the final revised guidelines require raised thresholds that exceed ¼ inch to be beveled on each side with a slope not steeper than 1:2. The final revised guidelines include an exception that exempts existing and altered thresholds which do not exceed ¾ inch and are beveled on each side from the requirement.

Exterior sliding doors typically have higher thresholds than other doors to provide a barrier for water and wind infiltration, and to prevent the doors from being lifted out of the tracks. Threshold heights for exterior sliding doors typically exceed 1 inch. The ¾ inch threshold requirement in the current guidelines is typically met by providing a special installation detail. In wood construction, the threshold may need to be set on the sub-floor, or the sub-floor material or thickness may need to change at the threshold. In concrete construction, the slab may need to be recessed at the door location. Adding a lightweight concrete floor topping on the structural floor can also raise the finish floor in relation to the threshold height. Changing the threshold requirement from ¾ inch to ½ inch will make the special installation detail slightly more difficult, but is not expected to add any quantifiable cost to the work.

Lower thresholds, whether ¾ inch or ½ inch, make it more difficult to prevent water and wind infiltration, and require special design consideration to be given to the detail at the juncture of exterior walls and floors where exterior sliding doors are provided. Changing the threshold requirement from ¾ inch to ½ inch may require some additional design consideration, but does not add to the cost of the sliding door or to the design solution. Where the design solution is too difficult or too costly, a swinging door can be used instead of a sliding door. Swinging doors must also meet the ½ inch threshold requirement, but threshold heights and profiles for swinging doors are more varied than for sliding doors. Swinging doors can meet the ½ inch threshold requirement without any special installation detail and provide greater protection against water and wind infiltration.

105

6.22   Door and Gate Surfaces

Table 6.22 shows the relevant text of the current guidelines and the final revised guidelines with respect to the technical requirement for door and gate surfaces.

Table 6.22 – Door and Gate Surfaces (text version)

Current Guidelines	Final Revised Guidelines
No requirement.	**404.1 General.** Doors, doorways, and gates that are part of an accessible route shall comply with 404. *404.2.10 Door and Gate Surface. Swinging door and gate surfaces within 10 inches (255 mm) of the finish floor or ground measured vertically shall have a smooth surface on the push side extending the full width of the door or gate. Parts creating horizontal or vertical joints in these surfaces shall be within 1/16 inch (1.6 mm) of the same plane as the other. Cavities created by added kick plates shall be capped. Exceptions: . . . 2. Tempered glass doors without stiles and having a bottom rail or shoe with the top leading edge tapered at 60 degrees minimum from the horizontal shall not be required to meet the 10 inch (255 mm) bottom smooth surface height requirement. . . . 4. Existing doors and gates without smooth surfaces within 10 inches (255 mm) of the finish floor or ground shall not be required to comply with 404.2.10 provided that if added kick plates are installed, cavities created by such kick plates are capped.*
Model Codes & Standards	
ICC/ANSI A117.1-1998: Section 404.2.10 has an equivalent requirement for door and gate surfaces and exception for tempered glass doors without stiles.	

The current guidelines do not contain any technical requirement for door surfaces. The final revised guidelines require a smooth surface on the bottom 10 inches of the push side of swinging doors so that individuals who use wheelchairs can open the door without creating a trap or pinch point. The revision is expected to have minimal impacts since wood, metal, and composite doors with flush surfaces meet the technical requirements. Doors with raised or inset panels 10 inches above the bottom of the door also meet the technical requirements. The final revised guidelines contain an exception that exempts tempered glass doors without stiles from the technical requirements. The exception requires the top rail to be beveled to the glass surface, which is a common detail on tempered glass doors. The final revised guidelines also contain an exception for existing doors.

6.23   Automatic Door Break-Out Openings

Table 6.23 shows the relevant text of the current guidelines and the final revised guidelines with respect to the technical requirement for automatic door break-out openings.

Table 6.23 – Automatic Door Break-Out Openings (text version)

Current Guidelines	Final Revised Guidelines
4.13.12 Automatic Doors and Power-Assisted Doors. If an automatic door is used, then it shall comply with ANSI/BHMA A156.10-1985. Slowly opening, low-powered, automatic doors shall comply with ANSI A156.19-1984. . . .	**404.1 General.** Doors, doorways, and gates that are part of an accessible route shall comply with 404. **404.3 Automatic and Power-Assisted Doors and Gates.** Automatic doors and automatic gates shall comply with 404.3. . . . **404.3.1 Clear Width.** Doorways shall provide a clear opening of 32 inches (815 mm) minimum in power-on and power-off mode. The minimum clear width for automatic door systems in a doorway shall be based on the clear opening provided by all leaves in the open position. ***404.3.6 Break Out Opening.*** *Where doors and gates without standby power are a part of a means of egress, the clear break out opening at swinging or sliding doors and gates shall be 32 inches (815 mm) minimum when operated in emergency mode.* **Exception:** Where manual swinging doors and gates comply with 404.2 and serve the same means of egress compliance with 404.3.6 shall not be required.
Model Codes & Standards	
IBC 2000: Sections 1003.3.1.1 and 1003.3.1.3.2 have an equivalent requirement for automatic door break-out openings. **IBC 2003:** Sections 1008.1.1 and 1008.1.3.2 have an equivalent requirement for automatic door break-out openings.	

107

The current guidelines do not contain any technical requirement for automatic door break out openings. The final revised guidelines require automatic doors that are part of a means of egress and that do not have standby power to have a 32 inch minimum clear break out opening when operated in emergency mode. The minimum clear opening width for automatic doors is measured with all leaves in the open position. Automatic bi-parting doors or pairs of swinging doors that provide a 32 inch minimum clear break out opening in emergency mode when both leaves are opened manually meet the technical requirement. The final revised guidelines include an exception that exempts automatic doors from the technical requirement for break-out openings when accessible manual swinging doors serve the same means of egress. The revision is expected to have minimal impacts since most automatic doors that are part of a means of egress meet the technical requirement.

6.24 Assistive Listening Systems

Table 6.24 shows the relevant text of the current guidelines and the final revised guidelines with respect to the technical requirements for assistive listening systems.

Table 6.24 – Assistive Listening Systems (text version)

Current Guidelines	Final Revised Guidelines
4.33.7 Types of Assistive Listening Systems. Assistive listening systems (ALS) are intended to augment standard public address and audio systems by providing signals which can be received directly by persons with special receivers or their own hearing aids and which eliminate or filter background noise. The type of assistive listening system appropriate for a particular application depends on the characteristics of the setting, the nature of the program, and the intended audience. Magnetic induction loops, infra-red and radio frequency systems are types of listening systems which are appropriate for various applications.	**706.1 General.** Assistive listening systems required in assembly areas shall comply with 706. *706.2 Receiver Jacks. Receivers required for use with an assistive listening system shall include a 1/8-inch (3.5 mm) standard mono jack.* *706.3 Receiver Hearing-Aid Compatibility. Receivers required to be hearing-aid compatible shall interface with telecoils in hearing aids through the provision of neckloops.* *706.4 Sound Pressure Level. Assistive listening systems shall be capable of providing a sound pressure level of 110 dB minimum and 118 dB maximum with a dynamic range on the volume control of 50 dB.* *706.5 Signal-to-Noise Ratio. The signal-to-noise ratio for internally generated noise in assistive listening systems shall be 18 dB minimum.* *706.6 Peak Clipping Level. Peak clipping shall not exceed 18 dB of*

Printed by Builder's Book, Inc., Bookstore · www.buildersbook.com

Current Guidelines	Final Revised Guidelines
	clipping relative to the peaks of speech.
Model Codes & Standards	
ICC/ANSI A117.1-1998: No specific requirements for assistive listening systems.	

The current guidelines do not contain specific technical requirements for assistive listening systems. The final revised guidelines require assistive listening systems to have standard mono jacks; and require hearing-aid compatible receivers to have neckloops to interface with telecoils in hearing aids. The final revised guidelines also specify sound level pressure, signal-to-noise ratio, and peak clipping level. The revision is expected to have minimal impacts since currently available assistive listening systems meet the technical requirements.

6.25 Automated Teller Machines and Fare Machines

Table 6.25 shows the relevant text of the current guidelines and the final revised guidelines with respect to the technical requirements for automated teller machines and fare machines.

Table 6.25 – Automated Teller Machines and Fare Machines (text version)

Current Guidelines	Final Revised Guidelines
4.34.1 General. Each automated teller machine required to be accessible by 4.1.3 shall be on an accessible route and shall comply with 4.34.	**707.1 General.** Automatic teller machines and fare machines shall comply with 707.
4.34.5 Equipment for Persons with Vision Impairments. *Instructions and all information for use shall be made accessible to and independently usable by persons with vision impairments.*	**707.3 Operable Parts.** Operable parts shall comply with 309. Unless a clear or correct key is provided, each operable part shall be able to be differentiated by sound or touch, without activation. . . .
10.3.1 New Construction. New stations in rapid rail, light rail, commuter rail, intercity bus, intercity rail, high speed rail, and other fixed guideway systems (e.g., automated guideway transit, monorails, etc.) shall comply with the following provisions, as applicable: . . .	**707.4 Privacy.** Automatic teller machines shall provide the opportunity for the same degree of privacy of input and output available to all individuals.
(7) Automatic fare vending, collection and adjustment (e.g., add fare) systems shall comply with . . . 4.34.5.	*707.5 Speech Output. Machines shall be speech enabled. Operating instructions and orientation, visible transaction prompts, user input verification, error messages, and all displayed information for full use shall be accessible to and independently usable by individuals with vision impairments. Speech shall be delivered through a mechanism that is*

Current Guidelines	Final Revised Guidelines
	readily available to all users, including but not limited to, an industry standard connector or a telephone handset. Speech shall be recorded or digitized human, or synthesized.
	***Exceptions: 1.** Audible tones shall be permitted instead of speech for visible output that is not displayed for security purposes, including but not limited to, asterisks representing personal identification numbers.*
	***2.** Advertisements and other similar information shall not be required to be audible unless they convey information that can be used in the transaction being conducted.*
	***3.** Where speech synthesis cannot be supported, dynamic alphabetic output shall not be required to be audible.*
	***707.5.1 User Control.** Speech shall be capable of being repeated or interrupted. Volume control shall be provided for the speech function.*
	***Exception:** Speech output for any single function shall be permitted to be automatically interrupted when a transaction is selected.*
	***707.5.2 Receipts.** Where receipts are provided, speech output devices shall provide audible balance inquiry information, error messages, and all other information on the printed receipt necessary to complete or verify the transaction.*
	***Exceptions: 1.** Machine location, date and time of transaction, customer account number, and the machine identifier shall not be required to be audible.*
	***2.** Information on printed receipts that duplicates information available on-screen shall not be required to be presented in the form of an audible receipt.*
	***3.** Printed copies of bank statements and checks shall not be required to be audible.*

Current Guidelines	Final Revised Guidelines
	707.6 Input. *Input devices shall comply with 707.6.* **707.6.1 Input Controls.** *At least one tactilely discernible input control shall be provided for each function. Where provided, key surfaces not on active areas of display screens, shall be raised above surrounding surfaces. Where membrane keys are the only method of input, each shall be tactilely discernable from surrounding surfaces and adjacent keys.* **707.6.2 Numeric Keys.** *Numeric keys shall be arranged in a 12-key ascending or descending telephone keypad layout. The number five key shall be tactilely distinct from the other keys.* **707.6.3 Function Keys.** *Function keys shall comply with 707.6.3.* **707.6.3.1 Contrast.** *Function keys shall contrast visually from background surfaces. Characters and symbols on key surfaces shall contrast visually from key surfaces. Visual contrast shall be either light-on-dark or dark-on-light.* ***Exception:*** *Tactile symbols required by 707.6.3.2 shall not be required to comply with 707.6.3.1.* **707.6.3.2 Tactile Symbols.** *Function key surfaces shall have tactile symbols as follows: Enter or Proceed key: raised circle; Clear or Correct key: raised left arrow; Cancel key: raised letter ex; Add Value key: raised plus sign; Decrease Value key: raised minus sign.* **707.7 Display Screen.** *The display screen shall comply with 707.7.* ***Exception:*** *Drive-up only automatic teller machines and fare machines*

Current Guidelines	Final Revised Guidelines
	shall not be required to comply with 707.7.1.
	707.7.1 Visibility. *The display screen shall be visible from a point located 40 inches (1015 mm) above the center of the clear floor space in front of the machine.*
	707.7.2 Characters. *Characters displayed on the screen shall be in a sans serif font. Characters shall be 3/16 inch (4.8 mm) high minimum based on the uppercase letter "I". Characters shall contrast with their background with either light characters on a dark background or dark characters on a light background.*
	707.8 Braille Instructions. *Braille instructions for initiating the speech mode shall be provided. Braille shall comply with 703.3.*
Model Codes & Standards	
ICC/ANSI A117.1-1998: Section 707 has similar requirements for automatic teller machines and fare machines.	

The current guidelines require instructions and all information for using automated teller machines and fare machines to be accessible to and independently usable by persons with vision impairments. Blind individuals and their organizations have entered into settlement agreements with major banks to implement the current guidelines by providing speech output and tactilely discernable input controls on automated teller machines. The manufacturers of automated teller machines have responded by making available equipment with these features. The final revised guidelines contain technical requirements for privacy, speech output, tactilely discernable input controls, display screens, and Braille instructions.

The Access Board held a public meeting in October 2000 to gather additional information on the capabilities of automated teller machines, especially with respect to speech output. Based on the meeting and supplemental comments from the banking industry, the final revised guidelines include several exceptions:

- Where the network cannot support speech synthesis, dynamic alphabetic output is not required to be audible.

- Audible tones are permitted instead of speech for visible output that is not displayed for security purposes, such as asterisks representing personal identification numbers.

112

- Advertisements are not required to be audible unless they convey information that can be used in the transaction being conducted.

- Speech output for any single function is permitted to be automatically interrupted when a transaction is selected.

- Information on printed receipts that duplicates information available during the transaction is not required to be presented in the form of an audible receipt.

- Information on printed receipts identifying machine location, machine number, date and time of transaction, and customer account number is not required to be audible.

- Printed copies of bank statements and checks are not required to be audible.

- Tactile symbols for the enter or proceed key, clear or correct key, cancel key, add value key, and decrease value key are not required to contrast visually from background surfaces.

The revision is expected to have minimal impacts since the technical requirements are consistent with current technology, and the exceptions address the concerns of the banking industry.

6.26   Wheelchair Space Overlap in Assembly Areas

Table 6.26 shows the relevant text of the current guidelines and the final revised guidelines with respect to the technical requirements for wheelchair space overlap in assembly areas.

Table 6.26 – Wheelchair Space Overlap in Assembly Areas (text version)

Current Guidelines	Final Revised Guidelines
4.3.3 Width. The minimum clear width of an accessible route shall be 36 in (915 mm) except at doors (see 4.13.5 and 4.13.6). . . .	**402.1 General.** Accessible routes shall comply with 402. **402.2 Components.** Accessible routes shall consist of one or more of the following components: walking surfaces with a running slope not steeper than 1:20, doorways, ramps, curb ramps excluding the flared sides, elevators, and platform lifts. All components of an accessible route shall comply with the applicable requirements of Chapter 4. **403.5.1 Clear Width.** Except as provided in 403.5.2 and 403.5.3, the clear width of walking surfaces shall be 36 inches (915 mm) minimum. . . .

113

	802.1.4 Approach. Wheelchair spaces shall adjoin accessible routes. Accessible routes shall not overlap wheelchair spaces.
	802.1.5 Overlap. Wheelchair spaces shall not overlap circulation paths.
Model Codes & Standards	
IBC 2000: Section 1008.7.6 prohibits obstructions in the required width of assembly aisles, except for handrails.	
IBC 2003: Section 1024.9.6 prohibits obstructions in the required width of assembly aisles, except for handrails.	

The current guidelines and the final revised guidelines require walkways that are part of an accessible route to have a 36 inch minimum clear width. The final revised guidelines specifically prohibit accessible routes from overlapping wheelchair spaces. This is consistent with the technical requirements for accessible routes, since the clear width of accessible routes cannot be obstructed by any object. The final revised guidelines also specifically prohibit wheelchair spaces from overlapping circulation paths. An advisory note clarifies that this prohibition applies only to the circulation path width required by applicable building codes and fire and life safety codes since the codes prohibit obstructions in the required width of assembly aisles.

The revision does not present any difficult design challenges and is expected to have minimal impacts. Where a main circulation path is located in front of a row of seats that contains a wheelchair space and the circulation path is wider than required by applicable building codes and fire and life safety codes, the wheelchair space may overlap the "extra" circulation path width. Where a main circulation path is located behind a row of seats that contains a wheelchair space and the wheelchair space is entered from the rear, the aisle in front of the row may need be to be wider in order not to block the required circulation path to the other seats in the row, or a mid-row opening may need to be provided to access the required circulation path to the other seats.

6.27 Visible Alarms in Hotel Guest Rooms with Communication Features

Table 6.27 shows the relevant text of the current guidelines and the final revised guidelines with respect to the technical requirement for visible alarms in hotel guest rooms with communication features.

Table 6.27 – Visible Alarms in Hotel Guest Rooms with Communication Features
(text version)

Current Guidelines	Final Revised Guidelines
9.3.1 General. In sleeping rooms required to comply with this section, auxiliary visual alarms shall be provided and shall comply with 4.28.4. . . .	**806.3 Guest Rooms with Communication Features.** Guest rooms required to provide communication features shall comply with 806.3.
4.28.4 Auxiliary Alarms. Units and	**806.3.1 Alarms.** Where emergency

114

sleeping accommodations shall have a visual alarm connected to the building emergency alarm system or shall have a standard 110-volt electrical receptacle into which such an alarm can be connected and a means by which a signal from the building emergency alarm system can trigger such an auxiliary alarm. When visual alarms are in place the signal shall be visible in all areas of the unit or room. Instructions for use of the auxiliary alarm or receptacle shall be provided.

warning systems are provided, alarms complying with 702 shall be provided.

702.1 General. Fire alarm systems shall have permanently installed audible and visible alarms complying with NFPA 72 (1999 or 2002 edition) (incorporated by reference, see "Referenced Standards" in Chapter 1) . . . In addition, alarms in guest rooms required to provided communication features shall comply with sections 4-3 and 4-4 of NFPA 72 (1999 edition) or sections 7.4 and 7.5 of NFPA 72 (2002 edition).

Model Codes & Standards
IBC 2000: Section 907.9.1.2 has an equivalent requirement for visible alarms in hotel guest rooms with communication features. **IBC 2003:** Section 907.9.1.3 has an equivalent requirement for visible alarms in hotel guest rooms with communication features.

The current guidelines require hotel guest rooms with communication features to provide either permanently installed visible alarms that are connected to the building fire alarm system, or portable visible alarms that are connected to a standard 110-volt electrical outlet and are activated by the building fire alarm system. People who are deaf or hard of hearing have reported that portable visible alarms used in hotel guest rooms are deficient because the alarms are not always activated by the building fire alarm system, and the alarms do not work when the building power source goes out in emergencies.

The final revised guidelines require hotel guest rooms with communication features to provide permanently installed visible alarms complying with the NFPA 72, National Fire Alarm Code (1999 or 2002 edition). The NFPA 72 contains technical requirements for visible alarms in sleeping areas, and requires combination smoke alarms and visible notification appliances that are connected to the building's electrical system. The revision is consistent with the model building codes and fire and life safety codes, which are adopted by all the States and require newly constructed hotels to provide hard-wired smoke alarms complying with the NFPA 72 in guest rooms, including combination visible notification devices in guest rooms for individuals with hearing impairments.

As discussed in Chapter 5.14, the final revised guidelines add a new exception for alterations to existing facilities that exempt existing fire alarm systems from providing visible alarms, unless the fire alarm system is upgraded or replaced, or a new fire system is installed. Hotels that alter guest rooms are not required to provide permanently installed visible alarms complying with the NFPA 72 if the existing fire alarm system has not been upgraded or replaced, or a new fire alarm system has not been installed.

115

CHAPTER 7: REVISIONS THAT HAVE MONETARY IMPACTS

7.0 Introduction

This chapter discusses revisions to the scoping and technical requirements that will have monetary impacts on the new construction and alterations of facilities. The relevant text of the current guidelines and the final revised guidelines is presented in tables. Unless otherwise noted, the current guidelines refer to ADAAG. The requirements are presented in the order in which they appear in the final revised guidelines. Scoping and technical requirements are presented together, where appropriate. The text of the current guidelines and the final revised guidelines is underlined to highlight the revisions in the scoping and technical requirements. Equivalent requirements in the International Building Code and the ICC/ANSI A117.1 Standard on Accessible and Usable Buildings and Facilities are also noted in the tables.

The unit cost is estimated for each revision that has monetary impacts. The unit cost is an estimated average cost and includes labor, overhead, and mark-up for construction contingencies. The facilities that will be primarily affected by the revisions are identified. The impacts of the revisions on alterations to existing facilities are also examined by answering these questions:

- Is the element or space typically altered?

- Is the element or space part of the "path of travel" serving a primary function area?

- Does alteration of the element or space involve technical infeasibility?

7.1 Location of Accessible Routes to Stages

Table 7.1 shows the relevant text of the current guidelines and the final revised guidelines with respect to the scoping requirement for the location of accessible routes to stages.

Table 7.1 – Accessible Routes to Stages

Current Guidelines	Final Revised Guidelines
4.33.5 Access to Performing Areas. *An accessible route shall connect wheelchair seating locations with performing areas, including stages, arena floors, dressing rooms, locker rooms, and other spaces used by performers.*	*206.2.6 Performance Areas.* *Where a circulation path directly connects a performance area to an assembly seating area, an accessible route shall directly connect the assembly seating area with the performance area. An accessible route shall be provided from performance areas to ancillary areas or facilities used by performers unless exempted by 206.2.3 Exceptions 1 through 7.*
Model Codes & Standards	
IBC 2000: Section 1104.5 has a similar requirement for accessible routes.	

116

IBC 2003: Section 1108.2.8 has an equivalent requirement for accessible routes to stages.

The current guidelines require an accessible route to connect the seating area and the stage. The final revised guidelines require the accessible route to directly connect the seating area and the stage, where a circulation path directly connects the seating area and the stage. The current guidelines and the final revised guidelines also require an accessible route to connect the stage and ancillary areas used by performers such as dressing rooms.

The final revised guidelines do not require an additional accessible route to be provided to the stage. Rather, the final revised guidelines specify where the accessible route to the stage, which is required by the current guidelines, must be located. All stages do not have circulation paths that directly connect to the seating area. Stages that regularly host live performances are likely to have direct connections. Where direct connections are provided, they usually consist of fixed or built-in stairs.

Where a circulation path directly connects the seating area and the stage, the design choices for providing an accessible route that directly connects both areas are largely a function of the size of the facility. Larger facilities can incorporate a ramp into the design of cross-aisles, calipers, or side stages to directly connect the seating area and the stage. A platform lift may be the only design solution for a smaller facility. Platform lifts raise aesthetic concerns when used in performing arts centers. These concerns can be addressed by locating the platform lift to the side of the seating area or the stage, or concealing the platform lift behind an enclosure.

The impacts of the revision on newly constructed facilities that provide a circulation path directly connecting the seating area and the stage will vary depending on the specific design of the facility.

- Facilities that would comply with the accessible route requirement in the current guidelines by providing a platform lift will not incur any additional costs other than for locating the platform lift near the seating area.

- Facilities that would comply with the accessible route requirement in the current guidelines by providing a ramp will not incur any additional costs other than for designing the ramp so that it directly connects the seating area and the stage.

- Facilities that would comply with the accessible route requirement in the current guidelines without providing a platform lift or a ramp will incur additional costs for a platform lift or a ramp to directly connect the seating area and the stage. The estimated average cost for a platform lift is $15,674. The costs for the ramp will depend on the design.

The 2000 edition of the International Building Code requires an accessible route to coincide with or be located in the same general area as the general circulation path, and has the same effect as the final revised guidelines when applied to stages. The 2003 edition of the International Building Code has an equivalent scoping requirement for accessible routes to stages. Facilities that are required to comply with the 2000 or 2003

117

edition of the International Building Code will not incur any additional costs to comply with the revised scoping requirement for the location of accessible routes to stages.

The revision will primarily affect newly constructed performing arts centers and auditoriums that have circulation paths directly connecting the seating area and the stage.

The impacts of the revision on alterations to existing facilities are examined below:

- *Is the element or space typically altered?*
  Circulation paths to existing stages are not typically altered.

- *Is the element or space part of the "path of travel" serving a primary function area?*
  If an existing stage is altered and there is no accessible route to the stage, then an accessible route would have to be provided to the stage to the extent that the costs of providing an accessible "path of travel" do not exceed 20 percent of the costs of the alterations to the stage. The costs for providing an accessible route to the stage would be incurred under the current guidelines. If a circulation path directly connects the seating area and the stage, then the costs for designing the accessible route to directly connect both areas would be attributable to the final revised guidelines.

- *Does alteration of the element or space involve technical infeasibility?*
  It may not be feasible to design a ramp to directly connect the seating area and the stage in existing facilities due to existing physical or site constraints. A platform lift may be the only design solution in existing facilities.

7.2 Standby Power for Platform Lifts

Table 7.2 shows the relevant text of the current guidelines and the final revised guidelines with respect to the scoping requirement for standby power for platform lifts.

118

Table 7.2 – Standby Power for Platform Lifts (text version)

Current Guidelines	Final Revised Guidelines
No requirement.	*207.2 Platform Lifts. Standby power shall be provided for platform lifts permitted by section 1003.2.13.4 of the International Building Code (2000 edition and 2001 Supplement) or section 1007 of the International Building Code (2003 edition) (incorporated by reference, see "Referenced Standards" in Chapter 1) to serve as a part of an accessible means of egress.*
Model Codes & Standards	
IBC 2000: No requirement. **IBC 2003:** Section 1007.5 has an equivalent requirement for standby power for platform lifts that are part of an accessible means of egress.	

The final revised guidelines require standby power to be provided for platform lifts that are permitted to serve as part of an accessible means of egress by the International Building Code. The International Building Code permits platform lifts to serve as part of an accessible means of egress in a limited number of places where platform lifts are allowed in new construction.

The impacts of the revision on newly constructed facilities that are permitted to use platform lifts will vary depending on the source of the standby power.

- Building codes and fire and life safety codes require certain facilities to provide a standby power source for fire protection systems. Where a building standby power source is provided, the facility will incur additional costs for wiring to connect the platform lift to the standby power circuit.

- Some platform lifts use a direct current (DC) power source. The platform lifts are charged by an external alternating current (AC) power source and are equipped with a battery for storing DC power. Facilities that use a platform lift with a DC power source will not incur any additional costs.

- Facilities that do not provide a standby power source or do not use a platform lift with a DC power source will incur additional costs for a back-up battery. The estimated average cost for a back-up battery with a 90 minute power supply is $2,353.

The 2003 edition of the International Building Code has an equivalent scoping requirement for standby power for platform lifts that are part of an accessible means of egress. Facilities that are required to comply with the 2003 edition of the International Building Code will not incur any additional costs to comply with the revised scoping requirement for standby power for platform lifts that serve as part of an accessible means of egress.

119

The revision will primarily affect newly constructed performing arts centers and auditoriums that use platform lifts to provide an accessible route to the stage. Platform lifts are rarely used in the other places permitted in new construction.

The revision will not impact alterations to existing facilities since accessible means of egress are not required in existing facilities that are altered.

7.3 Van Accessible Parking Spaces

Table 7.3.1 shows the relevant text of the current guidelines and the final revised guidelines with respect to the scoping and technical requirements for van accessible parking spaces.

Table 7.3.1 – Van Accessible Parking Spaces (text version)

Current Guidelines	Final Revised Guidelines
4.1.2 Accessible Sites and Exterior Facilities: New Construction. An accessible site shall meet the following minimum requirements: . . . (5) (b) *One in every eight accessible spaces but not less than one, shall be served by an access aisle 96 in (2440 mm) wide minimum and shall be designated "van accessible" as required by 4.6.4. . . .* **4.6.3 Parking Spaces.** Accessible parking spaces shall be at least 96 in (2440 mm) wide. . . . Two accessible parking spaces may share a common access aisle (see Fig. 9). . . . **4.6.4 Signage.** Accessible parking spaces shall be designated as reserved by a sign showing the symbol of accessibility. . . . Spaces complying with 4.1.2 (5) (b) shall have an additional sign "Van Accessible" mounted below the symbol of accessibility. **4.6.5 Vertical Clearance.** . . . At parking spaces complying with 4.1.2(5)(b), provide minimum vertical clearance of 98 in (2490 mm) at the parking space and along at least one vehicle access route to such spaces from site entrance(s) and exit(s).	*208.2.4 Van Parking Spaces. For every six or fraction of six parking spaces required by 208.2 to comply with 502, at least one shall be a van parking space complying with 502.* **502.2 Vehicle Spaces.** Car parking spaces shall be 96 inches (2440 mm) wide minimum and van parking spaces shall be 132 inches (3350 mm) wide minimum, shall be marked to define the width, and shall have an adjacent access aisle complying with 502.3. **Exception:** Van parking spaces shall be permitted to be 96 inches (2440 mm) wide minimum where the access aisle is 96 inches (2440 mm) wide minimum. **502.3 Access Aisle.** . . . Two parking spaces shall be permitted to share a common access aisle. **502.3.1 Width.** Access aisles serving car and van parking spaces shall be 60 inches (1525 mm) wide minimum. **502.3.2 Length.** Access aisles shall extend the full length of the parking spaces they serve. **502.3.3 Marking.** Access aisles shall be marked so as to discourage parking in them.

Current Guidelines	Final Revised Guidelines
	502.4 Floor or Ground Surfaces. Parking spaces and access aisles serving them shall comply with 302. Access aisles shall be at the same level as the parking spaces they serve. Changes in level are not permitted. **Exception:** Slopes not steeper than 1:48 shall be permitted.
	502.5 Vertical Clearance. Parking spaces for vans, access aisles, and vehicular routes serving them shall provide a vertical clearance of 98 inches (2490 mm) minimum.
	502.6 Identification. Parking space identification signs shall include the International Symbol of Accessibility complying with 703.7.2.1. Signs identifying van parking spaces shall contain the designation "van accessible." . . .

Model Codes & Standards

IBC 2000: Section 1106.4 has a similar requirement for the number of van accessible parking spaces.

IBC 2003: Section 1106.5 has an equivalent requirement for the number of van accessible parking spaces.

ICC/ANSI A117.1-1998: Section 502.2 has similar requirements for the size of van accessible parking spaces.

The current guidelines require one in every eight accessible parking spaces to be van accessible. The final revised guidelines require one in every six accessible parking spaces to be van accessible. Van accessible parking spaces are 3 feet wider than accessible parking spaces as shown in Table 7.3.2.

Table 7.3.2 – Parking Space Width in Feet (text version)

	Accessible Parking Space			Van Accessible Parking Space		
	Parking Space	Access Aisle	Total Width	Parking Space	Access Aisle	Total Width
Current Guidelines	8	5	13	8	8	16

121

Final Revised Guidelines	8	5	13	11	5	16
				or 8	or 8	16

The impacts of the revision on newly constructed parking facilities will vary depending on the size of the facility and work involved.

- Facilities with 600 or fewer parking spaces will not incur any additional costs, where van accessible parking spaces with 8 feet wide access aisles are provided and two van accessible parking spaces share a common access aisle.

- Facilities with 601 to 3200 parking spaces will have to widen one access aisle by 3 feet, where van accessible parking spaces with 8 feet wide access aisles are provided and two van accessible parking spaces share a common access aisle. For each additional 1800 parking spaces over 3200, an additional access aisle will have to be widened by 3 feet. The estimated average cost for widening an access aisle by 3 feet is $73 if only additional striping is needed, and $344 if additional paving and stripping is needed.

The 2003 edition of the International Building Code has an equivalent scoping requirement for van accessible parking spaces. Facilities that are required to comply with the 2003 edition of the International Building Code will not incur any additional costs to comply with the revised scoping requirement for van accessible parking spaces.

The revision will primarily affect newly constructed parking facilities with more than 600 parking spaces.

The impacts of the revision on alterations to existing parking facilities are examined below:

- *Is the element or space typically altered?*
  Resurfacing or restriping an existing parking facility is considered an alteration. If an existing parking facility is resurfaced or restriped and does not have the required number of accessible parking spaces, including van accessible parking spaces, then the required number of accessible parking spaces would have to be provided. Only the costs for providing van accessible parking spaces in addition to the number required under the current guidelines would be attributable to the final revised guidelines. Existing parking facilities will have to provide signs to identify the additional van accessible parking spaces required by the revised final guidelines. The estimated average cost for a sign is $50.

- *Is the element or space part of the "path of travel" serving a primary function area?*
  Parking spaces are part of the "path of travel" serving a primary function area. If a primary function area in an existing facility is altered and the parking facility serving the primary function area does not have any accessible parking spaces, then accessible parking spaces would have to

122

be provided to the extent the costs of providing an accessible "path of travel" do not exceed 20 percent of the costs of the alterations to the primary function area. Most of the costs for providing accessible parking spaces will be incurred under the current guidelines. Only the costs for providing van accessible parking spaces in addition to the number required under the current guidelines would be attributable to the final revised guidelines.

- *Does alteration of the element or space involve technical infeasibility?* Existing parking facilities are not required to increase the size of the facility to provide additional van accessible parking spaces. Where existing physical or site constraints limit the number of van accessible parking spaces that can be provided, a parking facility may need to provide one less parking space in order to provide an additional van accessible parking space. In existing multi-level parking garages with low ceilings and sloped floors, it may not be feasible to provide the required vertical clearance (98 inches minimum) or level surface (slopes not steeper than 1:48) for additional van accessible parking spaces because it would involve altering a load-bearing structural member which is an essential part of the structural frame, or existing physical or site constraints.

7.4 Ambulatory Accessible Toilet Compartments

Table 7.4 shows the relevant text of the current guidelines and the final revised guidelines with respect to the scoping and technical requirements for ambulatory accessible toilet compartments.

Table 7.4 – Ambulatory Accessible Toilet Compartments (text version)

Current Guidelines	Final Revised Guidelines
4.23.4 Water Closets. If toilet stalls are provided, then at least one shall be a standard toilet stall complying with 4.17; *where 6 or more stalls are provided, in addition to the stall complying with 4.17.3, at least one stall 36 in (915 mm) wide with an outward swing, self-closing door and parallel grab bars complying with Fig. 30 (d) and 4.26 shall be provided. . . .* [Note: Figure 30 (d) shows grab bars 42 inches long minimum, located 12 inches maximum from the rear wall.]	**213.3.1 Toilet Compartments.** Where toilet compartments are provided, at least one toilet compartment shall comply with 604.8.1. *In addition to the compartment required to comply with 604.8.1, at least one compartment shall comply with 604.8.2 where six or more toilet compartments are provided, or where the combination of urinals and water closets totals six or more fixtures.* **604.8.2.1 Size.** Ambulatory accessible compartments shall have a depth of 60 inches (1525 mm) minimum and a width of 35 inches (890 mm) minimum and 37 inches (940 mm) maximum. **604.8.2.3 Grab Bars.** Grab bars shall comply with 609. A side-wall grab bar complying with 604.5.1 shall be provided on both sides of the compartment.

123

	604.5.1 Side Wall. The side wall grab bar shall be 42 inches (1065 mm) long minimum, located 12 inches (305 mm) maximum from the rear wall and extending 54 inches (1370 mm) minimum from the rear wall.
Model Codes & Standards	
IBC 2000: Section 1108.2.2 has an equivalent requirement for ambulatory accessible toilet compartments.	
IBC 2003: Section 1109.2.2 has an equivalent requirement for ambulatory accessible toilet compartments.	

The current guidelines require at least one ambulatory accessible toilet compartment in toilet rooms where six or more toilet compartments are provided. The final revised guidelines require at least one ambulatory accessible toilet compartment in toilet rooms where six or more toilet compartments are provided, or where six or more water closets and urinals are provided.

The plumbing codes specify the minimum number of plumbing fixtures required in various types of facilities based on the number of occupants. The plumbing codes require separate toilet rooms to be provided for men and women, and usually specify that an equal number of the required plumbing fixtures be provided for each sex. In men's toilet rooms, the plumbing codes usually specify the required number of plumbing fixtures that must be urinals, or permit urinals to be substituted for water closets.

The final revised guidelines allow for parity in the scoping requirements for ambulatory accessible toilet compartments in men's and women's toilet rooms by including urinals in the plumbing fixture count. Under the final revised guidelines, if a women's toilet room has six water closets, and a men's toilet room in the same facility has four water closets and two urinals, both toilet rooms would be required to provide at least one ambulatory accessible toilet compartment. The current guidelines require the women's toilet room, but not the men's toilet room, to provide at least one ambulatory accessible toilet compartment.

The final revised guidelines require ambulatory accessible toilet compartments to be between 35 inches and 37 inches wide and at least 60 inches deep, and to have grab bars at least 42 inches long on each side of the compartment. The plumbing codes usually require toilet compartments to be at least 30 inches wide and 60 inches deep. The increase in the width of the ambulatory accessible toilet compartment will not add to construction costs. The only additional cost is for the two grab bars on the side walls of the ambulatory accessible toilet compartment. The estimated average cost for grab bars is $145.

The 2000 and 2003 editions of the International Building Code have an equivalent scoping requirement for ambulatory accessible toilet compartments. Facilities that are required to comply with the 2000 or 2003 editions of the International

Building Code will not incur any additional costs to comply with the revised scoping requirement for ambulatory accessible toilet compartments.

The revision will primarily affect newly constructed facilities with men's toilet rooms that have six or more water closets and urinals, but fewer than six toilet compartments.

The impacts of the revision on alterations to existing facilities are examined below:

- *Is the element or space typically altered?*
  Toilet compartments are not typically altered.

- *Is the element or space part of the "path of travel" serving a primary function area?*
  Toilet rooms are part of the "path of travel" serving a primary function area. If a primary function area in an existing facility is altered and the toilet rooms serving the primary function area are not accessible, then accessible toilet rooms would have to be provided to the extent the costs of providing an accessible "path of travel" does not exceed 20 percent of the costs of the alterations to the primary function area. Most of the costs for providing the accessible toilet rooms will be incurred under the current guidelines. Only the costs of providing an ambulatory accessible toilet compartment in men's toilet rooms with six or more water closets or urinals, but fewer than six water closets, would be attributable to the final revised guidelines.

- *Does alteration of the element or space involve technical infeasibility?*
  Adding grab bars to a toilet compartment to provide an ambulatory accessible toilet compartment will not usually involve technical infeasibility.

7.5 Public TTYS

Table 7.5 shows the relevant text of the current guidelines and the final revised guidelines with respect to the scoping requirements for public TTYs.

Table 7.5 – Public TTYs (text version)

Current Guidelines	Final Revised Guidelines
4.1.3 Accessible Buildings: New Construction. Accessible buildings and facilities shall meet the following minimum requirements: . . . (17) Public Telephones. . . . (c) The following shall be provided in accordance with 4.31.9.	**217.4 TTYs.** TTYs complying with 704.4 shall be provided in accordance with 217.4 ***217.4.1 Bank Requirement.*** *Where four or more public pay telephones are provided at a bank of telephones, at least one public TTY complying with 704.4 shall be provided at that bank.* ***Exception:*** *TTYs shall not be required at banks of telephones*

125

Current Guidelines	Final Revised Guidelines
(i) If four or more public pay telephones (including both interior and exterior telephones) are provided at a site of a private facility, and at least one is at an interior location, then at least one interior public text telephone (TTY) shall be provided. If an interior public pay telephone is provided in a public use area in a building of a public facility, at least one interior public text telephone (TTY) shall be provided in the building in a public use area.	*located within 200 feet (61 m) of, and on the same floor as, a bank containing a public TTY.*
	217.4.2 Floor Requirement. *TTYs in public buildings shall be provided in accordance with 217.4.2.1. TTYs in private buildings shall be provided in accordance with 217.4.2.2.*
(ii) If an interior public pay telephone is provided in a private facility that is a stadium or arena, a convention center, a hotel with a convention center, or a covered mall, at least one interior public text telephone (TTY) shall be provided in the facility. In stadiums, arenas, and convention centers which are public facilities, at least one public text telephone (TTY) shall be provided on each floor level having at least one interior public pay telephone.	**217.4.2.1 Public Buildings.** *Where at least one public pay telephone is provided on a floor of a public building, at least one public TTY shall be provided on that floor.*
	217.4.2.2 Private Buildings. *Where four or more public pay telephones are provided on a floor of a private building, at least one public TTY shall be provided on that floor.*
(iii) If a public pay telephone is located in or adjacent to a hospital emergency room, hospital recovery room, or hospital waiting room, one public text telephone (TTY) shall be provided at each such location.	**217.4.3 Building Requirement.** *TTYs in public buildings shall be provided in accordance with 217.4.3.1. TTYs in private buildings shall be provided in accordance with 217.4.3.2.*
(iv) If an interior public pay telephone is provided in the secured area of a detention or correctional facility subject to section 12, then at least one public text telephone (TTY) shall also be provided in at least one secured area.	**217.4.3.1 Public Buildings.** *Where at least one public pay telephone is provided in a public building, at least one public TTY shall be provided in the building. Where at least one public pay telephone is provided in a public use area of a public building, at least one public TTY shall be provided in the public building in a public use area.*
10.3.1 New Construction. New stations in rapid rail, light rail, commuter rail, intercity bus, intercity rail, high speed rail, and other fixed guideway systems (e.g., automated guideway transit, monorails, etc.) shall comply with the following provisions,	**217.4.3.2 Private Buildings.** *Where four or more public pay telephones are provided in a private building, at least one public TTY shall be provided in the building.*
	217.4.4 Exterior Site Requirement. *Where four or more public pay telephones are provided on an*

126

Current Guidelines	Final Revised Guidelines
as applicable: . . . (12) Text Telephones: . . . (a) *If an interior public pay telephone is provided in a transit facility (as defined by the Department of Transportation) at least one interior public text telephone shall be provided in the station.* (b) *Where four or more public pay telephones serve a particular entrance to a rail station and at least one is in an interior location, at least one interior public text telephone shall be provided to serve that entrance. Compliance with this section constitutes compliance with 4.1.3 (17) (c).* **10.4 Airports** **10.4.1 New Construction** (4) Where public pay telephones are provided, and at least one is at an interior location, a public text telephone (TTY) shall be provided in compliance with 4.31.9. Additionally, if four or more public pay telephones are located in any of the following locations, at least one public text telephone (TTY) shall also be provided in that location: (a) a main terminal outside the security areas; (b) a concourse within the security areas; or (c) a baggage claim area in a terminal. Compliance with this section constitutes compliance with 4.1.3 (17) (c).	*exterior site, at least one public TTY shall be provided on the site.* ***217.4.5 Rest Stops, Emergency Roadside Stops, and Service Plazas.*** *Where at least one public pay telephone is provided at a public rest stop, emergency roadside stop, or service plaza, at least one public TTY shall be provided.* **217.4.6 Hospitals.** Where at least one public pay telephone is provided serving a hospital emergency room, hospital recovery room, or hospital waiting room, at least one public TTY shall be provided at each location. ***217.4.7 Transportation Facilities.*** *In transportation facilities, in addition to the requirements of 217.4.1 through 217.4.4, where at least one public pay telephone serves a particular entrance to a bus or rail facility, at least one public TTY shall be provided to serve that entrance. In airports, in addition to the requirements of 217.4.1 through 217.4.4, where four or more public pay telephones are located in a terminal outside the security areas, a concourse within the security areas, or a baggage claim area in a terminal, at least one public TTY shall be provided in each location.* **217.4.8 Detention and Correctional Facilities.** In detention and correctional facilities, where at least one pay telephone is provided in a secured area used only by detainees or inmates and security personnel, at least one TTY shall be provided in at least one secured area.

Model Codes & Standards
IBC 2000: Section E1106.4 of Appendix E has equivalent requirements for public TTYs in private facilities.

Current Guidelines	Final Revised Guidelines
IBC 2003: Section E106.4 of Appendix E has equivalent requirements for public TTYs in private facilities and government facilities.	

The current guidelines and the final revised guidelines have scoping requirements for public TTYs in private facilities and government facilities.

The current guidelines require private facilities to provide at least one public TTY in an interior location, where four or more public pay telephones are provided on a site and at least one is in an interior location. The final revised guidelines require private facilities to provide at least one public TTY:

- In a building that has four or more public pay telephones; and

- On a floor that has four or more public pay telephones.

The current guidelines require government facilities to provide at least one public TTY in an interior location, where a public pay telephone is provided in a public use area in a building. The final revised guidelines require government facilities to provide at least one public TTY:

- In a building that has at least one public pay telephone (where a public pay telephone is provided in a public use area, a public TTY is required in a public use area); and

- On a floor that has at least one public pay telephone.

The final revised guidelines also require private facilities and government facilities to provide at least one public TTY:

- In a bank of four or more public pay telephones (banks of telephones located within 200 feet of, and on the same floor as, another bank of telephones containing a public TTY are exempt); and

- On an exterior site that has four or more public pay telephones.

The current guidelines and the final guidelines have additional scoping requirements for public TTYs in hospitals, airports, bus and rail stations, and detention and correctional facilities. The scoping requirements for public TTYs in these facilities are the same in the current guidelines and the final revised guidelines, except for bus and rail stations which are required to provide a public TTY at an entrance to the station where a public pay telephone is provided at the entrance under the final revised guidelines. The final revised guidelines also require a public TTY at public rest stops that have a public pay telephone. The estimated average cost for a public TTY is $2,320.

Appendix E to the 2000 edition of the International Building Code has equivalent scoping requirements for public TTYs in private facilities. Appendix E to the 2003 edition of the International Building Code has equivalent scoping requirements for public TTYs in privatee facilities and government facilities. State and local governments that adopt the International Building Code must specifically reference Appendix E in the adopting legislation or regulations to make the scoping requirements in that appendix mandatory. Facilities in jurisdictions where State or local governments have specifically referenced Appendix E in the legislation or regulations adopting the 2000 or 2003 editions of the International Building Code will not incur any additional costs to comply with the revised scoping requirements for public TTYs.

The revision will primarily affect newly constructed private facilities that have four or more public pay telephones on more than one floor of a building, or in a bank of telephones; newly constructed government facilities that have a public pay telephone on more than one floor of a building, or four or more public pay telephones in a bank of telephones; newly constructed bus and rail stations that have a public pay telephone at an entrance to the facility; and newly constructed public rest stops.

The impacts of the revisions on alterations to existing facilities are examined below:

- *Is the element or space typically altered?*
  If public pay telephones are replaced or new public pay telephones are added to an existing facility, public TTYs would have to be provided in accordance with the scoping requirements. Only the costs for providing public TTYs in addition to the number required under the current guidelines would be attributable to the final revised guidelines.

- *Is the element or space part of the "path of travel" serving a primary function area?*
  Public pay telephones are part of the "path of travel" serving a primary function area. If a primary function area in an existing facility is altered and the public pay telephones serving the primary function area are not accessible, then accessible public pay telephones would have to be provided to the extent the costs of providing an accessible "path of travel" does not exceed 20 percent of the costs of the alterations to the primary function area. The costs of providing wheelchair accessible public telephones and, depending on the number of public pay telephones provided at the site or the facility, a public TTY will be incurred under the current guidelines. Only the costs for providing public TTYs in addition to the number required under the current guidelines would be attributable to the final revised guidelines.

- *Does alteration of the element or space involve technical infeasibility?*
  Providing a public TTY in an existing facility will not usually involve technical infeasibility.

7.6 Operable Windows

129

Table 7.6 shows the relevant text of the current guidelines and the final revised guidelines with respect to the scoping and technical requirements for operable windows.

Table 7.6 – Operable Windows (text version)

Current Guidelines	Final Revised Guidelines
No requirement.	*229.1 General. Where glazed openings are provided in accessible rooms or spaces for operation by occupants, at least one opening shall comply with 309. Each glazed opening required by an administrative authority to be operable shall comply with 309.* *Exceptions: 1. Glazed openings in residential dwellings units required to comply with 809 shall not be required to comply with 229.* *2. Glazed openings in guest rooms required to provide communication features and in guest rooms required to comply with 206.5.3 shall not be required to comply with 229.* **309.1 General.** Operable parts shall comply with 309. **309.3 Height.** Operable parts shall be placed within one or more of the reach ranges specified in 308. [Note: The high forward or side reach is 48 inches maximum where the reach is unobstructed.] **309.4 Operation.** Operable parts shall be operable with one hand and shall not require tight grasping, pinching, or twisting of the wrist. The force required to activate operable parts shall be 5 pounds (22.2 N) maximum. . . .

Model Codes & Standards
IBC 2000: Section 1108.13.1 has an equivalent requirement for operable windows in accessible rooms in certain institutional and residential occupancies, including hotel guest rooms and patient sleeping rooms in hospitals and nursing homes. **IBC 2003:** Section 1109.13.1 has an equivalent requirement for operable windows in accessible rooms in certain institutional and residential occupancies, including hotel guest rooms and patient sleeping rooms in hospitals and nursing homes.

130

The current guidelines do not have any scoping requirement for operable windows. The final revised guidelines require that, where windows are provided in accessible rooms and are intended to be opened by the occupants, at least one window meet the technical requirements for operable parts. If a building code or fire or life safety code requires a window in an accessible room to be operable, then the window is required to meet the technical requirements for operable parts. The final revised guidelines contain an exception that exempts windows in dwelling units, and in hotel guest rooms that are not required to provide mobility features.

The technical requirements for operable parts require the parts to be no higher than 48 inches from the floor; and to be operable with one hand and not require tight grasping, pinching, or twisting of the wrist. The maximum force to activate an operable part is 5 pounds. Hardware that meets the technical requirements for operable parts is available for sliding or double hung windows. The estimated average cost for the hardware is $505 per window.

The 2000 and 2003 editions of the International Building Code have an equivalent scoping requirement for accessible rooms in certain institutional and residential occupancies, including hotel guest rooms and patient sleeping rooms in hospitals and nursing homes. Facilities that are required to comply with the 2000 or 2003 editions of the International Building Code will not incur any additional costs to comply with the revised scoping requirement for operable windows.

The revision will primarily affect newly constructed hotel guest rooms and patient sleeping rooms with mobility features. Windows in employee work areas are not required to be accessible. Windows in most other types of facilities are intended for use by service or maintenance personnel, and not the occupants.

The impacts of the revision on alterations to existing facilities are examined below:

- *Is the element or space typically altered?*
  Windows are not typically altered.

- *Is the element or space part of the "path of travel" serving a primary function area?*
  Windows are not part of the "path of travel" serving a primary function area.

- *Does alteration of the element or space involve technical infeasibilty?*
  Adding hardware to a window to meet the technical requirements for operable parts will not usually involve technical infeasibility.

7.7 Two-Way Communication Systems

Table 7.7 shows the relevant text of the current guidelines and the final revised guidelines with respect to the scoping and technical requirements for two-way communication systems.

131

Table 7.7 – Two-Way Communication Systems (text version)

Current Guidelines	Final Revised Guidelines
No requirement.	*230.1 General. Where a two-way communication system is provided to gain admittance to a building or facility or to restricted areas within a building or facility, the system shall comply with 708.* **708.1 General.** Two-way communication systems shall comply with 708. *708.2 Audible and Visual Indicators. The system shall provide both audible and visual signals.* **708.3 Handsets.** Handset cords, if provided, shall be 29 inches (735 mm) long minimum.
Model Codes & Standards	
IBC 2000: No requirement for two-way communication systems. **IBC 2003:** Section E105.7 of Appendix E has an equivalent scoping requirement for two-way communication systems, but ICC/ANSI A117.1-1998 has no technical requirement for such systems.	

The current guidelines do not have any scoping and technical requirements for two-way communication systems at entrances. The final revised guidelines require two-way communication systems used to gain admission to a facility (other than a residential facility) or a restricted area within a facility to be equipped with audible and visible signals. Two-way communication systems are typically used to allow visitors to announce their presence; and a person at an interior location such as a security desk or reception area to acknowledge receipt of the announcement and remotely admit the visitor. Most two-way communication systems currently in use provide audible signals only. The estimated average cost for adding visual signals to two-way communication systems is $1,392.

The revision will primarily affect newly constructed buildings that have two-way communication systems at entrances to restrict access by the public.

The impacts of the revision on alterations to existing facilities are examined below:

- *Is the element or space typically altered?*
  If a two-way communications system in an existing facility is replaced or a new two-way communications system is added, then the system would have to provide audible and visual signals.

132

- *Is the element or space part of the "path of travel" serving a primary function area?*
  Two-way communication systems are not addressed in the Department of Justice's regulations defining "path of travel."

- *Does alteration of the element or space involve technical infeasibility?*
  Providing audible and visual signals for a two-way communication system in an existing facility will not usually involve technical infeasibility.

7.8 Maneuvering Clearance or Standby Power for Automatic Doors

Table 7.8 shows the relevant text of the current guidelines and the final revised guidelines with respect to the technical requirement for maneuvering clearance or standby power for automatic doors.

Table 7.8 – Maneuvering Clearance or Standby Power for Automatic Doors (text version)

Current Guidelines	Final Revised Guidelines
4.13.6 Maneuvering Clearances at Doors. Minimum maneuvering clearances at doors that are not automatic or power-assisted shall be as shown in Fig. 25.	*404.3.2 Maneuvering Clearance.* . . . Clearances at automatic doors and gates without standby power and serving an accessible means of egress shall comply with 404.2.4. *Exception:* Where automatic doors and gates remain open in the power-off condition, compliance with 404.2.4 shall not be required.
Model Codes & Standards	
No requirement for maneuvering clearance or standby power for automatic doors.	

The current guidelines do not require maneuvering clearance at automatic doors. The final revised guidelines require automatic doors that serve as an accessible means of egress to either provide maneuvering clearance or to have standby power to operate the door in emergencies. The revision has limited application and will affect in-swinging automatic doors that serve small spaces with an occupant load of less than 50 persons.

Building codes and fire and life safety codes require certain facilities to provide a standby power source for fire protection systems. Where a building standby power source is provided, the facility will incur additional costs for wiring to connect the automatic door to the standby power circuit. The estimated average cost for a back-up battery with a 90 minute power supply is $2,353.

The revision will not impact alterations to existing facilities since accessible means of egress are not required in existing facilities that are altered.

7.9 Power Operated Doors for Platform Lifts

133

Table 7.9 shows the relevant text of the current guidelines and the final revised guidelines with respect to the technical requirement for power operated doors for platform lifts.

Table 7.9 – Power Operated Doors for Platform Lifts (text version)

Current Guidelines	Final Revised Guidelines
4.13.1 Doors. Doors required to be accessible by 4.1 shall comply with the requirements of 4.13. **4.13.6 Maneuvering Clearances at Doors.** Minimum maneuvering clearances at doors that are not automatic or power assisted shall be as shown in Fig.25.	*410.6 Doors and Gates. Platform lifts shall have low-energy power-operated doors or gates complying with 404.3. . . .* *Exception: Platform lifts serving two landings maximum and having doors or gates on opposite sides shall be permitted to have self-closing manual doors or gates.*
Model Codes & Standards	
ICC/ANSI A117.1-1998: Section 408.2 has a similar requirement for power operated doors on platform lifts.	

The current guidelines require doors on platform lifts to provide maneuvering clearance, or to be power operated. The final revised guidelines require platform lifts to provide power operated doors, but permit platform lifts that serve no more than two landings and that have doors on opposite sides to provide self-closing manual doors.

The revision has limited application and will affect platform lifts that serve more than two landings or that do not have self-closing manual doors on opposite sides. Platform lifts typically serve only two landings and have self-closing manual doors on opposite sides. The estimated average cost for power operated doors on platform lifts is $569. The 2000 and 2003 editions of the International Building Code reference the ICC/ANSI A117.1 standard which has a similar requirement for power operated doors on platform lifts. Facilities that are required to comply with the 2000 and 2003 editions of the International Building Code will not incur any additional costs to comply with the revised technical requirement for power operated doors for platform lifts.

The impacts of the revisions on alterations to existing facilities are examined below:

- *Is the element or space typically altered?*
  If a platform lift in an existing facility is replaced or a new platform lift is added, and the platform lift serves more than two landings or does not have self-closing manual doors on opposite sides, then the platform lift would have to provide power operated doors.

- *Is the element or space part of the "path of travel" to a primary function area?*
  If a primary function area in an existing facility is altered, and there is no accessible route to the primary function, and a platform lift is added to provide an accessible route, and the platform lift serves more than two

134

landings or does not have self-closing manual doors on opposite sides, then the platform lift would have to provide power operated doors to the extent the costs of providing an accessible "path of travel" does not exceed 20 percent of the costs of the alterations to the primary function area. The cost for providing the platform lift would be incurred under the current guidelines. Only the cost for providing power operated doors on the platform lift would be attributable to the final revised guidelines.

- *Does alteration of the element or space involve technical infeasibility?* Providing power operated doors for a platform lift in an existing facility will not usually involve technical infeasibility.

7.10 Water Closet Clearance in Toilet Rooms

Table 7.10.1 shows the relevant text of the current guidelines and the final revised guidelines with respect to the technical requirement for water closet clearance in toilet rooms.

Table 7.10.1 – Water Closet Clearance in Toilet Rooms (text version)

Current Guidelines	Final Revised Guidelines
4.16.2 Clear Floor Space. Clear floor space for water closets not in stalls shall comply with Fig. 28. . . . [Note: Figure 28 shows three configurations for the clearance around a water closet depending on the type of approach: (a) Where only a forward approach to the water closet is provided, the clearance is 48 inches minimum measured perpendicular from the side wall and 66 inches minimum measured perpendicular from the rear wall. A lavatory with knee and toe clearance and 18 inches minimum from the water closet centerline is permitted on the wall behind the water closet. (b) Where only a parallel approach to the water closet is provided, the clearance is 48 inches minimum measured perpendicular from the side wall and 56 inches minimum measured perpendicular from the rear wall. A lavatory with knee and toe clearance and 18 inches minimum from the water closet centerline is	**604.3 Clearance.** Clearances around water closets and in toilet compartments shall comply with 604.3. **604.3.1 Size.** *Clearance around a water closet shall be 60 inches (1525 mm) minimum measured perpendicular from the side wall and 56 inches (1420 mm) minimum measured perpendicular from the rear wall.* **604.3.2 Overlap.** The required clearance around the water closet shall be permitted to overlap the water closet, associated grab bars, dispensers, sanitary napkin disposal units, coat hooks, shelves, accessible routes, clear floor space and clearances required at other fixtures, and the turning space. *No other fixtures or obstructions shall be located within the required water closet clearance.* *Exception: In residential dwelling units, a lavatory complying with 606 shall be permitted on the rear wall 18 inches (455 mm) minimum from the water closet centerline where the*

135

Current Guidelines	Final Revised Guidelines
permitted on the wall behind the water closet. (c) Where both a forward approach and a parallel approach to the water closet are provided, the clearance is 60 inches minimum measured perpendicular from the side wall and 56 inches minimum measured perpendicular from the rear wall. No other fixture is permitted to overlap the water closet clearance.]	*clearance at the water closet is 66 inches (1675 mm) minimum measured perpendicular from the rear wall.*
Model Codes & Standards	
ICC/ANSI A117.1-1998: Section 604.3 has an equivalent requirement for water closet clearance in toilet rooms. Section 1002.5.2 specifies three configurations for the clearance around a water closet in toilet rooms in Type A dwelling units depending on the type of approach.	

The current guidelines specify three configurations for clearance around water closets in toilet rooms depending on the type of approach provided as shown in Table 7.10.2.

Table 7.10.2 – Current Guidelines: Water Closet Clearance (text version)

Approach Provided to Water Closet	Minimum Clearance in Inches Measured Perpendicular from	
	Side Wall	Rear Wall
Forward only	48	66
Parallel only	48	56
Both Forward & Parallel	60	56

Two of the configurations (forward approach only and parallel approach only) allow a lavatory located on the wall behind the water closet to overlap the water closet clearance, where the edge of the lavatory closest to the water closet is 18 inches minimum from the water closet centerline and there is knee and toe clearance under the lavatory.

The final revised guidelines specify only one configuration for clearance around a water closet in toilet rooms, which is the same as the configuration for both a forward and parallel approach under the current guidelines (i.e., 60 inches by 56 inches minimum). The final revised guidelines do not permit the lavatory to overlap the water closet clearance, but contain an exception for dwelling units that permits a lavatory to be located on the wall behind the water closet, where the edge of the lavatory closest to the water closet is 18 inches minimum from the water closet centerline, there is knee and toe clearance under the lavatory, and the minimum size of the water closet clearance is increased by 10 inches (from 56 to 66 inches) measured perpendicular to the rear wall.

136

The revised technical requirement for water closet clearance adds approximately 9 square feet to the size of the toilet room. Toilet rooms in dwelling units that use the exception permitting the lavatory to overlap the water closet clearance add approximately 4 square feet to the size of the toilet room. A new exception that has been added to the final revised guidelines permitting the toilet room door to swing into the clearance required around any fixture, where a clear floor space is provided within the toilet room beyond the arc of the door, results in at least a 7 square feet reduction in the required room size. This new exception eliminates the impacts that result from the change in the technical requirement for water closet clearance, where the toilet door swings into the toilet room.

The revision will impact toilet rooms with out-swinging doors. Toilet rooms are generally not designed with out-swinging doors because they obstruct circulation paths, are a potential hazard to passersby, and interfere with other adjacent doors. The notable exception is toilet rooms in patient sleeping rooms. In newly constructed dwelling units that have a toilet room with an out-swinging door, the estimated average cost for finishing an additional 4 square feet of space for the required water closet clearance is $286. In other newly constructed facilities that have a toilet room with an out-swinging door, the estimated average cost for finishing an additional 9 square feet of space for the required water closet clearance is $667.

The 2000 and 2003 editions of the International Building Code reference the ICC/ANSI A117.1-1998 standard which has an equivalent requirement for water closet clearance in toilet rooms, except for Type A dwelling units. For Type A dwelling units, the ICC/ANSI A117.1-1998 standard specifies three configurations for clearance around water closets in toilet rooms depending on the type of approach similar to the current guidelines. Except for Type A dwelling units, facilities that are required to comply with the 2000 or 2003 editions of the International Building Code will not incur any additional costs to comply with the revised technical requirement for water closet clearance in toilet rooms.

The impacts of the revision on alterations to existing facilities are examined below:

- *Is the element or space typically altered?*
  If a toilet room in an existing facility is altered, then the required 60 inches by 56 inches minimum clearance would have to be provided at the water closet.

- *Is the element or space part of the "path of travel" serving a primary function area?*
  Toilet rooms are part of the "path of travel" serving a primary function area If a primary function area in an existing facility is altered and the toilet rooms serving the primary function area are not accessible, then accessible toilet rooms would have to be provided to the extent the costs of providing an accessible "path of travel" does not exceed 20 percent of the costs of the alterations to the primary function area. Most of the costs for providing the accessible toilet rooms will be incurred under the current guidelines. Only the costs of providing the additional clearance in toilet

137

rooms with out-swinging doors would be attributable to the final revised guidelines.

- *Does alteration of the element or space involve technical infeasibility?*
  It may not be feasible to rearrange fixtures or walls in existing toilet rooms due to existing physical or site constraints. Where such conditions exist, compliance is required to the maximum extent feasible.

7.11   Shower Spray Controls

Table 7.11 shows the relevant text of the current guidelines and the final revised guidelines with respect to the technical requirement for shower spray controls.

Table 7.11 – Shower Spray Controls (text version)

Current Guidelines	Final Revised Guidelines
4.21.6 Shower Unit. A shower spray unit with a hose at least 60 in (1525 mm) long that can be used both as a fixed shower head and as a hand-held shower shall be provided.	**607.1 General.** Bathtubs shall comply with 607.
	607.6 Shower Spray Unit and Water. A shower spray unit with a hose 59 inches (1500 mm) long minimum that can be used both as a fixed-position shower head and as a hand-held shower shall be provided. *The shower spray unit shall have an on/off control with a non-positive shut-off.* If an adjustable-height shower head on a vertical bar is used, the bar shall be installed so as not to obstruct the use of grab bars. Bathtub shower spray units shall deliver water that is 120°F (49°C) maximum.
	608.1 General. Shower compartments shall comply with 608.
	608.6 Shower Spray Unit and Water. A shower spray unit with a hose 59 inches (1500 mm) long minimum that can be used both as a fixed-position shower head and as a hand-held shower shall be provided. *The shower spray unit shall have an on/off control with a non-positive shut-off.* If an adjustable-height shower head on a vertical bar is used, the bar shall be installed so as not to obstruct the use of grab bars. Shower spray units shall deliver water that is 120°F (49°C) maximum.

Printed by Builder's Book, Inc., Bookstore · www.buildersbook.com

	Exception: A fixed shower head located at 48 inches (1220 mm) above the shower finish floor shall be permitted instead of a hand-held spray unit in facilities that are not medical care facilities, long term care facilities, transient lodging, or residential dwelling units.
Model Codes & Standards	
No requirement for an on/off control on shower spray units.	

The current guidelines require a shower spray unit to be provided in accessible bathtubs and shower compartments. The final revised guidelines require the shower spray unit to have an on/off control. The difference between the estimated average cost for a fixed flow shower spray unit and a variable flow shower spray unit with an on/off control is $161.

The revision will primarily affect bathtubs and shower compartments in newly constructed hotel guest rooms, patient sleeping rooms, and dwelling units with mobility features.

The impacts of the revision on alterations to existing facilities are examined below:

- *Is the element or space typically altered?*
  If a shower spray unit is replaced in an existing facility, then the shower spay unit would have to provide an on/off control.

- *Is the element or space part of the "path of travel" serving a primary function area?*
  The final revised guidelines exempt dwelling units from the scoping requirement for alterations to primary function areas. Toilet rooms in other facilities are part of the "path of travel" serving a primary function area. If a primary function area in an existing facility is altered and the toilet rooms serving the primary function area are not accessible, then accessible toilet rooms would have to be provided to the extent the costs of providing an accessible "path of travel" does not exceed 20 percent of the costs of the alterations to the primary function area. Most of the costs for providing the accessible toilet rooms will be incurred under the current guidelines. If the toilet room has a bathtub or shower compartment, the additional cost for providing a shower spray unit with an on/off control would be attributable to the final guidelines.

- *Does alteration of the element or space involve technical infeasibility?*
  Providing a shower spray unit with an on/off control will not usually involve technical infeasibility.

7.12   Galley Kitchen Clearances

139

Table 7.12 shows the relevant text of the current guidelines and the final revised guidelines with respect to the technical requirements for galley kitchen clearances. The current guidelines refer to UFAS.

Table 7.12 – Galley Kitchen Clearances (text version)

Current Guidelines	Final Revised Guidelines
4.34.6 Kitchens. Accessible or adaptable kitchens and their components shall be on an accessible route and shall comply with the requirements of 4.34.6. **4.34.6.1 Clearance.** Clearances between all opposing base cabinets, counter tops, appliances, or walls shall be 40 in (1015 mm) minimum, except in U-shaped kitchens, where such clearance shall be 60 in (1525 mm) minimum.	*804.2 **Clearance.** Where a pass through kitchen is provided, clearances shall comply with 804.2.1. Where a U-shaped kitchen is provided, clearances shall comply with 804.2.2.* ***Exception:** Spaces that do not provide a cooktop or conventional range shall not be required to comply with 804.2.* *804.2.1 **Pass Through Kitchen.** In pass through kitchens where counters, appliances or cabinets are on two opposing sides, or where counters, appliances or cabinets are opposite a parallel wall, clearance between all opposing base cabinets, counter tops, appliances, or walls within kitchen work areas shall be 40 inches (1015 mm) minimum. Pass through kitchens shall have two entries.* *804.2.2 **U-Shaped.** In U-shaped kitchens enclosed on three contiguous sides, clearance between all opposing base cabinets, counter tops, appliances, or walls within kitchen work areas shall be 60 inches (1525 mm) minimum.*
Model Codes & Standards	
ICC/ANSI A 117.1-1998: Sections 804.2.1, 1002.12.1.,1 and 1002.12.1.2 have similar requirements for kitchen clearances.	

The current guidelines specify clearances between opposing base cabinets, counters, appliances, or walls based on the layout of the kitchen:

- "U-shaped" kitchens are required to have 60 inches minimum clearance between opposing base cabinets, counters, appliances, or walls. The current guidelines do not further describe what constitutes a "U-shaped" kitchen.

- All other kitchens are required to have 40 inches minimum clearance between opposing base cabinets, counters, appliances, or walls.

The final revised guidelines also specify clearances between opposing base cabinets, counters, appliances, or walls based on the layout of the kitchen:

- "U-shaped" kitchens, which are enclosed on three contiguous sides, are required to have 60 inches minimum clearance between opposing base cabinets, counters, appliances, or walls.

- "Pass through" kitchens, which have two entries, are required to have 40 inches minimum clearance between opposing base cabinets, counters, appliances, or walls.

- An exception exempts kitchens that do not have a cooktop or conventional range from the clearance requirements.

The revision will impact small "galley" kitchens with base cabinets, counters, and appliances on two opposing walls. The current guidelines require this "galley" kitchen to have 40 inches minimum clearance between the opposing base cabinets, counters, appliances, or walls. In multi-family residential facilities, kitchens, bathrooms, and closets are located along interior walls, and space constraints may limit adding a second entry to the kitchen. If a "galley" kitchen does not have two entries, the final revised guidelines require the kitchen to have 60 inches minimum clearance between the opposing base cabinets, counters, appliances, or walls. For a typical small "galley" kitchen that is 8 feet long, increasing the width of the kitchen to provide 60 inches clearance would add approximately 13 square feet to the kitchen. In a newly constructed residential facility, the estimated average cost for finishing an additional 13 square feet of kitchen space to provide the required clearance is $993.

The revision will primarily affect "galley" kitchens in newly constructed dwelling units with mobility features, and office buildings and hotel guest suites that have kitchens with a cooktop or conventional range.

The impacts of the revision on alterations to existing facilities are examined below:

- *Is the element or space typically altered?*
  If the base cabinets, counters, or walls in an existing "galley" kitchen are altered and the kitchen does not have two entries, then the required 60 inches minimum clearance would have to be provided between the opposing base cabinets, countertops, and appliances,

- *Is the element or space part of the "path of travel" serving a primary function area?*
  The final revised guidelines exempt dwelling units from the scoping requirement for alterations to primary function areas. Kitchens in other facilities are not part of the "path of travel" serving a primary function area.

141

- *Does alteration of the element or space involve technical infeasibility?*
  It may not be feasible to rearrange base counters, countertops, and walls in existing kitchens due to existing physical or site constraints. Where such conditions exist, compliance is required to the maximum extent feasible.

7.13   Hotel Guest Room Vanities

Table 7.13 shows the relevant text of the current guidelines and the final revised guidelines with respect to the technical requirement for vanities in hotel guest rooms with mobility features.

Table 7.13 – Hotel Guest Room Vanities (text version)

Current Guidelines	Final Revised Guidelines
No requirement.	*806.2.4.1 Vanity Counter Top Space. If vanity counter top space is provided in non-accessible guest toilet or bathing rooms, comparable vanity counter top space, in terms of size and proximity to the lavatory, shall also be provided in accessible guest toilet or bathing rooms.*
Model Codes & Standards	
No requirement for hotel guest room vanities.	

The current guidelines do not contain any technical requirement for vanities in hotel guest rooms with mobility features. One design approach for providing clearances around plumbing fixtures in hotel guest rooms with mobility features is to eliminate the vanity and to provide a wall-hung lavatory with knee and toe clearance. The final revised guidelines require that, where vanities are provided in other hotel guest rooms, comparable vanity counter top space be provided in hotel guest rooms with mobility features. For purposes of this assessment, it is assumed that the vanity provided in other hotel guest rooms is 6 feet long and 2 feet deep, and that the lavatory provided in hotel guest rooms with mobility features is 2 feet long and 2 feet deep. A vanity counter top space that is 4 feet long and 2 feet deep will have to be provided in hotel guest rooms with mobility features. The estimated average cost for 8 square feet of vanity counter top space is $144. Shelving may also be used to provide the comparable counter top space. Depending on the layout of the toilet room, up to 8 square feet would have to be added to the toilet room. In a newly constructed hotel, the estimated average cost for finishing an additional 8 square feet of toilet room is $608.

The impacts of the revision on alterations to existing facilities are examined below:

- *Is the element or space typically altered?*
  If a toilet room in an existing hotel guest room with mobility features is altered, and the toilet room does not have a vanity, and the toilet rooms in other hotel guest rooms have vanities, then equivalent vanity counter top space would have to be provided in the altered toilet room.

142

- *Is the element or space part of the "path of travel" serving a primary function area?*
  If an existing hotel guest room is altered to provide mobility features, **the toilet room serving the guest room will also typically be altered.**

- *Does alteration of the element or space involve technical infeasibility?*
  It may not be feasible to rearrange fixtures and walls in existing toilet rooms in hotel guestrooms to provide equivalent vanity counter top space due to existing physical or site constraints. Where such conditions exist, compliance is required to the maximum extent feasible.

7.14   Dwelling Units with Communication Features

Table 7.14 shows the relevant text of the current guidelines and the final revised guidelines with respect to the technical requirements for dwelling units with communication features.

Table 7.14 – Communication Features for Residential Dwelling Units (text version)

Current Guidelines	Final Revised Guidelines
No requirement.	**809.5 Residential Dwelling Units with Communication Features.** Residential dwelling units required to have communication features shall comply with 809.5. ***809.5.1 Building Fire Alarm System.** Where a building fire alarm system is provided, the system wiring shall be extended to a point within the residential dwelling unit in the vicinity of the residential dwelling unit smoke detection system.* ***809.5.1.1 Alarm Appliances.** Where visual alarm appliances are provided within a residential dwelling unit as part of the building fire alarm system, they shall comply with 702.* [Note: Section 702 references the NFPA 72, National Fire Alarm Code (1999 or 2002 edition).] **809.5.1.2 Activation.** All visual alarm appliances provided within the residential dwelling unit for building fire alarm notification shall be activated upon activation of the building fire alarm system in the portion of the building containing

143

Current Guidelines	Final Revised Guidelines
	the residential dwelling unit.

809.5.2 Residential Dwelling Unit Smoke Detection System. Residential dwelling unit smoke detection systems shall comply with NFPA 72 *(1999 or 2002 edition) (incorporated by reference, see "Referenced Standards" in Chapter 1).*

809.5.2.2 Activation. All visible alarm appliances provided within the residential dwelling unit for smoke detection notification shall be activated upon smoke detection.

809.5.3 Interconnection. The same visible alarm appliances shall be permitted to provide notification of residential dwelling unit smoke detection and building fire alarm activation.

809.5.4 Prohibited Use. Visible alarm appliances used to indicate residential dwelling unit smoke detection or building fire alarm activation shall not be used for any other purpose within the residential dwelling unit.

809.5.5 Residential Dwelling Unit Primary Entrance. *Communication features shall be provided at the residential dwelling unit primary entrance complying with 809.5.5.*

809.5.5.1 Notification. *A hard-wired electric doorbell shall be provided. A button or switch shall be provided outside the residential dwelling unit primary entrance. Activation of the button or switch shall initiate an audible tone and visible signal within the residential dwelling unit. Where visible doorbell signals are located in sleeping areas, they shall have controls to deactivate the signal.*

809.5.5.2 Identification. *A means for visually identifying a visitor without opening the residential dwelling unit entry*

144

Current Guidelines	Final Revised Guidelines
	door shall be provided and shall allow for a minimum 180 degree range of view.
	809.5.6 Site, Building, or Floor Entrance. *Where a system, including a closed-circuit system, permitting voice communication between a visitor and the occupant of the residential dwelling unit is provided, the system shall comply with 708.4.*
	708.4 Residential Dwelling Unit Communication Systems. *Communications systems between a residential dwelling unit and a site, building, or floor entrance shall comply with 708.4.*
	708.4.1 Common Use or Public Use System Interface. *The common use or public use system interface shall include the capability of supporting voice and TTY communication with the residential dwelling unit interface.*
	708.4.2 Residential Dwelling Unit Interface. *The residential dwelling unit system interface shall include a telephone jack capable of supporting voice and TTY communication with the common use or public use system interface.*

Model Codes & Standards
IBC 2000: No scoping requirement for dwelling units with communication features.
IBC 2003: No scoping requirement for dwelling units with communication features.
ICC/ANSI A117.1-1998: Sections 1004.1 through 1004.7 have similar technical requirements for dwelling units with communication features.

The current guidelines do not have any technical requirements for dwelling units with communication features. The final revised guidelines require newly constructed residential facilities to provide the following in dwelling units with communication features:

- **Where a building fire alarm system is provided, the system wiring is required to extend to the dwelling unit smoke detection system. The building fire alarm system and the dwelling unit smoke detection system**

145

are permitted to be interconnected. Visible alarm appliances are not required, but where they are provided, they are to be activated upon activation of the building fire alarm system in the portion of the building containing the dwelling unit and upon detection of smoke within the dwelling unit. There is no cost for connecting the building alarm system and the dwelling unit smoke detection system since this is a common practice permitted by the NFPA 72, National Fire Alarm Code.

- A hard-wired electric doorbell is required at the primary entrance to the dwelling unit that initiates an audible tone and visible signal within the dwelling unit when activated. Visible signals are not required in the sleeping area, but where provided there, a switch is required to turn off the signals. A door peephole is also required for identifying visitors. The estimated average cost for an electric doorbell with an audible tone and visible signal, and a door peephole is $322. If electric doorbells and door peepholes are provided for all the dwelling units in the facility, the estimated average cost for adding a visible signal to the doorbells in the dwelling units with communication features is $96.

- Where a voice communication system is provided at the entrance to the residential facility that permits communication between a visitor and the occupant of the dwelling unit, the system is required to have the capability of supporting voice and TTY communication at the public or common use side of the system, and a telephone jack capable of supporting voice and TTY communication at the dwelling unit side of the system. The costs will depend on the type of voice communication system used. Systems that are integrated with the telecommunications devices in the dwelling units and have built-in jacks to support TTY communication will not add any costs, other than the cost of the system. If TTY connections are added to the system, the estimated average cost is $353. Locating an electrical outlet near the system to supply power for a TTY adds no cost to new construction.

The revision will primarily affect Federal, State, and local government housing, which are required to provide communications features in 2 percent of newly constructed dwelling units.

The impacts of the revision on alterations to existing facilities are examined below:

- *Is the element or space typically altered?*
  The final revised guidelines have specific scoping requirements for alterations to Federal, State, and local government housing which are discussed in Chapter 6.17.

- *Is the element or space part of the "path of travel" serving a primary function area?*
  The final revised guidelines exempt dwelling units from the scoping requirement for alterations to primary function areas.

146

- *Does alteration of the element or space involve technical infeasibility?* Providing communication features in a dwelling unit will not usually involve technical infeasibility.

7.15   Summary

The impacts of the revisions discussed in this chapter on newly constructed facilities are summarized in Table 7.15.1.

Table 7.15.1 – Impacts on Newly Constructed Facilities (text version)

Revision & Facilities Primarily Affected	Current Guidelines	Final Revised Guidelines & International Building Code	Unit Cost
Accessible Routes to Stages Performing arts centers and auditoriums with permanent stairs directly connecting seating area and stage.	Accessible route required to connect seating area and stage.	Where circulation path directly connects seating area and stage, accessible route required to directly connect seating area and stage. **IBC 2000 & 2003:** Equivalent requirement.	Will vary from $0 to $15,674 depending on specific design of facility.
Standby Power for Platform Lifts Performing arts centers and auditoriums with platform lifts.	No requirement.	Where platform lift serves as part of accessible means of egress, standby power required. **IBC 2003:** Equivalent requirement.	Will vary from $0 to $2,353 depending on specific design of facility.
Van Accessible Parking Spaces Facilities with more than 600 parking spaces.	One in every 8 accessible parking spaces required to be van accessible.	One in every 6 accessible parking spaces required to be van accessible. **IBC 2003:** Equivalent requirement.	$73 to $344
Ambulatory Accessible Toilet Compartments Facilities with men's toilet rooms that have 6 or more water closets and urinals, but fewer than 6 toilet compartments.	Toilet rooms with 6 or more toilet compartments required to provide ambulatory accessible toilet compartment with grab bars.	Toilet rooms with 6 or more toilet compartments, or combination of 6 or more water closets and urinals, required to provide ambulatory accessible toilet compartment with grab bars.	$145

147

Revision & Facilities Primarily Affected	Current Guidelines	Final Revised Guidelines & International Building Code	Unit Cost
		IBC 2000 & 2003: Equivalent requirement.	
Public TTYs Private facilities with 4 or more public telephones on more than one floor. Government facilities with public telephone on more than one floor. Private facilities and government facilities with 4 or more public telephones in a bank. Private facilities and government facilities with 4 or more public telephones on an exterior site. Bus and rail stations with fewer than 4 public telephones at entrance. Public rest stops with public telephones.	Private facilities with 4 or more public telephones required to provide public TTY. Government facilities with public telephone in public use area of building, required to provide public TTY. Rail stations with 4 or more public telephones at entrance required to provide public TTY at entrance.	Private facilities required to provide public TTY in building with 4 or more public telephones, and on floor with 4 or more public telephones. Government facilities required to provide public TTY in building with public telephone and on floor with public telephone. Private and government facilities required to provide public TTY in bank of 4 or more public telephones. Banks of public telephones located within 200 feet of, and on the same floor as, another bank of telephones with public TTY exempt. Private and government facilities required to provide public TTY on exterior site with 4 or more public telephones. Bus or rail stations with public telephone at entrance required to provide public TTY at entrance. Public rest stops with public telephone required to provide public TTY. **IBC 2000 (Appendix E):**	$2,320

148

Revision & Facilities Primarily Affected	Current Guidelines	Final Revised Guidelines & International Building Code	Unit Cost
		Equivalent requirements for private facilities. **IBC 2003 (Appendix E):** Equivalent requirements for private facilities and government facilities.	
Operable Windows Hotels, and hospitals and nursing homes.	No requirement.	At least one operable window in accessible rooms required to comply with technical requirements for operable parts: 48 inches maximum reach range; operable with one hand; no tight grasping, pinching, or twisting of wrist; 5 pounds maximum force to activate. Employee work areas and dwelling units exempt. **IBC 2000 & 2003:** Equivalent requirement for hotel guest rooms and patient sleeping rooms with mobility features.	$505
Two-Way Communication Systems at Entrances Office buildings with two-way communication systems at entrances.	No requirement.	Two-way communication systems at entrances required to provide audible and visual signals.	$1,392
Maneuvering Clearance or Standby Power for Automatic Doors Facilities with in-swinging automatic	No requirement.	Automatic doors serving accessible means of egress required to provide maneuvering clearance or to have standby power.	Will vary depending on specific design of facility. $2,353 if back-up

Printed by Builder's Book, Inc., Bookstore · www.buildersbook.com

Revision & Facilities Primarily Affected	Current Guidelines	Final Revised Guidelines & International Building Code	Unit Cost
doors serving spaces with occupant load of fewer than 50 persons.			battery used.
Power-Operated Doors for Platform Lifts Facilities with platform lifts serving more than 2 landings, or without self-closing doors on opposite sides.	Doors required to provide maneuvering clearance or to be power-operated.	Doors on platform lifts required to be power-operated. Platform lifts serving only 2 landings and with self-closing doors on opposite sides exempt. **IBC 2000 & 2003:** Similar requirement.	Will vary depending on specific design of facility. $569 if power-operated door provided.
Water Closet Clearance in Single User Toilet Rooms Federal, State, and local government housing; hotels; hospitals and nursing homes; and office buildings.	Minimum clearance in accessible toilet rooms based on approach: Forward: 48 x 66 inches Parallel: 48 x 56 inches Both forward and parallel: 60 x 56 inches.	Minimum clearance in accessible toilet rooms: 60 x 56 inches. **IBC 2000 & 2003:** Equivalent requirement except for dwelling units.	$286 for dwelling units. $667 for other facilities.
Shower Spray Controls Federal, State, and local government housing; hotels; and hospitals and nursing homes.	Shower spray unit required in bathtubs and shower compartments in accessible toilet rooms and bathing rooms.	On/off control required on shower spray unit.	$161
Galley Kitchen Clearance Federal, State, and local government housing; hotels with suites that have kitchens with cooktops or conventional ranges; office buildings that have	Minimum clearance between opposing base cabinets, counter tops, appliances, or walls in accessible galley kitchens: 40 inches.	Minimum clearance between opposing base cabinets, counter tops, appliances, or walls in accessible galley kitchens where two entries not provided: 60 inches. Kitchens without cooktop or conventional range exempt.	$993

Revision & Facilities Primarily Affected	Current Guidelines	Final Revised Guidelines & International Building Code	Unit Cost
kitchens with cooktops or conventional ranges.			
Hotel Vanity Counter Top Space Hotels.	No requirement.	Comparable vanity counter top space required in hotel guest rooms with mobility features.	$752
Dwelling Units with Communication Features Federal, State, and local government housing.	No requirement.	Two percent of dwelling units required to provide communication features: building fire alarm system wiring extend to dwelling unit smoke detection system; door bell with audible and visible signals; door peep-hole. Where voice communication system provided at entry to facility, system required to have capacity to support TTY communication.	$96 for visual signal if doorbell & peep-hole provided. $322 for doorbell with visual signal & peephole. $353 for TTY connection if voice communication system at entry.

The impacts of the revisions on alterations to existing facilities will vary depending on whether the element or space is typically altered; whether the element or space is part of the "path of travel" serving a primary function area and whether the primary function area is altered; and whether alteration of the element or space involves technical infeasibility (i.e., altering a load-bearing structural member which is an essential part of the structural frame, or existing physical or site constraints). In addition, some of the revisions do not apply to existing facilities. The revisions that will have no or limited impacts on alterations to existing facilities are summarized in Table 7.15.2.

Table 7.15.2 – Revisions That Have No or Limited (text version) Impacts on Alterations to Existing Facilities

Revisions Do Not Apply to Existing Facilities	Elements and Spaces Not Typically Altered	Elements and Spaces Not Part of "Path of Travel"	Alteration of Elements or Spaces May Involve Technical Infeasibility
Standby power for platform lifts	Circulation paths to stages	Windows	Multi-level parking garages with low

Printed by Builder's Book, Inc., Bookstore · www.buildersbook.com

serving as part of accessible means of egress	Toilet compartments	Two-way communication systems	ceilings and sloped floors
Automatic doors serving accessible means of egress	Windows	Toilet rooms in dwelling units	Toilet rooms
			Kitchens
		Kitchens in dwelling units	
		Communication features in dwelling units	

Office buildings, hotels, hospitals and nursing homes, and Federal, State, and local government housing will be affected by many of the revisions and are likely to experience relatively higher costs than other types of facilities. The national costs of the revisions for the construction of these facilities are estimated in Chapter 8.

The impacts of some of the revisions will vary depending on the specific design of the facility. Most performing arts centers and auditoriums that have fixed or built-in stairs directly connecting the seating area and the stage would comply with the accessible route requirements in the current guidelines by providing a platform lift or ramp, and will have to locate the platform lift or design the ramp so that it directly connects the seating area and the stage. Performing arts centers and auditoriums that have fixed or built-in stairs directly connecting the seating area and the stage and would comply with the accessible route requirements in the current guidelines without providing a platform lift or ramp, will incur additional costs for a platform lift or ramp to directly connect the seating area and the stage. Performing arts centers, auditoriums, and other facilities with platform lifts that serve as part of an accessible means of egress, will have to connect the platform lift to the building standby power source, which many buildings are required to provide by the building codes or fire and life safety codes; or will have to provide a back-up battery for the platform lift if it does not use a direct current (DC) power source. Facilities with platform lifts that serve more than two landings, or that do not have self-closing doors on opposite sides, will have to provide power-operated doors. Most platform lifts serve only two landings, and have self closing doors on opposite sides. Facilities that have an in-swinging automatic door which serves a space with an occupant load of fewer than 50 persons and also serves as an accessible means of egress from the space, will have to provide maneuvering clearance at the door; or will have to connect the door to the building standby power source, which as noted above many buildings are required to provide; or will have to provide a back-up battery for the door. The International Building Code has equivalent requirements for these elements, except for automatic doors.

CHAPTER 8: NATIONAL COSTS FOR OFFICE BUILDINGS, HOTELS, HOSPITALS AND NURSING HOMES, AND GOVERMENT HOUSING

8.0 Introduction

This chapter estimates the national costs of revisions for the construction of office buildings, hotels, hospitals and nursing homes, and Federal, State, and local government housing. A preliminary analysis of the revisions that have monetary impacts in Chapter 7 shows that the new construction and alterations of these facilities will be affected by many of the revisions, and they are likely to experience relatively higher costs than other facilities. This chapter also addresses whether the final revised guidelines are an economically significant regulatory action.

Data is presented on construction projects for office buildings, hotels, hospitals and nursing homes, and Federal, State, and local government housing from:

- The December 2002 Dodge Construction Potentials Bulletin, which reports the number of construction projects started during 2002; the total floor area of the projects; and total value of the projects.

- The Census Bureau Annual Value of Construction Put in Place, which reports the value of construction work installed during 2002. Large non-residential construction projects usually take more than 12 months to complete. The Census Bureau Annual Value of Construction Put in Place includes not only construction projects started in 2002, but also construction projects started prior to 2002. The Census Bureau Annual Value of Construction Put in Place also counts certain costs not included in the Dodge Construction Potentials Bulletin. For these reasons, the values reported in the Census Bureau Annual Value of Construction Put in Place are generally higher than the values reported in the Dodge Construction Potentials Bulletin.

- Industry sources, where available, on the number and size of existing facilities, number and size of construction projects started and new facilities completed, and construction costs.

The Dodge Construction Potentials Bulletin includes alteration projects that cost $100,000 or more. The Dodge Construction Potentials Bulletin does not provide separate data on alteration projects. The Census Bureau Annual Value of Construction Put in Place also includes alteration work. Alteration work accounted for 38 percent of office building construction work; 23 percent of hotel construction work; 54 percent of hospital construction work; and 65 percent of Federal, State, and local government residential construction work installed in 2002. The assessment treats alteration projects the same as new construction projects, and assumes that the entire facility is altered and will be affected by revisions. However, if only a portion of an existing facility is altered, and the altered elements and spaces are not affected by the revisions, the assessment will overstate the national costs.

The average size and value of construction projects reported in the Dodge Construction Potentials Bulletin are compared to the data on existing facilities and new facilities.

153

- If the average size or value of construction projects reported in the Dodge Construction Potentials Bulletin is comparable to existing facilities or new facilities, the number of construction projects reported in the Dodge Construction Potentials Bulletin is considered representative of the number of facilities that will be affected by the revisions.

- If the average size or value of construction projects reported in the Dodge Construction Potentials Bulletin is extremely small compared to existing facilities or new facilities, the number of construction projects reported in the Dodge Construction Potentials Bulletin most likely represents a significant number of alteration projects involving work on only portions of existing facilities that may not be affected by the revisions.

- When the number of construction projects reported in the Dodge Construction Potentials Bulletin most likely represents a significant number of alteration projects involving work on only portions of existing facilities that may not be affected by the revisions, and appropriate industry data is available, then the industry data is used.

- When the number of construction projects reported in the Dodge Construction Potentials Bulletin most likely represents a significant number of alteration projects involving work on only portions of existing facilities that may not be affected by the revisions, and appropriate industry data is not available, then the total floor area or value of the construction projects reported in the Dodge Construction Potentials Bulletin is converted to an equivalent number of average size facilities.

- The Dodge Construction Potentials Bulletin does not include data on the total number of Federal, State, or local government residential construction projects, or the total floor area of the projects; and may underestimate the value of the projects. The Census Bureau Annual Value of Construction Put in Place is used to estimate the number of Federal, State, and local government dwelling units that will be affected by the revisions.

Assumptions are made about the percentage of facilities that will be affected by each revision. The assumptions are based on discussions with industry sources. The additional costs imposed by the revisions on newly constructed facilities are estimated and compared to the total construction costs for individual facilities. The national costs of the revisions for each type of facility are estimated based on the number of facilities that will be affected by the revisions.

As discussed in Chapter 2, the national costs of the revisions are measured against the current guidelines and the International Building Code. The current guidelines are the upper bound of the range of national costs, and assume that the facilities are not required to also comply with equivalent requirements in the International Building Code. The International Building Code is the lower bound of the range of national costs, and assumes that the facilities are required to also comply with equivalent requirements in the International Building Code. The International Building Code has been adopted in statewide by 28 States, and by

154

local governments in another 15 States. The actual national costs will be between the lower and upper bound of the range.

8.1 Office Buildings

8.1.1 Office Building Data

The Dodge Construction Potentials Bulletin reports that 23,100 construction projects for private office buildings were started in 2002; and 958 projects for government office buildings were started in 2002. Private office building construction projects totaled 150 million square feet valued at $19.0 billion (average project size: 6,500 sq. ft.; average project value: $825,000). Government office building construction projects totaled 10 million square feet valued at $2.6 billion (average project size: 10,400 sq. ft.; average project value: $2.6 million).

The Census Bureau Annual Value of Construction Put in Place reports that the value of private and government office building construction work installed during 2002 was $44.9 billion. New construction accounted for 62 percent of the work ($27.7 billion), and additions and alterations accounted for 38 percent of the work ($17.2 billion).

Cushman & Wakefield reports that in the second quarter of 2003 there was 19 million square feet of new office building space under construction in downtown areas, and 19 million square feet of new office building space under construction in suburban areas.

The Building Owners and Managers Association (BOMA) International conducts an annual survey of existing office buildings. The 2003 BOMA Experience Exchange Report included over 3,000 office buildings in the United States. The average size of private office buildings in downtown areas is 381,477 square feet (754 surveyed) and in suburban areas is 119,410 square feet (1,776 surveyed). The average size of government office buildings in downtown areas is 178,993 square feet (540 surveyed) and in suburban areas is 38,319 square feet (69 surveyed).

Since the average sizes of the construction projects reported in the Dodge Construction Potentials Bulletin (6,500 sq. ft. for private office buildings; 10,400 sq. ft. for government office buildings) are extremely small compared to the average sizes of existing office buildings surveyed in the 2003 BOMA Experience Exchange Report (381,447 sq. ft. (downtown area) and 119,410 sq. ft. (suburban area) for private office buildings; 178,993 sq. ft. (downtown area) and 38,319 sq. ft. (suburban area) for government office buildings), the total number of construction projects reported in the Dodge Construction Potentials Bulletin (24,058 projects) most likely represents a significant number of alteration projects involving work on only portions of existing facilities that may not be affected by the revisions. To estimate the national costs of the revisions for office buildings, the total square feet of office building construction reported in the Dodge Construction Potentials Bulletin (160 million sq. ft.) is converted to an equivalent number of average size office buildings. It is assumed that the total square feet of office building construction is equally divided between downtown areas and suburban areas.

155

The total square feet of office building construction is equivalent to 985 average size office buildings as shown in Table 8.1.1.

Table 8.1.1 – Office Building Construction:
Total Floor Area Equivalent to Average Size Office Buildings (text version)

Location	Number of Buildings & Average Size	Total Floor Area
Private Office Buildings		
Downtown Area	200 Buildings (380,000 sq. ft. per building)	76 million sq. ft
Suburban Area	625 Buildings (120,000 sq. ft. per building)	75 million sq. ft.
Government Office Buildings		
Downtown Area	30 Buildings (180,000 sq. ft. per building)	5 million sq. ft.
Suburban Area	130 Buildings (40,000 sq. ft. per building)	5 million sq. ft.
Total	985 Buildings	161 million sq. ft.

Office building construction costs vary widely and range from $100 to $200 or more per square foot. For purposes of this assessment, $140 per square foot is used to estimate the construction costs for office buildings. The total construction costs for the 985 office buildings in Table 8.1.1 is $22.6 billion compared to $21.6 billion in the Dodge Construction Potentials Bulletin as shown in Table 8.1.2.

Table 8.1.2 – Office Building Construction Costs (text version)

Location	Number of Buildings & Average Size	Construction Costs Per Building (Millions)	Total Construction Costs (Billions)
Private Office Buildings			
Downtown Area	200 Buildings (380,000 sq. ft. per building)	$53.2	$10.6
Suburban Area	625 Buildings (120,000 sq. ft. per building)	$16.8	$10.5
Government Office Buildings			
Downtown Area	30 Buildings (180,000 sq. ft. per building)	$25.2	$.8
Suburban Area	130 Buildings (40,000 sq. ft. per building)	$5.6	$.7
		Total (Billions)	$22.6

8.1.2 Revisions That Affect Office Buildings

Van Accessible Parking Spaces

Office buildings that have between 601 and 3,200 parking spaces will have to widen one access aisle from 5 feet to 8 feet. For each additional 1,800 parking spaces over 3,200, an additional access aisle will have to be widened by 3 feet. The 2003 BOMA Experience Exchange Report provides data on the average number of parking spaces per 1,000 square feet. Private office buildings (1,843 surveyed) have 1.96 parking spaces and government office buildings (507 surveyed) have 0.92 parking spaces per 1,000 square feet. Based on these ratios, private office buildings with more than 306,000 square feet and government offices with more than 625,000 square feet will have at least 601 parking spaces. As shown in Table 8.1.1, the only office building that meets these criteria is the average downtown private office building. The average downtown private office building will not have more than 3,200 parking spaces. Therefore, for purposes of this assessment, it is assumed that 100 percent of the downtown private office buildings (200 buildings) will have between 601 and 3,200 parking spaces.

Ambulatory Accessible Toilet Compartments

Men's toilet rooms with six or more water closets and urinals, but fewer than six toilet compartments, will have to provide an ambulatory accessible toilet compartment with grab bars. Plumbing codes typically specify the minimum number of plumbing fixtures required based on the type of building and occupant load. Plumbing fixtures are usually divided equally between men's and women's toilet rooms; and urinals are allowed to be provided in place of a certain number of water closets in men's toilet rooms. Plumbing fixtures are usually dispersed evenly among the floors in office buildings. For purposes of this assessment, it is assumed that 100 percent of the downtown private office buildings (200 buildings) and 100 percent of downtown government office buildings (30 buildings) will have men's toilet rooms with six or more water closets and urinals, but fewer than six toilet compartments. It is also assumed that the private office buildings will have 20 floors and the government office buildings will have 10 floors.

Public TTYs

Private office buildings are currently required to provide a public TTY in buildings with four or more public pay telephones. Under the final revised guidelines, private office buildings will have to provide a public TTY in buildings with four or more public pay telephones; on floors with four or more public pay telephones; and in banks with four or more public pay telephones. Banks of telephones located on the same floor within 200 feet from a bank with a public TTY are exempt from the requirement.

Government office buildings are currently required to provide a public TTY in buildings with a public pay telephone in a public use area. Under the final revised guidelines, government office buildings will have to provide a public TTY in buildings with a public pay telephone; on floors with a public pay telephone; and

157

in banks with four or more public pay telephones. Banks of telephones located on the same floor within 200 feet from a bank with a public TTY are exempt from the requirement.

For purposes of this assessment, it is assumed that 10 percent of private office buildings (83 buildings) will have four or more public pay telephones on two floors and will have to provide an additional public TTY. It is also assumed that 10 percent of government office buildings (16 buildings) will have a public pay telephone on two floors and will have to provide an additional public TTY.

Two-Way Communication Systems

Where two-way communication systems are provided to gain entry to an office building or a restricted area within the building, the system will have to provide audible and visible signals. Card-reader systems are more common than two-way communication systems in office buildings. Some card-reader systems also include a two-way communication system and will be affected by the final revised guidelines. For purposes of this assessment, it is assumed that 25 percent of private and government office buildings (250 buildings) will have a two-way communication system.

Water Closet Clearance

If an office building has a single-user toilet room with an out-swinging door, the toilet room will have to be increased by 9 square feet to provide the 60 inches by 56 inches minimum clearance around the water closet. Office buildings usually have multi-user toilet rooms. A single-user toilet room may be provided within office suites for executives, or for the convenience of employees or customers. Single-user toilet rooms usually have in-swinging doors. For purposes of this assessment, it is assumed that 25 percent of private and government office buildings (250 buildings) will have a single-user toilet room with an out-swinging door.

Galley Kitchen Clearance

If an office building has a galley kitchen with a cooktop or range that is enclosed on three sides, the kitchen will have to be increased by 13 square feet to provide 60 inches minimum clearance between the counters or walls. Kitchens in office buildings are usually equipped with a microwave oven. Cooktops or ranges are not usually provided in office building kitchens. For purposes of this assessment, it is assumed that 10 percent of private and government office buildings (100 buildings) will have a galley kitchen with a cooktop or range.

The revisions that affect office buildings are summarized in Table 8.1.3.

Table 8.1.3 – Revisions That Affect Office Buildings (text version)

Revision	Assumptions: Percentage (Number) of Office Buildings Affected	Costs Per Facility Compared to		
		Current Guidelines	IBC 2000	IBC 2003

Van Accessible Parking Spaces	100% (200) Downtown Private Office Buildings Have 601 – 3,200 Parking Spaces	$344	$344	$0
Ambulatory Accessible Toilet Compartments	100% (200) Downtown Private Office Buildings Have 20 Men's Toilet Rooms with 6 or More Water Closets and Urinals, but Fewer Than 6 Toilet Compartments	$2,900	$0	$0
	100% (30) Downtown Government Office Buildings Have 10 Men's Toilet Rooms with 6 or More Water Closets and Urinals, but Fewer Than 6 Toilet Compartments	$1,450	$0	$0
Public TTYs	10% (83) Private Office Buildings Have 4 or More Public Pay Telephones on 2 Floors	$2,320	$2,320	$2,320
	10% (16) Government Office Buildings Have 1 Public Pay Telephone on 2 Floors	$2,320	$2,320	$2,320
Two-Way Communication Systems	25% (250) Private and Government Office Buildings Have 1 Two-Way Communication System	$1,392	$1,392	$1,392
Water Closet Clearance	25% (250) Private and Government Office Buildings Have 1 Single-User Toilet Room with Out-Swinging Door	$667	$0	$0
Galley Kitchen Clearance	10% (100) Private and Government Office Buildings Have 1 Galley Kitchen with Cooktop or Range	$993	$993	$993

8.1.3 Additional Costs for Office Buildings

For purposes of estimating the additional costs of the revisions for the construction of individual office buildings, it is assumed that the downtown private office building is affected by all the revisions in Table 8.1.3; the downtown government office building is affected by all the revisions in Table 8.1.3, except for van accessible parking spaces; and the suburban private and government office buildings are affected by all the revisions in Table 8.1.3, except for van accessible parking spaces and ambulatory accessible toilet compartments. The additional costs of the revisions for the construction of individual office buildings are shown in Table 8.1.4.

Table 8.1.4 – Additional Costs for Office Buildings (text version)

Office Building & Construction Costs	Additional Costs Compared to (Percentage of Total Construction Costs)		
	Current Guidelines	IBC 2000	IBC 2003
Downtown Private $53.2 Million	$8,616 (0.02%)	$5,049 (0.01%)	$4,705 (0.01%)
Suburban Private	$5,372	$4,705	$4,705

159

$16.8 Million	(0.03%)	(0.03%)	(0.03%)
Downtown Government	$6,822	$4,705	$4,705
$25.2 Million	(0.03%)	(0.02%)	(0.02%)
Suburban Government	$5,372	$4,705	$4,705
$5.6 Million	(0.1%)	(0.08%)	(0.08%)

8.1.4　National Costs for Office Buildings

For purposes of estimating the national costs of the revisions for the construction of office buildings, the assumptions summarized in Table 8.1.3 regarding the number of office buildings affected by each revision are applied. The national costs for the construction of office buildings are shown in Table 8.1.5.

Table 8.1.5 – National Costs for Office Buildings (text version)

Revision	Assumptions: Number of Office Buildings Affected	National Costs Compared to		
		Current Guidelines Upper Bound	IBC 2000 Lower Bound	IBC 2003 Lower Bound
Van Accessible Parking Spaces	200 Downtown Private Office Buildings	$66,800	$66,800	$0
Ambulatory Accessible Toilet Compartments	200 Downtown Private Office Buildings	$580,000	$0	$0
	30 Downtown Government Office Buildings	$43,500	$0	$0
Public TTYs	100 Private and Government Office Buildings	$232,000	$232,000	$232,000
Two-Way Communication Systems	250 Private and Government Office Buildings	$348,000	$348,000	$348,000
Water Closet Clearance	250 Private and Government Office Buildings	$166,750	$0	$0
Galley Kitchen Clearance	100 Private and Government Office Buildings	$99,300	$99,300	$99,300
Total (Millions)		$1.5	$0.7	$0.7

8.2　Hotels

8.2.1　Hotel Data

The Dodge Construction Potentials Bulletin reports that 1,121 construction projects for hotels were started in 2002. Hotel construction projects totaled 9 million square feet valued at $4.4 billion (average project size: 35,150 sq. ft.; average project value: $4.0 million).

The Census Bureau Annual Value of Construction Put in Place reports that the value of hotel construction work installed during 2002 was $10.3 billion. New construction accounted for 77 percent of the work ($8.0 billion), and additions and alterations accounted for 23 percent of the work ($2.3 billion).

161

The American Hotel and Lodging Association (AHLA) issues an annual profile of the lodging industry. The 2003 AHLA Lodging Industry Profile provides data on the number of existing hotels as of the end of 2002. Lodging Econometrics provides data on the number of new hotels completed in 2001 and 2002. The data is shown in Table 8.2.1.

Table 8.2.1 – Hotels by Size (text version)

Size	Existing Hotels at End of 2002	New Hotels Completed in 2001 & 2002
Under 75 rooms	26,840 (57%)	753 (41%)
75 – 149 rooms	14,170 (30%)	810 (45%)
150 – 299 rooms	4,422 (10%)	193 (11%)
300 – 500 rooms	1,103 (2%)	38 (2%)
Over 500 rooms	505 (1%)	24 (1%)
Total	47,040 (100%)	1,818 (100%)

Lodging Econometrics reports that 631 new hotels were completed between July 2002 and July 2003, and another 528 new hotels were under construction at the end of July 2003.

Hotel guest rooms vary in size from 250 square feet for an economy hotel to 350 or more square feet for an upscale hotel. The total floor area of a hotel will depend on the other facilities provided, including restaurants, banquet and meeting rooms, and exercise rooms and pools. Hotel construction costs vary widely depending on location, class of hotel, and other facilities provided. The range of construction costs per room by hotel size is shown in Table 8.2.2.

Table 8.2.2 - Hotel Construction Costs per Room (text version)

Size	Range
Under 75 rooms	$28,000 - $38,000
75 – 149 rooms	$42,000 – $52,000
150 – 299 rooms	$55,000 – $70,000
300 – 500 rooms	$55,000 - $100,000
Over 500 rooms	$95,000 - $110,000

For purposes of this assessment, the middle of the range of construction costs and the
average number of guest rooms in hotels for each size group that were completed in 2001 and 2002 are used to estimate the total construction costs of hotels as shown in Table 8.2.3.

Table 8.2.3 – Hotel Construction Costs (text version)

Size	Average Number of Rooms in New	Construction Costs (Millions)

Printed by Builder's Book, Inc., Bookstore · www.buildersbook.com

	Hotels Completed in 2001 & 2002	
Under 75 rooms	56	$1.8
75 – 149 rooms	102	$4.8
150 – 299 rooms	207	$12.9
300 – 500 rooms	388	$30.1
Over 500 rooms	797	$81.7

The average size and value of hotel construction projects reported in the Dodge Construction Potentials Bulletin (35,100 sq. ft.; $4.0 million) are equivalent to a hotel with 75 to 149 guest rooms. The number of construction projects reported in the Dodge Construction Potentials Bulletin (1,121 projects) is considered representative of the number of hotels that will be affected by the revisions. It is assumed that the hotel construction projects have guest rooms in the same percentages as new hotels completed during 2001 and 2002 as shown in Table 8.2.4.

Table 8.2.4 – Hotel Construction Projects by Size (text version)

Size	Percentage of New Hotels Completed in 2001 & 2002	Hotel Construction Projects Started in 2002
Under 75 rooms	41%	460
75 – 149 rooms	45%	504
150 – 299 rooms	11%	123
300 – 500 rooms	2%	22
Over 500 rooms	1%	11
Total	100%	1,120

8.2.2   Revisions That Affect Hotels

Van Accessible Parking Spaces

Hotels that have between 601 and 3,200 parking spaces will have to widen one access aisle from 5 feet to 8 feet. For each additional 1,800 parking spaces over 3,200, an additional access aisle will have to be widened by 3 feet. For purposes of this assessment, it is assumed that 100 percent of hotels with 300 or more guest rooms (33 hotels) will have between 601 and 3,200 parking spaces.

Ambulatory Accessible Toilet Compartments

Men's toilet rooms with six or more water closets and urinals, but fewer than six toilet compartments, will have to provide an ambulatory accessible toilet compartment with grab bars. Plumbing codes typically specify the minimum number of plumbing fixtures required based on the type of building and occupant load. Plumbing fixtures are usually divided equally between men's and women's toilet rooms; and urinals are allowed to be provided in place of a certain number of water closets in men's toilet rooms. For purposes of this assessment, it is

163

assumed that 100 percent of hotels with 300 to 500 rooms (22 hotels) will have one men's toilet room with six or more water closets and urinals, but fewer than six toilet compartments. It is also assumed that 100 percent of hotels with over 500 rooms (11 hotels) will have two men's toilet rooms with six or more water closets and urinals, but fewer than six toilet compartments.

Public TTYs

Hotels are currently required to provide a public TTY in buildings with four or more public pay telephones. Under the final revised guidelines, hotels will have to provide a public TTY in buildings with four or more public pay telephones; on floors with four or more public pay telephones; and in banks with four or more public pay telephones. Banks of telephones located on the same floor within 200 feet from a bank with a public TTY are exempt from the requirement. For purposes of this assessment, it is assumed that 100 percent of hotels with 300 to 500 rooms (22 hotels) will have four or more public pay telephones on two floors and will have to provide an additional public TTY. It is also assumed that 100 percent of hotels with over 500 rooms (11 hotels) will have three banks of telephones with four or more public pay telephones and that the banks are not located within 200 feet on the same floor, and will have to provide two additional public TTYs.

Operable Windows

Where guest rooms with mobility features have windows that can be opened, at least one window per room will have to meet the technical requirements for operable parts. With the exception of single story motel type lodging, windows in hotels are typically fixed and do not open. For purposes of this assessment, it is assumed that 50 percent of hotels with under 75 guest rooms (230 hotels), and 25 percent of hotels with 75 to 149 guest rooms (126 hotels) will have windows that open.

Water Closet Clearance

If a bathroom in a guest room with mobility features has an out-swinging door, the bathroom will have to be increased by 9 square feet to provide the 60 inches by 56 inches minimum clearance around the water closet. Bathrooms usually have in-swinging doors. For purposes of this assessment, it is assumed that in 25 percent of hotels (281 hotels) guest rooms with mobility features will have bathrooms with an out-swinging door.

Shower Spray Controls

Bathtubs and showers in guest rooms with mobility features will have to provide an on/off control on hand held shower sprays. For purposes of this assessment, it is assumed that in 100 percent of hotels (1,120 hotels) hand held shower sprays in guest rooms with mobility features will need an on/off control.

Galley Kitchen Clearance

164

If a guest suite with mobility features has a galley kitchen with a cooktop or range and is enclosed on three sides, the kitchen will have to be increased by 13 square feet to provide 60 inches minimum clearance between the counters or walls. Extended stay hotels and suite hotels sometimes have kitchens with a cooktop or range. For purposes of this assessment, it is assumed that 5 percent of hotels with 75 to 149 rooms (23 hotels) will have a galley kitchen with a cooktop or range in guest suites with mobility features.

Vanity Counter Space

Guest rooms with mobility features will have to provide vanity counter space that is comparable to the counter space in other guest rooms. In some hotels, comparable vanity counter space is provided in guest rooms with mobility features, and in other hotels it is not. For purposes of this assessment, it is assumed that in 50 percent of hotels (561 hotels) guest rooms with mobility features will need to provide comparable vanity counter space.

The revisions that affect hotels are summarized in Table 8.2.5. The minimum number of guest rooms with mobility features is based on the highest number of guest rooms for the hotel size group. For example, the minimum number of guest rooms with mobility features for hotels with 75 to 149 guest rooms is based on 149 rooms. For hotels with over 500 guest rooms, the minimum number of guestrooms with mobility features is based on 800 rooms.

Table 8.2.5 – Revisions That Affect Hotels (text version)

Revision	Assumptions: Percentage (Number) of Hotels Affected	Costs Per Facility Compared to		
		Current Guidelines	IBC 2000	IBC 2003
Van Accessible Parking Spaces	100% (33) Hotels with 300 or More Rooms Have 601 – 3,200 Parking Spaces	$344	$344	$0
Ambulatory Accessible Toilet Compartments	100% (22) Hotels with 300 – 500 Rooms Have 1 Men's Toilet Rooms with 6 or More Water Closets and Urinals, but Fewer than 6 Toilet Compartments	$145	$0	$0
	100% (11) Hotels with over 500 Rooms Have 2 Men's Toilet Rooms with 6 or More Water Closets and Urinals, but Fewer than 6 Toilet Compartments	$290	$0	$0
Public TTYs	100% (22) Hotels with 300 – 500 Rooms Have 4 or More Public Pay Telephones on 2 Floors	$2,320	$2,320	$2,320
	100% (11) Hotels with over 500 Rooms Have 3 Banks with 4 or More Public Pay Telephones	$4,640	$4,640	$4,640

165

Operable Windows	50% (230) Hotels with under 75 Rooms Have Operable Windows in 4 Rooms with Mobility Features	$2,020	$0	$0
	25% (126) Hotels with 75 – 149 Rooms Have Operable Windows in 7 Rooms with Mobility Features	$3,535	$0	$0
Water Closet Clearance	25% (115) Hotels with under 75 Rooms Have Bathroom with Out-Swinging Door in 4 Rooms with Mobility Features	$2,668	$0	$0
	25% (126) Hotels with 75 -149 Rooms Have Bathroom with Out-Swinging Door in 7 Rooms with Mobility Features	$4,669	$0	$0
	25% (31) Hotels with 150 – 299 Rooms Have Bathroom with Out-Swinging Door in 10 Rooms with Mobility Features	$6,670	$0	$0
	25% (6) Hotels with 300 – 500 Rooms Have Bathroom with Out-Swinging Door in 13 Rooms with Mobility Features	$8,671	$0	$0
	25% (3) Hotels with over 500 Rooms Have Bathroom with Out-Swinging Door in 28 Rooms with Mobility Features	$18,676	$0	$0
Shower Spray Controls	100% (460) Hotels with under 75 Rooms Have to Provide Shower Spray Controls in 4 Rooms with Mobility Features	$644	$644	$644
	100% (504) Hotels with 75 -149 Rooms Have to Provide Shower Spray Controls in 7 Rooms with Mobility Features	$1,127	$1,127	$1,127
	100% (123) Hotels with 150 – 299 Rooms Have to Provide Shower Spray Controls in 10 Rooms with Mobility Features	$1,610	$1,610	$1,160
	100% (22) Hotels with 300 – 500 Rooms Have to Provide Shower Spray Controls in 13 Rooms with Mobility Features	$2,093	$2,093	$2,093
	100% (11) Hotels with over 500 Rooms Have to Provide Shower Spray Controls in 28 Rooms with Mobility Features	$4,508	$4,508	$4,508
Galley Kitchen Clearance	5% (23)Hotels with 75 – 149 rooms Have Galley Kitchen in 7 Rooms	$6,951	$6,951	$6,951

166

	with Mobility Features			
Vanity Counter Space	50% (230) Hotels with under 75 Rooms Have to Provide Vanity Counter Space in 4 Rooms with Mobility Features	$3,008	$3,008	$3,008
	50% (252) Hotels with 75 -149 Rooms Have to Provide Vanity Counter Space in 7 Rooms with Mobility Features	$5,264	$5,264	$5,264
	50% (62) Hotels with 150 – 299 Rooms Have to Provide Vanity Counter Space in 10 Rooms with Mobility Features	$7,520	$7,520	$7,520
	50% (11) Hotels with 300 – 500 Rooms Have to Provide Vanity Counter Space in 13 Rooms with Mobility Features	$9,776	$9,776	$9,776
	50% (6) Hotels with over 500 Rooms Have to Provide Vanity Counter Space in 28 Rooms with Mobility Features	$21,056	$21,056	$21,056

8.2.3 Additional Costs for Hotels

For purposes of estimating the additional costs of the revisions for the construction of individual hotels, the assumptions summarized in Table 8.2.5 are applied, except that it is assumed that each hotel is affected by water closet clearance and vanity counter space; each hotel with under 75 guest rooms is affected by operable windows; and each hotel with 75 to 149 guest rooms is affected by operable windows and galley kitchen clearance. The additional costs of the revisions for the construction of individual hotels are shown in Table 8.2.6.

167

Table 8.2.6 – Additional Costs for Hotels (text version)

Hotel & Construction Costs	Additional Costs Compared to (Percentage of Total Construction Costs)		
	Current Guidelines	IBC 2000	IBC 2003
Under 75 rooms $1.8 Million	$8,340 (0.5%)	$3,652 (0.2%)	$3,652 (0.2%)
75 – 149 rooms $4.8 Million	$21,546 (0.4%)	$13,342 (0.3%)	$13,342 (0.3%)
150 – 299 rooms $12.9 Million	$15,800 (0.1%)	$9,130 (0.07%)	$9,130 (0.07%)
300 – 500 rooms $30.1 Million	$23,349 (0.08%)	$14,533 (0.05%)	$14,189 (0.05%)
Over 500 rooms $81.7 Million	$49,514 (0.06%)	$30,548 (0.04%)	$30,204 (0.04%)

8.2.4 National Costs for Hotels

For purposes of estimating the national costs of the revisions for the construction of hotels, the assumptions summarized in Table 8.2.5 regarding the number of hotels affected by each revision are applied. The national costs for the construction of hotels are shown in Table 8.2.7.

Table 8.2.7 – National Costs for Hotels (text version)

Revision	Assumptions: Number of Hotels Affected	National Costs Compared to		
		Current Guidelines Upper Bound	IBC 2000 Lower Bound	IBC 2003 Lower Bound
Van Accessible Parking Spaces	33 Hotels with 300 or More Rooms	$11,352	$11,352	$0
Ambulatory Accessible Toilet Compartments	22 Hotels with 300 – 500 Rooms	$3,190	$0	$0
	11 Hotels with over 500 Rooms	$3,190	$0	$0
Public TTYs	22 Hotels with 300 – 500 Rooms	$51,040	$51,040	$51,040
	11 Hotels with over 500 Rooms	$51,040	$51,040	$51,040
Operable Windows	230 Hotels with under 75 Rooms	$464,600	$0	$0
	126 Hotels with 75 – 149 Rooms	$445,410	$0	$0
Water Closet Clearance	115 Hotels with under 75 Rooms	$306,820	$0	$0

168

	126 Hotels with 75 -149 Rooms	$588,294	$0	$0
	31 Hotels with 150 – 299 Rooms	$206,770	$0	$0
	6 Hotels with 300 – 500 Rooms	$68,671	$0	$0
	3 Hotels with over 500 Rooms	$56,028	$0	$0
Shower Spray Controls	460 Hotels with under 75Rooms	$296,240	$296,240	$296,240
	504 Hotels with 75 -149 Rooms	$568,008	$568,008	$568,008
	123 Hotels with 150 – 299 Rooms	$198,030	$198,030	$198,030
	22 Hotels with 300 – 500 Rooms	$46,046	$46,046	$46,046
	11 Hotels with over 500 Rooms	$49,588	$49,588	$49,588
Galley Kitchen Clearance	23 Hotels with 75 – 149 Rooms	$159,873	$159,873	$159,873
Vanity Counter Space	230 Hotels with under 75 Rooms	$691,840	$691,840	$691,840
	252 Hotels with 75 -149 Rooms	$1,326,528	$1,326,528	$1,326,528
	61 Hotels with 150 – 299 Rooms	$466,240	$466,240	$466,240
	11 Hotels with 300 – 500 Rooms	$107,536	$107,536	$107,536
	6 Hotels with over 500 Rooms	$126,336	$126,336	$126,336
	Total (Millions)	**$6.2**	**$4.1**	**$4.1**

8.3 Hospitals and Nursing Homes

8.3.1   Hospital and Nursing Home Data

The Dodge Construction Potentials Bulletin reports that 7,480 construction projects for hospitals and health care facilities were started in 2002. Hospital and health care construction projects totaled 97 million square feet valued at $15.9 billion (average project size: 12,190 sq. ft.; average project value: $2.1 million). The construction projects include freestanding outpatient facilities and other health care facilities that will not be affected by the revisions.

The Census Bureau Annual Value of Construction Put in Place reports that the value of hospital and health care facility construction work installed during 2002 was $27.6 billion. Hospital construction work alone was $17.0 billion. New construction accounted for 46 percent of the hospital work ($7.9 billion), and additions and alterations accounted for 54 percent of the hospital work ($9.1 billion).

169

The American Hospital Association (AHA) conducts an annual survey of existing hospitals. The 2003 AHA Hospital Statistics reports that there were 5,801 registered hospitals and 987,440 staffed beds in 2001 (average staffed beds per hospital: 170).

Modern Healthcare conducts an annual survey of hospital and health care facility construction, projects. The survey results for hospital and nursing home construction projects started in 2002 are shown in Table 8.3.1.

Table 8.3.1 – Hospital and Nursing Home (text version)
Construction Projects Started in 2002

Facility	Projects	Beds (New or Replacement)	Construction Costs (Billions)
Acute Care Hospital	1,207	124,710	$15.7
Specialty Hospital	177	5,399	$3.2
Rehabilitation Hospital	41	1,455	$.4
Nursing Home	64	5,159	$.6
Total	1,489	136,723	$19.9

The typical patient sleeping room has one bed and is 150 to 200 square feet, excluding the toilet room and closet. The total floor area of a hospital will depend on the facilities provided, including rooms for surgery and other procedures.

Hospital construction costs vary widely depending on location and facilities provided. Modern Healthcare provides data on the size and costs of hospital construction projects. A sample of projects under design or construction in 2003 included a new 80 bed hospital in Florida costing $80 million; a 130 bed addition to an existing hospital in Missouri, including seven operating rooms and 20 obstetrics suites, costing $137 million; and a new 170 bed hospital in Tennessee costing $80 million.

Since the construction projects in the Dodge Construction Potentials Bulletin include other health care facilities that will not be affected by the revisions, and the average value of the construction projects ($2.1 million) is extremely small compared to the sample of hospital construction projects in Modern Healthcare ($80 million to $137 million), the number of hospital and nursing home construction projects in the Modern Healthcare survey (1,425 hospital projects with 131,564 new or replacement beds valued at $19.3 billion; 64 nursing home projects with 5,159 new or replacement beds valued at $0.6 billion) is used for purposes of estimating the national costs of the revisions for hospitals and nursing homes. It is assumed that the patient sleeping rooms in hospitals have one bed and that 10 percent of the beds in rehabilitation hospitals specialize in treating conditions that affect mobility. It is also assumed that 50 percent of the patient sleeping rooms in nursing homes have one bed per room, and 50 percent have two beds per room. A minimum of 15,223 patient sleeping rooms with mobility features will be affected by the revisions as shown in Table 8.3.2.

170

Table 8.3.2 – Patient Sleeping Rooms with Mobility Features (text version)

Facility	Beds (New or Replacement)		Minimum Number Rooms with Mobility Features	
Acute Care Hospital		124,710	10%	12,471
Specialty Hospital		5,399	10%	540
Rehabilitation Hospital	(Mobility conditions)	146	100%	146
	(Other conditions)	1,309	10%	131
Nursing Home	(1 bed per room)	2,580	50%	1,290
	(2 beds per room)	2,580	50%	645
Total		136,723		15,223

8.3.2 Revisions That Affect Hospitals and Nursing Homes

Van Accessible Parking Spaces

Hospitals that have between 601 and 3,200 parking spaces will have to widen one access aisle from 5 feet to 8 feet. For each additional 1,800 parking spaces over 3,200, an additional access aisle will have to be widened by 3 feet. For purposes of this assessment, it is assumed that 100 percent of hospitals (1,425 hospitals) will have between 601 and 3,200 parking spaces. It is also assumed that nursing homes will not have more than 600 parking spaces.

Ambulatory Accessible Toilet Compartments

Men's toilet rooms with six or more water closets and urinals, but less than six toilet compartments, will have to provide an ambulatory accessible toilet compartment with grab bars. For purposes of this assessment, it is assumed that in hospitals and nursing homes men's toilet rooms will have less than six water closets and urinals.

Public TTYs

Hospitals are currently required to provide a public TTY near emergency rooms, recovery rooms, and waiting rooms if a public pay telephone is provided at any of these locations. The final revised guidelines do not change this requirement. For purposes of this assessment, it is assumed that hospitals will not have to provide any additional public TTYs than currently required.

Nursing homes are currently required to provide a public TTY in buildings with four or more public pay telephones. Under the final revised guidelines, nursing homes will have to provide a public TTY in buildings with four or more public pay telephones; on floors with four or more public pay telephones; and in banks with four or more public pay telephones. For purposes of this assessment, it is assumed that nursing homes will not have four or more public pay telephones on a floor or in a bank.

171

Operable Windows

Where patient sleeping rooms with mobility features have windows that can be opened, at least one window per room will have to meet the technical requirements for operable parts. Patient sleeping rooms in hospitals typically have fixed windows that do not open to control infection risks. Hospitals and nursing homes also typically provide fixed windows for energy and cost considerations. For purposes of this assessment, it is assumed that in hospitals patient sleeping rooms with mobility features will not have operable windows, and in nursing homes 50 percent of patient sleeping rooms with mobility features (968 rooms) will have operable windows.

Water Closet Clearance

Toilet rooms in patient sleeping rooms with mobility features usually have out-swinging doors and will have to be increased by 9 square feet to provide the 60 inches by 56 inches minimum clearance at the water closet. For purposes of this assessment, it is assumed that 100 percent of patient sleeping rooms with mobility features (15,223 rooms) will be impacted by this revision.

Shower Spray Controls

Bathtubs and showers in patient sleeping rooms with mobility features will have to provide an on/off control on hand held shower sprays. For purposes of this assessment, it is assumed that in 100 percent of patient sleeping rooms with mobility features (15,223 rooms) hand held shower sprays will need an on/off control.

The revisions that affect hospitals and nursing homes are summarized in Table 8.3.3.

Table 8.3.3 – Revisions That Affect Hospitals and Nursing Homes (text version)

Revision	Assumptions: Percentage (Number) of Hospitals and Nursing Homes/ Patient Sleeping Rooms with Mobility Features Affected	Costs Per Facility/Patient Sleeping Room Compared to		
		Current Guidelines	IBC 2000	IBC 2003
Van Accessible Parking Spaces	100% (1,425) Hospitals Have 601 – 3,200 Parking Spaces	$344	$344	$0
Operable Windows	50% (968) Patient Sleeping Rooms with Mobility Features in Nursing Homes Have Operable Windows	$505	$0	$0
Water Closet Clearance	100% (15,223) Patient Sleeping Rooms with Mobility Features Have Toilet Rooms with Out-Swinging Doors	$667	$0	$0
Shower Spray	100% (15,223) Patient Sleeping Rooms with Mobility Features Have	$161	$161	$161

| Controls | to Provide Shower Spray Controls | | | | | |

8.3.3 Additional Costs for Hospitals

For purposes of estimating the additional costs of the revisions for the construction of individual hospitals, the lower end of the hospital construction costs sampled in Modern Healthcare is used: a new hospital with 170 beds costing $80 million. The hospital is required to provide a minimum of 17 patient sleeping rooms with mobility features. It is assumed that the hospital is affected by all the revisions in Table 8.3.2, except for operable windows. The additional costs of the revisions for the construction of individual hospitals are $14,420 compared to the current guidelines, which is 0.02 percent of the total construction costs; and $3,081 compared to the 2000 edition of the International Building Code and $2,737 compared to the 2003 edition of the International Building Code, which are 0.00% of the total construction costs.

8.3.4 National Costs for Hospitals and Nursing Homes

For purposes of estimating the national costs of the revisions for the construction of hospitals and nursing rooms, the assumptions summarized in Table 8.3.2 regarding the number of facilities and patient sleeping rooms with mobility features affected by each revision are applied. The national costs of the revisions for the construction of hospitals and nursing homes are shown in Table 8.3.4.

Table 8.3.4 –National Costs for Hospitals and Nursing Homes (text version)

Revision	Assumptions: Number of Hospitals and Nursing Homes/ Patient Sleeping Rooms with Mobility Features Affected	National Costs Compared to		
		Current Guidelines Upper Bound	IBC 2000 Lower Bound	IBC 2003 Lower Bound
Van Accessible Parking Spaces	1,425 Hospitals	$490,200	$490,200	$0
Operable Windows	968 Patient Sleeping Rooms with Mobility Features	$488,840	$0	$0
Water Closet Clearance	15,223 Patient Sleeping Rooms with Mobility Features	$10,153,741	$0	$0
Shower Spray Controls	15,223 Patient Sleeping Rooms with Mobility Features	$2,450,903	$2,450,903	$2,450,903
Total (Millions)		$13.6	$2.9	$2.4

8.4 Federal, State, and Local Government Housing

8.4.1 Federal, State, and Local Government Housing Data

173

The Dodge Construction Potentials Bulletin reports that the value of residential construction projects started by Federal, State, and local governments in 2002 was $2.8 billion. The Dodge Construction Potentials Bulletin does not include data on the total number of the Federal, State, and local government residential construction projects, or the total floor area of the projects.

The Census Bureau Annual Value of Construction Put in Place reports that the value of residential construction work installed by Federal, State, and local governments during 2002 was $6.0 billion as shown in Table 8.4.1.

Table 8.4.1 – Value of Residential Construction Put in Place by Federal, State, and Local Governments in 2002 (Millions of Dollars) (text version)

Government	New Construction	Alteration	Total
Federal	$818	$617	$1,435
State and Local	$1,265	$3,327	$4,592
Total	$2,083	$3,944	$6,027

New construction accounted for 35 percent of the work ($2.0 billion), and additions and alterations accounted for 65 percent of the work ($4.0 billion). Ninety eight percent of the State and local government residential construction projects are multi-family residential facilities.

The Census Bureau Characteristics of New Housing Completed in 2002 provides the following information on rental units in privately owned multi-family residential facilities:

- 77 percent of multi-family residential construction projects are completed within 12 months.

- 47 percent of the units have two bedrooms, 33 percent have one bedroom, 17 percent have three or more bedrooms, and 2 percent are efficiencies.

- The median floor area is 1,070 square feet.

If the percentage of Federal, State, and local government multi-family residential construction projects completed within 12 months is equivalent to percentage of private multi-family construction projects completed within the same period (77 percent completed within 12 months), the values in the Dodge Construction Potentials Bulletin ($2.8 billion) and the Census Bureau Annual Value of Construction Put in Place ($6.0 Billion) should not differ so widely. The Dodge Construction Potentials Bulletin may underestimate the value of Federal, State, and local government residential construction, and the Census Bureau Annual Value of Construction Put in Place may be a better indicator of the number of dwelling units constructed or altered by Federal, State, and local governments. This assessment uses the Census Bureau Annual Value of Construction Put in Place to estimate the national costs for Federal, State, and local government housing.

174

Construction costs for multi-family residential facilities range from $100 to $120 per square foot. The lower range is used for purposes of this assessment. A two bedroom dwelling unit is assumed to be 1,000 square feet and cost $100,000 to construct. The annual value of residential new construction work by Federal, State, and local governments ($2.1 billion) is equivalent to 21,000 new two bedroom dwelling units. A minimum of 1,050 of the units are required to provide mobility features, and a minimum of 420 of the units are required to provide communication features as shown in Table 8.4.2.

Table 8.4.2 - Value of Residential New Construction Work Equivalent to New Two Bedroom Dwelling Units (text version)

Government	New Construction Work	Two Bedroom Units (Assume $100,000 per Unit)	Minimum Number Units with Mobility Features (5 Percent)	Minimum Number Units with Communication Features (2 Percent)
Federal	$0.8 Billion	8,000	400	160
State and Local	$1.3 Billion	13,000	650	260
Total	$2.1 Billion	21,000	1,050	420

For purposes of this assessment, it is assumed that it costs $50,000 to substantially alter a dwelling unit and that the annual value of residential alteration work by Federal, State, and local governments ($3.9 billion) is equivalent to 78,000 substantially altered dwelling units. A minimum of 3900 dwelling units are required to have mobility features, and a minimum of 1,560 dwelling units are required to have communication features as shown in Table 8.4.3.

Table 8.4.3 - Value of Residential Alteration Work Equivalent to Substantially Altered Two Bedroom Dwelling Units (text version)

Government	Alteration Work	Two Bedroom Units (Assume $50,000 per Unit)	Minimum Number Units with Mobility Features (5 Percent)	Minimum Number Units with Communication Features (2 Percent)
Federal	$0.6 Billion	12,000	600	240
State and Local	$3.3 Billion	66,000	3,300	1,320
Total	$3.9 Billion	78,000	3,900	1,560

8.4.2 Revisions That Affect Federal, State, and Local Government Housing

Water Closet Clearance

If a bathroom in a dwelling unit with mobility features has an out-swinging door, the bathroom will have to be increased by 4 square feet to provide the 60 inches

175

by 56 inches minimum clearance around the water closet. Bathrooms usually have in-swinging doors. For purposes of this assessment, it is assumed that 25 percent of dwelling units with mobility features (1,238 units) will have bathrooms with an out-swinging door.

Shower Spray Controls

Bathtubs and showers in dwelling units with mobility features will have to provide an on/off control on hand held shower sprays. For purposes of this assessment, it is assumed that hand held shower spray units in 100 percent of dwelling units with mobility features (4,950 units) will need an on/off control.

Galley Kitchen Clearance

If a dwelling unit with mobility features has a galley kitchen and the space is enclosed on three sides, the kitchen will have to be increased by 13 square feet to provide 60 inches minimum clearance between the counters or walls. For purposes of this assessment, it is assumed that 75 percent of dwelling units with mobility features (3,713 units) will have a galley kitchen and the space is enclosed on three sides.

Communication Features

Dwelling units required to provide communication features will have to provide a doorbell with audible and visible signals and a door peephole to identify visitors. For purposes of this assessment, it assumed that 50 percent of dwelling units required to provide communication features (990 units) will have doorbells with audible signals and door peepholes, and will need to add a visible signal to the doorbell; and that the other 50 percent (990 units) will not have doorbells or door peepholes, and will need doorbells with audible and visible signals and door peepholes. Where a voice communication system is provided to gain entry to a building with dwelling units required to provide communication features, the system will have to be capable of supporting TTY communication. For purposes of this assessment, it is assumed that 25 percent of dwelling units required to provide communication features (495 units) will be in a building where a voice communication system is provided to gain entry to the building.

The revisions that affect Federal, State, and local government housing are summarized in Table 8.4.4.

Table 8.4.4 – Revisions That Affect Federal, State, and Local Government Housing (text version)

Revision	Assumptions: Percentage (Number) of Dwelling Units with Mobility Features or Communication Features Affected	Costs per Dwelling Unit Compared to	
		Current Guidelines	IBC 2000 & 2003
Water Closet Clearance	25% (1,238) Dwelling Units with Mobility Features Have Bathrooms with Out-Swing Doors	$286	$286
Shower Spray	100% (4,950) Dwelling Units with	$161	$161

176

Controls	Mobility Features Have to Provide Shower Spray Controls		
Galley Kitchen Clearance	75% (3,713) Dwelling Units with Mobility Features Have Galley Kitchens	$993	$993
Doorbells with Audible and Visual Signals and Door Peepholes	50% (990) Dwelling Units with Communication Features Have Doorbells with Audible Signals and Door Peepholes	$96	$96
	50% (990) Dwelling Units with Communication Features Have No Doorbell or Door Peephole	$322	$322
Voice Communication System at Entry Support TTY Communication	25% (495) Dwelling Units with Communication Features in Facilities with Voice Communication System at Entry to Site, Building, or Floor	$353	$353

8.4.3 Additional Costs for Federal, State, and Local Government Housing

For purposes of estimating the additional costs of the revisions for the construction of Federal, State, and local government housing, the assumptions summarized in Table 8.4.4 are applied, except that it is assumed that each dwelling unit with mobility features is affected by water closet clearance and galley kitchen clearance. It is also assumed that each dwelling unit required to provide communication features will not have a doorbell or door peephole, and will be in buildings where a voice communication system is provided to gain entry to the building. Federal, State, and local governments usually construct or alter housing as part of a project consisting of a number of dwelling units located on a common site or several sites. The additional costs for dwelling units with mobility features and dwelling units with communication features will be incurred as part of the entire housing project costs. Since most of the additional costs for the revisions are for dwelling units with mobility features and a minimum of 5 percent (or one in 20) dwelling units is required to provide mobility features, the additional costs of the revisions are shown in Table 8.4.5 as a percentage of the total construction costs for a housing project with 20 dwelling units.

Table 8.4.5 – Additional Costs for Federal, State, and Local Government Housing (text version)

Dwelling Unit & Project Costs	Additional Costs Compared to (Percentage of Total Project Construction Costs)	
	Current Guidelines	IBC 2000 & 2003
Dwelling Unit with Mobility Features	$1,440	$1,440
Dwelling Unit with Communication Features	$675	$675
Project with 20 Dwelling Units $2 million	$2,115 (0.01%)	$2,115 (0.01%)

177

8.4.4 National Costs for Federal, State, and Local Government Housing

For purposes of estimating the national costs of the revisions for the construction of Federal, State, and local government housing, the assumptions summarized in Table 8.4.4 regarding the number of dwelling units with mobility features and dwelling units with communication features affected by each revision are applied. The national costs for the construction of Federal, State, and local government housing are shown in Table 8.4.6.

Table 8.4.6 – National Costs for Federal, State, and Local Government Housing (text version)

Revision	Assumptions: Number of Dwelling Units with Mobility Features or Communication Features Affected	National Costs Compared to	
		Current Guidelines Upper Bound	IBC 2000 & 2003 Lower Bound
Water Closet Clearance	1,238 Dwelling Units with Mobility Features	$354,068	$354,068
Shower Spray Controls	4,950 Dwelling Units with Mobility Features	$796,950	$796,950
Galley Kitchen Clearance	3,713 Dwelling Units with Mobility Features	$3,687,009	$3,687,009
Doorbells with Audible and Visual Signals and Door Peepholes	990 Dwelling Units with Communication Features That Have Doorbells with Audible Signals and Door Peepholes	$95,040	$95,040
	990 Dwelling Units with Communication Features That Have No Doorbell and No Door Peephole	$318,780	$318,780
Voice Communication System at Entry Support TTY Communication	495 Dwelling Units with Communication Features in Facilities That Have Voice Communication System at Entry to Site, Building, or Floor	$174,735	$174,735
	Total (Millions)	$5.4	$5.4

8.5 Other Large Facilities

Three of the revisions that have monetary impacts will affect the new construction and alterations of other large facilities. The three revisions are summarized in Table 8.5.1.

Table 8.5.1 – Revisions That Affect New Construction and Alterations of Other Large Facilities (text version)

Revision & Facilities Affected	Current Guidelines	Final Revised Guidelines &	Unit Cost

178

		International Building Code	
Van Accessible Parking Spaces Facilities with more than 600 parking spaces.	One in every 8 accessible parking spaces required to be van accessible.	One in every 6 accessible parking spaces required to be van accessible. **IBC 2003:** Equivalent requirement.	$344 for paving and striping 3 additional feet of access aisle in facilities with 601 to 3200 parking spaces $344 for each additional 1800 parking spaces over 3200
Ambulatory Accessible Toilet Compartments Facilities with men's toilet rooms that have 6 or more water closets and urinals, but fewer than 6 toilet compartments.	Toilet rooms with 6 or more toilet compartments required to provide ambulatory accessible toilet compartment with grab bars	Toilet rooms with 6 or more toilet compartments, or combination of 6 or more water closets and urinals, required to provide ambulatory accessible toilet compartment with grab bars. **IBC 2000 & 2003:** Equivalent requirement.	$145 for grab bars
Public TTYs Private facilities with 4 or more public telephones on more than one floor or in bank of telephones. Government facilities with public telephone on more than one floor, or 4 or more public telephones in bank of telephones. Bus and rail stations with fewer than 4 public telephones at	Private facilities with 4 or more public telephones required to provide public TTY. Government facilities with public telephone in public use area of building, required to provide public TTY. Rail stations with 4 or more public telephones at entrance required to provide public TTY at entrance.	Private facilities required to provide public TTY in building with 4 or more public telephones, and on floor with 4 or more public telephones. Government facilities required to provide public TTY in building with public telephone, and on floor with public telephone. Private facilities and government facilities required to provide public TTY in bank of 4 or more public telephones.	$2,320 for public TTY

179

entrance.		Banks of public telephones located within 200 feet of, and on the same floor as, another bank of telephones with public TTY exempt.	
Public rest stops with public telephones.			
		Private facilities and government facilities required to provide public TTY on exterior site with 4 or more public telephones.	
		Bus or rail stations with public telephone at entrance required to provide public TTY at entrance.	
		Public rest stops with public telephone required to provide public TTY.	
		IBC 2000 (Appendix E): Equivalent requirement for private facilities.	
		IBC 2003 (Appendix E): Equivalent requirement for private and government facilities.	

The costs of the three revisions for the construction of large office buildings, hotels, and hospitals are summarized in Tables 8.5.2 through 8.5.4.

Table 8.5.2 –Costs for Large Office Buildings (text version)

Revision	Facilities Affected Annually	National Costs (Millions)	Percentage of Facility Construction Costs
Compared to Current Guidelines (Upper Bound)			
Van Accessible Parking Spaces	200	$0.07	0.0006%
Ambulatory Accessible Toilet Compartments	230	$0.62	0.0058%
Public TTYs	99	$0.23	0.0044%
Total	230	$0.92	0.0104%

		Compared to IBC 2000 & 2003 (Lower Bound)	
Van Accessible Parking Spaces	200	$0.00	0.0000%
Ambulatory Accessible Toilet Compartments	230	$0.00	0.0000%
Public TTYs	99	$0.23	0.0044%
Total	230	$0.23	0.0044%

Table 8.5.3 – Costs for Large Hotels (text version)

Revision	Facilities Affected Annually	National Costs (Millions)	Percentage of Facility Construction Costs
Compared to Current Guidelines (Upper Bound)			
Van Accessible Parking Spaces	33	$0.01	0.0004% to 0.0011%
Ambulatory Accessible Toilet Compartments	33	$0.00	0.0004%
Public TTYs	33	$0.10	0.0057% to 0.0077%
Total	33	$0.11	0.0065% to 0.0093%
Compared to IBC 2000 & 2003 (Lower Bound)			
Van Accessible Parking Spaces	33	$0.00	0.0000%
Ambulatory Accessible Toilet Compartments	33	$0.00	0.0000%
Public TTYs	33	$0.10	0.0057% to 0.0077%
Total	33	$0.10	0.0057% to 0.0077%

Table 8.5.4 –Costs for Large Hospitals (text version)

Revision	Facilities Affected Annually	National Costs (Millions)	Percentage of Facility Construction Costs
Compared to Current Guidelines (Upper Bound)			
Van Accessible Parking Spaces	1,425	$0.49	0.0004%
Ambulatory Accessible Toilet Compartments	0	$0.00	0.0000%
Public TTYs	0	$0.00	0.0000%

181

Total	1,425	$0.49	0.0004%

Compared to IBC 2000 & 2003 (Lower Bound)			
Van Accessible Parking Spaces	1,425	$0.00	0.0000%
Ambulatory Accessible Toilet Compartments	0	$0.00	0.0000%
Public TTYs	0	$0.00	0.0000%
Total	1,425	$0.00	0.0000%

The costs of the three revisions for the construction of these large facilities are insignificant compared to the total construction costs of the facilities. This disaggregated analysis of the cost of the three revisions for the construction of these large facilities provides a defendable estimate of the costs of the revisions for the construction of other large facilities. The revisions discussed in Chapter 5 that reduce impacts will also offset the additional costs of the three revisions for the construction of some other larger facilities. For example, the additional costs for van accessible parking spaces, ambulatory accessible toilet compartments, and public TTYs will be offset in sports stadiums by the reduced scoping requirements for wheelchair spaces; in shopping malls by the deletion of the scoping requirement for detectable warnings at hazardous vehicular areas; in colleges and universities by the exception permitting the number of required receivers for assistive listening systems to be calculated based on the total number of seats in assembly areas in the building; and in high schools by the exception for accessible routes to small press boxes.

In addition, when compared to the International Building Code, the only costs are for public TTYs. In States that have adopted Appendix E to the International Building Code, which includes an equivalent requirement for public TTYs, there is no additional cost.

8.6 Economically Significant Regulatory Action

This chapter estimates the national costs of the revisions for the construction of facilities that are likely to experience relatively higher costs than other facilities as shown in Table 8.6.1.

Table 8.6.1 – National Costs for Facilities Likely to Experience Relatively Higher Costs (text version)

Facility	National Costs Compared to	
	Current Guidelines Upper Bound	IBC 2000 & 2003 Lower Bound
Office Buildings	$1.5 million	$0.7 million
Hotels	$6.2 million	$4.1 million
Hospitals & Nursing Homes	$13.6 million	$2.9 million
Government Housing	$5.4 million	$5.4 million
Total	$26.7 million	$13.1 million

182

The final revised guidelines will affect the new construction and alterations of other types of facilities not discussed in this chapter. The Dodge Construction Potentials Bulletin reports that the value of non-residential building construction projects started in 2002 was $152 billion. The Census Bureau Annual Value of Construction Put in Place reports that the value of non-residential building construction work, and Federal, State, and local government housing construction work installed in 2002 was $270 billion. In order to be considered an economically significant regulatory action with an annual effect on the economy of $100 million or more, the final revised guidelines would need to have impacts totaling from 0.04 percent to 0.07 percent of the construction costs reported in the Dodge Construction Potentials Bulletin and the Census Bureau Annual Value of Construction Put in Place. These impacts are insignificant for an individual facility, but when added together across the economy are economically significant.

In addition, there are benefits that result from this regulatory action that cannot be quantified, but are substantial. As discussed in Chapter 3, the harmonization of the final revised guidelines with the International Building Code and the ICC/ANSI A117.1 Standard for Accessible and Usable Buildings and Facilities will greatly facilitate compliance with the Americans with Disabilities Act and Architectural Barriers Act, and reduce the likelihood of mistakes that can result in litigation and costly retrofitting of facilities. As discussed in Chapter 5, the final revised guidelines also revise some existing scoping and technical requirements that will reduce the impacts on many facilities.

Because an extremely low threshold of impacts on individual facilities can render the final revised guidelines an economically significant regulatory action, and because the benefits of the final revised guidelines are unquantifiable but substantial, the Access Board has classified the final revised guidelines as an economically significant regulatory action.

CHAPTER 9: LEASED POSTAL FACILITIES

9.0 Introduction

The Architectural Barriers Act requires facilities leased by the Federal government to be accessible to individuals with disabilities. The General Services Administration, which is responsible for most of the leasing activity for the Federal government, requires leased facilities to comply with UFAS and ADAAG, and the final revised guidelines will have minimal impacts on its leasing activities.

The United States Postal Service (USPS), which leases about 27,000 postal facilities, issued standards for its leased facilities in 1986. The USPS surveyed 22 of its leased facilities in 2003 to assess the customer areas and employee areas compliance with the USPS' current standards and the final revised guidelines. The facilities are located in seven States, and range in size from 300 square feet to 20,000 square feet. The facilities have been occupied from 3 years to 50 years. The USPS considers the facilities representative of its current inventory of leased facilities. If an element did not comply with the USPS' current standards or the final revised guidelines, estimates were prepared for altering the element to bring it into compliance and the costs were assigned to either the USPS' current standards or the final revised guidelines. The costs for altering the facilities to comply with the final revised guidelines ranged from $950 for a 17,415 square feet facility that has been occupied for 17 years, to $45,058 for a 2,086 square feet facility that has been occupied for 48 years.

After the USPS adopts the final revised guidelines as standards, the USPS will need to alter its leased facilities to comply with the final revised guidelines when a new lease is entered into for a facility, including a previously occupied facility. The USPS used the costs for altering the 22 surveyed facilities to comply with the final revised guidelines as the basis for estimating the average cost for altering the 3,322 postal facilities whose lease terms, including options, expire during 2003 or 2004. The average cost was weighted to take into account the size of the facilities and the number of years the facilities have been occupied. The USPS estimated the average cost for altering the 3,332 facilities to comply with the final revised guidelines when new leases are entered into would be $9,234 per facility. The total annual costs for altering the facilities to comply with the final revised guidelines would be $15.3 million based on an average of 1,661 new leases entered into each year.

The final revised guidelines will also have impacts on postal facilities that are newly
constructed or altered by the USPS. In fiscal years 2000 to 2003, the USPS constructed or expanded an average of about 300 facilities per year, including about 200 leased facilities and 100 owned facilities. In fiscal year 2003, the USPS also conducted about 250 major alteration projects at existing facilities. The impacts on new construction and alteration projects will be minimal compared to the impacts on leased facilities.

The results of the USPS' survey are discussed in this chapter.

9.1 Customer Service Counters

The final revised guidelines require a portion of customer service counters in leased facilities to be accessible. Where a parallel approach is provided, the accessible portion of the counter must be at least 36 inches long and no higher than 36 inches. In existing facilities, if making a portion of the counter accessible would result in a reduction in the number of existing counters or existing mailboxes, an exception permits the accessible portion of the counter to be at least 24 inches long where a parallel approach is provided and the clear floor space is centered on the accessible portion of the counter. Where a forward approach is provided, the accessible portion of the counter must be at least 30 inches long and no higher than 36 inches, and knee and toe clearance must be provided under the counter.

The USPS' current standards do not specifically address customer service counters in leased facilities that are not newly constructed or altered. The USPS has designed modular customer service counters that comply with the final

184

revised guidelines, and currently installs the accessible counters in newly constructed or altered postal facilities.

Nineteen of the surveyed facilities do not currently have an accessible customer service counter. The estimates for removing an existing customer service counter and installing an accessible counter ranged from $1,620 to $11,350. For 11 facilities, the estimates were between $4,700 and $4,900. The highest estimate ($11,350) included a new roll-down gate over the customer service counter. The facilities assigned the costs for the accessible customer service counters to the final revised guidelines.

9.2 Van Accessible Parking Spaces

The final revised guidelines require one in every six accessible parking spaces to be van
accessible. The USPS' current standards do not contain any provisions for van accessible parking spaces in leased facilities.

Eight of the surveyed facilities do not provide parking spaces for customers. These facilities have parking available on the street which will not be affected by the final revised guidelines. Another facility, a modular unit that is a carrier annex to a main post office, does not have its own parking lot.

A van accessible parking space, including the access aisle, is 3 feet wider than an accessible parking space. Providing a van accessible parking space in an existing parking lot usually requires restriping some of the parking spaces. The number of parking spaces that need to be restriped will depend on the layout of the parking lot. Six of the surveyed facilities that provide parking spaces for customers estimated the costs for restriping the parking spaces to provide a van accessible parking space. The estimates for restriping the parking spaces ranged from $413 to $1,301. Three facilities assigned the costs for restriping the parking spaces to the final revised guidelines. One facility assigned the costs for restriping the parking spaces to the USPS' current standards because the existing pavement markings were faded. Two facilities will have to repave the existing accessible parking space to make it level and assigned all or most of the costs for repaving and restriping the parking space to the USPS' current standards.

Accessible parking spaces are identified by signs with the International Symbol of Accessibility; and van accessible parking spaces include the words "van accessible" on the signs. Eight of the surveyed facilities that provide parking spaces for customers estimated the costs for providing signs to identify the van accessible parking spaces. The estimates ranged from $113 for a wall mounted sign to $572 for a new pole and sign. Four facilities assigned the costs for providing signs to identify the van accessible parking spaces to the final revised guidelines; and four facilities assigned the costs for the signs to the USPS' current standards because the existing signs did not comply with the standards or needed to be replaced.

9.3 Letter Drops and Stamp Machines

The final revised guidelines require at least one of each type of depository, vending machine, and change machine to meet the technical requirements for operable parts, including 48 inches maximum for an unobstructed high forward or side reach. The USPS' current standards do not specifically address depositories, vending machines, and change machines in leased facilities that are not newly constructed or altered.

Twelve of the surveyed facilities have letter drops and stamp machines above the 48 inches maximum for an unobstructed high forward or side reach. The estimates for lowering the letters drops and stamp machines ranged from $150 to $1,600. Seven facilities assigned the costs for lowering the letter drops and stamp machines to the final revised guidelines, and five facilities assigned the costs to the USPS' current standards.

9.4 Other Customer Areas

Twelve of the surveyed facilities will have to make alterations to provide an accessible route to customer areas. The alterations included replacing curb ramps, sidewalks, and doorway landings; installing ramps; and widening doorways. The estimates for the alterations ranged from $993 to $10,800. The USPS' current standards require an accessible route to customer areas in leased facilities. Nine facilities assigned the costs for the alterations to provide an accessible route to customer areas to the USPS' current standards; two facilities assigned the costs to the final revised guidelines; and one facility assigned some costs to the USPS' current standards and other costs to the final revised guidelines.

The other alterations that will have to be made to customer areas include:

- *Parking Access Aisles* – Two facilities will have to replace built-up curb ramps in parking access aisles. The estimates for replacing the curb ramps ranged from $2,940 to $3,973. The USPS' current standards require parking access aisles in leased facilities to be level. The final revised guidelines specifically prohibit curb ramps from projecting into parking access aisles. The facilities assigned the costs for replacing the curb ramps to the final revised guidelines.

- *Post Office Boxes* – Two facilities reported they will have to relocate post office boxes. The estimates for relocating the post office boxes ranged from $320 to $1,134. The USPS current standards require at least 5 percent of post office boxes to be located in the second or third set of modules from the floor, approximately 12 to 36 inches above the floor. The final revised guidelines require at least 5 percent of mailboxes to comply with the technical requirements for operable parts, including 48 inches maximum for an unobstructed high forward or side reach and 15 inches minimum for an unobstructed low forward or side reach. The facilities assigned the costs for relocating the post office boxes to the final revised guidelines.

186

- *Writing Desks* – Fifteen facilities will have to replace writing desks in customer areas. The estimates for replacing the writing desks ranged from $1,300 to $2,290. The USPS' current standards require at least one writing desk to provide knee clearance and the top of the desk to be between 28 inches to 34 inches above the floor. The final revised guidelines require at least 5 percent of work surfaces to provide knee and toe clearance and the top of the surface to be between 28 inches to 34 inches above the floor. The facilities assigned the costs for replacing the writing desks to the USPS' current standards.

- *Doors* – Ten facilities reported they will have to replace door closers. One facility will also have to replace door hardware to comply with the USPS' current standards.

9.5 Employee Areas

The USPS' current standards require employee areas in leased facilities to comply with the requirements for substantially altered facilities. Substantially altered facilities are required to have at least one accessible route, one accessible entrance, and one accessible toilet room for each sex. Substantially altered facilities are also required to give consideration to providing accessible parking spaces, drinking fountains, storage, fire alarms, public telephones, seating, tables, and work surfaces.

The final revised guidelines do not differentiate between customer areas and employee areas in leased facilities covered by the Architectural Barriers Act. The final revised guidelines require an accessible route to primary function areas in leased facilities, and allow the USPS define what areas are primary function areas. Among the elements and spaces required to be accessible in leased facilities are: parking spaces, toilet rooms, drinking fountains, fire alarms, public telephones, and dining surfaces and work surfaces.

Only 13 of the 22 facilities surveyed their employee areas for accessibility. Three of the facilities will have to make alterations to provide an accessible route to the employee areas. The estimates for the alterations ranged from $2,000 to $13,675. The facilities assigned the costs for the alterations to provide an accessible route to employee areas to the final revised guidelines.

The other alterations that will have to be made to employee areas include:

- *Parking Spaces* – Five facilities will have to alter employee parking spaces to make them accessible. The estimates for altering the employee parking spaces ranged from $400 to $8,900. The facilities assigned the costs to the final revised guidelines.

- *Door Hardware* – Nine facilities will have to replace the door hardware in employee areas. The estimates for replacing the door hardware ranged from $100 to $2,200. Four facilities assigned all or part of the costs to the USPS' current standards, and five facilities assigned the costs to the final revised guidelines.

187

- *Drinking Fountains* – Nine facilities will have to provide an accessible drinking fountain in employee areas. The estimates for an accessible drinking fountain ranged from $2,000 to $2,450. One facility assigned the costs to the USPS' current standards, and eight facilities assigned the costs to the final revised guidelines.

- *Signs* – Three facilities will have to provide accessible signs in employee areas. The surveys do not provide any details about the signs. The estimates for the signs ranged from $200 to $500. The facilities assigned the costs to the final revised guidelines.

- *Other Elements and Spaces* – A facility will have to provide a ramp at an emergency egress door and assigned the costs ($8,100) to the USPS' current standards. A facility will have to alter a toilet room to make it accessible and assigned the costs ($9,594) to the USPS' current standards. A facility will have to alter a toilet room, a counter in a break room, and a locker to make them accessible and assigned some costs ($5,900) to the USPS' current standards and other costs ($250) to the final revised guidelines.

CHAPTER 10: SMALL ENTITIES

10.0   Introduction

The Regulatory Flexibility Act requires agencies to analyze the impacts of proposed and final rules on small entities, and alternatives to minimize any significant economic impacts on small entities. The analysis may be performed in conjunction with the regulatory assessment required by Executive Order 12866. If an agency determines after preliminary analysis that a rule is not expected to have a significant economic impact on a substantial number of small entities, the agency is not required to analyze alternatives to minimize any significant economic impacts on small entities. The agency must certify that the rule has no significant economic impact on a substantial number of small entities, and explain the factual basis for the determination.

10.1   Certification of No Significant Economic Impact

The Access Board prepared a regulatory assessment for the proposed rule. The regulatory assessment analyzed the impacts of the revisions in the proposed rule on the new construction and alterations of facilities by comparing the revisions to the current guidelines; the 1998 edition of the ICC/ANSI A117.1 Standard on Accessible and Usable Buildings and Facilities; and the new International Building Code, which was under development and was expected to be widely adopted by State and local governments. The revisions in the proposed rule added less than 0.5 percent to the total construction costs of the facilities examined, with the exception of large sports stadiums and arenas. Based on this analysis, the Access Board certified that the proposed rule was not expected to have a

188

significant economic impact on the new construction and alterations of facilities by a substantial number of small entities when the proposed rule was published in November 1999.

The Small Business Administration objected to the certification of no significant economic impact. The Small Business Administration noted that the ICC/ANSI A117.1 standard is a voluntary consensus standard, and there was no factual information presented in the regulatory assessment for the proposed rule showing the 1998 edition of the ICC/ANSI A117.1 standard had actually been adopted by State and local governments. Since the proposed rule was published in November 1999, the new International Building Code has been published. The International Building Code references the 1998 edition of the ICC/ANSI A117.1 standard for technical requirements. The International Building Code has been adopted statewide by 28 States and by local governments in another 15 States.

This assessment analyzes the impacts of the final revised guidelines by separately comparing the revisions to the current guidelines and to the International Building Code. The additional costs of the revisions for facilities that are likely to experience higher costs than other facilities are estimated in Chapter 8 with separate columns for the current guidelines and the International Building Code. The costs listed under the current guidelines column are the upper bound, and assume that the facilities are not required to comply with equivalent requirements in the International Building Code. The costs listed under the International Building Code column are the lower bound, and assume that the facilities are required to comply with equivalent requirements in the International Building Code. As shown in Table 10.1, the final revised guidelines add 0.01 to 0.5 percent to the total construction costs of the facilities compared to the current guidelines; and 0.00 to 0.3 percent to the total construction costs of the facilities compared to the International Building Code.

Table 10.1 – Costs of Final Revised Guidelines (text version)

Facility	Costs as Percentage of Total Construction Costs Compared to	
	Current Guidelines (Upper Bound)	IBC (Lower Bound)
Office Buildings	0.02 to 0.10 %	0.01 to 0.08 %
Hotels	0.06 to 0.50 %	0.04 to 0.30 %
Hospitals and Nursing Homes	0.02 %	0.00 %
Federal, State, and Local Government Housing	0.01 %	0.01 %

As discussed in Chapter 4, the Access Board has adopted alternatives in the final revised guidelines that eliminate costs that were estimated in the regulatory assessment for the proposed rule by:

- Adding a new scoping requirement for visible alarms in employee work areas that allows for such alarms to be provided as needed;

189

- Not increasing the scoping requirement for hotel guest rooms with communication features;

- Clarifying the scoping requirement for vertical dispersion of wheelchair spaces and modifying the scoping requirement for designated aisle seats in assembly areas; and

- Not adding new scoping requirements for equivalent vertical access and companion seats in assembly areas.

As discussed in Chapter 5, the final revised guidelines also reduce some existing scoping requirements and add new exceptions to some existing scoping and technical requirements that will benefit small entities. For example, small entities with four or fewer parking spaces are not required to provide signs identifying accessible parking spaces. Doctor's offices with clustered toilet rooms are not required to make each one accessible. High schools are not required to provide accessible routes to small press boxes.

The Small Business Administration requested the Access Board to analyze the impacts of the final revised guidelines on alterations to existing facilities. The impacts will be facility specific and will depend on the elements and spaces that are altered in an existing facility. Chapter 7 analyzes the impacts of the revisions that have monetary impacts on alterations to existing facilities by answering a series of questions about whether the element or space is typically altered; whether the element or space is part of the "path of travel" serving a primary function area; and whether the general exception for technical infeasibility may apply to alterations of the element or space. Chapter 8 includes alteration projects in the estimates of the national costs of the revisions for facilities that are likely to experience relatively higher costs than other facilities.

Finally, the Small Business Administration requested the Access Board to analyze the impacts of the final revised guidelines on the obligation of entities under the Americans with Disabilities Act to remove architectural and communication barriers in existing facilities, where it is readily achievable. As discussed in Chapter 2.6, the Department of Justice will revise the accessibility standards for the Americans with Disabilities Act after the Access Board publishes the final revised guidelines, and will address the effect of the revised standards on existing facilities subject to the barrier removal requirement. A statement has been added to the final revised guidelines to clarify that any determination to apply the revised scoping and technical requirements to existing facilities subject to the barrier removal requirement is solely with the discretion of the Department of Justice and is effective only to the extent required by regulations issued by the Department of Justice.

For the reasons stated above, the Access Board certifies that the final revised guidelines are not expected to have a significant economic impact on the new construction and alterations of facilities by a substantial number of small entities.

190